TWELFTH EDITION

D0036070

LANGUAGE AWARENESS

Readings for College Writers

Paul Eschholz, *University of Vermont*
Alfred Rosa, *University of Vermont*
Virginia Clark, *late of University of Vermont*

bedford/st.martin's
Macmillan Learning
Boston • New York

For Bedford/St. Martin's

VICE PRESIDENT, EDITORIAL, MACMILLAN LEARNING HUMANITIES: Edwin Hill
EDITORIAL DIRECTOR, ENGLISH: Karen S. Henry
SENIOR PUBLISHER FOR COMPOSITION, BUSINESS AND TECHNICAL WRITING,
    DEVELOPMENTAL WRITING: Leasa Burton
EXECUTIVE EDITOR: John Sullivan
SENIOR DEVELOPMENTAL EDITOR: Rachel Goldberg
EDITORIAL ASSISTANT: Evelyn Denham
PRODUCTION EDITOR: Lidia MacDonald-Carr
MEDIA PRODUCER: Sarah O'Connor
PRODUCTION SUPERVISOR: Robert Cherry
EXECUTIVE MARKETING MANAGER: Joy Fisher Williams
PROJECT MANAGEMENT: Cenveo Publisher Services
DIRECTOR OF RIGHTS AND PERMISSIONS: Hilary Newman
PHOTO EDITOR: Robin Fadool
PERMISSIONS ASSISTANT: Michael McCarty
TEXT PERMISSIONS MANAGER: Kalina Ingham
SENIOR ART DIRECTOR: Anna Palchik
COVER DESIGN: John Callahan
COVER IMAGE: Elizabeth Rosen
COMPOSITION: Cenveo ® Publisher Services
PRINTING AND BINDING: RR Donnelley and Sons

Manufactured in the United States of America.

1 0 9 8 7 6
f e d c b a

For *information, write:* Bedford/St. Martin's, 75 Arlington Street, Boston, MA 02116 (617-399-4000)

ISBN 978-1-4576-9797-5 (Student Edition)
ISBN 978-1-319-04410-7 (Instructor's Edition)

Acknowledgments

"The limits of my language means the limits of my world."
—Ludwig Wittgenstein

" 'Meow' means 'woof' in cat."
—George Carlin

"Because without our language, we have lost ourselves.
Who are we without our words?"
—Melina Marchetta

PREFACE

Since the first edition of *Language Awareness* appeared in 1974, its purpose has been twofold: to foster an appreciation of the richness, flexibility, and vitality of the English language and to help students to use their language more responsibly and effectively in speech and particularly in writing. Because of these purposes, *Language Awareness* has been used successfully in a variety of courses over the years. Its primary use, however, has been and continues to be in college composition courses. Clearly, many instructors believe as we do—that the study of language and the study of writing go hand in hand.

Because the study of language is so multifaceted, we cover a broad spectrum of topics, including language acquisition, regional dialects of American English, the relationship between language and culture, the language of new technologies, the language of prejudice, and the power of language in influencing advertising, politics, the media, and gender roles. Opening students' eyes to the power of language—its ability to shape and influence perceptions and cultural attitudes—is, we believe, one of the worthiest goals a writing class can pursue.

NEW TO THE TWELFTH EDITION

As in previous editions of *Language Awareness*, the selections in the twelfth edition are written primarily in nontechnical language on topics of current interest. Our questions and introductory material help students to understand those topics, providing clearly defined opportunities for thoughtful writing. Guided by comments and advice from hundreds of colleagues and students across the country who have used the previous editions, we have made some dramatic improvements in this twelfth edition.

New Selections

Almost half of the sixty-six professional selections in *Language Awareness* are new to this edition. We have retained many of the classic, informative, and well-written essays from earlier editions, such as Gordon Allport's "The Language of Prejudice," Helen Keller's "The Day Language Came into My Life," Martin Luther King Jr.'s "I Have a Dream," William Lutz's "The World of Doublespeak," Malcolm X's "Coming to an Awareness of Language," and Andrew Sullivan's "What's So Bad about Hate?"

The thirty-seven new selections, chosen for their insight and clear, thought-provoking writing, also reflect the language issues of an increasingly complex, multicultural America. Representing a wide variety of voices, the readings address a range of language concerns on issues from gender roles to deaf culture. New selections include Roxane Gay's "The Careless Language of Sexual Violence," Sherry Turkle's "The Tethered Self: Technology Reinvents Intimacy and Solitude," Sherman Alexie's "Superman and Me," Malala Yousafzai's "Address at the Youth Takeover of the United Nations," Annie Dillard's "Write Till You Drop," Steven Pinker's "Good Writing," Toni Morrison's "When Language Dies: 1993 Nobel Prize for Literature Lecture," and Sherryl Kleinman, Matthew B. Ezzell, and A. Corey Frost's "The Social Harms of 'Bitch.'" We believe that the new selections will spark student interest and bring currency to the otherwise class-proven essays retained from earlier editions.

New Thematic Chapter

Students and teachers, pleased with the relevancy of the thematic chapters in past editions of *Language Awareness*, asked us to provide a fresh new theme to prompt lively discussion. The result is Chapter 11, "The Language of Conflict: Argument, Apology, and Dignity," a thematic chapter that offers a collection of readings on the interplay between language and conflict, whether interpersonal or international. By analyzing the dynamics of current and past conflicts, we can come to better understand how our words affect others and their words us. The authors of the readings in this chapter have already begun to assess how we use language to confront, threaten, disrespect, or forgive one another. They offer in-depth looks at how to defuse tense situations through unexpected language; how labelling someone's actions and ideology can change how we perceive their threat; and how apology and forgiveness work, as well as how they can go wrong.

Current Language Controversies

Chapter 13, "Current Language Controversies," offers three new casebooks that ask questions about present-day language issues: "How Does Technology Impact Communication in Relationships?" looks at the effects of texting, e-mail, and other digital communication on our professional and personal communities. "How Does Language Work in

Advertising?" combines two timeless essays about the form and function of advertisements with two current analyses of how advertisers use
language to manipulate consumers. "Why Do We Lie?" begins with a
classification of types of lies and a look into the development of our
ability to lie at a young age, and it raises the additional questions of
the true effects of lying as well as why we do it in the first place. In
each casebook, the end-of-selection questions invite students to bring
the language concepts and ideas they have learned in the earlier core
chapters of *Language Awareness* to bear on the topics of the language
debates. At the end of each debate, a set of Writing Suggestions offers
students opportunities to join in the debate by extending their analyses
of individual articles and making connections among the various perspectives of the writers.

KEY FEATURES OF *LANGUAGE AWARENESS*

Class-Tested Topics

Instructors have told us that the chapters on "Understanding the
Power of Language," "Language Essentials," "Language Communities,"
"Writers on Writing," "Language that Manipulates," "Language that
Changed the World," "The Language of Discrimination," and "Language
and Gender" are indispensable in the courses they teach. Not only do the
readings in these chapters represent essential areas of language study, but
they also teach students useful ways to look at and write about the world
around them. Each of these chapters has been updated with new essays
that reflect recent trends, but they retain the spirit and purpose of their
predecessors.

Introductory Chapters on Reading and Writing

To supplement the study of language with instruction in reading and
writing, we have expanded our coverage of the twin tasks of reading and
writing. Based on years of classroom experience, these opening two chapters
provide students with the essentials of college reading and writing. The first
chapter, "Reading Critically," provides students with guidelines for critical
reading, demonstrates how they can get the most out of their reading by taking advantage of the apparatus accompanying each selection, and shows how
they can generate their own writing from the reading they do. The second
chapter, "Writing in College and Beyond," explores the world of academic
writing. Here students learn how to master the core elements that all instructors expect in academic essays, starting with an understanding of the writing
assignment itself, establishing a thesis, determining an organization, using
evidence, and culminating with documenting sources and avoiding plagiarism. Each step in the process is illustrated with a student essay in progress.

Chapter Introductions

Brief, one- to two-page chapter introductions discuss the key elements of each chapter's topic and why the topic is important to study. In addition, the introductions briefly discuss individual readings, explaining how they connect to larger language issues and how they relate to each other.

Student-Tested Headnotes, Journal Prompts, Questions, Activities, and Writing Suggestions

INFORMATIVE HEADNOTES. Headnotes preceding each selection discuss the content of the essay and provide pertinent information about the author and where and when the selection was first published.

"WRITING TO DISCOVER" JOURNAL PROMPTS. Each selection begins with a journal prompt designed to get students writing—before they start reading—about their own experiences with the language issues discussed in the selection. Students are then more likely to approach the selection with a critical eye. From time to time, class activities or writing assignments ask students to return to these journal writings and to reflect on them before proceeding with more formal writing tasks.

END-OF-SELECTION QUESTIONS. The "Thinking Critically about the Reading" questions at the end of each selection emphasize content and writing strategies. Content questions challenge students to develop a deeper understanding of ideas contained in the essay, in some cases by drawing connections to other readings or analyzing their own experiences. Other questions ask students to explore and analyze the writer's strategies in developing the selection to determine how effective writing achieves its aims.

LANGUAGE IN ACTION ACTIVITIES. The "Language in Action" activities that follow every selection in Chapters 4 through 12 give students a chance to analyze real-world examples of the language issues discussed by the essayists, with poems, cartoons, parodies, advertisements, photographs, letters to the editor, syndicated columns, and more. Designed to be completed either in class or at home in about twenty minutes, these activities ask students to take a hands-on approach to what they are learning from the essays and to give them a chance to demonstrate their growing language aptitude.

END-OF-SELECTION WRITING ASSIGNMENTS. To give students more opportunities to practice thinking and writing, we provide several Writing

Suggestions at the end of every selection in Chapters 4 through 13. Each assignment is designed to elicit a three- to five-page paper. Some assignments ask students to use their "Writing to Discover" journal entries as springboards for an extended essay; for others, students use their analytical skills to make critical connections among articles on the same topic; and some assignments ask students to do library or community-based research in order, for example, to examine the language used in local public documents, the language used in law offices, or campus slang.

Glossary of Rhetorical and Linguistic Terms

The Glossary of Rhetorical and Linguistic Terms includes definitions of key language terms and concepts as well as the standard terminology of rhetoric. References to glossary entries appear where needed in the questions that accompany each selection, allowing students to look up unfamiliar terms as they read.

Rhetorical Contents

At the end of the text, an alternate table of contents classifies the selections in *Language Awareness* according to the rhetorical strategies they exemplify (i.e., Comparison and Contrast, Definition, Illustration, Cause and Effect Analysis, and Argument), making it easier for instructors to assign readings that parallel the types of writing their students are doing.

GET THE MOST OUT OF YOUR COURSE WITH *LANGUAGE AWARENESS*

Bedford/St. Martin's offers resources and format choices that help you and your students get even more out of your book and course. To learn more about or to order any of the following products, contact your Bedford/St. Martin's sales representative, e-mail sales support (**sales_support@bfwpub.com**), or visit the website at **macmillanhighered .com/languageawareness/catalog**.

Select Value Packages

Add value to your text by packaging one of the following resources with *Language Awareness*. To learn more about package options for any of the following products, contact your Bedford/St. Martin's sales representative or visit **macmillanhighered.com/languageawareness/catalog**.

WRITER'S HELP 2.0 is a powerful online writing resource that helps students find answers whether they are searching for writing advice on their own or as part of an assignment.

- **Smart search**
  Built on research with more than 1,600 student writers, the smart search in *Writer's Help 2.0* provides reliable results even when students use novice terms, such as *flow* and *unstuck*.
- **Trusted content from our best-selling handbooks**
  Choose *Writer's Help 2.0 for Hacker Handbooks* or *Writer's Help 2.0 for Lunsford Handbooks* and ensure that students have clear advice and examples for all of their writing questions.
- **Adaptive exercises that engage students**
  Writer's Help 2.0 includes LearningCurve, game-like online quizzing that adapts to what students already know and helps them focus on what they need to learn.

Student access is packaged with *Language Awareness* at a significant discount. Order ISBN 978-1-319-06598-0 for *Writer's Help 2.0 for Hacker Handbooks* or ISBN 978-1-319-06599-7 for *Writer's Help 2.0 for Lunsford Handbooks* to ensure your students have easy access to online writing support. Students who rent a book or buy a used book can purchase access to *Writer's Help 2.0* at **macmillanhighered.com/writershelp2**.

Instructors may request free access by registering as an instructor at **macmillanhighered.com/writershelp2**. For technical support, visit **macmillanhighered.com/getsupport**.

PORTFOLIO KEEPING, THIRD EDITION, BY NEDRA REYNOLDS AND ELIZABETH DAVIS, provides all the information students need to use the portfolio method successfully in a writing course. *Portfolio Teaching*, a companion guide for instructors, provides the practical information instructors and writing program administrators need to use the portfolio method successfully in a writing course. To order *Portfolio Keeping* packaged with this text, contact your sale representative for a package ISBN.

Instructor Resources

macmillanhighered.com/languageawareness/catalog
You have a lot to do in your course. Bedford/St. Martin's wants to make it easy for you to find the support you need—and to get it quickly.

The Instructor's Manual for Language Awareness is available as a PDF that can be downloaded from the Bedford/St. Martin's online catalog at the URL above. In addition to chapter overviews and teaching tips, the instructor's manual includes classroom activities and discussions of each of the book's reading questions and Language in Action activities.

Teaching Central offers the entire list of Bedford/St. Martin's print and online professional resources in one place. You'll find landmark reference works, sourcebooks on pedagogical issues, award-winning collections, and practical advice for the classroom—all free for instructors. Visit **macmillanhighered.com/teachingcentral**.

Join Our Community! The Macmillan English Community is now Bedford/St. Martin's home for professional resources, featuring Bedford *Bits*, our popular blog site offering new ideas for the composition classroom and composition teachers. Connect and converse with a growing team of Bedford authors and top scholars who blog on *Bits*: Andrea Lunsford, Nancy Sommers, Steve Bernhardt, Traci Gardner, Barclay Barrios, Jack Solomon, Susan Bernstein, Elizabeth Wardle, Doug Downs, Elizabeth Losh, Jonathan Alexander, and Donna Winchell.

In addition, you'll find an expanding collection of additional resources that support your teaching.

- Sign up for webinars
- Download resources from our professional resource series that support your teaching
- Start a discussion
- Ask a question
- Follow your favorite members
- Review projects in the pipeline

Visit **community.macmillan.com** to join the conversation with your fellow teachers.

ACKNOWLEDGMENTS

We are grateful to the following reviewers, whose comments helped us shape this edition: Shavawn Berry, Arizona State University; Nicole Beveridge, Kingsborough Community College; Stacey Corbitt, Montana Tech of the University of Montana; Judi Crowe, Millikin University; Wade Edwards, Longwood University; Patrick Hunter, California State University-Northridge; Mary Catherine Kiliany, Robert Morris University; Robert Lively, Truckee Meadows Community College; Joseph Marmaud, Missouri Western State University; Marsha McSpadden, University of Alabama; Susan Morris, Creighton University; Cheryl Murray, Queens University of Charlotte; Erin Presley, Eastern Kentucky University; Henriette Recny, University at Buffalo; Ian Roberts, Missouri Western State University; Joseph Robertshaw, Youngstown State University; Mason Smith, Eastern Kentucky University; and Sara Yaklin, University of Toledo.

We would like to express our appreciation to the staff at Bedford/St. Martin's, especially Sarah Macomber for supporting us in our efforts to find innovative and engaging new readings and to update and energize our Language in Action activities so that they provide strong links between language study and real-world issues. Her assistant, Evelyn Denham, handled a number of important tasks and facilitated manuscript flow. Thanks go to Lidia MacDonald-Carr, our production editor; to Denise Quirk, our superlative copyeditor; and to Pablo D'Stair and Michael McCarty for clearing permissions. Our thanks also to Dr. Sarah Federman for preparing the Instructor's Manual for this new edition. Without our students at the University of Vermont over the years, a book such as *Language Awareness* would not have been possible. Their enthusiasm for language study and writing and their responses to materials included in this book have proved invaluable.

We thank our wives, Betsy and Maggie—without their assistance in finding meaningful essays and in reading proof and without their unflagging support, none of this would have been possible. Finally, we thank each other. Beginning in 1971 we have collaborated on many textbooks in language and writing, all of which have gone into multiple editions. With this twelfth edition of *Language Awareness*, we enter the forty-fifth year of working together. Ours must be one of the longest-running and most mutually satisfying writing partnerships in college textbook publishing. The journey has been invigorating and challenging as we have come to understand the complexities and joys of good writing and sought out new ways to help students become better writers.

PAUL ESCHHOLZ
ALFRED ROSA

Contents

PREFACE   v

1. READING CRITICALLY   1

GETTING THE MOST OUT OF YOUR READING   2

    1. Prepare Yourself to Read the Selection   2

    2. Read the Selection to Get an Overview of It   4

        Be Specific, NATALIE GOLDBERG   5

    3. Annotate the Selection with Marginal Notes   6

    4. Summarize the Selection in Your Own Words   9

    5. Analyze the Selection to Come to an Understanding of It   9

    6. Complete the "Language in Action" Activity to Discover
the Far-Reaching Connections between the Selection and
Language in the Real World   13

PRACTICE READING, ANNOTATING, AND ANALYZING   14

What's in a Name?, HENRY LOUIS GATES JR.   14

READING AS A WRITER   19

2. WRITING IN COLLEGE AND BEYOND   21

DEVELOPING AN EFFECTIVE WRITING PROCESS   21

    1. Understand Your Assignment   22

    2. Find a Subject and Topic   23

    3. Gather Ideas   27

    4. Formulate a Thesis   31

    5. Support Your Thesis with Evidence   32

    6. Determine Your Organization   34

    7. Write Your First Draft   35

    8. Revise   35

    9. Edit and Proofread   38

    10. Sample Student Essay Using Writing Process   39

The "Negro Revolt" in Me, REBEKAH SANDLIN (student essay)   39

3. WRITING WITH SOURCES   43

WHAT DOES IT MEAN TO WRITE WITH SOURCES?   43

WRITE WITH SOURCES   43

LEARN TO SUMMARIZE, PARAPHRASE, AND QUOTE FROM YOUR SOURCES   46
  Summary   47
  Paraphrase   48
  Direct Quotation   49

INTEGRATE BORROWED MATERIAL INTO YOUR TEXT   50

AVOID PLAGIARISM   53

A SAMPLE STUDENT ESSAY USING LIBRARY AND INTERNET SOURCES   57

The "Official English" Movement: Can America Proscribe Language
with a Clear Conscience?, JAKE JAMIESON (student essay)   58

4. UNDERSTANDING THE POWER OF LANGUAGE: HOW WE FIND OUR VOICES   65

Coming to an Awareness of Language, MALCOLM X   67

"I saw that the best thing I could do was get hold of a dictionary—to study, to learn some words."

The Day Language Came into My Life, HELEN KELLER   72

The celebrated deaf and blind writer recalls her discovery of language.

Superman and Me, SHERMAN ALEXIE   77

"I read with equal parts joy and desperation. I loved those books, but I also knew that love had only one purpose. I was trying to save my life."

Writing to Change the World, MARY PIPHER   82

"All writing is designed to change the world, at least a small part of the world, or in some small way, perhaps a change in a reader's mood or in his or her appreciation of a certain kind of beauty."

You Can Keep Quiet, You Can Emigrate, or You Can Stay Here
and Fight, EMILY PARKER   88

As Russian activists and bloggers take to the Web, their lives and families are threatened by the government they criticize.

Letter from Birmingham Jail, MARTIN LUTHER KING JR.   95

"For years now I have heard the word 'Wait!' It rings in the ear of every Negro with piercing familiarity. This 'Wait' has almost always meant 'Never.' We must come to see, with one of our distinguished jurists, that 'justice too long delayed is justice denied.'"

5. LANGUAGE ESSENTIALS: MAKING SENSE OF WORDS IN THE WORLD   111

Language and Thought, SUSANNE K. LANGER   112

"Language is the highest and most amazing achievement of the symbolistic human mind. The power it bestows is almost inestimable, for without it anything properly called 'thought' is impossible."

Words Don't Mean What They Mean, STEVEN PINKER   120

"Words let us say the things we want to say and also things we would be better off not having said."

Word Power for Babies, MELISSA FAY GREENE   126

A journalist and writer looks at the effects of the "word shortage" that low-income children experience and examines an innovative program devised to close the word gap.

Chunking, BEN ZIMMER   133

"In recent decades, the study of language acquisition and instruction has increasingly focused on 'chunking': how children learn language not so much on a word-by-word basis but in larger 'lexical chunks' or meaningful strings of words that are committed to memory."

Our Language Prejudices Don't Make No Sense, RAFFAELLA ZANUTTINI   137

"There is no single recipe for English; rather, there are a number of recipes."

Lost in Translation, LERA BORODITSKY   141

A Stanford University linguist sheds new light on the Sapir-Whorf hypothesis: "Do the languages we speak shape the way we think? Do they merely express thoughts, or do the structures in languages (without our knowledge or consent) shape the very thoughts we wish to express?"

6. LANGUAGE COMMUNITIES: WHERE DO WE BELONG?   147

Speech Communities, PAUL ROBERTS   148

Roberts defines and exemplifies both real and imagined speech communities, noting that how we speak says as much about us as what we say.

All-American Dialects, RICHARD LEDERER   159

"Each language is a great pie. Each slice of that pie is a dialect, and no single slice is the language. Do not try to change your language into the kind of English that nobody speaks. Be proud of your slice of the pie."

Losing the Language of Silence, LOU ANN WALKER   168

"What is it about sign language that makes people want to fight for it?"

Two Ways to Belong in America, BHARATI MUKHERJEE   174

In recounting a disagreement with her sister over the merits of citizenship, this Indian American writer comes to an insightful conclusion: "The price that the immigrant willingly pays, and that the exile avoids, is the trauma of self-transformation."

Mother Tongue, AMY TAN   179

"I spend a great deal of my time thinking about the power of language—the way it can evoke an emotion, a visual image, a complex idea, or a simple truth. Language is the tool of my trade. And I use them all—all the Englishes I grew up with."

Talk the Talk, ERIC C. MILLER   186

The author explores the history of the English-only movement and argues against an official language: "Language is an organic force, and difficult to control."

7. WRITERS ON WRITING: HOW AND WHY WE WRITE   195

Reading to Write, STEPHEN KING   196

"If you want to be a writer, you must do two things above all others: Read a lot and write a lot. There's no way around these two things that I'm aware of, no short cut."

Write Till You Drop, ANNIE DILLARD   202

"Write as if you were dying. At the same time, assume you write for an audience consisting solely of terminal patients. That is, after all, the case."

Good Writing, STEVEN PINKER   208

"Savoring good prose is not just a more effective way to develop a writerly ear than obeying a set of commandments; it's a more inviting one."

Shitty First Drafts, ANNE LAMOTT   221

"For me and most of the other writers I know, writing is not rapturous. In fact, the only way I can get anything written at all is to write really, really shitty first drafts."

The Maker's Eye: Revising Your Own Manuscripts,
DONALD M. MURRAY   226

Like most good writers, Murray knows that writing is rewriting.

Simplicity, WILLIAM ZINSSER   233

"If you find that writing is hard, it's because it *is* hard."

On Not Writing, BILL HAYES   239

A professional writer discusses his experience with writer's block and the need for creative rest.

8. Language That Manipulates: Politics, Propaganda, and Doublespeak   245

Propaganda: How Not to Be Bamboozled, DONNA WOOLFOLK CROSS   247

"If we are to continue to be a government 'by the people,' let us become informed about the methods and purposes of propaganda, so we can be the masters, not the slaves of our destiny."

Selection, Slanting, and Charged Language, NEWMAN P. BIRK AND GENEVIEVE B. BIRK   261

These scholars show how language can be manipulated to create particular impressions.

The Lost Art of the Unsent Angry Letter, MARIA KONNIKOVA   272

"We have more avenues to express immediate displeasure than ever before, and may thus find ourselves more likely to hit send or tweet when we would have done better to hit save or delete."

The World of Doublespeak, WILLIAM LUTZ   277

An English professor exposes the disguises of doublespeak, "language which pretends to communicate but doesn't."

Language That Silences, JASON STANLEY   289

"Words are misappropriated and meanings twisted. I believe that these tactics are not really about making substantive claims, but rather play the role of silencing. They are, if you will, linguistic strategies for stealing the voices of others."

Assassination and the American Language, ELLIOT ACKERMAN   294

A former CIA and military officer struggles with the contradictions inherent in the language of clandestine military actions, where "assassination" is prohibited but "targeted killings" still occur.

9. Language That Changed the World: Words That Made a Difference   299

I Have a Dream, MARTIN LUTHER KING JR.   301

The great civil rights leader gives voice to his dream of freedom and equality, "a dream deeply rooted in the American dream."

Inaugural Address, JOHN F. KENNEDY   309

"Let every nation know, whether it wishes us well or ill, that we shall pay any price, bear any burden, meet any hardship, support any friend, oppose any foe to assure the survival and success of liberty."

Address at the Youth Takeover of the United Nations, MALALA YOUSAFZAI   314

"Dear friends, on 9 October 2012, the Taliban shot me on the left side of my forehead. They shot my friends, too. They thought that the bullets would silence us, but they failed. And out of that silence came thousands of voices."

When Language Dies: 1993 Nobel Prize for Literature Lecture,
TONI MORRISON   319

> "We die. That may be the meaning of life. But we do language. That may be the measure of our lives."

The Perils of Indifference, ELIE WIESEL   327

> "In a way, to be indifferent to that suffering is what makes the human being inhuman. Indifference, after all, is more dangerous than anger or hatred."

A Modest Proposal, JONATHAN SWIFT   334

> This well-known satirical essay clearly outlines a plan to end hunger in eighteenth-century Ireland.

10. THE LANGUAGE OF DISCRIMINATION: HATE, PREJUDICE, AND STEREOTYPES   345

What's So Bad about Hate?, ANDREW SULLIVAN   347

> Legislating against hate crimes has become more and more common in the past decades. But, what does hate mean in this context, and can legislation really be effective?

The Language of Prejudice, GORDON ALLPORT   364

> What causes prejudice? This famous psychologist points to the workings of language for the answer.

The "F Word," FIROOZEH DUMAS   376

> An Iranian immigrant recounts the prejudice she witnessed and the difficulties she had as a child, a student, and a job-seeking college graduate with an "identifiably 'ethnic' name."

Why We Need to Tolerate Hate, WENDY KAMINER   382

> "People harbor biases; they always have and always will, and their right to believe in the inferiority or sinfulness of particular groups is the same as your right to believe in equality."

Twitter, Hate Speech, and the Costs of Keeping Quiet,
GREG LUKIANOFF   387

> "The idea that society achieves something positive by mandating that people with bad opinions must hide them, or discuss them only in forums of the like-minded, is not only extraordinarily naive, it can be dangerous. Bigots driven into echo chambers may only become more extreme."

Thugs. Students. Rioters. Fans: Media's Subtle Racism in Unrest Coverage,
AKIBA SOLOMON   393

> An essayist and editor analyzes the differences in language in reports of violence, unearthing the ways that words like "rioter" and "looter" become racially coded in the media.

What's Really Going on with the Word "Thug"—And Why I'm Not Ready to
Let It Go, MAISHA Z. JOHNSON   398

"Attitudes that villainize people of color, people defying gender norms,
and poor people are the same ones that target us for discrimination,
violence, and incarceration. And they're the same attitudes that can add
racist undertones to the word 'thug.'"

11. THE LANGUAGE OF CONFLICT: ARGUMENT, APOLOGY, AND DIGNITY   403

Sorry, Regrets, and More, EDWIN BATTISTELLA   406

This linguistics expert dissects variations of the apology and looks at
how the language of an apology shapes its reception—and its sincerity.

Dignity, DONNA HICKS   417

"When we are ignorant of the effects that our behavior has on others,
and if our culture perpetuates and enables that ignorance, we will
unknowingly do harm to one another."

The Dork Police: Further Adventures of Flex Cop, MICHAEL GARDNER   425

A veteran Cincinnati police sergeant describes the innovative verbal and
visual tactics he used to defuse tense confrontations with citizens: "We
experimented daily with ways of startling subjects into confusion in
order to interrupt their dangerous mental patterns and provide a space
for something more positive."

Regretlessly Yours: The No-Fault Apology, RICK REILLY   433

This Mad-Libs-style spoof of a standard "athletic apology" offers an
irreverent look at the way major sports figures frame their offenses and
attempt to excuse their bad behavior.

Tarring Opponents as Extremists Really Can Work, EMILY BADGER   437

An urban policy journalist exposes how labelling people as members of
a group can influence our perception of them—and how those labels
are exploited by politicians and policymakers to advance agendas.

Letting Go, AMY WESTERVELT   441

"It was a moment I'd read about—this sudden shift when the need to
forgive outweighs the drive for revenge."

12. LANGUAGE AND GENDER: POWER, ABUSE, EQUALITY   451

The Careless Language of Sexual Violence, ROXANE GAY   452

"When we're talking about race or religion or politics, it is often said
we need to speak carefully. These are difficult topics where we need to
be vigilant not only in what we say but how we express ourselves. That
same care, I would suggest, has to be extended to how we write about
violence, and sexual violence in particular."

Happy Feminist, CHIMAMANDA NGOZI ADICHIE   460

> A Nigerian writer discusses our society's discomfort in talking about gender issues and the need to reclaim terms like *feminist*: "Gender is not an easy conversation to have. It makes people uncomfortable, sometimes even irritable. Both men and women are resistant to talk about gender, or are quick to dismiss the problems of gender. Because thinking of changing the status quo is always uncomfortable."

The Social Harms of "Bitch," SHERRYL KLEINMAN, MATTHEW B. EZZELL, AND A. COREY FROST   465

> The authors examine what motivates women to adopt the epithet "bitch" and argue that the term is not harmless.

11 Words You Need to Teach Your Son Before He Turns 6, JOANNA SCHROEDER   470

> "As a parent, and someone who pays close attention to social issues around gender, I think it's crucial that we make a conscious choice to arm all of our kids with words that can give them important social skills or the ability to describe feelings."

"Bros Before Hos": The Guy Code, MICHAEL KIMMEL   477

> What does it mean to be a man today? A leading authority on men and masculinity describes the code and explores how language both reinforces it and discourages anyone from denying its demands.

The Internet Talks Like a Woman, BEN CRAIR   485

> This writer and editor analyzes research into how men and women use language online and finds that men tend to adopt women's communication styles rather than preserving their own offline habits.

13. CURRENT LANGUAGE CONTROVERSIES   491

How Does Technology Impact Communication in Relationships?   491

The Tethered Self: Technology Reinvents Intimacy and Solitude, SHERRY TURKLE   492

> "Technology is the architect of our intimacies, but this means that as we text, Twitter, e-mail, and spend time on Facebook, technology is not just doing things for us, but to us, changing the way we view ourselves and our relationships."

Keep Your Thumbs Still When I'm Talking to You, DAVID CARR   496

> "Add one more achievement to the digital revolution: It has made it fashionable to be rude."

Lost in Translation, ALISON J. STEIN   501

> A journalist extols the virtues of face-to-face communication over e-mail when it comes to communicating about sensitive issues.

How Does Language Work in Advertising?   506

The Hard Sell: Advertising in America, BILL BRYSON   507

> This journalist provides an entertaining behind-the-scenes look at the language involved in some of America's most successful advertising campaigns.

Weasel Words: The Art of Saying Nothing at All, WILLIAM LUTZ   520

> Words in advertisements often appear to be making a claim about a product's effectiveness or excellence when in fact they are not making a claim at all.

The Creepy Language Tricks Taco Bell Uses to Fool People into Eating There, KIERA BUTLER   531

> An editor teams up with a professor to analyze the hidden claims and associations in fast-food and upscale restaurant menus.

Is the "Natural" Label 100 Percent Misleading?, DEENA SHANKER   534

> "'Natural' currently means something different to every consumer. And, if that's really the case, how can it mean anything at all?"

Why Do We Lie?   540

The Truth about Lying, JUDITH VIORST   541

> A classification of different kinds of lies and a look at situations that seem to justify—or even necessitate—lying.

Learning to Lie, PO BRONSON   547

> "Although we think of truthfulness as a young child's paramount virtue, it turns out that lying is the more advanced skill. A child who is going to lie must recognize the truth, intellectually conceive of an alternate reality, and be able to convincingly sell that new reality to someone else."

Is Lying Bad for Us?, RICHARD GUNDERMAN   558

> "It has been estimated that the average American tells 11 lies per week. Is this bad for us?"

Psychology of Fraud: Why Good People Do Bad Things, CHANA JOFFE-WALT AND ALIX SPIEGEL   562

> This visual essay examines the psychology of fraud and the motivating factors that lead people to commit and collude in wrongdoing.

14. A BRIEF GUIDE TO WRITING A RESEARCH PAPER   577

ESTABLISH A REALISTIC SCHEDULE   578

LOCATE AND USE PRINT AND ONLINE SOURCES   579

  Conduct Keyword Searches   580
  Use Subject Directories to Define and Develop Your
  Research Topic   581

Evaluate Your Sources   582

Analyze Your Sources   584

Develop a Working Bibliography of Your Sources   585

Take Notes   587

Document Your Sources   588
      MLA In-Text Citations   589
      MLA List of Works Cited   590
      MLA Manuscript Format   600
      APA In-Text Citations   602
      APA List of References   603
      APA Manuscript Format   608

Glossary of Rhetorical and Linguistic Terms   610

Rhetorical Contents   619

Index of Authors and Titles   630

1

READING CRITICALLY

The readings in *Language Awareness* emphasize the crucial role language plays in virtually every aspect of our lives, and they reveal the essential elements of the writer's craft. As you read and study the selections in this text, you will discover the power of language in our world: You will become more aware of your own language usage and how it affects others, and, at the same time, you will become more sensitive to how the language of others affects you. An additional benefit of close, critical reading is that you will become more familiar with different types of writing and learn how good writers make decisions about writing strategies and techniques. All of these insights will help you become a more thoughtful, discerning reader and, equally important, a better writer.

As the word *critical* suggests, reading critically means questioning what you read in a thoughtful, organized way and with an alert, inquiring mind. Critical reading is a skill you need if you are truly to engage and understand the content of a piece of writing as well as the craft that shapes the writer's ideas into an effective, efficient, and presentable form. Never accept what you read simply because it's in print. Instead, scrutinize it, challenge it, and think about its meaning and significance.

Critical reading is also a skill that takes time and practice to acquire. While most of us learned before we got to college how to read for content and summarize what a writer said, not all of us learned how to analyze what we were reading. Reading critically is like engaging a writer in a conversation—asking for the meaning of a particular statement, questioning the definition of a crucial term, or demanding more evidence to support a generalization. In addition, critical reading requires asking ourselves why we like one piece of writing and not another, or why one argument is more believable or convincing than another.

As you learn more about reading thoughtfully and purposefully, you will come to a better understanding of both the content and the craft of any piece of writing. As an added bonus, learning to read critically will help you read your own work with more insight and, as a result, write more persuasively.

1

GETTING THE MOST OUT OF YOUR READING

Critical reading requires, first of all, that you commit time and effort. Second, it requires that you apply goodwill and energy to understanding and appreciating what you are reading, even if the subject matter does not immediately appeal to you. Remember, your mission is twofold: You must analyze and comprehend the content of what you are reading; and then you must understand the writer's methods to see firsthand the kinds of choices a writer makes in his or her writing.

To help you grow as a critical reader and to get the most out of what you read, use the following classroom-proven steps:

1. Prepare yourself to read the selection.
2. Read the selection to get an overview of it.
3. Annotate the selection with marginal notes.
4. Summarize the selection in your own words.
5. Analyze the selection to come to an understanding of it.
6. Complete the "Language in Action" activity to discover the far-reaching connections between the selection and language in the real world.

To demonstrate how these steps can work for you, we've applied them to an essay by the popular nonfiction writer Natalie Goldberg. Like the other selections in *Language Awareness,* Goldberg's essay "Be Specific" is accessible and speaks to an important contemporary language issue. She points to the importance of using specific names in speaking and writing, and she demonstrates how we give things their proper dignity and integrity when we name them.

1. Prepare Yourself to Read the Selection

Instead of diving into any given selection in *Language Awareness* or any other book, there are a few things that you can do that will prepare you to get the most out of what you will read. It's helpful, for example, to get a context for what you'll read. What's the essay about? What do you know about the writer's background and reputation? Where was the essay first published? Who was the intended audience for the essay? And, finally, how much do you already know about the subject of the reading selection? We encourage you to consider carefully the materials that precede each selection in this book. Each selection begins with a title, headnote, and journal prompt. From the **title** you often discover the writer's position on an issue or attitude toward the topic. On occasion, the title can give clues about the intended audience and the writer's purpose in writing the piece. The **headnote** contains a biographical note about the author followed by publication information and rhetorical highlights about the selection. In addition to information on the person's life and work, you'll read about his or her reputation and authority to write on the subject of the piece. The

publication information indicates when the essay was published and in what book or magazine it first appeared. This information, in turn, gives you insight about the intended audience. The **rhetorical highlights** direct your attention to one or more aspects of how the selection was written. Finally, the Writing to Discover **journal prompt** encourages you to collect your thoughts and opinions about the topic or related issues before you commence reading. The journal prompt makes it easy to keep a record of your own knowledge or thinking on a topic before you see what the writer has to offer.

To understand how these context-building materials can work for you, carefully review the following informational materials that accompany Natalie Goldberg's essay "Be Specific."

Be Specific
Title

NATALIE GOLDBERG

Born in 1948, author Natalie Goldberg is a teacher of writing who has conducted writing workshops across the country. In addition to her classes and workshops, Goldberg shares her love of writing in her books; she has made writing about writing her speciality. Her first and best known work, *Writing Down the Bones: Freeing the Writer Within*, was published in 1986. Goldberg's advice to would-be writers is practical and pithy, on the one hand, and mystical or spiritual in its call to writers to know and become more connected to the environment. In short, as one reviewer observed, "Goldberg teaches us not only how to write better, but how to live better." *Writing Down the Bones* was followed by five more books about writing: *Wild Mind: Living the Writer's Life* (1990), *Thunder and Lightning: Cracking Open the Writer's Craft* (2000), *Old Friend from Far Away: The Practice of Writing Memoir* (2008) and *The True Secret of Writing: Connecting Life with Language* (2014). Altogether, more than a million copies of these books are now in print. Goldberg has also written fiction: the novel *Banana Rose* (1995), and the autobiography: *Long Quiet Highway: Waking Up in America* (1993) and *The Great Failure: A Bartender, a Monk, and My Unlikely Path to Truth* (2004).

Headnote

Biographical information

"Be Specific" is taken from Goldberg's *Writing Down the Bones* and is representative of the book as a whole. Notice the ways in which Goldberg demonstrates her advice to be specific, to use names whenever possible. Which of her many examples resonates best with you?

Publication information

Rhetorical highlight

WRITING TO DISCOVER: *Suppose someone says to you, "I   Journal walked in the woods today." What do you envision? Write down what   prompt you see in your mind's eye. Now suppose someone says, "I walked in the redwood forest today." Again, write what you see. What's different about your two descriptions, and why?*

From reading these preliminary materials, what expectations do you have for the selection itself? How does this knowledge equip you to engage the selection before you actually read it? From the *title* you probably inferred that Goldberg will explain what she means by the command "be specific" and what is to be gained by following this advice. Her purpose clearly is to give advice to writers. The *biographical note* reveals that Goldberg has written a number of books detailing her own experiences with writing as well as giving advice to aspiring writers of all ages, and that she has taught writing courses and conducted writing workshops for many years. This experience gives her the knowledge and authority to write on this topic. The *publication information* indicates that the subject of Goldberg's essay is an argument in favor of being specific in writing. Because the selection was first published as part of her book *Writing Down the Bones: Freeing the Writer Within*, Goldberg can anticipate that readers, who we can assume are looking for writing advice, will be open to her argument. The *rhetorical highlight* alerts you to be mindful of how Goldberg practices what she's preaching in her own writing and prompts you to consider her examples. Finally, the *journal prompt*—a hands-on exercise in specificity—asks you to describe in writing the visuals conjured up in your mind by two statements and to draw conclusions about any differences you note in your responses.

It's always a good practice to take several minutes before reading a selection to reflect on what you already know about a particular issue and where you stand on it and why. After reading Goldberg's essay, you can compare your own experiences with being specific—or being unspecific—in writing with those of Goldberg.

2. Read the Selection to Get an Overview of It

Always read the selection at least twice, no matter how long it is. The first reading gives you a chance to get acquainted with the essay and to form first impressions. With the first reading you want to get an overall sense of what the writer is saying, keeping in mind the essay's title and what you learned about the writer in the headnote. The essay will offer you information, ideas, and arguments—some you may have expected; some you may not have. As you read, you may find yourself questioning or modifying your sense of what the writer is saying. Resist the urge to annotate at this point; instead, concentrate on the content, on the main points of what's being said. Now read Natalie Goldberg's essay.

Be Specific

NATALIE GOLDBERG

Be specific. Don't say "fruit." Tell what kind of fruit—"It is a pomegranate." Give things the dignity of their names. Just as with human beings, it is rude to say, "Hey, girl, get in line." That "girl" has a name. (As a matter of fact, if she's at least twenty years old, she's a woman, not a "girl" at all.) Things, too, have names. It is much better to say "the geranium in the window" than "the flower in the window." "Geranium"—that one word gives us a much more specific picture. It penetrates more deeply into the beingness of that flower. It immediately gives us the scene by the window—red petals, green circular leaves, all straining toward sunlight.

About ten years ago I decided I had to learn the names of plants and flowers in my environment. I bought a book on them and walked down the tree-lined streets of Boulder, examining leaf, bark, and seed, trying to match them up with their descriptions and names in the book. Maple, elm, oak, locust. I usually tried to cheat by asking people working in their yards the names of the flowers and trees growing there. I was amazed how few people had any idea of the names of the live beings inhabiting their little plot of land.

When we know the name of something, it brings us closer to the ground. It takes the blur out of our mind; it connects us to the earth. If I walk down the street and see "dogwood," "forsythia," I feel more friendly toward the environment. I am noticing what is around me and can name it. It makes me more awake.

If you read the poems of William Carlos Williams, you will see how specific he is about plants, trees, flowers—chicory, daisy, locust, poplar, quince, primrose, black-eyed Susan, lilacs—each has its own integrity. Williams says, "Write what's in front of your nose." It's good for us to know what is in front of our noses. Not just "daisy," but how the flower is in the season we are looking at it—"The dayseye hugging the earth/in August . . . brownedged,/green and pointed scales/armor his yellow."* Continue to hone your awareness: to the name, to the month, to the day, and finally to the moment.

Williams also says: "No idea, but in things." Study what is "in front of your nose." By saying "geranium" instead of "flower," you are penetrating more deeply into the present and being there. The closer we can get to what's in front of our nose, the more it can teach us everything. "To see the World in a Grain of Sand, and a heaven in a Wild Flower . . . "** 5

In writing groups and classes too, it is good to quickly learn the names of all the other group members. It helps to ground you in the group and make you more attentive to each other's work.

---

* William Carlos Williams, "Daisy," in *The Collected Earlier Poems* (New York: New Directions, 1938). [Goldberg's note.]

** William Blake, "The Auguries of Innocence." [Goldberg's note.]

Learn the names of everything: birds, cheese, tractors, cars, buildings. A writer is all at once everything—an architect, French cook, farmer—and at the same time, a writer is none of these things.

3. Annotate the Selection with Marginal Notes

Some students find it valuable to capture their first impressions, thoughts, or reactions immediately after they've finished reading a selection. If you keep a reading journal, record your ideas in a paragraph or two. You are now ready for the second reading of the essay, this time with pencil or pen in hand to annotate the text.

As you read the essay a second time, engage it—highlight key passages and make marginal annotations. Your second reading will be quite different from your first, because you already know what the essay is about, where it is going, and how it gets there. Now you can relate the parts of the essay more accurately to the whole. Use the second reading to test your first impressions against the words on the page, developing and deepening your sense of the writer's argument. Because you already have a general understanding of the essay's content and structure, you can focus on the writer's purpose and means of achieving it. You can look for features of organization and style that you can learn from and adapt to your own work.

One question that students frequently ask us is "What should I annotate?" When you annotate a text, you should do more than simply underline or highlight what you think are the important points to remember. Instead, as you read, write down your thoughts, reactions, and questions in the margins or on a separate piece of paper. Think of your annotations as an opportunity to have a conversation with the writer of the essay.

Mark what you believe to be the selection's main point when you find it stated directly. Look for the pattern or patterns of development the author uses to explore and support that point, and record the information. If you disagree with a statement or conclusion, object in the margin: "No!" If you're not convinced by the writer's claims or evidence, indicate that response: "Why?" or "Who says?" or "Explain." If you are impressed by an argument or turn of phrase, compliment the writer: "Good point." If there are any words that you do not recognize or that seem to you to be used in a questionable way, circle them so that you can look them up in a dictionary.

Jot down whatever marginal notes come naturally to you. Most readers combine brief responses written in the margins with their own system of underlining, circling, highlighting, stars, vertical lines, and question marks.

Remember that there are no hard-and-fast rules for which elements you annotate. Choose a method of annotation that works best for you and that will make sense to you when you go back to recollect your thoughts and responses to the essay. When annotating a text, don't be

---

How to Annotate a Text

Here are some suggestions of elements you may want to mark to help you keep a record of your responses as you read:

- Memorable statements of important points
- Key terms or concepts
- Central issues or themes
- Examples that support a main point
- Unfamiliar words
- Questions you have about a point or passage
- Your responses to a specific point or passage

---

timid. Mark up your book as much as you like, or jot down as many responses in your notebook as you think will be helpful. Don't let annotating become burdensome. A word or phrase is usually as good as a sentence. Notice how one of our students used marginal annotations to record her responses to Goldberg's text.

Be specific. Don't say "fruit." Tell what kind of fruit—"It is a pomegranate." Give things the dignity of their names. Just as with human beings, it is rude to say, "Hey, girl, get in line." That "girl" has a name. (As a matter of fact, if she's at least twenty years old, she's a woman, not a "girl" at all.) Things, too, have names. It is much better to say "the geranium in the window" than "the flower in the window." "Geranium"—that one word gives us a much more specific picture. It penetrates more deeply into the beingness of that flower. It immediately gives us the scene by the window—red petals, green circular leaves, all straining toward sunlight.

I agree — tho my grandma calls her friends "the girls" — ?

I think I do pay more attn. when people call me by name.

About ten years ago I decided I had to learn the names of plants and flowers in my environment. I bought a book on them and walked down the tree-lined streets of Boulder, examining leaf, bark, and seed, trying to match them up with their descriptions and names in the book. Maple, elm, oak, locust. I usually tried to cheat by asking people working in their yards the names

She's practicing what she preaches — but that's a LOT of work …

I doubt I could tell the difference between a maple and an elm.

of the flowers and trees growing there. I was amazed how few people had any idea of the names of the live beings inhabiting their little plot of land.

When we know the name of something, it brings us closer to the ground. It takes the blur out of our mind; it connects us to the earth. If I walk down the street and see "dogwood," "forsythia," I feel more friendly toward the environment. I am noticing what is around me and can name it. It makes me more awake.

If you read the poems of William Carlos Williams, you will see how specific he is about plants, trees, flowers—chicory, daisy, locust, poplar, quince, primrose, black-eyed Susan, lilacs—each has its own integrity. Williams says, "Write what's in front of your nose." It's good for us to know what is in front of our noses. Not just "daisy," but how the flower is in the season we are looking at it—"The dayseye hugging the earth/in August . . . brownedged,/green and pointed scales/armor his yellow." Continue to hone your awareness: to the name, to the month, to the day, and finally to the moment.

Williams also says: "No idea, but in things." Study what is "in front of your nose." By saying "geranium" instead of "flower," you are penetrating more deeply into the present and being there. The closer we can get to what's in front of our nose, the more it can teach us everything. "To see the World in a Grain of Sand, and a heaven in a Wild Flower . . . "

In writing groups and classes too, it is good to quickly learn the names of all the other group members. It helps to ground you in the group and make you more attentive to each other's work.

Learn the names of everything: birds, cheese, tractors, cars, buildings. A writer is all at once everything—an architect, French cook, farmer—and at the same time, a writer is none of these things.

Handwritten margin notes:

THESIS

Interesting—wonder if it's true. (How could you test it?)

Is Williams a really famous poet? LOOK THIS UP. Why does she keep quoting him?

I know I couldn't name all the people in my writing class. (Wonder if it would make a difference.)

Not sure what she means here. How can a writer be "all" and "none" of these things??

4. Summarize the Selection in Your Own Words

After carefully annotating the selection, you will find it worthwhile to summarize what the writer has said, to see how the main points work together to give support to the writer's thesis. An efficient way to do this is to make a simple paragraph-by-paragraph outline of what you've read. Try to capture the essence of each paragraph in a single sentence. Such an outline enables you to understand how the essay works, to see what the writer's position is and how he or she has structured the essay and organized the main ideas.

Consider the following paragraph-by-paragraph outline one of our students made after reading Goldberg's essay:

Paragraph 1: Goldberg announces her topic and demonstrates the power of names with the example of the geranium.

Paragraph 2: She recounts how she went about learning the names of plants and trees in her Colorado neighborhood.

Paragraph 3: She explains how knowing the names of things makes her feel connected to the world around her.

Paragraph 4: She uses the example of poet William Carlos Williams to support her point about the power of names.

Paragraph 5: She continues with the example of Williams to broaden the discussion of what it means to "penetrate more deeply" into the world that is "in front of your nose."

Paragraph 6: She says that knowing the names of people in your writing group or class creates community.

Paragraph 7: She advises writers to "learn the names of everything" as a way of being "at once everything" and "at the same time . . . none of these things."

With your paragraph-by-paragraph outline in hand, you are now ready to analyze the reading.

5. Analyze the Selection to Come to an Understanding of It

After reading the essay a second time and annotating it, you are ready to analyze it, to probe for a deeper understanding of and appreciation for what the writer has done. In analyzing an essay, you will examine its basic parts methodically to see the significance of each part and understand how they relate to one another. One of the best ways to analyze an essay is to answer a basic set of questions—questions that require you to do some critical thinking about the essay's content and form.

Each essay in *Language Awareness* is followed by a set of "Thinking Critically about the Reading" questions similar to the ones suggested here

---

Questions to Help You Analyze What You Read

1. What is the writer's main point or thesis?

2. To whom is the essay addressed? To a general audience with little or no background knowledge of the subject? To a specialized group familiar with the topic? To those who are likely to agree or disagree with the argument?

3. What is the writer's purpose in addressing this audience?

4. What is the writer's attitude toward the subject of the essay — positive, critical, objective, ironic, hostile?

5. What assumptions, if any, does the writer make about the subject and/or the audience? Are these assumptions explicit (stated) or implicit (unstated)?

6. What kinds of evidence does the writer use to support his or her thesis — personal experience, expert opinions, statistics? Does the writer supply enough evidence to support his or her position? Is the evidence reliable, specific, and up-to-date?

7. Does the writer address opposing views on the issue?

8. How is the essay organized and developed? Does the writer's strategy of development suit his or her subject and purpose?

9. How effective is the essay? Is the writer convincing about his or her position?

---

but more specific to the essay. These questions help you analyze both the content of an essay and the writer's craft. In answering each of these questions, always look for details from the selection itself to support your position.

Having read and reread Goldberg's essay and studied the student annotations to the text, consider the following set of student answers to the key questions listed above. Are there places where you would have answered the questions differently? Explain.

1. What is the writer's main point or thesis?

Goldberg wants to tell her readers why it's important for people, especially writers, to be specific and to learn the names of everything in their part of the world. She states her main point in paragraph 3: "When we know the name of something, it brings us closer to the ground. It takes the blur out of our mind; it connects us to the earth." In short, being specific in what we call things makes us see, think, and write more clearly.

2. *To whom is the essay addressed? To a general audience with little or no background knowledge of the subject? To a specialized group familiar with the topic? To those who are likely to agree or disagree with the argument?*

Goldberg's intended audience seems to be writers who are looking for advice. In paragraph 4, she quotes William Carlos Williams: "Write what's in front of your nose." In paragraph 6, Goldberg stresses the importance of knowing classmates' or group members' names and how this knowledge "helps to ground you in the group and make you more attentive to each other's work." In her final paragraph Goldberg acknowledges her audience of writers by emphasizing the writer's duty to learn the names of everything.

3. *What is the writer's purpose in addressing this audience?*

Goldberg's purpose is to give her readers some direct advice about writing and life: "Be specific." More specifically(!), she advises her readers to give people and things names and to create a specific time context (month, day, moment, etc.) for what they're describing ("Not just 'daisy,' but how the flower is in the season we are looking at it . . .").

4. *What is the writer's attitude toward the subject of the essay—positive, critical, objective, ironic, hostile?*

Goldberg is enthusiastic and extremely positive about the importance of naming things. She believes that "[w]hen we know the name of something, it brings us closer to the ground. It takes the blur out of our mind; it connects us to the earth" and makes us more "awake" to the environment; it allows us to "[penetrate] more deeply" into what is in front of us and to learn from it, and it grounds us and makes us more attentive in a group. She's excited to share her own experiences with learning the names of things.

5. *What assumptions, if any, does the writer make about the subject and/ or the audience? Are these assumptions explicit (stated) or implicit (unstated)?*

Goldberg makes several key assumptions in this essay:
- The title assumes that readers will be comfortable with commands.
- The examples of "pomegranate," "geranium," "maple," "elm," "oak," "locust," "dogwood," and "forsythia" assume that readers have a basic knowledge of fruits, flowers, and trees—or that they'll be motivated enough to look them up.
- The reference to the poet William Carlos Williams assumes that the audience will know who he is and perhaps be familiar with his poetry—or, again, that they will be motivated enough to look him up. Goldberg's footnotes, however, show that she does not assume readers will recognize the poem "Daisy" (4) or "The Auguries of Innocence," quoted in paragraph 5.
- Goldberg assumes that readers, after learning the names of the plants, flowers, trees, and people in their environment, will have experiences similar to the ones she has had: "I feel more friendly toward the environment. I am noticing what is around me and can name it. It makes me more awake" (3).

6. *What kinds of evidence does the writer use — personal experience, expert opinions, statistics? Does the writer supply enough evidence to support his or her position? Is the evidence reliable, specific, and up-to-date?*

To support her claim that writers need to be specific, Goldberg uses the examples of "fruit/pomegranate," "girl/[name]," and "flower/geranium" in her opening paragraph — hoping that her readers will agree that the specific terms are better than the general ones. She follows these examples with personal experience: She explains how she went about learning the names of plants and flowers in Boulder, Colorado, and shares what she felt as a result. In paragraphs 4 and 5, Goldberg cites the poetry of William Carlos Williams as evidence that specific language creates great poems.

It is difficult to say whether this evidence is enough. Assuming her readers are beginning writers eager to learn, as she seems to have intended, it is probably safe to say that her evidence will be convincing. If a less receptive audience or an audience of nonwriters were reading the essay, though, more evidence or a different kind (maybe examples of how being specific helps in everyday life) might be needed.

7. *Does the writer address opposing views on the issue?*

While Goldberg does not directly address opposing views, she does discuss what happens when writers or speakers are *not* specific. For example, in paragraph 1 she says that calling someone "girl" instead of calling her by name can be rude, which is another way of saying that it denies that person her dignity — a pretty serious charge. In addition, when she tells us how knowing the names of things brings us closer to our environment, she implies that not knowing these names actually makes us feel disconnected from the world around us — something no one wants to feel.

8. *How is the essay organized and developed? Does the writer's strategy of development suit his or her subject and purpose?*

Goldberg organizes her essay in a straightforward and logical manner. She introduces her topic with her central directive, "Be specific," and then immediately shows through three examples what happens when a writer is specific. She organizes the examples in the body of her essay — paragraphs 2 through 6 — by telling how she learned to be more specific, quoting William Carlos Williams's advice to "Write what's in front of your nose," and advising us that we should learn the names of people in the groups and classes we belong to. Goldberg concludes her essay where she began, by directing us to "Learn the names of everything." In learning the names of everything, she reminds us that "A writer is all at once everything — an architect, French cook, farmer — and at the same time, a writer is none of these things." Although it seems paradoxical at first, this statement, when you stop to think about it, is very empowering — you're not really an architect or a French cook or a farmer, but, when you write, you get to experience the world the way they do.

9. *How effective is the essay? Is the writer convincing about his or her position?*

Goldberg's essay is effective because it serves her purpose very well. She raises her readers' awareness of the value of names and demonstrates why it is so important to give things their names in order to understand our world and to write effectively about it. Her argument about being specific is convincing — after reading the essay, it's difficult to look at a flower and not wonder, at least, whether it's a tulip, poppy, daffodil, rose, or something else. Goldberg offers practical advice on how each of us can get started learning the names of things, be they the names of the other people in our class or the names of the plants, trees, and flowers on our campus.

6. Complete the "Language in Action" Activity to Discover the Far-Reaching Connections between the Selection and Language in the Real World

The "Language in Action" activities that accompany each selection in *Language Awareness* give you an opportunity to work with real world examples of language issues or concepts discussed in the selections, with exercises, cartoons, advertisements, photographs, poems, movie reviews, parodies, essay excerpts, syndicated columns, letters to the editor and more. Designed to be completed either in class or at home in about fifteen to twenty minutes, these activities invite you to take a hands-on approach to what you're learning from the essays and give you a chance to demonstrate your growing language aptitude. Consider the following activity that accompanied the Goldberg essay:

LANGUAGE IN ACTION

A useful exercise in learning to be more specific in our writing is to see the words we use for people, places, things, and ideas as being positioned somewhere on what might be called a "ladder of abstraction." In the following chart, notice how the words progress from more general to more specific.

More General	General	Specific	More Specific
Organism	Plant	Flower	Iris
Vehicle	Car	Chevrolet	1958 Chevrolet Impala

Using the examples above as models, try to fill in the missing parts of the following ladder of abstraction:

More General	General	Specific	More Specific
Writing instrument	_____	Fountain pen	Waterman fountain pen
_____	Sandwich	Corned beef sandwich	Reuben
Fruit	Dessert	Pie	_____
American	_____	Navaho	Laguna Pueblo

	Reference book	Dictionary	_____
_____			
School	_____	Technical high school	_____
Medicine	Oral medicine	Gel capsule	_____

After filling in the blanks yourself, compare your answers with those of your classmates. Now compare them to those provided by one of our students and discuss the variety of possible answers:

Line 1: Pen

Line 2: Lunch food

Line 3: Blueberry pie

Line 4: Native American

Line 5: Book, *American Heritage Dictionary of the English Language*

Line 6: High school, Essex Junction Technical Education Center

Line 7: Tylenol Gel Caps

PRACTICE READING, ANNOTATING, AND ANALYZING

Before you read the following essay, think about its title, the biographical and rhetorical information in the headnote, and the journal prompt. Make some marginal notes of your expectations for the essay, and write out a response to the journal prompt. Then, as you read the essay itself for the first time, try not to stop; take it all in as if in one breath. The second time, however, pause to annotate key points in the text, using the marginal rules we have provided alongside each paragraph. As you read, remember the nine basic questions we listed earlier on page 10.

What's in a Name?

Title: _____
_____
_____

HENRY LOUIS GATES JR.

The preeminent African American scholar of our time, Henry Louis Gates Jr. is the Alphonse Fletcher University Professor and director of the W. E. B. Du Bois Institute for African and African American Research at Harvard University. Among his impressive list of publications are *Figures in Black: Words, Signs and the "Racial" Self* (1987), *The Signifying Monkey: A Theory of Afro-American Literary Criticism* (1988), *Loose Canons: Notes on Culture Wars* (1992), *The Future of the Race* (1997), and *Thirteen Ways*

Biographical note: _____
_____
_____
_____
_____

of Looking at a Black Man (1999). His most recent books are *Mr. Jefferson and Miss Wheatley* (2003) and *Finding Oprah's Roots: Finding Your Own* (2007). In 2011, Gates published *Life Upon These Shores: Looking at African American History*. His *Colored People: A Memoir* (1994) recollects in a wonderful prose style his youth growing up in Piedmont, West Virginia, and his emerging sexual and racial awareness. Gates first enrolled at Potomac State College and later transferred to Yale, where he studied history. With the assistance of an Andrew W. Mellon Foundation Fellowship and a Ford Foundation Fellowship, he pursued advanced degrees in English at Clare College at the University of Cambridge. He has been honored with a MacArthur Foundation Fellowship, inclusion on *Time* magazine's "25 Most Influential Americans" list, a National Humanities Medal, and election to the American Academy of Arts and Letters.

Publication information: _____

In "What's in a Name?," excerpted from a longer article published in the fall 1989 issue of *Dissent* magazine, Gates tells the story of an early encounter with the language of prejudice. In learning how one of the "bynames" used by white people to define African Americans robs them of their identity, he feels the sting of racism firsthand. Notice how Gates's use of dialogue gives immediacy and poignancy to his narration.

Rhetorical highlight: ____

WRITING TO DISCOVER: *Reflect on racially charged language you have heard. For example, has anyone ever used a racial or ethnic epithet to refer to you? When did you first become aware that such terms existed? How do you feel about being characterized or defined by your race or ethnicity? If you yourself have ever used such terms, what was your intent in using them? What was the response of others?*

Journal prompt: _____

The question of color takes up much space in these pages, but the question of color, especially in this country, operates to hide the graver questions of the self.

— JAMES BALDWIN, 1961

*Epigraphs:*____

...blood, darky, Tar Baby, Kaffir, shine...moor, blacka-moor, Jim Crow, spooks....quadroon, meriney, red bone, high yellow...Mammy, porch monkey, home, homeboy, George spearchucker, schwarze, Leroy, Smokey...mouli, buck, Ethiopian, brother, sistah...

— TREY ELLIS, 1989

I had forgotten the incident completely, until I read Trey Ellis's essay, "Remember My Name," in a recent issue of the *Village Voice*[1] (June 13, 1989). But there, in the middle of an extended italicized list of the bynames of "the race" ("the race" or "our people" being the terms my parents used in polite or reverential discourse, "jigaboo" or "nigger" more commonly used in anger, jest, or pure disgust), it was: "George." Now the events of that very brief exchange return to mind so vividly that I wonder why I had forgotten it.

My father and I were walking home at dusk from his second job. He "moonlighted" as a janitor in the evenings for the telephone company. Every day but Saturday, he would come home at 3:30 from his regular job at the paper mill, wash up, eat supper, then at 4:30 head downtown to his second job. He used to make jokes frequently about a union official who moonlighted. I never got the joke, but he and his friends thought it was hilarious. All I knew was that my family always ate well, that my brother and I had new clothes to wear, and that all of the white people in Piedmont, West Virginia, treated my parents with an odd mixture of resentment and respect that even we understood at the time had something directly to do with a small but certain measure of financial security.

He had left a little early that evening because I was with him and I had to be in bed early. I could not have been more than five or six, and we had stopped off at the Cut-Rate Drug Store (where no black person in town but my father could sit down to eat, and eat off real plates with real silverware) so that I could buy some caramel ice cream, two scoops in a wafer cone, please, which I was busy licking when Mr. Wilson walked by.

Mr. Wilson was a very quiet man, whose stony, brooding, silent manner seemed designed to scare off any overtures of friendship, even from white people. He was Irish, as was one-third of our village (another third being Italian), the more affluent among whom sent their children to "Catholic School" across the bridge in Maryland. He had white straight hair, like my Uncle Joe, whom he uncannily resembled, and he carried a black worn metal lunch pail, the kind that Riley[2] carried on the television show. My father always spoke to him, and for reasons that we never did understand, he always spoke to my father.

Para. 1._____

Para. 2._____

Para. 3._____

Para. 4._____

---

1. *Village Voice:* a nationally distributed weekly newspaper published in New York City.
2. A character on the U.S. television show *The Life of Riley,* a blue-collar, ethnic sitcom popular in the 1950s.

"Hello, Mr. Wilson," I heard my father say.   Para. 5–8
"Hello, George."
I stopped licking my ice cream cone, and asked my Dad
in a loud voice why Mr. Wilson had called him "George."
"Doesn't he know your name, Daddy? Why don't you
tell him your name? Your name isn't George."
For a moment I tried to think of who Mr. Wilson was
mixing Pop up with. But we didn't have any Georges among
the colored people in Piedmont; nor were there colored
Georges living in the neighboring towns and working at the
mill.
"Tell him your name, Daddy."   Para. 10–14
"He knows my name, boy," my father said after a long
pause. "He calls all colored people George."
A long silence ensued. It was "one of those things," as
my Mom would put it. Even then, that early, I knew when
I was in the presence of "one of those things," one of those
things that provided a glimpse, through a rent[3] curtain, at
another world that we could not affect but that affected us.
There would be a painful moment of silence, and you would
wait for it to give way to a discussion of a black superstar such
as Sugar Ray[4] or Jackie Robinson.[5]
"Nobody hits better in a clutch than Jackie Robinson."
"That's right. Nobody."
I never again looked Mr. Wilson in the eye.   Para. 15. ____

Once you have read and reread Gates's essay and annotated the text,
write out answers to the six Thinking Critically about the Reading questions as well as the Language in Action activity found below. Then compare your answers with those of the other students in class.

THINKING CRITICALLY ABOUT THE READING

1. In the epigraph to this essay, Gates presents two quotations, one by James
    Baldwin. What do you think Baldwin meant when he wrote, "The question
    of color, especially in this country [America], operates to hide the graver
    questions of self"? How does this statement relate to the theme of Gates's
    essay?

---

3. torn.
4. Walker Smith Jr. (1921–1989), American professional boxer and six-time world
champion.
5. (1919–1972): The first black baseball player in the National League.

2. In his opening paragraph, Gates refers to the other quotation in the epigraph—a list of bynames used to refer to African Americans that appeared in an article by Trey Ellis—and states that his reading of this article triggered a childhood memory for him. How did you first feel after reading Ellis's list of bynames for African Americans? What did you find offensive about these racial slurs? Explain.

3. Later in his opening paragraph Gates reveals that "'the race' or 'our people' [were] the terms my parents used in polite or reverential discourse, 'jigaboo' or 'nigger' more commonly used in anger, jest, or pure disgust." Why does Gates make so much of Mr. Wilson's use of "George" when his own parents used words so much more obviously offensive? What do you see as the essential difference between white people using Trey Ellis's list of terms to refer to people of color and African Americans using the same terms to refer to themselves? Explain.

4. Gates describes Mr. Wilson and provides some background information about him in paragraph 4. What do you think is Gates's purpose in providing this information? (Glossary: *Description*)

5. Explain what happens in paragraph 12. What is "one of those things," as Gates's mother put it? In what ways is "one of those things" really Gates's purpose in telling his story? Why does Gates say, "I never again looked Mr. Wilson in the eye" (15)?

6. In paragraphs 5 and 6, Gates uses dialogue to capture the key exchange between his father and Mr. Wilson. What does this dialogue add to his narration? (Glossary: *Narration*) What would have been lost if Gates had simply described the conversation between the two men?

LANGUAGE IN ACTION

Comment on the importance of one's name as revealed in the following Ann Landers column. Ann Landers is the pen name created for advice columnist Ruth Crowley in 1943 and later used by Eppie Lederer for her "Ask Ann Landers" syndicated lifestyle advice column that was featured in newspapers across the country from 1955 to 2002. Though fictional, Ann Landers became an institution and cultural icon for the era.

Refusal to Use Name Is the Ultimate Insult

DEAR ANN LANDERS: Boy, when you're wrong, you're really wrong. Apparently, you have never been the victim of a hostile, nasty, passive-aggressive person who refuses to address you by name. Well, I have.

My husband's mother has never called me by my name in the 21 years I've been married to her son. Nor has she ever said "please" or "thank you," unless someone else is within hearing distance. My husband's children by his first wife are the same way. The people they care about are always referred to by name, but the rest of us are not called anything.

> If you still think this is a "psychological glitch," as you said in a recent column, try speaking to someone across the room without addressing that person by name. To be nameless and talked at is the ultimate put-down, and I wish you had said so. — "Hey You" in Florida
>
> **DEAR FLORIDA:** Sorry I let you down. Your mother-in-law's refusal to call you by name is, I am sure, rooted in hostility. Many years ago, Dr. Will Menninger said, "The sweetest sound in any language is the sound of your own name." It can also be a valuable sales tool. My former husband, one of the world's best salesmen, said if you want to make a sale, get the customer's name, use it when you make your pitch, and he will be half sold. His own record as a salesman proved him right.

What is the meaning of Dr. Will Menninger's statement: "The sweetest sound in any language is the sound of your own name"?

READING AS A WRITER

Reading and writing are the two sides of the same coin: Active critical reading is a means to help you become a better writer. By reading we can begin to see how other writers have communicated their experiences, ideas, thoughts, and feelings in their writing. We can study how they have used the various elements of the essay — thesis, unity, organization, beginnings and endings, paragraphs, transitions, effective sentences, word choice, tone, and figurative language — to say what they wanted to say. By studying the style, technique, and rhetorical strategies of other writers, we learn how we might effectively do the same. The more we read and write, the more we begin to read as writers and, in turn, to write knowing what readers expect.

What does it mean to read as a writer? Most of us have not been taught to read with a writer's eye, to ask why we like one piece of writing and not another. Likewise, most of us do not ask ourselves why one piece of writing is more believable or convincing than another. When you learn to read with a writer's eye, you begin to answer these important questions and, in the process, come to appreciate what is involved in selecting and focusing a subject as well as the craftsmanship involved in writing — how a writer selects descriptive details, uses an unobtrusive organizational pattern, opts for fresh and lively language, chooses representative and persuasive examples, and emphasizes important points with sentence variety.

On one level, reading stimulates your thinking by providing you with subjects to write about. After reading Amy Tan's essay "Mother Tongue," Helen Keller's "The Day Language Came into My Life," or Malcolm X's "Coming to an Awareness of Language," you might, for example, be inspired to write about a powerful language experience you have had and how that experience, in retrospect, was a "turning point" in your life.

On a second level, reading provides you with information, ideas, and perspectives for developing your own paper. In this way, you respond to what you read, using material from what you've read in an essay. For example, after reading Richard Lederer's essay on regional language differences in America, you might want to elaborate on what he has written, drawing on your own experiences and either agreeing with his examples or generating better ones for the area of the country in which you were raised. You could also qualify his argument for the preservation of these language differences or take issue with it. The three mini-debates in Chapter 13, "Current Language Controversies," offer you the opportunity to read extensively about focused topics — "How Does Technology Impact Communication in Relationships?," "How Does Language Work in Advertising?, and "Why Do We Lie?" — and to use the information and opinions expressed in these essays as resources for your own thesis-driven paper.

On a third level, active reading can increase your awareness of how others' writing affects you, thus making you more sensitive to how your own writing will affect your readers. For example, if you have been impressed by an author who uses convincing evidence to support each of her claims, you might be more likely to back up your own claims carefully. If you have been impressed by an apt turn of phrase or absorbed by a writer's new idea, you may be less inclined to feed your readers dull, worn out, and trite phrases. More to the point, however, the active reading that you will be encouraged to do in *Language Awareness* will help you to recognize and analyze the essential elements of the essay. When you see, for example, how a writer like Susanne K. Langer uses a strong thesis statement, about how language separates humans from the rest of the animal kingdom, to control the parts of her essay, you can better appreciate the importance of having a clear thesis statement in your writing. When you see the way Bharati Mukherjee uses transitions to link key phrases with important ideas so that readers can recognize clearly how the parts of her essay are meant to flow together, you have a better idea of how to achieve such coherence in your own writing. And when you see the way Donna Woolfolk Cross uses a division and classification organizational plan to differentiate clearly the various categories of propaganda, you see a powerful way in which you too can organize an essay using this method of development.

Finally, another important reason to master the skills of critical reading is that you will be your own first reader and critic for everything you write. How well you are able to scrutinize your own drafts will powerfully affect how well you revise them, and revising well is crucial to writing well. Reading others' writing with a critical eye is a useful and important practice; the more you read, the more practice you will have in sharpening your skills. The more sensitive you become to the content and style decisions made by the writers in *Language Awareness,* the more skilled you will be at making similar decisions in your own writing.

2

WRITING IN COLLEGE AND BEYOND

Nothing is more important to your success in school and in the workplace than learning to write well. You've heard it so often you've probably become numb to the advice. Let's ask the big question, however. Why is writing well so important? The simple answer is that no activity develops your ability to think better than writing does. Writing allows you to develop your thoughts and to "see" and reflect critically on what you think: In that sense, writing also involves its twin sister, reading. Writing well often means organizing your thoughts into a compelling argument and engaging readers by using concise, specific language. Small wonder, then, that academic programs and employers in all fields are constantly looking for people who can read and write well. Simply put, the ability to read and write well is a strong indication of a good mind.

College is a practical training ground for learning to write and think well. Whenever you write in college, you are writing as a member of a community of scholars, teachers, and students. By questioning, researching, and writing in company with other members of the college community, you come both to understand college material and to demonstrate your knowledge of it. In college, with the help of instructors, you will write essays, analyses, term papers, reports, reviews of research, critiques, and summaries. What you learn now will be fundamental, not only to your education, but also to your later success, no matter what career you intend to pursue.

DEVELOPING AN EFFECTIVE WRITING PROCESS

Writers cannot rely on inspiration alone to produce effective writing. Good writers follow a writing *process*: They analyze their assignment, gather ideas, draft, revise, edit, and proofread. It is worth remembering, however, that the writing process is rarely as simple and straightforward as it might appear to be. Often the process is recursive, moving back and forth among different stages. Moreover, writing is

21

personal—no two people go about it exactly the same way. Still, it is possible to describe basic guidelines for developing a writing process, thereby allowing you to devise your own reliable method for undertaking a writing task.

1. Understand Your Assignment

Much of your college writing will be done in response to specific assignments from your instructors or research questions that you develop in consultation with your teachers. Your environmental studies professor, for example, may ask you to write a report on significant new research on carbon dioxide emissions and global warming; your American history professor may ask you to write an analysis of the long-term effects of Japanese Americans' internment during World War II. From the outset you need to understand precisely what your instructor is asking you to do. The keys to understanding assignments such as these are *subject* words (words that focus on content) and *direction* words (words that indicate your purpose for and method of development in writing). For example, consider what you are being asked to do in each of the following assignments:

> Tell about an experience you have had that dramatically revealed to you the importance of being accurate and precise in your use of language.

> Many languages are lost over time because speakers of those languages die. When a language is lost, the particular culture embodied in the language is also lost. Using an extinct language and culture as an example, explain how the language embodies a culture and exactly what is lost when a language becomes extinct.

> Advocates of the English-only movement want to see English adopted as our country's official language. Argue for or against the philosophy behind this movement.

In the first example above, the subject words are *experience* and *importance of being accurate and precise in your use of language*. The direction word is *tell*, which means that you must share the details of the experience so that your readers can appreciate them as if they were there, sharing the experience. The content words in the second example are *languages, culture*, and *extinct language and culture*. The direction word is *explain*. In the third example, the content words are *English-only movement* and *our country's official language*. The direction word is *argue*. In each case the subject words limit and focus the content, and the direction words dictate how you will approach this content in writing.

The words *tell, explain,* and *argue* are only a few of the direction words that are commonly found in academic writing assignments. The following list of additional direction words and their meanings will help you better understand your writing assignments and what is expected of you.

Direction Words

Analyze: take apart and examine closely

Categorize: place into meaningful groups

Compare: look for differences, stress similarities

Contrast: look for similarities, stress differences

Critique: point out positive and negative features

Define: provide the meaning for a term or concept

Describe: give detailed sensory perceptions for a person, a place, or an event

Evaluate: judge according to some established standard

Identify: recognize or single out

Illustrate: show through examples

Interpret: explain the meaning of a document, an action, an event, or a behavior

Prove: demonstrate truth by logic, fact, or example

Synthesize: bring together or make meaningful connections among elements

---

After reading an assignment several times, check with your instructor if you are still unsure about what is being asked of you. He or she will be glad to clear up any possible confusion before you start writing. Be sure, as well, that you understand any additional requirements of the assignment, such as length or format.

2. Find a Subject and Topic

Although your instructor will sometimes give you specific writing assignments, you will often be asked to choose your own subject and topic. In a course in which you are using *Language Awareness,* you would in this case first select a broad subject within the area of language studies that you think you may enjoy writing about, such as professional jargon, dialects, political speeches, advertising language, or propaganda. A language issue that you have experienced firsthand (discrimination, for example) or something you've read may bring other subjects to mind. In the student essay that concludes this chapter, Rebekah Sandlin revisits her own racial prejudices as an elementary school student and what she has learned from them. You might also consider a language-related issue that involves your career ambitions, such as the areas of business (avoiding exaggerated advertising claims), law (eliminating obscure legal language), nursing (communicating effectively with patients), or journalism (reporting the news objectively). Another option is to list some subjects you enjoy discussing with friends and that you can approach from a language perspective: music (gender bias in rap lyrics), work (decoding insurance policies and medical benefits), and college life (speech codes on campus).

Next, try to narrow your general subject until you arrive at a topic that you think will be both interesting to your readers and appropriate for the length of your paper (and the time you have to write it). The following chart shows how the general areas of jargon, journalism, and television commercials might be narrowed to a specific essay topic. (If you're having trouble coming up with general subjects or specific topics, try some of the discovery techniques discussed in Step 3 (pp. 27–30).

General Subject Area	Narrowed Topic	Specific Essay Topic
Jargon	Medical jargon	Medical jargon used between doctors and terminally ill patients
Journalism	Slanted language in newswriting	Slanted language in newspapers' coverage of international events
Television commercials	Hidden messages in television commercials	Hidden messages in television commercials on children's Saturday morning programs

USE THE WRITING SUGGESTIONS IN *LANGUAGE AWARENESS*. As far as writing about the subjects and topics discussed in *Language Awareness* is concerned, there is no shortage of ideas and approaches at your disposal. There are at least two Writing Suggestions at the end of every selection in the book. If you have the freedom to choose your own subject and topic, and the approach you take, you may want to use one of the suggestions as a springboard for your own creativity. If, on the other hand, you are assigned a Writing Suggestion, be sure you understand what is being asked of you. If you are unclear about the assignment or you want to widen or narrow its focus or change its intent in any way, be sure to do so in consultation with your instructor. You can and should be creative in using even an assigned suggestion, maybe even using it as a starting point for your own research and thesis, but again get your instructor's approval before starting your paper so no misunderstandings result.

DETERMINE YOUR PURPOSE. All effective writing springs from a clear purpose. Most good writing seeks specifically to accomplish any one of the following three purposes:

- To express thoughts and feelings about life experiences
- To inform readers by explaining something about the world around them
- To persuade readers to adopt some belief or take some action

In *expressive writing*, or writing from experience, you put your thoughts and feelings before all other concerns. When Malcolm X shows his frustration at not having appropriate language to express himself (Chapter 4) and when Amy Tan describes how her mother's use of English shaped her own approach to writing (Chapter 6), each one is writing from experience. In each case, the writer has clarified an important life experience and has conveyed what he or she learned from it.

Informative writing focuses on telling the reader something about the outside world. In informative writing, you report, explain, analyze, define, classify, compare, describe a process, or examine causes and effects. When Paul Roberts explains the formation of speech communities (Chapter 6), he is writing to inform.

Argumentative writing seeks to influence readers' thinking and attitudes toward a subject and, in some cases, to move them to a particular course of action. Such persuasive writing uses logical reasoning, authoritative evidence, and testimony, and it sometimes includes emotionally charged language and examples. In writing their arguments, Greg Lukianoff (Chapter 10) uses logical reasoning, evidence, and examples to make the case that hate speech serves a constructive purpose and Kiera Butler (Chapter 13) uses current examples from actual menus to show how restaurants manipulate customers' impressions.

KNOW YOUR AUDIENCE.   The best writers always keep their audience in mind. Once they have decided on a topic and a purpose, writers present their material in a way that empathizes with their readers, addresses their difficulties and concerns, and appeals to their rational and emotional faculties. Based on knowledge of their audience, writers make conscious decisions on content, sentence structure, and word choice.

Writing for an Academic Audience   Academic writing most often employs the conventions of formal standard English, or the language of educated professionals. Rather than being heavy or stuffy, good academic writing is lively and engaging and holds the reader's attention by presenting interesting ideas supported with relevant facts, statistics, and detailed information. Informal writing, usually freer and simpler in form, is typically used in notes, journal entries, e-mail, text messages, instant messaging, and the like.

In order not to lessen the importance of your ideas and your credibility, be sure that informal writing does not carry over into your academic writing. Always keeping your audience and purpose in mind will help you achieve an appropriate style.

When you write, your audience might be an individual (your instructor), a group (the students in your class), a specialized group (art history majors), or a general readership (readers of your student newspaper). To help identify your audience, ask yourself the questions posed on page 27.

Using Discipline-Specific Language   The point of discipline-specific language, sometimes referred to as professional language or even jargon, is not to make a speaker or writer sound like a scientist, or a humanities scholar, or a geologist. Rather, discipline-specific language provides a kind of "shorthand" means of expressing complex concepts. Its proper use will grow from your knowledge of the discipline, from the reading you have done in the field, and from the hours you have spent in the company of your teachers and peers.

While the meaning of some disciplinary language will become clear to you from context as you read and discuss course material, some of it, left undefined, will present a stumbling block to your understanding of the material. Glossaries of disciplinary terms exist for most disciplines: Make use of them. Also, never be shy about asking your instructor or more experienced classmates for help when you're unsure of the meaning of a term.

Considering Opposing Arguments   You will likely not have trouble convincing those who agree with your argument from the outset, but what about those who are skeptical or think differently from you? You need to discover who these people are by talking with them or by reading what they have written. Do your research, be reasonable, and find common ground where possible, but take issue where you must. To refute an opposing argument, you can present evidence showing that the opposition's data or evidence is incomplete or distorted, that its reasoning is faulty, or that its conclusions do not fit the evidence.

Formal versus Informal Writing

Formal Writing	*Informal Writing*
Uses standard English, the language of public discourse typical of newspapers, magazines, books, and speeches	Uses nonstandard English, slang, colloquial expressions (*anyways, dude, freaked out*), and shorthand (*OMG, IMHO, GR8*)
Uses mostly third person	Uses first and second person most often

Avoids most abbreviations (*Professor, brothers, miles per gallon, Internet, digital video recorder*)	Uses abbreviations and acronyms (*Prof., bros., mpg, Net, DVR*)
Uses an impersonal tone (*The speaker took questions from the audience at the end of her lecture.*)	Uses an informal tone (*It was great the way she answered questions at the end of her talk.*)
Uses longer, more complex sentences	Uses shorter, simpler sentences
Adheres to the rules and conventions of proper grammar	Takes a casual approach to the rules and conventions of proper grammar

Questions about Audience

- Who are my readers? Are they a specialized or a general group?
- What do I know about my audience's age, gender, education, religious affiliation, economic status, and political views?
- What does my audience know about my subject? Are they experts or novices?
- What does my audience need to know about my topic in order to understand my discussion of it?
- Will my audience be interested, open-minded, resistant, or hostile to what I have to say?
- Do I need to explain any specialized language so that my audience can understand my subject? Is there any language that I should avoid?
- What do I want my audience to do as a result of reading my essay?

3. Gather Ideas

Ideas and information (facts and details) lie at the heart of good prose. Ideas grow out of information; information supports ideas. Before you begin to draft, gather as many ideas as possible and as much information as you can about your topic in order to inform and stimulate your readers intellectually.

Most writers use one or more discovery techniques to help them gather information, zero-in on a specific topic, or find connections among ideas. In addition to your reading and discussing writing ideas with your classmates and friends, you may want to experiment with some of the discovery techniques explained below.

KEEPING A JOURNAL.   Many writers use a journal to record thoughts and observations that might be mined for future writing projects. They have learned not to rely on their memories to retain ideas, facts, and statistics they have heard or read about. Writers also use journals to keep all kinds of lists: lists of questions they would like answers to; lists of issues that concern them; lists of topics they would like to write about someday.

To aid your journal writing as you use this text, each reading selection in *Language Awareness* begins with a journal prompt called "Writing to Discover." The purpose of each prompt is to get you thinking and writing about your own experiences with the language issues discussed in the selection before you start reading. You thus have the opportunity to discover what you already know about a particular topic and to explore your observations, feelings, and opinions about it. The writing you do at this point is something you can always return to after reading each piece.

FREEWRITING.   Journals are also useful if you want to freewrite. *Freewriting* is simply writing for a brief uninterrupted period of time—say, ten or fifteen minutes—on anything that comes to your mind. It is a way to get your mind working and to ease into a writing task. Start with a blank sheet of paper or computer screen and write about the general subject you are considering. Write as quickly as you can, don't stop for any reason, and don't worry about punctuation, grammar, or spelling. Write as though you were talking to your best friend, and let your writing take you in any direction. If you run out of ideas, don't stop; just repeat the last few things you wrote over and over again, and you'll be surprised—more ideas will begin to emerge. Just as regular exercise gets you in shape, regular freewriting will help you feel more natural and comfortable when writing.

OPEN-ENDED WRITING.   A useful extension of freewriting is a discovery strategy called open-ended writing. Follow the same directions for freewriting but also stop every ten minutes or so to evaluate what you have written. Analyze your freewriting and identify ideas, issues, expressions, phrases, and terms that show relationships and themes, and that may also engender questions about your material. Copy only those related elements onto a new sheet of paper and begin freewriting again. By repeating the process at least several times, following your freewrites with analysis each time, you will inevitably deepen your thinking about your topic and get closer to being able to write your first draft.

BRAINSTORMING. Another good way to generate ideas and information about a topic is to *brainstorm*—to list everything you know about a topic, freely associating one idea with another. Don't worry about order or level of importance. Try to capture everything that comes to mind because you never know what might prove valuable later on. Write quickly, but if you get stalled, reread what you have written; doing so will help you move in new directions. Keep your list handy so that you can add to it over the course of several days. Here, for example, is a student's brainstorming list on why Martin Luther King Jr.'s speech, "I Have a Dream," has endured:

> *Why "I Have a Dream" Is Memorable*
>
> *civil rights demonstration in Washington, D.C., delivered on steps of Lincoln Memorial*
>
> *repetition of "I have a dream"*
>
> *references to the Bible, spirituals*
>
> *"bad check" metaphor*
>
> *other memorable figures of speech*
>
> *200,000 people*
>
> *reminds me of other great American documents and speeches — Declaration of Independence and Gettysburg Address*
>
> *refers to various parts of the country*
>
> *embraces all races and religions*
>
> *sermon format*
>
> *displays energy and passion*

ASKING QUESTIONS. *Asking questions* about a particular topic or experience may help you generate information before you start to write. If you are writing about a personal experience, for example, asking questions may refresh your memory about the details and circumstances of the incident or help you discover why the experience is still so memorable. The newspaper reporter's five Ws and an H — Who? What? Where? When? Why? and How? — are excellent questions to start with. One student, for example, developed the following questions to help her explore an experience of verbal abuse:

> *1. Who was involved in the abusive situation?*
>
> *2. What specific language was used?*
>
> *3. Where did the abuse most often take place?*
>
> *4. When did the verbal abuse first occur?*
>
> *5. Why did the abusive situation get started? Why did it continue?*
>
> *6. How did I feel about the abuse as it was happening? How do I feel about it now?*

As the student jotted down answers to these questions, other questions came to mind, such as, *What did I try to do after the verbal abuse occurred? Did I seek help from anyone else? How can I help others who are being verbally abused?* Before long, the student had recalled enough information for a rough draft about her experience.

CLUSTERING. Another strategy for generating ideas and gathering information is *clustering*. Put your topic, or a key word or phrase about your topic, in the center of a sheet of paper and draw a circle around it. (The student example below shows the topic "Hospital jargon at summer job" in the center.) Draw three or more lines out from this circle, and jot down main ideas about your topic, drawing a circle around each one. Repeat the process by drawing lines from the main-idea circles and adding examples, details, or questions you have. You may wind up pursuing one line of thought through many add-on circles before beginning a new cluster.

One advantage of clustering is that it allows you to sort your ideas and information into meaningful groups right from the start. As you carefully sort your ideas and information, you may begin to see an organizational plan for your writing. In the following example, the student's clustering is based on the experiences he had while working one summer in a hospital emergency room. Does the clustering provide any clues to how he might organize his essay?

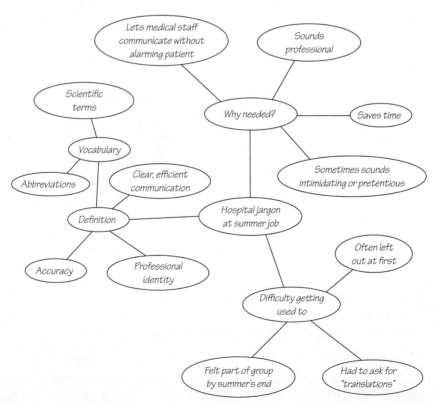

4. Formulate a Thesis

The thesis of an essay is its main idea, the major point the writer is trying to make. A thesis should be

- The most important point you make about your topic
- More general than the ideas and facts used to support it
- Focused enough to be covered in the space allotted for the essay

The thesis is often expressed in one or two sentences called a *thesis statement*. Here's an example of a thesis statement about television news programs:

> The so-called serious news programs are becoming too like tabloid news shows in both their content and their presentation.

A thesis statement should not be a question but rather an assertion. If you find yourself writing a question for a thesis statement, answer the question first—this answer will be your thesis statement.

An effective strategy for developing a thesis statement is to begin by writing, "What I want to say is that . . ."

> *What I want to say is that* unless language barriers between patients and health care providers are bridged, many patients' lives in our most culturally diverse cities will be endangered.

Later you can delete the formulaic opening, and you will be left with a thesis statement.

To determine whether your thesis is too general or too specific, think hard about how easy it will be to present data—that is, facts, statistics, names, examples or illustrations, and opinions of authorities—to support it. If you stray too far in either direction, your task will become much more difficult. A thesis statement that is too general will leave you overwhelmed by the number of issues you must address. For example, the statement "Political attack speeches damage the American political system" would lead to the question "How?" To answer it, you would probably have to include information about national politics, free speech, libel, character assassination, abusive language, the fallacy of ad hominem arguments, and so on. To cover all of this in the time and space you have for a typical college paper would mean taking shortcuts, and your paper would be ineffective. On the other hand, too specific a thesis statement would leave you with too little information to present. "Governor Wright's speech implies that Senator Smith's personal life is a disgrace" does not leave you with any opportunity to develop an argument. An appropriate thesis statement like "Political attack speeches have harmed politicians' images and turned off voters in Big City's mayoral elections over the past decade" leaves room for argument but can still be proven by examining poll responses, voter turnout records, and other evidence.

The thesis statement is usually presented near the beginning of the essay. One common practice in shorter college papers is to position the thesis statement as the final sentence of the first paragraph.

Is Your Thesis Solid?

Once you have a possible thesis statement in mind, ask yourself the following questions:

- Does my thesis statement take a clear position on an issue? (Could I imagine someone agreeing or disagreeing with it? If not, it might be a statement of fact, instead of an arguable thesis.)
- Will I be able to find evidence that supports my position? Where? What kinds? (If you're unsure, it wouldn't hurt to take a look at a few secondary sources at this point.)
- Will I be able to make my claim and present sufficient evidence to support it in a paper of the assigned length, and by the due date? (If not, you might need to scale back your claim to something more manageable.)

---

5. Support Your Thesis with Evidence

The types of evidence you use in your academic writing will be determined to some extent by the discipline in which you are working. For example, for a research project in psychology on the prejudice shown toward people with unusual names, you will almost certainly rely heavily on published studies from peer-reviewed journals. Depending on the assignment, however, you might also devise an experiment of your own or interview people with unusual names to gather firsthand accounts of their experiences. For an argument essay on the same topic in a composition course, as in many courses in the humanities, languages, and literatures, you would cite a wide range of sources, perhaps including—but not limited to—peer-reviewed journals. Depending on the assignment, you might also include your own experience and informal observations.

To support her argument on book banning, one student derives most of her evidence from an array of experts, as in the following example, where she cites scholar Henry Reichman:

> Henry Reichman writes that in 1990, Frank Mosca's *All-American Boys* (1983) and Nancy Garden's *Annie on My Mind* (1982), two books with gay themes, were donated to high schools in Contra Costa, California; at three of these high schools, the books were seized by administrators and then "lost" (53).

PRIMARY AND SECONDARY SOURCES. In general, researchers and writers work with two types of evidence: primary sources and secondary sources.

Primary sources in the humanities and languages/literatures are works that grow out of and are close to a time, place, or culture under study. These can include documents such as letters, speeches, interviews, manuscripts, diaries, treaties, maps; creative written works such as novels, plays, poems, songs, and autobiographies; and three-dimensional artifacts such as paintings, sculptures, pottery, weaving, buildings, tools, and furniture. Primary sources in the social, natural, and applied sciences are the factual reports and descriptions of discoveries, experiments, surveys, and clinical trials.

Secondary sources in the humanities and languages/literatures restate, analyze, and interpret primary sources. Common secondary sources include analyses, critiques, histories, and commentaries in the form of books, articles, encyclopedia entries, and documentaries. Secondary sources in the sciences analyze and interpret discoveries and experiments and often comment on the validity of the research models and methods and the value of those discoveries and experiments.

Writing in a specific discipline requires that you use the most authoritative and reliable source materials available for that discipline. Your instructors can help you in this regard by either providing you with a list of resources commonly used in their fields or directing you to such a list in your library or on the Internet. Many academic libraries include helpful subject study guides on their home pages as well.

For a brief guide to finding, evaluating, and documenting sources in print and online, see pages 582–584.

FACTS, STATISTICS, EXAMPLES, AND EXPERT TESTIMONY. The evidence you use in your academic writing should place a high value on facts and statistics, examples and illustrations, and the testimony of experts. You must be accurate in your use of facts and statistics, and you must check and double-check that you have cited them correctly. Be sure that you carefully consider the examples and illustrations you use to support your thesis: Use those that work best with your subject and the audience you have in mind. Finally, be selective in citing the works and comments of experts in your discipline. If you choose wisely, the works of respected scholars and experts will be immediately recognizable to others familiar with the subject area, and your argument will have a much better chance of succeeding.

The following passage illustrates how student Jake Jamieson uses examples in his paper on the Official English movement:

> Ed Morales, the author of *Living in Spanglish*, reports that the mayor of Bogota, New Jersey, called for a boycott of McDonald's restaurants after the "company displayed a billboard advertising a new iced coffee drink in Spanish," calling "the ad . . . 'offensive' and 'divisive' because it sends a message that Hispanic immigrants do not need to learn English" (par. 2–3).

6. Determine Your Organization

There are several organizational patterns you might follow in drafting an essay. Most of you are already familiar with the most common one — *chronological order.* In this pattern, which is often used to narrate a story, explain a process, or relate a series of events, you start with the earliest event or step and move forward in time.

In a comparison-and-contrast essay, you might follow a *block* pattern or a *point-by-point* organization. In a block pattern, a writer provides all the information about one subject, followed by a block of comparable information about the other subject. In a point-by-point comparison, on the other hand, the writer starts by comparing both subjects in terms of a particular point, then compares both on a second point, and so on. In an essay comparing two dialects of American English, for example, you could follow the block pattern, covering all the characteristics of one dialect and then all the characteristics of the other. Alternatively, you could organize your material in terms of defining characteristics (for example, geographical range; characteristics of speakers; linguistic traits), filling in the details for each dialect in turn.

Other patterns of organization include moving from *the general to the specific,* from *smallest to largest,* from *least important to most important,* or from *the usual to the unusual.* In an essay about medical jargon, for instance, you might cover its general characteristics first and then move to specifics, or you might begin with what is most usual (or commonly known) about doctors' language and then discuss what is unusual about it. Whatever order you choose, keep in mind that what you present first and last will probably stay in the reader's mind the longest.

After you choose an organizational pattern, jot down the main ideas in your essay. In other words, make a scratch outline. As you add more information and ideas to your scratch outline, you may want to develop a formal, more detailed outline of your paper. In writing a formal outline, follow these rules:

1. Include the title of your essay, a statement of purpose, and the thesis statement.
2. Write in complete sentences unless your meaning is immediately clear from a phrase.
3. If you divide any category, make sure there are at least two subcategories. The reason for this is simple: You cannot divide something into fewer than two parts.
4. Observe the traditional conventions of formal outlining. Notice how each new level of specificity is given a new letter or number designation.

Title:
Purpose:
Thesis:
I.
   A.
   B.
      1.
      2.
         a.
         b.
         c.
II.

7. Write Your First Draft

Sometimes we are so eager to get on with the writing of a first draft that we begin before we are ready, and the results are disappointing. Before beginning to write, therefore, ask yourself, "Have I done enough prewriting? Is there a point to what I want to say?" If you have done a thorough job of gathering ideas and information, if you think you can accomplish the purpose of your paper, and if you are comfortable with your organizational plan, your answers will be "yes."

If, however, you feel uneasy, review the various prewriting steps to try to resolve the problem. Do you need to gather more information? Sharpen your thesis? Rethink your purpose? Refine your organization? Now is the time to think about these issues, to evaluate and clarify your writing plan. Time spent at this juncture is time well spent because it will not only improve your paper but will save you time and effort later on.

As you write, don't be discouraged if you do not find the most appropriate language for your ideas or if your ideas do not flow easily. Push ahead with the writing, realizing that you will be able to revise the material later, adding information and clarifications wherever necessary. Be sure to keep your audience in mind as you write, so that your diction and coverage stay at the appropriate level. Remember also to bridge all the logical and emotional leaps for your audience. Rereading what you have already written as you go along will help you to further develop your ideas and tie them together. Once completed, a first draft will give you a sense of accomplishment. You will see that you have something to work with, something to build on and improve during the revision process.

8. Revise

After you complete your first draft, you will need to revise it. During the revision stage of the writing process, you will focus on the large issues of thesis, purpose, evidence, organization, and paragraph structure to make sure that your writing says what you want it to say. First, though, it is crucial that you set your draft aside for a while. Then you can come back to it with a fresh eye and some objectivity. When you do, resist the temptation to plunge immediately into a second draft: Scattered changes will not necessarily improve the piece. Instead, try to look at your writing as a whole and to tackle your writing problems systematically. Use the following guidelines:

- Make revisions on a hard copy of your paper. (Triple-space your draft so that you can make changes more easily.)
- Read your paper aloud, listening for parts that do not make sense.
- Ask a fellow student to read your essay and critique it.

A Brief Guide to Peer Critiquing

When critiquing someone else's paper:

- Read the essay carefully. Read it to yourself first, and then, if possible, have the writer read it to you at the beginning of the session. Some flaws become obvious when read aloud.
- Ask the writer to state his or her purpose for writing and to identify the thesis statement within the paper itself.
- Be positive, but be honest. Never denigrate the paper's content or the writer's effort, but do your best to identify how the writer can improve the paper through revision.
- Try to address the most important issues first. Think about the thesis and the organization of the paper before moving on to more specific topics like word choice.
- Do not be dismissive, and do not dictate changes. Ask questions that encourage the writer to reconsider parts of the paper that you find confusing or ineffective.

When someone critiques your work:

- Give your reviewer a copy of your paper before your meeting.
- Listen carefully to your reviewer, and try not to discuss or argue each issue. Record comments, and evaluate them later.

- Do not get defensive or explain what you wanted to say if the reviewer misunderstands what you meant. Try to understand the reviewer's point of view, and learn what you need to revise to clear up the misunderstanding.
- Consider every suggestion, but only use the ones that make sense to you in your revision.
- Be sure to thank your reviewer for his or her effort on your behalf.

One way to begin the revision process is to compare the earlier outline of your first draft to an outline of how it actually came out. This will help you see, in abbreviated form, the organization and flow of the essential components of your essay and perhaps detect flaws in reasoning.

Another method you can use in revising is to start with large-scale issues, such as your overall structure, and then concentrate on finer and finer points. As you examine your essay, ask yourself about what you have written and address the large elements of your essay: thesis, purpose, organization, paragraphs, and evidence.

Revising the Large Elements of an Essay

- Is my topic specific enough?
- Does my thesis statement identify my topic and make an assertion about it?
- Is my essay organized the best way, given my purpose?
- Are my paragraphs adequately developed, and does each support my thesis?
- Have I accomplished my purpose?
- How effective is my beginning? My ending?
- Is my title effective?

Once you have addressed the major problems in your essay by writing a second draft, you should be ready to turn your attention to the finer elements of sentence structure, word choice, and usage.

Revising Sentence - Level Elements

- Do my sentences convey my thoughts clearly, and do they emphasize the most important parts of my thinking?
- Are my sentences stylistically varied?
- Is my choice of words fresh and forceful, or is my writing weighed down by clichés and unnecessary wordiness?
- Have I made any errors of usage?

Finally, if you find yourself dissatisfied with specific elements of your draft, look at several essays in *Language Awareness* to see how other writers have dealt with the particular situation you are confronting. For example, if you don't like the way the essay starts, find some beginnings you think are particularly effective; if your paragraphs don't seem to flow into one another, examine how various writers use transitions; if an example seems unconvincing, examine the way other writers include details, anecdotes, facts, and statistics to strengthen their illustrations. Remember that the readings in the text are there as a resource for you as you write.

9. Edit and Proofread

Now that you have revised in order to make your essay "right," it is time to think about making it "correct." During the editing stage of the writing process, check your writing for errors in grammar, punctuation, capitalization, spelling, and manuscript format. Both your dictionary and your college handbook will help you answer specific editing questions about your paper.

Addressing Common Editing Problems and Errors

- Do my verbs agree in number with their subjects?
- Do my pronouns have clear antecedents—that is, do they clearly refer to specific nouns earlier in my sentences?
- Do I have any sentence fragments, comma splices, or run-on sentences?
- Have I made any unnecessary shifts in person, tense, or number?
- Have I used the comma properly in all instances?
- Have I checked for misspellings, mistakes in capitalization, and typos?

- Have I inadvertently confused words like *their, they're,* and *there* or *it's* and *its?*
- Have I followed the prescribed guidelines for formatting my manuscript?

Having revised and edited your essay, you are ready to print your final copy. Be sure to proofread your work before submitting it to your instructor. Even though you may have used your computer's spell checker, you might find that you have typed *worm* instead of *word,* or *form* instead of *from.* Also check to see that your essay is properly line spaced and that the text is legible.

10. Sample Student Essay Using Writing Process

The following essay was written by Rebekah Sandlin while she was a student at Miami University in Oxford, Ohio. After Rebekah read the essays in the chapter on prejudice, stereotypes, and language, her instructor, Linda Parks, asked her to write about a personal experience with biased language and how that language affected her. Rebekah vividly remembered an experience she had in the third grade, when she used the phrase "just like a nigger" to mock a classmate. Using that experience as the starting point of her essay, she then traces a series of subsequent encounters she had with the word *nigger* and recounts her resulting personal growth. By the end of her essay, Rebekah makes it clear to her readers why she felt compelled to tell her story.

Sandlin 1

Rebekah Sandlin

English 111 sec. BD

October 23, 2015

Paper #3

The "Negro Revolt" in Me

She said "seven" when the answer was clearly "ten." We were in the third grade and had been studying multiplication for a few weeks. Our teacher, Mrs. Jones, reminded Monica that "we are multiplying now, not adding. Five times two will always be ten" I laughed at Monica. How did she not know the answer to five times two? We had been over it and practiced it so many times. My laughter encouraged the other kids in the

Brief introductory anecdote captures readers' attention.

Sandlin 2

class to join in with me. Within seconds the laughing had escalated into pointing fingers and calling her stupid. That's when "it" happened. That's when I said what I will always regret for the rest of my life. I said, "Just like a nigger."

Playing on her weaknesses in math, laughing at her, encouraging the rest of the class to point at her, and calling her the most degrading word in history still eats at my insides. The class stopped laughing. Monica cried. Mrs. Jones gasped and yanked me into the hallway where she scolded me for a good half an hour. That is how I learned that language could be used as a dangerous tool. That's when I learned about prejudice and its effects on people. That's how it happened. This is how it has affected my life.

> Writer introduces the main point (thesis) of the story (narrative) she's about to write.

Mrs. Jones sent me home with a note explaining my "behavior" in class. I remember being terribly afraid to give that note to my mom. I felt guilty, confused, and embarrassed, but I wasn't sure why I felt that way. No one had taken the time to explain to me why the word had such a negative connotation. No one told me that blacks were once treated terribly wrong or that they were used as slaves. No one told me about the interracial rapes that occurred on plantations or about the children being taken and sold to rich white landowners. No one told me about them being denied an education and proper shelter. No one told me. I was just a small white girl living in a predominately white city and going to a predominately white school. I knew nothing about diversity and equal rights for everyone. I knew nothing.

> Writer uses chronological organization.

My mom sat me down at the kitchen table and asked me how I could have said such a terrible thing. "Where did you learn that word?" she asked. She sounded furious and embarrassed. She kept asking me where I had heard the word and who taught it to me. Before I had a chance to respond she knew the answer. My dad was on the phone in

Sandlin 3

the next room talking to his father. He was laughing and he said, "just like a nigger." My mom lowered her head and whispered, "go to your room." I quietly got up and obeyed her command. I'm not sure what she said to him, but I could hear their mumbled fighting through the vents. I pressed my ear to the vent on the floor to try and make sense of my mother's cries. It was no use. Two hours later they came upstairs to give me one of their "you did something wrong" speeches. Except this speech was different from most. It began with an apology and an attempt to justify my father's words.

It started with a story. My dad grew up on a tobacco farm in southern Georgia. His family hired blacks to work out in the fields. "No," he reassured, "they weren't slaves. We paid them." His family was prejudiced toward blacks. Their language and actions rubbed off onto my dad. The only difference was that my dad learned that what he said and how he treated blacks was wrong. Through growing up and living in integrated working environments, he learned how "not to act" in the presence of a black person. However, when he talked to his father he still acted and talked like he was prejudiced. He said that he didn't understand why he did it other than he desperately wanted to be accepted by his own father. He admitted that he was wrong and told me that I was lucky because I was going to learn the "real way" to treat people. He promised to never use the word again as long as I promised to do the same thing. I agreed.

I was in the fifth grade the next time I heard the word used. Ironically, I was in a math class again. Except this time I didn't say it, someone else did. Unlike Monica, this girl didn't cry. Instead, she gave an evil glare. I was the one that stood up to say something in her defense. I yelled at Dan and told him that what he had said was rude and degrading. "How would you like it if someone called you honky?"

Powerful use of dialogue, especially her father speaking on the phone— show, don't tell.

Writer introduces her father's story within her own story.

"I was in the fifth grade" signals the passage of time and orients readers to new incident.

Sandlin 4

I screamed. He hauled off and hit me right in the arm! He called me a

"nigger-lover."

The teacher broke it up, and we were sent to the principal's office.

I was suspended for using vulgar language. I had used the word "honky."

Dan was given a warning and sent back to class. I had plenty of time to

think about what I had done wrong while I waited in the office for my

mom to come and pick me up. No matter how hard I tried, I couldn't see

what I had done wrong. That girl did not want to be called a nigger. I

was just trying to show him what it would feel like if someone had said

something like that to him. My mom did not agree with me. I learned

an important lesson that day. Using bad words to stop other bad words

is like using violence to stop violence — it doesn't work. My mom was

supportive and said that she respected what I was trying to do but next

time I should use better sense. I didn't want there to be a next time.

> Writer gives her narrative purpose by sharing what she learned about language and prejudice from her experiences.

THINKING CRITICALLY ABOUT THE STUDENT ESSAY

1. What is Sandlin's thesis? Why do you think she stated her thesis where she did?

2. How does Sandlin use stories to structure her essay? How does she balance narrative with analysis and reflection of the events she experienced?

3. Do you agree with Sandlin's assessment of the times when she used derogatory language? If not, why not?

4. How would you have ended this essay, if you were the one writing it?

WRITING WITH SOURCES

WHAT DOES IT MEAN TO WRITE WITH SOURCES?

Some of the writing you do in college will be experiential—that is, based on your personal experiences—but many of your college assignments will call upon you to do some research, to write with sources. While most of us have had some experience with basic research practices—locating and evaluating print and online sources, taking notes from those sources, and documenting those sources—we have not learned how to integrate these sources effectively and purposefully into our papers. (For more information on basic research and documentation practices, see Chapter 14, "A Brief Guide to Writing a Research Paper," pp. 577–609.) Your purpose in writing with sources is not to present a collection of quotations that show you can report what others have said about your topic. Your goal is to analyze, evaluate, and synthesize the materials you have researched so that you can take ownership of your topic. You learn how to view the results of research from your own perspective and arrive at an informed opinion of your topic. In short, you become a participant in a conversation with your sources about your topic.

To help you on your way, this chapter provides advice on (1) summarizing, paraphrasing, and quoting sources, (2) integrating summaries, paraphrases, and quotations into the text of your paper using signal phrases, and (3) avoiding plagiarism when writing with sources. In addition, one student paper models different ways of engaging meaningfully with outside sources and of reflecting that engagement in writing.

WRITE WITH SOURCES

Each time that you introduce an outside source into your paper, be sure that you are using that source in a purposeful way. Outside sources can be used to

- support your thesis and main points with statements from noted authorities,
- offer memorable wording of key terms or ideas,
- extend your ideas by introducing new information, and
- articulate opposing positions for you to argue against.

Consider Joseph P. Kahn's use of two outside sources in the following passage from his May 5, 2011, article in the *Boston Globe* entitled "What Does Friend Mean Now?":

> What we mean when we talk about friends and friendships these days has many of us baffled. Experts who track the changing meaning of language agree that our common reference points are becoming less fixed as the lines blur between the virtual and the real, the face-to-face and Facebooked. Between what may feel good to hear—or quantify, in the case of online connections—and what squares with the reality of interpersonal relationships. "The meanings of words derive from how we use them—and clearly as the world changes, we apply words in different ways," says Lera Boroditsky, a Stanford University psychology professor and language expert. Before online interaction became a routine part of daily life, she adds, "You saw friends in person or spoke to them on the phone. Today there's a real change in how we interact, and our language is struggling to keep up."
>
> MIT sociologist Sherry Turkle, who studies technology and its cultural impact, maintains that "friend" has become "contested terrain" linguistically as social media sites alter the term's very DNA. "It calls into question how many friends we have and what they are," says Turkle, author of *Alone Together: Why We Expect More from Technology and Less from Each Other*. "You can have 3,000 friends who look at your photos and what you've published, but only 100 who know about your heart." The challenge, she contends, is to avoid confusing virtual friendship with the real deal. "Friendship is about letting something happen between two people that's surprising and new," says Turkle, whereas social networking "gives the illusion of companionship without the demands of intimacy. It's friendship on demand, when I want it."

Here Kahn quotes two language authorities—Lera Boroditsky of Stanford University and Sherry Turkle of MIT—to support his main point that the meaning of *friends* and *friendships* "are becoming less fixed as the lines blur between the virtual and the real."

In the following passage from "Why the U.S. Needs an Official Language," Mauro E. Mujica uses outside sources to present the position that he will ultimately argue against.

> Historically, the need to speak and understand English has served as an important incentive for immigrants to learn the language and assimilate into the mainstream of American society. For the last 30 years, this idea has been turned on its head. Expecting immigrants to learn English has been called "racist." Marta Jimenez, an attorney for the Mexican American Legal Defense and Educational Fund, speaks of "the historical use of English in the United States as a tool of oppression."
>
> Groups such as the National Association for Bilingual Education complain about the "restrictive goal" of having immigrant children learn in English. The former mayor of Miami, Maurice Ferre, dismissed the idea of even a bilingual future for the city. "We're talking about Spanish

as a main form of communication, as an official language," he averred.
"Not on the way to English."

Perhaps this change is best illustrated in the evolving views of the
League of United Latin American Citizens (LULAC). Started in 1929,
the group was originally pro-English and pro-assimilation. One of the
founding aims and purposes of LULAC was "to foster the acquisition
and facile use of the Official Language of our country that we may
hereby equip ourselves and our families for the fullest enjoyment of our
rights and privileges and the efficient discharge of our duties and obli-
gations to this, our country." By the 1980s the executive director of
LULAC Arnoldo Torres, could proudly proclaim, "We cannot assimilate and we won't!"

By letting the opposition articulate their position themselves, Mujica
reduces the possibility of being criticized for misrepresenting his opponents while at the same time sets himself up to give strong voice to his
belief that the United States should declare English its official language.

Sometimes source material is too long and detailed to be quoted
directly in its entirety. In such cases, a writer will choose to summarize or
paraphrase the material in his or her own words before introducing it in
an essay. For example, notice how Janet Holmes summarizes two lengthy
reports about male-female discourse in the workplace for use in her essay
"Women Talk Too Much" that appeared in *Language Myths* in 1999.

Despite the widespread belief that women talk more than men, most
of the available evidence suggests just the opposite. When women and
men are together, it is the men who talk most. Two Canadian researchers, Deborah James and Janice Drakich, reviewed sixty three studies
which examined the amount of talk used by American women and men
in different contexts. Women talked more than men in only two studies.

In New Zealand, too, research suggests that men generally dominate the talking time. Margaret Franken compared the amount of talk
used by female and male "experts" assisting a female TV host to interview well-known public figures. In a situation where each of three interviewers was entitled to a third of the interviewers' talking time, the men
took more than half on every occasion.

Here Holmes introduces each summary with a signal phrase — "Two
Canadian researchers, Deborah James and Janice Drakich, reviewed" and
"Margaret Franken compared." Holmes concludes each summary with a
pointed statement of the researchers' conclusion.

Finally, the following passage comes from the article "Creeper!
Rando! Sketchball!" that appeared in the *New York Times* on October
29, 2010. Here writer Ben Zimmer uses representative quotations from
three University of North Carolina students, all enrolled in a grammar of
current English class, to speak to his claim that "terms like *creeper*, *rando*,
and *sketchball* come in handy as women deal with men who may try to give
them unwanted attention."

In interviews I conducted with [Professor Connie C.] Eble's students, one recurring theme that emerged was the impact of technology and social media on the need to patrol social boundaries. "With Facebook and texting," Natasha Duarte said, "it's easier to contact someone you're interested in, even if you only met them once and don't really know them. To the person receiving them, these texts and Facebook friend requests or wall posts can seem premature and unwarranted, or sketchy."

Facebook in particular lends itself to "stalkerish" behavior, Christina Clark explained, and indeed the compound verb *Facebook stalk* (meaning "excessively or surreptitiously peruse another's Facebook profile") shows up in the latest slang lists. "People put things on Facebook a lot of the time to show off pictures of themselves and to meet new people, but some of these new people are undesirables," Clark said. "Unfortunately, it can be hard to filter these people out without feeling unkind, so this information is available to them, and often it is alarming if they seem to be looking through pictures or constantly trying to find out what you're up to. These people then become stalkers or 'creepers.'"

Lilly Kantarakias said she believes that the shift to technologically mediated exchanges among students is leading to a "loss of intimacy" and that this failure to engage in human contact is responsible for the rise in all of the "sketchy" talk. "People have lost both their sense of communication and social-interaction skills," Kantarakias said. "We know only how to judge people off of a Facebook page or we easily misinterpret texts or e-mails. You can see it in the way people walk around campus, texting on their cells, being completely oblivious to the hundreds of people surrounding them. We've become lazy with our speech and our social profiling of fellow human beings."

By letting the three representative female students articulate their own views on the impact of technology and social media on one's social boundaries, Zimmer demonstrates that he is not discussing an isolated problem. Each student is able to speak to the issue from personal experience. Collectively, they help Zimmer make his point convincingly.

LEARN TO SUMMARIZE, PARAPHRASE, AND QUOTE FROM YOUR SOURCES

When taking notes from your sources, you must decide whether to summarize, paraphrase, or quote directly. The approach you take is largely determined by the content of the source passage and the way you envision using it in your paper. Each of these techniques—summarizing, paraphrasing, and quoting—will help you better incorporate source material into your essays. Making use of all three of these techniques, rather than relying on only one or two, will keep your text varied and interesting. In most cases it is better to summarize or paraphrase material from sources—which by definition means using your own words—instead of quoting verbatim (word for word). Capturing an idea in your own words ensures that you have thought about and understood what your source is saying. All the examples in the following discussion are taken from essays in *Language Awareness* unless otherwise noted, and page numbers refer to pages in this text.

Summary

When you *summarize* material from one of your sources, you capture in condensed form the essential idea of a passage, an article, or an entire chapter. Summaries are particularly useful when you are working with lengthy, detailed arguments or long passages of narrative or descriptive background information in which the details are not germane to the overall thrust of your paper. You simply want to capture the essence of the passage because you are confident that your readers will readily understand the point being made or do not need to be convinced about its validity. Because you are distilling information, a summary is always shorter than the original; often a chapter or more can be reduced to a paragraph, or several paragraphs to a sentence or two. Remember in writing a summary you should use your own wording.

Consider the following paragraphs from Gordon Allport's "The Language of Prejudice" which appears on pages 364–373 of this text.

> Some labels such as "blind man," are exceedingly salient and powerful. They tend to prevent alternative classification, or even cross-classification. Ethnic labels are often of this type, particularly if they refer to some highly visible feature, e.g., Negro, Oriental. They resemble the labels that point to some outstanding incapacity—*feeble-minded, cripple, blind man.* Let us call such symbols "labels of primary potency." These symbols act like shrieking sirens, deafening us to all finer discriminations that we might otherwise perceive. Even though the blindness of one man and the darkness of pigmentation of another may be defining attributes for some purposes, they are irrelevant and "noisy" for others.
>
> Most people are unaware of this basic law of language—that every label applied to a given person refers properly only to one aspect of his nature. You may correctly say that a certain man is *human, a philanthropist, a Chinese, a physician, an athlete.* A given person may be all of these; but the chances are that *Chinese* stands out in your mind as the symbol of primary potency. Yet neither this nor any other classificatory label can refer to the whole of a man's nature. (Only his proper name can do so.)

A student wishing to capture the gist of Allport's point without repeating his detailed explanation wrote the following summary on page 48.

SUMMARY NOTE CARD

Labels of primacy potency

Allport warns about the dangers of using labels — especially ethnic

labels — because of their power to distort our perceptions of other human

beings.

Allport, 365

Paraphrase

When you *paraphrase* material from a source, you restate the information in your own words instead of quoting directly. Unlike a summary, which gives a brief overview of the essential information in the original, a paraphrase seeks to maintain the same level of detail as the original to aid readers in understanding or believing the information presented. A paraphrase presents the original information in approximately the same number of words but with different wording. To put it another way, your paraphrase should accurately present ideas in the original, but it should not use the same words or sentence structure as the original. Even though you are using your own words in a paraphrase, it's important to remember that you are borrowing ideas and therefore must acknowledge the source of these ideas with a citation.

How would you paraphrase the following passage from "Selection, Slanting, and Charged Language" by Newman P. and Genevieve B. Birk, which appears on pages 261–269 of this text?

> When we put our knowledge into words, a second process of selection, the process of slanting, takes place. Just as there is something, a rather mysterious principle of selection, which chooses for us what we will notice, and what will then become our knowledge, there is also a principle which operates, with or without our awareness, to select certain facts and feelings from our store of knowledge, and to choose the words and the emphasis that we shall use to communicate our meaning.

The following note card illustrates how one student paraphrased this passage:

PARAPHRASE NOTE CARD

Slanting

Every time we communicate information and ideas, we engage in a secondary process known as slanting. An even earlier selection process, that of acquiring knowledge, remains something of a mystery because who can say why we notice what we do and why it becomes a part of what we know. Slanting, a conscious or subconscious process, further selects the facts and emotions we convey; it finds not only the words we use but also the way we emphasize them when we communicate.

Newman P. Birk, Genevieve B. Birk,
"Selection, Slanting, and Charged Language," 262

Notice how carefully the student captures the essence of the Birks' ideas in her own words as well as her own sentence structures. Capturing an idea in your own words demonstrates that you have thought about and understood what your source is saying.

Direct Quotation

When you *quote* a source directly, you copy the words of your source exactly, putting all quoted material in quotation marks. When you make a quotation note card, check the passage carefully for accuracy, including punctuation and capitalization. Be selective about what you choose to quote. Reserve direct quotation for important ideas stated memorably, for especially clear explanations by authorities, and for arguments by proponents of a particular position in their own words.

Consider, for example, the following passage quoted directly from William Zinsser's essay "Simplicity," on page 233 of this text, emphasizing the importance—and current rarity—of clear, concise writing.

On occasion you'll find a useful passage with some memorable wording in it. Avoid the temptation to quote the whole passage; instead, try combining summary or paraphrase with direct quotation.

QUOTATION NOTE CARD

Wordiness

"Clutter is the disease of American writing. We are a society strangling in unnecessary words, circular constructions, pompous frills, and meaningless jargon."

William Zinsser, "Simplicity," 233

Consider the following paragraph from Martin Luther King Jr.'s "Letter from Birmingham Jail" (p. 95), addressed ostensibly to eight white clergymen who had published a letter about civil disorder in the Birmingham *Post-Herald*.

> You express a great deal of anxiety over our willingness to break laws. This is certainly a legitimate concern. Since we so diligently urge people to obey the Supreme Court's decision of 1954 outlawing segregation in the public schools, at first glance it may seem rather paradoxical for us consciously to break laws. One may well ask: "How can you advocate breaking some laws and obeying others?" The answer lies in the fact that there are two types of laws: just and unjust. I would be the first to advocate obeying just laws. One has not only a legal but moral responsibility to obey just laws. Conversely, one has a moral responsibility to disobey unjust laws. I would agree with St. Augustine that "an unjust law is no law at all."

Notice how the student's note on the following page has quotation marks carefully added around all the words that were borrowed directly.

INTEGRATE BORROWED MATERIAL INTO YOUR TEXT

Being familiar with the material in your notes will help you decide how to integrate your sources into your drafts. Though it is not necessary to use all of your notes, nor to use them all at once in your first draft, you do need to know which ones support your thesis, extend your ideas, offer

QUOTATION AND SUMMARY NOTE CARD

> ### Just and unjust laws
>
> *MLK is quick to answer his fellow clergy who question his "willingness to break laws." He addresses their concerns by explaining that there are "just and unjust" laws. King strongly believes that we all have a "legal" and "moral responsibility to obey just laws" as well as "a moral responsibility to disobey unjust laws."*
>
> *Martin Luther King Jr., "Letter from Birmingham Jail," 99*

better wording of your ideas, and reveal the opinions of noted authorities. Occasionally you will want to use notes that include ideas contrary to your own so that you can rebut them in your own argument. Once you have analyzed your notes, you may even alter your thesis slightly in light of the information and ideas you have discovered.

Whenever you want to use borrowed material, be it a quotation, a paraphrase, or summary, your goal always is to integrate these sources smoothly and logically so as not to disrupt the flow of your paper or confuse your readers. It is best to introduce borrowed material with a *signal phrase*, which alerts readers that borrowed information is about to be presented.

SELECTING APPROPRIATE SIGNAL PHRASES. A signal phrase minimally consists of the author's name and a verb (e.g., *Michael Pollan contends*). Signal phrases help readers better follow your train of thought. When you integrate a quote, paraphrase, or summary into your paper, vary your signal phrases and choose verbs for the signal phrases that accurately convey the tone and intent of the writer you are citing. If a writer is arguing, use the verb *argues* (or *asserts, claims,* or *contends*); if a writer is contesting a particular position or fact, use the verb *contests* (or *denies, disputes, refutes,* or *rejects*). Verbs that are specific to the situation in your paper will bring your readers into the intellectual debate (and avoid the monotony of all-purpose verbs like *says* or *writes*). The following examples illustrate how you can vary signal phrases to add precision and interest to your writing:

Malcolm X confesses that "trying to write simple English, I not only wasn't articulate, I wasn't even functional" (p. 68).

Using a series of vivid examples, Stephen Pinker reminds us why "we sheathe our words in politeness and innuendo and other forms of doublespeak" (p. 123).

Anne Lamott encourages aspiring writers to give up their fears of first drafts because "few writers really know what they are doing until they've done it" (p. 222).

"Hate, like much of human feeling, is not rational," argues Andrew Sullivan, "but it usually has its reasons. And it cannot be understood, let alone condemned, without knowing them" (p. 253).

Sherry Turkle asserts that "Often, our new digital connections offer the illusion of companionship without the demands of friendship" (p. 493).

Sherman Alexie explains how he struggled with his peers' and teachers' expectations, because to them, "a smart Indian is a dangerous person, widely feared and ridiculed by Indians and non-Indians alike" (p. 79).

Other verbs that you should keep in mind when constructing signal phrases include the following:

acknowledges	compares	grants	reasons
adds	confirms	implies	reports
admits	declares	insists	responds
believes	endorses	points out	suggests

Well-chosen signal phrases help you integrate quotations, paraphrases, and summaries into the flow of your paper. Besides, signal phrases let your reader know who is speaking and, in the case of summaries and paraphrases, exactly where your ideas end and someone else's begin. Never confuse your reader with a quotation that appears suddenly without introduction. Unannounced quotations leave your reader wondering how the quoted material relates to the point you are trying to make. Look at the following example from the first draft of a student's paper on the pros and cons of social networking on Facebook. The quotation is from Daniel Lyons' article "The High Price of Facebook," which appeared May 15, 2010, on *Newsweek.com*.

Unannounced Quotation

Many Facebook users worry that the privacy settings are not clear enough to protect people. "I also suspect that whatever Facebook has done so far to invade our privacy, it's only the beginning. Which is why I'm considering deactivating my account. Facebook is a handy site, but I'm freaked out by the idea that my information is in the hands of people I don't trust. That's too high a price to pay" (Lyons). But we should remember that every time a privacy setting is changed, Web sites like Gizmodo.com and Slate.com alert users to the changes. Viral copy-and-paste status updates start circulating on Facebook notifying users of the privacy changes and the need to make updates to your profile if necessary. All of the criticisms Facebook is subjected to due to its rapid growth and evolution are overblown because users who are not satisfied with their level of privacy can simply delete personal information from their profiles, or routinely check their privacy settings.

In the following revision, the student integrates the quotation into the text by means of a signal phrase and in a number of other ways as well. By giving the name of the writer being quoted, referring to his authority on the subject, and noting that the writer is speaking from experience, the student provides more context so that the reader can better understand how this quotation fits into the discussion.

Integrated Quotation

Many Facebook users worry that the privacy settings are not clear enough to protect people. Tech-savvy commentator Daniel Lyons, a senior editor at *Forbes* magazine, has joined the chorus of critics. He warns, "I also suspect that whatever Facebook has done so far to invade our privacy, it's only the beginning. Which is why I'm considering deactivating my account. Facebook is a handy site, but I'm freaked out by the idea that my information is in the hands of people I don't trust. That's too high a price to pay" (Lyons). But we should remember that every time a privacy setting is changed, Web sites like Gizmodo.com and Slate.com alert users to the changes. Viral copy-and-paste status updates start circulating on Facebook notifying users of the privacy changes and the need to make updates to your profile if necessary. All of the criticisms Facebook is subjected to due to its rapid growth and evolution are overblown because users who are not satisfied with their level of privacy can simply delete personal information from their profiles or routinely check their privacy settings.

AVOID PLAGIARISM

The importance of honesty and accuracy in working with outside sources—whether print, digital, or personal interview or correspondence—cannot be stressed enough. In working closely with the ideas and words of others, intellectual honesty demands that we distinguish between what we borrow—acknowledging it with a citation—and what is our own. Any material borrowed word for word must be placed within quotation marks and be properly cited. Any idea, explanation, or argument you have paraphrased or summarized must be properly cited, and it must be clear where the paraphrase or summary begins and ends. In short, to use someone else's ideas, whether in their original form or in an altered form, without proper acknowledgment is to be guilty of **plagiarism**.

You must acknowledge and document the source of your information whenever you do any of the following:

- quote a source exactly, word for word
- paraphrase or summarize information and ideas from a source
- cite statistics, tables, charts, graphs, or other visuals

You do *not* need to document the following types of information:

- your own observations, experiences, ideas, and opinions
- factual information available in a number of reference works (information known as "common knowledge")
- proverbs, sayings, or familiar quotations

For a discussion of MLA style for in-text documentation practices, see pages 589–590.

The Council of Writing Program Administrators offers the following helpful definition of *plagiarism* in academic settings for administrators, faculty, and students: "In an instructional setting, plagiarism occurs when a writer deliberately uses someone else's language, ideas, or other (not common knowledge) material without acknowledging its source."

Accusations of plagiarism can be upheld even if plagiarism is unintentional. A little attention and effort can help to eliminate this possibility. While taking notes, check and recheck all direct quotations against the wording of the original, and be sure you've labeled them clearly as quotations. Double-check your paraphrases to be sure that you have not used the writer's wording or sentence structure.

While writing your paper, make sure that you put quotation marks around material taken verbatim, and double-check the text against your note card—or, better yet, against the original—to make sure that the quotation is accurate. When using paraphrases or summaries, be sure to cite the source.

The sections that follow provide examples of appropriate use of quotation, paraphrase, and summary.

USING QUOTATION MARKS FOR LANGUAGE BORROWED DIRECTLY. Again, when you use another person's exact words or sentences, you must enclose the borrowed language in quotation marks. Even if you cite the source, you are guilty of plagiarism if you fail to use quotation marks. The following example demonstrates both plagiarism and a correct citation for a direct quotation.

Original Source

In the last decade, Standards departments have become more tolerant of sex and foul language, but they have cracked down on violence and become more insistent about the politically correct presentation of minorities. Lately, however, they seem to be swinging wildly back and forth between allowing everything and allowing nothing.

—TAD FRIEND, "You Can't Say That: The Networks Play
Word Games," *New Yorker* Nov. 19, 2001, page 45.

Plagiarism

In the last decade, Standards departments have become more tolerant of sex and foul language, but, according to social commentator Tad Friend, they have cracked down on violence and become more insistent about the politically correct presentation of minorities. Lately, however, they seem to be swinging wildly back and forth between allowing everything and allowing nothing (45).

Correct Citation of Borrowed Words in Quotation Marks

"In the last decade, Standards departments have become more tolerant of sex and foul language," according to social commentator Tad Friend, "but they have cracked down on violence and become more insistent about the politically correct presentation of minorities. Lately, however, they seem to be swinging wildly back and forth between allowing everything and allowing nothing" (45).

USING YOUR OWN WORDS IN PARAPHRASE AND SUMMARY. When summarizing or paraphrasing a source, you must use your own language. It is not enough simply to change a word here or there; you must restate the idea(s) from the original *in your own words*, using your own style and sentence structure. In the following example, notice how plagiarism can occur when care is not taken in the wording or sentence structure of a paraphrase.

Original Source

Stereotypes are a kind of gossip about the world, a gossip that makes us prejudge people before we ever lay eyes on them. Hence it is not surprising that stereotypes have something to do with the dark world of prejudice. Explore most prejudices (note that the word means prejudgment) and you will find a cruel stereotype at the core of each one.
—ROBERT L. HEILBRONER, "Don't Let Stereotypes Warp Your Judgment," *Reader's Digest* Jan. 1962, page 254.

Unacceptably Close Wording

According to Heilbroner, we prejudge other people even before we have seen them when we think in stereotypes. That stereotypes are related to the ugly world of prejudice should not surprise anyone. If you explore the heart of most prejudices — beliefs that literally prejudge — you will discover a mean stereotype lurking (254).

Unacceptably Close Sentence Structure

Heilbroner believes that stereotypes are images of people, images that enable people to prejudge other people before they have seen them. Therefore, no one should find it surprising that stereotypes are somehow related to the ugly world of prejudice. Examine most prejudices (the word literally means prejudgment) and you will uncover a vicious stereotype at the center of each (254).

Acceptable Paraphrase

Heilbroner believes that there is a link between stereotypes and the hurtful practice of prejudice. Stereotypes make for easy conversation, a kind of shorthand that enables people to find fault with others before ever meeting them. Most human prejudices, according to Heilbroner, have an ugly stereotype lurking somewhere inside them (254).

Finally, as you proofread your final draft, check your citations one last time. If at any time while you are taking notes or writing your paper you have a question about plagiarism, consult your instructor for clarification and guidance before proceeding.

Preventing Plagiarism

Questions to Ask about Direct Quotations

- Do quotation marks clearly indicate the language that I borrowed verbatim (word for word)?
- Is the language of the quotation accurate, with no missing or misquoted words or phrases?
- Do the brackets or ellipsis marks clearly indicate any changes or omissions I have introduced?
- Does a signal phrase naming the author introduce each quotation? If not, is the author's name in the parenthetical citation?
- Does a parenthetical page citation follow each quotation?

Questions to Ask about Summaries and Paraphrases

- Is each summary and paraphrase written in my own words and style?
- Does each summary and paraphrase accurately represent the opinion, position, or reasoning of the original writer?
- Does each summary and paraphrase start with a signal phrase so that readers know where my borrowed material begins?
- Does each summary and paraphrase conclude with a parenthetical page citation?

Questions to Ask about Facts and Statistics

- Do I use a signal phrase or some other marker to introduce each fact or statistic that is not common knowledge so that readers know where the borrowed material begins?
- Is each fact or statistic that is not common knowledge clearly documented with a parenthetical page citation?

A SAMPLE STUDENT ESSAY USING LIBRARY AND INTERNET SOURCES

Jake Jamieson wrote the following essay while he was a student at the University of Vermont and has updated it for inclusion in this book. His assignment was to write an argument, and he was free to choose his own topic from among the language issues covered in class. After considering a number of possible topics and doing some preliminary searches on several of them, Jamieson decided to tackle the issue of legislating English as the official language for the United States. As one who believes in the old axiom "if it isn't broken, don't fix it," Jamieson was intrigued by the sup porters of the Official English movement, who feel the need to fix a system that seems to be working just fine. As you read, notice how he uses outside sources to set out the various pieces of the Official English position and then uses his own thinking and examples as well as experts who support him to undercut that position. Throughout his essay Jamieson uses MLA-style in-text citations together with a list of works cited.

Jamieson 1

Jake Jamieson

Professor A. Rosa

Written Expression 001

12 April 2015

The "Official English" Movement:

Can America Proscribe Language with a Clear Conscience?

Many people think of the United States as a giant cultural "melting pot" where people from other countries come together and bathe in the warm waters of assimilation. In this scenario the newly arrived immigrants readily adopt American cultural ways and learn to speak English. For others, however, this serene picture of the melting pot analogy does not ring true. These people see the melting pot as a giant cauldron into which immigrants are tossed; here their cultures, values, and backgrounds are boiled away in the scalding waters of discrimination. At the center of the discussion about immigrants and assimilation is language: Should immigrants be required to learn English or should accommodations be made so they can continue to use their native languages?

Those who argue that the melting pot analogy is valid believe that immigrants who come to America do so willingly and should be expected to become a part of its culture instead of hanging on to their past. For them, the expectation that immigrants will celebrate this country's holidays, dress as Americans dress, embrace American values, and, most importantly, speak English is not unreasonable. They believe that assimilation offers the only way for everyone in this country to live together in harmony and the only way to dissipate the tensions that inevitably arise when cultures clash. One major problem with this argument, however, is that there is no agreement on what exactly constitutes the "American way" of doing things.

Marginal notes:

Title: Writer introduces subject and provides focus.

Writer sets context for discussion, identifies central problem of the "Official English" language debate.

Thesis question: Writer states the key question to be addressed in paper.

Writer introduces a major problem with assimilation model.

Jamieson 2

Not everyone in America is of the same religious persuasion or has the same set of values, and different people affect vastly different styles of dress. There are so many sets of variables that it would be hard to defend the argument that there is only one culture in the United States. Currently, the one common denominator in America is that the overwhelming majority of us speak English, and because of this a major movement is being staged in favor of making English the country's "official" language while it is still the country's national and common language. Making English America's "official" language would change the ground rules and expectations surrounding immigrant assimilation. According to columnist and social commentator Charles Krauthammer, making English the "official" language has important implications:

> "Official" means the language of the government and its institutions. "Official" makes clear our expectations of accultura-tion. "Official" means that every citizen, upon entering America's most sacred political space, the voting booth, should minimally be able to identify the words President and Vice President and county commissioner and judge. The immigrant, of course, has the right to speak whatever he wants. But he must understand that when he comes to the U.S., swears allegiance and accepts its bounty, he undertakes to join its civic culture. In English. (495)

Many reasons are given to support the notion that making English the official language of the land is a good idea and that it is exactly what this country needs, especially in the face of the growing diversity of languages in metropolitan areas. Economics is a major reason. As Mauro E. Mujica, chairman and CEO of U.S. English, reports, "Los Angeles County spent $3.3 million, 15 percent of the entire election budget, to print election ballots in seven languages and hire multilingual poll workers for the March 2002 primary. The county also spends $265 per day for each of the 420 full-time court interpreters" (par. 16).

Opposition argument: English as the common denominator in America—time to act.

Quotation: Writer quotes Krauthammer to present the "Official English" perspective.

Writer indents long quotation according to MLA style.

Writer uses MLA in-text citation format which includes introductory signal phrase and parenthetical paragraph number to integrate a quotation about the economic impact of not having English as the nation's official language.

Supporters of Official English contend that all government
communication must be in English. Because communication is absolutely
necessary for democracy to survive, they believe that the only way to
ensure the existence of our nation is to make sure a common language
exists. Making English official would ensure that all government business,
from ballots to official forms to judicial hearings, would have to be
conducted in English. From this vantage point championing English as
our national language is not hostile at all because as Mujica asserts,
"Parents around the world know that English is the global language and
that their children need to learn it to succeed. English is the language
of business, higher education, diplomacy, aviation, the Internet, science,
popular music, entertainment, and international travel" (par. 3).
Political and cultural commentator Greg Lewis echoes Mujica's sentiments
when he boldly states, "to succeed in America . . . it's important to
speak, read, and understand English as most Americans speak it. There's
nothing cruel or unfair in that; it's just the way it is" (par. 5).

> Writer presents the opposition argument favoring Official English.

For those who do not subscribe to this way of thinking, however,
this type of legislation is anything but a welcoming act or invitation to
participate. Many of them, like Myriam Marquez, readily acknowledge the
importance of English but fear that "talking in Spanish — or any other
language, for that matter — is some sort of litmus test used to gauge
American patriotism" (497). Others suggest that anyone attempting to
regulate language is treading dangerously close to the First Amendment
and must have a hidden agenda of some type. Why, it is asked, make a
language official when it is already firmly entrenched and widely used in
this country without legislation to mandate it? For many, the answer is
plain and simple — discrimination.

> Writer introduces the anti-Official English position.

This tendency of Official English proponents to put down other
languages is one that shows up again and again, even though they
maintain that they have nothing against other languages or the people

Jamieson 4

who speak them. If there is no malice intended toward other languages,
why is the use of any language other than English tantamount to lunacy
according to an almost constant barrage of literature and editorial opinion?
Ed Morales, the author of *Living in Spanglish*, reports that the mayor of
Bogota, New Jersey, called for a boycott of McDonald's restaurants after
the "company displayed a billboard advertising a new iced coffee drink in
Spanish," calling "the ad . . . 'offensive' and 'divisive' because it sends a
message that Hispanic immigrants do not need to learn English" (par. 2–3).
Now, according to this mindset, not only is speaking any language other
than English offensive, but it is also irrational and bewildering. What is
this world coming to when businesses want to attract new customers using
Spanish or people just want to speak and make transactions in their native
language? Why do they refuse to change and become more like us? Why
can't immigrants see that speaking English is quite simply the right way
to go? These and many other questions like them are implied by Official
English proponents when they discuss the issue.

> Quotation:
> Writer cites
> author Morales
> to support
> claim about
> official English
> proponents.

> Writer asks
> a series of
> rhetorical
> questions.

The scariest prospect of all is that this opinion is quickly gaining
popularity all around the country. It appears to be most prevalent in
areas with high concentrations of Spanish-speaking residents. To date the
English Language Unity Act and one amendment to the Constitution have
been proposed in the House and Senate. There are more than twenty-eight
states — including Arizona, Missouri, North Dakota, Florida, California,
Virginia, and New Hampshire — that have made English their official
language, and more are debating the issue at this time. An especially
disturbing fact about this debate — and it was front and center in 2010
during the discussions and protests about what to do with America's over
12.5 million illegal immigrants — is that Official English laws always seem
to be linked to anti-immigration legislation, such as proposals to limit
immigration or to restrict government benefits to immigrants.

> Writer updates
> readers on
> the status of
> Official English
> legislation.

Jamieson 5

Although Official English proponents maintain that their bid for

language legislation is in the best interest of immigrants, the facts

tend to show otherwise. University of Texas professor Robert D. King

strongly believes that "language does not threaten American unity." He

recommends that "we relax and luxuriate in our linguistic richness and

our traditional tolerance of language differences" (492). A decision has

to be made in this country about what kind of message we will send

to the rest of the world. Do we plan to allow everyone in this country

the freedom of speech that we profess to cherish, or will we decide to

reserve it only for those who speak English? Will we hold firm to our

belief that everyone is deserving of life, liberty, and the pursuit of

happiness in this country? Or will we show the world that we believe

in these things only when they pertain to ourselves and people like us?

"The irony," as Hispanic columnist Myriam Marquez observes, "is that

English-only laws directed at government have done little to change the

inevitable multi-cultural flavor of America" ("English-Only Laws" A10).

> Writer cites University of Texas professor to assure readers that the United States does not need to make English the nation's official language.

> Writer concludes with an observation by an Hispanic journalist about the impact of English-only legislation to date.

Jamieson 6

Works Cited

"'English Language Unity Act' Will Encourage Common Language."

    EnglishFirst.org. 18 Mar. 2011. Web. 22 Feb. 2012.

King, Robert D. "Should English Be the Law?" *Language Awareness*. 11th

    ed. Eds. Paul Eschholz, Alfred Rosa, and Virginia Clark. Boston:

    Bedford, 2013. 483-92. Print.

Krauthammer, Charles. "In Plain English: Let's Make It Official." *Language*

    Awareness. 11th ed. Eds. Paul Eschholz, Alfred Rosa, and Virginia

    Clark. Boston: Bedford, 2013. 493-95. Print.

Lewis, Greg. "An Open Letter to Diversity's Victims." *WashingtonDispatch*

    .com. 12 Aug. 2003. Web. 22 Feb. 2012.

Marquez, Myriam. "English-Only Laws Serve to Appease Those Who Fear

    the Inevitable." *Orlando Sentinel* 10 July 2000: A10. Print.

---. "Why and When We Speak Spanish in Public." *Language Awareness*.

    11th ed. Eds. Paul Eschholz, Alfred Rosa, and Virginia Clark. Boston:

    Bedford, 2013. 496-97. Print.

Morales, Ed. "English-only Debate Turns Absurd." *Progressive.org*. 19 July

    2006. Web. 23 Feb. 2012.

Mujica, Mauro E. "Why the U.S. Needs an Official Language." *WorldandI*

    .com. Dec. 2003. Web. 23 Feb. 2012.

The heading *Works Cited* is centered at the top on page.

Writer uses MLA style for his list of works cited. The list begins on a new page. Entries are presented in alphabetical order by authors' last names. The first line of each entry begins at the left margin; subsequent lines are indented five spaces. Double space within entries as well as between entries.

The correct MLA forms for various other kinds of publications are given on pages 590–594.

4

UNDERSTANDING THE POWER OF LANGUAGE: HOW WE FIND OUR VOICES

Most of us accept language as we accept the air we breathe; we cannot get along without it, and we take it for granted almost all of the time. Many days we find ourselves on language overload, bombarded by a steady stream of verbal and written messages—some invited, others not—but how much do we really know about language? How well do we understand how language works? Few of us are aware of the extent to which language is used to mislead and manipulate. Still fewer of us are fully conscious of the ways, subtle and not, in which our use of language may affect others. And even fewer of us recognize that our very perceptions of the world are influenced, and our thoughts at least partially shaped, by language. However, we are also the beneficiaries of language far more than we are its victims. Language is one of humankind's greatest achievements and most important resources, and it is a subject endlessly fascinating in itself.

If it is true that we are all in some sense prisoners of language, it is equally true that liberation begins with an awareness of that fact. Chapter 4, "Understanding the Power of Language," presents five essays in which individuals tell of their language struggles and their triumphs. In "Coming to an Awareness of Language," Malcolm X relates how he came to understand the power of words while serving time in the Norfolk Prison Colony. He remembers his frustration and feelings of inadequacy when he recognized the limitations of his slang-filled street talk. Not one to sit around and drown in self-pity, Malcolm X charted a course that empowered and liberated his mind. Next, we read the inspiring story of Helen Keller, a woman who broke the chains of blindness and deafness and connected to the world around her. In "The Day Language Came into My Life," Keller recounts the day she, with the help of her teacher Anne Mansfield Sullivan, discovered "everything had a name, and each name gave birth to a new thought." In the third essay, "Superman and Me," Sherman Alexie describes his experience of learning to read and write as an Indian boy at a reservation school: "I refused to fail. I was smart. I was arrogant. I was lucky." In the fourth essay, "Writing to Change the World," Mary Pipher tells of first reading *The Diary of Anne Frank* as an adolescent. She uses this experience as a jumping-off point to discuss the power of the written word to advance social, political, and economic change. Next, Emily Parker explores the danger to free expression in Russia, where political journalists and activists are routinely threatened and even brutally harmed or killed. In "You Can Keep Silent, You Can Emigrate, or You Can Stay Here and Fight," she tells the stories of Oleg Kashin and Alexey Navalny, who have risked their safety to speak out against government corruption. And in the final selection, "Letter from Birmingham Jail," Martin Luther King Jr. demonstrates the power of written language. Through carefully crafted emotional and logical appeals, King argues that nonviolent direct action can put an end to prejudice, hatred, and bigotry in the United States. Many historians credit King's letter with changing the course of the civil rights movement in the 1960s, successfully culminating in the landmark Civil Rights Act of 1964 and the Voting Rights Act of 1965.

Coming to an Awareness of Language

MALCOLM X

On February 21, 1965, Malcolm X, the Black Muslim leader, was shot to death as he addressed an afternoon rally in Harlem. He was thirty-nine years old. In the course of his brief life, he had risen from a world of thieving, pimping, and drug pushing to become one of the most articulate and powerful African Americans in the United States during the early 1960s. In 1992 his life was reexamined in Spike Lee's film *Malcolm X*. With the assistance of the late Alex Haley, the author of *Roots*, Malcolm X told his story in *The Autobiography of Malcolm X* (1964), a moving account of his search for fulfillment. This selection is taken from the *Autobiography*.

All of us have been in situations in which we have felt somehow betrayed by our language, unable to find just the right words to express ourselves. "Words," as lexicographer Bergen Evans has said, "are the tools for the job of saying what you want to say." As our repertoire of words expands so does our ability to express ourselves — to articulate clearly our thoughts, feelings, hopes, fears, likes, and dislikes. Frustration at not being able to express himself in the letters he wrote drove Malcolm X to the dictionary, where he discovered the power of words.

WRITING TO DISCOVER: *Write about a time when someone told you that it is important to have a good vocabulary. What did you think when you heard this advice? Why do you think people believe that vocabulary is important? How would you assess your own vocabulary?*

I've never been one for inaction. Everything I've ever felt strongly about, I've done something about. I guess that's why, unable to do anything else, I soon began writing to people I had known in the hustling world, such as Sammy the Pimp, John Hughes, the gambling house owner, the thief Jumpsteady, and several dope peddlers. I wrote them all about Allah and Islam and Mr. Elijah Muhammad. I had no idea where most of them lived. I addressed their letters in care of the Harlem or Roxbury bars and clubs where I'd known them.

I never got a single reply. The average hustler and criminal was too uneducated to write a letter. I have known many slick sharp-looking hustlers, who would have you think they had an interest in Wall Street; privately, they would get someone else to read a letter if they received one. Besides, neither would I have replied to anyone writing me something as wild as "the white man is the devil."

What certainly went on the Harlem and Roxbury wires was that Detroit Red was going crazy in stir,[1] or else he was trying some hype to shake up the warden's office.

---

1. Slang for being in jail.

During the years that I stayed in the Norfolk Prison Colony, never did any official directly say anything to me about those letters, although, of course, they all passed through the prison censorship. I'm sure, however, they monitored what I wrote to add to the files which every state and federal prison keeps on the conversion of Negro inmates by the teachings of Mr. Elijah Muhammad.

But at that time, I felt that the real reason was that the white man   5
knew that he was the devil.

Later on, I even wrote to the Mayor of Boston, to the Governor of Massachusetts, and to Harry S. Truman. They never answered; they probably never even saw my letters. I handscratched to them how the white man's society was responsible for the black man's condition in this wilderness of North America.

Anyone who has read a great deal can imagine the new world that opened.

It was because of my letters that I happened to stumble upon starting to acquire some kind of homemade education.

I became increasingly frustrated at not being able to express what I wanted to convey in letters that I wrote, especially those to Mr. Elijah Muhammad. In the street, I had been the most articulate hustler out there—I had commanded attention when I said something. But now, trying to write simple English, I not only wasn't articulate, I wasn't even functional. How would I sound writing in slang, the way I would *say* it, something such as, "Look daddy, let me pull your coat about a cat. Elijah Muhammad—"

Many who today hear me somewhere in person, or on television, or those who read something I've said, will think I went to school far beyond the eighth grade. This impression is due entirely to my prison studies.

It had really begun back in the Charlestown Prison, when Bimbi first   10
made me feel envy of his stock of knowledge. Bimbi had always taken charge of any conversation he was in, and I had tried to emulate him. But every book I picked up had few sentences which didn't contain anywhere from one to nearly all of the words that might as well have been in Chinese. When I just skipped those words, of course, I really ended up with little idea of what the book said. So I had come to the Norfolk Prison Colony still going through only book-reading motions. Pretty soon, I would have quit even these motions, unless I had received the motivation that I did.

I saw that the best thing I could do was get hold of a dictionary—to study, to learn some words. I was lucky enough to reason also that I should try to improve my penmanship. It was sad. I couldn't even write in a straight line. It was both ideas together that moved me to request a dictionary along with some tablets and pencils from the Norfolk Prison Colony school.

I spent two days just rifling uncertainly through the dictionary's pages. I'd never realized so many words existed! I didn't know *which* words I needed to learn. Finally, just to start some kind of action, I began copying.

In my slow, painstaking, ragged handwriting, I copied into my tablet everything printed on that first page, down to the punctuation marks.

I believe it took me a day. Then, aloud, I read back, to myself, everything I'd written on the tablet. Over and over, aloud, to myself, I read my own handwriting.

I woke up the next morning, thinking about those words—immensely   15
proud to realize that not only had I written so much at one time, but I'd written words that I never knew were in the world. Moreover, with a little effort, I also could remember what many of these words meant. I reviewed the words whose meanings I didn't remember. Funny thing, from the dictionary's first page right now, that "aardvark" springs to my mind. The dictionary had a picture of it, a long-tailed, long-eared, burrowing African mammal, which lives off termites caught by sticking out its tongue as an anteater does for ants.

I was so fascinated that I went on—I copied the dictionary's next page. And the same experience came when I studied that. With every succeeding page, I also learned of people and places and events from history. Actually the dictionary is like a miniature encyclopedia. Finally the dictionary's A section had filled a whole tablet—and I went on into the B's. That was the way I started copying what eventually became the entire dictionary. It went a lot faster after so much practice helped me pick up handwriting speed. Between what I wrote in my tablet, and writing letters, during the rest of my time in prison I would guess I wrote a million words.

I suppose it was inevitable that as my word-base broadened, I could for the first time pick up a book and read and now begin to understand what the book was saying. Anyone who has read a great deal can imagine the new world that opened. Let me tell you something: from then until I left that prison, in every free moment I had, if I was not reading in the library, I was reading on my bunk. You couldn't have gotten me out of books with a wedge. Between Mr. Muhammad's teachings, my correspondence, my visitors . . . and my reading of books, months passed without my even thinking about being imprisoned. In fact, up to then, I never had been so truly free in my life.

THINKING CRITICALLY ABOUT THE READING

1. What motivated Malcolm X "to acquire some kind of homemade education" (7)?

2. Malcolm X narrates his experience as a prisoner using the first-person pronoun *I*. Why is the first person particularly appropriate? What would be lost or gained had he told his story using the third-person pronoun *he*? (Glossary: *Point of View*)

3. For many, *vocabulary building* means learning strange, multisyllabic, difficult-to-spell words. But acquiring an effective vocabulary does not need to be any of these things. What, for you, constitutes an effective vocabulary? How would you characterize Malcolm X's vocabulary in this selection? Do you find his word choice appropriate for his purpose? (Glossary: *Purpose*) Explain.

4. In paragraph 8, Malcolm X remembers thinking how he would "sound writing in slang" and feeling inadequate because he recognized how slang or street talk limited his options. (Glossary: *Slang*) In what kinds of situations is slang useful and appropriate? When is Standard English more appropriate? (Glossary: *Standard English*)

5. In paragraph 8, Malcolm X describes himself as having been "the most articulate hustler out there" but in writing he says he "wasn't even functional." What differences between speaking and writing could account for such a discrepancy? How does the tone of this essay help you understand Malcolm X's dilemma? (Glossary: *Tone*)

6. What is the nature of the freedom that Malcolm X refers to in the final sentence? In what sense is language liberating? Is it possible for people to be "prisoners" of their own language? Explain.

LANGUAGE IN ACTION

Many newspapers carry regular vocabulary-building columns, and the *Reader's Digest* has for many years included a section called "It Pays to Enrich Your Word Power." You might enjoy taking the following quiz, which is excerpted from *Reader's Digest*.

It Pays to Enrich Your Word Power

Zeus and his thunderbolts, Thor and his hammer, Medusa and her power to turn flesh into stone: these are all fascinating figures in mythology and folklore. Associated with such legends are words we use today, including the 10 selected below.

1. **panic** *n.* —A: pain. B: relief. C: mess. D: fear.

2. **bacchanal** (*BAK ih NAL*) *n.*—A: drunken party. B: graduation ceremony. C: backache remedy. D: victory parade.

3. **puckish** *adj.*—A: wrinkly. A: B: quirky. C: quarrelsome. D: mischievous.

4. **cyclopean** (*SIGH klo PEA en*) *adj.*—A: wise. B: gigantic. C: wealthy. D: repetitious.

5. **hector** *v.*—A: to curse. B: bully. C: disown. D: injure.

6. **cupidity** (*kyoo PID ih tee*) *n.*—A: thankfulness. B: ignorance. C: abundance. D: desire.

7. **mnemonic** (*knee MON ik*) *adj.*—pertaining to A: memory. B: speech. C: hearing. D: sight.

8. **stygian** (*STIJ ee an*) *adj.*—A: stingy. B: hellish. C: uncompromising. D: dirty.

9. **narcissistic** *adj.*—A: indecisive. B: very sleepy. C: very vain. D: just.

10. **zephyr** (*ZEF er*) *n.*—A: breeze. B: dog. C: horse. D: tornado.

ANSWERS:

1. **panic**—*[D]* Fear; widespread terror; as, An outbreak of Ebola led to *panic* in the small village. *Pan,* frightening Greek god of nature.

2. **bacchanal**—*[A]* Drunken party; orgy; as, Complaints to the police broke up the *bacchanal. Bacchus,* Roman god of wine.

3. **puckish**—*[D]* Mischievous; prankish. *Puck,* a trickloving sprite or fairy.

4. **cyclopean**—*[B]* Gigantic; huge; as, the *cyclopean* home runs of Mark McGwire. *Cyclopes,* a race of fierce, oneeyed giants.

5. **hector**—*[B]* To bully; threaten. *Hector,* Trojan leader slain by Achilles and portrayed as a bragging menace in some dramas.

6. **cupidity**—*[D]* Strong desire. *Cupid,* Roman god of love.

7. **mnemonic**—*[A]* Pertaining to memory; as, "Spring forward and fall back" is a *mnemonic* spur to change time twice a year. *Mnemosyne,* Greek goddess of memory.

8. **stygian**—*[B]* Hellish; dark and gloomy. *Styx,* a river in Hades.

9. **narcissistic**—*[C]* Very vain; self-loving; as, The *narcissistic* actress preened for the photographers. *Narcissus,* a youth who fell in love with his own reflection.

10. **zephyr**—*[A]* Soft breeze; as, The storm tapered off to a *zephyr. Zephyrus,* gentle Greek god of the west wind.

Are you familiar with most of the words on the quiz? Did some of the answers surprise you? In your opinion, is the level of difficulty appropriate for the *Reader's Digest* audience? What does the continuing popularity of vocabulary-building features suggest about the attitudes of many Americans toward language?

WRITING SUGGESTIONS

1. All of us have been in situations in which our ability to use language seemed inadequate—for example, when taking an exam; being interviewed for a job; giving directions; or expressing sympathy, anger, or grief. Write a brief essay in which you recount one such frustrating incident in your life. Before beginning to write, review your reactions to Malcolm X's frustrations with his limited vocabulary. Share your experiences with your classmates.

2. Malcolm X solved the problem of his own illiteracy by carefully studying the dictionary. Would this be a viable solution to the national problem of illiteracy? Are there more practical alternatives to Malcolm X's approach? What, for example, is being done in your community to combat illiteracy? What are some of the more successful approaches being used in other parts of the country? Write a brief essay about the problem of illiteracy. In addition to using your library for research, you may want to check out the Internet to see what it has to offer.

The Day Language Came into My Life

HELEN KELLER

Helen Keller (1880–1968) became blind and deaf at the age of eighteen months as a result of a disease. As a child, then, Keller became accustomed to her limited world, for it was all that she knew. She experienced only certain fundamental sensations, such as the warmth of the sun on her face, and few emotions, such as anger and bitterness. It wasn't until she was almost seven years old that her family hired Anne Sullivan, a young woman who would turn out to be an extraordinary teacher, to help her. As Keller learned to communicate and think, the world opened up to her. She recorded her experiences in an autobiography, *The Story of My Life* (1903), from which the following selection is taken.

Helen Keller is in a unique position to remind us of what it is like to pass from the "fog" of prethought into the world where "everything had a name, and each name gave birth to a new thought." Her experiences as a deaf and blind child also raise a number of questions about the relationship between language and thought, emotions, ideas, and memory. Over time, Keller's acquisition of language allowed her to assume all the advantages of her birthright. Her rapid intellectual and emotional growth as a result of language suggests that we, too, have the potential to achieve a greater measure of our humanity by further refining our language abilities.

WRITING TO DISCOVER: *Consider what your life would be like today if you had been born without the ability to understand language or to speak or if you had suddenly lost the ability to use language later in life. Write about those aspects of your life that you think would be affected most severely.*

The most important day I remember in all my life is the one on which my teacher, Anne Mansfield Sullivan, came to me. I am filled with wonder when I consider the immeasurable contrast between the two lives which it connects. It was the third of March 1887, three months before I was seven years old.

On the afternoon of that eventful day, I stood on the porch, dumb, expectant. I guessed vaguely from my mother's signs and from the hurrying to and fro in the house that something unusual was about to happen, so I went to the door and waited on the steps. The afternoon sun penetrated the mass of honeysuckle that covered the porch and fell on my upturned face. My fingers lingered almost unconsciously on the familiar leaves and blossoms which had just come forth to greet the sweet southern spring. I did not know what the future held of marvel or surprise for me. Anger and bitterness had preyed upon me continually for weeks and a deep languor had succeeded this passionate struggle.

Have you ever been at sea in a dense fog, when it seemed as if a tangible white darkness shut you in, and the great ship, tense and anxious, groped her way toward the shore with plummet and sounding-line, and you waited with beating heart for something to happen? I was like that ship before my education began, only I was without compass or sounding-line and had no way of knowing how near the harbor was. "Light! give me light!" was the wordless cry of my soul, and the light of love shone on me in that very hour.

I felt approaching footsteps. I stretched out my hand as I supposed to my mother. Someone took it, and I was caught up and held close in the arms of her who had come to reveal all things to me, and, more than all things else, to love me.

The morning after my teacher came she led me into her room and gave   5
me a doll. The little blind children at the Perkins Institution had sent it and Laura Bridgman had dressed it; but I did not know this until afterward. When I had played with it a little while, Miss Sullivan slowly spelled into my hand the word "d-o-l-l." I was at once interested in this finger play and tried to imitate it. When I finally succeeded in making the letters correctly I was flushed with childhood pleasure and pride. Running downstairs to my mother I held up my hand and made the letters for doll. I did not know that I was spelling a word or even that words existed; I was simply making my fingers go in monkeylike imitation. In the days that followed I learned to spell in this uncomprehending way a great many words, among them *pin*, *hat, cup* and a few verbs like *sit, stand* and *walk*. But my teacher had been with me several weeks before I understood that everything has a name.

One day, while I was playing with my new doll, Miss Sullivan put my big rag doll into my lap also, spelled "d-o-l-l" and tried to make me understand that "d-o-l-l" applied to both. Earlier in the day we had had a tussle over the words "m-u-g" and "w-a-t-e-r." Miss Sullivan had tried to impress it upon me that "m-u-g" is *mug* and that "w-a-t-e-r" is *water*, but I persisted in confounding the two. In despair she had dropped the subject for the time, only to renew it at the first opportunity. I became impatient at her repeated attempts and, seizing the new doll, I dashed it upon the floor. I was keenly delighted when I felt the fragments of the broken doll at my feet. Neither sorrow nor regret followed my passion-ate outburst. I had not loved the doll. In the still, dark world in which I lived there was no strong sentiment or tenderness. I felt my teacher sweep the fragments to one side of the hearth, and I had a sense of satisfaction that the cause of my discomfort was removed. She brought me my hat, and I knew I was going out into the warm sunshine. This thought, if a wordless sensation may be called a thought, made me hop and skip with pleasure.

We walked down the path to the well-house, attracted by the fra-grance of the honeysuckle with which it was covered. Some one was draw-ing water and my teacher placed my hand under the spout. As the cool stream gushed over one hand she spelled into the other the word *water*, first slowly, then rapidly. I stood still, my whole attention fixed upon the motions of her fingers. Suddenly I felt a misty consciousness as of

I knew then that "w-a-t-e-r" meant the wonderful cool something that was flowing over my hand.

something forgotten—a thrill of returning thought; and somehow the mystery of language was revealed to me. I knew then that "w-a-t-e-r" meant the wonderful cool something that was flowing over my hand. The living word awakened my soul, gave it light, hope, joy, set it free! There were barriers still, it is true, but barriers that could in time be swept away.

I left the well-house eager to learn. Everything had a name, and each name gave birth to a new thought. As we returned to the house every object which I touched seemed to quiver with life. That was because I saw everything with the strange, new sight that had come to me. On entering the door I remembered the doll I had broken. I felt my way to the hearth and picked up the pieces. I tried vainly to put them together. Then my eyes filled with tears; for I realized what I had done, and for the first time I felt repentance and sorrow.

I learned a great many new words that day. I do not remember what they all were; but I do know that *mother, father, sister, teacher* were among them—words that were to make the world blossom for me, "like Aaron's rod, with flowers." It would have been difficult to find a happier child than I was as I lay in my crib at the close of that eventful day and lived over the joys it had brought me, and for the first time longed for a new day to come.

THINKING CRITICALLY ABOUT THE READING

1. In paragraph 6, Keller writes, "One day, while I was playing with my new doll, Miss Sullivan put my big rag doll into my lap also, spelled 'd-o-l-l' and tried to make me understand that 'd-o-l-l' applied to both." Why do you think Miss Sullivan placed a different doll in her lap? What essential fact about language did the action demonstrate to Keller?

2. In paragraph 6, Keller also tells us that in trying to learn the difference between "m-u-g" and "w-a-t-e-r" she "persisted in confounding the two" terms. In a letter to her home institution, Sullivan elaborated on this confusion, revealing that it was caused by Keller thinking that both words meant "drink." How in paragraph 7 does Keller finally come to understand these words? What does she come to understand about the relationship between them?

3. In paragraph 8, after the experience at the well, Keller comes to believe that "everything had a name, and each name gave birth to a new thought." Reflect on that statement. Does she mean that the process of naming leads to thinking?

4. Keller realized that over time words would make her world open up for her. Identify the parts of speech of her first words. In what ways do these parts of speech open up one's world? Explain how these words or parts of speech provide insights into the nature of writing. How does Keller's early language use compare with her use of English in her essay?

5. While it is fairly easy to see how Keller could learn the names of concrete items, it may be more difficult for us to understand how she learned about her emotions. What does her difficulty in coming to terms with abstractions—such as love, bitterness, frustration, repentance, sorrow—tell us as writers about the strategies we need to use to effectively convey emotions and feelings to our readers? In considering your answer, examine the diction Keller uses in her essay. (Glossary: *Diction*)

LANGUAGE IN ACTION

In paragraph 3, Keller uses figurative language—the metaphor of being lost in a fog—to explain her feeling of helplessness and her frustration at not being able to communicate. (Glossary: *Figures of Speech*) Metaphors and similes—brief, imaginative comparisons that highlight the similarities between things that are basically dissimilar—can be extremely helpful when trying to communicate a new concept or a strange or difficult feeling. Create a metaphor (implied comparison) or a simile (implicit comparison introduced by *like* or *as*) that would be helpful in describing each item in the following list. The first one has been completed for you to illustrate the process.

1. Skyscraper: The skyscraper sparkled in the sunlight like a huge glass needle. (Simile)

   The skyscraper, a huge glass needle, sparkled in the sunlight. (Metaphor)
2. Sound of an explosion
3. Happy person
4. Greasy French fries
5. Disagreeable roommate
6. Cold wind
7. Crowded elevator
8. Loneliness
9. Slow-moving car
10. Rainy day

Compare your metaphors and similes with those written by other members of your class. Which metaphors and similes for each item on the list seem to work best? Why? Do any seem tired or clichéd?

WRITING SUGGESTIONS

1. It could be said that we process our world in terms of our language. Using a variety of examples from your own experience, write an essay illustrating the validity of this observation. For example, aside from the photographs you took on your last vacation, your trip exists only in the words you use to describe it, whether in conversations or in writing.
2. Helen Keller explains that she felt no remorse when she shattered her doll. "In the still, dark world in which I lived there was no strong sentiment or

tenderness" (6) she recalls. However, once she understood that things had names, Keller was able to feel repentance and sorrow. In your own words, try to describe why you think her feelings changed. Before you begin to write, you may want to reread your Writing to Discover entry for the Keller article. You may also want to discuss this issue with classmates or your instructor and do some research of your own into the ways language alters perception among people who are blind or deaf.

Superman and Me

SHERMAN ALEXIE

Born in 1966, Native American poet, novelist, and filmmaker Sherman Alexie grew up on the Spokane Indian Reservation in Wellpinit, Washington. As Alexie's autobiographical writing attests, it was difficult growing up an Indian kid in America, let alone on a reservation afflicted by poverty and addiction. Alexie also dealt with a seizure condition that drew ridicule from his peers, kept him from many typical rites of passage, and immersed him in a world of books. Distinguishing himself academically by refusing to remain passive and submissive, he earned a place in a high school off the reservation where he became not only the school's sole Indian student but also the president of his class and star player of its basketball team. College proved to be more difficult, and Alexie's anxiety led him to struggle with alcoholism, as his father had. Amid this struggle he attended Gonzaga University before transferring to Washington State University, where he earned a B.A. in American studies. Alexie quit drinking at the age of twenty-three and has remained sober since.

Alexie's work, drawn from many of these experiences, explores themes of Indian poverty and isolation, violence and addiction, tenacity and resistance, while indicting the long history of racism in American society. Alexie is known for writing the critically acclaimed film *Smoke Signals* (1998) and the novels *The Lone Ranger and Tonto Fist Fight in Heaven* (1993), which won a PEN/Hemingway Award, and *War Dances* (2010), which won a PEN/Faulkner Award, and he has more-recently gained an audience among young readers with his *The Absolutely True Diary of a Part-Time Indian* (2007), which won a National Book Award for Young People's Literature.

Like the partly autobiographical *Diary of a Part-Time Indian*, the essay included here, which first appeared in the 1997 anthology *The Most Wonderful Books: Writers on Discovering the Pleasures of Reading*, reflects on Alexie's learning process. For Alexie, his early literacy experience led to the desire to learn and to find a voice that could save his own life as well as the lives of his people. He was on a quest to prove not only that writing was not, as he puts it, "something beyond Indians," but that Indians had something worthwhile to say, something worth preserving.

WRITING TO DISCOVER: *Think about a time when you felt particularly dismissed or unheard in conversation. How did you react? Did you feel like you had any authority to make yourself heard? What role do you think one's ability to read and write well play in being able to "fight back"?*

I learned to read with a Superman comic book. Simple enough, I suppose. I cannot recall which particular Superman comic book I read, nor can I remember which villain he fought in that issue. I cannot remember the plot, nor the means by which I obtained the comic book. What I can remember is this: I was 3 years old, a Spokane Indian boy living with his family on the Spokane Indian Reservation in eastern Washington state. We were poor by most standards, but one of my parents usually managed to find some minimum-wage job or another, which made us middle-class by reservation standards. I had a brother and three sisters. We lived on a combination of irregular paychecks, hope, fear and government surplus food.

My father, who is one of the few Indians who went to Catholic school on purpose, was an avid reader of westerns, spy thrillers, murder mysteries, gangster epics, basketball player biographies and anything else he could find. He bought his books by the pound at Dutch's Pawn Shop, Goodwill, Salvation Army and Value Village. When he had extra money, he bought new novels at supermarkets, convenience stores and hospital gift shops. Our house was filled with books. They were stacked in crazy piles in the bathroom, bedrooms and living room. In a fit of unemployment-inspired creative energy, my father built a set of bookshelves and soon filled them with a random assortment of books about the Kennedy assassination, Watergate, the Vietnam War and the entire 23-book series of the Apache westerns. My father loved books, and since I loved my father with an aching devotion, I decided to love books as well.

I can remember picking up my father's books before I could read. The words themselves were mostly foreign, but I still remember the exact moment when I first understood, with a sudden clarity, the purpose of a paragraph. I didn't have the vocabulary to say "paragraph," but I realized that a paragraph was a fence that held words. The words inside a paragraph worked together for a common purpose. They had some specific reason for being inside the same fence. This knowledge delighted me. I began to think of everything in terms of paragraphs. Our reservation was a small paragraph within the United States. My family's house was a paragraph, distinct from the other paragraphs of the LeBrets to the north, the Fords to our south and the Tribal School to the west. Inside our house, each family member existed as a separate paragraph but still had genetics and common experiences to link us. Now, using this logic, I can see my changed family as an essay of seven paragraphs: mother, father, older brother, the deceased sister, my younger twin sisters and our adopted little brother.

At the same time I was seeing the world in paragraphs, I also picked up that Superman comic book. Each panel, complete with picture, dialogue and narrative was a three-dimensional paragraph. In one panel, Superman breaks through a door. His suit is red, blue and yellow. The brown door shatters into many pieces. I look at the narrative above the picture. I cannot read the words, but I assume it tells me that "Superman is breaking down the door." Aloud, I pretend to read the words and say, "Superman is breaking down the door." Words, dialogue, also float out of Superman's mouth. Because he is breaking down the door, I assume he says, "I am breaking down the door." Once again, I pretend to read the words and say aloud, "I am breaking down the door." In this way, I learned to read.

This might be an interesting story all by itself. A little Indian boy 5 teaches himself to read at an early age and advances quickly. He reads "Grapes of Wrath" in kindergarten when other children are struggling through "Dick and Jane." If he'd been anything but an Indian boy living on the reservation, he might have been called a prodigy. But he is an Indian boy living on the reservation and is simply an oddity. He grows into a man who often speaks of his childhood in the third-person, as if it will somehow dull the pain and make him sound more modest about his talents.

A smart Indian is a dangerous person, widely feared and ridiculed by Indians and non-Indians alike. I fought with my classmates on a daily basis. They wanted me to stay quiet when the non-Indian teacher asked for answers, for volunteers, for help. We were Indian children who were expected to be stupid. Most lived up to those expectations inside the classroom but subverted them on the outside. They struggled with basic reading in school but could remember how to sing a few dozen powwow songs. They were monosyllabic in front of their non-Indian teachers but could tell complicated stories and jokes at the dinner table. They submissively ducked their heads when confronted by a non-Indian adult but would slug it out with the Indian bully who was 10 years older. As Indian children, we were expected to fail in the non-Indian world. Those who failed were ceremonially accepted by other Indians and appropriately pitied by non-Indians.

> **A smart Indian is a dangerous person, widely feared and ridiculed by Indians and non-Indians alike.**

I refused to fail. I was smart. I was arrogant. I was lucky. I read books late into the night, until I could barely keep my eyes open. I read books at recess, then during lunch, and in the few minutes left after I had finished my classroom assignments. I read books in the car when my family traveled to powwows or basketball games. In shopping malls, I ran to the bookstores and read bits and pieces of as many books as I could. I read the books my father brought home from the pawnshops and secondhand. I read the books I borrowed from the library. I read the backs of cereal boxes. I read the newspaper. I read the bulletins posted on the walls of the school, the clinic, the tribal offices, the post office. I read junk mail. I read auto-repair manuals. I read magazines. I read anything that had words and paragraphs. I read with equal parts joy and desperation. I loved those books, but I also knew that love had only one purpose. I was trying to save my life.

Despite all the books I read, I am still surprised I became a writer. I was going to be a pediatrician. These days, I write novels, short stories, and poems. I visit schools and teach creative writing to Indian kids. In all my years in the reservation school system, I was never taught how to write poetry, short stories or novels. I was certainly never taught that Indians wrote poetry, short stories and novels. Writing was something beyond Indians. I cannot recall a single time that a guest teacher visited the reservation. There must have been visiting teachers. Who were they? Where are they now? Do they exist? I visit the schools as often as possible. The Indian kids crowd the classroom. Many are writing their own poems, short stories and novels. They have read my books. They have read many other books. They look at me with bright eyes and arrogant wonder. They are trying to save their lives. Then there are the sullen and already defeated Indian kids who sit in the back rows and ignore me with theatrical precision. The pages of their notebooks are empty. They carry neither pencil nor pen. They stare out the window. They refuse and resist. "Books," I say to them. "Books," I say. I throw my weight against their locked doors. The door holds. I am smart. I am arrogant. I am lucky. I am trying to save our lives.

THINKING CRITICALLY ABOUT THE READING

1. In the first two paragraphs of Alexie's essay, we learn a great deal about his family through items listed in a series. What do we learn, either explicitly or through inference? Why would Alexie disclose such personal information in list form? What effect does this choice have on the reader?

2. In his third paragraph, Alexie calls a paragraph "a fence that held words." How does Alexie describe his response to his newfound knowledge? How does it become personally significant for him? Why do you think Alexie might choose the word "fence"?

3. In paragraph 5, Alexie actually draws attention to his own grammar by noting that he is writing in the third person. What effect does Alexie suggest writing in the third person has on him? On readers? In what ways might this passage change if written in first or second person?

4. Alexie writes in paragraph 6 that "a smart Indian is a dangerous person, widely feared and ridiculed by Indians and non-Indians alike." Why do you think Alexie calls a "smart Indian" dangerous? What or who has given him that idea? Would his sentiment differ if he replaced the word "Indian" with another of his own identities (male, heterosexual, etc.)?

5. Alexie emphasizes several times that through writing he is "trying to save lives." Why do you think he characterizes reading and writing in this way? What metaphors or other figures of speech does he use to emphasize the dire importance of reading and writing?

LANGUAGE IN ACTION

Sherman Alexie read many traditional books, and he also reports reading voraciously all sorts of texts you wouldn't expect a child to pick up as reading material:

> I read the backs of cereal boxes. I read the newspaper. I read the bulletins posted on the walls of the school, the clinic, the tribal offices, the post office. I read junk mail. I read auto-repair manuals. I read magazines. I read anything that had words and paragraphs.

Bring a text like this to class and examine it carefully, thinking of it as a text to learn from, and consider how it changes when taken as seriously as a work of literature. What can you learn about the world from your text? Consider not just its content, but its language, structure, and even its design. What would you have learned if you had read it as a child? What do you take from this text that you couldn't find in the kinds of books you might read for school?

WRITING SUGGESTIONS

1. Through the first four paragraphs of his essay, Alexie tells a literacy narrative, a short story describing the process by which he learned to read. After spending some time thinking about your own early experiences with books (learning to read; your first favorite book; being read to by a parent or sibling) or later literacy developments (encountering a book that changed the way you thought; encountering a book that you could not get through or one that you couldn't put down), write a few paragraphs detailing your own literacy narrative. What have been the turning points in your life as a reader and a writer? What has made you think of yourself as "good" or "bad" at reading or writing?

2. Although Alexie's work looks at the marginalization many Indians feel in relation to white culture, there is something universal to his essay. Alexie writes in the essay's last paragraph: "Then there are the sullen and already defeated Indian kids who sit in the back rows and ignore me with theatrical precision. The pages of their notebooks are empty. They carry neither pencil nor pen. They stare out the window. They refuse and resist. 'Books,' I say to them. 'Books,' I say. I throw my weight against their locked doors." Of course, not only "Indian kids" feel "sullen and already defeated" and "refuse and resist" their teachers' efforts. In fact, recent research suggests that more and more students and teachers are feeling defeated in the face of an American education system that focuses on standardized testing. Spend some time researching criticisms of standardized testing as well as the benefits. Choose a position in relationship to testing and discuss the effect this test-centered system seems to be having on students. In what ways are students' individual needs being met or ignored? In what ways does standardization ensure or discourage the kind of engagement with the world through reading and writing that Alexie explores?

Writing to Change the World

Mary Pipher

Psychologist, educator, author, and family therapist, Mary Pipher was born in 1947 in Springfield, Missouri, and grew up in Beaver City, Nebraska. She did her undergraduate work in cultural anthropology at the University of California, Berkeley, graduating in 1969, and received her Ph.D. in clinical psychology from the University of Nebraska in 1977. Pipher is the author of eight books including the hugely popular *Hunger Pains: The Modern Woman's Tragic Quest for Thinness* (1997); *Reviving Ophelia: Saving the Selves of Adolescent Girls* (1994), which was on the *New York Times* bestseller list for 26 weeks; *The Shelter of Each Other: Rebuilding Our Families to Enrich Our Lives* (1996); *Seeking Peace: Chronicles of the Worst Buddhist in the World* (2009); and *The Green Boat: Reviving Ourselves in our Capsized Culture* (2013).

The following selection is taken from *Writing to Change the World* (2006), which was inspired by a workshop Pipher taught at the University of Nebraska's National Summer Writer's Conference. In the book, Pipher uses the epiphany she had while first reading *The Diary of Anne Frank* as a twelve-year-old to launch into an exploration of the truly incredible power of the written word. Pipher's reflections on the power of writing to change the world gives readers a fresh take on the old adage, "The pen is mightier than the sword."

WRITING TO DISCOVER: *Name two or three of the most memorable books you have read. What about these books moved you or made such an impression upon you? Did any of these books change the way you view the world? If so, explain how.*

The first book to change my view of the universe was *The Diary of Anne Frank*. I read Anne's diary when I was a twelve-year-old, in Beaver City, Nebraska. Before I read it, I had been able to ignore the existence of evil. I knew a school had burned down in Chicago, and that children had died there. I had seen grown-ups lose their tempers, and I had encountered bullies and nasty school-mates. I had a vague sense that there were criminals—jewel thieves, bank robbers, and Al Capone–style gangsters—in Kansas City and Chicago. After reading the diary, I realized that there were adults who would systematically kill children. My comprehension of the human race expanded to include a hero like Anne, but also to include the villains who killed her. When I read Anne Frank's diary, I lost my spiritual innocence.

In September 2003, when I was fifty-five years old, I visited the Holocaust Museum, in Washington, D.C., to view the Anne Frank exhibit. I looked at the cover of her little plaid diary, and at the pages of her writing, at her family pictures. Miep Gies, Otto Frank's employee who brought food to the family, spoke on video about the people who hid in the attic. She said that Anne had always wanted to know the truth about what was going on. Others would believe the sugarcoated version of Miep's stories, but Anne would follow her to the door and ask, "What is really happening?"

The museum showed a short film clip of Anne dressed in white, her long hair dark and shiny. She is waving exuberantly from a balcony at a wedding party that is parading down the street. There are just a few seconds of film, captured by a filmmaker at the wedding who must have been entranced by her enthusiasm. The footage is haunting. Anne's wave seems directed at all of us, her small body casting a shadow across decades.

At the end of the exhibit, attendees hear the voice of a young girl reading Anne's essay, "Give," a piece inspired by her experience of passing beggars on the street. She wonders if people who live in cozy houses have any idea of the life of beggars. She offers hope: "How wonderful it is that no one has to wait, but can start right now to gradually change the world." She suggests action: "Give whatever you have to give, you can always give something, even if it is a simple act of kindness." And she ends with "The world has plenty of room, riches, money and beauty. God has created enough for each and every one of us. Let us begin by dividing it more fairly."

Even though Anne Frank was ultimately murdered, she managed, in   5 her brief and circumscribed life, to tell the truth and bequeath the gift of hope. She searched for beauty and joy even in the harsh, frightened world of the attic in which her family hid from the Nazis. Her writing has lived on to give us all a sense of the potential largesse of the human soul, even in worst-case scenarios. It also reminds us that, behind the statistics about war and genocide, there are thousands of good people who have a responsibility to help.

All writing is designed to change the world, at least a small part of the world, or in some small way, perhaps a change in a reader's mood or in his or her appreciation of a certain kind of beauty. Writing to improve the world can be assessed by the goals of its writers and/or by its effects on the world. Most likely, Mary Oliver did not write her poem "Wild Geese" to inspire environmental activists and yet environmentalists have found it inspirational. Bob Dylan claims he had no intention of composing a protest song when he penned "Blowin' in the Wind," but it became the anthem for many of the causes of the last half of the twentieth century. On the other hand, musicians like Tori Amos, the Indigo Girls, and the band Ozomatli do hope to influence their listeners in specific ways, and they succeed. Looking back, Rachel Carson, in *Silent Spring*, satisfies both intent and effect: she wrote the book to stop the use of certain pesticides, and, following its publication, DDT was banned in the United States.

My dad told me about a rule that he and other soldiers followed in the Pacific during World War II. It was called the Law of 26, and it postulates that for every result you expect from an action there will be twenty-six results you do not expect. Certainly this law applies to writing. Sometimes a book intended to have one effect has quite another. For example, Upton Sinclair wrote *The Jungle* to call attention to the exploitation of the immigrant labor force and their working conditions in factories, yet it led to an outcry over unsanitary conditions in the meat industry and helped establish uniform standards for beef processing and inspection nationwide.

All writing to effect change need not be great literature. Some of it is art, of course, such as Walt Whitman's "I Hear America Singing" or Abraham Lincoln's Gettysburg Address. Some of it is relatively straightforward such as *Rampage: The Social Roots of School Shooting* by Katherine Newman, David Harding, and Cybelle Fox. And some of it is both artful and straightforward. For example, in *The Age of Missing Information*, Bill McKibben has a clever idea that he executes beautifully: he compares what he learns from a week in the mountains to what he learns from watching a week's worth of cable television. On the mountaintop, McKibben experiences himself as small yet connected to something large and awe-inspiring. He comes down from the mountain calm and clear-thinking. Watching cable for a week, he hears over and over that he has unmet needs, that he is grossly inadequate, yet he still is the center of the universe, deserving of everything he wants. McKibben ended the week feeling unfocused, agitated, and alone.

Change writers trust that readers can handle multiple points of view, contradictions, unresolved questions, and nuance.

Many effective writers are not stylists, but they manage to convey a very clear message. Their writing is not directed toward sophisticates or literary critics. It is designed to influence cousin Shirley, farmer Dale, coworker Jan, Dr. Lisa, neighbor Carol, businessman Carl, or voter Sylvia. Expository writing for ordinary people calls for a variety of talent—storytelling skills, clarity, and the ability to connect. Whether they are working on an op-ed piece, a speech, or a poem, skilled writers exercise creativity and conscious control. They labor to make the important interesting, and even compelling, to readers.

Change writers hope that readers will join them in what Charles Johnson calls "an invitation to struggle." Whereas writers of propaganda encourage readers to accept certain answers, writers who want to transform their readers encourage the asking of questions. Propaganda invites passive agreement; change writing invites original thought, openheartedness, and engagement. Change writers trust that readers can handle multiple points of view, contradictions, unresolved questions, and nuance. If, as André Gide wrote, "Tyranny is the absence of complexity," then change writers are founders of democracies.

10

Good writing astonishes its writer first. My favorite example of this phenomenon is Leo Tolstoy's *Anna Karenina*. Tolstoy planned to write a novel that condemned adultery, and his intention was to make the adulteress an unsympathetic character. But when he came to truly understand Anna as he wrote the book, he fell in love with her, and, a hundred years later, so do his readers. Empathy can turn contempt into love.

THINKING CRITICALLY ABOUT THE READING

1. What do you think Pipher means when she says, "I lost my spiritual innocence" while reading *The Diary of Anne Frank* as a twelve-year-old?

2. In paragraphs 2 through 4 Pipher tells of visiting the Holocaust Museum in Washington, D.C., to view the Anne Frank exhibit. Why do you suppose Pipher chose to tell her readers about the parts of the exhibit that she does? What insights into Anne's character does Pipher give us?

3. Pipher believes that "all writing is designed to change the world" (6). What examples does she provide to support her claim? Did you find her examples convincing? If you were writing an argument along similar lines as Pipher, what examples of change writing would you choose to support this claim, and why?

4. According to Pipher, what talents do writers of good expository prose possess? Do you agree? How well does Pipher exhibit these talents in this essay? Explain.

5. What are the key differences between change writing and propaganda, according to Pipher? What accounts for the power of each of these types of writing? Which type do you think is more powerful in the long run?

LANGUAGE IN ACTION

Over the years, communities throughout the United States have banned or censored many classic works of literature. The American Library Association keeps track of attempts to ban books and publishes a list of the most frequently challenged books each year. Consider for a moment the following frequently banned books, many of which you have probably heard of if not read:

The Scarlet Letter—Nathaniel Hawthorne

The Adventures of Huckleberry Finn—Mark Twain

The Catcher in the Rye—J. D. Salinger

To Kill a Mockingbird—Harper Lee

Bridge to Terabithia—Katherine Paterson

The Lord of the Flies—William Golding

Anne Frank: The Diary of a Young Girl—Anne Frank

The Grapes of Wrath—John Steinbeck

The Color Purple—Alice Walker

Harry Potter series—J. K. Rowling

Slaughterhouse Five—Kurt Vonnegut

The Bluest Eye—Toni Morrison

The Prince of Tides—Pat Conroy

Blubber—Judy Blume

I Know Why the Caged Bird Sings—Maya Angelou

The Absolutely True Diary of a Part-Time Indian—Sherman Alexie

Heather Has Two Mommies—Leslea Newman

Persepolis—Marjane Satrapi

Gone with the Wind—Margaret Mitchell

What do you think motivates communities to ban books from libraries and schools? Select one of the titles from the list above that you have read and explain what people might have found objectionable about the book. Share your analysis with your class. On what grounds might someone object to the various books on this list? Do you think there is ever a legitimate reason for banning a book? What do book banning and censorship tell us about the power of the written word?

WRITING SUGGESTIONS

1. In her opening sentence Pipher tells us that "the first book to change my view of the universe was *The Diary of Anne Frank*." What was the first book that caused you to view the world differently? Write an essay about that book, describing in detail the impact that it had on you when you first read. Consider the book as an adult; how have your thoughts on it changed? You may find it helpful to review what you wrote in response to the Writing to Discover prompt for this selection on page 82 before starting to write.

2. In his memoir *Growing Up*, newspaper reporter and columnist Russell Baker recalls a moment during his eleventh-grade English class when he discovered that "my words had the power to make people laugh." Baker's teacher Mr. Fleagle wanted to make a point about essay writing by reading a student paper to the class. As Fleagle started to read, Baker—prepared for the worst—was suddenly surprised: "He was reading *my words* out loud to the entire class. What's more, the entire class was listening. Listening attentively. Then somebody laughed, then the entire class was laughing, and not in contempt and ridicule, but with open-hearted enjoyment." Have you ever considered that your writing has the power to inform, to entertain, to educate, or to persuade your peers? Write an essay in which you recount when you, or someone close to you, discovered that writing has power. Be sure to identify the purpose of that piece of writing, and which audience it was trying to influence.

3. Pipher mentions several examples of change writing, from the literary (Walt Whitman's "I Hear America Singing") to the political (the Gettysburg Address) to the sociological (Katherine Newman, David Harding, and Cybelle Fox's book about the history of school shootings). What type of change writing do you think exerts the most power? If you were to embark on a writing project intended to change the world in some capacity, what issue or issues would you address? Would you focus on a national or global problem? Or would you advocate for change on a personal level? Would you compose an inspiring poem, or would you choose to draft a clear, hard-nosed proposal? Describe the topic you would most want to address and the medium you would choose to convey your ideas.

4. *The Diary of Anne Frank* is a very powerful piece of change writing, read by millions of students each year. It reminds us of the importance of pursuing kindness and justice in the world. Ironically, despite its international audience and wide reach, the book was not written for others. As its title attests, the book is a diary, a journal of private thoughts, a repository for young Anne's expressions of wonder, frustration, anxiety, and hope. Pipher calls the diary change writing, but does it matter that Anne Frank never intended for anyone to read it? Write an essay in which you consider whether a private journal or diary can, in fact, be change writing.

You Can Keep Quiet, You Can Emigrate, or You Can Stay Here and Fight

EMILY PARKER

Emily Parker graduated with honors from Brown University with a double major in international relations and comparative literature and has an M.A. in East Asian studies from Harvard University. After completing her graduate studies, Parker worked as a writer and editor for the *Wall Street Journal* and as an editor for the *New York Times*. Parker also worked for Secretary of State Hillary Clinton as a member of her policy planning staff. While working for the Department of State, she served as an advisor on issues related to Internet freedom and open government.

Building on her passion about the role of new media in government, Parker is now the digital diplomacy advisor and a senior fellow at the New America Foundation. She has also created three projects on digital diplomacy, including Code4Country, an open coding marathon that convenes software developers in the United States and Russia to foster transparency in government through technology. She is also a former fellow at the Council on Foreign Relations and Asia Society's Center on U.S.-China Relations, as well as a Global Policy Fellow at Carnegie Moscow Center. At the latter she began to research the role of blogging and social media in Russia, which laid the foundation for the following selection.

The selection below is an excerpt from Parker's book *Now I Know Who My Comrades Are: Voices from the Internet Underground* (2015), which explores the role of technology in challenging the oppression of citizens under authoritarian regimes across the globe. The excerpt below deals with the challenges — and grave dangers — of being a journalist in twenty-first-century Russia.

WRITING TO DISCOVER: *Think about the role new media plays in your life. Do you have a Facebook account? Are you on Instagram or Twitter or Tumblr? Choose one platform on which to reflect and then reread all of your entries for the past month. Have you written anything controversial? Try to imagine yourself as a government official assigned to monitor your accounts, and flag any questionable activity.*

What [Russian anti-corruption campaigner, lawyer, and political activist] Alexey Navalny was doing in Russia, essentially a combination of investigative journalism and whistle-blowing, was not only unusual, it was incredibly dangerous. Challenging official corruption could have deadly consequences. One of the most notorious cases was that of the attorney Sergei Magnitsky, who accused Russian officials of stealing from the government. He was held without trial for eleven months, during which time he fell ill and was denied medical treatment. In 2009 he died in a Russian jail.

After his death Magnitsky became an international cause célèbre. In June 2012 the U.S. House Foreign Affairs Committee passed a bipartisan bill called the Sergei Magnitsky Rule of Law Accountability Act. Shortly thereafter, the Senate Foreign Relations Committee also passed the bill. It imposes banking and visa restrictions on Russian officials who are implicated in human rights abuses. Former House Committee on Foreign Affairs Chairman Ileana Ros-Lehtinen said that corruption in Russia is "widely accepted as normal and a way of life. . . . Tragically, those who challenge the authorities and take on this forbidden subject are dealt with harshly, and several of those who have investigated it have been assaulted, jailed, and even killed." In November 2012 the bill passed through the U.S. House of Representatives. In December President Obama signed the bill into law. Russia responded swiftly and angrily by passing a ban on U.S. adoptions of Russian children.

Although Russian apathy did have some fear at its root, most Russians had long ago given up on challenging the rich and powerful. As a result, the individuals who did push the envelope became vulnerable targets of abuse. Those individuals were ruthlessly punished, and the punishers often got off scot-free. Often it was unclear who commissioned the violence. There was a strong but silent undercurrent of violence and lawlessness that streamed through daily life. It was everywhere and nowhere, easy to ignore and impossible to forget.

One summer evening I was accompanying Veronika [Belenkaya, research assistant,] back to her apartment in Moscow. Veronika lived near Belorusskaya Square, which has a little foundation and cafés where we would enjoy wine or coffee outdoors. We weren't far from the square when we came upon an ordinary if somewhat run-down apartment building that had a dark red door. Veronika called my attention to a small Russian plaque next to the door. This was nothing unusual: Moscow is dotted with plaques commemorating poets, writers, and various wartime heroes, and Veronika loved to point them out.

Underneath this particular plaque were two wilted white roses. We stopped walking, and I casually peered at its message. It said, "This is the building in which Anna Politkovskaya lived and was viciously murdered."

Politkovskaya was a journalist and human rights activist who was   5
fiercely critical of Vladimir Putin and the Chechen conflict. She wrote for *Novaya Gazeta*, a prominent opposition newspaper, and made powerful enemies in both the Kremlin and Chechnya. Politkovskaya's editor, Yuri Shcekochikhin, had died of poisoning, and Politkovskaya herself was the target of constant death threats. In 2004 she flew to North Ossetia to cover the tragedy in Beslan, where children in a school were being held hostage by terrorists.

The cautious Politkovskaya took her own food on the plane and accepted only a cup of tea. Apparently, that was all it took. She fell into a coma and was taken to Moscow, where doctors determined that she had been poisoned by a toxin that damaged her kidneys, liver, and endocrine system. Thus, as the journalist and author Masha Gessen observed, Politkovskaya "was effectively prevented from covering and investigating the tragedy in Beslan." Politkovskaya never fully recovered from the poisoning and continued to have health problems.

On October 7, 2006, she was shot to death in the elevator of the very building Veronika and I were facing. Her death, which drew gasps of horror from around the world, happened to take place on Putin's fifty-fourth birthday. According to Gessen, the day after Politkovskaya's death, Putin sent his own birthday wishes to a figure skater and a popular actor, but didn't make any public comment about the murder. Three days later, he met with German chancellor Angela Merkel in Dresden. When he got out of his car, he found a picket line of some thirty people holding signs with the word KILLER.

At the press conference that followed his meeting with Merkel, Putin apparently had no choice but to comment on Politkovskaya's death. He did say that the murder was "an unacceptable crime that cannot go unpunished."

He acknowledged that Politkovskaya was a harsh critic of the Russian government, then added, "Her ability to influence political life in Russia was extremely insignificant." Eventually an accomplice to the murder was sentenced to prison. In 2013 five suspects in the case went on a trial that Politkovskaya's children called "illegitimate."

On the same street as Politkovskaya's building was a pharmacy and a store 10 that appeared to sell men's underwear. The only reminder of what happened there is a little black sign, put up by the opposition activist and former chess champion Garry Kasparov, that many Russians don't stop to read.

Russia is a notoriously dangerous place for journalists, largely because so many crimes against them go unpunished.

Russia is a notoriously dangerous place for journalists, largely because so many crimes against them go unpunished. "The impunity the masterminds enjoy—this is the main part of the mechanism, which breeds new murders," said Sergey Sokolov, deputy editor of the *Novaya Gazeta*. In 2012 the Committee to Protect Journalists ranked Russia ninth on its "impunity index"—the list of countries where journalists' murderers roam free. At the time, Russia had sixteen unsolved journalist murders.

Oleg Kashin, the popular blogger and *Kommersant* writer, returned home late one night to find two men waiting for him outside his house. One was holding a bouquet of flowers. They proceeded to beat him with their fists and metal objects. Kashin's jaw and leg were broken, his skull was fractured, and his fingers were partially torn off. His editor at *Kommersant* interpreted the damage to his hands as a clear attempt to get him to stop writing.

Like Politkovskaya, Kashin had an assortment of enemies. He covered the environmentalist and resident group protests against the cutting down of Khimki Forest in order to make room for a highway between Moscow and St. Petersburg. Backed by powerful figures, it appeared as if the federal project would yield dividends for the Khimki administration and its mayor, Vladimir Strelchenko.

One of the highway's strongest critics, the journalist Mikhail Beketov, was beaten nearly to death in 2008. Beketov had defended the forest, which was home to old trees and wild animals, and he also suggested that local officials were profiting from the project. Local officials were not happy. Beketov received phone threats. His dog was killed. His car was blown up. And then he was severely beaten and left lying in the snow. Like Kashin's, his hands had also been bashed.

If that wasn't bad enough, in 2010 a judge found Beketov guilty of   15
slandering Strelchenko by accusing him of involvement in blowing up Beketov's car. Beketov was fined a small amount, which was then suspended. His own brutal attack went unpunished, and he died in 2013.

In Kashin's case, there were various possible motives for the beating. One theory was that his attack was linked to his blog post about Andrei Turchak, the governor of the Pskov region, which argued that he had gotten his position through his Kremlin ties. Turchak had threatened Kashin months before the attack.

Another theory, and the one Kashin himself believed, was that he was attacked for crossing Nashi, an ultranationalist youth group founded by the Kremlin. He was highly critical of their violent tactics, claiming that they were launching attacks and beating up the opposition. He questioned their impunity and the fact that they were not being tried for their violence.

I first met Kashin in a small, dimly lit Starbucks on Moscow's bustling Tverskaya Street. It was a few months after his attack. He was determinedly cheerful, although he looked vaguely lost. He was missing some of his teeth, and one of his fingers had been amputated. He told me that President Medvedev had promised to catch the killers. In fact, President Medvedev had tweeted, "I have ordered the office of the Prosecutor General and the Interior Ministry to take the case of the attempted murder of the journalist Kashin under special control. The criminals must be found and punished."

"I feel optimism about journalism in Russia," Kashin told me, while I tried not to look at his mutilated hand. "I think the Kremlin understands that a kind of a new perestroika is needed." Then he ended our meeting rather abruptly, and I walked him outside. A young guy on the street inexplicably took a cell phone photo of him. I realized that Kashin's bodyguards were sitting in a weathered-looking car, waiting in the dark. He told me they were being paid for by the Russian government. Neither Kashin's attackers nor those who commissioned the beating have yet been brought to justice.

If this is what can happen to journalists in Russia, imagine the possible   20
fate of someone like Navalny. Not only was he trying to reveal corruption, but he wanted someone to pay for it. As a result of Navalny's anticorruption campaigns, corporations and individuals stood to lose real money. Many speculated that his days were numbered. He has a wife and small children, and he was known to keep guns in the house.

The one silver lining was that at least his disappearance wouldn't go unnoticed. In 2010 Navalny's blog had about fifty thousand daily readers. He had begun to attract the attention of the Western media. Navalny knew he was striking a nerve. People were sick of corruption, and now someone was offering the possibility of making things at least a little better. He still wasn't the most popular blogger in Russia, but he was well on the way to becoming the most powerful.

Fame alone, however, won't protect you in Russia. The disgraced businessman Mikhail Khodorkovsky, whose arrest generated great controversy throughout Russia and the world, was still behind bars. The first time I spoke with Navalny, I asked him if he was afraid. He didn't pause. "I know how easily people are killed in Russia," he said. "But in the end, it's a question of choice. You can keep silent, you can emigrate, or you can stay here and fight."

And a fight it would be. Not only was he putting himself in danger, but his activities started to cause trouble for his family. In 2011 he told me that his family had two very small shops, of which Navalny was cofounder and part owner. He believes that his activities led the authorities to constantly check the stores' licenses and certificates. "It's not a problem for me, but it's a problem for our parents," he said. "Not a big problem but it's, you know, annoying."

His wife, Julia, supported his activities, but his parents worried. Navalny finally had to have a frank conversation with his family. He told them squarely, "There will be a date when I will be arrested. So just consider it as a fact. Stop discussing. Just be prepared." He said that conversation brought a sense of relief, and it became "taboo" for the family to pester him about his safety.

This is not to say that his mother slept more easily. "Unfortunately, I was stupid enough, and I showed her how to Google me on the Internet," he told me. He said she knows how to find all mentions of him on blogs and Twitter. "She reads everything which was written about me. And half of it is a kind of, 'he will be killed.'"   25

Still, Navalny was emboldened by the knowledge that he wasn't alone. The first time we spoke, he said proudly, "I feel the support of the people, and the support of the bloggers who are ready to join me in my action."

THINKING CRITICALLY ABOUT THE READING

1. In paragraph 4, Parker comments on a "little black sign" inconspicuously placed on a shabby apartment building. It commemorates the assassination of Russian journalist Anna Politkovskaya, stating simply: "This is the building in which Anna Politkovskaya lived and was viciously murdered." How does this placard compare to your own experience with commemorative plaques? Compared to the story Parker tells about Politkovskaya's life and death, does "viciously murdered" seem sufficient? How might you have written the placard differently?

2. Parker calls Russia a "notoriously dangerous place for journalism" (12). Why were the journalists Parker interviews considered dangerous? How does Parker characterize the retaliation that they suffered?

3. In depicting a contemporary Russia that allows for such brutality against its own citizens, what stylistic choices or additional details within the narrative does Parker include to reaffirm the nation's modernity? Why do you think she includes such details?

4. In the United States we, as citizens, prize free speech and the freedom of the press as hallmarks of our society. Based on the descriptions in this article, what seem to be hallmarks of Russian society? Of its citizens? Of its government? Thinking reflectively, how might you censor your response if you were writing inside Russian territory?

5. In paragraph 23, Parker quotes Alexey Navalny, who suggests Russian journalists have three choices: "You can stay silent, you can emigrate, or you can stay here and fight." He is a blogger and whistleblower who had around fifty thousand daily readers at the time this essay was published, which Parker suggests may protect him from reprisal. How do you think new media could play a role in stopping both corruption and violence against critical reporting? What new media in particular do you think affords the most protections and why?

LANGUAGE IN ACTION

Chapter 2, Article 29, of the Russian constitution states,

1. Everyone shall be guaranteed the freedom of ideas and speech.

2. Propaganda or campaigning inciting social, racial, national or religious hatred and strife is impermissible. The propaganda of social, racial, national, religious or language superiority is forbidden.

3. No one may be coerced into expressing one's views and convictions or into renouncing them.

4. Everyone shall have the right to seek, get, transfer, produce and disseminate information by any lawful means. The list of information constituting the state secret shall be established by the federal law.

5. The freedom of the mass media shall be guaranteed. Censorship shall be prohibited.

Where in the language of this excerpt, if anywhere, does the Russian government justify or leave itself open to the possibility of coercing and physically combating those who criticize its decisions? What does this discrepancy say about where true freedom of speech comes from? *Can* a government-granted right be located in words, or does it only begin there? Consider whether the American freedom of speech is guaranteed by the First Amendment, or by the common ideals of the American government and people. There seems to be a great discrepancy between the law and what actually happens in Russian society. Is it possible that the same discrepancies exist in ours?

WRITING SUGGESTIONS

1. The injustices perpetrated against journalists daring to write freely in countries like Russia likely raises our ire as readers, but does that ire compel us to want all speech protected? Should it? Although hate crimes have existed in the United States from its inception, hate speech is a relatively new concept. If one researches the history of hate speech in the United States compared to that in other democratic nations in Europe, we find that while hate speech is protected under free speech in the United States, other countries outlaw hate speech and symbolism (swastikas, Holocaust denial, speech that promotes hatred on the basis of race, sexual orientation, etc.). Write an essay in which you argue whether or not free speech should protect hate speech in the United States. To better understand the issue and support your claims, read about hate speech in the United States and about restrictions on hate speech in Europe. (You might start with readings in Chapter 10, particularly Andrew Sullivan's "What's So Bad about Hate?," Wendy Kaminer's "Why We Need to Tolerate Hate," and Greg Lukianoff's "Twitter, Hate Speech, and the Costs of Keeping Quiet.")

2. In 2012, the three members of the all-female Russian punk band Pussy Riot were arrested on charges of "hooliganism" and inciting "religious hatred" when performing in Moscow's Christ the Savior cathedral. The group members have been outspoken critics of Vladmir Putin, and their arrest was largely political. Like writers and bloggers, artists and musicians often engage with politics. Spend time reading the lyrics of protest songs or the lyrics of an artist whose work has been tagged with a "parental advisory" label for its political content (e.g., N.W.A.). Focusing on one or two of the songs you've found, write an essay that addresses not only what makes these works controversial but also what makes them effective: Where have they been performed? How have they been used? Spend time analyzing the artistry of these works as well as their controversial nature: what makes the song effective? How do the lyrics craft an argument or engage with a politically controversial topic?

Letter from Birmingham Jail

MARTIN LUTHER KING JR.

Martin Luther King Jr. was born in 1929 in Atlanta, Georgia. The son of a Baptist minister, he was himself ordained at the age of eighteen and went on to study at Morehouse College, Crozer Theological Seminary, Boston University, and Chicago Theological Seminary. He first came to prominence in 1955, in Montgomery, Alabama, when he led a successful boycott against the city's segregated bus system. As the first president of the Southern Christian Leadership Conference, King promoted a policy of massive but nonviolent resistance to racial injustice, organized and led many civil rights demonstrations, and spoke out against the military draft and the Vietnam War. In 1964 he was awarded the Nobel Peace Prize. King's books include *Stride Toward Freedom* (1958) and *Why We Can't Wait* (1964). America lost a powerfully articulate and gifted leader when he was assassinated in Memphis, Tennessee, in 1968.

On Good Friday in 1963, the Reverend Martin Luther King Jr. led a march into downtown Birmingham, Alabama, to protest racial segregation by Birmingham's city government and local retailers. King and his fellow marchers met fierce opposition from the local police. They were arrested and jailed. King was detained for eight days. During this time King wrote his now-landmark letter from Birmingham Jail in response to a published statement by eight moderate white clergymen from Alabama who were horrified by the trouble in the streets and disagreed with King's fundamental strategy of nonviolent direct action. Historians agree that King's "Letter from Birmingham Jail" changed the political landscape in America, effectively marking a turning point of the civil rights movement and continuing to provide inspiration to the struggle for equal rights everywhere.

WRITING TO DISCOVER: *If you were to encounter an injustice in your world, how would you deal with it? Would you take direct action to confront the injustice? Would you seek some legal solution to the problem? Or would you ignore the injustice in hopes that it would go away? Is there any scenario you can imagine in which you would resort to violence? Explain.*

My Dear Fellow Clergymen:

While confined here in the Birmingham city jail, I came across your recent statement calling my present activities "unwise and untimely." Seldom do I pause to answer criticism of my work and ideas. If I sought to answer all the criticisms that cross my desk, my secretaries would have little time for anything other than such correspondence in the course of the day, and I would have no time for constructive work. But since I feel that you are men of genuine good will and that your criticisms are sincerely set forth, I want to try to answer your statement in what I hope will be patient and reasonable terms.

I think I should indicate why I am here in Birmingham, since you have been influenced by the view which argues against "outsiders coming in."

Injustice anywhere is a threat to justice everywhere.

I have the honor of serving as president of the Southern Christian Leadership Conference, an organization operating in every southern state, with headquarters in Atlanta, Georgia. We have some eighty-five affiliated organizations across the South, and one of them is the Alabama Christian Movement for Human Rights. Frequently we share staff, educational, and financial resources with our affiliates. Several months ago the affiliate here in Birmingham asked us to be on call to engage in a nonviolent direct-action program if such were deemed necessary. We readily consented, and when the hour came we lived up to our promise. So I, along with several members of my staff, am here because I was invited here. I am here because I have organizational ties here.

But more basically, I am in Birmingham because injustice is here. Just as the prophets of the eighth century B.C. left their villages and carried their "thus saith the Lord" far beyond the boundaries of their home towns, and just as the Apostle Paul left his village of Tarsus and carried the gospel of Jesus Christ to the far corners of the Greco-Roman world, so am I compelled to carry the gospel of freedom beyond my own home town. Like Paul, I must constantly respond to the Macedonian call for aid.

Moreover, I am cognizant of the interrelatedness of all communities and states. I cannot sit idly by in Atlanta and not be concerned about what happens in Birmingham. Injustice anywhere is a threat to justice everywhere. We are caught in an inescapable network of mutuality, tied in a single garment of destiny. Whatever affects one directly, affects all indirectly. Never again can we afford to live with the narrow, provincial, "outside agitator" idea. Anyone who lives inside the United States can never be considered an outsider anywhere within its bounds.

You deplore the demonstrations taking place in Birmingham. But 5 your statement, I am sorry to say, fails to express a similar concern for the conditions that brought about the demonstrations. I am sure that none of you would want to rest content with the superficial kind of social analysis that deals merely with effects and does not grapple with underlying causes. It is unfortunate that demonstrations are taking place in Birmingham, but it is even more unfortunate that the city's white power structure left the Negro community with no alternative.

In any nonviolent campaign there are four basic steps: collection of the facts to determine whether injustices exist; negotiation; self-purification; and direct action. We have gone through all these steps in Birmingham. There can be no gainsaying the fact that racial injustice engulfs this community. Birmingham is probably the most thoroughly segregated city in the United States. Its ugly record of brutality is widely known. Negroes have experienced grossly unjust treatment in courts. There have been more unsolved bombings of Negro homes and churches in Birmingham than in any other city in the nation. These are the hard, brutal facts of the case. On the basis of these conditions, Negro leaders sought to negotiate with the city fathers. But the latter consistently refused to engage in good-faith negotiation.

Then, last September, came the opportunity to talk with leaders of Birmingham's economic community. In the course of the negotiations, certain promises were made by the merchants—for example, to remove the stores' humiliating racial signs. On the basis of these promises, the Reverend Fred Shuttlesworth and the leaders of the Alabama Christian Movement for Human Rights agreed to a moratorium on all demonstrations. As the weeks and months went by, we realized that we were the victims of a broken promise. A few signs, briefly removed, returned; the others remained.

As in so many past experiences, our hopes had been blasted, and the shadow of deep disappointment settled upon us. We had no alternative except to prepare for direct action, whereby we would present our very bodies as means of laying our case before the conscience of the local and the national community. Mindful of the difficulties involved, we decided to undertake a process of self-purification. We began a series of workshops on nonviolence, and we repeatedly asked ourselves: "Are you able to accept blows without retaliating?" "Are you able to endure the ordeal of jail?" We decided to schedule our direct-action program for the Easter season, realizing that except for Christmas, this is the main shopping period of the year. Knowing that a strong economic-withdrawal program would be the by-product of direct action, we felt that this would be the best time to bring pressure to bear on the merchants for the needed change.

Then it occurred to us that Birmingham's mayoral election was coming up in March, and we speedily decided to postpone action until after election day. When we discovered that the Commissioner of Public Safety, Eugene "Bull" Connor, had piled up enough votes to be in the run-off, we decided again to postpone action until the day after the run-off so that the demonstrations could not be used to cloud the issues. Like many others, we waited to see Mr. Connor defeated, and to this end we endured postponement after postponement. Having aided in this community need, we felt that our direct-action program could be delayed no longer.

You may well ask, "Why direct action? Why sit-ins, marches, and so   10
forth? Isn't negotiation a better path?" You are quite right in calling for negotiation. Indeed, this is the very purpose of direct action. Nonviolent direct action seeks to create such a crisis and foster such a tension that a community which has constantly refused to negotiate is forced to confront the issue. It seeks so to dramatize the issue that it can no longer be ignored.

My citing the creation of tension as part of the work of the nonviolent-resister may sound rather shocking. But I must confess that I am not afraid of the word "tension." I have earnestly opposed violent tension, but there is a type of constructive, nonviolent tension which is necessary for growth. Just as Socrates[1] felt that it was necessary to create a tension in the mind so that individuals could rise from the bondage of myths and half-truths to the unfettered realm of creative analysis and objective appraisal, so must we see the need for nonviolent gadflies to create the kind of tension in society that will help men rise from the dark depths of prejudice and racism to the majestic heights of understanding and brotherhood.

The purpose of our direct-action program is to create a situation so crisis-packed that it will inevitably open the door to negotiation. I therefore concur with you in your call for negotiation. Too long has our beloved Southland been bogged down in a tragic effort to live in monologue rather than dialogue.

One of the basic points in your statement is that the action that I and my associates have taken in Birmingham is untimely. Some have asked: "Why didn't you give the new city administration time to act?" The only answer that I can give to this query is that the new Birmingham administration must be prodded about as much as the outgoing one, before it will act. We are sadly mistaken if we feel that the election of Albert Boutwell as mayor will bring the millennium to Birmingham. While Mr. Boutwell is a much more gentle person than Mr. Connor, they are both segregationists, dedicated to maintenance of the status quo. I have hoped that Mr. Boutwell will be reasonable enough to see the futility of massive resistance to desegregation. But he will not see this without pressure from devotees of civil rights. My friends, I must say to you that we have not made a single gain in civil rights without determined legal and nonviolent pressure. Lamentably, it is an historical fact that privileged groups seldom give up their privileges voluntarily. Individuals may see the moral light and voluntarily give up their unjust posture; but, as Reinhold Niebuhr[2] has reminded us, groups tend to be more immoral than individuals.

We know through painful experience that freedom is never voluntarily given by the oppressor; it must be demanded by the oppressed. Frankly, I have yet to engage in a direct-action campaign that was "well timed" in the view of those who have not suffered unduly from the disease of segregation. For years now I have heard the word "Wait!" It rings in the ear of every Negro with piercing familiarity. This "Wait" has almost always meant "Never." We must come to see, with one of our distinguished jurists, that "justice too long delayed is justice denied."

---

1. The greatest of the ancient Greek philosphers, Socrates was sentenced to death because he persisted in raising difficult questions of authority.

2. Niebuhr (1892–1971), an American theologian, attempted to establish a practical code of social ethics based in religious conviction.

We have waited for more than 340 years for our constitutional and God-given rights. The nations of Asia and Africa are moving with jetlike speed toward gaining political independence, but we still creep at horse-and-buggy pace toward gaining a cup of coffee at a lunch counter. Perhaps it is easy for those who have never felt the stinging darts of segregation to say, "Wait." But when you have seen vicious mobs lynch your mothers and fathers at will and drown your sisters and brothers at whim; when you have seen hate-filled policemen curse, kick, and even kill your black brothers and sisters; when you see the vast majority of your twenty million Negro brothers smothering in an airtight cage of poverty in the midst of an affluent society; when you suddenly find your tongue twisted and your speech stammering as you seek to explain to your six-year-old daughter why she can't go to the public amusement park that has just been advertised on television, and see tears welling up in her eyes when she is told that Funtown is closed to colored children, and see ominous clouds of inferiority beginning to form in her little mental sky, and see her beginning to distort her personality by developing an unconscious bitterness toward white people; when you have to concoct an answer for a five-year-old son who is asking, "Daddy, why do white people treat colored people so mean?"; when you take a cross-country drive and find it necessary to sleep night after night in the uncomfortable corners of your automobile because no motel will accept you; when you are humiliated day in and day out by nagging signs reading "white" and "colored"; when your first name becomes "nigger," your middle name becomes "boy" (however old you are) and your last name becomes "John," and your wife and mother are never given the respected title "Mrs."; when you are harried by day and haunted by night by the fact that you are a Negro, living constantly at tiptoe stance, never quite knowing what to expect next, and are plagued with inner fears and outer resentments; when you are forever fighting a degenerating sense of "nobodiness"—then you will understand why we find it difficult to wait. There comes a time when the cup of endurance runs over, and men are no longer willing to be plunged into the abyss of despair. I hope, sirs, you can understand our legitimate and unavoidable impatience.

You express a great deal of anxiety over our willingness to break laws.   15 This is certainly a legitimate concern. Since we so diligently urge people to obey the Supreme Court's decision of 1954 outlawing segregation in the public schools, at first glance it may seem rather paradoxical for us consciously to break laws. One may well ask: "How can you advocate breaking some laws and obeying others?" The answer lies in the fact that there are two types of laws: just and unjust. I would be the first to advocate obeying just laws. One has not only a legal but a moral responsibility to obey just laws. Conversely, one has a moral responsibility to disobey unjust laws. I would agree with St. Augustine[3] that "an unjust law is no law at all."

---

3. An early bishop of the Christian church, St. Augustine (354–430) is considered the founder of theology.

Now, what is the difference between the two? How does one determine whether a law is just or unjust? A just law is a manmade code that squares with the moral law or the law of God. An unjust law is a code that is out of harmony with the moral law. To put it in the terms of St. Thomas Aquinas[4]: An unjust law is a human law that is not rooted in eternal law and natural law. Any law that uplifts human personality is just. Any law that degrades human personality is unjust. All segregation statutes are unjust because segregation distorts the soul and damages the personality. It gives the segregator a false sense of superiority and the segregated a false sense of inferiority. Segregation, to use the terminology of the Jewish philosopher Martin Buber, substitutes an "I-it" relationship for an "I-thou" relationship and ends up relegating persons to the status of things. Hence segregation is not only politically, economically, and sociologically unsound, it is morally wrong and sinful. Paul Tillich[5] has said that sin is separation. Is not segregation an existential expression of man's tragic separation, his awful estrangement, his terrible sinfulness? Thus it is that I can urge men to obey the 1954 decision of the Supreme Court, for it is morally right; and I can urge them to disobey segregation ordinances, for they are morally wrong.

Let us consider a more concrete example of just and unjust laws. An unjust law is a code that a numerical or power majority group compels a minority group to obey but does not make binding on itself. This is *difference* made legal. By the same token, a just law is a code that a majority compels a minority to follow and that it is willing to follow itself. This is *sameness* made legal.

Let me give another explanation. A law is unjust if it is inflicted on a minority that, as a result of being denied the right to vote, had no part in enacting or devising the law. Who can say that the legislature of Alabama which set up that state's segregation laws was democratically elected? Throughout Alabama all sorts of devious methods are used to prevent Negroes from becoming registered voters, and there are some counties in which, even though Negroes constitute a majority of the population, not a single Negro is registered. Can any law enacted under such circumstances be considered democratically structured?

Sometimes a law is just on its face and unjust in its application. For instance, I have been arrested on a charge of parading without a permit. Now, there is nothing wrong in having an ordinance which requires a permit for a parade. But such an ordinance becomes unjust when it is used to maintain segregation and to deny citizens the First Amendment privilege of peaceful assembly and protest.

---

4. The wide-embracing Christian teachings of medieval philosopher St. Thomas Aquinas (1225–1274) have been applied to every realm of human activity.

5. Tillich (1886–1965) and Buber (1878–1965) are both important figures in twentieth-century religious thought.

God, and without this hard work, time itself becomes an ally of the forces of social stagnation. We must use time creatively, in the knowledge that the time is always ripe to do right. Now is the time to make real the promise of democracy and transform our pending national elegy into a creative psalm of brotherhood. Now is the time to lift our national policy from the quicksand of racial injustice to the solid rock of human dignity.

You speak of our activity in Birmingham as extreme. At first I was rather disappointed that fellow clergymen would see my nonviolent efforts as those of an extremist. I began thinking about the fact that I stand in the middle of two opposing forces in the Negro community. One is a force of complacency, made up in part of Negroes who, as a result of long years of oppression, are so drained of self-respect and a sense of "somebodiness" that they have adjusted to segregation; and in part of a few middle-class Negroes who, because of a degree of academic and economic security and because in some ways they profit by segregation, have become insensitive to the problems of the masses. The other force is one of bitterness and hatred, and it comes perilously close to advocating violence. It is expressed in the various black nationalist groups that are springing up across the nation, the largest and best-known being Elijah Muhammad's Muslim movement. Nourished by the Negro's frustration over the continued existence of racial discrimination, this movement is made up of people who have lost faith in America, who have absolutely repudiated Christianity, and who have concluded that the white man is an incorrigible "devil."

I have tried to stand between these two forces, saying that we need emulate neither the "do-nothingism" of the complacent nor the hatred and despair of the black nationalist. For there is the more excellent way of love and nonviolent protest. I am grateful to God that, through the influence of the Negro church, the way of nonviolence became an integral part of our struggle.

If this philosophy had not emerged, by now many streets of the South would, I am convinced, be flowing with blood. And I am further convinced that if our white brothers dismiss as "rabble-rousers" and "outside agitors" those of us who employ nonviolent direct action, and if they refuse to support our nonviolent efforts, millions of Negroes will, out of frustration and despair, seek solace and security in black-nationalist ideologies—a development that would inevitably lead to a frightening racial nightmare.

Oppressed people cannot remain oppressed forever. The yearning for freedom eventually manifests itself, and that is what has happened to the American Negro. Something within has reminded him of his birthright of freedom, and something without has reminded him that it can be gained. Consciously or unconsciously, he has been caught up by the *Zeitgeist,*[9] and with his black brothers of Africa and his brown and yellow brothers of Asia, South America, and the Caribbean, the United States Negro is moving with a sense of great urgency toward the promised land of racial

30

---

9. *Zeitgeist:* German word for "the spirit of the times."

justice. If one recognizes this vital urge that has engulfed the Negro community, one should readily understand why public demonstrations are
taking place. The Negro has many pent-up resentments and latent frustrations, and he must release them. So let him march; let him make prayer
pilgrimages to the city hall; let him go on freedom rides—and try to
understand why he must do so. If his repressed emotions are not released
in nonviolent ways, they will seek expression through violence; this is not
a threat but a fact of history. So I have not said to my people, "Get rid of
your discontent." Rather, I have tried to say that this normal and healthy
discontent can be channeled into the creative outlet of nonviolent direct
action. And now this approach is being termed extremist.

But though I was initially disappointed at being categorized as an
extremist, as I continued to think about the matter I gradually gained a
measure of satisfaction from the label. Was not Jesus an extremist for love:
"Love your enemies, bless them that curse you, do good to them that hate
you, and pray for them which despitefully use you, and persecute you." Was
not Amos an extremist for justice: "Let justice roll down like waters and
righteousness like an ever-flowing stream." Was not Paul an extremist for
the Christian gospel: "I bear in my body the marks of the Lord Jesus." Was
not Martin Luther an extremist: "Here I stand; I cannot do otherwise, so
help me God." And John Bunyan: "I will stay in jail to the end of my days
before I make a butchery of my conscience." And Abraham Lincoln: "This
nation cannot survive half slave and half free." And Thomas Jefferson: "We
hold these truths to be self-evident, that all men are created equal. . . ."
So the question is not whether we will be extremists, but what kind of
extremists we will be. Will we be extremists for hate or for love? Will we be
extremists for the preservation of injustice or for the extension of justice?
In that dramatic scene on Calvary's hill three men were crucified. We must
never forget that all three were crucified for the same crime—the crime of
extremism. Two were extremists for immorality, and thus fell below their
environment. The other, Jesus Christ, was an extremist for love, truth, and
goodness, and thereby rose above his environment. Perhaps the South, the
nation, and the world are in dire need of creative extremists.

I had hoped that the white moderate would see this need. Perhaps
I was too optimistic; perhaps I expected too much. I suppose I should
have realized that few members of the oppressor race can understand
the deep groans and passionate yearnings of the oppressed race, and still
fewer have the vision to see that injustice must be rooted out by strong,
persistent, and determined action. I am thankful, however, that some of
our white brothers in the South have grasped the meaning of this social
revolution and committed themselves to it. They are still all too few
in quantity, but they are big in quality. Some—such as Ralph McGill,
Lillian Smith, Harry Golden, James McBride Dabbs, Ann Braden, and
Sarah Patton Boyle—have written about our struggle in eloquent and
prophetic terms. Others have marched with us down nameless streets of

the South. They have languished in filthy, roach-infested jails, suffering the abuse and brutality of policemen who view them as "dirty nigger-lovers." Unlike so many of their moderate brothers and sisters, they have recognized the urgency of the moment and sensed the need for powerful "action" antidotes to combat the disease of segregation.

Let me take note of my other major disappointment. I have been so greatly disappointed with the white church and its leadership. Of course, there are some notable exceptions. I am not unmindful of the fact that each of you has taken some significant stands on this issue. I commend you, Reverend Stallings, for your Christian stand on this past Sunday, in welcoming Negroes to your worship service on a nonsegregated basis. I commend the Catholic leaders of this state for integrating Spring Hill College several years ago.

But despite these notable exceptions, I must honestly reiterate that I have been disappointed with the church. I do not say this as one of those negative critics who can always find something wrong with the church. I say this as a minister of the gospel, who loves the church; who was nurtured in its bosom; who has been sustained by its spiritual blessings and who will remain true to it as long as the cord of life shall lengthen.

When I was suddenly catapulted into the leadership of the bus protest in Montgomery, Alabama, a few years ago, I felt we would be supported by the white church. I felt that the white ministers, priests, and rabbis of the South would be among our strongest allies. Instead, some have been outright opponents, refusing to understand the freedom movement and misrepresenting its leaders; all too many others have been more cautious than courageous and have remained silent behind the anesthetizing security of stained-glass windows. 35

In spite of my shattered dreams, I came to Birmingham with the hope that the white religious leadership of this community would see the justice of our cause and, with deep moral concern, would serve as the channel through which our just grievances could reach the power structure. I had hoped that each of you would understand. But again I have been disappointed. . . .

There was a time when the church was very powerful—in the time when the early Christians rejoiced at being deemed worthy to suffer for what they believed. In those days the church was not merely a thermometer that recorded the ideas and principles of popular opinion; it was a thermostat that transformed the mores of society. Whenever the early Christians entered a town, the people in power became disturbed and immediately sought to convict the Christians for being "disturbers of the peace" and "outside agitators." But the Christians pressed on, in the conviction that they were "a colony of heaven," called to obey God rather than man. Small in number, they were big in commitment. They were too God-intoxicated to be "astronomically intimidated." By their effort and example they brought an end to such ancient evils as infanticide and gladitorial contests.

Things are different now. So often the contemporary church is a weak, ineffectual voice with an uncertain sound. So often it is an arch-defender of the status quo. Far from being disturbed by the presence of the church, the power structure of the average community is consoled by the church's silent—and often even vocal—sanction of things as they are.

But the judgment of God is upon the church as never before. If today's church does not recapture the sacrificial spirit of the early church, it will lose its authenticity, forfeit the loyalty of millions, and be dismissed as an irrelevant social club with no meaning for the twentieth century. Every day I meet young people whose disappointment with the church has turned into outright disgust.

Perhaps I have once again been too optimistic. Is organized reli-   40 gion too inextricably bound to the status quo to save our nation and the world? Perhaps I must turn my faith to the inner spiritual church, the church within the church, as the true *ekklesia*[10] and the hope of the world. But again I am thankful to God that some noble souls from the ranks of organized religion have broken loose from the paralyzing chains of conformity and joined us as active partners in the struggle for freedom. They have left their secure congregations and walked the streets of Albany, Georgia, with us. They have gone down the highways of the South on torturous rides for freedom. Yes, they have gone to jail with us. Some have been dismissed from their churches, have lost the support of their bishops and fellow ministers. But they have acted in the faith that right defeated is stronger than evil triumphant. Their witness has been the spiritual salt that has preserved the true meaning of the gospel in these troubled times. They have carved a tunnel of hope through the dark mountain of disappointment.

I hope the church as a whole will meet the challenge of this decisive hour. But even if the church does not come to the aid of justice, I have no despair about the future. I have no fear about the outcome of our struggle in Birmingham, even if our motives are at present misunderstood. We will reach the goal of freedom in Birmingham and all over the nation, because the goal of America is freedom. Abused and scorned though we may be, our destiny is tied up with America's destiny. Before the pilgrims landed at Plymouth, we were here. Before the pen of Jefferson etched the majestic words of the Declaration of Independence across the pages of history, we were here. For more than two centuries our forebears labored in this country without wages; they made cotton king; they built the homes of their masters while suffering gross injustice and shameful humiliation—and yet out of a bottomless vitality they continued to thrive and develop. If the inexpressible cruelties of slavery could not stop us, the opposition we now face will surely fail. We will win our freedom because the sacred heritage of our nation and the eternal will of God are embodied in our echoing demands.

---

10. *ekklesia:* word referring to the early Church and its spirit; from the Greek New Testament.

Before closing I feel impelled to mention one other point in your statement that has troubled me profoundly. You warmly commended the Birmingham police force for keeping "order" and "preventing violence." I doubt that you would have so warmly commended the police force if you had seen its dogs sinking their teeth into unarmed, nonviolent Negroes. I doubt that you would so quickly commend the policemen if you were to observe their ugly and inhumane treatment of Negroes here in the city jail; if you were to watch them push and curse old Negro women and young Negro girls; if you were to see them slap and kick old Negro men and young boys; if you were to observe them, as they did on two occasions, refuse to give us food because we wanted to sing our grace together. I cannot join you in your praise of the Birmingham police department.

It is true that the police have exercised a degree of discipline in handling the demonstrators. In this sense they have conducted themselves rather "nonviolently" in public. But for what purpose? To preserve the evil system of segregation. Over the past few years I have consistently preached that nonviolence demands that the means we use must be as pure as the ends we seek. I have tried to make clear that it is wrong to use immoral means to attain moral ends. But now I must affirm that it is just as wrong, or perhaps even more so, to use moral means to preserve immoral ends. Perhaps Mr. Connor and his policemen have been rather nonviolent in public, as was Chief Pritchett in Albany, Georgia, but they have used the moral means of nonviolence to maintain the immoral end of racial injustice. As T. S. Eliot has said, "The last temptation is the greatest treason: To do the right deed for the wrong reason."

I wish you had commended the Negro sit-inners and demonstrators of Birmingham for their sublime courage, their willingness to suffer, and their amazing discipline in the midst of great provocation. One day the South will recognize its real heroes. They will be the James Merediths,[11] with the noble sense of purpose that enables them to face jeering and hostile mobs, and with the agonizing loneliness that characterizes the life of the pioneer. They will be old, oppressed, battered Negro women, symbolized in a seventy-two-year-old woman in Montgomery, Alabama, who rose up with a sense of dignity and with her people decided not to ride segregated buses, and who responded with ungrammatical profundity to one who inquired about her weariness: "My feets is tired, but my soul is at rest." They will be the young high school and college students, the young ministers of the gospel and a host of their elders, courageously and nonviolently sitting in at lunch counters and willingly going to jail for conscience' sake. One day the South will know that when these disinherited children of God sat down at lunch counters, they were in reality standing up for what is best in the American dream and for the most sacred values in our Judaeo-Christian

---

11. In 1961 James Meredith became the first black student to enroll at the University of Mississippi, sparking considerable controversy and confrontation.

heritage, thereby bringing our nation back to those great wells of democracy which were dug deep by the founding fathers in their formulation of the Constitution and the Declaration of Independence.

Never before have I written so long a letter. I'm afraid it is much too 45 long to take your precious time. I can assure you that it would have been much shorter if I had been writing from a comfortable desk, but what else can one do when he is alone in a narrow jail cell, other than write long letters, think long thoughts, and pray long prayers?

If I have said anything in this letter that overstates the truth and indicates an unreasonable impatience, I beg you to forgive me. If I have said anything that understates the truth and indicates my having a patience that allows me to settle for anything less than brotherhood, I beg God to forgive me.

I hope this letter finds you strong in the faith. I also hope that circumstances will soon make it possible for me to meet each of you, not as an integrationist or a civil-rights leader but as a fellow clergyman and a Christian brother. Let us all hope that the dark clouds of racial prejudice will soon pass away and the deep fog of misunderstanding will be lifted from our fear-drenched communities, and in some not too distant tomorrow the radiant stars of love and brotherhood will shine over our great nation with all their scintillating beauty.

Yours for the cause of Peace and Brotherhood,

MARTIN LUTHER KING, JR.

THINKING CRITICALLY ABOUT THE READING

1. King's letter was written in response to a published statement by eight white clergymen (see p. 109). What specific criticism did these men level at King and his followers? How does King respond to each objection?

2. King says that he advocates nonviolent resistance. What are the four basic steps of any nonviolent campaign? Why does King believe that the time for negotiations has passed?

3. According to King, what does the word *wait* (13) mean to the black community?

4. What does King see as the key difference between just and unjust laws? Explain.

5. The white clergy label King an *extremist* (30). What does this word mean to you? How does King turn being labeled an "extremist" to his advantage?

6. Why is King disappointed with the white church? What does he want the white clergy to do? In what ways has the church skirted its responsibilities to African Americans?

7. King says that he "stand[s] in the middle of two opposing forces in the Negro community" (27). What are those forces, and why does he see himself between them?

LANGUAGE IN ACTION

Here is the letter written by eight white Alabama clergymen that Martin Luther King Jr. responded to in his "Letter from Birmingham Jail":

> We the undersigned clergymen are among those who, in January, issued "An Appeal for Law and Order and Common Sense," in dealing with racial problems in Alabama. We expressed understanding that honest convictions in racial matters could properly be pursued in the courts, but urged that decisions of those courts should in the meantime be peacefully obeyed.
>
> Since that time there had been some evidence of increased forbearance and a willingness to face facts. Responsible citizens have undertaken to work on various problems which cause racial friction and unrest. In Birmingham, recent public events have given indication that we will have opportunity for a new constructive and realistic approach to racial problems.
>
> However, we are now confronted by a series of demonstrations by some of our Negro citizens, directed and led in part by outsiders. We recognize the natural impatience of people who feel that their hopes are slow in being realized. But we are convinced that these demonstrations are unwise and untimely.
>
> We agree rather with certain local Negro leadership which has called for honest and open negotiation of racial issues in our area. And we believe this kind of facing of issues can best be accomplished by citizens of our own metropolitan area, white and Negro, meeting with their knowledge and experience of the local situation. All of us need to face that responsibility and find proper channels for its accomplishment.
>
> Just as we formerly pointed out that "hatred and violence have no sanction in our religious and political traditions," we also point out that such actions as incite to hatred and violence, however technically peaceful those actions may be, have not contributed to the resolution of our local problems. We do not believe that these days of new hope are days when extreme measures are justified in Birmingham.
>
> We commend the community as a whole, and the local news media and law enforcement officials in particular, on the calm manner in which these demonstrations have been handled. We urge the public to continue to show restraint should the demonstrations continue, and the law enforcement officials to remain calm and continue to protect our city from violence.
>
> We further strongly urge our own Negro community to withdraw support from these demonstrations, and to unite locally in working peacefully for a better Birmingham. When rights are consistently denied, a cause should be pressed in the courts and in negotiations among local leaders, and not in the streets. We appeal to both our white and Negro citizenry to observe the principles of law and order and common sense.

What do you see in the language of this letter than might have caused King to take action, when so many other letters crossed his desk without reply? What might have seemed especially alarming to him?

In one color, underline the adjectives that refer to the rights activism of King. In another, underline the adjectives that the clergymen use to describe the "ideal" action, and which, by implication, comprise the opposite of King's approach. How do both groups of words urge citizens to see things the clergymen's way, and how does King use these sets of adjectives to direct his reply?

WRITING SUGGESTIONS

1. In paragraph 4, King boldly states, "Injustice anywhere is a threat to justice everywhere. We are caught in an inescapable network of mutuality, tied in a single garment of destiny. Whatever affects one directly, affects all indirectly." Write an essay in which you explore the truth in King's statement, using social and economic injustices that you see around you as examples.

2. King advocates nonviolent resistance as a way of confronting oppression. What other means of confronting oppression were available to him? What are the strengths and weaknesses of those alternatives? Write an essay in which you assess the effectiveness of nonviolent resistance in the light of its alternatives. Is nonviolent direct action still realistic or viable today? You may find it helpful to review what you wrote in response to the Writing to Discover prompt for this selection.

5

LANGUAGE ESSENTIALS: MAKING SENSE OF WORDS IN THE WORLD

In "Language Essentials," six writers explore some language fundamentals that give us a greater understanding and appreciation for the miracle of language that we all share. In "Language and Thought," philosopher Susanne K. Langer explains how language separates humans from the rest of the animal kingdom. She demonstrates the power of language and shows "without it anything properly called 'thought' is impossible." While we might celebrate the remarkable resilience and flexibility of the English language, it can also tie us in knots, as Steven Pinker explains in "Words Don't Mean What They Mean." Pinker's essay is full of examples of how we all participate in an elaborate "linguistic dance" with each other whenever we try to communicate.

The following four selections are written by a new generation of scholars and researchers. Their works attest to an endless fascination we have for language study and to a recognition of how much still needs to be done filling in the gaps in our understanding. Journalist Melissa Fay Greene explores the importance of early exposure to spoken language—and the consequences of the "word gap" that develops when infants don't hear enough of it—in "Word Power for Babies." In "Chunking," Ben Zimmer explains the theory that instead of learning the lexicon, or word-horde, of a language word by word as we assume is normal practice, we may in fact learn it in chunks or groups of words. The theory is somewhat controversial, but we're already applying it to the pedagogy of learning a second language. In "Our Language Prejudices Don't Make No Sense," Raffaella Zanuttini argues that our assumptions about correct language often come from false assumptions, many of which are based on racial, ethnic, and socioeconomic prejudice. But, says Zanuttini, there is no factual basis for a single, correct version of English—different varieties of English are no more right or wrong than are different recipes for a common dish. Finally, Lera Boroditsky, in "Lost in Translation," reexamines one of the oldest and most intriguing of all theories of the interaction of language and the brain, the Sapir-Whorf hypothesis, also known as the linguistic relativity hypothesis. She and her fellow researchers have found new evidence that sheds light on the question: Does the language we speak shape reality, or does reality shape our language? Or, does it work both ways? Surely you will find her international explorations and the examples she brings to bear on the question fascinating.

Language and Thought

SUSANNE K. LANGER

Susanne K. Langer was born in New York City in 1895 and attended Radcliffe College. There she studied philosophy, an interest she maintained until her death in 1985. She stayed in Cambridge, Massachusetts, as a tutor at Harvard University from 1927 to 1942. Langer then taught at the University of Delaware, Columbia University, and Connecticut College, where she remained from 1954 until the end of her distinguished teaching career. Her books include *Philosophy in a New Key: A Study of the Symbolism of Reason, Rite, and Art* (1942), *Feeling and Form* (1953), and *Mind: An Essay in Human Feeling* (1967).

In the following essay, which originally appeared in *Ms.* magazine, Langer explores how language separates humans from the rest of the animal kingdom. She contends that the use of symbols—in addition to the use of signs that animals also use—frees humans not only to react to their environment but also to think about it. Moreover, symbols allow us to create imagery and ideas not directly related to the real world, so that we can plan, imagine, and communicate abstractions—to do, in essence, the things that make us human.

WRITING TO DISCOVER: *Young children must often communicate—and be communicated to—without the use of language. To a child, for example, a danger sticker on a bottle can mean "don't touch," and a green traffic light might mean "the car will start again." Think back to your own childhood experiences. Write about how communication took place without language. What associations were you able to make?*

A symbol is not the same thing as a sign; that is a fact that psychologists and philosophers often overlook. All intelligent animals use signs; so do we. To them as well as to us sounds and smells and motions are signs of food, danger, the presence of other beings, or of rain or storm. Furthermore, some animals not only attend to signs but produce them for the benefit of others. Dogs bark at the door to be let in; rabbits thump to call each other; the cooing of doves and the growl of a wolf defending his kill are unequivocal signs of feelings and intentions to be reckoned with by other creatures.

We use signs just as animals do, though with considerably more elaboration. We stop at red lights and go on green; we answer calls and bells, watch the sky for coming storms, read trouble or promise or anger in each other's eyes. That is animal intelligence raised to the human level. Those of us who are dog lovers can probably all tell wonderful stories of how high our dogs have sometimes risen in the scale of clever sign interpretation and sign using.

A sign is anything that announces the existence or the imminence of some event, the presence of a thing or a person, or a change in the state of affairs. There are signs of the weather, signs of danger, signs of future good or evil, signs of what the past has been. In every case a sign is closely bound up with something to be noted or expected in experience. It is always a part of the situation to which it refers, though the reference may be remote in space and time. In so far as we are led to note or expect the signified event we are making correct use of a sign. This is the essence of rational behavior, which animals show in varying degrees. It is entirely realistic, being closely bound up with the actual objective course of history—learned by experience, and cashed in or voided by further experience.

If man had kept to the straight and narrow path of sign using, he would be like the other animals, though perhaps a little brighter. He would not talk, but grunt and gesticulate the point. He would make his wishes known, give warnings, perhaps develop a social system like that of bees and ants, with such a wonderful efficiency of communal enterprise that all men would have plenty to eat, warm apartments—all exactly alike and perfectly convenient—to live in, and everybody could and would sit in the sun or by the fire, as the climate demanded, not talking but just basking, with every want satisfied, most of his life. The young would romp and make love, the old would sleep, the middle-aged would do the routine work almost unconsciously and eat a great deal. But that would be the life of a social, superintelligent, purely sign-using animal.

To us who are human, it does not sound very glorious. We want to   5
go places and do things, own all sorts of gadgets that we do not absolutely need, and when we sit down to take it easy we want to talk. Rights and property, social position, special talents and virtues, and above all our ideas, are what we live for. We have gone off on a tangent that takes us far away from the mere biological cycle that animal generations accomplish; and that is because we can use not only signs but symbols.

A symbol differs from a sign in that it does not announce the presence of the object, the being, condition, or whatnot, which is its meaning, but merely *brings this thing to mind*. It is not a mere "substitute sign" to which we react as though it were the object itself. The fact is that our reaction to hearing a person's name is quite different from our reaction to the person himself. There are certain rare cases where a symbol stands directly for its meaning: in religious experience, for instance, the Host is not only a symbol but a Presence. But symbols in the ordinary sense are not mystic. They are the same sort of thing that ordinary signs are; only they do not call our attention to something necessarily present or to be physically dealt with—they call up merely a conception of the thing they "mean."

The difference between a sign and a symbol is, in brief, that a sign causes us to think or act *in face* of the thing signified, whereas a symbol causes us to think *about* the thing symbolized. Therein lies the great importance of symbolism for human life, its power to make this life so different from any other animal biography that generations of men have found it incredible to suppose that they were of purely zoological origin. A sign is always embedded in reality, in a present that emerges from the actual past and stretches to the future; but a symbol may be divorced from reality altogether. It may refer to what is not the case, to a mere idea, a figment, a dream. It serves, therefore, to liberate thought from the immediate stimuli of a physically present world; and that liberation marks the essential difference between human and nonhuman mentality. Animals think, but they think *of* and *at* things; men think primarily *about* things. Words, pictures, and memory images are symbols that may be combined and varied in a thousand ways. The result is a symbolic structure whose meaning is a complex of all their respective meanings, and this kaleidoscope of *ideas* is the typical product of the human brain that we call the "stream of thought."

The process of transforming all direct experience into imagery or into that supreme mode of symbolic expression, language, has so completely taken possession of the human mind that it is not only a special talent but a dominant, organic need. All our sense impressions leave their traces in our memory not only as signs disposing our practical reactions in the future but also as symbols, images representing our *ideas* of things; and the tendency to manipulate ideas, to combine and abstract, mix and extend them by playing with symbols, is man's outstanding characteristic. It seems to be what his brain most naturally and spontaneously does. Therefore his primitive mental function is not judging reality, but *dreaming his desires.*

Dreaming is apparently a basic function of human brains, for it is free and unexhausting like our metabolism, heartbeat, and breath. It is easier to dream than not to dream, as it is easier to breathe than to refrain from breathing. The symbolic character of dreams is fairly well established. Symbol mongering, on this ineffectual, uncritical level, seems to be instinctive, the fulfillment of an elementary need rather than the purposeful exercise of a high and difficult talent.

The special power of man's mind rests on the evolution of this   10
special activity, not on any transcendently high development of animal intelligence. We are not immeasurably higher than other animals; we are different. We have a biological need and with it a biological gift that they do not share.

Because man has not only the ability but the constant need of *conceiving* what has happened to him, what surrounds him, what is demanded of him—in short, of symbolizing nature, himself, and his hopes and fears—he has a constant and crying need of *expression.* What he cannot express, he cannot conceive; what he cannot conceive is chaos, and fills him with terror.

If we bear in mind this all-important craving for expression, we get a new picture of man's behavior; for from this trait spring his powers and his weaknesses. The process of symbolic transformation that all our experiences undergo is nothing more nor less than the process of *conception*, underlying the human faculties of abstraction and imagination.

When we are faced with a strange or difficult situation, we cannot react directly, as other creatures do, with flight, aggression, or any such simple instinctive pattern. Our whole reaction depends on how we manage to conceive the situation—whether we cast it in a definite dramatic form, whether we see it as a disaster, a challenge, a fulfillment of doom, or a fiat of the Divine Will. In words or dreamlike images, in artistic or religious or even in cynical form, we must *construe* the events of life. There is great virtue in the figure of speech, "I can *make* nothing of it," to express a failure to understand something. Thought and memory are processes of *making* the thought content and the memory image; the pattern of our ideas is given by the symbols through which we express them. And in the course of manipulating those symbols we inevitably distort the original experience, as we abstract certain features of it, embroider and reinforce those features with other ideas, until the conception we project on the screen of memory is quite different from anything in our real history.

Conception is a necessary and elementary process; what we do with our conceptions is another story. That is the entire history of human culture—of intelligence and morality, folly and superstition, ritual, language, and the arts—all the phenomena that set man apart from, and above, the rest of the animal kingdom. As the religious mind has to make all human history a drama of sin and salvation in order to define its own moral attitudes, so a scientist wrestles with the mere presentation of "the facts" before he can reason about them. The process of *envisaging* facts, values, hopes, and fears underlies our whole behavior pattern; and this process is reflected in the evolution of an extraordinary phenomenon found always, and only, in human societies—the phenomenon of language.

Language is the highest and most amazing achievement of the symbolistic human mind. The power it bestows is almost inestimable, for without it anything properly called "thought" is impossible. The birth of language is the dawn of humanity. The line between man and beast—between the highest ape and the lowest savage—is the language line. Whether the primitive Neanderthal man was anthropoid or human depends less on his cranial capacity, his upright posture, or even his use of tools and fire, than on one issue we shall probably never be able to settle—whether or not he spoke.

In all physical traits and practical responses, such as skills and visual judgments, we can find a certain continuity between animal and human

15

mentality. Sign using is an ever evolving, ever improving function through-out the whole animal kingdom, from the lowly worm that shrinks into his hole at the sound of an approaching foot, to the dog obeying his master's command, and even to the learned scientist who watches the movements of an index needle.

The continuity of the sign-using talent has led psychologists to the belief that language is evolved from the vocal expressions, grunts and coos and cries, whereby animals vent their feelings or signal their fellows; that man has elaborated this sort of communion to the point where it makes a perfect exchange of ideas possible.

I do not believe that this doctrine of the origin of language is correct. The essence of language is symbolic, not signific; we use it first and most vitally to formulate and hold ideas in our own minds. Conception, not social control, is its first and foremost benefit.

The essence of language is symbolic, not signific; we use it first and most vitally to formulate and hold ideas in our own minds.

Watch a young child, who is learning to speak, play with a toy; he says the name of the object, e.g.: "Horsey! horsey! horsey!" over and over again, looks at the object, moves it, always saying the name to himself or to the world at large. It's quite a time before he talks to anyone in par-ticular; he talks first of all to himself. This is his way of forming and fixing the *conception* of the object in his mind, and around this conception all his knowledge of it grows. *Names* are the essence of language; for the *name* is what abstracts the conception of the horse from the horse itself, and lets the mere idea recur at the speaking of the name. This permits the conception gathered from one horse experience to be exemplified again by another instance of a horse, so that the notion embodied in the name is a general notion.

To this end, the baby uses a word long before he *asks* for the object; when he wants his horsey he is likely to cry and fret, because he is reacting to an actual environment, not forming ideas. He uses the animal language of *signs* for his wants; talking is still a purely symbolic process—its prac-tical value has not really impressed him yet. 20

Language need not be vocal; it may be purely visual, like written lan-guage, or even tactual, like the deaf-mute system of speech; but it *must be denotative*. The sounds, intended or unintended, whereby animals com-municate do not constitute a language because they are signs, not names. They never fall into an organic pattern, a meaningful syntax of even the most rudimentary sort, as all language seems to do with a sort of driving necessity. That is because signs refer to actual situations, in which things have obvious relations to each other that require only to be noted; but symbols refer to ideas, which are not physically there for inspection, so their connections and features have to be represented. This gives all true language a natural tendency toward growth and development, which seems almost like a life of its own. Languages are not invented; they grow with our need for expression.

In contrast, animal "speech" never has a structure. It is merely an emotional response. Apes may greet their ration of yams with a shout of "Nga!" But they do not say "Nga" between meals. If they could *talk about* their yams instead of just saluting them, they would be the most primitive men instead of the most anthropoid of beasts. They would have ideas, and tell each other things true and false, rational or irrational; they would make plans and invent laws and sing their own praises, as men do.

THINKING CRITICALLY ABOUT THE READING

1. What is Langer's thesis in this essay? Where does she state it? (Glossary: *Thesis*)

2. Define what Langer refers to as a *sign*. Define *symbol*. (Glossary: *Definition* and *Symbol*) Why is the distinction between the two so important?

3. What examples of signs and symbols does Langer provide? (Glossary: *Examples*) How effective do you find her examples? What examples of signs and symbols can you provide?

4. What is the essential difference between the way animals "think" and the way humans think? How has that changed human mental function at an organic level? How has the biological change affected our development in relation to animals?

5. In paragraph 11, Langer states: "What [man] cannot express, he cannot conceive; what he cannot conceive is chaos, and fills him with terror." Review the first ten paragraphs of the essay. How does Langer prepare the reader to accept this abstract and bold statement? (Glossary: *Concrete/Abstract* and *Organization*)

6. What does Langer mean when she says, "In words or dreamlike images . . . we must *construe* the events of life" (13)? How does this claim relate to the process of conception?

LANGUAGE IN ACTION

Review what Langer has to say about signs and symbols, particularly the differences she draws between them in paragraphs 6 and 7. Then examine the following graphics. What does each graphic mean? Which ones are signs, and which are symbols? Be prepared to defend your conclusions in a classroom discussion.

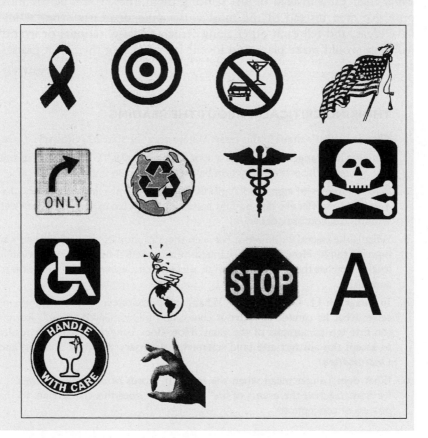

WRITING SUGGESTIONS

1. Using symbols for expression need not involve explicit use of language. Within the framework of a particular society, many methods of symbolic communication are possible. When you walk across campus, for example, what do you want to communicate to others even if you do not speak to anyone? How do you communicate this message? For instance, how does your facial expression, clothing, hairstyle, or jewelry serve as a symbol? Write an essay in which you describe and analyze the nonlanguage symbols you use to communicate.

2. It has often been said that language reveals the character of the person using it. Write an essay in which you analyze the character of a particular writer based on his or her use of language. You may want to comment on a writer in this text whose article you have read, such as Langer. Consider such areas as vocabulary range, sentence variety, slang, correct grammar, technical language, and tone. What do these elements tell you about the character of the person? (Glossary: *Slang, Technical Language,* and *Tone*)

3. Research recent experiments involving animal communication. Some experiments, for example, reveal the gorilla's use of sign language; others show that dolphins have complex communication systems that we are only beginning to understand. Write a paper in which you summarize the research and discuss how it relates to Langer's ideas about human and animal use of signs and symbols. Did you find any evidence that certain animals can use basic symbols? Is there a possibility that gorillas and dolphins can think *about* things rather than simply *of* and *at* them?

Words Don't Mean What They Mean

Steven Pinker

Internationally recognized language and cognition scholar and researcher Steven Pinker was born in Montreal, Canada, in 1954. He immigrated to the United States shortly after receiving his B.A. from McGill University in 1976. After earning a doctorate from Harvard University in 1979, Pinker taught psychology at Harvard, Stanford University, and the Massachusetts Institute of Technology, where he directed the Center for Cognitive Neuroscience. Currently, he is the Johnstone Family Professor in the Department of Psychology at Harvard University. Since publishing *Language Learnability and Language Development* in 1984, Pinker has written extensively on language development in children. He has what one critic writing in the *New York Times Book Review* calls "that facility, so rare among scientists, of making the most difficult material . . . accessible to the average reader." The popularity of Pinker's books *The Language Instinct* (1994), *How the Mind Works* (1997), *Words and Rules: The Ingredients of Language* (1999), *The Blank Slate: The Modern Denial of Human Nature* (2002), *The Stuff of Thought: Language As a Window into Human Nature* (2007), and *The Better Angels of Our Nature: Why Violence Has Declined* (2011) attests to the public's genuine interest in human nature and language.

In the following article, adapted from *The Stuff of Thought* and first published in the September 6, 2007, issue of *Time*, Pinker discusses how phrases convey different meanings in different contexts and how this flexibility can both help and hinder human communication and relationships. Pinker uses a number of examples from a wide range of endeavors to illustrate his points about words and the ways they work.

WRITING TO DISCOVER: *Have you ever found yourself in a conversation in which the words that were being spoken to you didn't mean what you supposed they meant? For example, if someone were to say "That's really nice" sarcastically, and you missed the sarcastic tone, you'd miss the meaning entirely. Describe such a situation that you've been in, and explain the difference in meaning between the words being spoken and the intended meaning.*

In the movie *Tootsie*, the character played by Dustin Hoffman is disguised as a woman and is speaking to a beautiful young actress played by Jessica Lange. During a session of late-night girl talk, Lange's character says, "You know what I wish? That a guy could be honest enough to walk up to me and say, 'I could lay a big line on you, but the simple truth is I find you very interesting, and I'd really like to make love to you.' Wouldn't that be a relief?"

Later in the movie, a twist of fate throws them together at a cocktail party, this time with Hoffman's character dressed as a man. The actress doesn't recognize him, and he tries out the speech on her. Before he can even finish, she throws a glass of wine in his face and storms away.

When people talk, they lay lines on each other, do a lot of role playing, sidestep, shilly-shally and engage in all manner of vagueness and innuendo. We do this and expect others to do it, yet at the same time we profess to long for the plain truth, for people to say what they mean, simple as that. Such hypocrisy is a human universal.

Sexual come-ons are a classic example. "Would you like to come up and see my etchings?" has been recognized as a double entendre for so long that by 1939, James Thurber could draw a cartoon of a hapless man in an apartment lobby saying to his date, "You wait here, and I'll bring the etchings down."

The veiled threat also has a stereotype: the Mafia wiseguy offering   5
protection with the soft sell, "Nice store you got there. Would be a real shame if something happened to it." Traffic cops sometimes face not-so-innocent questions like, "Gee, Officer, is there some way I could pay the fine right here?" And anyone who has sat through a fund-raising dinner is familiar with euphemistic schnorring like, "We're counting on you to show leadership."

Why don't people just say what they mean? The reason is that conversational partners are not modems downloading information into each other's brains. People are very, very touchy about their relationships. Whenever you speak to someone, you are presuming the two of you have a certain degree of familiarity—which your words might alter. So every sentence has to do two things at once: convey a message and continue to negotiate that relationship.

The clearest example is ordinary politeness. When you are at a dinner party and want the salt, you don't blurt out, "Gimme the salt." Rather, you use what linguists call a whimperative, as in "Do you think you could pass the salt?" or "If you could pass the salt, that would be awesome."

Taken literally, these sentences are inane. The second is an overstatement, and the answer to the first is obvious. Fortunately, the hearer assumes that the speaker is rational and listens between the lines. Yes, your point is to request the salt, but you're doing it in such a way that first takes care to establish what linguists call "felicity conditions," or the prerequisites to making a sensible request. The underlying rationale is that the hearer not be given a command but simply be asked or advised about one of the necessary conditions for passing the salt. Your goal is to have your need satisfied without treating the listener as a flunky who can be bossed around at will.

Warm acquaintances go out of their way not to look as if they are presuming a dominant-subordinate relationship but rather one of equals. It works the other way too. When people are in a subordinate relationship (like a driver with police), they can't sound as if they are presuming anything more than that, so any bribe must be veiled. Fund raisers, simulating an atmosphere of warm friendship with their donors, also can't break the spell with a bald businesslike proposition.

It is in the arena of sexual relationships, however, that the linguistic dance can be its most elaborate. In an episode of *Seinfeld,* George is asked by his date if he would like to come up for coffee. He declines, explaining that caffeine keeps him up at night. Later he slaps his forehead: " 'Coffee' doesn't mean coffee! 'Coffee' means sex!" The moment is funny, but it's also a reminder of just how carefully romantic partners must always tread. Make too blatant a request, as in *Tootsie,* and the hearer is offended; too subtle, as in *Seinfeld,* and it can go over the hearer's head.

In the political arena, miscalibrated speech can lead to more serious consequences than wine in the face or a slap on the forehead. In 1980, Wanda Brandstetter, a lobbyist for the National Organization for Women (NOW), tried to get an Illinois state representative to vote for the Equal Rights Amendment (ERA) by handing him a business card on which she had written, "Mr. Swanstrom, the offer for help in your election, plus $1,000 for your campaign for the pro-ERA vote." A prosecutor called the note a "contract for bribery," and the jury agreed.

So how do lobbyists in Gucci Gulch bribe legislators today? They do it with innuendo. If Brandstetter had said, "As you know, Mr. Swanstrom, NOW has a history of contributing to political campaigns. And it has contributed more to candidates with a voting record that is compatible with our goals. These days one of our goals is the ratification of the ERA," she would have avoided a fine, probation and community service.

Indirect speech has a long history in diplomacy, too. In the wake of the Six-Day War in 1967, the U.N. Security Council passed its famous Resolution 242, which called for the "withdrawal of Israeli armed forces from territories occupied in the recent conflict." The wording is ambiguous. Does it mean "some of the territories" or "all of the territories"? In some ways it was best not to ask, since the phrasing was palatable to Israel and its allies only under the former interpretation and to concerned Arab states and their allies only under the latter. Unfortunately, for 40 years partisans have been debating the semantics of Resolution 242, and the Israeli-Arab conflict remains unresolved, to put it mildly.

That's not to say such calculated ambiguity never works for diplomats. After all, the language of an agreement has to be acceptable not just to leaders but to their citizens. Reasonable leaders might thus come to an understanding between themselves, while each exploits the ambiguities of the deal to sell it to their country's more bellicose factions. What's more, diplomats can gamble that times will change and circumstances will bring the two sides together, at which point they can resolve the vagueness amicably.

When all else fails, as it often does, nations can sort out their problems without any words at all—and often without fighting either. In these cases, they may fall back on communicating through what's known as authority ranking, also known as power, status, autonomy and dominance. The logic of authority ranking is "Don't mess with me." Its biological roots are in the dominance hierarchies that are widespread in the animal kingdom. One animal claims the right to a contested resource based on size,

> **Words let us say the things we want to say and also things we would be better off not having said.**

strength, seniority or allies, and the other animal cedes it when the outcome of the battle can be predicted and both sides have a stake in not getting bloodied in a fight whose winner is a forgone conclusion. Such sword-rattling gestures as a larger military power's conducting "naval exercises" in the waters off the coast of a weaker foe are based on just this kind of preemptive reminder of strength.

People often speak of indirect speech as a means of saving face. What we're referring to is not just a matter of hurt feelings but a social currency with real value. The expressive power of words helps us guard this prized asset, but only as long as we're careful. Words let us say the things we want to say and also things we would be better off not having said. They let us know the things we need to know, and also things we wish we didn't. Language is a window into human nature, but it is also a fistula, an open wound through which we're exposed to an infectious world. It's not surprising that we sheathe our words in politeness and innuendo and other forms of doublespeak.

THINKING CRITICALLY ABOUT THE READING

1. Pinker opens his essay with an extended example from the movie *Tootsie*. What point about language does this example illustrate?

2. Pinker creates a number of categories for the ways in which people "lay lines on each other, do a lot of role playing, sidestep, shilly-shally and engage in all manner of vagueness and innuendo" (3). Explain these categories and provide an example of your own for each. In your opinion, do any of the categories overlap?

3. What do you think Pinker means when he says, "Such hypocrisy is a human universal" (3)? Do you believe that this hypocrisy is necessary? What would need to change for us to speak the "plain truth" to each other?

4. Why, according to Pinker, do people have so much trouble conversing? How is a conversation between two humans different from a conversation between two modems?

5. What are "felicity conditions" (8)? Describe several situations in which you have used "felicity conditions." Have you ever tried but failed to establish these conditions? Explain what happened.

6. Explain what "indirect speech" (13) is. Why do you think people resort to indirect speech? Why is it not surprising that indirect speech has a long history in the arenas of politics and diplomacy?

LANGUAGE IN ACTION

Read the following English folktale, which is taken from Joseph Jacob's 1890 book *English Fairy Tales*. What do you learn about the nature of words from this story? Explain. How do you think Steven Pinker would respond to this folktale?

From "Master of all Masters"

A girl once went to a fair to be hired as a servant. At last a funny-looking old gentleman engaged her and took her home to his house. When she got there he told her he had something to teach her for in his house he had his own names for things.

He said to her: "What will you call me?"
"Master or Mister or whatever you please, sir."
"You must call me 'Master of Masters.' And what would you call this?" pointing to his bed.
"Bed or couch or whatever you please, sir."
"No, that's my 'barnacle.' And what do you call these?" said he, pointing to his pants.
"Breeches or trousers or whatever you please, sir."
"You must call them 'squibs and crackers.' And what do you call her?" pointing to the cat.
"Kit or cat or whatever you please, sir."
"You must call her 'white-faced simminy.' And this now," showing the fire, "what would you call this?"
"Fire or flame or whatever you please, sir."
"You must call it 'hot cockalorum,' and what this?" he went on, pointing to the water.
"Water or wet or whatever you please, sir."
"No, 'pandalorum' is its name. And what do you call this?" asked he, as he pointed to the house.
"House or cottage or whatever you please, sir."
"You must call it 'high topper mountain.'"

That very night the servant woke her master up in a fright and said: "Master of all masters, get out of your barnacle and put on your squibs and crackers. For white-face simminy has got a spark of hot cockalorum on its tail, and unless you get some pandalorum high topper mountain will be all on hot cockalorum." . . . That's all.

WRITING SUGGESTIONS

1. According to Pinker, "It is in the arena of sexual relationships . . . that the linguistic dance can be most elaborate." He supports this claim with examples from an episode of *Seinfeld* and the movie *Tootsie*. What exactly is the "linguistic dance" to which he refers? Does your own experience or that

of your friends with the language used in any dating relationship support or contradict Pinker's claim? How would you characterize conversations in these relationships? Write an essay in which you examine the language between partners in dating relationships. You may find it helpful to compare their language with that of other relationships; for example, is their language as indirect as that of nondating friends?

2. What does Pinker mean when he says, "Language is a window into human nature, but it is also a fistula, an open wound through which we're exposed to an infectious world" (16)? In what ways can language be considered an "open wound"? Why do you suppose that Pinker is not surprised "that we sheathe our words in politeness and innuendo and other forms of doublespeak" (16)? What evidence does he provide to justify his lack of surprise? Are you convinced? Why or why not? Write a paper in which you explore the meaning of Pinker's concluding remarks about language.

Word Power for Babies

MELISSA FAY GREENE

Melissa Fay Greene is an award-winning journalist, nonfiction writer, and mother of nine. Raised in Ohio, where she also earned her B.A. in English from Oberlin College in 1975, she and her family now live in Georgia, where Greene was born. She is the author of five books of nonfiction, including *Praying for Sheetrock* (1991), *The Temple Bombing* (1996), *Last Man Out* (2003), *There Is No Me Without You: One Woman's Odyssey to Rescue Her Country's Children* (2006), and the memoir *No Biking in the House Without a Helmet* (2011). Her work has won a number of awards, including a Guggenheim Fellowship (2015), two National Book Award nominations, a National Book Critics Circle Award nomination, and the ACLU National Civil Liberties Award, among others.

While Greene's first four works address the identity politics of race and class, her most recent work is a memoir of parenthood and parenting. In *No Biking in the House Without a Helmet*, Greene offers a warm, honest, and often hilarious portrayal of parenting, along with her husband, Don Samuel, the couple's nine children, four by birth and five by adoption. Four of the family's five adoptees hail from Ethiopia, the country whose HIV/AIDS-induced orphan crisis was the subject of *There Is No Me Without You*. In the following selection, which first appeared in *Reader's Digest* in 2014, Greene studies the ways in which exposure to words can build babies' brains and equip them with both language skills and the expectation of success later in life.

WRITING TO DISCOVER: *What memories do you have of being read to or learning rhymes and songs? What was your first favorite book? How do you think your early experiences with words might have shaped how you approached more difficult reading and writing later on?*

Babies need a few basic things to get started: mother's milk, or something like it; love, attention, and playtime; clean clothes; and a safe place to sleep. All over the world, high- or low-income, desert or forest, highrise or countryside, doting parents give their babies these essentials. But educational researchers have uncovered something else babies need, and this they're not getting equally up and down the income scale. The missing element is not an heirloom-quality cherrywood changing table, an all-leather car seat with cup holder, or an ergonomic Scandinavian stroller (none of which has been linked to positive life outcomes anyway). The missing element costs nothing and is as plentiful as air, yet the devastating lack of it hampers brain development.

Many low-income American children are suffering from a shortage of words—songs, nursery rhymes, storybooks, chitchat, everyday stuff. How can that be? All parents issue directives— "Time for your bath" or "Let's put on your jammies." In low-income families, where parents often have had less education and limited access to parenting guidance, that's usually the end of it; while in wealthier families, directives are only a small part of an ongoing conversation. "Let's put on your jammies. Your jammies are so soft! What color are these jammies? They're yellow. And look at these little animals on your jammies. What are those? Those are ducks! 'Quack, quack, quack,' say the ducks!" All that babbling isn't silliness; it's mind-building. Words streaming from radio or television, or from parents or caregivers chatting on cell phones, are of no benefit, however—a finding that merits attention from *all* parents.

In many low-income families, warm and loving parents may struggle desperately to provide all the other basics, without a clue that their relative silence—and the lack of bedtime stories, picture books, and lullabies—hurts the babies.

Beginning in the 1990s, researchers at Rice and Columbia Universities reported eye-opening findings about how many more words middle-class and affluent kids hear day in and out. Using interview techniques and tracking devices including "word pedometers," they've determined that well-off children hear 30 million more words in the first three years of life.

The deficit has astounding and bitter consequences. More than any   5 other strand in the lives of poor children, the 30-million-word gap has been linked to poor school performance, a failure to learn to read, a failure to graduate from high school, and an inability to prepare for and to enjoy career success.

Tammy Edwards, 31, grew up on the South Shore of Long Island, on the Poospatuck Reservation, a shady village of about 100 families affiliated with the Unkechaug Nation. It's a windy beach town, the asphalt roads and scruffy grass yards giving way to

Many low-income American children are suffering from a shortage of words—songs, nursery rhymes, storybooks, chitchat, everyday stuff.

sand dunes and parcels of tangled coastal forest. Massive maple and pine trees rustle with sea breezes. In summer, it looks like a vacation town, full of barefoot kids with Popsicles and folks relaxing on their porches. But it's also a poor town, with high unemployment; more than a quarter of the households are below the poverty line. Out-of-work men linger in the streets. Smoke shops dominate the retail scene, most operating out of trailers, and some men— in desperation—freelance, flagging down cars to sell individual packs of cigarettes. Four or five families anchor their mobile homes on the same half acre of land and hang up their laundry and raise their children together in the common yard.

Tammy Edwards is a kind and serious young woman who works two jobs while caring for her aging father and young daughter in her mobile home. When exhausted, she might take a moment to smooth back her thick hair and secure it with bobby pins, maybe glancing out the window and quickly tallying how many tasks lie ahead before nightfall. When a bit of humor comes her way, for instance when watching her five-year-old, Ayanah, dance, Edwards's face lights up with an enormous, disbelieving, happy smile.

She's used to being on her own. "My mother died when I was 11, and my father couldn't really take care of me," she says. She grew up moving from house to house on the reservation, where everyone calls everyone else Cousin; in fact, her grandfather was a chief. "The Unkechaug Nation is my family," she says.

But though Tammy grew up feeling loved, she, like millions of young Americans, heard too few words. "We didn't have many books," she says. "They had a Christmas program for the kids on the reservation, and one year, I won a set of encyclopedias. I was so happy! It felt like winning a whole bunch of money. Afterward, folks would come to me to ask if they could borrow one to do a project. I was happy to share. I graduated high school and got a certificate in medical billing and a certification in home health care. I took a little bit of college, but my grades weren't too good. I had thought about becoming a teacher."

Edwards has big dreams for Ayanah, an ebullient girl whose   10
Native American name is Bright Star. And she is lucky because help was nearby.

"At 18 months, every child still has the potential to invent Facebook,"

By the time a child enters school, it may be too late to close the 30-million-word gap.

says Sarah E. Walzer, chief executive officer of an extraordinary nonprofit called the Parent-Child Home Program (PCHP). A former legal counsel in the US. Department of Health and Human Services, Walzer is a slight, fast-talking woman in her early 50s, with flyaway graying brown hair and a gentle smile. She has devoted her career to trying to level the playing field for poor children.

In the PCHP program, she explains, literacy specialists make home visits to help parents and very young toddlers close the word gap—because by the time a child enters school, it may be too late to catch up.

"Here's a child on his first day of kindergarten," Walzer says. "His teacher tells the class, 'You can pick out a book from the shelf and take it back to your seat.' But this child has never held a book before. He doesn't know how to handle it, how to turn the pages. He doesn't know how to get pleasure from it. He's failing his first day of kindergarten."

From there it gets worse. "The data show that a child who is behind in kindergarten will be behind in third grade, behind in sixth grade, and at high risk of not completing high school," she says.

To address the lag, some states mandated pre-K for four-year-olds. But the low-income four-year-olds were ill-equipped for pre-K too. Federally funded programs like Head Start reached out to children as young as three, but—to the alarm of experts—even the three-year-olds were behind national standards.

Today, it's widely accepted that the best time to start engaging in verbal interaction—to share rhymes and songs and picture books—is at a child's birth. The American Academy of Pediatrics recently stated that advocacy for early reading would become part of all well-baby checkups.

"Our job is to get there before the word gap magnifies," Walzer says. To put parents at ease, the early-literacy specialists often come from the communities in which they're working, and 25 percent of them are parent-graduates of the program. They visit up to twice a week for two years, with the idea of having fun together, using not only the books, puzzles, and toys provided by the program but also everything available. A visitor will demonstrate how to make sorting laundry a learning experience and how a trip to the grocery isn't really complete without naming fruits and vegetables, shapes and colors.

It's a simple strategy, and it works: "Children who go through our program graduate from high school at rates 20 percent higher than those of their national peer group," Walzer says. Currently the Parent-Child Home Program serves 7,000 families in 12 states. New York, where Tammy Edwards lives, is one of them.

In 2010, Helen Fechter, a PCHP specialist who works within Edwards's school district, reached out to Tammy Edwards personally. One of Fechter's first contacts on the Poospatuck Reservation, Edwards had never heard of the program—nor of the importance of early language enrichment—but she was open to learning more.

"Helen told me that introducing a child to reading at 18 months will help them going into school," Edwards says. "I had ordered a set of picture books for Ayanah but never took the time out to actually sit down with her. I was really happy to have to set a date to do it."

Edwards's experience confirms another of Walzer's observations: "The half hour the visitor spends with a parent and young child is a refuge. The visitor relays, 'No matter what the house looks like, no matter what's going on with the rest of your life, let's enjoy this time of reading and playing with your beautiful child.'"

Edwards soon learned that her basic reading skills were more than adequate to meet her daughter's needs. "We have clients who cannot read at all," Walzer says. "We assure them that their knowledge of the world will enrich their child's experience. You can spend half an hour on two pages of a picture book, enjoying all the details. You can make up the story."

"Ayanah's first book was *Clifford the Big Red Dog*," Edwards says. "Oh my goodness, she loved that dog! She was 18 months old and had a favorite book. She still talks about that book. She's in Head Start now and doing really well She loves all books so much! If she sees a book she feels like reading, like the Dora the Explorer books, she just picks it up."

"I like Dora!" Ayanah agrees. "And Diego. Diego is Dora's cousin. Dora is a big girl like me. I like the *Frozen* book. I like books about frogs. I like books about the ones that have long necks, named giraffes. Also horses. Chickens. And birds. I like books about birds."

As Tammy Edwards began referring friends on the reservation to PCHP, more and more parents opened their doors. Helen Fechter became such a regular at Poospatuck that, today, as she drives through the village, everyone waves. "I feel like a celebrity," Fechter says.

To date, 23 families have participated in PCHP as a result of Edwards's   25
endorsement. And when Ayanah graduated from the program, Edwards went through training to become an early-literacy specialist herself.

In November 2012, PCHP named her a Parent Literacy Champion and gave her a $1,000 scholarship. Edwards plans to go back to school to earn her teaching certification.

Recently, Edwards visited with two-and-a-half-year-old Jailah Overton and Jailah's mother, Shavon, to introduce a new book. Jailah was all dressed up in a gray-and-pink top, her round clean face glowed, and her hair had been tightly woven and braided with little white beads. Her mother couldn't stop smiling with pride and excitement as she sat down with her daughter for their lesson. Ayanah, now five, tagged along to help and chose one of her favorite books to share: *Are You My Mother?* by P. D. Eastman.

Jailah listened intensely as Edwards read the classic plight of the baby bird who hatches while his mother is off hunting for food. Off he treks in search of her, asking a dog, a kitten, a hen, a cow, and a steam shovel if any of them is his mother. Jailah looked captivated, probably as awed by the importance of this momentous half hour as by the page-turning plot.

"'Are you my mother?' he said to the cow," read Edwards, "'How could I be your mother?' said the cow. 'I am a cow,'" A little worried, Jailah glanced at her own mother for reassurance.

Suddenly Ayanah intervened, feeling she could do a better job of   30
holding the book and turning the pages. Edwards smiled and read on.

"Just then, the mother came back to the tree!" she read with excitement.

"She came back!" echoed Jailah's mother. Jailah scrunched up her little face in glee.

"Look, who is that?" asked Edwards, drawing Jailah back to the book.

"That's the mommy bird —that's her mommy!" explained Ayanah.

"'Yes, I know who you are,' said the baby bird," read Edwards. Jailah   35
gazed up into the faces of Edwards, Ayanah, and her mother and then back to the page, taking in all the great news. "'You are my mother!'"

At this, Jailah, overcome, collapsed sideways into her mother's lap.

At the end of the two-year program, Walzer says, some parents grow anxious. A parent will say to a home visitor, "I don't mind if you don't bring any more books or puzzles, but can you please keep coming?" The visitor will say, "We still have some time left, but you need to know that you have done all of this, not me; you are the one who has been educating your child."

"Pretty early on," Walzer says, "usually within the first week or two, when the child comes out with a new word or completes a rhyme, a parent will say, 'I had no idea my child could be so smart.' That's the moment that changes the whole trajectory because when parents have high expectations, their children tend to succeed. The parent starts saying, 'You are so smart, you're going to graduate from high school. You are going to college.'"

THINKING CRITICALLY ABOUT THE READING

1. According to Greene, what causes the "30-million-word gap" (5)? How might Greene's metaphor of words as free and "plentiful as air" (1) help her make her point in the essay?

2. Greene quotes Sarah Walzer, chief executive officer of the Parent-Child Home Program (PCHP), who asserts that "at 18 months, every child still has the potential to invent Facebook (11)." Does she mean this literally or figuratively? Why do you think she chooses Facebook as her example? How do you think Greene expects readers to react to this statement?

3. How does Walzer use the image of a book to describe children's early literacy deficit? What effect do you think this image has on readers?

4. How does the language gap Greene describes widen as children develop? What does the literacy research Walzer mentions suggest about relationship of language and literacy to academic and future life success?

5. How does PCHP worker Helen Fechter describe her reception on the reservation after having worked with several families? What does her ability to earn their trust and respect suggest about the perception of language and literacy within the community?

6. Characterize Jailah's reactions to P. D. Eastman's *Are You My Mother?* as described at the end of the selection. Why do you think Greene chooses to end the essay in this way? What does the quotation from Walzer add to Jailah's story?

LANGUAGE IN ACTION

Using the suggestions for parents in Greene's article and other suggestions you may find by searching for "30-million-word gap" online, draft a poster advertisement, Internet meme, infographic, commercial, or radio spot offering parents specific ideas for how to talk more to their children. Your public service announcement should illuminate not only *how* to add to a home's word count, but also *why* it's important.

As you compose your announcement, consider how the language of persuasion differs from language meant only to inform. How can you adapt Greene's approach in order to convince parents to change? What do you focus on? How can you present scientific findings in a way that both holds attention and conveys the message quickly?

WRITING SUGGESTIONS

1. As this article makes clear, language and literacy abilities help to define our success, including our ability to graduate from high school. Recently, a 2013 study conducted at Emory University has found that reading novels affects brain connectivity. As neuroscientist and researcher Gregory Berns has put it, the study suggests that "stories shape our lives and in some cases help define a person." Consider a story that has had a profound effect on you, and, in a short essay modeling Greene's use of description, discuss how that story has shaped or helped to define you. When did you first encounter it? How did it change you? How might it help others?

2. The end of the essay suggests that high expectations have a profound impact on both parents and children. As Walzer explains, as the child succeeds, parents feel more confident not only in their child's future success but also in themselves, as evidenced by Edwards's newfound ambition. Do you agree with Walzer's assessment that parents in the program had "no idea" their children could be so smart? Why, in your opinion, would parents like Edwards have that impression? Write an essay in which you discuss the relationship between language and literacy skills, parent-child bonding, and confidence building. How do those elements combine in the profound effects of the "30-million-word gap"?

Chunking

Ben Zimmer

Ben Zimmer was born in 1971 and graduated from Yale University in 1992 with a B.A. in linguistics. He has also studied linguistic anthropology at the University of Chicago. From 2006 to 2008 Zimmer was an editor for American dictionaries for Oxford University Press and was a consultant to the *Oxford English Dictionary*. From March 2010 to February 2011, he wrote the "On Language" column made popular by the late William Safire. Zimmer is now the executive producer of the *Visual Thesaurus* and *Vocabulary.com*. Zimmer's work has been reprinted in two blog anthologies, *Far from the Madding Gerund* (2006) and *Ultimate Blogs* (2008). He has also written for *Slate* and the *Boston Globe* and can be followed on Twitter.

In the following selection, which first appeared in the *New York Times* on September 16, 2010, Zimmer describes the language acquisition theory known as "chunking." As Zimmer says, however, "not everyone is on board" with the theory and how it is now being used by some instructors to teach English as a second language.

WRITING TO DISCOVER: *Some people complain that when we run into a friend and ask, "Hey, how are you?," we really don't ask that question to find out how the person is, that we don't mean the question literally, and that we are simply using a canned phrase as a way of saying hello. Have you found yourself using similarly prefabricated phrases as a shorthand method of speaking and writing? If so, what kind of response do you usually receive?*

My ebullient 4-year-old son, Blake, is a big fan of the CDs and DVDs that the band They Might Be Giants recently produced for the kiddie market. He'll gleefully sing along to "Seven," a catchy tune from their 2008 album "Here Come the 123s" that tells of a house overrun by anthropomorphic number sevens. The first one is greeted at the door: "Oh, there's the doorbell. Let's see who's out there. Oh, it's a seven. Hello, Seven. Won't you come in, Seven? Make yourself at home."

Despite the song's playful surrealism (more and more sevens arrive, filling up the living room), the opening lines are routine and formulaic. The polite ritual of answering the door and inviting a guest into your house relies on certain fixed phrases in English: "Won't you come in?" "Make yourself at home."

As Blake learned these pleasantries through the song and its video, I wondered how much—or how little—his grasp of basic linguistic etiquette is grounded in the syntactical rules that structure how words are combined in English. An idiom like "Make yourself at home" is rather tricky if you stop to think about it: the imperative verb "make" is followed by a second-person reflexive pronoun ("yourself") and an adverbial phrase ("at home"), but it's difficult to break the phrase into its components. Instead, we grasp the whole thing at once.

Ritualized moments of everyday communication—greeting someone, answering a telephone call, wishing someone a happy birthday—are full of these canned phrases that we learn to perform with rote precision at an early age. Words work as social lubricants in such situations, and a language learner like Blake is primarily getting a handle on the pragmatics of set phrases in English, or how they create concrete effects in real-life interactions. The abstract rules of sentence structure are secondary.

> **[I]t becomes clearer just how "chunky" the language is, with certain words showing undeniable attractions to certain others.**

In recent decades, the study of language acquisition and instruction has increasingly focused on "chunking": how children learn language not so much on a word-by-word basis but in larger "lexical chunks" or meaningful strings of words that are committed to memory. Chunks may consist of fixed idioms or conventional speech routines, but they can also simply be combinations of words that appear together frequently, in patterns that are known as "collocations." In the 1960s, the linguist Michael Halliday pointed out that we tend to talk of "strong tea" instead of "powerful tea," even though the phrases make equal sense. Rain, on the other hand, is much more likely to be described as "heavy" than "strong."

A native speaker picks up thousands of chunks like "heavy rain" or "make yourself at home" in childhood, and psycholinguistic research suggests that these phrases are stored and processed in the brain as individual units. As the University of Nottingham linguist Norbert Schmitt has explained, it is much less taxing cognitively to have a set of ready-made lexical chunks at our disposal than to have to work through all the possibilities of word selection and sequencing every time we open our mouths.

Cognitive studies of chunking have been bolstered by computer-driven analysis of usage patterns in large databases of texts called "corpora." As linguists and lexicographers build bigger and bigger corpora (a major-league corpus now contains billions of words, thanks to readily available online texts), it becomes clearer just how "chunky" the language is, with certain words showing undeniable attractions to certain others.

Many English-language teachers have been eager to apply corpus findings in the classroom to zero in on salient chunks rather than individual vocabulary words. This is especially so among teachers of English as a second language, since it's mainly the knowledge of chunks that allows nonnative speakers to advance toward nativelike fluency. In his 1993 book, *The Lexical Approach,* Michael Lewis set out a program of action, and the trend has continued in such recent works as *From Corpus to Classroom: Language Use and Language Teaching* and *Teaching Chunks of Language: From Noticing to Remembering.*

Not everyone is on board, however. Michael Swan, a British writer on language pedagogy, has emerged as a prominent critic of the lexical-chunk approach. Though he acknowledges, as he told me in an e-mail, that "high-priority chunks need to be taught," he worries that "the 'new toy' effect can mean that formulaic expressions get more attention than they deserve, and other aspects of language—ordinary vocabulary, grammar, pronunciation and skills—get sidelined."

Swan also finds it unrealistic to expect that teaching chunks will pro-   10
duce nativelike proficiency in language learners. "Native English speakers have tens or hundreds of thousands—estimates vary—of these formulae at their command," he says. "A student could learn 10 a day for years and still not approach native-speaker competence."

Besides, Swan warns, "overemphasizing 'scripts' in our teaching can lead to a phrase-book approach, where formulaic learning is privileged and the more generative parts of language—in particular the grammatical system—are backgrounded." Formulaic language is all well and good when talking about the familiar and the recurrent, he argues, but it is inadequate for dealing with novel ideas and situations, where the more open-ended aspects of language are paramount.

The methodology of the chunking approach is still open to this type of criticism, but data-driven reliance on corpus research will most likely dominate English instruction in coming years. Lexical chunks have entered the house of language teaching, and they're making themselves at home.

THINKING CRITICALLY ABOUT THE READING

1. What do the terms "chunking" and "collocation" mean in your own words? With what "lexical chunks" are you familiar?

2. What are "corpora" and how do they help teachers of English as a second language?

3. What are the arguments against using chunking as an approach to teaching a language? Do you agree or disagree with those arguments? Why or why not?

4. Does Zimmer think that the opponents of lexical chunking will prevail or does he believe that the chunking approach to language acquisition will dominate in the years ahead? Explain.

5. Why was the chunking approach to teaching and learning a language not available until recently? Explain.

LANGUAGE IN ACTION

Linguists tell us that we cannot identify expressions as chunks with any certainty unless we have corpora at our disposal to check their validity. We can, however, use our intuition and perhaps come close to identifying chunks in the language used around us. Try, for example, to identify chunks used in the following passage by bracketing them. Compare your choices with others in your class and discuss your choices.

The basketball game was a stunning success for our team. We had endured devastating injuries in the previous contests this season and we weren't sure how our team would rise to the occasion on Saturday night. Playing as a team made all the difference, however, as did Coach Taylor's strategy for the game. By cleverly using his bench and making timely player substitutions he was able to keep the Wildcats off balance throughout most of the game. Coach Taylor's use of the clock in the waning moments of the game deserves special attention and may be the explanation of how we finally snatched victory from the jaws of defeat.

WRITING SUGGESTIONS

1. Write an essay in support of or opposition to the use of chunking as a way of teaching vocabulary to students of English as a second language. You might want to begin your research with the two writers that Zimmer cites, Michael Lewis and Michael Swan, and go into more depth about the specific goals and strategies of teachers using chunking.

2. In his famous essay "Politics and the English Language," George Orwell took a critical approach to the use of prefabricated phrases of the kind that we now refer to as "chunks," particularly in political speeches and texts. Read his essay, which you can find online, and write one of your own in which you analyze his concerns in light of what you now know about teaching vocabulary using such prefabricated expressions.

Our Language Prejudices Don't Make No Sense

Raffaella Zanuttini

Raffaella Zanuttini, a native of Italy and a polyglot, is a professor of linguistics at Yale University. As Zanuttini explains on her personal Web site, her interest in linguistics stems from the fact that it "studies a component of human nature with methods that approach scientific rigor." In 2011, Zanuttini founded the Yale Grammatical Diversity Project, a research group that studies and documents grammatical diversity in North American English. Her research is rooted in combatting social prejudices based on speech, such as those discussed in the essay included here. She notes that her teaching, like her research, seeks to emphasize "grammatical richness" and the "complexity of each variety" of English spoken. In 2014, Zanuttini was awarded a National Science Foundation Grant to study the small regional variations in the syntax of North American English. She also serves as a Fellow in the Public Voices Fellowship program at Yale, reinforcing her commitment to shedding light on the many varieties of English.

The essay below, first published in *Pacific Standard* magazine on October 22, 2014, draws on her research and teaching to combat "false assumption[s] about language," which she suggests are often used to justify prejudice. As Zanuttini explains here, negatively judging certain varieties of English "amounts to a negative judgment on the people who speak that variety," and she exhorts her readers to think more broadly about what they consider to be "acceptable" English.

WRITING TO DISCOVER: *Think of your own background, the region you grew up in, and your own understanding of your family's social class. Do you find yourself judging others for their "poor" grammar or way of speaking? Have others judged you for the way you speak?*

There are some things you just don't say in polite society. You don't make overtly racist comments. You don't insult the poor. You do your best not to offend others' political sensibilities. But there is one type of comment that does not seem to be marked as inappropriate, though it certainly is potentially hurtful as it reflects an underlying negative attitude toward others—and a false assumption about language.

Here's how it often goes: "I can't stand it when people say *aks* instead of *ask*—it sounds so stupid!" "It drives me crazy when people use double negatives, like *I didn't see no one, or Didn't nobody get hurt*. That just doesn't make any sense!"

There is no scientific basis for such negative comments. Both the alternation between [sk] and [ks] (an instance of what linguists call metathesis) and the presence of multiple negative elements within a sentence with the reading of a single negation (or negative concord) are natural phenomena that are found across human languages. Negative concord is part of the grammar of Russian and Italian, among many other languages, for example, and was also part of the grammar of Old English and Middle English. We don't hear people getting upset about the fact that the Italian *Non ho visto nessuno* (literally "not (I) have seen no one") contains two negative elements—it is simply accepted as part of the grammar of this language, as it should be. Yet people get upset about negative concord in English. Why?

There is no single recipe for English; rather, there are a number of recipes.

It's because we associate these linguistic features with speakers who occupy a low position on the socio-economic scale. We think of negative concord as something used by certain black speakers, certain speakers of Appalachian English, and working-class people more generally. These groups have low prestige in American society and, by association, the variety of English they speak has low prestige—to some, it even sounds stupid, or illogical. But there is nothing illogical with negative concord as a strategy for expressing sentential negation; if it rubs us the wrong way, it's because of who uses it in English. In fact, those who don't look down on these groups, don't look down on the way they speak, either. Young people who love hip-hop music and admire its performers borrow negative concord into their own variety of English to sound cool and gain street cred; whether a variety sounds stupid or cool is a reflection of how we feel about the people who use it.

To be sure, many would argue that [aks] or negative concord raise   5
eyebrows not because of a negative attitude, but simply because they are not part of the grammar of English. English is not Italian—or Russian—after all. In this line of thinking, we object to these linguistic features because they represent a violation of the rules of English grammar. There is a major flaw in this reasoning, however: it presumes that there is a single grammar of English. There isn't.

Think of grammar as a recipe that allows us to form the sentences of the language we speak—a mental recipe that tells us how to form, pronounce, and interpret the sentences of our language. There is no single recipe for English; rather, there are a number of recipes. They have a lot in common, but are also slightly different from one another. They give rise to different varieties of English. Such varieties align with many factors, including age, ethnic or social identity, and geographical location—there is no doubt that English speakers in London, Sydney, and Los Angeles have slightly different recipes and thus speak different varieties of English.

In every country, one of these varieties emerges as the variety of prestige—the one that people need to use in job interviews, in formal occasions, on television, and more generally to climb the socio-economic ladder. Schools teach the recipe (or grammar) of this prestige variety; in doing so, they empower children, by giving them access to economic opportunities. But this doesn't mean that the other varieties are stupid, illogical, or nonsensical, or that they are a distortion of the prestige variety, or "bad grammar." They are simply different; they reflect mental grammars that differ minimally from one another, within limits imposed by general properties of human language. When we say that they are cool or illogical, we are expressing a judgment on the people who speak them—and if the judgment is negative, it amounts to a negative judgment on the people who speak that variety.

How should we think of different varieties of the same language? Following an analogy in Mark Baker's book *The Atoms of Language: The Mind's Hidden Rules of Grammar*, I suggest that we think about varieties of the same language the way we think about varieties of bread. Different kinds of bread are the overt reflection of recipes that differ minimally from one another. There is no bread that is stupid, illogical, or a distortion of another, but there might be types of bread that we feel are more appropriate—or even required by convention—for certain situations, and types of bread found in certain places and not in others, or associated with certain ethnic groups or social classes.

Similarly, no variety of English is a distortion of another; there are   10
some that are appropriate—or even required by convention—for certain situations, and some that are found in certain places and not in others, or associated with certain ethnic groups or social classes. But just as we wouldn't say that biscuits, baguette, pita, or challah are illogical or stupid, or distortions from "proper bread," similarly we shouldn't think that African-American English or Appalachian English or the English of Boston's North End are illogical or stupid, or distortions from "proper English." The recipes are simply different, and we should consider ourselves fortunate and appreciate the varieties that they yield. No one wants to live in a homogeneous white bread world.

THINKING CRITICALLY ABOUT THE READING

1. Why do you think Zanuttini mentions both race and poverty in the essay's second paragraph? How does one's use of language relate to these identity categories?

2. Do you think Zanuttini would like grammar-based judgments to be included on the list of "things you just don't say in polite society" (1)? Why or why not? How likely do you think this is?

3. Zanuttini asks readers to "think of grammar as a recipe" (6) and linguistic differences as varieties of bread. How does Zanuttini explain these metaphors? What does she hope thinking of grammar in this way will accomplish? How might it still carry the suggestion that some recipes or breads are better than others? Could you think of another metaphor to describe how we speak?

4. With what groups of speakers does Zanuttini argue that we associate "negative concord" (3)? What types of stigmas and judgments does this association create among those who speak a more prestigious variety of English? What does Zanuttini suggest we learn about "prestige" speakers from their judgments against "negative concord"?

5. Zanuttini concludes her essay by asserting: "No one wants to live in a homogeneous white bread world." Does "white bread" refer only to language as a recipe or variety of bread? What connotative meanings does the phrase carry? What is Zanuttini implying here, and why do you think she chooses not to spell it out?

LANGUAGE IN ACTION

Although plenty of people say that texting is ruining language, texting conventions might instead be creating a new variety of English. Make a quick list of conventions or goals of texting English that differentiate it from "proper English." Then, do a grammatical analysis of the text messages in your phone. Check for examples of "metathesis" or "negative concord" (see paragraph 3 of Zanuttini's article). What other errors do you see? Try to recall how you reacted to the errors when you first received the texts. Did you notice any of them and see them as *errors*? Or did the errors make sense in the context of texting, and therefore not seem like errors at all? Did any of them cause you to make assumptions about the background of the text writer?

WRITING SUGGESTIONS

1. Zanuttini names three groups of English speakers typically targeted by language prejudice: African Americans, Appalachians, and those of Boston's North End. What other groups can you think of? Choose one of these groups or one of your own, and do some research to test Zanuttini's contention that these varieties of English are considered "illogical or stupid, or distortions" of a proper English. You might search on Tumblr and/or Twitter for hashtags such as black English, Ebonics, hillbilly, redneck, Boston accent, bahstahn. What did you find? Are some of the entries more racist or classist than others? Choose one group and write a report of your own research. Be sure to comment on whether or not you see Zanuttini's research bear out online and the problems that arise from such representations.

2. Animated sitcoms for an adult audience often contain satirical social commentary, much of which comes in the form of exaggerated stereotypes. Choose an animated sitcom such as *The Simpsons, Family Guy, King of the Hill, American Dad, South Park*, or *Bob's Burgers* and watch a few episodes to consider how each character's variety of English affects her or his treatment in the show. Are characters stereotyped based on the variety of English they use? Does their language use help to perpetuate a stereotype? Do any of these characters break stereotypes associated with their language use—for instance, does a character with a typically mocked Southern accent become the voice of reason? Choose a single character and write a critical analysis of how his/her use of language perpetuates or resists stereotypes—or possibly does both at the same time.

Lost in Translation

LERA BORODITSKY

Lera Boroditsky was born about 1976 in Belarus. She earned her B.A. degree with honors from Northwestern University in 1996 and her doctorate in cognitive psychology from Stanford University in 2001. She focuses her research on a very old question in language study: whether or not the languages we speak shape the way we think, often referred to as the Sapir-Whorf hypothesis. She has found evidence that suggests that the differing ways people think and see the world may stem from the differing syntactical and lexical structures of their languages. For her work, Boroditsky has been awarded a National Science Foundation Career Award and the Marr Prize from the Cognitive Science Society. In 2002 she was named a Searle Scholar in a program administered by the Kinship Foundation, and in 2011 she was named an *Utne Reader* visionary.

"Lost in Translation," first published in the *Wall Street Journal* on July 24, 2010, explains the work she and her colleagues are now doing to reexamine the Sapir-Whorf hypothesis, or linguistic relativity hypothesis, that language might indeed shape reality, an idea she says "was for a long time considered untestable at best and more often simply crazy and wrong."

WRITING TO DISCOVER: *Do you think you shape your language or your language shapes you? Or both? What do you mean by "shape"? What if you speak more than one language?*

Do the languages we speak shape the way we think? Do they merely express thoughts, or do the structures in languages (without our knowledge or consent) shape the very thoughts we wish to express?

Take "Humpty Dumpty sat on a . . ." Even this snippet of a nursery rhyme reveals how much languages can differ from one another. In English, we have to mark the verb for tense; in this case, we say "sat" rather than "sit." In Indonesian you need not (in fact, you can't) change the verb to mark tense.

In Russian, you would have to mark tense and also gender, changing the verb if Mrs. Dumpty did the sitting. You would also have to decide if the sitting event was completed or not. If our ovoid hero sat on the wall for the entire time he was meant to, it would be a different form of the verb than if, say, he had a great fall.

In Turkish, you would have to include in the verb how you acquired this information. For example, if you saw the chubby fellow on the wall with your own eyes, you'd use one form of the verb, but if you had simply read or heard about it, you'd use a different form.

Do English, Indonesian, Russian and Turkish speakers end up attend-   5
ing to, understanding, and remembering their experiences differently
simply because they speak different languages?

These questions touch on all the major controversies in the study of
mind, with important implications for politics, law and religion. Yet very
little empirical work had been done on these questions until recently. The
idea that language might shape thought was for a long time considered
untestable at best and more often simply crazy and wrong. Now, a flurry
of new cognitive science research is showing that in fact, language does
profoundly influence how we see the world.

The question of whether languages shape the way we think goes back
centuries; Charlemagne proclaimed that "to have a second language is to
have a second soul." But the idea went out of favor with scientists when
Noam Chomsky's theories of language gained popularity in the 1960s
and '70s. Dr. Chomsky proposed that there is a universal grammar for all
human languages—essentially, that languages don't really differ from one
another in significant ways. And because languages didn't differ from one
another, the theory went, it made no sense to ask whether linguistic differences led to differences in thinking.

The search for linguistic universals yielded interesting data on languages, but after decades of work, not a single proposed universal has
withstood scrutiny. Instead, as linguists probed deeper into the world's
languages (7,000 or so, only a fraction of them analyzed), innumerable
unpredictable differences emerged.

Of course, just because people talk differently doesn't necessarily
mean they think differently. In the past decade, cognitive scientists have
begun to measure not just how people talk, but also how they think,
asking whether our understanding of even such fundamental domains of
experience as space, time and causality could be constructed by language.

For example, in Pormpuraaw, a remote Aboriginal community in   10
Australia, the indigenous languages don't use terms like "left" and "right."
Instead, everything is talked about in terms of absolute cardinal directions (north, south, east, west), which means you say things like, "There's
an ant on your southwest leg." To say hello in Pormpuraaw, one asks,
"Where are you going?," and an appropriate response might be, "A long
way to the south-southwest. How about you?" If you don't know which
way is which, you literally can't get past hello.

About a third of the world's languages (spoken in all kinds of physical
environments) rely on absolute directions for space. As a result of this constant linguistic training, speakers of such languages are remarkably good
at staying oriented and keeping track of where they are, even in unfamiliar
landscapes. They perform navigational feats scientists once thought were
beyond human capabilities. This is a big difference, a fundamentally different way of conceptualizing space, trained by language.

Differences in how people think about space don't end there. People rely on their spatial knowledge to build many other more complex or abstract representations including time, number, musical pitch, kinship relations, morality and, emotions. So if Pormpuraawans think differently about space, do they also think differently about other things, like time?

To find out, my colleague Alice Gaby and I traveled to Australia and gave Pormpuraawans sets of pictures that showed temporal progressions (for example, pictures of a man at different ages, or a crocodile growing, or a banana being eaten). Their job was to arrange the shuffled photos on the ground to show the correct temporal order. We tested each person in two separate sittings, each time facing in a different cardinal direction. When asked to do this, English speakers arrange time from left to right. Hebrew speakers do it from right to left (because Hebrew is written from right to left).

Pormpuraawans, we found, arranged time from east to west. That is, seated facing south, time went left to right. When facing north, right to left. When facing east, toward the body, and so on. Of course, we never told any of our participants which direction they faced. The Pormpuraawans not only knew that already, but they also spontaneously used this spatial orientation to construct their representations of time. And many other ways to organize time exist in the world's languages. In Mandarin, the future can be below and the past above. In Aymara, spoken in South America, the future is behind and the past in front.

In addition to space and time, languages also shape how we understand causality. For example, English likes to describe events in terms of agents doing things. English speakers tend to say things like "John broke the vase" even for accidents. Speakers of Spanish or Japanese would be more likely to say "the vase broke itself." Such differences between languages have profound consequences for how their speakers understand events, construct notions of causality and agency, what they remember as eyewitnesses and how much they blame and punish others.

In studies conducted by Caitlin Fausey at Stanford, speakers of English, Spanish and Japanese watched videos of two people popping balloons, breaking eggs, and spilling drinks either intentionally or accidentally. Later everyone got a surprise memory test: For each event, can you remember who did it? She discovered a striking cross-linguistic difference in eyewitness memory. Spanish and Japanese speakers did not remember the agents of accidental events as well as did English speakers. Mind you, they remembered the agents of intentional events (for which their language would mention the agent) just fine. But for accidental events, when one wouldn't normally mention the agent in Spanish or Japanese, they didn't encode or remember the agent as well.

In another study, English speakers watched the video of Janet Jackson's infamous "wardrobe malfunction" (a wonderful nonagentive coinage

15

introduced into the English language by Justin Timberlake), accompanied by one of two written reports. The reports were identical except in the last sentence where one used the agentive phrase "ripped the costume" while the other said "the costume ripped." Even though everyone watched the same video and witnessed the ripping with their own eyes, language mattered. Not only did people who read "ripped the costume" blame Justin Timberlake more, they also levied a whopping 53 percent more in fines.

Beyond space, time and causality, patterns in language have been shown to shape many other domains of thought. Russian speakers, who make an extra distinction between light and dark blues in their language, are better able to visually discriminate shades of blue. The Piraha, a tribe in the Amazon in Brazil, whose language eschews number words in favor of terms like few and many, are not able to keep track of exact quantities. And Shakespeare, it turns out, was wrong about roses: Roses by many other names (as told to blindfolded subjects) do not smell as sweet.

Patterns in language offer a window on a culture's dispositions and priorities. For example, English sentence structures focus on agents, and in our criminal-justice system, justice has been done when we've found the transgressor and punished him or her accordingly (rather than finding the victims and restituting appropriately, an alternative approach to justice). So does the language shape cultural values, or does the influence go the other way, or both?

Languages, of course, are human creations, tools we invent and hone   20
to suit our needs. Simply showing that speakers of different languages think differently doesn't tell us whether it's language that shapes thought or the other way around. To demonstrate the causal role of language, what's needed are studies that directly manipulate language and look for effects in cognition.

One of the key advances in recent years has been the demonstration of precisely this causal link. It turns out that if you change how people talk, that changes how they think. If people learn another language, they inadvertently also learn a new way of looking at the world. When bilingual people switch from one language to another, they start thinking differently, too. And if you take away people's ability to use language in what should be a simple nonlinguistic task, their

The languages we speak not only reflect or express our thoughts, but also shape the very thoughts we wish to express.

performance can change dramatically, sometimes making them look no smarter than rats or infants. (For example, in recent studies, MIT students were shown dots on a screen and asked to say how many there were. If they were allowed to count normally, they did great. If they simultaneously did a nonlinguistic task—like banging out rhythms—they still did great. But if they did a verbal task when shown the dots—like repeating the words spoken in a news report—their counting fell apart. In other words, they needed their language skills to count.)

All this new research shows us that the languages we speak not only reflect or express our thoughts, but also shape the very thoughts we wish to express. The structures that exist in our languages profoundly shape how we construct reality, and help make us as smart and sophisticated as we are.

Language is a uniquely human gift. When we study language, we are uncovering in part what makes us human, getting a peek at the very nature of human nature. As we uncover how languages and their speakers differ from one another, we discover that human natures too can differ dramatically, depending on the languages we speak. The next steps are to understand the mechanisms through which languages help us construct the incredibly complex knowledge systems we have. Understanding how knowledge is built will allow us to create ideas that go beyond the currently thinkable. This research cuts right to the fundamental questions we all ask about ourselves. How do we come to be the way we are? Why do we think the way we do? An important part of the answer, it turns out, is in the languages we speak.

THINKING CRITICALLY ABOUT THE READING

1. Why according to Boroditsky is it difficult to believe in Chomsky's theory of language universals?

2. In paragraph 10 Boroditsky discusses some language-thought peculiarities (for us as English speakers) that exist in the Pormpuraaw community of Australia. In what areas of human experience do researchers find differences?

3. What relationship does Boroditsky point to between English speakers' priority for an agent-based language structure and our criminal justice system? Does knowing about this connection make you more or less optimistic about the recent turn to giving more attention to victims' rights in our society? Explain.

4. Boroditsky says in paragraph 20, "Simply showing that speakers of different languages think differently doesn't tell us whether it's language that shapes thought or the other way around." What does she say researchers now need to do?

5. Why are people who speak more than one language important to language-thought researchers?

6. In your own words, explain why the language-thinking connection is so important for us to understand.

LANGUAGE IN ACTION

Those in the class who know more than one language may want to offer for discussion instances or examples of where the languages they know differ in structure and/or meaning when referring to the same things, ideas, people, and experiences. For example, the Italian term *allegro* ("lively, brisk, rapid") is a musical direction used to indicate a passage that should be played fast and musicians know that it should not be played as fast as a passage marked *presto* ("fast, rapid"). *Allegro ma non troppo* ("fast but not too fast") makes yet another distinction. Musicians learn these terms and there is a common understanding of just how fast the music should be played, although the musicians might agree to make even finer adjustments for particular compositions and passages within them. Here is an example of how a native Czech speaker used the syntax of his language but superimposed it on English: "He talked behind my back right in front of me," which might mean "he talked critically of me but in a way that I could hear."

WRITING SUGGESTIONS

1. The larger context for Boroditsky's research is the linguistic relativity hypothesis, also known as the Sapir-Whorf hypothesis. Write an essay explaining the hypothesis and its development throughout history. Who were Edward Sapir and Benjamin Lee Whorf, and what differing views did they have on the idea that language shapes reality? What impact did Noam Chomsky's ideas about language universals have on the theory and what positions have prominent linguists taken in the last three to four decades? Be sure to offer your own evaluation of the hypothesis.

2. Write an essay describing the major arguments linguists have made for and against the linguistic relativity hypothesis. How are younger linguists, in addition to Lera Boroditsky, now seeking to prove or disprove the hypothesis?

6

LANGUAGE COMMUNITIES: WHERE DO WE BELONG?

We reveal ourselves—where we come from, who we are, and who we'd like to be—in the language we use every day. At the same time, our use of language shapes us: In writing, speaking, or text messaging, we evolve as individuals in communication with other language users, exchanging signs and meanings and exploring new ways of defining ourselves and our place in the world. In this chapter we offer a collection of five readings that provide different perspectives on the speech communities to which we belong and how these communities, in turn, shape how we use language.

In the first reading, Paul Roberts writes about how speech communities form based on such factors as age, geography, and social class, and how the language patterns we learn in our speech communities affect how the world perceives (and receives) us. In "All-American Dialects," Richard Lederer focuses on the regional varieties or dialects of English that are spoken throughout the United States. Specifically, he explores the current state of these geographical speech communities, which he and others believe are rapidly disappearing because of the pressure from the homogenizing effects of mass media. In "Losing the Language of Silence," Lou Ann Walker addresses the complex effects of new assistive devices, like cochlear implants, on the deaf community as a way of illustrating larger questions about the future of deaf culture. She looks at the ways in which deaf children are caught between the demands of a hearing world and the need for connection, and she argues that American Sign Language is far from outmoded. In "Two Ways to Belong in America," Bharati Mukherjee reflects on her experience coming to America from India and how she chose to become an American citizen. In contrast to her expatriate Indian sister, Mukherjee needed "to put roots down, to vote and make the difference that I can." In time she realized that "the price that the immigrant willingly pays, and that the exile avoids, is the trauma of self-transformation." In "Mother Tongue," Amy Tan recounts her experiences growing up in a bilingual world, with one foot firmly planted in the English-speaking community of school and books and the other in her neighborhood community where she heard Chinese as well as the limited or "broken" English spoken by her immigrant mother. Finally, in "Talk the Talk," Eric C. Miller sheds light on both sides of the "English-only" debate in the United States. Miller gives a historical, political, and cultural look at the issue and concludes that American unity is not in fact threatened by linguistic diversity.

Speech Communities

PAUL ROBERTS

Paul Roberts (1917–1967) was a linguist, teacher, and writer. Born in California, he received his B.A. from San Jose State University and his M.A. and Ph.D. from the University of California at Berkeley. After teaching at San Jose State and then Cornell University, Roberts became director of language at the Center of American Studies in Rome. His books include *Understanding Grammar* (1954), *Patterns of English* (1956), *Understanding English* (1958), *English Sentences* (1962), and *English Syntax* (1964).

In the following selection from *Understanding English*, Roberts writes about the development of speech variations within the United States that are based on what he identifies as "speech communities." These communities—which sometimes have their own dialects, their own jargon, and their own codes, meanings, and pronunciations—are formed by a variety of factors, according to Roberts, including "age, geography, education, occupation, social position."

WRITING TO DISCOVER: *Think about your own way of speaking. What factors do you believe are the most powerful influences on your own use of English—for example, your family, the region you grew up in, your peers? Do you have more than one way of speaking, depending on whom you are with or where you are?*

Imagine a village of a thousand people all speaking the same language and never hearing any language other than their own. As the decades pass and generation succeeds generation, it will not be very apparent to the speakers of the language that any considerable language change is going on. Oldsters may occasionally be conscious of and annoyed by the speech forms of youngsters. They will notice new words, new expressions, "bad" pronunciations, but will ordinarily put these down to the irresponsibility of youth, and decide piously that the language of the younger generation will revert to decency when the generation grows up.

It doesn't revert, though. The new expressions and the new pronunciations persist, and presently there is another younger generation with its own new expressions and its own pronunciations. And thus the language changes. If members of the village could speak to one another across five hundred years, they would probably find themselves unable to communicate.

Now suppose that the village divides itself and half the people move away. They move across the river or over a mountain and form a new village. Suppose the separation is so complete that the people of New Village have no contact with the people of Old Village. The language of both villages will change, drifting away from the language of their common ancestors. But the drift will not be in the same direction. In both villages there will be new expressions and new pronunciations, but not the same ones. In the course of time the languages of Old Village and New Village will be mutually unintelligible with the language they both started with. They will also be mutually unintelligible with one another.

An interesting thing—and one for which there is no perfectly clear explanation—is that the rate of change will not ordinarily be the same for both villages. The language of Old Village changes faster than the language of New Village. One might expect that the opposite would be true—that the emigrants, placed in new surroundings and new conditions, would undergo more rapid language changes. But history reports otherwise. American English, for example, despite the violence and agony and confusion to which the demands of a new continent have subjected it, is probably essentially closer to the language of Shakespeare than London English is.

Suppose one thing more. Suppose Old Village is divided sharply into   5 an upper class and a lower class. The sons and daughters of the upper class go to preparatory school and then to the university; the children of the lower class go to work. The upper-class people learn to read and write and develop a flowering literature; the lower-class people remain illiterate. Dialects develop, and the speech of the two classes steadily diverges. One might suppose that most of the change would go on among the illiterate, that the upper-class people, conscious of their heritage, would tend to preserve the forms and pronunciations of their ancestors. Not so. The opposite is true. In speech, the educated tend to be radical and the uneducated conservative. In England one finds Elizabethan forms and sounds not among Oxford and Cambridge graduates but among the people of backward villages.

A village is a fairly simple kind of speech community—a group of people steadily in communication with one another, steadily hearing one another's speech. But the village is by no means the basic unit. Within the simplest village there are many smaller units—groupings based on age, class, occupation. All these groups play intricately on one another and against one another, and a language that seems at first a coherent whole will turn out on inspection to be composed of many differing parts. Some forces tend to make these parts diverge, other forces hold them together. Thus the language continues in tension.

THE SPEECH COMMUNITIES OF THE CHILD

The child's first speech community is ordinarily his family. The child learns whatever kind of language the family speaks—or, more precisely, whatever kind of language it speaks to him. The child's language learning, now and later, is governed by two obvious motives: the desire to communicate and the desire to be admired. He imitates what he hears. More or less successful imitations usually bring action and reward and tend to be repeated. Unsuccessful ones usually don't bring action and reward and tend to be discarded.

But since language is a complicated business it is sometimes the unsuccessful imitations that bring the reward. The child, making a stab at the word *mother*, comes out with *muzzer*. The family decides that this is just too cute for anything and beams and repeats *muzzer*, and the child, feeling that he's scored a bull's eye, goes on saying *muzzer* long after he has mastered *other* and *brother*. Baby talk is not so much invented by the child as sponsored by the parent.

Eventually the child moves out of the family and into another speech community—other children of his neighborhood. He goes to kindergarten and immediately encounters speech habits that conflict with those he has learned. If he goes to school and talks about his *muzzer*, it will be borne in on him by his colleagues that the word is not well chosen. Even *mother* may not pass muster, and he may discover that he gets better results and is altogether happier if he refers to his female parent as his ma or even his old lady.

Children coming together in a kindergarten class bring with them   10
language that is different because it is learned in different homes. It is all to some degree unsuccessfully learned, consisting of not quite perfect imitations of the original. In school all this speech coalesces, differences tend to be ironed out, and the result differs from the original parental speech and differs in pretty much the same way.

The pressures on the child to conform to the speech of his age group, his speech community, are enormous. He may admire his teacher and love his mother, he may even—and even consciously—wish to speak as they do. But he *has* to speak like the rest of the class. If he does not, life becomes intolerable.

The speech changes that go on when the child goes to school are often most distressing to parents. Your little Bertram, at home, has never heard anything but the most elegant English. You send him to school, and what happens? He comes home saying things like "I done real good in school today, Mom." But Bertram really has no choice in the matter. If Clarence and Elbert and the rest of the fellows customarily say "I done real good," then Bertram might as well go around with three noses as say things like "I did very nicely."

Individuals differ of course, and not all children react to the speech community in the same way. Some tend to imitate and others tend to force imitation. But all to some degree have their speech modified by forces over which neither they nor their parents nor their teachers have any real control.

Individuals differ too in their sensitivity to language. For some, language is always a rather embarrassing problem. They steadily make boners, saying the right thing in the wrong place or the wrong way. They have a hard time fitting in. Others tend to change their language slowly, sticking stoutly to their way of saying things, even though their way differs from that of the majority. Still others adopt new language habits almost automatically, responding quickly to whatever speech environment they encounter.

Indeed some children of five or six have been observed to speak two   15
or more different dialects without much awareness that they are doing so. Most commonly, they will speak in one way at home and in another on the playground. At home they say, "I did very nicely" and "I haven't any"; these become at school, "I done real good" and "I ain't got none."

THE CLASS AS A SPEECH COMMUNITY

Throughout the school years, or at least through the American secondary school, the individual's most important speech community is his age group, his class. Here is where the real power lies. The rule is conformity above all things, and the group uses its power ruthlessly on those who do not conform. Language is one of the chief means by which the school group seeks to establish its entity, and in the high school this is done more or less consciously. The obvious feature is high school slang, picked up from the radio, from other schools, sometimes invented, changing with bewildering speed. Nothing is more satisfactory than to speak today's slang; nothing more futile than to use yesterday's.

There can be few tasks more frustrating than that of the secondary school teacher charged with the responsibility of brushing off and polishing up the speech habits of the younger generation. Efforts to make *real* into *really*, *ain't* into *am not*, *I seen him* into *I saw him*, *he don't* into *he doesn't* meet at best with polite indifference, at worst with mischievous counterattack.

The writer can remember from his own high school days when the class, a crashingly witty bunch, took to pronouncing the word *sure* as *sewer*. "Have you prepared your lesson, Arnold?" Miss Driscoll would ask. "Sewer, Miss Driscoll," Arnold would reply. "I think," said Miss Driscoll, who was pretty quick on her feet too, "that you must mean 'sewerly,' since the construction calls for the adverb not the adjective." We were delighted with the suggestion and went about saying "sewerly" until the very blackboards were nauseated. Miss Driscoll must have wished often that she had let it lay.

CONFRONTING THE ADULT WORLD

When the high school class graduates, the speech community disinte-grates as the students fit themselves into new ones. For the first time in the experience of most of the students the speech ways of adult communities begin to exercise real force. For some people the adjustment is a relatively simple one. A boy going to work in a garage may have a good deal of new lingo to pick up, and he may find that the speech that seemed so racy and won such approval in the corridors of Springfield High leaves his more adult associates merely bored. But a normal person will adapt himself without trouble.

For others in other situations settling into new speech communities   20 may be more difficult. The person going into college, into the business world, into scrubbed society may find that he has to think about and work on his speech habits in order not to make a fool of himself too often.

College is a particularly complicated problem. Not only does the freshman confront upperclassmen not particularly disposed to find the speech of Springfield High particularly cute, but the adult world, as rep-resented chiefly by the faculty, becomes increasingly more immediate. The problems of success, of earning a living, of marriage, of attaining a satis-factory adult life loom larger, and they all bring language problems with them. Adaptation is necessary, and the student adapts.

The student adapts, but the adult world adapts too. The thousands of boys and girls coming out of the high schools each spring are affected by the speech of the adult communities into which they move, but they also affect that speech. The new pronunciation habits, developing grammatical features, different vocabulary do by no means all give way before the dis-approval of elders. Some of them stay. Elders, sometimes to their dismay, find themselves changing their speech habits under the bombardment of those of their juniors. And then of course the juniors eventually become the elders, and there is no one left to disapprove.

THE SPACE DIMENSION

Speech communities are formed by many features besides that of age. Most obvious is geography. Our country was originally settled by people coming from different parts of England. They spoke different dialects to begin with and as a result regional speech differences existed from the start in the different parts of the country. As speakers of other languages came to America and learned English, they left their mark on the speech of the sections in which they settled. With the westward movement, new pio-neers streamed out through the mountain passes and down river valleys, taking the different dialects west and modifying them by new mixtures in new environments.

Today we are all more or less conscious of certain dialect differences in our country. We speak of the "southern accent," the "Brooklyn accent," the "New England accent." Until a few years ago it was often said that American English was divided into three dialects: Southern American (south of the Mason-Dixon line); Eastern American (east of the Connecticut River); and Western American. This description suggests certain gross differences all right, but recent research shows that it is a gross oversimplification.

The starting point of American dialects is the original group of colonies.   25 We had a New England settlement, centering in Massachusetts; a Middle Atlantic settlement, centering in Pennsylvania; a southern settlement, centering in Virginia and the Carolinas. These colonies were different in speech to begin with, since the settlers came from different parts of England. Their differences were increased as the colonies lived for a century and a half or so with only thin communication with either Mother England or each other. By the time of the Revolution the dialects were well established. Within each group there were of course subgroups. Richmond speech differed markedly from that of Savannah. But Savannah and Richmond were more like each other than they were like Philadelphia or Boston.

> **We speak of America as the melting pot, but the speech communities of this continent are very far from having melted into one.**

The Western movement began shortly after the Revolution, and dialects followed geography. The New Englanders moved mostly into upper New York State and the Great Lakes region. The Middle Atlantic colonists went down the Shenandoah Valley and eventually into the heart of the Midwest. The southerners opened up Kentucky and Tennessee, later the lower Mississippi Valley, later still Texas and much of the Southwest. Thus new speech communities were formed, related to the old ones of the seaboard, but each developing new characteristics as lines of settlement crossed.

New complications were added before and after the Revolution by the great waves of immigration of people from countries other than England: Swedes in Delaware, Dutch in New York, Germans and Scots-Irish in Pennsylvania, Irish in New England, Poles and Greeks and Italians and Portuguese. The bringing in of black slaves had an important effect on the speech of the South and later on the whole country. The Spanish in California and the Southwest added their mark. In [the twentieth and twenty-first centuries], movement of peoples goes on: the trek of southern blacks to northern and western cities, the migration of people from Arkansas, Oklahoma, and Texas to California. All these have shaped and are shaping American speech.

We speak of America as the melting pot, but the speech communities of this continent are very far from having melted into one. Linguists today can trace very clearly the movements of the early settlers in the still-living speech of their descendants. They can follow an eighteenth century speech community west, showing how it crossed this pass and followed that river, threw out an offshoot here, left a pocket there, merged with another group, halted, split, moved on once more. If all other historical evidence were destroyed, the history of the country could still be reconstructed from the speech of modern America.

SOCIAL DIFFERENCES

The third great shaper of speech communities is social class. This has been, and is, more important in England than in America. In England, class differences have often been more prominent than those of age or place. If you were the blacksmith's boy, you might know the son of the local baronet, but you didn't speak his language. You spoke the language of your social group, and he that of his, and over the centuries these social dialects remained widely separated.

England in the twentieth century has been much democratized, but the language differences are far from having disappeared. One can still tell much about a person's family, his school background, his general position in life by the way he speaks. Social lines are hard to cross, and language is perhaps the greatest barrier. You may make a million pounds and own several cars and a place in the country, but your vowels and consonants and nouns and verbs and sentence patterns will still proclaim to the world that you're not a part of the upper crust.   30

In America, of course, social distinctions have never been so sharp as they are in England. We find it somewhat easier to rise in the world, to move into social environments unknown to our parents. This is possible, partly, because speech differences are slighter; conversely, speech differences are slighter because this is possible. But speech differences do exist. If you've spent all your life driving a cab in Philly and, having inherited a fortune, move to San Francisco's Nob Hill, you will find that your language is different, perhaps embarrassingly so, from that of your new acquaintances.

Language differences on the social plane in America are likely to correlate with education or occupation rather than with birth—simply because education and occupation in America do not depend so much on birth as they do in other countries. A child without family connection can get himself educated at Harvard, Yale, or Princeton. In doing so, he acquires the speech habits of the Ivy League and gives up those of his parents.

Exceptions abound. But in general there is a clear difference between the speech habits of the college graduate and those of the high-school graduate. The cab driver does not talk like the Standard Oil executive, the college professor like the carnival pitch man, or an Illinois merchant like a sailor shipping out of New Orleans. New York's Madison Avenue and

Third Avenue are only a few blocks apart, but they are widely separated in language. And both are different from Broadway.

It should be added that the whole trend of modern life is to reduce rather than to accentuate these differences. In a country where college education becomes increasingly everybody's chance, where executives and refrigerator salesmen and farmers play golf together, where a college professor may drive a cab in the summertime to keep his family alive, it becomes harder and harder to guess a person's education, income, and social status by the way he talks. But it would be absurd to say that language gives no clue at all.

GOOD AND BAD

Speech communities, then, are formed by many features: age, geography, education, occupation, social position. Young people speak differently from old people, Kansans differently from Virginians, Yale graduates differently from Dannemora graduates. Now let us pose a delicate question: aren't some of these speech communities better than others? That is, isn't better language heard in some than in others?   35

Well, yes, of course. One speech community is always better than all the rest. This is the group in which one happens to find oneself. The writer would answer unhesitatingly that the noblest, loveliest, purest English is that heard in the Men's Faculty Club of San Jose State College, San Jose, California. He would admit, of course, that the speech of some of the younger members leaves something to be desired; that certain recent immigrants from Harvard, Michigan, and other foreign parts need to work on the laughable oddities lingering in their speech; and that members of certain departments tend to introduce a lot of queer terms that can only be described as jargon. But in general the English of the Faculty Club is ennobling and sweet.

As a practical matter, good English is whatever English is spoken by the group in which one moves contentedly and at ease. To the bum on Main Street in Los Angeles, good English is the language of other L.A. bums. Should he wander onto the campus of UCLA, he would find the talk there unpleasant, confusing, and comical. He might agree, if pressed, that the college man speaks "correctly" and he doesn't. But in his heart he knows better. He wouldn't talk like them college jerks if you paid him.

If you admire the language of other speech communities more than you do your own, the reasonable hypothesis is that you are dissatisfied with the community itself. It is not precisely other speech that attracts you but the people who use this speech. Conversely, if some language strikes you as unpleasant or foolish or rough, it is presumably because the speakers themselves seem so.

To many people, the sentence "Where is he at?" sounds bad. It is bad, they would say, in and of itself. The sounds are bad. But this is very hard to prove, If "Where is he at?" is bad because it has bad sound combinations, then presumably "Where is the cat?" or "Where is my hat?" are just as bad, yet no one thinks them so. Well, then, "Where is he at?" is bad because it uses too many words. One gets the same meaning from "Where is he?" so why add the *at*? True. Then "He going with us?" is a better sentence than "Is he going with us?" You don't really need the *is*, so why put it in?

Certainly there are some features of language to which we can apply   40 the terms *good* and *bad*, *better* and *worse*. Clarity is usually better than obscurity; precision is better than vagueness. But these are not often what we have in mind when we speak of good and bad English. If we like the speech of upper-class Englishmen, the presumption is that we admire upper-class Englishmen — their characters, culture, habits of mind. Their sounds and words simply come to connote the people themselves and become admirable therefore. If we heard the same sounds and words from people who were distasteful to us, we would find the speech ugly.

This is not to say that correctness and incorrectness do not exist in speech. They obviously do, but they are relative to the speech community — or communities — in which one operates. As a practical matter, correct speech is that which sounds normal or natural to one's comrades. Incorrect speech is that which evokes in them discomfort or hostility or disdain.

THINKING CRITICALLY ABOUT THE READING

1. Why does Roberts begin with a discussion of "the village"? Is he referring literally to villages, or does "the village" stand for something else? What does his extended example of "Old Village" and "New Village" (3–5) illustrate? (Glossary: *Beginnings and Endings; Examples*)

2. Roberts writes: "Baby talk is not so much invented by the child as sponsored by the parent" (8). Explain what he means by this. What are the most basic, and motivational, factors in a child's language learning?

3. When children go to school, they move into an entirely new speech community, where, according to Roberts, their speech is modified "by forces over which neither they nor their parents nor their teachers have any real control" (13). What are these forces? What are some of the ways in which the new speech community asserts itself and establishes its own identity?

4. "We speak of America as the melting pot, but the speech communities of this continent are very far from having melted into one" (28), writes Roberts. What factors have contributed to, and continue to foster, the multiplicity of speech communities across the United States?

5. According to Roberts, the impact in England of social class on shaping speech communities differs considerably from the impact of class on speech communities in the United States. What factors contribute to this difference? Do you think these differences are as relevant today as Roberts assumed they were when he wrote *Understanding English*?

6. Roberts asks the provocative question: "Aren't some of these speech communities better than others?" (35). What do you think he means by this? Is he referring to the language of the community, or the community members themselves? What kind of value judgments do you think we make about others based on their particular way of speaking?

LANGUAGE IN ACTION

In his 1995 memoir, *Dreams from My Father: A Story of Race and Inheritance*, then senator Barack Obama writes:

> I learned to slip back and forth between my black and white worlds, understanding that each possessed its own language and customs and structures of meaning, convinced that with a bit of translation on my part the two worlds would eventually cohere. Still, the feeling that something wasn't quite right stayed with me, a warning that sounded whenever a white girl mentioned in the middle of conversation how much she liked Stevie Wonder or when a woman in the supermarket asked me if I played basketball; or when the school principal told me I was cool. I did like Stevie Wonder, I did love basketball, and I tried my best to be cool at all times. So why did such comments set me on edge?

Why do you think Obama was "set on edge" by the kinds of comments he mentions toward the end of the passage? Can you sympathize with his position? Do you believe that it's possible to make different language communities to which one belongs "eventually cohere"? Why or why not?

WRITING SUGGESTIONS

1. We are often simultaneous members of more than one speech community, especially as we move into young adulthood and are introduced to groups outside of our family. Each of these groups can have its own demands, rules of membership, culture, and identity, to which we must adapt with chameleonlike skill. Write about your own experience moving between or among groups, identifying the most influential groups on your life and what demands were made on you in order to belong. What did you have to do to adapt to each group? How did the groups differ? Were they mutually exclusive, or did they overlap on occasion? Do you consider any one of the groups to be superior to the other, or were they simply equal, but different? If it helps you organize your thinking, make a sketch or a map of your communities. Write an essay in which you discuss what you discover.

2. Roberts writes:

> If you admire the language of other speech communities more than you do your own, the reasonable hypothesis is that you are dissatisfied with the community itself. It is not precisely the other speech that attracts you but the people who use this speech. Conversely, if some language strikes you as unpleasant or foolish or rough, it is presumably because the speakers themselves seem so (38).

Write an essay that supports or refutes his argument, providing examples from your own experience as evidence.

All-American Dialects

RICHARD LEDERER

Born in 1938, Richard Lederer has been a lifelong student of language. He holds degrees from Haverford College, Harvard University, and the University of New Hampshire and for twenty-seven years taught English at St. Paul's School in Concord, New Hampshire. Anyone who has read one of his over thirty-five books will understand why he has been referred to as "Conan the Grammarian" and "America's wittiest verbalist." Lederer loves language and enjoys writing about its marvelous richness and about how Americans use language. He has written over thirty-five books including *Anguished English* (1987), *Crazy English* (1989), *The Play of Words* (1990), *Adventures of a Verbivore* (1994), *Nothing Risque, Nothing Gained* (1995), *The Bride of Anguished English* (2002), *A Man of My Words: Reflections on the English Language* (2003), *Word Wizard: Super Bloopers, Rich Reflections, and Other Acts of Word Magic* (2006), and *Presidential Trivia: The Feats, Fates, Families, Foibles, and Firsts of Our American Presidents* (2007). In addition to writing books, Lederer pens a weekly syndicated column called "Looking at Language" for newspapers and magazines throughout the country. He is the "Grammar Grappler" for *Writer's Digest*, the language commentator for National Public Radio, and cohost of *A Way with Words*, a weekly radio program out of San Diego, where he currently lives.

The following essay was first published in *USA Today* magazine in July 2009. Lederer discusses, using multiple examples, regional dialects or speech communities and how they differ one from another in vocabulary, pronunciation, and grammar. Like John Steinbeck before him, Lederer fears that regional speech is rapidly disappearing. He fervently hopes that "American English does not turn into a bland, homogenized, pasteurized, assembly line product."

WRITING TO DISCOVER: *What part of the country did you grow up in? Do you think of yourself as speaking English with a regional "accent"? Are you proud of the way you and your friends and neighbors speak? How do you view speakers from other parts of the United States? Do you readily recognize regional differences in the way English is spoken?*

I have tongue and will travel, so I run around the country speaking to groups of teachers, students, librarians, women's clubbers, guild professionals, and corporate clients. These good people go to all the trouble of putting together meetings and conferences, and I walk in, share my thoughts about language in their lives, and imbibe their collective energy and synergy. I will go anywhere to spread the word about words and, in venturing from California to Manhattan Island, from the redwood forest to the Gulf Stream waters, I hear America singing. We are teeming nations within a nation, a country that is like a world. We talk in melodies of infinite variety; we dance to their sundry measure and lyrics.

Midway through John Steinbeck's epic *The Grapes of Wrath*, young Ivy observes, "Ever'body says words different. Arkansas folks says 'em different, and Oklahomy folks says 'em different, and we seen a lady from Massachusetts, an' she said 'em differentest of all. Couldn't hardly make out what she was sayin'."

One aspect of American rugged individualism is that not all of us say the same word in the same way. Sometimes, we do not even use the same name for the same object. I was born and grew up in Philadelphia a coon's age, a blue moon, a month of Sundays ago—when Hector was a pup. Phillufia, or Philly, which is what we kids called the city, was where the epicurean delight made with cold cuts, cheese, tomatoes, pickles, and onions stuffed into a long, hard-crusted Italian bread loaf was invented. The creation of that sandwich took place in the Italian pushcart section of the city, known as Hog Island. Some linguists contend that it was but a short leap from Hog Island to hoagie, while others claim that the label hoagie arose because only a hog had the appetite or technique to eat one properly.

As a young man, I moved to northern New England (N'Hampsha, to be specific), where the same sandwich designed to be a meal in itself is called a grinder—because you need a good set of grinders to chew it. Yet, my travels around the country have revealed that the hoagie or grinder is called at least a dozen other names—a bomber, Garibaldi (after the Italian liberator), hero, Italian sandwich, rocket, sub, submarine (which is what they call it in California, where I now live), torpedo, wedge, wedgie, and, in the deep South, a poor-boy (usually pronounced poh-boy).

In Philadelphia, we washed down our hoagies with soda. In New England, we did it with tonic and, by that word, I do not mean medicine. Soda and tonic in other parts are known as pop, soda pop, a soft drink, Coke, and quinine.   5

In northern New England, they take the term milk shake quite literally. To many residing in that corner of the country, a milk shake consists of milk mixed with flavored syrup—and nothing more—shaken up until foamy. If you live in Rhode Island or in southern Massachusetts and you want ice cream in your milk drink, you ask for a cabinet (named after the square wooden cabinet in which the mixer was encased). If you live farther north, you order a velvet or a frappe (from the French *frapper*, "to ice").

Clear—or is it clean or plumb?—across the nation, Americans sure do talk different. What do you call those flat, doughy things you often eat for breakfast—battercakes, flannel cakes, flapjacks, fritters, griddle cakes, or pancakes? Is that simple strip of grass between the street and the sidewalk a berm, boulevard, boulevard strip, city strip, devil strip, green belt, the parking, the parking strip, parkway, sidewalk plot, strip, swale, tree bank, or tree lawn? Is the part of the highway that separates the northbound from the southbound lanes the centerline, center strip, mall, medial strip, median strip, medium strip, or neutral ground? Is it a cock horse, dandle, hicky horse, horse, horse tilt, ridy horse, seesaw, teeter, teeterboard, teetering board, teetering horse, teeter-totter, tilt, tilting board, tinter, tinter board, or tippity bounce? Do fishermen employ an angledog, angleworm, baitworm, earthworm, eaceworm, fishworm, mudworm, rainworm, or redworm? Is a larger worm a dew worm, night crawler, night walker, or town worm? Is it a crabfish, clawfish, craw, crawdab, crawdad, crawdaddy, crawfish, crawler, crayfish, creekcrab, crowfish, freshwater lobster, ghost shrimp, mudbug, spiny lobster, or yabby? Depends where you live and who or whom it is you are talking to.

I figger, figure, guess, imagine, opine, reckon, and suspect that my being bullheaded, contrary, headstrong, muley, mulish, ornery, otsny, pigheaded, set, sot, stubborn, or utsy about this whole matter of dialects makes you sick to, in, or at your stomach. I assure you, though, that when it comes to American dialects, I'm not speaking fahdoodle, flumadiddle, flummydiddle, or flurriddiddle—translation, nonsense. I am no all-thumbs-and-no-fingers, all-knees-and-elbows, all-left-feet, antigoddling, bumfuzzled, discombobulated, flusterated, or foozled bumpkin, clodhopper, country jake, hayseed, hick, hillbilly, hoosier, jackpine savage, mossback, mountain-boomer, pumpkin-husker, rail-splitter, rube, sodbuster, stump farmer, swamp angel, yahoo, or yokel.

The biblical book of Judges tells of how one group of speakers used the word *shibboleth*, Hebrew for "stream," as a military password. The Gileadites had defeated the Ephraimites in battle and were holding some narrow places on the Jordan River that the fleeing Ephraimites had to cross to get home. In those days, it was hard to tell one kind of soldier from another because they did not wear uniforms. The Gileadites knew that the Ephraimites spoke a slightly different dialect of Hebrew and could be recognized by their inability to pronounce an initial "sh" sound. Thus, each time a soldier wanted to cross the river, "the men of Gilead said unto him, Art thou an Ephraimite? If he said, Nay, then they said unto him, Say now Shibboleth, and he said Sibboleth: for he could not frame to pronounce it right. Then they took him and slew him at the passages of Jordan: and there fell at that time of the Ephraimites forty and two thousand."

During World War II, some American officers adapted the strategy of the Old Testament Gileadites. Knowing that many Japanese have difficulty pronouncing the letter "L," these officers instructed their sentries to use only passwords that had L's in them, such as lallapalooza. The closest the Japanese got to the sentries was rarraparooza.

10

These days, English speakers do not get slaughtered for pronouncing their words differently from other English speakers, but the way those words sound can be labeled "funny" or "quaint" or "out of touch." In the George Bernard Shaw play "Pygmalion," Prof. Henry Higgins rails at Liza Doolittle and her cockney accent: "A woman who utters such depressing and disgusting sounds has no right to be anywhere—no right to live. Remember that you are a human being with a soul and the divine gift of articulate speech: that your native language is the language of Shakespeare and Milton and the Bible; and don't sit there crooning like a bilious pigeon!"

Most of us are aware that large numbers of people in the U.S. speak very differently than we do. Most of us tend to feel that the way "we" talk is right, and the way "they" talk is weird. "They," of course, refers to anyone who differs from "us." If you ask most adults what a dialect is, they will tell you it is what somebody else in another region passes off as English. These regions tend to be exotic places like Mississippi or Texas—or Brooklyn, where oil is a rank of nobility and earl is a black, slippery substance.

It is reported that many Southerners reacted to the elections of Jimmy Carter (Georgia) and Bill Clinton (Arkansas) by saying, "Well, at last we have a president who talks without an accent." Actually, Southerners, like everyone else, do speak with an accent, as witness these tongue-in-cheek entries in our Dictionary of Southernisms: ah (organ for seeing); are (60 minutes); arn (ferrous metal); ass (frozen water); ast (questioned); bane (small, kidney-shaped vegetable); bar (seek and receive a loan); bold (heated in water); card (one who lacks courage); farst (a lot of trees); fur (distance); har (to employ); hep (to assist); hire yew (a greeting); paw tree (verse); rat (opposite of lef); reckanize (to see); tarred (exhausted); t'mar (the day following t'day); thang (item); thank (to cogitate); and y'all (a bunch of "you's").

When I visited Alexandria, Louisiana, a local pastor offered me proof that y'all has biblical origins, especially in the letters of the apostle Paul: "We give thanks to God always for you all, making mention of you in our prayers" (First Epistle to the Thessalonians, 1:2) and "First, I thank my God through Jesus Christ for you all" (First Epistle to the Romans, 1:8). "Obviously," the good reverend told me, "Saint Paul was a Southerner," before adding, "Thank you, Yankee visitor, for appreciating our beloved Southernspeak. We couldn't talk without it."

An anonymous poem that I came upon in Louisville, Kentucky, clarifies the plural use of the one-syllable pronoun y'all: 15

> Y'all gather 'round from far and near,
> Both city folk and rural,
> And listen while I tell you this:
> The pronoun y'all is plural.

If I should utter, "Y'all come down,
Or we-all shall be lonely,"
I mean at least a couple of folks
And not one person only.

If I should say to Hiram Jones,
"I think that y'all are lazy,"
Or "Will y'all let me use y'all's knife?"
He'd think that I was crazy.

Don't think I mean to criticize
Or that I'm full of gall,
But when we speak of one alone,
We all say "you," not "y'all."

We all have accents. Many New Englanders drop the r in cart and farm and say "caht" and "fahm." Thus, the Midwesterner's "park the car in Harvard Yard" becomes the New Englander's "pahk the cah in Hahvahd Yahd." Those r's, though, are not lost. A number of upper Northeasterners, including the famous Kennedy family of Massachusetts, add "r" to words, such as "idear" and "Cuber," when those words come before a vowel or at the end of a sentence.

I.D. BY SPEECH PATTERN

When an amnesia victim appeared at a truck stop in Missouri in the fall of 1987, authorities tried in vain to discover her identity. Even after three months, police "ran into a brick wall," according to the *Columbia Daily Tribune*. Then, linguist Donald Lance of the University of Missouri-Columbia was called in to analyze her speech. After only a few sentences, Lance recognized the woman's West Pennsylvania dialect, and, within one month, police in Pittsburgh located her family. Among the clues used to pinpoint the woman's origin was the West Pennsylvanian use of "greezy" instead of "greasy," and "teeter-totter" rather than "seesaw." Dialectologists know that people who pronounce the word as "greezy" usually live south of a line that wiggles across the northern parts of New Jersey, Pennsylvania, Ohio, Indiana, and Illinois.

Linguist Roger Shuy writes about the reactions of Illinois residents in a 1962 survey of regional pronunciations, including the soundings of "greasy": "The northern Illinois informants felt the southern pronunciation was crude and ugly; it made them think of a very messy, dirty, sticky, smelly frying pan. To the southern and midland speakers, however, the northern pronunciation connoted a messy, dirty, sticky, smelly skillet."

Using the tools of his trade, Shuy was able to profile accurately Ted Kaczynski, the elusive Unabomber who terrorized the nation through the 1990s. Culling linguistic evidence from Kaczynski's "Manifesto," published in *The New York Times*, and the notes and letters accompanying the bombs, Shuy deduced the Unabomber's geographical origin, religious background, age, and education level.

Among the clues were the Unabomber's use of "sierras" to mean   20 "mountains," an indication that the writer had spent some time living in Northern California. In his manifesto, Kaczynski used expressions common to a person who was a young adult in the 1960s — "Holy Robots," "working stiff," and "playing footsy." His employment of sociological terms, such as "other directed," and his many references to "individual drives" suggested an acquaintance with the sociology in vogue during that decade, particularly that of David Reisman. The complexity of Kaczynski's sentence structure, including the subjunctive mood, and the learned-ness of his vocabulary, such as the words "surrogate," "sublimate," "overspecialization," and "tautology," pointed to someone highly educated.

All these conclusions were verified when Kaczynski was captured: He was in his early 50s, had grown up in Chicago and lived for a time in Northern California, and was well educated, having once been a university professor.

Face facts; we all speak some sort of dialect. When you learn language, you learn it as a dialect; if you do not speak a dialect, you do not speak. Dialect is not a label for careless, unlettered, nonstandard speech. A dialect is not something to be avoided or cured. Each language is a great pie. Each slice of that pie is a dialect, and no single slice is the language. Do not try to change your language into the kind of English that nobody really speaks. Be proud of your slice of the pie.

When you learn language, you learn it as a dialect; if you do not speak a dialect, you do not speak.

In the early 1960s, writer John Steinbeck decided to rediscover America in a camper with his French poodle, Charlie. He reported on his observations in a book called *Travels with Charlie* and included these thoughts on dialects: "One of my purposes was to listen, to hear speech, accent, speech rhythms, overtones, and emphasis. For speech is so much more than words and sentences. I did listen everywhere. It seemed to me that regional speech is in the process of disappearing, not gone but going. Forty years of radio and twenty years of television must have this impact. Communications must destroy localness by a slow, inevitable process."

I can remember a time when I almost could pinpoint a man's place of origin by his speech. That is growing more difficult and, in some foreseeable future, will become impossible. It is a rare house or building that is not rigged with spiky combers of the air. Radio and television speech becomes standardized, perhaps better English than we ever have used. Just as our bread—mixed and baked, packaged, and sold without benefit of accident or human frailty—is uniformly good and uniformly tasteless, so will our speech become one speech.

Forty years have passed since Steinbeck's trip, and the hum and buzz   25 of electronic voices have since permeated almost every home across our nation. Formerly, the psalmist tells us, "The voice of the turtle was heard in the land"—now, though, it is the voice of the broadcaster, with his or her immaculately groomed diction. Let us hope that American English does not turn into a bland, homogenized, pasteurized, assembly line product. May our bodacious language remain tasty and nourishing—full of flavor, variety, and local ingredients.

THINKING CRITICALLY ABOUT THE READING

1. How does Lederer use the writer John Steinbeck to introduce the subject of his essay? How does he bring the essay full circle by returning to Steinbeck in his conclusion? Did you find this beginning and ending effective? Explain why or why not.

2. What function do paragraphs 3 through 8 serve in the context on Lederer's essay? Why do you suppose that Lederer provides as many examples of vocabulary differences as he does?

3. How does Lederer illustrate the idea that Americans don't all sound the same when they speak, that there are pronunciation differences? Which examples of these pronunciation differences did you find most effective and interesting? Explain why.

4. Lederer explains how linguist Roger Shuy was able to profile correctly the Unabomber Ted Kaczynski. What did you find most interesting about Shuy's contextual analysis of Kaczynski's "Manifesto"? Explain.

5. How effective did you find Lederer's pie analogy to explain a language and its various dialects?

6. According to Lederer, what accounts for the gradual disappearance of regional speech differences? What do we risk losing as American English becomes more uniform and homogenized?

LANGUAGE IN ACTION

In paragraphs 3 through 7, Lederer identifies a number of everyday items—a large sandwich designed to be a meal in itself, a carbonated drink, the part of a highway that separates the northbound from the southbound lanes, a worm used for bait, and a freshwater shellfish with claws, for example—that are called by different names in different parts of the country.

To see what your vocabulary may reveal about your regional or cultural origins, age, sex, and occupation, let's do a mini-dialect vocabulary survey similar to much longer ones used by field investigators preparing the *Linguistic Atlas of New England* and other regional atlases. For each of the following familiar, everyday items, circle the word or words you actually use (don't circle words you've heard used by your parents, grandparents, or friends). If the word you use is not listed, provide it in the space alongside the item. Before beginning, please list the places where you have lived as well as the length of time you lived in each location.

1. Round, flat confection with hole in center, made with baking powder: *crull, cruller, doughnut, fatcake, fried cake, cake doughnut, raised doughnut,* _____

2. Center of a peach: *pit, seed, stone, kernel, heart,* _____

3. Large open plastic container for scrub water: *pail, bucket,* _____

4. Family word for mother: *ma, mama, mammy, maw, mom, mommer, mommy, mother,* _____

5. Over a sink: *faucet, hydrant, spicket, spigot, tap,* _____

6. Policeman: *cop, policeman, copper, fuzz, dick, officer, bull,* _____

7. Place where packaged groceries can be purchased: *grocery store, general store, supermarket, store, delicatessen, grocery, market, food market, food store, supermart,* _____

8. A white lumpy cheese: *clabber cheese, cottage cheese, curd cheese, curd(s), Dutch cheese, homemade cheese, pot cheese, smearcase, cream cheese,* _____

9. Holds small objects together: *rubber band, rubber binder, elastic binder, gum binder, elastic band,* _____

10. Become ill with a cold: *catch a cold, catch cold, get a cold, take cold, take a cold, come down with a cold,* _____

Discuss your answers with your classmates. Did you discover any regional patterns of usage among your classmates? Did other patterns emerge? Were there any items for which you use a different word or words than either your parents or grandparents?

WRITING SUGGESTIONS

1. As Lederer points out, "Most of us are aware that large numbers of people in the U.S. speak very differently than we do. Most of us tend to feel that the way 'we' talk is right, and the way 'they' talk is weird" (12). Do you agree with Lederer? Write an essay in which you discuss how you feel about the way you and your family, friends, and neighbors speak English. In what ways is the way you speak English tied up with your identity, who you are? Before you start writing you may find it helpful to review your response to the journal prompt for this selection.

2. Lederer notes that in the early 1960s author John Steinbeck bemoaned the fact that "regional speech is in the process of disappearing, not gone but going" (23). Lederer himself dreads the day when "our speech [will] become one speech" (24). What do you think would be lost if there were no dialects in the United States? What, if anything, would be gained? If you could wave a wand and make every person in the United States a speaker of Standard American dialect, the uninflected speech of radio and television news anchors that casts an aura of authority and refinement, would you? Write an essay in which you argue for or against Lederer's hope that "American English does not turn into a bland, homogenized, pasteurized, assembly line product. May our bodacious language remain tasty and nourishing—full of flavor, variety, and local ingredients" (25).

Losing the Language of Silence

LOU ANN WALKER

Born in the Midwest in 1952, Lou Ann Walker is one of three hearing daughters born to "profoundly, prelingually deaf" parents. A graduate of Harvard University, Walker is a writer, editor, and professor in the Creative Writing and Literature program at Stony Brook University's Southampton campus. In addition to serving as editor-in-chief of *TSR: The Southampton Review*, she has written for notable publications such as the *New York Times*, the *New York Times Magazine*, *Allure*, and *Esquire*, among others. Her memoir, *A Loss for Words: The Story of Deafness in a Family* (1987), won a Christopher Award, a Christian award for creative works that "affirm the highest values of the human spirit." She has also won a Rotary Foundation award, a National Endowment of the Arts grant, and a Marguerite Higgins Reporting Award.

As the oldest hearing child in her family, Walker often served as her parents' interpreter, confronting firsthand people's condescending and even cruel reactions to her parents' deafness, which she recounts in *A Loss for Words*. The essay included here reveals her personal interest in how cochlear implants and oralism are affecting the deaf community at large and her family in particular, as well as her sense that the fight to preserve American Sign Language is "not so much about the absence of hearing as about the presence of a language."

WRITING TO DISCOVER: *Do you know any signed communication—formal or otherwise? How and why was it introduced to you? When and how do you use it, if at all?*

Every day, thousands of people drive the expressway past a mysterious and imposing turreted brick Victorian in the Bronx. Visitors to St. Joseph's School for the Deaf remark how disconcerting it must be to teach with trucks roaring by constantly. Hearing people's annoyance at loud distractions? The basis for long-standing jokes in the deaf world. The real noise at this and New York's other 4,201 schools is about deaf culture's fight for survival. Once again, the eloquent language of signing is under attack.

St. Joseph's is feeling the impact of the cochlear-implant boom later than other places. Until five years ago, no hospital in the Bronx was doing the implant. "Then it exploded here," says Dr. Patricia Martin, the school's executive director. "About one third of our children have cochlear implants. I think the deaf community as we know it is going to be different. Many say the cochlear implant is the demise of deaf culture."

Hearing loss is the most prevalent sensory loss in the United States. One in 1,000 babies is born profoundly deaf, according to the Deafness Research Foundation. Another two out of 1,000 have a hearing loss correctable by hearing aids. The National Institute on Deafness and Other Communication Disorders points out that "an implant does not restore normal hearing." Cochlear implants bypass damaged portions of the ear and directly stimulate the auditory nerve. Signals generated by the implant are sent by way of the auditory nerve to

I'm hearing, but American Sign Language (ASL) was my first language.

the brain. Hearing through a cochlear implant is different from normal hearing and takes time to learn. "Some cochlear implants are extremely successful," Martin says. "But people with implants are still deaf. Just because you have a prosthesis doesn't mean you're not an amputee. Whether or not people want to be part of a deaf community is a choice."

My own parents are profoundly, prelingually deaf—deaf before the age of two. I'm hearing, but American Sign Language (ASL) was my first language. I signed for myself as I talked to people at St. Joseph's about the conflicts over deaf culture. Many parents are resistant to letting children with implants learn ASL; teachers are discouraged from using it, with oral and lip-reading instruction now favored. More deaf children are being mainstreamed into public-school classrooms. But not all children succeed with implants, and if they are unable to acquire enough tools to communicate, they fall behind. The battles over ASL are not so much about the absence of hearing as about the presence of a language.

What is it about sign language that makes people want to fight for it? 5 Robert Pinsky wrote a poem in collaboration with deaf students depicting ASL as "a language, full of grace . . . visible, invisible, dark, and clear." It is a language of extraordinary intimacy. If French is the language of lovers and German the language of commerce, then perhaps sign is the language of humans connecting. You can't sign to someone if you're standing next to that person. You have to look full-on at each other—watch each other's faces and necks, shoulders and elbows, hips and knees. You have to stand a bit farther back than you do with spoken language so that you can take in the entirety of the person, and take in that entirety you must. A mother cannot stir the soup and shout over her shoulder for her child to finish homework. Instead, she puts down the spoon, goes to find the child, faces the child, and signs. She watches the child's response carefully and responds to what the child is doing or not doing, saying or not saying.

The emphasis in sign language is on visual creativity. Whereas a hearing teenager might frequently repeat "like" and "so," deaf people encourage each other to play with the language, expand the poetry in everyday speech. A turbulent plane ride isn't "like so bouncing, like I thought I would toss my lunch, like that plane just dropped." No, this jet cruising at top speed hit clouds, bounced, swirled, swooped up, down, overhead bins popping open, clothing tumbling onto heads, tray table wobbling, stomach so tense, so nervous. In sign, articles and prepositions that have nothing to do with setting up the visual field are thrown out. Instead of telling a story in a linear way, several events are related at once. The deaf storyteller holds onto the stomach while relating the actual movement of the aircraft. People speak of the music of sign. Yet I see it more as a painting—it's the complexity of the painting you take in, the totality of the Matisse, the Monet. Signing is about playing with negative space as much as with positive.

Not long after St. Joseph's was established, Alexander Graham Bell and Edward Miner Gallaudet, founder of what is now Gallaudet University, in Washington, D.C., embarked on a bitter feud. Bell advocated oralism; Gallaudet, the use of sign. Both men had mothers who were deaf. Within two decades of the 1880 Milan Conference, where Bell campaigned that deaf people should not be teachers of the deaf, many programs around the world, and particularly in the U.S., had become oral. Children were required to focus on speaking and lip reading, and not allowed to sign.

For much of the twentieth century, oralism took precedence. But that doesn't mean that deaf people weren't signing to each other all the time. In hallways, in dormitories, behind buildings—these were the places of forbidden pleasures. In public, deaf people's signs were often small, constrained. Too often, hearing people stared. Or sniffed, repelled by the physicality of the signs. Deaf clubs where people congregated to trade stories, gossip—those were the places of freedom. The deaf-power movement came into being in the late sixties, and by the eighties there was a truce. Oralists and manualists agreed to disagree. Signing even became chic; hearing parents enrolled their hearing babies in sign programs—or learned signing themselves to promote early language acquisition.

The recent resurgence of oralism seems to have taken culturally deaf people by surprise. Organizations such as the Deafness Research Foundation now talk about "conquering deafness," stinging terms to some deaf people, given the eugenics laws through the twenties and the 1,600 deaf people exterminated in Nazi Germany.

A few years ago, St. Joseph's had a student enrollment of 130—now   10
it's 110. "In ten years, I don't know: Will we be open?" asks Amy Sincoff, the St. Joseph's librarian. " We hope as long as we can—not only for our jobs. For the deaf culture." She speaks of an implanted boy who was mainstreamed. "He couldn't function. It was too hearing."

How can there be such a thing as too hearing? For a deaf person used to signing, the rhythms of communication are off. In a deaf class, someone points to where one's attention should fall. Heads turn. Hearing people often don't look at what is germane—out of politesse, or simply because they don't need to. If everyone is looking in different directions, how can you know what's going on? Think of a playground—children dashing off to swing, then running back into tight groups, heads together, making jokes. Those heads are too close for a person relying on lip reading.

A deaf person's ability to read faces is so refined that he or she can parse every blink. Hearing people say one thing, but their faces often indicate different thoughts. Deaf children can tell when a mainstream teacher is miffed at the interruption of class for speech lessons. They sense the teacher's annoyance at having an extra person in the classroom if the student has an interpreter. Even the architecture of a classroom works to the deaf student's disadvantage; often, filing cabinets are too high for clear sight lines, and desks are arranged so that students turn their backs to one another.

Some kids know how to use their "otherness" to their advantage. One deaf girl who was mainstreamed in high school was brilliant at manipulating her state-mandated interpreter to help her become popular. She sprinkled her conversation with curse words—the interpreter is required by code to say everything the deaf person signs. The kids laughed. She was a social star.

A St. Joseph's display case labeled PROGRESS holds a smattering of once-bright technological advances: a tie-clip hearing aid circa the fifties; a "Phonic Ear" from the sixties; an eyeglass aid from the seventies. So many of the kids in the school, Sincoff says, toss their external cochlear-implant devices into a backpack. "Just like they used to with those," she says, pointing at the case.

There is a sign I love: two fists at the forehead that suddenly whoosh   15
out, hands expanding into encompassing arcs. The translation: "Mind expanded." Or, "New world opening up." Or, "I suddenly take in so much more than I ever could before." As someone who lives in the world of words and signs, I support whatever will give a child as much language as possible. I am for cochlear implants and I am for sign language. I wish so many people didn't see those two as mutually exclusive.

The ferocity of attachment to the language of signing in the deaf world keeps growing. This past November, my mild-mannered 80-year-old deaf father drove an hour and a half from his home to Purdue University to take part in a—yes, silent—protest against the exclusive use of oralism. In orange letters on his black T-shirt:

STOP LANGUAGE OPPRESSION
DEAF BABIES AND CHILDREN
HAVE A RIGHT TO
AMERICAN SIGN LANGUAGE

When I question him as to why he went to the protest, he says, "I simply want people to honor the way your mother and I speak." Someone once asked my father what the best thing about being deaf was. His answer? "Being deaf."

THINKING CRITICALLY ABOUT THE READING

1. What is the "real noise" at St. Joseph's School for the Deaf? How do cochlear implants pose a threat to American Sign Language (ASL) and why? What is Walker's position in this debate?

2. How does poet Robert Pinsky describe ASL (5)? Why might poetry best describe the language?

3. Walker calls ASL "the language of humans connecting" (5). Aren't all languages a means for human connection? How does she explain this characterization? What makes ASL different?

4. In paragraph 6 Walker explains that unlike those who are hearing, "deaf people encourage each other to play with the language, expand the poetry in everyday speech," and then goes on to explain that ASL is best likened to music or painting in how it makes meaning. How does signing differ in its emphasis and organization of stories? What examples does she give of deaf storytelling?

5. What is at stake for deaf students and the deaf community if ASL is phased out of use? How does Walker suggest students will suffer if "oralism" is used exclusively?

6. What does Walker mean by "too hearing" (10-11)? How might mainstream classrooms remain too hearing for deaf students?

7. How have deaf people been treated historically? Has it changed over time? How does the push for oralism as well as language like "conquering deafness" suggest that a prejudice against difference remains?

LANGUAGE IN ACTION

Though Walker doesn't mention the word audism specifically, can you guess, based on the poster below and on words like sexism and racism, what it might mean and why anyone might want to stop it?

Analyze this poster as a form of protest against audism. How does the fact that sign language is visual instead of aural make traditional forms of protest complicated? How might that complication be used to the protestors' advantage? Imagine coming across a silent demonstration like the one Walker describes her father attending (16). How would you react? Do you imagine you'd more easily ignore it, or would the silence itself be enough to get your attention?

WRITING SUGGESTIONS

1. Unlike others who have likened ASL storytelling to poetry or music, Walker sees it "more as a painting—it's the complexity of the painting you take in, the totality" of it (6), which her brief description of how a deaf person might describe a turbulent plane ride attempts to convey. How does the story work? How does it convey turbulence? What aspects of the ride are most central to the story and why? After you analyze how ASL might paint the story of such a trip, think about how you might convey the same "poetry in everyday speech." Spend some time observing this week and try to "paint" the story of one simple experience in words, using the kinds of vivid images Walker describes. Because the experience needs to be fresh in your mind to really engage with the assignment, do not retell an old story or memory. In fact, it's best to work with an everyday experience. For example, you might re-imagine your wait in line for coffee, a spat you had with a friend, or lunch with a parent. Try to take in all you can about your surroundings and convey the experience as a series of images. Consider, for example, what part of the experience you should privilege, how you might change order and sentence structure, the effect of fragments or run-on sentences, and the type of word-images that might convey tone or mood, etc., as you "paint."

2. Fundamentally, Walker's essay is about the right to use the language of one's own choosing and how denying one's language, to some degree, denies an aspect of one's identity. Although most of us are likely hearing individuals and cannot experience the world as a deaf person does, we can consider how restrictions on personal expression deny us access to the life we would choose. To catch a glimpse of this denial, try to "go dark" on electronic communication for a day or two and keep a journal of the experience. Instead of participating and responding through social media, texting, email (aside from what is necessary to complete your coursework)—or any forum that you regularly use to live your digital life—record some of the conversations you would have participated in and what you would have added to them as you watch them unfold. Record any events or plans you risked missing out on because you could not respond, too. Then write a few reflective paragraphs about the experience. How did the restrictions on digital communication affect you? What was it like to "hear" conversations without being able to participate?

Two Ways to Belong in America

BHARATI MUKHERJEE

The prominent Indian American writer and university professor Bharati Mukherjee was born into an aristocratic family in Calcutta (now Kolkata), India, in 1940. After India's independence, her family relocated to England because of her father's work. She returned to India in the 1950s where she earned her bachelor's degree at the University of Calcutta in 1959 and a master's degree from the University of Baroda in 1961. Later she pursued her long-held desire to become a writer by earning a master of fine arts degree at the University of Iowa and eventually a doctorate in English and comparative literature. After she married an American, Clark Blaise, the couple moved to Canada, where they lived for fourteen years until legislation there against South Asians led them to move back to the United States. Before joining the faculty at the University of California, Berkeley, Mukherjee taught at McGill University, Skidmore College, Queens College, and City University of New York. Currently her work centers on writing and the themes of immigration, particularly concerning women, immigration policy, immigrant communities, and cultural alienation. With her husband, she has authored *Days and Nights in Calcutta* (1977) and *The Sorrow and the Terror: The Haunting Legacy of the Air India Tragedy* (1987). In addition, she has published seven novels including *The Tiger's Daughter* (1971), *Wife* (1975), *Darkness* (1985), *Jasmine* (1989), *The Holder of the World* (1993), and *The Tree Bride* (2004); two collections of short stories, *Darkness* (1985) and *The Middleman and Other Stories* (1988), for which she won the National Book Critics Circle Award; and two works of nonfiction, *Political Culture and Leadership in India* (1991) and *Regionalism in Indian Perspective* (1992).

The following essay was first published in the *New York Times* in 1996 in response to new legislation championed by the then vice president, Al Gore, that gave expedited citizenship for legal immigrants living in the United States. As you read Mukherjee's essay, notice the way she has organized her presentation of the contrasting views that she and her sister have toward the various aspects of living as either a legal immigrant or a citizen in the United States.

WRITING TO DISCOVER: *The word immigrant has many connotations. What associations does the word have for you? If you were to move to another country, how do you think it would feel to be considered an immigrant?*

This is a tale of two sisters from Calcutta, Mira and Bharati, who have lived in the United States for some thirty-five years, but who find themselves on different sides in the current debate over the status of immigrants. I am an American citizen and she is not. I am moved that thousands of long-term residents are finally taking the oath of citizenship. She is not.

Mira arrived in Detroit in 1960 to study child psychology and pre-school education. I followed her a year later to study creative writing at the University of Iowa. When we left India, we were almost identical in appearance and attitude. We dressed alike, in saris; we expressed identical views on politics, social issues, love and marriage in the same Calcutta convent-school accent. We would endure our two years in America, secure our degrees, then return to India to marry the grooms of our father's choosing.

Instead, Mira married an Indian student in 1962 who was getting his business administration degree at Wayne State University. They soon acquired the labor certifications necessary for the green card of hassle-free residence and employment.

Mira still lives in Detroit, works in the Southfield, Michigan, school system, and has become nationally recognized for her contributions in the fields of preschool education and parent-teacher relationships. After thirty-six years as a legal immigrant in this country, she clings passionately to her Indian citizenship and hopes to go home to India when she retires.

In Iowa City in 1963, I married a fellow student, an American of   5 Canadian parentage. Because of the accident of his North Dakota birth, I bypassed labor-certification requirements and the race-related "quota" system that favored the applicant's country of origin over his or her merit. I was prepared for (and even welcomed) the emotional strain that came with marrying outside my ethnic community. In thirty-three years of marriage, we have lived in every part of North America. By choosing a husband who was not my father's selection, I was opting for fluidity, self-invention, blue jeans and T-shirts, and renouncing three thousand years (at least) of caste-observant, "pure culture" marriage in the Mukherjee family. My books have often been read as unapologetic (and in some quarters overenthusiastic) texts for cultural and psychological "mongreliza-tion." It's a word I celebrate.

Mira and I have stayed sisterly close by phone. In our regular Sunday morning conversations, we are unguardedly affectionate. I am her only blood relative on this continent. We expect to see each other through the looming crises of aging and ill health without being asked. Long before Vice President Gore's "Citizenship USA" drive, we'd had our polite arguments over the ethics of retaining an overseas citizenship while expecting the permanent protection and economic benefits that come with living and working in America.

Like well-raised sisters, we never said what was really on our minds, but we probably pitied one another. She, for the lack of structure in my life, the erasure of Indianness, the absence of an unvarying daily core.

I, for the narrowness of her perspective, her uninvolvement with the mythic depths or the superficial pop culture of this society. But, now, with the scapegoating of "aliens" (documented or illegal) on the increase, and the targeting of long-term legal immigrants like Mira for new scrutiny and new self-consciousness, she and I find ourselves unable to maintain the same polite discretion. We were always unacknowledged adversaries, and we are now, more than ever, sisters.

"I feel used," Mira raged on the phone the other night. "I feel manipulated and discarded. This is such an unfair way to treat a person who was invited to stay and work here because of her talent. My employer went to the INS and petitioned for the labor certification. For over thirty years, I've invested my creativity and professional skills into the improvement of *this* country's preschool system. I've obeyed all the rules, I've paid my taxes, I love my work, I love my students, I love the friends I've made. How dare America now change its rules in midstream? If America wants to make new rules curtailing benefits of legal immigrants, they should apply only to immigrants who arrive after those rules are already in place."

In one family, from two sisters alike as peas in a pod, there could not be a wider divergence of immigrant experience.

To my ears, it sounded like the description of a long-enduring, comfortable yet loveless marriage, without risk or recklessness. Have we the right to demand, and to expect, that we be loved? (That, to me, is the subtext of the arguments by immigration advocates.) My sister is an expatriate, professionally generous and creative, socially courteous and gracious, and that's as far as her Americanization can go. She is here to maintain an identity, not to transform it.

I asked her if she would follow the example of others who have decided to become citizens because of the anti-immigration bills in Congress. And here, she surprised me. "If America wants to play the manipulative game, I'll play it too," she snapped. "I'll become a U.S. citizen for now, then change back to Indian when I'm ready to go home. I feel some kind of irrational attachment to India that I don't to America. Until all this hysteria against legal immigrants, I was totally happy. Having my green card meant I could visit any place in the world I wanted to and then come back to a job that's satisfying and that I do very well."   10

In one family, from two sisters alike as peas in a pod, there could not be a wider divergence of immigrant experience. America spoke to me — I married it — I embraced the demotion from expatriate aristocrat to immigrant nobody, surrendering those thousands of years of "pure culture," the saris, the delightfully accented English. She retained them all. Which of us is the freak?

Mira's voice, I realize, is the voice not just of the immigrant South Asian community but of an immigrant community of the millions who have stayed rooted in one job, one city, one house, one ancestral culture, one cuisine, for the entirety of their productive years. She speaks for greater numbers than I possibly can. Only the fluency of her English and the anger, rather than fear, born of confidence from her education, differentiate her from the seamstresses, the domestics, the technicians, the shop owners, the millions of hardworking but effectively silenced documented immigrants as well as their less fortunate "illegal" brothers and sisters.

Nearly twenty years ago, when I was living in my husband's ancestral homeland of Canada, I was always well-employed but never allowed to feel part of the local Quebec or larger Canadian society. Then, through a Green Paper that invited a national referendum on the unwanted side effects of "nontraditional" immigration, the Government officially turned against its immigrant communities, particularly those from South Asia.

I felt then the same sense of betrayal that Mira feels now. I will never forget the pain of that sudden turning, and the casual racist outbursts the Green Paper elicited. That sense of betrayal had its desired effect and drove me, and thousands like me, from the country.

Mira and I differ, however, in the ways in which we hope to interact   15
with the country that we have chosen to live in. She is happier to live in America as an expatriate Indian than as an immigrant American. I need to feel like a part of the community I have adopted (as I tried to feel in Canada as well). I need to put roots down, to vote and make the difference that I can. The price that the immigrant willingly pays, and that the exile avoids, is the trauma of self-transformation.

THINKING CRITICALLY ABOUT THE READING

1. What is Mukherjee's thesis? (Glossary: *Thesis*) Where does she present it? How has Mukherjee organized her essay? (Glossary: *Comparison and Contrast*)

2. What arguments does Mukherjee make for becoming an American citizen? What arguments does her sister make for retaining her Indian citizenship? Which sister do you think made the "right" decision? Explain.

3. Mukherjee chooses to let her sister Mira speak for herself in this essay. What do you think would have been lost had she spoken for her sister, simply reporting what Mira felt and believed as an immigrant in the United States? Explain. Why do you think Mukherjee's sister feels "used" by attempts to change American laws regarding social security benefits for noncitizens?

4. Mukherjee uses the word *mongrelization* in paragraph 5. What do you think she means by this word, and why does she celebrate it?

5. What do you think Mukherjee's sister means when she says in paragraph 10, "If America wants to play the manipulative game, I'll play it too"? How do you react to her decision and to her possible plans if and when she eventually returns to India? Explain.

6. At the end of paragraph 11 Mukherjee asks a question. How does she answer it? How would you answer it? Do you, like Mukherjee, "need to feel like a part of the community I have adopted" (15). What does Mukherjee mean when she says in paragraph 15, "The price that the immigrant willingly pays, and that the exile avoids, is the trauma of self-transformation"?

LANGUAGE IN ACTION

Another Indian American writer, Jhumpa Lahiri, writes about her experience growing up in the United States with dual identities in an essay titled "My Two Lives." In it, she explains the struggle she had in making sense of her combined cultures, especially as a child. She writes:

> According to my parents I was not American, nor would I ever be no matter how hard I tried. I felt doomed by their pronouncement, misunderstood and gradually defiant. In spite of the first lessons of arithmetic, one plus one did not equal two but zero, my conflicting selves always canceling each other out.

Discuss whether or not you see the conclusions Lahiri makes (or is told to make) about her identity in the ways that Bharati Mukherjee and her sister view their immigrant experiences. How might the concept of "conflicting selves canceling each other out" resonate with the Mukherjee sisters? How do they attempt to resolve that conflict? How would you?

WRITING SUGGESTIONS

1. In paragraph 7 Mukherjee writes about the relationship that she had with her sister by saying that "we never said what was really on our minds, but we probably pitied one another." These types of differences are played out on a larger scale when immigrants who have transformed themselves into Americans are confronted by those who have chosen to retain their ethnic identity, and these tensions often lead to name-calling and aggressive prejudice. Such situations exist within the Latino, African American, and Southeast Asian American communities and perhaps among all immigrant groups. Write an essay comparing and contrasting the choices of lifestyle that members of an ethnic or cultural community you are familiar with make as they try to find a comfortable place in American society.

2. Mukherjee presents her sister's reasons for not becoming a citizen and supports them with statements that her sister has made. Imagine that you are Mira Mukherjee. Write a counterargument to the one presented by your sister that gives your reasons for remaining an Indian citizen. Consider that you have already broken with tradition by marrying a man "not of your father's choosing" but also that the "trauma of self-transformation" that your sister raises in the conclusion of her essay is much deeper and more complicated than she has represented it. Can you say that you are holding on to tradition when you are not? Can you engage in a challenging self-transformation if it is not genuinely motivated?

Mother Tongue

AMY TAN

Amy Tan was born in Oakland, California, in 1952, to Chinese immigrant parents. Growing up in a bilingual world, Tan became interested in languages at an early age. At San Jose State University she earned a B.A. in English in 1973 and a master's in linguistics the following year. Tan worked as a child language development specialist and a freelance speech writer for corporate executives before she began writing stories for her own personal enjoyment and therapy. These stories resulted in her first book, *The Joy Luck Club* (1989), a tightly woven novel about four Chinese mothers and their American-born daughters. This novel was a finalist for the National Book Award and later adapted into a commercially successful film. Tan has written five other novels including *The Kitchen God's Wife* (1991), *The Hundred Secret Senses* (1995), *The Bonesetter's Daughter* (2001), *Saving Fish from Drowning* (2005), and *The Valley of Amazement* (2012); a collection of nonfiction essays, *The Opposite of Fate: A Book of Musings* (2003); and two children's books, *The Moon Lady* (1992) and *Sagwa, the Chinese Siamese Cat* (1994). Tan currently resides in Sausalito, California.

The following essay was first delivered as a speech and later published in the fall 1990 issue of the *Threepenny Review*. Here Tan explains how she wrote *The Joy Luck Club* and communicated with her mother, using "all the Englishes I grew up with." She explores the limitations of growing up in a household where she heard "broken" English spoken by her immigrant parents.

WRITING TO DISCOVER: *What is your cultural identity? Do you consider yourself an American, or do you identify with another culture? To what extent is your cultural identity tied to language? Explain.*

I am not a scholar of English or literature. I cannot give you much more than personal opinions on the English language and its variations in this country or others.

I am a writer. And by that definition, I am someone who has always loved language. I am fascinated by language in daily life. I spend a great deal of my time thinking about the power of language—the way it can evoke an emotion, a visual image, a complex idea, or a simple truth. Language is the tool of my trade. And I use them all—all the Englishes I grew up with.

Recently, I was made keenly aware of the different Englishes I do use. I was giving a talk to a large group of people, the same talk I had already given to half a dozen other groups. The nature of the talk was about my writing, my life, and my book *The Joy Luck Club*. The talk was going along well enough, until I remembered one major difference that made the whole talk sound wrong. My mother was in the room. And it was perhaps the first time she had heard me give a lengthy speech, using the kind of English I have never used with her. I was saying things like "The intersection of memory upon imagination" and "There is an aspect of my fiction that relates to thus-and-thus"—a speech filled with carefully wrought grammatical phrases, burdened, it suddenly seemed to me, with nominalized forms, past perfect tenses, conditional phrases, all the forms of standard English that I had learned in school and through books, the forms of English I did not use at home with my mother.

Just last week, I was walking down the street with my mother, and I again found myself conscious of the English I was using, the English I do use with her. We were talking about the price of new and used furniture and I heard myself saying this: "Not waste money that way." My husband was with us as well, and he didn't notice any switch in my English. And then I realized why. It's because over the twenty years we've been together I've often used that same kind of English with him, and sometimes he even uses it with me. It has become our language of intimacy, a different sort of English that relates to family talk, the language I grew up with.

Language is the tool of my trade. And I use them all—all the Englishes I grew up with.

So you'll have some idea of what this family talk I heard sounds like, I'll quote what my mother said during a recent conversation which I videotaped and then transcribed. During this conversation, my mother was talking about a political gangster in Shanghai who had the same last name as her family's, Du, and how the gangster in his early years wanted to be adopted by her family, which was rich by comparison. Later, the gangster became more powerful, far richer than my mother's family, and one day showed up at my mother's wedding to pay his respects. Here's what she said in part:

"Du Yusong having business like fruit stand. Like off the street kind. He is Du like Du Zong—but not Tsung-ming Island people. The local people call putong, the river east side, he belong to that side local people. That man want to ask Du Zong father take him in like become own family. Du Zong father wasn't look down on him, but didn't take seriously, until that man big like become a mafia. Now important person, very hard to inviting him. Chinese way, came only to show respect, don't stay for dinner. Respect for making big celebration, he shows up. Mean gives lots of respect. Chinese custom. Chinese social life that way. If too important won't have to stay too long. He come to my wedding. I didn't see, I heard it. I gone to boy's side, they have YMCA dinner. Chinese age I was nineteen."

You should know that my mother's expressive command of English belies how much she actually understands. She reads the *Forbes* report, listens to *Wall Street Week*, converses daily with her stockbroker, reads all of Shirley MacLaine's books with ease—all kinds of things I can't begin to understand. Yet some of my friends tell me they understand 50 percent of what my mother says. Some say they understand 80 to 90 percent. Some say they understand none of it, as if she were speaking pure Chinese. But to me, my mother's English is perfectly clear, perfectly natural. It's my mother tongue. Her language, as I hear it, is vivid, direct, full of observation and imagery. That was the language that helped shape the way I saw things, expressed things, made sense of the world.

Lately, I've been giving more thought to the kind of English my mother speaks. Like others, I have described it to people as "broken" or "fractured" English. But I wince when I say that. It has always bothered me that I can think of no way to describe it other than "broken," as if it were damaged and needed to be fixed, as if it lacked a certain wholeness and soundness. I've heard other terms used, "limited English," for example. But they seem just as bad, as if everything is limited, including people's perceptions of the limited English speaker.

I know this for a fact, because when I was growing up, my mother's "limited" English limited *my* perception of her. I was ashamed of her English. I believed that her English reflected the quality of what she had to say. That is, because she expressed them imperfectly her thoughts were imperfect. And I had plenty of empirical evidence to support me: the fact that people in department stores, at banks, and at restaurants did not take her seriously, did not give her good service, pretended not to understand her, or even acted as if they did not hear her.

My mother has long realized the limitations of her English as well. When I was fifteen, she used to have me call people on the phone to pretend I was she. In this guise, I was forced to ask for information or even to complain and yell at people who had been rude to her. One time it was a call to her stockbroker in New York. She had cashed out her small portfolio and it just so happened we were going to go to New York the next week, our very first trip outside California. I had to get on the phone and say in an adolescent voice that was not very convincing, "This is Mrs. Tan."

And my mother was standing in the back whispering loudly, "Why he don't send me check, already two weeks late. So mad he lie to me, losing me money."

And then I said in perfect English, "Yes, I'm getting rather concerned. You had agreed to send the check two weeks ago, but it hasn't arrived."

Then she began to talk more loudly. "What he want, I come to New York tell him front of his boss, you cheating me?" And I was trying to calm her down, make her be quiet, while telling the stockbroker, "I can't tolerate any more excuses. If I don't receive the check immediately, I am going to have to speak to your manager when I'm in New York next week." And sure enough, the following week there we were in front of this astonished stockbroker, and I was sitting there red-faced and quiet, and

10

my mother, the real Mrs. Tan, was shouting at his boss in her impeccable broken English.

We used a similar routine just five days ago, for a situation that was far less humorous. My mother had gone to the hospital for an appointment, to find out about a benign brain tumor a CAT scan had revealed a month ago. She said she had spoken very good English, her best English, no mistakes. Still, she said, the hospital did not apologize when they said they had lost the CAT scan and she had come for nothing. She said they did not seem to have any sympathy when she told them she was anxious to know the exact diagnosis, since her husband and son had both died of brain tumors. She said they would not give her any more information until the next time and she would have to make another appointment for that. So she said she would not leave until the doctor called her daughter. She wouldn't budge. And when the doctor finally called her daughter, me, who spoke in perfect English—lo and behold—we had assurances the CAT scan would be found, promises that a conference call on Monday would be held, and apologies for any suffering my mother had gone through for a most regrettable mistake.

I think my mother's English almost had an effect on limiting my pos-   15
sibilities in life as well. Sociologists and linguists probably will tell you that a person's developing language skills are more influenced by peers. But I do think that the language spoken in the family, especially in immigrant families which are more insular, plays a large role in shaping the language of the child. And I believe that it affected my results on achievement tests, IQ tests, and the SAT. While my English skills were never judged as poor, compared to math, English could not be considered my strong suit. In grade school I did moderately well, getting perhaps B's, sometimes B-pluses, in English and scoring perhaps in the sixtieth or seventieth percentile on achievement tests. But those scores were not good enough to override the opinion that my true abilities lay in math and science, because in those areas I achieved A's and scored in the ninetieth percentile or higher.

This was understandable. Math is precise; there is only one correct answer. Whereas, for me at least, the answers on English tests were always a judgment call, a matter of opinion and personal experience. Those tests were constructed around items like fill-in-the-blank sentence completion, such as "Even though Tom was____, Mary thought he was____." And the correct answer always seemed to be the most bland combinations of thoughts, for example, "Even though Tom was shy, Mary thought he was charming," with the grammatical structure "even though" limiting the correct answer to some sort of semantic opposites, so you wouldn't get answers like, "Even though Tom was foolish, Mary thought he was ridiculous." Well, according to my mother, there were very few limitations as to what Tom could have been and what Mary might have thought of him. So I never did well on tests like that.

The same was true with word analogies, pairs of words, in which you were supposed to find some sort of logical, semantic relationship—for example, " 'sunset' is to 'nightfall' as ____ is to ____." And here you would be presented with a list of four possible pairs, one of which showed the same kind of relationship: "red" is to "stoplight," "bus" is to "arrival," "chills" is to "fever," "yawn" is to "boring." Well, I could never think that way. I knew what the tests were asking, but I could not block out of my mind the images already created by the first pair, "sunset is to nightfall"—and I would see a burst of colors against a darkening sky, the moon rising, the lowering of a curtain of stars. And all the other pairs of words—red, bus, stoplight, boring—just threw up a mass of confusing images, making it impossible for me to sort out something as logical as saying: "A sunset precedes nightfall" is the same as "a chill precedes a fever." The only way I would have gotten that answer right would have been to imagine an associative situation, for example, my being disobedient and staying out past sunset, catching a chill at night, which turns into feverish pneumonia as punishment, which indeed did happen to me.

I have been thinking about all this lately, about my mother's English, about achievement tests. Because lately I've been asked, as a writer, why there are not more Asian Americans represented in American literature. Why are there few Asian Americans enrolled in creative writing programs? Why do so many Chinese students go into engineering? Well, these are broad sociological questions I can't begin to answer. But I have noticed in surveys—in fact, just last week—that Asian students, as a whole, always do significantly better on math achievement tests than in English. And this makes me think that there are other Asian-American students whose English spoken in the home might also be described as "broken" or "limited." And perhaps they also have teachers who are steering them away from writing and into math and science, which is what happened to me.

Fortunately, I happen to be rebellious in nature and enjoy the challenge of disproving assumptions made about me. I became an English major my first year in college, after being enrolled as pre-med. I started writing nonfiction as a freelancer the week after I was told by my former boss that writing was my worst skill and I should hone my talents toward account management.

But it wasn't until 1985 that I finally began to write fiction. And at first I wrote using what I thought to be wittily crafted sentences, sentences that would finally prove I had mastery over the English language. Here's an example from the first draft of a story that later made its way into *The Joy Luck Club*, but without this line: "That was my mental quandary in its nascent state." A terrible line, which I can barely pronounce.

Fortunately, for reasons I won't get into today, I later decided I should envision a reader for the stories I would write. And the reader I decided upon was my mother, because these were stories about mothers.

20

So with this reader in mind — and in fact she did read my early drafts — I began to write stories using all the Englishes I grew up with: the English I spoke to my mother, which for lack of a better term might be described as "simple"; the English she used with me, which for lack of a better term might be described as "broken"; my translation of her Chinese, which could certainly be described as "watered down"; and what I imagined to be her translation of her Chinese if she could speak in perfect English, her internal language, and for that I sought to preserve the essence, but neither an English nor a Chinese structure. I wanted to capture what language ability tests can never reveal: her intent, her passion, her imagery, the rhythms of her speech and the nature of her thoughts.

Apart from what any critic had to say about my writing, I knew I had succeeded where it counted when my mother finished reading my book, and gave me her verdict: "So easy to read."

THINKING CRITICALLY ABOUT THE READING

1. How effectively do the first two paragraphs function as an introduction to this essay? What are your expectations about the essay after Tan reveals her qualifications with language and literature?

2. What specifically are the different Englishes that Tan grew up with? How was each English used?

3. To give readers some idea of what the "family talk" Tan heard while growing up sounded like, Tan quotes her mother's story in paragraph 6. What did you think of Tan's mother after reading this paragraph? Did you understand everything the first time you read it, or did you have to reread portions to make sure you got it?

4. Why do you suppose Tan recounts the story of her mother's stockbroker and her mother's dealings with the hospital in paragraphs 10 through 14?

5. What does Tan mean when she writes, "I think my mother's English almost had an effect on limiting my possibilities in life" (15)?

6. In paragraphs 16 and 17 Tan discusses her difficulties with questions on English tests that called for "fill-in-the-blank sentence completion" and facility with "word analogies." Why do you suppose such questions vexed her? Explain.

LANGUAGE IN ACTION

When we listen to people speak, we readily notice if someone is using nonstandard English. We also recognize conversational or informal standard English. On occasion, we hear people using what might be called hyper- or super-standard English, speech that sounds too formal or proper for everyday conversation. In the following sets of sentences, classify each sentence as being (1) nonstandard English, (2) informal standard English, or (3) super-standard English.

1. a. If I was going to do that, I would start right now.
   b. If I were going to do that, I would start right now.
   c. Were I to do that, I would start right now.
   d. I would start right now, if I was going to do that.
2. a. He's not as smart as she.
   b. He's not so smart as she.
   c. He ain't as smart as her.
   d. He not as smart as her.

Discuss what words or word forms in the sentences that helped you label each one.

WRITING SUGGESTIONS

1. Do you believe that the English spoken at home while you were growing up had any effect on how well you did in school or in your community at large? Using Tan's essay as a model, write an essay exploring the "Englishes" you grew up with and how they affected your performance in and out of school.

2. Write an essay in which you explore the main differences between public language — that is, language used in school, workplace, and government settings — and private language — that is, language used in familial or other intimate relationships.

Talk the Talk

ERIC C. MILLER

Eric C. Miller earned his Ph.D. at the Pennsylvania State University and is an assistant professor in communication studies at Bloomsburg University of Pennsylvania, where he teaches courses in public speaking, argument and analysis, and studies in propaganda. His work has been published in *Aeon* and *Journal of Communication and Religion*, and he is a regular contributor to *Religion Dispatches*.

According to Miller's blog, in the classroom he strives to help students understand that rhetoric is not "a synonym for insincere or deceptive speech," but a theory and practice that shapes how we speak and what we know. From this perspective, Miller encourages his students not just to become better speakers but to think seriously about what they want to say and the words they choose. Miller wants to help students understand that the language they use operates within larger webs of social meaning. His courses focus on civic engagement and he encourages students "to realize their potential as thinkers and citizens."

The following essay analyzes the debate about whether or not English should be lawfully declared the official language of the United States. Miller suggests that these ongoing debates have common rhetorical roots in how political parties work "to create certain impressions in the minds of others." In the case of the English-only debate, each side, he suggests, uses the language that most appeals to its supporters to define the relationship between language and the country's unity and national identity.

WRITING TO DISCOVER: *How do you define "unity" in the United States? What brings the country's citizens together and helps them understand themselves as American? What role does language—English or otherwise—play in creating or disrupting that unity?*

"English-only" advocacy in the United States dates at least as far back as 1919, when President Theodore Roosevelt declared: "We have room for but one language in this country, and that is the English language, for we intend to see that the crucible turns our people out as Americans, of American nationality, and not as dwellers in a polyglot boarding house." For Roosevelt, the connection between language and citizenship was explicit and unqualified—if Americans didn't speak English, they weren't Americans.

The California senator S. I. Hayakawa introduced the first "English Language Amendment" (ELA) in 1981, seeking to declare English the official language of the US, while overturning any state or federal statutes requiring the use of other languages. Though this amendment died in Congress, it reappeared in various iterations over time, passing the House in 1996, and finding Senate approval 10 years later, as part of an immigration reform bill that itself failed to become law. Despite these setbacks, the English-only movement remains active, and in 2010, a business man named Tim James ran for governor of Alabama with a campaign promise that the State Driver's Examinations would be offered exclusively in English. Thirty-one states—including Alabama—have now declared English their only official language and in 2012 both major political parties endorsed the English language in their official platforms, the Democrats touting "enhanced opportunities for English-language learning and immigrant integration," while the Republicans said they "support English as the nation's official language."

In 1997, citing the most recent Census data, the historical linguist Robert D. King noted that 94 percent of people in the US speak English willingly, making a law totally unnecessary. Mauro E. Mujica, chairman of the advocacy group "US English," countered that the figure is actually 97 percent, and so the law is just common sense. These days, the numbers are similar. Census data published in 2011 shows that about 79 percent of people in the US speak only English at home. A further 16 percent claim to speak English "well" or "very well." Such congruence casts suspicion on the premise that the "official" demarcation is *just* about the need for clear communication. In truth, for many English-only advocates, language has become a stand-in for less palatable sentiments, the fear of changing racial demographics among them.

It has become impolitic to attack a rising Mexican-American population on purely racial grounds, but it remains acceptable to criticize "illegal immigration," policy and language standards. The tactic is neither new nor particularly subtle. Writing in 1753, Benjamin Franklin fretted about the increasing German population by noting that these immigrants are "generally the most ignorant Stupid Sort of their own Nation" and that "they will soon out number us, that all the advantages we have will not, in My Opinion, be able to preserve our language, and even our government will become precarious."

Then, as now, such attitudes support the linguist John Nist's claim in   5
1966 that language is used "primarily as a means of communion rather than as a means of communication." Commonality of speech creates a web of connections that hold a people together. Language is a national identity, to be preserved and protected, generally by the expulsion of *others*. This might even override considerations of race, as the black cultural theorist Frantz Fanon noted in his book *Peau noire, masques blancs* (1952), published as *Black Skin, White Masks* in 1967: "The Negro of the Antilles will be proportionately whiter—that is, he will come closer to being a real human being—in direct ratio to his mastery of the French language."

As Fanon argued—and Tim James understood—otherness is multi-faceted, and should not be theorised on any one face to the detriment of all the rest. European immigrants, for example, have a long history of cold reception in the US, their foreign tongues or dialects revealing them as *other* even when their skin tone did not. For German, Polish, Swedish and Irish émigrés, their perceived humanity in America always increased in direct ratio to their mastery of English. For Hayakawa, author of the first ELA legislation, co-founder of US English, and a Canadian immigrant of Japanese ancestry himself, this reality was acknowledged, if slightly spun.

Writing for *USA Today* in 1989, Hayakawa stressed that English proficiency was necessary if immigrants were to compete and succeed in US markets. Supporting migrants and their children to maintain their mother tongue is, he suggested, a racist policy, as it presumes that certain immigrants are incapable of learning English. "Brown people," he wrote, "like Mexicans and Puerto Ricans; red people, like American Indians; and yellow people, like the Japanese and Chinese, are assumed not to be smart enough to learn English. No provision is made, however, for non-English-speaking French-Canadians in Maine or Vermont, or Yiddish-speaking Hasidic Jews in Brooklyn, who are white and thus presumed to be able to learn English without difficulty." Having spent several years living in Maine myself, I can testify that the northern part of the state does feature exit ramps marked "Sortie." But the point is well-taken.

African-Americans and other minority groups hailing *from* the US might well object to Hayawaka's point—and Fanon's. Speaking English, they might argue, does not guarantee *humanity* in the eyes of individuals or—perhaps more importantly—systems. Being able to communicate in English with police officers, for instance, has not kept young black males from filling the rosters of the US penal complex.

In 1996, the English-only debate acquired a new racially inflected dimension, when a school board in Oakland, California passed a resolution to permit use of Black Urban Vernacular—also known as "Ebonics"—in the curriculum. Since many of the district's children came from households that spoke this way, the board reasoned, it would be conducive to learning if teachers taught in a language the kids would understand. They further argued that, since Ebonics was structured and spoken like any other language, its place in school texts was no more or less arbitrary than Standard English or Spanish. Critics of the plan argued that Ebonics was nothing more than substandard English. It was also irrelevant to the world of employment, so adopting it in the classroom essentially doomed students to lives in the poor neighborhoods where they grew up. The opposition won out and Ebonics was dropped.

The case of Ebonics offers a twist on Fanon's explicit alignment of racial and language differences, because the ideal of a "Standard English" that will unify people across the US, is always and everywhere undermined by the simple reality of regional dialects (as occurs in other countries as   10 well). The English spoken in Georgia, for instance, is very different from that spoken in Massachusetts. Midwesterners in Wisconsin and Illinois use pronunciations and phrases that sound comical to west Texans, and vice versa. But while these variations on a Standard English help to fix regional identities, they do not create the types of problems associated with "urban" dialects.

Ebonics was deeply entangled with white perceptions of black otherness, relating to race, class, morality and violence, thus draping it with an added layer of threat. Even in southern states, a white police officer is more likely to identify with a black driver who speaks regional English in an accent they share, than with one speaking the widely stereotyped urban style. In other words, the *other* who speaks *like me* is more likely to win my favor than the *other* who compounds his otherness by speaking other than me.

While Ebonics might be a perfectly intelligible form of English to those who speak it, it goes against the grain of a white-dominated society in which belonging means talking the talk of Standard English. Never mind that ceding one's language preference effectively means capitulating to the forces of power and oppression. Or that adopting Standard English might feel unreal—using language as a conscious, even self-conscious, performance.

We wear the masks we think other people want to see.

Fanon titled his book *Black Skin, White Masks*, drawing attention to the performative aspects of language use, while the sociologist Erving Goffman, in *The Presentation of Self in Everyday Life* (1959), suggested that all people assume "roles" much like actors on the stage, engineering their self-presentations to create certain impressions in the minds of others. They take up "masks," in other words, to *fashion* themselves for public reception.

One prerequisite of being an American, as we have seen, is the ability to speak English. This chimes with Goffman's observation that: "A status, a position, a social place is not a material thing, to be possessed and then displayed; it is a pattern of appropriate conduct, coherent, embellished, and well-articulated. Performed with ease or clumsiness, awareness or not, guile or good faith, it is none the less something that must be enacted and portrayed, something that must be realized." For Goffman, inclusion and acceptance are goals we work toward, perhaps sacrificing our "true" selves to achieve. We wear the masks we think other people want to see.

Such thinking feeds directly into a more basic question of US identity: are we a "melting pot" or a "salad bowl"? Should those who come to US shores assimilate to US culture, or maintain their distinctive cultural markers? The question however is too simplistic: it essentializes both the issue and the nation. To the extent that America has a national culture, it has been shaped by elements that immigrants brought with them. To a

15

significant degree, these were absorbed into an expanding American-ness. While being absorbed, however, they maintained traces of their ancestry. Fidelity to a migrant past is not inherently threatening to a national future

It would be false to think that there is no price to be paid for those migrants who cannot communicate in English. Here as elsewhere, people who are isolated by language tend—much like poor people, or victims of sexual assault, for example—to get blamed for their condition. Immigrants to the US who cannot or will not learn to speak English are necessarily isolated from their English-speaking fellows. The non-speaker is powerless to contest whatever conclusions they draw. Like the ageing Japanese "picture brides" in Julie Otsuka's novel *The Buddha in the Attic* (2011), the non-speaker can find himself increasingly withdrawn from public life.

> **It would be false to think that there is no price to be paid for those migrants who cannot communicate in English.**

One promising avenue for integrating non-speakers comes in the form of bilingual immersion education. In southern California, home to a broad diversity of ethnicities and languages, such programs are proliferating. Recently, the Garden Grove unified school district proposed the state's first Vietnamese immersion program, geared to accommodating families worried about losing their culture—via their children—to a homogenized American-ness. Such programs offer a strong rejoinder to the absolutist stance of English-only advocates such as Mujica, who struck a heavy-handed chord during his most recent Congressional testimony, saying (in his slow Chilean drawl): "I know firsthand how important it is to know English to succeed in the United States. I have lived this issue, and it is incomprehensible to me that anyone would oppose legislation which codifies the language policy for this country."

But it is unclear how Official English would solve Mujica's problem. Instead of making life easier for new immigrants—assuming this is a goal—such a law would likely just bar them from even more opportunities. Likewise, since non-speakers would be further stigmatized, their nativist detractors could claim legal vindication for every exclusionary push. *This is Alabama*, they might say, *we speak English*.

Language is an organic force, and difficult to control. The troublesome example of official French policy in Quebec offers a cautionary tale. The US is so much larger, home to hundreds of millions of people and their myriad cultural traditions. Enforcement brings other problems, too, not least ideological ones; many supporters of Official English are political conservatives, critically opposed to government intervention in the lives of citizens. If imposition is to be avoided as a rule, then federal speech codes must surely qualify. And since laws are valid only to the degree that they can be enforced, language law is bound to be tenuous at best.

If the English language were under threat, matters might be different. But any honest appraisal of the situation in the US must concede that it   20 simply is not. At the close of his excellent 1997 essay on the subject, Robert D. King said that Americans are "not even close to the danger point," and that we can "relax and luxuriate in our linguistic richness and our traditional tolerance of language differences." Dismissing the idea that language was a threat to unity, he concluded: "Benign neglect is a good policy for any country when it comes to language, and it's a good policy for America."

Almost two decades later, I see no reason to disagree.

THINKING CRITICALLY ABOUT THE READING

1. How old is the English-only debate in politics? Does noting the debate's long history help support Miller's argument against a formal law? Why or why not?

2. Miller writes that both Democrats and Republicans "endorsed the English language in their official platforms" (2), but notes that their reasons differ. He cites that the Democrats noted "enhanced opportunities for English-language learning and immigrant integration" while Republicans said merely that they "support English as the nation's official language." How do these statements differ rhetorically, according to Miller? What does he imply about conservatives? About liberals? Do his implications reveal his own political bias?

3. Miller writes: "In truth, for many English-only advocates, language has become a stand-in for less palatable sentiments" (3). What does the word "palatable" mean here? To what types of sentiments does Miller refer?

4. How does our "white-dominated society" define the terms "other" and "race," according to Miller? How does he suggest the terms are manipulated to support arguments in favor of an English-only law?

5. How does Miller explain the idea that language use is a type of performance "to create certain impressions in the minds of others" (13)? What examples of this does he offer?

6. How does Miller use the idea that "language is an organic force, and difficult to control" (19) to argue against endorsing an English-only law? In what ways does Miller suggest such a law isn't really about language use, but about excluding certain groups of people? What problems and barriers would such a law present for immigrants seeking work, for example?

LANGUAGE IN ACTION

In recent years, the issue of immigration has been closely tied to the learning of English. Many people believe that English should be declared America's "official" language and that the business of the government ought to be carried out in English. They believe that people should be strongly urged—if not required—to learn English and that a common language would be a unifying force in a country that is growing increasingly diverse. Others believe that there is no need to legislate English as the country's official language and that immigrants should be encouraged to maintain traditional culture, cuisine, and language. As a class, brainstorm a list of the three most compelling reasons for encouraging/ requiring new immigrants to learn English. What are three important reasons for not encouraging/requiring new immigrants to learn the dominant language? Does Jeff Parker's cartoon cause you to have second thoughts on the issue of an official language? Explain.

"THEY SAY THEY'RE BUILDING A WALL BECAUSE TOO MANY OF US ENTER ILLEGALLY AND WON'T LEARN THEIR LANGUAGE OR ASSIMILATE INTO THEIR CULTURE..."

WRITING SUGGESTIONS

1. Conduct some research into the English-only debate, using magazines, journals, and online publications. Using Miller's rhetorical analysis as a model for your own, select an article from your research to analyze. (Even if the position you take disagrees with Miller's argument or with your own stance, you can model his analytical strategies.) Write an essay analyzing the article you selected. What inconsistencies can you identify in the article's logic? How does the article's arguments and language reveal underlying biases?

2. Miller's essay suggests that the words we use reflect and shape how we think and who we are. By extension, minor shifts and distinctions in word use can say volumes about a person or platform. For example, while Democrats "tout . . . 'enhanced opportunities for English-language learning and immigrant integration,'" Republicans simply state that they "'support English as the nation's official language.'" Although these statements take the same side in the debate, their wording indicates different values and different reasons for

the same goal. Because language operates within a larger network of meaning, small distinctions in related words often convey very different things. Choose a pair of terms from the following or come up with your own to research: "transgender" vs. "tranny"/"feminist" vs. "feminazi"/"gay marriage" vs. "marriage equality"/"undocumented workers" vs. "illegals"/"criminal" vs. "thug"/"perpetrator" vs. "accused." Read a few blogs or short essays that use one term or the other, and be sure to read about both terms, from both sides. Write an essay that uses the language you've researched to talk about the larger debate at hand. For instance, what different rhetoric and reasoning do you find from users of the term "gay marriage" vs. "marriage equality"? What strategies and language does each side use to make its points? Discuss how their language affects how they think and defines who they are to their audience.

7

WRITERS ON WRITING:
HOW AND WHY WE WRITE

Learning to write well is a demanding and difficult pursuit, but the ability to express exactly what you mean is one of the most enjoyable and rewarding skills you can possess. And, as with any sought-after goal, there is plenty of help available for the aspiring writer. In this chapter, we have gathered some of the best of that advice, offered by professional writers and respected teachers of writing.

The essays included in this chapter are based on current research and thinking on how writers go about their work. We begin with best-selling author Stephen King's "Reading to Write," wherein he supports the need to be an active and critical reader, much as we have done in Chapter 1, if you wish to become an effective writer. The rest of the essays in this section look more deeply into the writer's tool bag. Annie Dillard exhorts writers to hold nothing back in their writing. Her essay is a challenge to her readers to write novels, write about what fascinates them, and, above all, write right now. In "Good Writing," the renowned Harvard psychologist and linguist Steven Pinker reverse-engineers several pieces of writing in order to discover what makes them successful. His close reading of these pieces uncovers common elements that he argues are essential to good writing. Popular novelist and teacher of writing Anne Lamott recognizes that even though writers may start out with firm purpose and clear thinking, rough drafts are inevitably messy affairs. In "The Maker's Eye: Revising Your Own Manuscripts," the late Donald M. Murray recognizes the need to produce a first draft, no matter how messy, so as to move to the real job of writing. For him, as for almost all practicing writers, writing is revising. Next, we offer another take on the need to achieve clarity in your writing. In his essay "Simplicity," one of America's leading experts on writing, William Zinsser, offers the following support: "Writing is hard work. A clear sentence is no accident. Very few sentences come out right the first time, or even the third time. Remember this in moments of despair. If you find that writing is hard, it's because it *is* hard." Finally, Bill Hayes pushes back against the common wisdom and argues that writing, like fitness training, requires taking some time off. All these writing experts are worth reading not just once but again and again as you develop your own skills, confidence, and authority as a writer.

Reading to Write

Stephen King

Born in 1947, Stephen King is a 1970 graduate of the University of Maine. He worked as a janitor in a knitting mill, a laundry worker, and a high school English teacher before he struck it big with his writing. Today, many people consider King's name synonymous with the macabre; he is, beyond dispute, the most successful writer of horror fiction today. He has written dozens of novels and hundreds of short stories, novellas, and screenplays, among other works. His books have sold well over 300 million copies worldwide, and many of his novels have been made into popular motion pictures, including *Stand by Me, Misery, The Green Mile*, and *Dreamcatcher*. His fiction, starting with *Carrie* in 1974, includes *Salem's Lot* (1975), *The Shining* (1977), *The Dead Zone* (1979), *Christine* (1983), *Pet Sematary* (1983), *The Dark Half* (1989), *The Girl Who Loved Tom Gordon* (1999), *From a Buick 8* (2002), *Everything's Eventual: Five Dark Tales* (2002), *The Colorado Kid* (2005), *Cell* (2006), *Lisey's Story* (2006), *Duma Key* (2008), *Under the Dome* (2009), *11/22/63* (2011), *The Wind Through the Keyhole* (2012), *Mile 81* (2012), and *The Bazaar of Bad Dreams* (2015), a collection of stories accompanied by revelatory notes on how the story came about. Other works include *Danse Macabre* (1980), a nonfiction look at horror in the media, and *On Writing: A Memoir of the Craft* (2000).

In the following passage taken from *On Writing*, King discusses the importance of reading in learning to write. Reading, in his words, "offers you a constantly growing knowledge of what has been done and what hasn't, what is trite and what is fresh, what works and what just lies there dying (or dead) on the page."

WRITING TO DISCOVER: *In your opinion, are reading and writing connected in some way? If the two activities are related, what is the nature of that relationship? Do you have to be a reader to be a good writer, or is writing an activity that can be learned quite apart from reading?*

If you want to be a writer, you must do two things above all others: Read a lot and write a lot. There's no way around these two things that I'm aware of, no shortcut.

I'm a slow reader, but I usually get through seventy or eighty books a year, mostly fiction. I don't read in order to study the craft; I read because I like to read. It's what I do at night, kicked back in my blue chair. Similarly, I don't read fiction to study the art of fiction, but simply because I like stories. Yet there is a learning process going on. Every book you pick up has its own lesson or lessons, and quite often the bad books have more to teach than the good ones.

When I was in the eighth grade, I happened upon a paperback novel by Murray Leinster, a science fiction pulp writer who did most of his work during the forties and fifties, when magazines like *Amazing Stories* paid a penny a word. I had read other books by Mr. Leinster, enough to know that the quality of his writing was uneven. This particular tale, which was about mining in the asteroid belt, was one of his less successful efforts. Only that's too kind. It was terrible, actually, a story populated by paper-thin characters and driven by outlandish plot developments. Worst of all (or so it seemed to me at the time), Leinster had fallen in love with the word *zestful*. Characters watched the approach of ore bearing asteroids with *zestful smiles*. Characters sat down to supper aboard their mining ship with *zestful anticipation*. Near the end of the book, the hero swept the large-breasted, blonde heroine into a *zestful embrace*. For me, it was the literary equivalent of a smallpox vaccination: I have never, so far as I know, used the word *zestful* in a novel or a story. God willing, I never will.

Asteroid Miners (which wasn't the title, but that's close enough) was an important book in my life as a reader. Almost everyone can remember losing his or her virginity, and most writers can remember the first book he/she put down thinking: *I can do better than this, Hell, I* am *doing better than this!* What could be more encouraging to the struggling writer than to realize his/her work is unquestionably better than that of someone who actually got paid for his/her stuff?

If you want to be a writer, you must do two things above all others: Read a lot and write a lot.

One learns most clearly what not to do by reading bad prose—one   5
novel like *Asteroid Miners* (or *Valley of the Dolls, Flowers in the Attic*, and *The Bridges of Madison County*, to name just a few) is worth a semester at a good writing school, even with the superstar guest lecturers thrown in. Good writing, on the other hand, teaches the learning writer about style, graceful narration, plot development, the creation of believable characters, and truth-telling. A novel like *The Grapes of Wrath* may fill a new writer with feelings of despair and good old-fashioned jealousy—"I'll never be able to write anything that good, not if I live to be a thousand"—but such feelings can also serve as a spur, goading the writer to work harder and aim higher. Being swept away by a combination of great story and great writing—of being flattened, in fact—is part of every writer's necessary formation. You cannot hope to sweep someone else away by the force of your writing until it has been done to you.

So we read to experience the mediocre and the outright rotten; such experience helps us to recognize those things when they begin to creep into our own work, and to steer clear of them. We also read in order to measure ourselves against the good and the great, to get a sense of all that can be done. And we read in order to experience different styles.

You may find yourself adopting a style you find particularly exciting, and there's nothing wrong with that. When I read Ray Bradbury as a kid, I wrote like Ray Bradbury—everything green and wondrous and seen through a lens smeared with the grease of nostalgia. When I read James M. Cain, everything I wrote came out clipped and stripped and hard-boiled. When I read Lovecraft, my prose became luxurious and Byzantine. I wrote stories in my teenage years where all these styles merged, creating a kind of hilarious stew. This sort of stylistic blending is a necessary part of developing one's own style, but it doesn't occur in a vacuum. You have to read widely, constantly refining (and redefining) your own work as you do so. It's hard for me to believe that people who read very little (or not at all in some cases) should presume to write and expect people to like what they have written, but I know it's true. If I had a nickel for every person who ever told me he/she wanted to become a writer but "didn't have time to read," I could buy myself a pretty good steak dinner. Can I be blunt on this subject? If you don't have time to read, you don't have the time (or the tools) to write. Simple as that.

Reading is the creative center of a writer's life. I take a book with me everywhere I go, and find there are all sorts of opportunities to dip in. The trick is to teach yourself to read in small sips as well as in long swallows. Waiting rooms were made for books—of course! But so are theater lobbies before the show, long and boring checkout lines, and everyone's favorite, the john. You can even read while you're driving, thanks to the audiobook revolution. Of the books I read each year, anywhere from six to a dozen are on tape. As for all the wonderful radio you will be missing, come on—how many times can you listen to Deep Purple sing "Highway Star"?

Reading at meals is considered rude in polite society, but if you expect   10
to succeed as a writer, rudeness should be the second-to-least of your concerns. The least of all should be polite society and what it expects. If you intend to write as truthfully as you can, your days as a member of polite society are numbered, anyway.

Where else can you read? There's always the treadmill, or whatever you use down at the local health club to get aerobic. I try to spend an hour doing that every day, and I think I'd go mad without a good novel to keep me company. Most exercise facilities (at home as well as outside it) are now equipped with TVs, but TV—while working out or anywhere else—really is about the last thing an aspiring writer needs. If you feel you must have the news analyst blowhards on CNN while you exercise, or the stock market blowhards on MSNBC, or the sports blowhards on ESPN, it's time for you to question how serious you really are about becoming a writer. You must be prepared to do some serious turning inward toward the life of the imagination, and that means, I'm afraid, that Geraldo, Keith Olbermann, and Jay Leno must go. Reading takes time, and the glass teat takes too much of it.

Once weaned from the ephemeral craving for TV, most people will find they enjoy the time they spend reading. I'd like to suggest that turning off that endlessly quacking box is apt to improve the quality of your life as well as the quality of your writing. And how much of a sacrifice are we talking about here? How many *Frasier* and *ER* reruns does it take to make one American life complete? How many Richard Simmons infomercials? How many whiteboy/fatboy Beltway insiders on CNN? Oh man, don't get me started. Jerry-Springer-Dr.-Dre-Judge-Judy-Jerry-Falwell-Donny-and-Marie, I rest my case.

When my son Owen was seven or so, he fell in love with Bruce Springsteen's E Street Band, particularly with Clarence Clemons, the band's burly sax player. Owen decided he wanted to learn to play like Clarence. My wife and I were amused and delighted by this ambition. We were also hopeful, as any parent would be, that our kid would turn out to be talented, perhaps even some sort of prodigy. We got Owen a tenor saxophone for Christmas and lessons with Gordon Bowie, one of the local music men. Then we crossed our fingers and hoped for the best.

Seven months later I suggested to my wife that it was time to discontinue the sax lessons, if Owen concurred. Owen did, and with palpable relief—he hadn't wanted to say it himself, especially not after asking for the sax in the first place, but seven months had been long enough for him to realize that, while he might love Clarence Clemons's big sound, the saxophone was simply not for him—God had not given him that particular talent.

I knew, not because Owen stopped practicing, but because he was   15
practicing only during the periods Mr. Bowie had set for him: half an hour after school four days a week, plus an hour on the weekends. Owen mastered the scales and the notes—nothing wrong with his memory, his lungs, or his eye-hand coordination—but we never heard him taking off, surprising himself with something new, blissing himself out. And as soon as his practice time was over, it was back into the case with the horn, and there it stayed until the next lesson or practice time. What this suggested to me was that when it came to the sax and my son, there was never going to be any real playtime; it was all going to be rehearsal. That's no good. If there's no joy in it, it's just no good. It's best to go on to some other area, where the deposits of talent may be richer and the fun quotient higher.

Talent renders the whole idea of rehearsal meaningless; when you find something at which you are talented, you do it (whatever *it* is) until your fingers bleed or your eyes are ready to fall out of your head. Even when no one is listening (or reading, or watching), every outing is a bravura performance, because you as the creator are happy. Perhaps even ecstatic. That goes for reading and writing as well as for playing a musical instrument, hitting a baseball, or running the four-forty. The sort of strenuous reading and writing program I advocate—four to six hours a day, every day—will not seem strenuous if you really enjoy doing these things and have an aptitude for them; in fact, you may be following such a program already. If you feel you need permission to do all the reading and writing your little heart desires, however, consider it hereby granted by yours truly.

The real importance of reading is that it creates an ease and intimacy with the process of writing; one comes to the country of the writer with one's papers and identification pretty much in order. Constant reading will pull you into a place (a mind-set, if you like the phrase) where you can write eagerly and without self-consciousness. It also offers you a constantly growing knowledge of what has been done and what hasn't, what is trite and what is fresh, what works and what just lies there dying (or dead) on the page. The more you read, the less apt you are to make a fool of yourself with your pen or word processor.

THINKING CRITICALLY ABOUT THE READING

1. What does King mean when he writes that reading a bad novel is "worth a semester at a good writing school, even with the superstar guest lecturers thrown in" (5)? Do you take his observation seriously? Why or why not?

2. In paragraph 3, King berates the author Murray Leinster for his repeated use of the word *zestful*. He says he himself has, as far as he knows, never used the word. Why do you suppose he doesn't like the word? Have you ever used it in your own writing? Explain. (Glossary: *Diction*)

3. In paragraph 7 King says that "we read in order to experience different styles." What examples does he use to support this statement? If you have learned from someone else's style, what exactly was it that you learned? (Glossary: *Evidence*)

4. Authors, especially those as famous as King, are very much sought after as guests on television shows, at writing conferences, and at celebrity and charity events. Why does King believe that it is incompatible for one to be both a member of polite society and an author? Do you agree with him? Why or why not?

5. King does not like TV. What does he find wrong with it, especially for writers?

6. Admittedly, not everyone who wants to write well also aspires to be a great novelist. What value, if any, does King's advice about reading and writing have for you as a college student? Explain.

LANGUAGE IN ACTION

King closes paragraph 11 with the observation that "Reading takes time, and the glass teat takes too much of it." Identify your own "glass teat." Perhaps you're less inclined to turn to television, and more attached to your smart phone. Try detaching from it in a substantial way for twenty-four hours.

While you're disconnected, do what King describes and fill your spare moments with reading—a good book, a lousy book, whatever sort of book will hold your interest. Carry that book with you, turning to it when you might otherwise distract yourself, and observe how your thinking changes. Does increasing the amount of time you spend reading actually do what King suggests it does? Do you find you have more access to language, and more inclination and ability to write? After twenty-four hours steeped in a book and disconnected from other media, try writing something inspired by the style of that writer. Can you identify specific ways your impulses with language have changed?

WRITING SUGGESTIONS

1. King shares with his readers both his reading and writing experiences and the way they have influenced and shaped his development as a writer. Each of us has also been influenced by the reading and writing we have done. Some of us have done a lot of reading and writing in and out of school while others have not done as much as we would have liked. Write an essay explaining what your experiences have been with reading and writing and especially how your reading has influenced your writing and vice versa. Here are some of the many questions you might want to address in your essay: What writers have you envied and wanted to imitate? What subjects have interested you? What style of writing do you favor? What style annoys you? Have your tastes changed? What particular texts have had a great influence on your thinking and outlook?

2. King seems to be especially averse to watching television. Is it the medium, the types of programs aired, or a combination that annoys him? After all, consider that movies and miniseries made from his novels have appeared on television. Why do you suppose he finds pleasure in reading and not television? Does the same relationship between reading and writing take place between watching television and writing? Write an essay in which you argue against his rejection of television or in which you, like King, take issue with it and with those programs you find a waste of time.

Write Till You Drop

ANNIE DILLARD

Annie Dillard, born in 1945, has published frequently in a variety of different forms, including nonfiction narratives, novels, poetry, memoir, and even texts for musical compositions. Educated at Hollins College, a small private college in Virginia, Dillard began her successful career as writer with the collection of poems *Tickets for a Prayer Wheel* (1974), followed by the nonfiction narrative *Pilgrim at Tinker Creek* (1975), which won the Pulitzer Prize. Among her numerous other publications are *The Writing Life* (1989), *The Living* (1992), *For the Time Being* (1999), and *The Maytrees* (2007). Although many critics and readers find a strong sense of ethics in her writing, Dillard herself has said, "I don't write at all about ethics. . . . The kind of art I write is shockingly uncommitted." According to one critic, "Dillard's world is one where we're always blinking in wonder, doing double takes, and being tossed head over heels as the sacred pops up to surprise us." The exploration of the "sacred" could be considered a key trait of Dillard's writings.

In this article, originally published in the *New York Times* on May 28, 1989, Dillard writes that the business of the writer is to find his or her own special subject to write about. The writer needs a special, perhaps unique, perspective that no one else will write. Only that one writer can bring that idea to the world.

WRITING TO DISCOVER: *What have you learned about or experienced that you find interesting but struggle to understand? What interests or experiences of yours don't often come up in the books and articles you've read? What would you most like to read about those experiences? What could you write about them yourself?*

People love pretty much the same things best. A writer looking for subjects inquires not after what he loves best, but after what he alone loves at all. Strange seizures beset us. Frank Conroy loves his yo-yo tricks, Emily Dickinson her slant of light; Richard Selzer loves the glistening peritoneum, Faulkner the muddy bottom of a little girl's drawers visible when she's up a pear tree. "Each student of the ferns," I once read, "will have his own list of plants that for some reason or another stir his emotions."

Why do you never find anything written about that idiosyncratic thought you advert to, about your fascination with something no one else understands? Because it is up to you. There is something you find interesting, for a reason hard to explain. It is hard to explain because you have never read it on any page; there you begin. You were made and set here to give voice to this, your own astonishment.

Write as if you were dying. At the same time, assume you write for an audience consisting solely of terminal patients. That is, after all, the case.

What would you begin writing if you knew you would die soon? What could you say to a dying person that would not enrage by its triviality?

Write about winter in the summer. Describe Norway as Ibsen did, from a desk in Italy; describe Dublin as James Joyce did, from a desk in Paris. Willa Cather wrote her prairie novels in New York City; Mark Twain wrote "Huckleberry Finn" in Hartford. Recently scholars learned that Walt Whitman rarely left his room.

The writer studies literature, not the world. She lives in the world; she 5 cannot miss it. If she has ever bought a hamburger, or taken a commercial airplane flight, she spares her readers a report of her experience. She is careful of what she reads, for that is what she will write. She is careful of what she learns, because that is what she will know.

The writer knows her field—what has been done, what could be done, the limits—the way a tennis player knows the court. And like that expert, she, too, plays the edges. That is where the exhilaration is. She hits up the line. In writing, she can push the edges. Beyond this limit, here, the reader must recoil. Reason balks, poetry snaps; some madness enters, or strain. Now gingerly, can she enlarge it, can she nudge the bounds? And enclose what wild power?

A well-known writer got collared by a university student who asked, "Do you think I could be a writer?"

"Well," the writer said, "I don't know. . . . Do you like sentences?"

The writer could see the student's amazement. Sentences? Do I like sentences? I am 20 years old and do I like sentences? If he had liked sentences, of course, he could begin, like a joyful painter I knew. I asked him how he came to be a painter. He said, "I liked the smell of the paint."

Hemingway studied, as models, the novels of Knut Hamsun and Ivan 10 Turgenev. Isaac Bashevis Singer, as it happened, also chose Hamsun and Turgenev as models. Ralph Ellison studied Hemingway and Gertrude Stein. Thoreau loved Homer; Eudora Welty loved Chekhov. Faulkner described his debt to Sherwood Anderson and Joyce; E. M. Forster, his debt to Jane Austen and Proust. By contrast, if you ask a 21-year-old poet whose poetry he likes, he might say, unblushing, "Nobody's." He has not yet understood that poets like poetry, and novelists like novels; he himself likes only the role, the thought of himself in a hat. Rembrandt and Shakespeare, Bohr and Gauguin, possessed powerful hearts, not powerful wills. They loved the range of materials they used. The work's possibilities excited them; the field's complexities fired their imaginations. The caring suggested the tasks; the tasks suggested the schedules. They learned their fields and then loved them. They worked, respectfully, out of their love and knowledge, and they produced complex bodies of work that endure. Then, and only then, the world harassed them with some sort of wretched hat, which, if they were still living, they knocked away as well as they could, to keep at their tasks.

It makes more sense to write one big book—a novel or nonfiction narrative—than to write many stories or essays. Into a long, ambitious project you can fit or pour all you possess and learn. A project that takes five years will accumulate those years' inventions and richnesses. Much of those years' reading will feed the work. Further, writing sentences is difficult whatever their subject. It is no less difficult to write sentences in a recipe than sentences in "Moby-Dick." So you might as well write "Moby-Dick." Similarly, since every original work requires a unique form, it is more prudent to struggle with the outcome of only one form—that of a long work—than to struggle with the many forms of a collection.

Every book has an intrinsic impossibility, which its writer discovers as soon as his first excitement dwindles. The problem is structural; it is insoluble; it is why no one can ever write this book. Complex stories, essays and poems have this problem, too—the prohibitive structural defect the writer wishes he had never noticed. He writes it in spite of that. He finds ways to minimize the difficulty; he strengthens other virtues; he cantilevers the whole narrative out into thin air and it holds. Why are we reading, if not in hope of beauty laid bare, life heightened and its deepest mystery probed? Can the writer isolate and vivify all in experience that most deeply engages our intellects and our hearts? Can the writer renew our hopes for literary forms? Why are we reading, if not in hope that the writer will magnify and dramatize our days, will illuminate and inspire us with wisdom, courage and the hope of meaningfulness, and press upon our minds the deepest mysteries, so we may feel again their majesty and power? What do we ever know that is higher than that power which, from time to time, seizes our lives, and which reveals us startlingly to ourselves as creatures set down here bewildered? Why does death so catch us by surprise, and why love? We still and always want waking. If we are reading for these things, why would anyone read books with advertising slogans and brand names in them? Why would anyone write such books? We should mass half-dressed in long lines like tribesmen and shake gourds at each other, to wake up; instead we watch television and miss the show.

No manipulation is possible in a work of art, but every miracle is. Those artists who dabble in eternity, or who aim never to manipulate but only to lay out hard truths, grow accustomed to miracles. Their sureness is hard won. "Given a large canvas," said Veronese, "I enriched it as I saw fit."

The sensation of writing a book is the sensation of spinning, blinded by love and daring. It is the sensation of a stunt pilot's turning barrel rolls, or an inchworm's blind rearing from a stem in search of a route. At its worst, it feels like alligator wrestling, at the level of the sentence.

At its best, the sensation of writing is that of any unmerited grace. It is handed to you, but only if you look for it. You search, you break your fists, your back, your brain, and then—and only then—it is handed to you. From the corner of your eye you see motion. Something is moving through the air and headed your way. It is a parcel bound in ribbons and bows; it has two white wings. It flies directly at you; you can read your name on it. If it were a baseball, you would hit it out of the park. It is that

15

one pitch in a thousand you see in slow motion; its wings beat slowly as a hawk's.

One line of a poem, the poet said—only one line, but thank God for that one line—drops from the ceiling. Thornton Wilder cited this unnamed writer of sonnets: one line of a sonnet falls from the ceiling, and you **At its best, the sensation of writing is that of any unmerited grace. It is handed to you, but only if you look for it.** tap in the others around it with a jeweler's hammer. Nobody whispers it in your ear. It is like something you memorized once and forgot. Now it comes back and rips away your breath. You find and finger a phrase at a time; you lay it down as if with tongs, restraining your strength, and wait suspended and fierce until the next one finds you: yes, this; and yes, praise be, then this.

Einstein likened the generation of a new idea to a chicken's laying an egg: "Kieks—auf einmal ist es da." Cheep—and all at once there it is. Of course, Einstein was not above playing to the crowd.

Push it. Examine all things intensely and relentlessly. Probe and search each object in a piece of art; do not leave it, do not course over it, as if it were understood, but instead follow it down until you see it in the mystery of its own specificity and strength. Giacometti's drawings and paintings show his bewilderment and persistence. If he had not acknowledged his bewilderment, he would not have persisted. A master of drawing, Rico Lebrun, discovered that "the draftsman must aggress; only by persistent assault will the live image capitulate and give up its secret to an unrelenting line." Who but an artist fierce to know—not fierce to seem to know—would suppose that a live image possessed a secret? The artist is willing to give all his or her strength and life to probing with blunt instruments those same secrets no one can describe any way but with the instruments' faint tracks.

Admire the world for never ending on you as you would admire an opponent, without taking your eyes off him, or walking away.

One of the few things I know about writing is this: spend it all, shoot it, play it, lose it, all, right away, every time. Do not hoard what seems good for a later place in the book, or for another book; give it, give it all, give it now. The impulse to save something good for a better place later is the signal to spend it now. Something more will arise for later, something better. These things fill from behind, from beneath, like well water. Similarly, the impulse to keep to yourself what you have learned is not only shameful, it is destructive. Anything you do not give freely and abundantly becomes lost to you. You open your safe and find ashes.

After Michelangelo died, someone found in his studio a piece of paper on which he had written a note to his apprentice, in the handwriting of his old age: "Draw, Antonio, draw, Antonio, draw and do not waste time."

THINKING CRITICALLY ABOUT THE READING

1. Why does Dillard say "Write as if you were dying" (3)? In what ways could that be said about any activity worth doing? Are there circumstances in which this is bad advice? Explain.

2. In paragraph 4, Dillard recounts a series of writers who wrote their works while physically distant from what they were writing about. What is the benefit of physical distance? What does it ask of the writer?

3. What does Dillard mean by saying of a would-be poet that he "likes the thought of himself in a hat" (10)? What does the metaphor of a hat suggest?

4. Dillard writes about famous writers and the role models they had for their own writing. Which writers do you admire and consider role models for your own writing? Why? If you cannot think of a particular writer, approach the question by asking what kinds of writing you enjoy reading, and why? What is it that makes that writing good?

5. Dillard argues that a writer should write long works—books—rather than short works, such as short story collections. Do you agree or disagree? Why? How does the fact that Dillard has written both—long works and collections—affect your interpretation of her advice?

6. Dillard states that the writer writes, ". . . in hope of beauty laid bare" (12). What does she mean by that? How is beauty connected to language, and not just visual appearance?

LANGUAGE IN ACTION

Dillard poses "Do you like sentences?" as one of the most essential questions for an aspiring writer. Sentences are one place to begin to understand the mystery of good writing. Read the following sentences, and mark the ones that seem especially captivating to you. Notice if you laugh out loud, feel particularly tense, or feel emotionally connected to the speaker.

It was a fine cry—loud and long—but it had no bottom and it had no top, just circles and circles of sorrow.

—TONI MORRISON, *Sula*

This private estate was far enough away from the explosion so that its bamboos, pines, laurel, and maples were still alive, and the green place invited refugees—partly because they believed that if the Americans came back, they would bomb only buildings; partly because the foliage seemed a center of coolness and life, and the estate's exquisitely precise rock gardens, with their quiet pools and arching bridges, were very Japanese, normal, secure; and also partly (according to some who were there) because of an irresistible, atavistic urge to hide under leaves.

—JOHN HERSEY, *Hiroshima*

For what do we live, but to make sport for our neighbors, and laugh at them in our turn?

—JANE AUSTEN, *Pride and Prejudice*

> In many ways he was like America itself, big and strong, full of good intentions, a roll of fat jiggling at his belly, slow of foot but always plodding along, always there when you needed him, a believer in the virtues of simplicity and directness and hard labor.
>
> —TIM O'BRIEN, *The Things They Carried*
>
> I took a deep breath and listened to the old brag of my heart; I am, I am, I am.
>
> —SYLVIA PLATH, *The Bell Jar*

What do these sentences have in common? Do you like short sentences? Do you like long, winding sentences with lots of punctuation? Do you like a lot of adjectives and adverbs? Or do you like straightforward sentences? What is it specifically that you like about the sentences you picked?

Try to write sentences of your own that are structurally similar. The content doesn't have to be the same, but try putting the parts of speech—the nouns, the verbs, the adjectives—in more or less the same slots. What do you learn about writing by modeling your sentences on some you admire? Do you admire the sentences that you wrote, too? If not, why not? What's missing?

WRITING SUGGESTIONS

1. Dillard says, "You were made and set here to give voice to this, your own astonishment" (2). What do you consider your astonishment? Write an essay in which you describe to what extent you have—or have not—given voice to your own astonishment, and examine your own reasons for that. Be specific.

2. Dillard reports that "Einstein likened the generation of a new idea to a chicken's laying an egg: 'Kieks—auf einmal ist es da.' Cheep—and all at once there it is" (17). On the other hand, Thomas Edison allegedly said, "Genius is one percent inspiration, ninety-nine percent perspiration." Is "sudden inspiration" more common than old-fashioned hard work ("perspiration")? Is one more valuable than the other? Are there disciplines or fields in which one is more effective than the other? Write an essay about the generation of great ideas. You might conduct research about the history of the generation of great ideas and see if your analysis bears out in real-life cases.

Good Writing

Steven Pinker

Born in 1954, Steven Pinker is the Johnstone Family Professor in the Department of Psychology at Harvard University. Raised in the English-speaking Jewish community of Montreal, Canada, Pinker attended McGill University, receiving his B.A. in 1976. Just three years later, Pinker earned a Ph.D. at Harvard University. Pinker has taught psychology at Harvard, Stanford University, and the Massachusetts Institute of Technology, where he directed the Center for Cognitive Neuroscience. Since publishing *Language Learnability and Language Development* in 1984, Pinker has written extensively on language development in children. He has what one critic writing in the *New York Times Book Review* calls "that facility, so rare among scientists, of making the most difficult material . . . accessible to the average reader." Pinker has published numerous books, including *The Language Instinct* (1994), *How the Mind Works* (1997), *The Blank Slate: The Modern Denial of Human Nature* (2002), *The Stuff of Thought: Language as a Window into Human Nature* (2007), and *The Better Angels of Our Nature: Why Violence Has Declined* (2011). His most recent book is *Sense of Style: The Thinking Person's Guide to Writing in the 21st Century* (2014), from which this excerpt is taken.

The term "reverse engineering" is frequently used in a technical context, meaning to look at a finished product, such as computer hardware or software, and take it apart to see how it was constructed. Pinker employs the process with works of writing and dissects their language, examining word choice, syntax, figurative language—even the rhythm and pronunciation of the words. He demonstrates that effective writing does not follow just one set of rules, and that all of us, with a heightened awareness of language, can become better writers.

WRITING TO DISCOVER: *Who are some of your favorite writers? What is it about their writing that you particularly enjoy? Then think of your own writing—your vocabulary, your sense of how to write a sentence, your use of language. Describe your own writing style. Do you think you write like your favorite writers? Why or why not?*

"Education is an admirable thing," wrote Oscar Wilde, "but it is well to remember from time to time that nothing that is worth knowing can be taught." In dark moments while writing this book, I sometimes feared that Wilde might be right. When I polled some accomplished writers about which style manuals they had consulted during their apprenticeships, the most common answer I got was "none." Writing, they said, just came naturally to them.

I'd be the last to doubt that good writers are blessed with an innate dose of fluency with syntax and memory for words. But no one is born with skills in English composition per se. Those skills may not have come from stylebooks, but they must have come from somewhere.

That somewhere is the writing of other writers. Good writers are avid readers. They have absorbed a vast inventory of words, idioms, constructions, tropes, and rhetorical tricks, and with them a sensitivity to how they mesh and how they clash. This is the elusive "ear" of a skilled writer—the tacit sense of style which every honest stylebook, echoing Wilde, confesses cannot be explicitly taught. Biographers of great authors always try to track down the books their subjects read when they were young, because they know these sources hold the key to their development as writers.

I would not have written this book if I did not believe, contra Wilde, that many principles of style really can be taught. But the starting point for becoming a good writer is to be a good reader. Writers acquire their technique by spotting, savoring, and reverse-engineering examples of good prose. The goal of this chapter is to provide a glimpse of how that is done. I have picked four passages of twenty-first-century prose, diverse in style and content, and will think aloud as I try to understand what makes them work. My intent is not to honor these passages as if I were bestowing a prize, nor to hold them up as models for you to emulate. It's to illustrate, via a peek into my stream of consciousness, the habit of lingering over good writing wherever you find it and reflecting on what makes it good.

Savoring good prose is not just a more effective way to develop a writerly ear than obeying a set of commandments; it's a more inviting one. Much advice on style is stern and censorious. A recent bestseller advocated "zero tolerance" for errors and brandished the words *horror satanic, ghastly*, and *plummeting standards* on its first page. The classic manuals, **Writers acquire their technique by spotting, savoring, and reverse engineering examples of good prose.** written by starchy Englishmen and rock-ribbed Yankees, try to take all the fun out of writing, grimly adjuring the writer to avoid offbeat words, figures of speech, and playful alliteration. A famous piece of advice from this school crosses the line from the grim to the infanticidal: "Whenever you feel an impulse to perpetrate a piece of exceptionally fine writing, obey it—wholeheartedly—and delete it before sending your manuscript to press. *Murder your darlings*"?

An aspiring writer could be forgiven for thinking that learning to write is like negotiating an obstacle course in boot camp, with a sergeant barking at you for every errant footfall. Why not think of it instead as a form of pleasurable mastery, like cooking or photography? Perfecting the craft is a lifelong calling, and mistakes are part of the game. Though the quest for improvement may be informed by lessons and honed by practice, it must first be kindled by a delight in the best work of the masters and a desire to approach their excellence.

We are going to die, and that makes us the lucky ones. Most people are never going to die because they are never going to be born. The potential people who could have been here in my place but who will in fact never see the light of day outnumber the sand grains of Arabia. Certainly those unborn ghosts include greater poets than Keats, scientists greater than Newton. We know this because the set of possible people allowed by our DNA so massively exceeds the set of actual people. In the teeth of these stupefying odds it is you and I, in our ordinariness, that are here.

In the opening lines of Richard Dawkins's *Unweaving the Rainbow*, the uncompromising atheist and tireless advocate of science explains why his worldview does not, as the romantic and the religious fear, extinguish a sense of wonder or an appreciation of life.

We are going to die, and that makes us the lucky ones. Good writing starts strong. Not with a cliché ("Since the dawn of time"), not with a banality ("Recently, scholars have been increasingly concerned with the question of . . ."), but with a contentful observation that provokes curiosity. The reader of *Unweaving the Rainbow* opens the book and is walloped with a reminder of the most dreadful fact we know, and on its heels a paradoxical elaboration. We're lucky because we'll die? Who wouldn't want to find out how this mystery will be solved? The starkness of the paradox is reinforced by the diction and meter: short, simple words, a stressed monosyllable followed by six iambic feet.

Most people are never going to die. The resolution to the paradox—that a bad thing, dying, implies a good thing, having lived—is explained with parallel constructions: *never going to die . . . never going to be born.* The next sentence restates the contrast, also in parallel language, but avoids the tedium of repeating words yet again by juxtaposing familiar idioms that have the same rhythm: *been here in my place . . . see the light of day.*

the sand grains of Arabia. A touch of the poetic, better suited to the   10
grandeur that Dawkins seeks to invoke than a colorless adjective like *massive* or *enormous.* The expression is snatched from the brink of cliché by its variant wording (*sand grains* rather than *sands*) and by its vaguely exotic feel. The phrase *sands of Arabia*, though common in the early nineteenth century, has plunged in popularity ever since, and there is no longer even a place that is commonly called Arabia; we refer to it as Saudi Arabia or the Arabian Peninsula.

unborn ghosts. A vivid image to convey the abstract notion of a mathematically possible combination of genes, and a wily repurposing of a supernatural concept to advance a naturalistic argument.

greater poets than Keats, scientists greater than Newton. Parallel wording is a powerful trope, but after dying and being born, being here in my place and seeing the light of day, enough is enough. To avoid monotony Dawkins inverts the structure of one of the lines in this couplet. The phrase subtly alludes to another meditation on unrealized genius, "Some mute inglorious Milton here may rest," from Thomas Gray's "Elegy Written in a Country Churchyard."

In the teeth of these stupefying odds. The idiom brings to mind the menacing gape of a predator, reinforcing our gratitude for being alive: to come into existence we narrowly escaped a mortal threat, namely the high odds against it. How high? Every writer faces the challenge of finding a superlative in the English word-hoard that has not been inflated by hyperbole and overuse. *In the teeth of these incredible odds? In the teeth of these awesome odds?* Meh. Dawkins has found a superlative—to render into a stupor, to make stupid—that still has the power to impress.

Good writing can flip the way the world is perceived, like the silhouette in psychology textbooks which oscillates between a goblet and two faces. In six sentences Dawkins has flipped the way we think of death, and has stated a rationalist's case for an appreciation of life in words so stirring that many humanists I know have asked that it be read at their funerals.

> What is it that makes a person the very person that she is, herself alone and not another, an integrity of identity that persists over time, undergoing changes and yet still continuing to be—until she does not continue any longer, at least not unproblematically?
>
> I stare at the picture of a small child at a summer's picnic, clutching her big sister's hand with one tiny hand while in the other she has a precarious hold on a big slice of watermelon that she appears to be struggling to have intersect with the small *o* of her mouth. That child is me. But why is she me? I have no memory at all of that summer's day, no privileged knowledge of whether that child succeeded in getting the watermelon into her mouth. It's true that a smooth series of contiguous physical events can be traced from her body to mine, so that we would want to say that her body *is* mine; and perhaps bodily identity is all that our personal identity consists in. But bodily persistence over time, too, presents philosophical dilemmas. The series of contiguous physical events has rendered the child's body so different from the one I glance down on at this moment; the very atoms that composed her body no longer compose mine. And if our bodies are dissimilar, our points of view are even more so. Mine would be as inaccessible to her—just let *her* try to figure out [Spinoza's] *Ethics*—as hers is now to me. Her thought processes, prelinguistic, would largely elude me.
>
> Yet she is me, that tiny determined thing in the frilly white pinafore. She has continued to exist, survived her childhood illnesses, the near-drowning in a rip current on Rockaway Beach at the age of twelve, other dramas. There are presumably adventures that she—that is that I—can't undergo and still continue to be herself. Would I then be someone else or would I just no longer be? Were I to lose all sense of myself—were schizophrenia or demonic possession, a coma or progressive dementia to remove me from myself—would it be I who would be undergoing those trials, or would I have quit the premises? Would there then be someone else, or would there be no one?

Is death one of those adventures from which I can't emerge as myself? The sister whose hand I am clutching in the picture is dead. I wonder every day whether she still exists. A person whom one has loved seems altogether too significant a thing to simply vanish altogether from the world. A person whom one loves *is* a world, just as one knows oneself to be a world. How can worlds like these simply cease altogether? But if my sister does exist, then *what* is she, and what makes that thing that she now is identical with the beautiful girl laughing at her little sister on that forgotten day?

In this passage from *Betraying Spinoza*, the philosopher and novelist   15
Rebecca Newberger Goldstein (to whom I am married) explains the philosophical puzzle of personal identity, one of the problems that engaged the Dutch-Jewish thinker who is the subject of her book. Like her fellow humanist Dawkins, Goldstein analyzes the vertiginous enigma of existence and death, but their styles could not be more different—a reminder of the diverse ways that the resources of language can be deployed to illuminate a topic. Dawkins's could fairly be called masculine, with its confrontational opening, its cold abstractions, its aggressive imagery, its glorification of alpha males. Goldstein's is personal, evocative, reflective, yet intellectually just as rigorous.

at least not unproblematically. The categories of grammar reflect the building blocks of thought—time, space, causality, matter—and a philosophical wordsmith can play with them to awaken her readers to metaphysical conundrums. Here we have an adverb, *unproblematically*, modifying the verb *continue*, an ellipsis for *continue* to be. Ordinarily to be is not the kind of verb that can be modified by an adverb. To be or not *to be*—it's hard to see shades of gray there. The unexpected adverb puts an array of metaphysical, theological, and personal questions on the table before us.

a big slice of watermelon that she appears to be struggling to have intersect with the small o of her mouth. Good writing is understood with the mind's eye. The unusual description of the familiar act of eating in terms of its geometry—a piece of fruit intersecting with an *o*—forces the reader to pause and conjure a mental image of the act rather than skating over a verbal summary. We find the little girl in the photograph endearing not because the author has stooped to telling us so with words like *cute* or *adorable* but because we can see her childlike mannerisms for ourselves—as the author herself is doing when pondering the little alien who somehow is her. We see the clumsiness of a small hand manipulating an adult-sized object; the determination to master a challenge we take for granted; the out-of-sync mouth anticipating the sweet, juicy reward. The geometric language also prepares us for the prelinguistic thinking that Goldstein introduces in the next paragraph: we regress to an age at which "to eat" and even "to put in your mouth" are abstractions, several levels removed from the physical challenge of making an object intersect with a body part.

That child is me. But why is she me? . . . [My point of view] would be as inaccessible to her . . . as hers is now to me. . . . There are presumably adventures that she—that is that I—can't undergo and still continue to be herself. Would I then be someone else? Goldstein repeatedly juxtaposes nouns and pronouns in the first and third person: *that child . . . me; she . . . I . . . herself; I. . . . someone else.* The syntactic confusion about which grammatical person belongs in which phrase reflects our intellectual confusion about the very meaning of the concept "person." She also plays with *to be,* the quintessentially existential verb, to engage our existential puzzlement: *Would I then be someone else or would I just no longer be? . . . Would there then be someone else, or would there be no one?*

frilly white pinafore. The use of an old-fashioned word for an old-fashioned garment helps date the snapshot for us, without the cliché *faded photograph.*

The sister whose hand I am clutching in the picture is dead. After eighteen   20
sentences that mix wistful nostalgia with abstract philosophizing, the reverie is punctured by a stark revelation. However painful it must have been to predicate the harsh word *dead* of a beloved sister, no euphemism—*has passed away, is no longer with us*—could have ended that sentence. The topic of the discussion is how we struggle to reconcile the indubitable fact of death with our incomprehension of the possibility that a person can no longer exist. Our linguistic ancestors parlayed that incomprehension into euphemisms like *passed on* in which death consists of a journey to a remote location. Had Goldstein settled for these weasel words, she would have undermined her analysis before it began.

I wonder every day whether she still exists. A person whom one has loved seems altogether too significant a thing to simply vanish altogether from the world. A person whom one loves is a world, just as one knows oneself to be a world. How can worlds like these simply cease altogether? This passage fills my eyes every time I read it, and not just because it is about a sister-in-law I will never meet. With a spare restatement of what philosophers call the hard problem of consciousness (*A person . . . is a world, just as one knows oneself to be a world*), Goldstein creates an effect that is richly emotional. The puzzlement in having to make sense of this abstract philosophical conundrum mingles with the poignancy of having to come to terms with the loss of someone we love. It is not just the selfish realization that we have been robbed of their third-person company, but the unselfish realization that they have been robbed of their first-person experience.

The passage also reminds us of the overlap in techniques for writing fiction and nonfiction. The interweaving of the personal and the philosophical in this excerpt is being used as an expository device, to help us understand the issues that Spinoza wrote about. But it is also a theme that runs through Goldstein's fiction, namely that the obsessions of academic philosophy—personal identity, consciousness, truth, will, meaning, morality — are of a piece with the obsessions of human beings as they try to make sense of their lives.

MAURICE SENDAK, AUTHOR OF SPLENDID NIGHTMARES, DIES AT 83

Maurice Sendak, widely considered the most important children's book artist of the 20th century, who wrenched the picture book out of the safe, sanitized world of the nursery and plunged it into the dark, terrifying, and hauntingly beautiful recesses of the human psyche, died on Tuesday in Danbury, Conn. . . .

Roundly praised, intermittently censored, and occasionally eaten, Mr. Sendak's books were essential ingredients of childhood for the generation born after 1960 or thereabouts, and in turn for their children.

PAULINE PHILLIPS, FLINTY ADVISER TO MILLIONS AS DEAR ABBY, DIES AT 94

Dear Abby: My wife sleeps in the raw. Then she showers, brushes her teeth and fixes our breakfast — still in the buff. We're newlyweds and there are just the two of us, so I suppose there's really nothing wrong with it. What do you think? — Ed

Dear Ed: It's O.K. with me. But tell her to put on an apron when she's frying bacon.

Pauline Phillips, a California housewife who nearly 60 years ago, seeking something more meaningful than mah-jongg, transformed herself into the syndicated columnist Dear Abby — and in so doing became a trusted, tart-tongued adviser to tens of millions — died on Wednesday in Minneapolis . . . .

With her comic and flinty yet fundamentally sympathetic voice, Mrs. Phillips helped wrestle the advice column from its weepy Victorian past into a hard-nosed 20th-century present. . . .

Dear Abby: Our son married a girl when he was in the service. They were married in February and she had an 8 1/2-pound baby girl in August. She said the baby was premature. Can an 8 1/2-pound baby be this premature? — Wanting to Know

Dear Wanting: The baby was on time. The wedding was late. Forget it.

Mrs. Phillips began her life as the columnist Abigail Van Buren in 1956. She quickly became known for her astringent, often genteelly risqué, replies to queries that included the marital, the medical, and sometimes both at once.

HELEN GURLEY BROWN, WHO GAVE "SINGLE GIRL" A LIFE IN FULL, DIES AT 90

Helen Gurley Brown, who as the author of *Sex and the Single Girl* shocked early-1960s America with the news that unmarried women not only had sex but thoroughly enjoyed it — and who as the editor of *Cosmopolitan* magazine spent the next three decades telling those women precisely how to enjoy it even more—died on Monday in Manhattan. She was 90, though parts of her were considerably younger. . . .

As *Cosmopolitan's* editor from 1965 until 1997, Ms. Brown was widely credited with being the first to introduce frank discussions of sex into magazines for women. The look of women's magazines today—a sea of voluptuous models and titillating cover lines—is due in no small part to her influence.

My third selection, also related to death, showcases yet another tone and style, and stands as further proof that good writing does not fit into a single formula. With deadpan wit, an affection for eccentricity, and a deft use of the English lexicon, the linguist and journalist Margalit Fox has perfected the art of the obituary.

plunged [the picture book] into the dark, terrifying, and hauntingly beau- 25
tiful recesses of the human psyche; a trusted, tart-tongued adviser to tens of mil-
lions; a sea of voluptuous models and titillating cover lines. When you have to capture a life in just eight hundred words, you have to choose those words carefully. Fox has found some mots justes and packed them into readable phrases which put the lie to the lazy excuse that you can't sum up a complex subject—in this case a life's accomplishments—in just a few words.

Roundly praised, intermittently censored, and occasionally eaten. This is a zeugma: the intentional juxtaposition of different senses of a single word. In this list, the word *books* is being used in the sense of both their narrative content (which can be *praised* or *censored*) and their physical form (which can be *eaten*). Along with putting a smile on the reader's face, the zeugma subtly teases the bluenoses who objected to the nudity in Sendak's drawings by juxtaposing their censorship with the innocence of the books' readership.

and in turn for their children. A simple phrase that tells a story—a generation of children grew up with such fond memories of Sendak's books that they read them to their own children—and that serves as an understated tribute to the great artist.

Dear Abby: My wife sleeps in the raw. Beginning the obit with a bang, this sample column instantly brings a pang of nostalgia to the millions of readers who grew up reading Dear Abby, and graphically introduces her life's work to those who did not. We see for ourselves, rather than having to be told about, the offbeat problems, the waggish replies, the (for her time) liberal sensibility.

Dear Abby: Our son married a girl when he was in the service. The deliberate use of surprising transitions—colons, dashes, block quotations—is one of the hallmarks of lively prose. A lesser writer might have introduced this with the plodding "Here is another example of a column by Mrs. Phillips," but Fox interrupts her narration without warning to redirect our gaze to Phillips in her prime. A writer, like a cinematographer, manipulates the viewer's perspective on an ongoing story, with the verbal equivalent of camera angles and quick cuts.

the marital, the medical, and sometimes both at once. Killjoy style 30 manuals tell writers to avoid alliteration, but good prose is enlivened with moments of poetry, like this line with its pleasing meter and its impish pairing of *marital* and *medical*.

She was 90, though parts of her were considerably younger. A sly twist on the formulaic reporting and ponderous tone of conventional obituaries. We soon learn that Brown was a champion of women's sexual self-definition, so we understand the innuendo about cosmetic surgery as good-natured rather than catty—as a joke that Brown herself would have enjoyed.

hauntingly, flinty, tart-tongued, weepy, hard-nosed, astringent, genteelly, risqué, voluptuous, titillating. In selecting these uncommon adjectives and adverbs, Fox defies two of the commonest advisories in the stylebooks: Write with nouns and verbs, not adjectives and adverbs, and Never use an uncommon, fancy word when a common, plain one will do.

But the rules are badly stated. It's certainly true that a lot of turgid prose is stuffed with polysyllabic Latinisms (*cessation* for *end, eventuate in for cause*) and flabby adjectives (is *contributive to* instead of *contributes to, is determinative of* instead of *determines*). And showing off with fancy words you barely understand can make you look pompous and occasionally ridiculous. But a skilled writer can enliven and sometimes electrify her prose with the judicious insertion of a surprising word. According to studies of writing quality, a varied vocabulary and the use of unusual words are two of the features, that distinguish sprightly prose from mush.

The best words not only pinpoint an idea better than any alternative but echo it in their sound and articulation, a phenomenon called phonesthetics, the feeling of sound. It's no coincidence that *haunting* means "haunting" and *tart* means "tart," rather than the other way around; just listen to your voice and sense your muscles as you articulate them. *Voluptuous* has a voluptuous give-and-take between the lips and the tongue, and *titillating* also gives the tongue a workout while titillating the ear with a coincidental but unignorable overlap with a naughty word. These associations make *a sea of voluptuous models and titillating cover lines* more lively than a *sea of sexy models and provocative cover lines. And a sea of pulchritudinous models* would have served as a lesson on how not to choose words: the ugly *pulchritude* sounds like the opposite of what it means, and it is one of those words that no one ever uses unless they are trying to show off.

But sometimes even show-off words can work. In her obituary of 35 the journalist Mike McGrady, who masterminded a 1979 literary hoax in which a deliberately awful bodice ripper became an international best-seller, Fox wrote, "*Naked Came the Stranger* was written by 25 *Newsday* journalists in an era when newsrooms were arguably more relaxed and inarguably more bibulous." The playful *bibulous*, "tending to drink too much," is related to *beverage* and *imbibe* and calls to mind babbling, hobbling, bubbling, and burbling. Readers who want to become writers should read with a dictionary at hand (several are available as smartphone apps), and writers should not hesitate to send their readers there *if* the word is dead-on in meaning, evocative in sound, and not so obscure that the reader will never see it again. (You can probably do without *maieutic*, *propaedeutic*, and *subdoxastic*.) I write with a thesaurus, mindful of the advice I once read in a bicycle repair manual on how to squeeze a dent out of a rim with Vise-Grip pliers: "Do *not* get carried away with the destructive potential of this tool."

> From the early years of the twentieth century to well past its middle age, nearly every black family in the American South, which meant nearly every black family in America, had a decision to make. There were sharecroppers losing at settlement. Typists wanting to work in an office. Yard boys scared that a single gesture near the planter's wife could leave them hanging from an oak tree. They were all stuck in a caste system as hard and unyielding as the red Georgia clay, and they each had a decision before them. In this, they were not unlike anyone who ever longed to cross the Atlantic or the Rio Grande.
>
> It was during the First World War that a silent pilgrimage took its first steps within the borders of this country. The fever rose without warning or notice or much in the way of understanding by those outside its reach. It would not end until the 1970s and would set into motion changes in the North and South that no one, not even the people doing the leaving, could have imagined at the start of it or dreamed would take a lifetime to play out.
>
> Historians would come to call it the Great Migration. It would become perhaps the biggest underreported story of the twentieth century. . . .
>
> The actions of the people in this book were both universal and distinctly American. Their migration was a response to an economic and social structure not of their making. They did what humans have done for centuries when life became untenable—what the pilgrims did under the tyranny of British rule, what the Scotch-Irish did in Oklahoma when the land turned to dust, what the Irish did when there was nothing to eat, what the European Jews did during the spread of Nazism, what the landless in Russia, Italy, China, and elsewhere did when something better across the ocean called to them. What binds these stories together was the back-against-the-wall, reluctant yet hopeful search for something better, any place but where they were. They did what human beings looking for freedom, throughout history, have often done.
>
> They left.

In *The Warmth of Other Suns*, the journalist Isabel Wilkerson ensured that the story of the Great Migration would be underreported no longer. Calling it "great" is no exaggeration. The movement of millions of African

Americans from the Deep South to Northern cities set off the civil rights movement, redrew the urban landscape, rewrote the agenda of American politics and education, and transformed American culture and, with it, world culture.

Wilkerson not only rectifies the world's ignorance about the Great Migration, but with twelve hundred interviews and crystalline prose she makes us understand it in its full human reality. We live in an era of social science, and have become accustomed to understanding the social world in terms of "forces," "pressures," "processes," and "developments." It is easy to forget that those "forces" are statistical summaries of the deeds of millions of men and women who act on their beliefs in pursuit of their desires. The habit of submerging the individual into abstractions can lead not only to bad science (it's not as if the "social forces" obeyed Newton's laws) but to dehumanization. We are apt to think, "I (and my kind) choose to do things for reasons; he (and his kind) are part of a social process." This was a moral of Orwell's essay "Politics and the English Language," which warned against dehumanizing abstraction: "Millions of peasants are robbed of their farms and sent trudging along the roads with no more than they can carry: this is called *transfer of population* or *rectification of frontiers.*" With an allergy to abstraction and a phobia of cliché, Wilkerson trains a magnifying glass on the historical blob called "the Great Migration" and reveals the humanity of the people who compose it.

From the early years of the twentieth century to well past its middle age. Not even the chronology is described in conventional language: the century is an aging person, a contemporary of the story's protagonists.

Typists wanting to work in an office. Not "denial of economic opportunities." By invoking a moderately skilled occupation from an earlier era, Wilkerson invites us to imagine the desperation of a woman who has acquired a proficiency that could lift her from the cotton fields to a professional office but who is denied the chance because of the color of her skin.

Yard boys scared that a single gesture near the planter's wife could leave them hanging from an oak tree. Not "oppression," not "the threat of violence," not even "lynching," but a horrific physical image. We even see what kind of tree it is.

as hard and unyielding as the red Georgia clay. Once again prose is brought to life with a snatch of poetry, as in this simile with its sensual image, its whiff of allusion (I think of Martin Luther King's "red hills of Georgia"), and its lyrical anapest meter.

anyone who ever longed to cross the Atlantic or the Rio Grande. Not "immigrants from Europe or Mexico." Once again the people are not sociological categories. The author forces us to visualize bodies in motion and to remember the motives that pulled them along.

what the pilgrims did . . . what the Scotch-Irish did . . . what the European Jews did . . . what the landless in Russia, Italy, China, and elsewhere did. Wilkerson begins the paragraph by stating that the actions of her protagonists are universal, but she does not rest with that generalization. She nominates the Great Migration for inclusion in a list of storied emigrations (expressed in pleasingly parallel syntax), whose descendants doubtless include many of her readers. Those readers are implicitly invited to apply their respect for their ancestors' courage and sacrifice to the forgotten pilgrims of the Great Migration.

when the land turned to dust, not "the Dust Bowl"; *when there was nothing to eat*, not "the Potato Famine"; *the landless*, not "the peasants." Wilkerson will not allow us to snooze through a recitation of familiar verbiage. Fresh wording and concrete images force us to keep updating the virtual reality display in our minds.

They left. Among the many dumb rules of paragraphing foisted on   45
students in composition courses is the one that says that a paragraph may not consist of a single sentence. Wilkerson ends a richly descriptive introductory chapter with a paragraph composed of exactly two syllables. The abrupt ending and the expanse of blankness at the bottom of the page mirror the finality of the decision to move and the uncertainty of the life that lay ahead. Good writing finishes strong.

The authors of the four passages share a number of practices: an insistence on fresh wording and concrete imagery over familiar verbiage and abstract summary; an attention to the readers' vantage point and the target of their gaze; the judicious placement of an uncommon word or idiom against a backdrop of simple nouns and verbs; the use of parallel syntax; the occasional planned surprise; the presentation of a telling detail that obviates an explicit pronouncement; the use of meter and sound that resonate with the meaning and mood.

The authors also share an attitude: they do not hide the passion and relish that drive them to tell us about their subjects. They write as if they have something important to say. But no, that doesn't capture it. They write as if they have something important to show. And that, we shall see, is a key ingredient in the sense of style.

THINKING CRITICALLY ABOUT THE READING

1. Pinker says, "Good writers are avid readers" (3). Why is this? What parallels can you draw in other pursuits (for instance, teaching or cooking)?

2. As Pinker examines the passage from Richard Dawkins's *Unweaving the Rainbow*, he examines how Dawkins sometimes comes close to using a cliché but then changes the wording slightly, avoiding the cliché. What advantage does that strategy give Dawkins in his writing? What effect does it have on the reader?

3. In paragraph 18, Pinker refers to Dawkins's writing as "masculine." What does he mean by this? By implication, what would "feminine" writing look like? Do you agree with Pinker's distinction between masculine and feminine writing? Why or why not?

4. Pinker writes about what he terms an "overlap in techniques for writing fiction and nonfiction" (26), by which he implies that there are other aspects for writing fiction and nonfiction that are different. What might those differences be, and why do they exist?

5. Pinker at one point appears to criticize George Orwell for the advice he gives in "Politics and the English Language" against using fancy words when shorter, simpler words will do. What is the basis of that criticism? Do you agree with Pinker or with Orwell?

6. Explain the effect of the two words "They left" at the end of the introduction to *The Warmth of Other Suns* by Isabel Wilkerson (53). Why does Pinker think a two-word sentence can be a paragraph? In what circumstances might using such a short sentence as a complete paragraph be a problem? (You might consider as part of your response Sherman Alexie's definition of a paragraph in "Superman and Me" as "a fence that held words," p. 78).

7. Consider the conclusion in which Pinker argues what constitutes good writing. Do you agree or disagree with him? Why?

LANGUAGE IN ACTION

Steven Pinker's essay includes passages written by others, followed by analysis of what makes that passage's writing particularly good. In his analysis, he begins paragraphs with short, italicized phrases from the piece of writing to indicate which part he will discuss next, and focuses both on what each part is doing as a piece of writing and the emotional or intellectual impact it has on the reader.

Following Pinker's model, write a brief analysis of the first six paragraphs of the Annie Dillard's "Write Till You Drop" on pages 202–203. Pick out specific passages, italicize them, and try to both name the writing technique Dillard uses and the effect it has on you as a reader. How does Dillard's work hold up to the kind of close attention to writing that Pinker would give it?

WRITING SUGGESTIONS

1. Pinker is a Harvard-trained psychologist who has ascended to the highest ranks of academia, yet this work, like much of his writing, is intended to be read by the general public. Write an essay in which you reverse engineer Pinker's own use of language in this excerpt and show how he explains difficult concepts to a non-academic audience. Be sure to examine Pinker's word choice, tone, sentence structures, allusions, use of figurative language, and so on.

2. Pinker begins this chapter from his book *Sense of Style* by relaying his experience that most accomplished writers did not learn to write from style manuals but from the writings of others. Choose an accomplished writer, living or dead, and research how he or she developed as a writer. Write an essay in which you explain which writers influenced the writing style, subject matter, attitudes towards language, and intended audience of your chosen writer.

Shitty First Drafts

ANNE LAMOTT

Born in San Francisco in 1954, Anne Lamott is a graduate of Goucher College in Baltimore and is the author of six novels, including *Rosie* (1983), *Crooked Little Heart* (1997), *All New People* (2000), and *Blue Shoes* (2002). She has also been the food reviewer for *California* magazine, a book reviewer for *Mademoiselle*, and a regular contributor to *Salon's* "Mothers Who Think." Her nonfiction books include *Operating Instructions: A Journal of My Son's First Year* (1993), in which she describes her adventures as a single parent; *Traveling Mercies: Some Thoughts on Faith* (1999), in which she charts her journey toward faith in God; *Plan B: Further Thoughts on Faith* (2005); *Grace (Eventually): Thoughts on Faith* (2007); with her son Sam, *Some Assembly Required: A Journal of My Son's First Son* (2012); and *Small Victories: Spotting Improbable Moments of Grace* (2014).

In the following selection, taken from Lamott's popular book about writing, *Bird by Bird* (1994), she argues for the need to let go and write those "shitty first drafts" that lead to clarity and sometimes brilliance in our second and third drafts.

WRITING TO DISCOVER: *Many professional writers view first drafts as something they have to do before they can begin the real work of writing— revision. How do you view the writing of your first drafts? What patterns, if any, do you see in your writing behavior when working on first drafts? Is the work liberating? Restricting? Pleasant? Unpleasant? Explain in a paragraph or two.*

↓ thesis

Now, practically even better news than that of short assignments is the idea of shitty first drafts. All good writers write them. This is how they end up with good second drafts and terrific third drafts. People tend to look at successful writers, writers who are getting their books published and maybe even doing well financially, and think that they sit down at their desks every morning feeling like a million dollars, feeling great about who they are and how much talent they have and what a great story they have to tell; that they take in a few deep breaths, push back their sleeves, roll their necks a few times to get all the cricks out, and dive in, typing fully formed passages as fast as a court reporter. But this is just the fantasy of the uninitiated. I know some very great writers, writers you love who write beautifully and have made a great deal of money, and not one of them sits down routinely feeling wildly enthusiastic and confident. Not one of them writes elegant first drafts. All right, one of them does, but we do not like her very much. We do not think that she has a rich inner life or that God likes her or can even stand her. (Although when I mentioned this to my priest friend Tom, he said you can safely assume you've created God in your own image when it turns out that God hates all the same people you do.)

Very few writers really know what they are doing until they've done it. Nor do they go about their business feeling dewy and thrilled. They do not type a few stiff warm-up sentences and then find themselves bounding along like huskies across the snow. One writer I know tells me that he sits down every morning and says to himself nicely, "It's not like you don't have a choice, because you do—you can either type or kill yourself." We all often feel like we are pulling teeth, even those writers whose prose ends up being the most natural and fluid. The right words and sentences just do not come pouring out like ticker tape most of the time. Now, Muriel Spark is said to have felt that she was taking dictation from God every morning—sitting there, one supposes, plugged into a Dictaphone, typing away, humming. But this is a very hostile and aggressive position. One might hope for bad things to rain down on a person like this.

Very few writers really know what they are doing until they've done it.

For me and most of the other writers I know, writing is not rapturous. In fact, the only way I can get anything written at all is to write really, really shitty first drafts.

The first draft is the child's draft, where you let it all pour out and then let it romp all over the place, knowing that no one is going to see it and that you can shape it later. You just let this childlike part of you channel whatever voices and visions come through and onto the page. If one of the characters wants to say, "Well, so what, Mr. Poopy Pants?," you let her. No one is going to see it. If the kid wants to get into really sentimental, weepy, emotional territory, you let him. Just get it all down on paper, because there may be something great in those six crazy pages that you would never have gotten to by more rational, grown-up means. There may be something in the very last line of the very last paragraph on page six that you just love, that is so beautiful or wild that you now know what you're supposed to be writing about, more or less, or in what direction you might go—but there was no way to get to this without first getting through the first five and a half pages.

I used to write food reviews for *California* magazine before it folded. (My writing food reviews had nothing to do with the magazine folding, although every single review did cause a couple of canceled subscriptions. Some readers took umbrage at my comparing mounds of vegetable puree with various ex-presidents' brains.) These reviews always took two days to write. First I'd go to a restaurant several times with a few opinionated, articulate friends in tow. I'd sit there writing down everything anyone said that was at all interesting or funny. Then on the following Monday I'd sit down at my desk with my notes, and try to write the review. Even after I'd been doing this for years, panic would set in. I'd try to write a lead, but instead I'd write a couple of dreadful sentences, XX them out, try again, XX everything out, and then feel despair and worry settle on my chest like an x-ray apron. It's over, I'd think, calmly. I'm not going to be able to get the magic to work this time. I'm ruined. I'm through. I'm toast. Maybe, I'd think, I can get my old job back as a clerk-typist. But probably not.

5

I'd get up and study my teeth in the mirror for a while. Then I'd stop, remember to breathe, make a few phone calls, hit the kitchen and chow down. Eventually I'd go back and sit down at my desk, and *sigh* for the next ten minutes. Finally I would pick up my one-inch picture frame, stare into it as if for the answer, and every time the answer would come: all I had to do was to write a really shitty first draft of, say, the opening paragraph. And no one was going to see it.

So I'd start writing without reining myself in. It was almost just typing, just making my fingers move. And the writing would be terrible. I'd write a lead paragraph that was a whole page, even though the entire review could only be three pages long, and then I'd start writing up descriptions of the food, one dish at a time, bird by bird, and the critics would be sitting on my shoulders, commenting like cartoon characters. They'd be pretending to snore, or rolling their eyes at my overwrought descriptions, no matter how hard I tried to tone those descriptions down, no matter how conscious I was of what a friend said to me gently in my early days of restaurant reviewing. "Annie," she said, "it is just a piece of *chicken*. It is just a bit of *cake*."

But because by then I had been writing for so long, I would eventually let myself trust the process—sort of, more or less. I'd write a first draft that was maybe twice as long as it should be, with a self-indulgent and boring beginning, stupefying descriptions of the meal, lots of quotes from my black-humored friends that made them sound more like the Manson girls than food lovers, and no ending to speak of. The whole thing would be so long and incoherent and hideous that for the rest of the day I'd obsess about getting creamed by a car before I could write a decent second draft. I'd worry that people would read what I'd written and believe that the accident had really been a suicide, that I had panicked because my talent was waning and my mind was shot.

The next day, though, I'd sit down, go through it all with a colored pen, take out everything I possibly could, find a new lead somewhere on the second page, figure out a kicky place to end it, and then write a second draft. It always turned out fine, sometimes even funny and weird and helpful. I'd go over it one more time and mail it in.

Then, a month later, when it was time for another review, the whole process would start again, complete with the fears that people would find my first draft before I could rewrite it.

THINKING CRITICALLY ABOUT THE READING

1. What is Lamott's thesis, and where is her statement of the thesis? (Glossary: *Thesis*)

2. Lamott says that the perceptions most people have of how writers work is different from the reality of the work itself. She refers to this in paragraph 1 as "the fantasy of the uninitiated." What does she mean?

3. In paragraph 7 Lamott refers to a time when, through experience, she "eventually let [herself] trust the process—sort of, more or less." She is referring

to the writing process, of course, but why "more or less"? Do you think her wariness is personal, or is she speaking for all writers in this regard? Explain.

4. From what Lamott has to say, is writing a first draft more about content or psychology? Do you agree in regard to your own first drafts? Explain.

5. Lamott adds humor to her argument for "shitty first drafts." Give some examples. Do her attempts at humor add or detract from the points she makes? Explain.

6. In paragraph 5, Lamott offers a narrative of her experiences writing a food review in which she refers to an almost ritualistic set of behaviors. What is her purpose in telling her readers this story and the difficulties she has? (Glossary: *Narration*) Is it helpful for us to know this information? Explain.

7. What do you think of Lamott's use of the word *shitty* in her title and in the essay itself? Is it in keeping with the tone of her essay? (Glossary: *Tone*) Are you offended by her use of the word? Why or why not? What would be lost or gained if she used a different word?

LANGUAGE IN ACTION

In his 1990 book *The Play of Words*, Richard Lederer presents the following activity called "Verbs with Verve." What do you learn about the power of verbs from this exercise? Explain.

> Researchers showed groups of test subjects a picture of an automobile accident and then asked this question: "How fast were the cars going when they———?" The blank was variously filled in with *bumped, contacted, hit, collided,* or *smashed.* Groups that were asked "How fast were the cars going when they smashed?" responded with the highest estimates of speed.
>
> All of which proves that verbs create specific images in the mind's eye. Because verbs are the words in a sentence that express action and movement, they are the spark plugs of effective style. The more specific the verbs you choose in your speaking and writing, the more sparky will be the images you flash on the minds of your listeners and readers.
>
> Suppose you write, "'No,' she said and left the room." Grammatically there is nothing wrong with this sentence. But because the verbs *say* and *leave* are among the most general and colorless in the English language, you have missed the chance to create a vivid word picture. Consider the alternatives:

Said		*Left*	
apologized	jabbered	backed	sauntered
asserted	minced	bolted	skipped
blubbered	mumbled	bounced	staggered
blurted	murmured	crawled	stamped
boasted	shrieked	darted	stole
cackled	sighed	flew	strode
commanded	slurred	hobbled	strutted

drawled	snapped	lurched	stumbled
giggled	sobbed	marched	tiptoed
groaned	whispered	plodded	wandered
gurgled	whooped	pranced	whirled

If you had chosen from among these vivid verbs and had crafted the sentence "'No,' she sobbed, and stumbled out of the room," you would have created a powerful picture of someone quite distraught.

Here are brief descriptions of twenty different people. Choosing from the two lists of synonyms for *said* and *left*, fill in the blanks of the sentence "'No,' he/she _____, and _____ out of the room." Select the pair of verbs that best create the most vivid picture of each person described. Throughout your answers try to use as many different verbs as you can:

1. an angry person
2. a baby
3. a braggart
4. a child
5. a clown
6. a confused person
7. a cowboy/cowgirl
8. someone crying
9. a drunkard
10. an embarrassed person
11. an excited person
12. a frightened person
13. a happy person
14. someone in a hurry
15. an injured person
16. a military officer
17. a sneaky person
18. a timid person
19. a tired person
20. a witch

WRITING SUGGESTIONS

1. In order to become a better writer, it is essential to be conscious of what you do as a writer. In other words, you need to reflect on what you are thinking and feeling at each stage of the writing process. Lamott has done just this in writing her essay. Think about what you do at other stages of the writing process—prewriting (gathering information, selecting evidence, checking on the reliability of sources, separating facts from opinions), revising, editing, and proofreading, for example. Write an essay modeled on Lamott's in which you narrate an experience you have had with a particular type of writing or assignment.

2. Lamott's essay is about appearances versus reality. Write an essay in which you set the record straight by exposing the myths or misperceptions people have about a particular job, place, thing, or situation. Naturally, you need to ask yourself how much of an "inside story" you can reveal based on actual experiences you have had. In other words, you know that being a lifeguard is not as romantic as most people think because you have been one. Try to create the same informative but lighthearted tone that Lamott does in her essay by paying particular attention to the language you use.

The Maker's Eye: Revising Your Own Manuscripts

DONALD M. MURRAY

Born in Boston, Massachusetts, Donald M. Murray (1924–2006) taught writing for many years at the University of New Hampshire, his alma mater. He served as an editor at *Time* magazine, and he won the Pulitzer Prize in 1954 for editorials that appeared in the *Boston Globe*. Murray's published works include novels, short stories, poetry, and sourcebooks for teachers of writing, like *A Writer Teaches Writing: A Complete Revision* (1985), *The Craft of Revision* (1991), and *Learning by Teaching* (1982), in which he explores aspects of the writing process. *Write to Learn* (8th ed., 2005), a textbook for college composition courses, is based on Murray's belief that writers learn to write by writing, by taking a piece of writing through the whole process, from invention to revision. In the last decades of his life, Murray produced a weekly column entitled "Now and Then" for the *Boston Globe*.

In the following essay, first published in the *Writer* in October 1973 and later revised for this text, Murray discusses the importance of revision to the work of the writer. Most professional writers live by the maxim that "writing is rewriting." And to rewrite or revise effectively, we need to become better readers of our own work, open to discovering new meanings, and sensitive to our use of language. Murray draws on the experiences of many writers to make a compelling argument for careful revising and editing.

WRITING TO DISCOVER: *Thinking back on your education to date, what did you think you had to do when teachers asked you to revise a piece of your writing? How did the request to revise make you feel? Write about your earliest memories of revising some of your writing. What kinds of changes do you remember making?*

When students complete a first draft, they consider the job of writing done — and their teachers too often agree. When professional writers complete a first draft, they usually feel that they are at the start of the writing process. When a draft is completed, the job of writing can begin.

That difference in attitude is the difference between amateur and professional, inexperience and experience, journeyman and craftsman. Peter F. Drucker, the prolific business writer, calls his first draft "the zero draft" — after that he can start counting. Most writers share the feeling that the first draft, and all of those which follow, are opportunities to discover what they have to say and how best they can say it.

To produce a progression of drafts, each of which says more and says it more clearly, the writer has to develop a special kind of reading skill.

In school we are taught to decode what appears on the page as finished writing. Writers, however, face a different category of possibility and responsibility when they read their own drafts. To them the words on the page are never finished. Each can be changed and rearranged, can set off a chain reaction of confusion or clarified meaning. This is a different kind of reading which is possibly more difficult and certainly more exciting.

When a draft is completed, the job of writing can begin.

Writers must learn to be their own best enemy. They must accept the criticism of others and be suspicious of it; they must accept the praise of others and be even more suspicious of it. Writers cannot depend on others. They must detach themselves from their own pages so that they can apply both their caring and their craft to their own work.

Such detachment is not easy. Science-fiction writer Ray Bradbury supposedly puts each manuscript away for a year to the day and then rereads it as a stranger. Not many writers have the discipline or the time to do this. We must read when our judgment may be at its worst, when we are close to the euphoric moment of creation.   5

Then the writer, counsels novelist Nancy Hale, "should be critical of everything that seems to him most delightful in his style. He should excise what he most admires, because he wouldn't thus admire it if he weren't . . . in a sense protecting it from criticism." John Ciardi, the poet, adds, "The last act of the writing must be to become one's own reader. It is, I suppose, a schizophrenic process, to begin passionately and to end critically, to begin hot and to end cold; and, more important, to be passion-hot and critic-cold at the same time."

Most people think that the principal problem is that writers are too proud of what they have written. Actually, a greater problem for most professional writers is one shared by the majority of students. They are overly critical, think everything is dreadful, tear up page after page, never complete a draft, see the task as hopeless.

The writer must learn to read critically but constructively, to cut what is bad, to reveal what is good. Eleanor Estes, the children's book author, explains: "The writer must survey his work critically, coolly, as though he were a stranger to it. He must be willing to prune, expertly and hard-heartedly. At the end of each revision, a manuscript may look . . . worked over, torn apart, pinned together, added to, deleted from, words changed and words changed back. Yet the book must maintain its original freshness and spontaneity."

Most readers underestimate the amount of rewriting it usually takes to produce spontaneous reading. This is a great disadvantage to the student writer, who sees only a finished product and never watches the craftsman who takes the necessary step back, studies the work carefully, returns to the task, steps back, returns, steps back, again and again. Anthony Burgess, one of the most prolific writers in the English-speaking world, admits, "I might revise a page twenty times." Roald Dahl, the popular children's writer, states, "By the time I'm nearing the end of a story, the first part will have been reread and altered and corrected at least 150 times. . . . Good writing is essentially rewriting. I am positive of this."

Rewriting isn't virtuous. It isn't something that ought to be done. It is 10 simply something that most writers find they have to do to discover what they have to say and how to say it. It is a condition of the writer's life.

There are, however, a few writers who do little formal rewriting, primarily because they have the capacity and experience to create and review a large number of invisible drafts in their minds before they approach the page. And some writers slowly produce finished pages, performing all the tasks of revision simultaneously, page by page, rather than draft by draft. But it is still possible to see the sequence followed by most writers most of the time in rereading their own work.

Most writers scan their drafts first, reading as quickly as possible to catch the larger problems of subject and form, and then move in closer and closer as they read and write, reread and rewrite.

The first thing writers look for in their drafts is *information*. They know that a good piece of writing is built from specific, accurate, and interesting information. The writer must have an abundance of information from which to construct a readable piece of writing.

Next writers look for *meaning* in the information. The specifics must build to a pattern of significance. Each piece of specific information must carry the reader toward meaning.

Writers reading their own drafts are aware of *audience*. They put them- 15 selves in the reader's situation and make sure that they deliver information which a reader wants to know or needs to know in a manner which is easily digested. Writers try to be sure that they anticipate and answer the questions a critical reader will ask when reading the piece of writing.

Writers make sure that the *form* is appropriate to the subject and the audience. Form, or genre, is the vehicle which carries meaning to the reader, but form cannot be selected until the writer has adequate information to discover its significance and an audience which needs or wants that meaning.

Once writers are sure the form is appropriate, they must then look at the *structure*, the order of what they have written. Good writing is built on a solid framework of logic, argument, narrative, or motivation which runs through the entire piece of writing and holds it together. This is the time when many writers find it most effective to outline as a way of visualizing the hidden spine by which the piece of writing is supported.

The element on which writers may spend a majority of their time is *development*. Each section of a piece of writing must be adequately developed. It must give readers enough information so that they are satisfied. How much information is enough? That's as difficult as asking how much garlic belongs in a salad. It must be done to taste, but most beginning writers underdevelop, underestimating the reader's hunger for information.

As writers solve development problems, they often have to consider questions of *dimension*. There must be a pleasing and effective proportion among all the parts of the piece of writing. There is a continual process of subtracting and adding to keep the piece of writing in balance.

Finally, writers have to listen to their own voices. *Voice* is the force   20
which drives a piece of writing forward. It is an expression of the writer's authority and concern. It is what is between the words on the page, what glues the piece of writing together. A good piece of writing is always marked by a consistent, individual voice.

As writers read and reread, write and rewrite, they move closer and closer to the page until they are doing line-by-line editing. Writers read their own pages with infinite care. Each sentence, each line, each clause, each phrase, each word, each mark of punctuation, each section of white space between the type has to contribute to the clarification of meaning.

Slowly the writer moves from word to word, looking through language to see the subject. As a word is changed, cut, or added, as a construction is rearranged, all the words used before that moment and all those that follow that moment must be considered and reconsidered.

Writers often read aloud at this stage of the editing process, muttering or whispering to themselves, calling on the ear's experience with language. Does this sound right—or that? Writers edit, shifting back and forth from eye to page to ear to page. I find I must do this careful editing in short runs, no more than fifteen or twenty minutes at a stretch, or I become too kind with myself. I begin to see what I hope is on the page, not what actually is on the page.

This sounds tedious if you haven't done it, but actually it is fun. Making something right is immensely satisfying, for writers begin to learn what they are writing about by writing. Language leads them to meaning, and there is the joy of discovery, of understanding, of making meaning clear as the writer employs the technical skills of language.

Words have double meanings, even triple and quadruple meanings.   25
Each word has its own potential of connotation and denotation. And when writers rub one word against the other, they are often rewarded with a sudden insight, an unexpected clarification.

The maker's eye moves back and forth from word to phrase to sentence to paragraph to sentence to phrase to word. The maker's eye sees the need for variety and balance, for a firmer structure, for a more appropriate form. It peers into the interior of the paragraph, looking for coherence, unity, and emphasis, which make meaning clear.

I learned something about this process when my first bifocals were prescribed. I had ordered a larger section of the reading portion of the glass because of my work, but even so, I could not contain my eyes within this new limit of vision. And I still find myself taking off my glasses and bending my nose toward the page, for my eyes unconsciously flick back and forth across the page, back to another page, forward to still another, as I try to see each evolving line in relation to every other line.

When does this process end? Most writers agree with the great Russian writer Tolstoy, who said, "I scarcely ever reread my published writings, if by chance I come across a page, it always strikes me: all this must be rewritten; this is how I should have written it."

The maker's eye is never satisfied, for each word has the potential to ignite new meaning. This article has been twice written all the way through the writing process. . . . Now it is to be republished in a book. The editors made a few small suggestions, and then I read it with my maker's eye. Now it has been re-edited, re-revised, re-read, and re-re-edited, for each piece of writing to the writer is full of potential and alternatives.

A piece of writing is never finished. It is delivered to a deadline, torn   30 out of the typewriter on demand, sent off with a sense of accomplishment and shame and pride and frustration. If only there were a couple more days, time for just another run at it, perhaps then. . . .

THINKING CRITICALLY ABOUT THE READING

1. What are the essential differences between revising and editing? What types of language concerns are dealt with at each stage? Why is it important to revise before editing?

2. According to Murray, at what point(s) in the writing process do writers become concerned about the individual words they are using? What do you think Murray means when he says in paragraph 24 that "language leads [writers] to meaning"?

3. How does Murray define *information* and *meaning* (13–14)? Why is the distinction between the two terms important?

4. The phrase "the maker's eye" appears in Murray's title and in several places throughout the essay. What do you suppose he means by this? Consider how the maker's eye could be different from the reader's eye.

5. According to Murray, when is a piece of writing finished? What, for him, is the function of deadlines?

6. What does Murray see as the connection between reading and writing? How does reading help the writer? What should writers be looking for in their reading? What kinds of writing techniques or strategies does Murray use in his essay? Why should we read a novel or magazine article differently than we would a draft of one of our own essays?

7. According to Murray, writers look for information, meaning, audience, form, structure, development, dimension, and voice in their drafts. What rationale or logic do you see, if any, in the way Murray has ordered these items? Are these the kinds of concerns you have when reading your drafts? Explain.

8. Murray notes that writers often reach a stage in their editing where they read aloud, "muttering or whispering to themselves, calling on the ear's experience with language" (23). What exactly do you think writers are listening for when

they read aloud? Try reading several paragraphs of Murray's essay aloud. Explain what you learned about his writing. Have you ever read your own writing aloud? If so, what did you discover?

LANGUAGE IN ACTION

Carefully read the opening four paragraphs of Annie Dillard's "Living Like Weasels," which is taken from *Teaching a Stone to Talk* (1982). Using two different color pens, first circle the subject and underline the verb in each main clause in one color, and then circle the subject and underline the verb in each subordinate clause with the other. What does this exercise reveal about Dillard's diction (nouns and verbs) and sentence structure? (Glossary: *Diction*)

A weasel is wild. Who knows what he thinks? He sleeps in his underground den, his tail draped over his nose. Sometimes he lives in his den for two days without leaving. Outside, he stalks rabbits, mice, muskrats, and birds, killing more bodies than he can eat warm, and often dragging the carcasses home. Obedient to instinct, he bites his prey at the neck, either splitting the jugular vein at the throat or crunching the brain at the base of the skull, and he does not let go. One naturalist refused to kill a weasel who was socketed into his hand deeply as a rattlesnake. The man could in no way pry the tiny weasel off, and he had to walk half a mile to water, the weasel dangling from his palm, and soak him off like a stubborn label.

And once, says Ernest Thompson Seton — once, a man shot an eagle out of the sky. He examined the eagle and found the dry skull of a weasel fixed by the jaws to his throat. The supposition is that the eagle had pounced on the weasel and the weasel swiveled and bit as instinct taught him, tooth to neck, and nearly won. I would like to have seen that eagle from the air a few weeks or months before he was shot: was the whole weasel still attached to his feathered throat, a fur pendant? Or did the eagle eat what he could reach, gutting the living weasel with his talons before his breast, bending his beak, cleaning the beautiful airborne bones?

I have been reading about weasels because I saw one last week. I startled a weasel who startled me, and we exchanged a long glance.

Twenty minutes from my house, through the woods by the quarry and across the highway, is Hollins Pond, a remarkable piece of shallowness, where I like to go at sunset and sit on a tree trunk. Hollins Pond is also called Murray's Pond; it covers two acres of bottomland near Tinker Creek with six inches of water and six thousand lily pads. In winter, brown-and-white steers stand in the middle of it, merely dampening their hooves; from the distant shore they look like miracle itself, complete with miracle's nonchalance. Now, in summer, the steers are gone. The water lilies have blossomed and spread to a green horizontal plane that is terra firma to plodding blackbirds, and tremulous ceiling to black leeches, crayfish, and carp.

WRITING SUGGESTIONS

1. Why do you suppose teachers report that revision is the most difficult stage in the writing process for their students? What is it about revision that makes it difficult, or at least makes people perceive it as being difficult? Write an essay in which you explore your own experiences with revision. You may find it helpful to review what you wrote for the Writing to Discover prompt at the beginning of this essay.

2. Writing about pressing social issues usually requires a clear statement of a particular problem and the precise definition of critical terms. For example, if you were writing about the increasing number of people being kept alive by machines, you would need to examine the debate surrounding the legal and medical definitions of the word *death*. Debates continue about the meanings of other controversial terms, such as *morality, minority* (ethnic), *alcoholism, racism, sexual harassment, life* (as in the abortion issue), *pornography, liberal, gay, censorship, conservative, remedial, insanity, literacy, political correctness, assisted suicide, lying, high crimes and misdemeanors,* and *kidnapping* (as in custody disputes). Select one of these words or one of your own. After carefully researching some of the controversial people, situations, and events surrounding your word, write an essay in which you discuss the problems associated with the term and its definition.

Simplicity

WILLIAM ZINSSER

William Zinsser died in May 2015, leaving a legacy of works from more than seventy years as a writer. Born in New York City in 1922, Zinsser was educated at Princeton University. After serving in the Army in World War II, he worked at the *New York Herald Tribune* as an editor, writer, and critic. During the 1970s he taught a popular course in nonfiction at Yale University, and from 1979 to 1987 he was general editor of the Book-of-the-Month Club. Zinsser wrote more than a dozen books, including *The City Dwellers* (1962), *Pop Goes America* (1966), and *Spring Training* (1989), and three widely used books on writing: *Writing with a Word Processor* 1983), *Writing to Learn* (1993), and *On Writing Well* (first published in 1976; the thirtieth anniversary edition was released in 2006). In his later years, he taught journalism at Columbia University and the New School University, and his freelance writing regularly appeared in some of the leading American magazines.

The following selection is taken from *On Writing Well*. This book grew out of Zinsser's many years of experience as a professional writer and teacher. In this essay, Zinsser exposes what he believes is the writer's number one problem—"clutter." He sees Americans "strangling in unnecessary words, circular constructions, pompous frills, and meaningless jargon." His solution is simple: Writers must know what they want to say and must be thinking clearly as they start to compose. Then self-discipline and hard work are necessary to achieve clear, simple prose. No matter what your experience as a writer has been, you will find Zinsser's observations sound and his advice practical.

WRITING TO DISCOVER: *Some people view writing as "thinking on paper." They believe that by seeing something written on a page they are better able to "see what they think." Write about the relationship, for you, between writing and thinking. Are you one of those people who likes to "see" ideas on paper while trying to work things out? Or do you like to think through ideas before writing about them?*

Clutter is the disease of American writing. We are a society strangling in unnecessary words, circular constructions, pompous frills and meaningless jargon.

Who can understand the clotted language of everyday American commerce: the memo, the corporation report, the business letter, the notice from the bank explaining its latest "simplified" statement? What member of an insurance or medical plan can decipher the brochure explaining his costs and benefits? What father or mother can put together a child's toy from the instructions on the box? Our national tendency is to inflate and

233

thereby sound important. The airline pilot who announces that he is presently anticipating experiencing considerable precipitation wouldn't think of saying it may rain. The sentence is too simple—there must be something wrong with it.

But the secret of good writing is to strip every sentence to its cleanest components. Every word that serves no function, every long word that could be a short word, every adverb that carries the same meaning that's already in the verb, every passive construction that leaves the reader unsure of who is doing what—these are the thousand and one adulterants that weaken the strength of a sentence. And they usually occur in proportion to education and rank.

During the 1960s the president of my university wrote a letter to mollify the alumni after a spell of campus unrest. "You are probably aware," he began, "that we have been experiencing very considerable potentially explosive expressions of dissatisfaction on issues only partially related." He meant that the students had been hassling them about different things. I was far more upset by the president's English than by the students' potentially explosive expressions of dissatisfaction. I would have preferred the presidential approach taken by Franklin D. Roosevelt when he tried to convert into English his own government's memos, such as this blackout order of 1942:

> **Clear thinking becomes clear writing; one can't exist without the other.**

> Such preparations shall be made as will completely obscure all Federal buildings and non-Federal buildings occupied by the Federal government during an air raid for any period of time from visibility by reason of internal or external illumination.

"Tell them," Roosevelt said, "that in buildings where they have to keep the work going to put something across the windows."   5

Simplify, simplify. Thoreau said it, as we are so often reminded, and no American writer more consistently practiced what he preached. Open *Walden* to any page and you will find a man saying in a plain and orderly way what is on his mind:

> I went to the woods because I wished to live deliberately, to front only the essential facts of life, and see if I could not learn what it had to teach, and not, when I came to die, discover that I had not lived.

How can the rest of us achieve such enviable freedom from clutter? The answer is to clear our heads of clutter. Clear thinking becomes clear writing; one can't exist without the other. It's impossible for a muddy thinker to write good English. He may get away with it for a paragraph or two, but soon the reader will be lost, and there's no sin so grave, for the reader will not easily be lured back.

Who is this elusive creature, the reader? The reader is someone with an attention span of about 30 seconds—a person assailed by many forces competing for attention. At one time those forces were relatively few: newspapers, magazines, radio, spouse, children, pets. Today they also include a galaxy of electronic devices for receiving entertainment and information—television, VCRs, DVDs, CDs, video games, the Internet, e-mail, cell phones, BlackBerries, iPods—as well as a fitness program, a pool, a lawn and that most potent of competitors, sleep. The man or woman snoozing in a chair with a magazine or a book is a person who was being given too much unnecessary trouble by the writer.

It won't do to say that the reader is too dumb or too lazy to keep pace with the train of thought. If the reader is lost, it's usually because the writer hasn't been careful enough. That carelessness can take any number of forms. Perhaps a sentence is so excessively cluttered that the reader, hacking through the verbiage, simply doesn't know what it means. Perhaps a sentence has been so shoddily constructed that the reader could read it in several ways. Perhaps the writer has switched pronouns in mid-sentence, or has switched tenses, so the reader loses track of who is talking or when the action took place. Perhaps Sentence B is not a logical sequel to Sentence A; the writer, in whose head the connection is clear, hasn't bothered to provide the missing link. Perhaps the writer has used a word incorrectly by not taking the trouble to look it up.

Faced with such obstacles, readers are at first tenacious. They blame themselves—they obviously missed something, and they go back over the mystifying sentence, or over the whole paragraph, piecing it out like an ancient rune, making guesses and moving on. But they won't do that for long. The writer is making them work too hard, and they will look for one who is better at the craft.   10

Writers must therefore constantly ask: what am I trying to say? Surprisingly often they don't know. Then they must look at what they have written and ask: have I said it? Is it clear to someone encountering the subject for the first time? If it's not, some fuzz has worked its way into the machinery. The clear writer is someone clearheaded enough to see this stuff for what it is: fuzz.

I don't mean that some people are born clearheaded and are therefore natural writers, whereas others are naturally fuzzy and will never write well. Thinking clearly is a conscious act that writers must force on themselves, as if they were working on any other project that requires logic: making a shopping list or doing an algebra problem. Good writing doesn't come naturally, though most people seem to think it does. Professional writers are constantly bearded by people who say they'd like to "try a little writing sometime"—meaning when they retire from their real profession, like insurance or real estate, which is hard. Or they say, "I could write a book about that." I doubt it.

Writing is hard work. A clear sentence is no accident. Very few sentences come out right the first time, or even the third time. Remember this in moments of despair. If you find that writing is hard, it's because it *is* hard.

THINKING CRITICALLY ABOUT THE READING

1. What exactly is clutter? When do words qualify as clutter, and when do they not?

2. In paragraph 2, Zinsser states that "Our national tendency is to inflate and thereby sound important." What do you think he means by *inflate*? Provide several examples to illustrate how people use language to inflate.

3. In paragraph 9, Zinsser lists some of the language-based obstacles that a reader may encounter in carelessly constructed prose. Which of these problems most tries your patience? Why?

4. One would hope that education would help in the battle against clutter, but, as Zinsser notes, wordiness "usually occur[s] in proportion to education and rank" (3). Do your own experiences or observations support Zinsser's claim? Discuss.

5. What assumptions does Zinsser make about readers? According to Zinsser, what responsibilities do writers have to readers? How do these responsibilities manifest themselves in Zinsser's writing?

6. Zinsser believes that writers need to ask themselves two questions—"What am I trying to say?" and "Have I said it?"—constantly as they write (11). How would these questions help you eliminate clutter from your own writing? Give some examples from one of your essays.

7. In order "to strip every sentence to its cleanest components," we need to be sensitive to the words we use and know how they function within our sentences. For each of the "adulterants that weaken the strength of a sentence," which Zinsser identifies in paragraph 3, provide an example from your own writing.

8. Zinsser knows that sentence variety is an important feature of good writing. Locate several examples of the short sentences (seven or fewer words) he uses in this essay, and explain how each relates in length, meaning, and impact to the sentences around it.

LANGUAGE IN ACTION

The following two pages show a passage from Zinsser's final manuscript for this essay as it was published in the first edition of *On Writing Well*. Carefully study the manuscript, and discuss how Zinsser eliminated clutter in his own prose. Then, using Zinsser as a model, judiciously eliminate the clutter from several paragraphs in one of your papers.

5 --

is too dumb or too lazy to keep pace with the ~~writer's~~ train
of thought. My sympathies are ~~entirely~~ with him. ~~) He's not
so dumb.~~ (If the reader is lost, it is generally because the
writer ~~of the article~~ has not been careful enough to keep
him on the ~~proper~~ path.

This carelessness can take any number of ~~different~~ forms.
Perhaps a sentence is so excessively ~~long and~~ cluttered that
the reader, hacking his way through ~~all~~ the verbiage, simply
doesn't know what it ~~the writer~~ means. Perhaps a sentence has
been so shoddily constructed that the reader could read it in
any of several ~~two or three different~~ ways. ~~He thinks he knows what
the writer is trying to say, but he's not sure.~~ Perhaps the
writer has switched pronouns in mid-sentence, or ~~perhaps he~~
has switched tenses, so the reader loses track of who is
talking ~~to whom~~ or ~~exactly~~ when the action took place. Perhaps Sentence B is not a logical sequel to Sentence A -- the
writer, in whose head the connection is ~~perfectly~~ clear, has
not bothered to provide ~~given enough thought to providing~~ the missing link. Perhaps the writer has used an important word incorrectly by not
taking the trouble to look it up ~~and make sure.~~ He may think
that "sanguine" and "sanguinary" mean the same thing, but)
~~I can assure you that~~ (the difference is a bloody big one ~~to the
reader.~~ The reader ~~He~~ can only ~~try to~~ infer ~~what~~ (speaking of big differences) what the writer is trying to imply.

Faced with these ~~such a variety of~~ obstacles, the reader
is at first a remarkably tenacious bird. He ~~tends to~~ blames
himself. ~~He~~ obviously missed something, ~~he thinks,~~ and he goes
back over the mystifying sentence, or over the whole paragraph,
piecing it out like an ancient rune, making guesses and moving
on. But he won't do this for long. ~~He will soon run out of
patience.~~ (The writer is making him work too hard ~~-- harder
than he should have to work --~~ (and the reader will look for
one ~~a writer~~ who is better at his craft.

6 --

The writer must therefore constantly ask himself: What am I trying to say? ~~in this sentence?~~ Surprisingly often, he doesn't know. ~~And~~ Then he must look at what he has ~~just~~ written and ask: Have I said it? Is it clear to someone ^encountering^ ~~who is coming upon~~ the subject for the first time? If it's not, ~~clear,~~ it is because some fuzz has worked its way into the machinery. The clear writer is a person ~~who is~~ clear-headed enough to see this stuff for what it is: fuzz.

I don't mean ~~to suggest~~ that some people are born clear-headed and are therefore natural writers, whereas ^others^ ~~other people~~ are naturally fuzzy and will ~~therefore~~ never write well. Thinking clearly is ^a^ ~~an entirely~~ conscious act that the writer must ^force^ ~~keep forcing~~ upon himself, just as if he were ^embarking^ ~~starting~~ out on any other ~~kind of~~ project that ^requires^ ~~calls for~~ logic: adding up a laundry list or doing an algebra problem ~~or playing chess.~~ Good writing doesn't ~~just~~ come naturally, though most people obviously think ^it does.^ ~~it's as easy as walking.~~ The professional

WRITING SUGGESTIONS

1. Each of the essays in Chapter 7, "Writers on Writing," is concerned with the importance of writing well, of using language effectively and responsibly. Write an essay in which you explore one of the common themes (audience, revision, diction, simplicity) that is emphasized in two or more of the selections.

2. Zinsser begins his essay with the following claim: "Clutter is the disease of American writing. We are a society strangling in unnecessary words, circular constructions, pompous frills and meaningless jargon." Write an essay supporting or refuting his claim. Most important, document his view, and yours, with examples drawn from contemporary nonfiction writing—essays, advertisements, academic writing, and other forms of public prose. Try to use examples that have been published recently.

On Not Writing

BILL HAYES

> Bill Hayes, born in 1961, is a frequent contributor to the *New York Times*, from which this article is reprinted. It was published as part of series called Draft, which covers art and writing. Hayes is a recipient of a Guggenheim Fellowship in nonfiction. He has been a Visiting Scholar at the American Academy in Rome, the recipient of a Leon Levy Foundation grant, and a resident writer at Blue Mountain Center. He combines his interest in writing with an interest in photography. His published works include *Sleep Demons: An Insomniac's Memoirs* (2002), *Five Quarts: A Personal and Natural History of Blood* (2006), and *The Anatomist: A True Story of Gray's Anatomy* (2009). One critic said his most recent nonfiction book had "the flavor and pace of a novel," and another critic noted that Hayes "pays eloquent tribute to two masterpieces: the human body and the book detailing it."
>
> In this article, which was published on August 23, 2014, Hayes writes that he needed to take a break from writing. He speaks of his hiatus from writing not as a permanent departure, but merely as a rest in which to recharge his energies. But there is a danger—after all, how long can one not write and still consider oneself a writer? Hayes examines this problem from the perspective of an accomplished professional writer; however, it's not hard to apply his lesson to almost any other creative impulse one might have, either on an amateur or a professional level.

WRITING TO DISCOVER: *Have you ever experienced writer's block, in which you cannot write even though you know you should (or you need to!)? What techniques did you use to overcome that block?*

I started writing this essay five years ago, and then I stopped. That I was not able to finish the piece did not strike me at the time as ironic but as further proof that whatever I once had in me—juice, talent, will—was gone. In any case, completing it would have made moot the very point I was attempting to make: Not writing can be good for one's writing; indeed, it can make one a better writer.

I hadn't given up writing deliberately, and I cannot pinpoint a particular day when my not-writing period started, any more than one can say the moment when one is overtaken by sleep: It's only after you wake that you realize how long you were out. Nor did I feel blocked at first. Lines would come to me then slip away, like a dog that loses interest in how you are petting it and seeks another hand. This goes both ways. When I lost interest in them, the lines gradually stopped coming. Before I knew it, two years had passed with scarcely a word.

I didn't miss it, yet at the same time I felt something missing: A phantom voice, one might say. I had been pursuing writing since I was a kid, had published pieces in many places, and written three books back to back. I was nearing 50. To have silence and neither deadlines nor expectations for the first time in decades was sort of nice—and sort of troubling. Can one call oneself a writer when not-writing is what one actually does, day after day after day?

Fitness training today is generally built upon six major concepts ... and each of these, I found, has a correlative in writing.

I never lied. If someone asked, I'd say I was not working on anything, and no, had nothing on the back burner, in the oven, cooking, percolating or marinating. (What's with all the food metaphors anyway?) I wasn't hungry either.

At a party one night, a very artistic looking young man with an Errol Flynn mustache warned me that I must not take a break for too long. "It won't come back," he said gravely. "I stopped writing in 1999, and now I can barely write a press release."

I can't say this didn't scare me a bit. What if I really never wrote or published again?

I wouldn't be in bad company, I told myself. After "Joe Gould's Secret," Joseph Mitchell published nothing new in his remaining 31 years. E.M. Forster published no more novels between "A Passage to India" and his death 46 years later. And then there were those hall of fame figures: J.D. Salinger, who published nothing for the last half of his life, and Harper Lee, whose post-Mockingbird silence should be enough to canonize her, the patron saint of not-artists of any discipline.

But let's be real: I'm not them, and not-writing is not a way to support oneself. So I got a job (not writing-related), then moved to a new city, found another job, this time in fund-raising for a nonprofit organization, and eventually enrolled in a course to become a certified personal fitness trainer. Classes were held in the basement of a gym. I did it for fun, and more pragmatically, as a Plan B, a way to support myself if I got laid off (a real possibility). But it was there, unexpectedly, that I found my way back to writing full time, a framework for moving forward and validation for what I had done instinctively.

Fitness training today is generally built upon six major concepts (though they may go by different terms, depending upon the certifying agency), and each of these, I found, has a correlative in writing.

First, there is the Principle of Specificity. This states that what you train for is what you get: If it is strength you want, train for strength. In short, be specific. Writing 101, right? It's all in the details.

Next: The Overload Principle, training a part of the body above the level to which it is accustomed. You must provide constant stimuli so the body never gets used to a given task; otherwise, expect no change. So too

5

10

with writing: Push yourself, try new things—creative cross-training, I call it.

This leads to the Principle of Progression. Once you master new tasks, move on. Don't get stuck—whether on a paragraph or an exercise regimen. If you do, this will lead to Accommodation. With no new demands placed upon it, the body reaches homeostasis—not a good place to find oneself. Here, everything flattens out. So, don't get too comfortable; it will show on the page as clearly as in the mirror.

When stimuli are removed, gains are reversed—use it or lose it, the Principle of Reversibility. Just as movement in any form is better than none at all—walk around the block if you can't make it to Spin class—one must do something, anything, to keep the creative motor running. After I stopped writing, for instance, I bought a camera and started taking photographs instead.

And finally, the Rest Principle, the tenet that gave me particular solace. To make fitness gains, whether in strength, speed, stamina or whatever your aim (see Principle of Specificity), you must take ample time to recover.

I had been working out as long as I had been writing, so this last principle was not new to me. Overtraining without taking days off can lead to injuries, chronic fatigue and, frankly, pain. But I had never observed this rule very strictly when it came to working on a piece of writing. Just as the body needs time to rest, so too does an essay, story, chapter, poem, book or a single page.

In some cases, it is not just the writing that needs a breather but the writer, too. On this matter, I quote from a National Council on Strength and Fitness training manual, one of the textbooks we used in our personal training course. Here, fatigue is defined as "an inability to contract despite continued neural stimulation" (what a bodybuilder might call a failure to flex, you and I might call writer's block, in other words).

"As the rate of motor unit fatigue increases," the manual goes on, "the effect becomes more pronounced, causing performance to decline proportionately to the level of fatigue. Periods of recovery enable a working tissue to avoid fatigue for longer periods of time. . . . During the recovery period, the muscle fibers can rebuild their energy reserves, fix any damage resulting from the production of force, and fully return to normal pre-exertion levels."

Translation: Don't work through the pain; it will only hurt. Give yourself sufficient time to refresh.

How long should this period be? What is true for muscle fibers is true for creative ones as well. My rule of thumb in fitness training is 2-to-1: For every two days of intense workouts, a day off. However, "in cases of sustained high-level output," according to my manual, full recovery may take longer. This is what had happened with me. I needed a really, really long rest.

Then I woke one day, and a line came to me. It didn't slip away this   20
time but stayed put. I followed it, like a path. It led to another, then
another. Soon, pieces started lining up in my head, like cabs idling curb-
side, ready to go where I wanted to take them. But it wasn't so much that
pages started getting written that made me realize that my not-writing
period had come to an end. Instead, my perspective had shifted.

Writing is not measured in page counts, I now believe, any more than
a writer is defined by publication credits. To be a writer is to make a commitment to the long haul, as one does (especially as one gets older) to
keeping fit and healthy for as long a run as possible. For me, this means
staying active physically and creatively, switching it up, remaining curious and interested in learning new skills (upon finishing this piece, for
instance, I'm going on my final open-water dive to become a certified
scuba diver), and of course giving myself ample periods of rest, days or
even weeks off. I know that the writer in me, like the lifelong fitness devo-
tee, will be better off.

THINKING CRITICALLY ABOUT THE READING

1. In paragraph 1, Hayes states, "Not writing can be good for one's writing;
   indeed, it can make one a better writer." He also mentions a number of well-
   known writers who did not write for years, even decades, after some of their
   best work. In your opinion, do these observations sound like an evasion or a
   rationalization, or do they ring true? Why or why not? What is the point of
   such references and observations?

2. Hayes writes from the perspective of a man with several career and job choices
   available to him, which allow him to take an extended break from writing if
   he needs one. How do you think his advice might apply to someone, like a
   journalist or a student, for whom taking a break is not necessarily an option
   without jeopardizing a career or a semester's grades? What advice do you
   think Hayes would have for a writer in that position?

3. Hayes uses an analogy to describe his experiences: comparing physical fitness
   training with writing. In your opinion, does this analogy work? Are there
   problems with the analogy that Hayes overlooks or avoids? Explain.

4. Hayes says, "Then I woke one day, and a line came to me" (20). What about
   this comment seems almost mystical—a miracle that seems to have come out
   of nowhere? Where do you think Hayes finds the trust that eventually—perhaps after years—he creative impulse will return?

5. Hayes concludes his article with the comment that he intends to become a
   certified scuba diver. In your opinion, how much is diversity of experience an
   important element in creativity? What kinds of experiences seem most fruitful
   for a writer?

LANGUAGE IN ACTION

In his essay, Bill Hayes mentions the Principle of Specificity: "This states that what you train for is what you get: If it is strength you want, train for strength. In short, be specific. Writing 101, right? It's all in the details (10)."

As a student in a writing or language course, you, too, are training for something. Look at the syllabus for your course, or the course or department Web site, and find the language that indicates what it is, specifically, that you're training for. That is, look at the outcomes of the course, but look also at the kinds of work you're doing daily and weekly. What "muscles" are you building as a writer and a student? What does the course set out to help you improve, and what do you feel you most need to work on yourself? How can you keep up that kind of writing fitness once the course is over?

WRITING SUGGESTIONS

1. Hayes uses the six components of physical fitness training to create an analogy with the writing process. Write an essay in which you use another set of components—the steps of administering CPR, for instance, or even the steps involved in tying a shoelace—to illustrate the writing process. Be certain to address specifically each of the different components.

2. Hayes is an accomplished writer, but he is also an accomplished photographer. In what ways does having a creative mind move across limits of form, such as art, writing, dance, photography, music, fashion, and so on? Write an essay in which you discuss the ability of the creative mind to work in different ways. Why do you think such mental and creative "cross-training" might be useful? Can you see any disadvantages to working across different forms or disciplines? In what ways might similar boundary-crossing work to the advantage of those in other fields—say, medicine or engineering?

8

LANGUAGE THAT MANIPULATES: POLITICS, PROPAGANDA, AND DOUBLESPEAK

Political language can be deliberately manipulated to mislead, deceive, or cover up. In the wake of the war in Vietnam, the Watergate scandal and subsequent resignation of President Nixon, the Iran-Contra affair, the Clinton-Lewinsky scandal, and the wars in Iraq and Afghanistan, Americans have grown cynical about their political leaders' promises and programs. As presidential campaigns seem to get started earlier and earlier, we are fed a daily diet of political language. Political speech saturates print and electronic media, in an ever-shorter news cycle (and perhaps the disappearance of a news cycle altogether). Fiery sound bites and seemingly spontaneous one-liners are presented as though they contained an entire argument or philosophy. Our politicians are savvy about the time constraints in news media, and their speechwriters make sure that long speeches have at least a few headline-grabbing quotes that might win them wide, albeit brief, coverage. But in the end, we are left wondering what we can believe and who we can trust among our politicians if they don't uphold the promises they make.

In "Language That Manipulates: Politics, Propaganda, and Doublespeak," we present six essays to help you think critically about the political language that you hear every day so that you can function as a responsible citizen. In the first essay, "Propaganda: How Not to Be Bamboozled," Donna Woolfolk Cross takes the mystery out of the oft-misunderstood word *propaganda* as she identifies and defines thirteen of the rhetorical devices the propagandist uses to manipulate language for political purposes. Her examples and advice, in turn, will help you to detect those nasty "tricks" and not to be misled by the silver tongues of politicians. In "Selection, Slanting, and Charged Language," Newman and Genevieve Birk give us a crash course on how the language people use subtly shapes perceptions. They introduce us to three simple but powerful concepts— selecting, slanting, and charging—that when understood, will change forever the way we view political speech. Maria Konnikova reflects on the cathartic role played by unsent correspondence and speculates on how this may be changing in our digital age. She argues that, although we have more avenues to vent displeasure, we may find ourselves less satisfied by a hastily posted tweet than a letter stuck in a drawer to gather dust. In "The World of Doublespeak," political watchdog and language expert William Lutz examines the language of the government and corporate bureaucrat, "language which pretends to communicate but doesn't." His examples illustrate how language can be used deliberately to "mislead, distort, deceive, inflate, circumvent, obfuscate." In "Language That Silences," Jason Stanley brings the idea of silencing into view. He argues that one of the most insidious and harmful types of propaganda is that which makes counterarguments difficult or impossible to mount. When debate is stifled and trust lost, we are all rendered helpless and faith in our institutions is lost. Finally, in "Assassination and the American Language," Elliot Ackerman explores the implications of U.S. Executive Order 12333, which forbids assassination, in the context of U.S. military operations in Afghanistan and drone warfare more broadly. He points out how U.S. wars violate this order, and argues that when we avoid the word "assassination," Americans are fooling only themselves.

Propaganda: How Not to Be Bamboozled

Donna Woolfolk Cross

Donna Woolfolk Cross graduated from the University of Pennsylvania in 1969 and went on to receive her M.A. from the University of California, Los Angeles. A former professor of English at Onondaga Community College in Syracuse, New York, Cross has written extensively about language that manipulates, including the books *Mediaspeak: How Television Makes Up Your Mind* (1981) and *Word Abuse: How the Words We Use Use Us* (1979), which won an award from the National Council of Teachers of English. More recently she wrote *Pope Joan: A Novel* (2009). Her early work as a writer of advertising copy influences her teaching and writing. In an interview she remarked, "I was horrified to discover that first-year college students were completely unaware of—and, therefore, unable to defend themselves against—the most obvious ploys of admen and politicians. . . . We tend to think of language as something we use; we are much less often aware of the way we are used by language. The only defense is to become wise to the ways of words."

Although most people are against propaganda in principle, few know exactly what it is and how it works. In the following essay, which first appeared in *Speaking of Words: A Language Reader* (1977), Cross takes the mystery out of propaganda. She starts by providing a definition of it, and then she classifies the tricks of the propagandist into thirteen major categories. Cross's essay is chock-full of useful advice on how not to be manipulated by propaganda.

WRITING TO DISCOVER: *What do you think of when you hear the word propaganda? What kinds of people, organizations, or issues do you associate with it? Write about why you think people use propaganda.*

Propaganda. If an opinion poll were taken tomorrow, we can be sure that nearly everyone would be against it because it *sounds* so bad. When we say, "Oh, that's just propaganda," it means, to most people, "That's a pack of lies." But really, propaganda is simply a means of persuasion and so it can be put to work for good causes as well as bad—to persuade people to give to charity, for example, or to love their neighbors, or to stop polluting the environment.

For good or evil, propaganda pervades our daily lives, helping to shape our attitudes on a thousand subjects. Propaganda probably determines the brand of toothpaste you use, the movies you see, the candidates you elect when you get to the polls. Propaganda works by tricking us, by momentarily distracting the eye while the rabbit pops out from beneath the cloth. Propaganda works best with an uncritical audience. Joseph Goebbels, propaganda minister in Nazi Germany, once defined his work as "the conquest of the masses." The masses would not have been conquered, however, if they had known how to challenge and to question, how to make distinctions between propaganda and reasonable argument.

People are bamboozled mainly because they don't recognize propaganda when they see it. They need to be informed about the various devices that can be used to mislead and deceive—about the propagandist's overflowing bag of tricks. The following, then, are some common pitfalls for the unwary.

I. NAME-CALLING

As its title suggests, this device consists of labeling people or ideas with words of bad connotation, literally, "calling them names." Here the propagandist tries to arouse our contempt so we will dismiss the "bad name" person or idea without examining its merits.

Bad names have played a tremendously important role in the history of the world. They have ruined reputations and ended lives, sent people to prison and to war, and just generally made us mad at each other for centuries.

Name-calling can be used against policies, practices, beliefs and ideals, as well as against individuals, groups, races, nations. Name-calling is at work when we hear a candidate for office described as a "foolish idealist" or a "two-faced liar" or when an incumbent's policies are denounced as "reckless," "reactionary," or just plain "stupid." Some of the most effective names a public figure can be called are ones that may not denote anything specific: "Congresswoman Jane Doe is a *bleeding heart!*" (Did she vote for funds to help paraplegics?) or "The senator is a *tool of Washington!*" (Did he happen to agree with the president?) Senator Yakalot uses name-calling when he denounces his opponent's "radical policies" and calls them (and him) "socialist," "pinko," and part of a "heartless plot." He also uses it when he calls cars "puddle-jumpers," "can openers," and "motorized baby buggies."

For good or evil, propaganda pervades our daily lives, helping to shape our attitudes on a thousand subjects.

The point here is that when the propagandist uses name-calling, he doesn't want us to think—merely to react, blindly, unquestioningly. So the best defense against being taken in by name-calling is to stop and ask, "Forgetting the bad name attached to it, what are the merits of the idea itself? What does this name really mean, anyway?"

2. GLITTERING GENERALITIES

Glittering generalities are really name-calling in reverse. Name-calling uses words with bad connotations; glittering generalities are words with good connotations—"virtue words," as the Institute for Propaganda

Analysis has called them. The Institute explains that while name-calling tries to get us to *reject* and *condemn* someone or something without examining the evidence, glittering generalities try to get us to *accept* and *agree* without examining the evidence.

We believe in, fight for, live by "virtue words" which we feel deeply about: "justice," "motherhood," "the American way," "our Constitutional rights," "our Christian heritage." These sound good, but when we examine them closely, they turn out to have no specific, definable meaning. They just make us feel good. Senator Yakalot uses glittering generalities when he says, "I stand for all that is good in America, for our American way and our American birthright." But what exactly *is* "good for America"? How can we define our "American birthright"? Just what parts of the American society and culture does "our American way" refer to?

We often make the mistake of assuming we are personally unaffected by   10 glittering generalities. The next time you find yourself assuming that, listen to a political candidate's speech on TV and see how often the use of glittering generalities elicits cheers and applause. That's the danger of propaganda; it *works*. Once again, our defense against it is to ask questions: Forgetting the virtue words attached to it, what are the merits of the idea itself? What does "Americanism" (or "freedom" or "truth") really *mean* here? . . .

Both name-calling and glittering generalities work by stirring our emotions in the hope that this will cloud our thinking. Another approach that propaganda uses is to create a distraction, a "red herring," that will make people forget or ignore the real issues. There are several different kinds of "red herrings" that can be used to distract attention.

3. PLAIN-FOLKS APPEAL

"Plain folks" is the device by which a speaker tries to win our confidence and support by appearing to be a person like ourselves—"just one of the plain folks." The plain-folks appeal is at work when candidates go around shaking hands with factory workers, kissing babies in supermarkets, and sampling pasta with Italians, fried chicken with Southerners, bagels and blintzes with Jews. "Now I'm a businessman like yourselves" is a plain-folks appeal, as is "I've been a farm boy all my life." Senator Yakalot tries the plain-folks appeal when he says, "I'm just a small-town boy like you fine people." The use of such expressions once prompted Lyndon Johnson to quip, "Whenever I hear someone say, 'I'm just an old country lawyer,' the first thing I reach for is my wallet to make sure it's still there."

The irrelevancy of the plain-folks appeal is obvious: even if the man *is* "one of us" (which may not be true at all), that doesn't mean that his ideas and programs are sound—or even that he honestly has our best interests at heart. As with glittering generalities, the danger here is that we may mistakenly assume we are immune to this appeal. But propagandists wouldn't use it unless it had been proved to work. You can protect yourself by asking, "Aside from his 'nice guy next door' image, what does this man stand for? Are his ideas and his past record really supportive of my best interests?"

4. ARGUMENTUM AD POPULUM (STROKING)

Argumentum ad populum means "argument to the people" or "telling the people what they want to hear." The colloquial term from the Watergate era is "stroking," which conjures up pictures of small animals or children being stroked or soothed with compliments until they come to like the person doing the complimenting—and, by extension, his or her ideas.

We all like to hear nice things about ourselves and the group we   15
belong to—we like to be liked—so it stands to reason that we will respond warmly to a person who tells us we are "hard-working taxpayers" or "the most generous, free-spirited nation in the world." Politicians tell farmers they are the "backbone of the American economy" and college students that they are the "leaders and policy makers of tomorrow." Commercial advertisers use stroking more insidiously by asking a question which invites a flattering answer: "What kind of a man reads *Playboy?*" (Does he really drive a Porsche and own $10,000 worth of sound equipment?) Senator Yakalot is stroking his audience when he calls them the "decent law-abiding citizens that are the great pulsing heart and the life blood of this, our beloved country," and when he repeatedly refers to them as "you fine people," "you wonderful folks."

Obviously, the intent here is to sidetrack us from thinking critically about the man and his ideas. Our own good qualities have nothing to do with the issue at hand. Ask yourself, "Apart from the nice things he has to say about me (and my church, my nation, my ethnic group, my neighbors), what does the candidate stand for? Are his or her ideas in my best interests?"

5. ARGUMENTUM AD HOMINEM

Argumentum ad hominem means "argument to the man" and that's exactly what it is. When a propagandist uses *argumentum ad hominem*, he wants to distract our attention from the issue under consideration with personal attacks on the people involved. For example, when Lincoln issued the Emancipation Proclamation, some people responded by calling him the "baboon." But Lincoln's long arms and awkward carriage had nothing to do with the merits of the Proclamation or the question of whether or not slavery should be abolished.

Today *argumentum ad hominem* is still widely used and very effective. You may or may not support the Equal Rights Amendment, but you should be sure your judgment is based on the merits of the idea itself, and not the result of someone's denunciation of the people who support the ERA as "fanatics" or "lesbians" or "frustrated old maids." Senator Yakalot is using *argumentum ad hominem* when he dismisses the idea of using smaller automobiles with a reference to the personal appearance of one of its supporters, Congresswoman Doris Schlepp. Refuse to be waylaid by *argumentum ad hominem* and ask, "Do the personal qualities of the person being discussed have anything to do with the issue at hand? Leaving him or her aside, how good is the idea itself?"

6. TRANSFER (GUILT OR GLORY BY ASSOCIATION)

In *argumentum ad hominem,* an attempt is made to associate negative aspects of a person's character or personal appearance with an issue or idea he supports. The transfer device uses this same process of association to make us accept or condemn a given person or idea.

A better name for the transfer device is guilt (or glory) by association.   20
In glory by association, the propagandist tries to transfer the positive feelings of something we love and respect to the group or idea he wants us to accept. "This bill for a new dam is in the best tradition of this country, the land of Lincoln, Jefferson, and Washington," is glory by association at work. Lincoln, Jefferson, and Washington were great leaders that most of us revere and respect, but they have no logical connection to the proposal under consideration—the bill to build a new dam. Senator Yakalot uses glory by association when he says full-sized cars "have always been as American as Mom's apple pie or a Sunday drive in the country."

The process works equally well in reverse, when guilt by association is used to transfer our dislike or disapproval of one idea or group to some other idea or group that the propagandist wants us to reject and condemn. "John Doe says we need to make some changes in the way our government operates; well, that's exactly what the Ku Klux Klan has said, so there's a meeting of great minds!" That's guilt by association for you; there's no logical connection between John Doe and the Ku Klux Klan apart from the one the propagandist is trying to create in our minds. He wants to distract our attention from John Doe and get us thinking (and worrying) about the Ku Klux Klan and its politics of violence. (Of course, there are sometimes legitimate associations between the two things; if John Doe had been a *member* of the Ku Klux Klan, it would be reasonable and fair to draw a connection between the man and his group.) Senator Yakalot tries to trick his audience with guilt by association when he remarks that "the words 'community' and 'communism' look an awful lot alike!" He does it again when he mentions that Mr. Stu Pott "sports a Fidel Castro beard."

How can we learn to spot the transfer device and distinguish between fair and unfair associations? We can teach ourselves to *suspend judgment* until we have answered these questions: "Is there any legitimate connection between the idea under discussion and the thing it is associated with? Leaving the transfer device out of the picture, what are the merits of the idea by itself?"

7. BANDWAGON

Ever hear of the small, ratlike animal called the lemming? Lemmings are arctic rodents with a very odd habit: periodically, for reasons no one entirely knows, they mass together in a large herd and commit suicide by rushing into deep water and drowning themselves. They all run in together, blindly, and not one of them ever seems to stop and ask, "*Why am I doing this? Is this really what I want to do?*" and thus save itself from destruction. Obviously, lemmings are driven to perform their strange mass suicide rites by common instinct. People choose to "follow the herd" for more complex reasons, yet we are still all too often the unwitting victims of the bandwagon appeal.

Essentially, the bandwagon urges us to support an action or an opinion because it is popular—because "everyone else is doing it." This call to "get on the bandwagon" appeals to the strong desire in most of us to be one of the crowd, not to be left out or alone. Advertising makes extensive use of the bandwagon appeal ("join the Pepsi people"), but so do politicians ("Let us join together in this great cause"). Senator Yakalot uses the bandwagon appeal when he says that "More and more citizens are rallying to my cause every day," and asks his audience to "join them—and me—in our fight for America."

One of the ways we can see the bandwagon appeal at work is in the over-   25
whelming success of various fashions and trends which capture the interest (and the money) of thousands of people for a short time, then disappear suddenly and completely. For a year or two in the fifties, every child in North America wanted a coonskin cap so they could be like Davy Crockett; no one wanted to be left out. After that there was the hula-hoop craze that helped to dislocate the hips of thousands of Americans. [In the 1970s], what made millions of people rush out to buy their very own "pet rocks"?

The problem here is obvious: just because everyone's doing it doesn't mean that *we* should too. Group approval does not prove that something is true or is worth doing. Large numbers of people have supported actions we now condemn. [Within the last century], Hitler and Mussolini rose to absolute and catastrophically repressive rule in two of the most sophisticated and cultured countries of Europe. When they came into power they were welled up by massive popular support from millions of people who didn't want to be "left out" at a great historical moment.

Once the mass begins to move—on the bandwagon—it becomes harder and harder to perceive the leader *riding* the bandwagon. So don't be a lemming, rushing blindly on to destruction because "everyone else is doing it." Stop and ask, "Where is this bandwagon headed? Never mind about everybody else, is this what is best for *me*?" . . .

As we have seen, propaganda can appeal to us by arousing our emotions or distracting our attention from the real issues at hand. But there's a third way that propaganda can be put to work against us—by the use of faulty logic. This approach is really more insidious than the others because it gives the appearance of reasonable, fair argument. It is only when we look more closely that the holes in the logical fiber show up. The following are some of the devices that make use of faulty logic to distort and mislead.

8. FAULTY CAUSE AND EFFECT

As the name suggests, this device sets up a cause-and-effect relationship that may not be true. The Latin name for this logical fallacy is *post hoc ergo propter hoc,* which means "after this, therefore because of this." But just because one thing happened after another doesn't mean that one *caused* the other.

An example of false cause-and-effect reasoning is offered by the story 30 (probably invented) of the woman aboard the ship *Titanic*. She woke up from a nap and, feeling seasick, looked around for a call button to summon the steward to bring her some medication. She finally located a small button on one of the walls of her cabin and pushed it. A split second later, the *Titanic* grazed an iceberg in the terrible crash that was to send the entire ship to its destruction. The woman screamed and said, "Oh, God, what have I done? What have I done?" The humor of that anecdote comes from the absurdity of the woman's assumption that pushing the small red button resulted in the destruction of a ship weighing several hundred tons: "It happened after I pushed it, therefore it must be *because* I pushed it"—*post hoc ergo propter hoc* reasoning. There is, of course, no cause-and-effect relationship there.

The false cause-and-effect fallacy is used very often by political candidates. "After I came to office, the rate of inflation dropped to 6 percent." But did the person do anything to cause the lower rate of inflation or was it the result of other conditions? Would the rate of inflation have dropped anyway, even if he hadn't come to office? Senator Yakalot uses false cause and effect when he says "our forefathers who made this country great never had free hot meal handouts! And look what they did for our country!" He does it again when he concludes that "driving full-sized cars means a better car safety record on our American roads today."

False cause-and-effect reasoning is terribly persuasive because it seems so logical. Its appeal is apparently to experience. We swallowed X product—and the headache went away. We elected Y official and unemployment went down. Many people think, "There *must* be a connection." But causality is an immensely complex phenomenon; you need a good deal of evidence to prove that an event that follows another in time was "therefore" caused by the first event.

Don't be taken in by false cause and effect; be sure to ask, "Is there enough evidence to prove that this cause led to that effect? Could there have been any *other* causes?"

9. FALSE ANALOGY

An analogy is a comparison between two ideas, events, or things. But comparisons can be fairly made only when the things being compared are alike in significant ways. When they are not, false analogy is the result.

A famous example of this is the old proverb "Don't change horses in the middle of a stream," often used as an analogy to convince voters not to change administrations in the middle of a war or other crisis. But the analogy is misleading because there are so many differences between the things compared. In what ways is a war or political crisis like a stream? Is the president or head of state really very much like a horse? And is a nation of millions of people comparable to a man trying to get across a stream? Analogy is false and unfair when it compares two things that have little in common and assumes that they are identical. Senator Yakalot tries to hoodwink his listeners with false analogy when he says, "Trying to take Americans out of the kind of cars they love is as undemocratic as trying to deprive them of the right to vote."

Of course, analogies can be drawn that are reasonable and fair. It would be reasonable, for example, to compare the results of busing in one small Southern city with the possible results in another, *if* the towns have the same kind of history, population, and school policy. We can decide for ourselves whether an analogy is false or fair by asking, "Are the things being compared truly alike in significant ways? Do the differences between them affect the comparison?"

10. BEGGING THE QUESTION

Actually, the name of this device is rather misleading, because it does not appear in the form of a question. Begging the question occurs when, in discussing a questionable or debatable point, a person assumes as already established the very point that he is trying to prove. For example, "No thinking citizen could approve such a completely unacceptable policy as this one." But isn't the question of whether or not the policy *is* acceptable the very point to be established? Senator Yakalot begs the question when he announces that his opponent's plan won't work "because it is unworkable."

35

We can protect ourselves against this kind of faulty logic by asking, "What is assumed in this statement? Is the assumption reasonable, or does it need more proof?"

11. THE TWO-EXTREMES FALLACY (FALSE DILEMMA)

Linguists have long noted that the English language tends to view reality in sets of two extremes or polar opposites. In English, things are either black or white, tall or short, up or down, front or back, left or right, good or bad, guilty or not guilty. We can ask for a "straightforward yes-or-no answer" to a question, the understanding being that we will not accept or consider anything in between. In fact, reality cannot always be dissected along such strict lines. There may be (usually are) *more* than just two possibilities or extremes to consider. We are often told to "listen to both sides of the argument." But who's to say that every argument has only two sides? Can't there be a third—even a fourth or fifth—point of view?

The two-extremes fallacy is at work in this statement by Lenin, the   40 great Marxist leader: "You cannot eliminate *one* basic assumption, one substantial part of this philosophy of Marxism (it is as if it were a block of steel), without abandoning truth, without falling into the arms of bourgeois-reactionary falsehood." In other words, if we don't agree 100 percent with every premise of Marxism, we must be placed at the opposite end of the political-economic spectrum—for Lenin, "bourgeois-reactionary falsehood." If we are not entirely *with* him, we must be against him; those are the only two possibilities open to us. Of course, this is a logical fallacy; in real life there are any number of political positions one can maintain *between* the two extremes of Marxism and capitalism. Senator Yakalot uses the two-extremes fallacy in the same way as Lenin when he tells his audience that "in this world a man's either for private enterprise or he's for socialism."

One of the most famous examples of the two-extremes fallacy in recent history is the slogan, "America: Love it or leave it," with its implicit suggestion that we either accept everything just as it is in America today without complaint—or get out. Again, it should be obvious that there is a whole range of action and belief between those two extremes.

Don't be duped; stop and ask, "Are those really the only two options I can choose from? Are there other alternatives not mentioned that deserve consideration?"

12. CARD STACKING

Some questions are so multifaceted and complex that no one can make an intelligent decision about them without considering a wide variety of evidence. One selection of facts could make us feel one way and another selection could make us feel just the opposite. Card stacking is a device of propaganda which selects only the facts that support the propagandist's point of view, and ignores all the others. For example, a candidate could be made to look like a legislative dynamo if you say, "Representative McNerd introduced more new bills than any other member of the Congress," and neglect to mention that most of them were so preposterous that they were laughed off the floor.

Senator Yakalot engages in card stacking when he talks about the proposal to use smaller cars. He talks only about jobs without mentioning the cost to the taxpayers or the very real—though still denied—threat of depletion of resources. He says he wants to help his countrymen keep their jobs, but doesn't mention that the corporations that offer the jobs will also make large profits. He praises the "American chrome industry," overlooking the fact that most chrome is imported. And so on.

The best protection against card stacking is to take the "Yes, but . . ."   45
attitude. This device of propaganda is not untrue, but then again it is not the *whole* truth. So ask yourself, "Is this person leaving something out that I should know about? Is there some other information that should be brought to bear on this question?" . . .

So far, we have considered approaches that the propagandist can use to influence our thinking: appealing to our emotions, distracting our attention, and misleading us with logic that may appear to be reasonable but is in fact faulty and deceiving. But there is another approach that is probably the most common propaganda trick of them all.

13. TESTIMONIAL

The testimonial device consists in having some loved or respected person give a statement of support (testimonial) for a given product or idea. The problem is that the person being quoted may *not* be an expert in the field; in fact, he may know nothing at all about it. Using the name of a man who is skilled and famous in one field to give a testimonial for something in another field is unfair and unreasonable.

Senator Yakalot tries to mislead his audience with testimonial when he tells them that "full-sized cars have been praised by great Americans like John Wayne and Jack Jones, as well as by leading experts on car safety and comfort."

Testimonial is used extensively in TV ads, where it often appears in such bizarre forms as Joe Namath's endorsement of a pantyhose brand. Here, of course, the "authority" giving the testimonial not only is no expert about pantyhose, but obviously stands to gain something (money!) by making the testimonial.

When celebrities endorse a political candidate, they may not be mak-   50
ing money by doing so, but we should still question whether they are in
any better position to judge than we ourselves. Too often we are willing
to let others we like or respect make our decisions *for us,* while we follow
along acquiescently. And this is the purpose of testimonial—to get us to
agree and accept *without* stopping to think. Be sure to ask, "Is there any
reason to believe that this person (or organization or publication or whatever) has any more knowledge or information than I do on this subject?
What does the idea amount to on its own merits, without the benefit of
testimonial?"

The cornerstone of democratic society is reliance upon an informed
and educated electorate. To be fully effective citizens we need to be able
to challenge and to question wisely. A dangerous feeling of indifference
toward our political processes exists today. We often abandon our right, our
duty, to criticize and evaluate by dismissing *all* politicians as "crooked,"
all new bills and proposals as "just more government bureaucracy." But
there are important distinctions to be made, and this kind of apathy can
be fatal to democracy.

If we are to be led, let us not be led blindly, but critically, intelligently,
with our eyes open. If we are to continue to be a government "by the
people," let us become informed about the methods and purposes of propaganda, so we can be the masters, not the slaves of our destiny.

THINKING CRITICALLY ABOUT THE READING

1. According to Cross, what is propaganda? Who uses propaganda? Why is it
   used? (Glossary: *Propaganda*)

2. Why does Cross believe that it is necessary for people in a democratic society
   to become informed about the methods and practices of propaganda? What is
   her advice for dealing with propaganda?

3. What is a "red herring," and why do people use this technique? What is "begging the question"? (Glossary: *Logical Fallacies*)

4. What, according to Cross, is the most common propaganda trick? Provide
   some examples of it from your own experience.

5. How does Cross use examples in her essay? (Glossary: *Examples*) What do
   you think of the examples from Senator Yakalot? What, if anything, does this
   hypothetical senator add to the essay? Which other examples do you find most
   effective? Least effective? Explain why.

6. In her discussion of the bandwagon appeal (23–28), Cross uses the analogy
   of the lemmings. How does the analogy work? Why is it not a false analogy?
   (Glossary: *Analogy*) How do analogies help you, as a writer, explain your
   subject to readers?

LANGUAGE IN ACTION

At the beginning of her essay, Cross claims that propaganda "can be put to work for good causes as well as bad." Consider the following advertisements for the U.S. Postal Service's breast-cancer-stamp campaign and for the University of Vermont's Direct Service Programs. How would you characterize the appeal of each? What propaganda techniques does each use? Do you ever find appeals such as these objectionable? Why or why not? In what situations do you think it would be acceptable for you to use propaganda devices in your own writing?

Women Helping Battered Women

Summer or Fall Semester

Internships

Join the fight against domestic violence! You will work in a friendly, supportive environment. You will do challenging work for a worthwhile cause. You will have lots of learning opportunities. We need reliable people who are committed to social justice. You will need good communication skills, an open mind, and the ability to work somewhat independently.

We are now accepting applications.

Internships will be offered in the following programs:

Shelter Services
Hotline Program
Children's Shelter Services
Children's Playgroup Program
Development and Fundraising

Work Study Positions available in all the above programs as well as in
the financial and administrative programs.

All interns in Direct Service Programs have to complete the full Volunteer Training. The next trainings will be in May and September. Call now for more information: 658-3131.

WRITING SUGGESTIONS

1. Using several of the devices described by Cross, write a piece of propaganda. You may want to persuade your classmates to join a particular campus organization, support a controversial movement or issue, or vote for a particular candidate in an election.

2. Cross acknowledges in paragraph 1 that propaganda is "simply a means of persuasion," but she quickly cautions that people need to recognize propaganda and be alert to its potential to mislead or deceive. Write an essay for your campus newspaper arguing for a "short course" on propaganda recognition at your school. You might want to consider the following questions in your essay: How do propaganda and argumentation differ? Do both always

have the same intended effect? What could happen to people who don't recognize or understand propaganda when they encounter it?

3. Using Cross's list of propaganda devices, write an essay analyzing several newspaper editorials, political speeches, public-service advertising campaigns, or comparable examples of contemporary prose. What did you learn about the people or organizations as a result of your analysis? How were their positions on issues or their purposes expressed? Which propaganda devices did they use? After reading Cross's essay, did you find yourself "buying" the propaganda or recognizing and questioning it? Submit the original editorials, speeches, or advertisements with your essay.

Selection, Slanting, and Charged Language

Newman P. Birk and Genevieve B. Birk

The more we learn about language and how it works, the more abundantly clear it becomes that our language shapes our perceptions of the world. Because most people have eyes to see, ears to hear, noses to smell, tongues to taste, and skin to feel, it seems as though our perceptions of reality should be pretty similar. We know, however, that this is not the case, and language, it seems, makes a big difference in how we perceive our world. In effect, language acts as a filter, heightening certain perceptions, dimming others, and totally voiding still others.

In the following selection from their book *Understanding and Using Language* (1972), Newman and Genevieve Birk discuss how we use words, especially the tremendous powers that slanted and charged language wields. As a writer, you will be particularly interested to learn just how important your choice of words is. After reading what the Birks have to say, you'll never read another editorial, watch another commercial, or listen to another politician in quite the same way.

WRITING TO DISCOVER: *Choose three different people and write a description of a person, an object, or an event from each of their perspectives. Consider how each would relate to the subject you chose, what details each would focus on, and the attitude each would have toward that subject.*

A. THE PRINCIPLE OF SELECTION

Before it is expressed in words, our knowledge, both inside and outside, is influenced by the principle of selection. What we know or observe depends on what we notice; that is, what we select, consciously or unconsciously, as worthy of notice or attention. As we observe, the principle of selection determines which facts we take in.

Suppose, for example, that three people, a lumberjack, an artist, and a tree surgeon, are examining a large tree in the forest. Since the tree itself is a complicated object, the number of particulars or facts about it that one could observe would be very great indeed. Which of these facts a particular observer will notice will be a matter of selection, a selection that is determined by his interests and purposes. A lumberjack might be interested in the best way to cut the tree down, cut it up and transport it to the lumber mill. His interest would then determine his principle of selection in observing and thinking about the tree. The artist might consider painting a picture of the tree, and his purpose would furnish his principle of selection. The tree surgeon's professional interest in the physical health of the tree might establish a principle of selection for him. If each man were now required to

261

write an exhaustive, detailed report on everything he observed about the tree, the facts supplied by each would differ, for each would report those facts that his particular principle of selection led him to notice.[1]

The principle of selection holds not only for the specific facts that people observe but also for the facts they remember. A student suddenly embarrassed may remember nothing of the next ten minutes of class discussion but may have a vivid recollection of the sensation of the blood mounting, as he blushed, up his face and into his ears. In both noticing and remembering, the principle of selection applies, and it is influenced not only by our special interest and point of view but by our whole mental state of the moment.

The principle of selection then serves as a kind of sieve or screen through which our knowledge passes before it becomes our knowledge. Since we can't notice everything about a complicated object or situation or action or state of our own consciousness, what we do notice is determined by whatever principle of selection is operating for us at the time we gain the knowledge.

It is important to remember that what is true of the way the principle   5 of selection works for us is true also for the way it works for others. Even before we or other people put knowledge into words to express meaning, that knowledge has been screened or selected. Before an historian or an economist writes a book, or before a reporter writes a news article, the facts that each is to present have been sifted through the screen of a principle of selection. Before one person passes on knowledge to another, that knowledge has already been selected and shaped, intentionally or unintentionally, by the mind of the communicator.

B. THE PRINCIPLE OF SLANTING

When we put our knowledge into words, a second process of selection, the process of slanting, takes place. Just as there is something, a rather mysterious principle of selection, which chooses for us what we will notice, and what will then become our knowledge, there is also a principle which operates, with or without our awareness, to select certain facts and feelings from our store of knowledge, and to choose the words and emphasis that we shall use to communicate our meaning.[2] Slanting may be defined as the process of selecting (1) knowledge—factual and attitudinal; (2) words; and (3) emphasis, to achieve the intention of the

---

1. Of course, all three observers would probably report a good many facts in common—the height of the tree, for example, and the size of the trunk. The point we wish to make is that each observer would give us a different impression of the tree because of the different principle of selection that guided his observation.

2. Notice that the "principle of selection" is at work as *we take in* knowledge, and that slanting occurs *as we express* our knowledge in words.

communicator. Slanting is present in some degree in all communication: one may *slant for* (favorable slanting), *slant against* (unfavorable slanting), or *slant both ways* (balanced slanting). . . .

C. SLANTING BY USE OF EMPHASIS

Slanting by use of the devices of emphasis is unavoidable,[3] for emphasis is simply the giving of stress to subject matter, and so indicating what is important and what is less important. In speech, for example, if we say that Socrates was *a wise old man*, we can give several slightly different meanings, one by stressing *wise*, another by stressing *old*, another by giving equal stress to *wise* and *old*, and still another by giving chief stress to *man*. Each different stress gives a different slant (favorable or unfavorable or balanced) to the statement because it conveys a different attitude toward Socrates or a different judgment of him. Connectives and word order also slant by the emphasis they give: consider the difference in slanting or emphasis produced by *old but wise, old and wise, wise but old*. In writing, we cannot indicate subtle stresses on words as clearly as in speech, but we can achieve our emphasis and so can slant by the use of more complex patterns of word order, by choice of connectives, by underlining heavily stressed words, and by marks of punctuation that indicate short or long pauses and so give light or heavy emphasis. Question marks, quotation marks, and exclamation points can also contribute to slanting.[4] It is impossible either in speech or in writing to put two facts together without giving some slight emphasis or slant. For example, if we have in mind only two facts about a man, his awkwardness and his strength, we subtly slant those facts favorably or unfavorably in whatever way we may choose to join them.

More Favorable Slanting	*Less Favorable Slanting*
He is awkward and strong.	He is strong and awkward.
He is awkward but strong.	He is strong but awkward.
Although he is somewhat awkward, he is very strong.	He may be strong, but he's very awkward.

With more facts and in longer passages it is possible to maintain a delicate balance by alternating favorable emphasis and so producing a balanced effect.

---

3. When emphasis is present—and we can think of no instance in the use of language in which it is not—it necessarily influences the meaning by playing a part in the favorable, unfavorable, or balanced slant of the communicator. We are likely to emphasize by voice stress, even when we answer *yes* or *no* to simple questions.

4. Consider the slanting achieved by punctuation in the following sentences: He called the Senator an honest man? *He* called the Senator an honest man? He called the Senator an honest man! He said one more such "honest" senator would corrupt the state.

All communication, then, is in some degree slanted by the *emphasis* of the communicator.

D. SLANTING BY SELECTION OF FACTS

To illustrate the technique of slanting by selection of facts, we shall examine three passages of informative writing which achieve different effects simply by the selection and emphasis of material. Each passage is made up of true statements or facts about a dog, yet the reader is given three different impressions. The first passage is an example of objective writing or balanced slanting, the second is slanted unfavorably, and the third is slanted favorably.

1. Balanced Presentation

Our dog, Toddy, sold to us as a cocker, produces various reactions in various people. Those who come to the back door she usually growls and barks at (a milkman has said that he is afraid of her); those who come to the front door, she whines at and paws; also she tries to lick people's faces unless we have forestalled her by putting a newspaper in her mouth. (Some of our friends encourage these actions; others discourage them. Mrs. Firmly, one friend, slaps the dog with a newspaper and says, "I know how hard dogs are to train.") Toddy knows and responds to a number of words and phrases, and guests sometimes remark that she is a "very intelligent dog." She has fleas in the summer, and she sheds, at times copiously, the year round. Her blonde hairs are conspicuous when they are on people's clothing or on rugs or furniture. Her color and her large brown eyes frequently produce favorable comment. An expert on cockers would say that her ears are too short and set too high and that she is at least six pounds too heavy.

The passage above is made up of facts, verifiable facts,[5] deliberately   10
selected and emphasized to produce a *balanced* impression. Of course not all the facts about the dog have been given—to supply *all* the facts on any subject, even such a comparatively simple one, would be an almost impossible task. Both favorable and unfavorable facts are used, however, and an effort has been made to alternate favorable and unfavorable details so that neither will receive greater emphasis by position, proportion, or grammatical structure.

---

5. *Verifiable facts* are facts that can be checked and agreed upon and proved to be true by people who wish to verify them. That a particular theme received a failing grade is a verifiable fact; one needs merely to see the theme with the grade on it. That the instructor should have failed the theme is not, strictly speaking, a verifiable fact, but a matter of opinion. That women on the average live longer than men is a verifiable fact; that they live better is a matter of opinion, *a value judgment.*

2. Facts Slanted Against

That dog put her paws on my white dress as soon as I came in the door, and she made so much noise that it was two minutes before she had quieted down enough for us to talk and hear each other. Then the gas man came and she did a great deal of barking. And her hairs are on the rug and on the furniture. If you wear a dark dress they stick to it like lint. When Mrs. Firmly came in, she actually hit the dog with a newspaper to make it stay down, and she made some remark about training dogs. I wish the Birks would take the hint or get rid of that noisy, short-eared, overweight "cocker" of theirs.

This unfavorably slanted version is based on the same facts, but now these facts have been selected and given a new emphasis. The speaker, using her selected facts to give her impression of the dog, is quite possibly unaware of her negative slanting.

Now for a favorably slanted version:

3. Facts Slanted For

What a lively and responsible dog! When I walked in the door, there she was with a newspaper in her mouth, whining and standing on her hind legs and wagging her tail all at the same time. And what an intelligent dog. If you suggest going for a walk, she will get her collar from the kitchen and hand it to you, and she brings Mrs. Birk's slippers whenever Mrs. Birk says she is "tired" or mentions slippers. At a command she catches balls, rolls over, "speaks," or stands on her hind feet and twirls around. She sits up and balances a piece of bread on her nose until she is told to take it; then she tosses it up and catches it. If you are eating something, she sits up in front of you and "begs" with those big dark brown eyes set in that light, buff-colored face of hers. When I got up to go and told her I was leaving, she rolled her eyes at me and sat up like a squirrel. She certainly is a lively and intelligent dog.

Speaker 3, like Speaker 2, is selecting from the "facts" summarized in balanced version 1, and is emphasizing his facts to communicate his impression.

All three passages are examples of *reporting* (i.e., consist only of verifiable facts), yet they give three very different impressions of the same dog because of the different ways the speakers slanted the facts. Some people say that figures don't lie, and many people believe that if they have the "facts," they have the "truth." Yet if we carefully examine the ways of thought and language, we see that any knowledge that comes to us through words has been subjected to the double screening of the principle of selection and the slanting of language. . . .

Wise listeners and readers realize that the double screening that is pro- 15 duced by the principle of selection and by slanting takes place even when people honestly try to report the facts as they know them. (Speakers 2 and 3, for instance, probably thought of themselves as simply giving information about a dog and were not deliberately trying to mislead.) Wise listeners and readers know too that deliberate manipulators of language, by mere selection and emphasis, can make their slanted facts appear to support almost any cause.

In arriving at opinions and values we cannot always be sure that the facts that sift into our minds through language are representative and relevant and true. We need to remember that much of our information about politics, governmental activities, business conditions, and foreign affairs comes to us selected and slanted. More than we realize, our opinions on these matters may depend on what newspaper we read or what news commentator we listen to. Worthwhile opinions call for knowledge of reliable facts and reasonable arguments for and against—and such opinions include beliefs about morality and truth and religion as well as about public affairs. Because complex subjects involve knowing and dealing with many facts on both sides, reliable judgments are at best difficult to arrive at. If we want to be fairminded, we must be willing to subject our opinions to continual testing by new knowledge, and must realize that after all they *are* opinions, more or less trustworthy. Their trustworthiness will depend on the representativeness of our facts, on the quality of our reasoning, and on the standard of values that we choose to apply.

We shall not give here a passage illustrating the unscrupulous slanting of facts. Such a passage would also include irrelevant facts and false statements presented as facts, along with various subtle distortions of fact. Yet to the uninformed reader the passage would be indistinguishable from a passage intended to give a fair account. If two passages (2 and 3) of casual and unintentional slanting of facts about a dog can give such contradictory impressions of a simple subject, the reader can imagine what a skilled and designing manipulation of facts and statistics could do to mislead an uninformed reader about a really complex subject. An example of such manipulation might be the account of the United States that Soviet propaganda has supplied to the average Russian. Such propaganda, however, would go beyond the mere slanting of the facts: it would clothe the selected facts in charged words and would make use of the many other devices of slanting that appear in charged language.

E. SLANTING BY USE OF CHARGED WORDS

In the passages describing the dog Toddy, we were illustrating the technique of slanting by the selection and emphasis of facts. Though the facts selected had to be expressed in words, the words chosen were as factual as possible, and it was the selection and emphasis of facts and not of words that was mainly responsible for the two distinctly different impressions of the dog. In the passages below we are demonstrating another way of slanting—by the use of charged words. This time the accounts are very similar in the facts they contain; the different impressions of the subject, Corlyn, are produced not by different facts but by the subtle selection of charged words.

The passages were written by a clever student who was told to choose as his subject a person in action, and to write two descriptions, each using the "same facts." The instructions required that one description be slanted positively and the other negatively, so that the first would make the reader favorably inclined toward the person and the action, and the second would make him unfavorably inclined.

Here is the favorably charged description. Read it carefully and form   20
your opinion of the person before you go on to read the second description.

Corlyn

Corlyn paused at the entrance to the room and glanced about. A well-cut black dress draped subtly about her slender form. Her long blonde hair gave her chiseled features the simple frame they required. She smiled an engaging smile as she accepted a cigarette from her escort. As he lit it for her she looked over the flame and into his eyes. Corlyn had that rare talent of making every male feel that he was the only man in the world.

She took his arm and they descended the steps into the room. She walked with an effortless grace and spoke with equal ease. They each took a cup of coffee and joined a group of friends near the fire. The flickering light danced across her face and lent an ethereal quality to her beauty. The good conversation, the crackling logs, and the stimulating coffee gave her a feeling of internal warmth. Her eyes danced with each leap of the flames.

Taken by itself this passage might seem just a description of an attractive girl. The favorable slanting by use of charged words has been done so skillfully that it is inconspicuous. Now we turn to the unfavorable slanted description of the "same" girl in the "same" actions:

Corlyn

Corlyn halted at the entrance to the room and looked around. A plain black dress hung on her thin frame. Her stringy bleached hair accentuated her harsh features. She smiled an inane smile as she took a cigarette from her escort. As he lit it for her she stared over the lighter and into his eyes. Corlyn had a habit of making every male feel that he was the last man on earth.

She grasped his arm and they walked down the steps and into the room. Her pace was fast and ungainly, as was her speed. They each reached for some coffee and broke into a group of acquaintances near the fire. The flickering light played across her face and revealed every flaw. The loud talk, the fire, and the coffee she had gulped down made her feel hot. Her eyes grew more red with each leap of the flames.

When the reader compares these two descriptions, he can see how charged words influence the reader's attitude. One needs to read the two descriptions several times to appreciate all the subtle differences between them. Words, some rather heavily charged, others innocent-looking but lightly charged, work together to carry to the reader a judgment of a person and a situation. If the reader had seen only the first description of Corlyn, he might well have thought that he had formed his "own judgment on the basis of the facts." And the examples just given only begin to suggest the techniques that may be used in heavily charged language. For one thing, the two descriptions of Corlyn contain no really good example of the use of charged abstractions; for another, the writer was obliged by the assignment to use the same set of facts and so could not slant by selecting his material.

F. SLANTING AND CHARGED LANGUAGE

. . . When slanting of facts, or words, or emphasis, or any combination of the three *significantly influences* feelings toward, or judgments about, a subject, the language used is charged language. . . .

Of course communications vary in the amount of charge they carry and in their effect on different people; what is very favorably charged for one person may have little or no charge, or may even be adversely charged, for others. It is sometimes hard to distinguish between charged and uncharged expression. But it is safe to say that whenever we wish to convey any kind of inner knowledge—feelings, attitudes, judgments, values—we are obliged to convey that attitudinal meaning through the medium of charged language; and when we wish to understand the inside knowledge of others, we have to interpret the charged language that they choose, or are obliged to use. Charged language, then, is the natural and necessary medium for the communication of charged or attitudinal meaning. At times we have difficulty in living with it, but we should have even greater difficulty in living without it.

Some of the difficulties in living with charged language are caused   25
by its use in dishonest propaganda, in some editorials, in many political speeches, in most advertising, in certain kinds of effusive salesmanship, and in blatantly insincere, or exaggerated, or sentimental expressions of emotion. Other difficulties are caused by the misunderstandings and misinterpretations that charged language produces. A charged phrase misinterpreted in a love letter; a charged word spoken in haste or in anger; an acrimonious argument about religion or politics or athletics or fraternities; the frustrating uncertainty produced by the effort to understand the complex attitudinal meaning in a poem or play or a short story—these troubles, all growing out of the use of charged language, may give us the feeling that Robert Louis Stevenson expressed when he said, "The battle goes sore against us to the going down of the sun."

But however charged language is abused and whatever misunderstandings it may cause, we still have to live with it—and even by it. It shapes our attitudes and values even without our conscious knowledge; it gives purpose to, and guides, our actions; through it we establish and maintain relations with other people and by means of it we exert our greatest influence on them. Without charged language, life would be but half life. The relatively uncharged language of bare factual statement, though it serves its informative purpose well and is much less open to abuse and to misunderstanding, can describe only the bare land of factual knowledge; to communicate knowledge of the turbulencies and the calms and the deep currents of the sea of inner experience we must use charged language.

THINKING CRITICALLY ABOUT THE READING

1. What is the Birks' purpose in this essay? (Glossary: *Purpose*) Do they seem more intent on explaining or on arguing their position? Point to specific language they use that led you to your conclusion. (Glossary: *Diction*)

2. How do the Birks organize their essay? (Glossary: *Organization*) Do you think the organizational pattern is appropriate given their subject matter and purpose? Explain.

3. According to the Birks, how is slanting different from the principle of selection? What devices can a speaker or writer use to slant knowledge? When is it appropriate, if at all, to slant language?

4. Do you find the examples about Toddy the dog and Corlyn particularly helpful? (Glossary: *Examples*) Why or why not? What would have been lost, if anything, had the examples not been included?

5. Why is it important for writers and others to be aware of charged words? What can happen if you use charged language unknowingly? What are some of the difficulties in living in a world with charged language?

6. The Birks wrote this essay in 1972, when people were not as sensitive to sexist language as they are today. (Glossary: *Sexist Language*) Reread several pages of their essay, paying particular attention to the Birks' use of pronouns and to the gender of the people in their examples. Suggest ways in which the Birks' diction could be changed so as to eliminate any sexist language.

LANGUAGE IN ACTION

According to the editors of *Newsweek*, the March 8, 1999, "Voices of the Century: Americans at War" issue "generated more than two hundred passionate responses from civilians and veterans." The following five letters are representative of those the editors received and published in the issue of March 29, 1999. Carefully read each letter, looking for slanting and charged language. Point out the verifiable facts you find. How do you know these facts are verifiable?

Kudos for your March 8 issue, "Voices of the Century: Americans at War." This issue surely ranks among the best magazines ever published. As a military historian, I gained a better perspective of this turbulent century from this single issue than from many other sources combined. The first-person accounts are the genius of the issue. And your selection of storytellers was truly inspired. The "Voices of the Century" is so powerful that I will urge all of my friends to read it, buying copies for those who are not subscribers. Many persons today, especially those born after WWII, do not comprehend or appreciate the defining events of this century. How can we be more confident that they will be aware of our vital past when making important social and political decisions during the next century? I have great confidence in the American spirit and will, but this missing perspective is my principal concern as I leave this nation to the ministry of my daughters, my grandchildren, and their generation. Why not publish "Voices of the Century" as a booklet and make it readily available to all young people? Why not urge every school system to make it required reading prior to graduation from high school?

—ALAN R. McKIE, Springfield, VA

Your March 8 war issue was a powerfully illustrated essay of the men and women who have served our country and the people of other lands in so many capacities. But it was the photos that touched my soul and made me cry all over again for the human loss, *my* loss. As I stared at the pictures of the injured, dead, dying, and crying, I felt as though I were intruding on their private hell. God bless all of them, and my sincere thanks for a free America.

—DEBORAH AMES, Sparks, NV

I arrived in this country at 15 as a Jewish refugee from Nazism. I became an American soldier at 19 and a U.S. Foreign Service officer at 29. As a witness to much of the history covered in your special issue, I wanted to congratulate *Newsweek* on a superb job. In your excellent introduction, I found only one word with which I take issue: that "after the war Rosie and her cohort *happily* went back to the joys of motherhood and built the baby boom." Rosie and her cohort were forced back into their traditional gender roles, and it took the women's movement another generation or two to win back the gains achieved during the war.

—LUCIAN HEICHLER, Frederick, MD

Editor's note: The word "happily" was carefully chosen. Contemporary surveys indicated that most of the American women who joined the work force because of World War II were glad to get back to family life when it was over.

On the cover of your "Americans at War" issue, you have the accompanying text "From WWI to Vietnam: The Grunts and the Great Men—In Their Own Words." In each of these wars, the grunts *were* the great men.

—PAULA S. McGUIRE, Charlotte, NC

Your March 8 issue was painful for me and other members of my family as a result of the photograph you included on page 62 showing a wounded soldier being dragged from the line of fire during the Tet Offensive. My family had previously confirmed with the photographer that the soldier was my youngest brother, Marine Cpl. Robert Mack Harrelson. His bullet-riddled body fought hard to survive and, with the assistance of many excellent, caring members of our U.S. Military Medical Staff, he was able to regain some degree of normalcy after his return. But the injuries he received were too great to overcome, resulting in the military funeral he had requested. The rekindled grief brought on by your photo is keenly felt throughout our large family, and especially so by our dear 85-year-old mother, who still speaks of Bob as though he might reappear at any time. In spite of the photo, I sincerely congratulate your fine publication for reminding the world of the tragedy of war.

—LOWELL L. HARRELSON, Bay Minette, AL

WRITING SUGGESTIONS

1. Describe a day at your school or university. Begin with details that help you create a single dominant impression. Be careful to select only details that support the attitude and meaning you wish to convey. Once you've finished, compare your essay with those of your peers. In what ways do the essays differ? How are they the same? How does this writing exercise reinforce the Birks' discussion of the principle of selection?

2. When used only positively or only negatively, charged words can alienate the reader and bring the author's reliability into question. Consider the Birks' two examples of Corlyn. In the first example Corlyn can do no wrong, and in the second she can do nothing right. Using these two examples as a guide, write your own multiparagraph description of a person you know well. Decide on the overall impression you want to convey to your readers, and use charged words—both positive and negative—to create that impression.

3. Find a newspaper or magazine editorial on a subject that you have strong opinions about. Analyze the writer's selection of facts and use of charged language. How well does the writer present different viewpoints? Is the editorial convincing? Why or why not? After researching the topic further in your library or on the Internet, write a letter to the editor in response to the editorial. In your letter, use information from your research to make a point about the subject. Also comment on any charged or slanted language the editor used. Mail your letter to the editor.

The Lost Art of the Unsent Angry Letter

MARIA KONNIKOVA

Maria Konnikova, born in 1984, is a magna cum laude graduate of Harvard University who recently received her doctorate in psychology from Columbia University. Konnikova is originally from Moscow but came to the United States at the age of four. She is a frequently published writer whose works have appeared in publications such as the *Atlantic*, the *New York Times*, the *Boston Globe*, and the *Wall Street Journal*; her work has also appeared in the online magazine *Slate*. She is a frequent contributor to *Scientific American*. Her book *Mastermind: How to Think Like Sherlock Holmes* (2013) was a *New York Times* best seller, and she has recently published a new book, *The Confidence Game: Why We Fall for It . . . Every Time* (2015). Konnikova is a recipient of the 2015 Harvard Medical School Media Fellowship and is a Schachter Writing Fellow at Columbia University's Motivation Science Center.

The following article, which originally appeared as an op-ed piece in the *New York Times* on March 22, 2014, argues that there is value in the unsent angry letter. But in today's world of email, online posts, tweets, and other formats, all too often we might press the "send," "post," or "tweet" button before reconsidering our words. The result may be more vitriol and negativity online than would be if it weren't so easy to send out those angry words.

WRITING TO DISCOVER: *Write an angry letter of your own without any intention of sending it. It can be directed to whoever or whatever in your life is causing you pain, grief, or unhappiness. Your letter should be filled with detailed reasons for your anger, and you can express yourself however you wish. Do not send the letter! Put it aside for a day or two, and re-read it. Do you feel differently about the issue now than you did when you wrote the letter? Which parts of the letter are still valid? How did the act of writing the letter help you deal with your anger?*

Whenever Abraham Lincoln felt the urge to tell someone off, he would compose what he called a "hot letter." He'd pile all of his anger into a note, "put it aside until his emotions cooled down," Doris Kearns Goodwin once explained on NPR, "and then write: 'Never sent. Never signed.'" Which meant that Gen. George G. Meade, for one, would never hear from his commander in chief that Lincoln blamed him for letting Robert E. Lee escape after Gettysburg.

Lincoln was hardly unique. Among public figures who need to think twice about their choice of words, the unsent angry letter has a venerable tradition. Its purpose is twofold. It serves as a type of emotional catharsis, a way to let it all out without the repercussions of true engagement. And it acts as a strategic catharsis, an exercise in saying what you really think, which Mark Twain (himself a notable non-sender of correspondence) believed provided "unallowable frankness & freedom."

Harry S. Truman once almost informed the treasurer of the United States that "I don't think that the financial advisor of God Himself would be able to understand what the financial position of the Government of the United States is, by reading your statement." In 1922, Winston Churchill nearly warned Prime Minister David Lloyd George that when it came to Iraq, "we are paying eight millions a year for the privilege of living on an ungrateful volcano out of which we are in no circumstances to get any-thing worth having." Mark Twain all but chastised Russians for being too passive when it came to the czar's abuses, writing, "Apparently none of them can bear to think of losing the present hell entirely, they merely want the temperature cooled down a little."

Its purpose is twofold. It serves as a type of emotional catharsis, a way to let it all out without the repercussions of true engagement. And it acts as a strategic catharsis, an exercise in saying what you really think.

But while it may be the unsent mail of politicians and writers that is saved for posterity, that doesn't mean that they somehow hold a monopoly on the practice. Lovers carry on impassioned correspondence that the beloved never sees; family members vent their mutual frustrations. We rail against the imbecile who elbowed past us on the subway platform.

Personally, when I'm working on an article with an editor, I have a habit of using the "track changes" feature in Microsoft Word for writing retorts to suggested editorial changes. I then cool off and promptly delete the comments—and, usually, make the changes. (As far as I know, the uncensored me hasn't made it into a final version.)

In some ways, little has changed in the art of the unsent letter since Lincoln thought better of excoriating Meade. We may have switched the format from paper to screen, but the process is largely the same. You feel angry. And you construct a retort—only to find yourself thinking better of taking it any further. Emotions cooled, you proceed in a more reason-able, and reasoned, fashion. It's the opposite of the glib rejoinder that you think of just a bit too late and never quite get to say.

But it strikes me that in other, perhaps more fundamental, respects, the art of the unsent angry letter has changed beyond recognition in the world of social media. For one thing, the Internet has made the enterprise far more public. Truman, Lincoln and Churchill would file away their unsent correspondence. No one outside their inner circle would read what they had written. Now we have the option of writing what should have been our unsent words for all the world to see. There are threads on reddit and many a Web site devoted to those notes you'd send if only you were braver, not to mention the habit of sites like Thought Catalog of phrasing entire articles as letters that were never sent.

Want to express your frustration with your ex? Just submit a piece called "An Open Letter to the Girl I Loved and Lost," and hope that she sees it and recognizes herself. You, of course, have taken none of the risk of sending it to her directly.

A tweet about "that person," a post about "restaurant employees who should know better"; you put in just enough detail to make the insinuation fairly obvious, but not enough that, if caught, you couldn't deny the whole thing. It's public shaming with an escape hatch. Does knowing that we can expect a collective response to our indignation make it more satisfying?

Not really. Though we create a safety net, we may end up tangled all   10
the same. We have more avenues to express immediate displeasure than ever before, and may thus find ourselves more likely to hit send or tweet when we would have done better to hit save or delete. The ease of venting drowns out the possibility of recanting, and the speed of it all prevents a deeper consideration of what exactly we should say and why, precisely, we should say it.

When Lincoln wanted to voice his displeasure, he had to find a secretary or, at the very least, a pen. That process alone was a way of exercising self-control—twice over. It allowed him not only to express his thoughts in private (so as not to express them by mistake in public), but also to determine which was which: the anger that should be voiced versus the anger that should be kept quiet.

Now we need only click a reply button to rattle off our displeasures. And in the heat of the moment, we find the line between an appropriate response and one that needs a cooling-off period blurring. We toss our reflexive anger out there, but we do it publicly, without the private buffer that once would have let us separate what needed to be said from what needed only to be felt. It's especially true when we see similarly angry commentary coming from others. Our own fury begins to feel more socially appropriate.

We may also find ourselves feeling less satisfied. Because the angry email (or tweet or text or whatnot) takes so much less effort to compose than a pen-and-paper letter, it may in the end offer us a less cathartic experience, in just the same way that pressing the end call button on your cellphone will never be quite the same as slamming down an old-fashioned receiver.

Perhaps that's why we see so much vitriol online, so many anonymous, bitter comments, so many imprudent tweets and messy posts. Because creating them is less cathartic, you feel the need to do it more often. When your emotions never quite cool, they keep coming out in other ways.

But even though a degree of depth and consideration may well have   15
been lost along with the art of the unsent letter, something was also lost with those old letters that weren't sent because their would-be sender overthought their appropriateness. I'd have loved for Truman to have actually

sent this one off to the red-baiting Republican senator from Wisconsin, Joseph R. McCarthy: "You are not even fit to have a hand in the operation of the Government of the United States. I am very sure that the people of Wisconsin are extremely sorry that they are represented by a person who has as little sense of responsibility as you have."

Truman may have ended up regretting lashing out, but at least he would have had the satisfaction of knowing that he'd told off one of the blights of the American political scene when so many kept quiet. What survived as a "hot letter" would have made for quite the viral email.

THINKING CRITICALLY ABOUT THE READING

1. Konnikova begins her article by recounting how President Abraham Lincoln would write angry letters and then not send them. Why would she start the article with a figure such as Lincoln, as opposed to Harry Truman, whom she mentions later?

2. What does Konnikova mean when she states that the unsent angry letter provides a "catharsis" (2)? What are the two different types of catharsis she describes?

3. How has the art of the unsent angry letter changed from the past to today? What has been lost because of those changes? What might be gained?

4. At one point, Konnikova discusses the idea of posting ambiguous statements ("a tweet about 'that person,'" for instance) that can allow for anonymity or plausible deniability. Can such ambiguous statements provide the sense of catharsis that Konnikova associates with unsent letters? Why or why not?

5. Konnikova points out that sometimes it might have been better if the angry letter had been sent. She cites, for example, that Harry Truman should have sent the infamous Senator Joe McCarthy a letter excoriating him for his red-baiting tactics (15). Does her argument for sending such letters contradict her overall point in this article? Why or why not? Where would you draw the line between a letter that should be sent and one that should remain unsent?

LANGUAGE IN ACTION

Locate one of the Web sites that Konnikova mentions in paragraph 7 that allow you to submit or post an "unsent" letter, such as thought-catalog.com or ourunsentletters.com. Try to identify what the conventions are for these letters. What does the new, online art of the lost letter look like? How have commenters reacted to the lost letter? Konnikova analyzes some of the differences she sees between these new letters and the old, but what do you notice that she doesn't mention? What examples do you find to prove or disprove her points?

WRITING SUGGESTIONS

1. Konnikova states, "But it strikes me that in other, perhaps more fundamental, respects, the art of the unsent angry letter has changed beyond recognition in the world of social media" (7). Write an essay in which you examine how the format of a letter can determine not only how something is written but also what is written. Is what we write by hand substantially different from what we type on a keyboard or a phone? Why or why not? What other factors might be at play in any differences in content? (You might wish to research Marshall McLuhan's book, *The Medium Is the Message* [1967], for additional thoughts on this idea.)

2. Of the unsent angry letter, Konnikova writes, "It serves as a type of emotional catharsis, a way to let it all out without the repercussions of true engagement. And it acts as a strategic catharsis, an exercise in saying what you really think." Write an essay in which you discuss the relationship between emotional and strategic catharsis. In what ways does "letting it all out" lead to figuring out how to "say what you really think"? Does the strategic side—figuring out *how* to express yourself on top of *what* you have to say—have an emotional component of its own? Write an essay about the role of writing and its ability to create catharsis. Consider how writing might serve as a form of mental healing—releasing negative thoughts and emotions—as well as serving practical goals.

The World of Doublespeak

WILLIAM LUTZ

Born in Racine, Wisconsin, in 1940, William Lutz was a professor of English at Rutgers University from 1971 until his retirement in 2006 and was editor of the *Quarterly Review of Doublespeak* for fourteen years. Through his book *Doublespeak: From Revenue Enhancement to Terminal Living* (1980), Lutz first awakened Americans to how people in important positions were manipulating language. As chair of the National Council of Teachers of English's Committee on Public Doublespeak, Lutz has been a watchdog of public officials who use language to "mislead, distort, deceive, inflate, circumvent, obfuscate." Each year the committee presents the Orwell Awards, recognizing the most outrageous uses of public doublespeak in the worlds of government and business. Lutz's books include *The New Doublespeak: Why No One Knows What Anyone's Saying Anymore* (1997) and *Doublespeak Defined: Cut through the Bull**** and Get to the Point* (1999).

In the following essay, which first appeared in Christopher Ricks's and Leonard Michaels's anthology *State of the Language* (1990), Lutz examines doublespeak, "language which pretends to communicate but doesn't, language which makes the bad seem good, the negative appear positive, the unpleasant attractive, or at least tolerable." He identifies the various types of doublespeak and cautions us about the possible serious effects that doublespeak can have on our thinking.

WRITING TO DISCOVER: *Have you ever heard or read language that you thought was deliberately evasive, language that manipulated your perception of reality, or, worse yet, language that communicated nothing? Jot down your thoughts about such language. For example, what kinds of language do people use to talk about death, cancer, mental illness, firing a person, killing someone, or ending a relationship? Do you think evasive or manipulative language is ever justified? Explain.*

Farmers no longer have cows, pigs, chickens, or other animals on their farms; according to the U.S. Department of Agriculture, farmers have "grain-consuming animal units" (which, according to the Tax Reform Act of 1986, are kept in "single-purpose agricultural structures," not pig pens and chicken coops). Attentive observers of the English language also learned recently that the multibillion dollar stock market crash of 1987 was simply a "fourth quarter equity retreat"; that airplanes don't crash, they just have "uncontrolled contact with the ground"; that janitors are really "environmental technicians"; that it was a "diagnostic misadventure of a high magnitude" which caused the death of a patient in a Philadelphia hospital, not medical malpractice; and that President Reagan wasn't really unconscious while he underwent minor surgery, he was just in a "non-decision-making form." In other words, doublespeak continues to spread as the official language of public discourse.

Doublespeak is a blanket term for language which pretends to communicate but doesn't, language which makes the bad seem good, the negative appear positive, the unpleasant attractive, or at least tolerable. It is language which avoids, shifts, or denies responsibility, language which is at variance with its real or its purported meaning. It is language which conceals or prevents thought. Basic to doublespeak is incongruity, the incongruity between what is said, or left unsaid, and what really is: between the word and the referent, between seem and be, between the essential function of language, communication, and what doublespeak does—mislead, distort, deceive, inflate, circumvent, obfuscate.

When shopping, we are asked to check our packages at the desk "for our convenience," when it's not for our convenience at all but for the store's "program to reduce inventory shrinkage." We see advertisements for "pre-owned," "experienced," or "previously distinguished" cars, for "genuine imitation leather," "virgin vinyl," or "real counterfeit diamonds." Television offers not reruns but "encore telecasts." There are no slums or ghettos, just the "inner city" or "substandard housing" where the "disadvantaged," "economically nonaffluent," or "fiscal underachievers" live. Nonprofit organizations don't make a profit, they have "negative deficits" or "revenue excesses." In the world of doublespeak dying is "terminal living."

> **In other words, doublespeak continues to spread as the official language of public discourse.**

We know that a toothbrush is still a toothbrush even if the advertisements on television call it a "home plaque removal instrument," and even that "nutritional avoidance therapy" means a diet. But who would guess that a "volume-related production schedule adjustment" means closing an entire factory in the doublespeak of General Motors, or that "advanced downward adjustments" means budget cuts in the doublespeak of Caspar Weinberger[1], or that "energetic disassembly" means an explosion in a nuclear power plant in the doublespeak of the nuclear power industry?

The euphemism, an inoffensive or positive word or phrase designed   5
to avoid a harsh, unpleasant, or distasteful reality, can at times be doublespeak. But the euphemism can also be a tactful word or phrase; for ex-ample, "passed away" functions not just to protect the feelings of another person but also to express our concern for another's grief. This use of the euphemism is not doublespeak but the language of courtesy. A euphemism used to mislead or deceive, however, becomes doublespeak.

---

1. Caspar Weinberger (1917–2006), prominent Republican politician and businessman, served as Secretary of Defense under President Ronald Reagan.

In 1984, the U.S. State Department announced that in its annual reports on the status of human rights in countries around the world it would no longer use the word "killing." Instead, it would use the phrase "unlawful or arbitrary deprivation of life." Thus the State Department avoids discussing government-sanctioned killings in countries that the United States supports and has certified as respecting human rights.

The Pentagon also avoids unpleasant realities when it refers to bombs and artillery shells which fall on civilian targets as "incontinent ordnance" or killing the enemy as "servicing the target." In 1977 the Pentagon tried to slip funding for the neutron bomb unnoticed into an appropriations bill by calling it an "enhanced radiation device." And in 1971 the CIA gave us that most famous of examples of doublespeak when it used the phrase "eliminate with extreme prejudice" to refer to the execution of a suspected double agent in Vietnam.

Jargon, the specialized language of a trade or profession, allows colleagues to communicate with each other clearly, efficiently, and quickly. Indeed, it is a mark of membership to be able to use and understand the group's jargon. But it can also be doublespeak—pretentious, obscure, and esoteric terminology used to make the simple appear complex, and not to express but impress. In the doublespeak of jargon, smelling something becomes "organoleptic analysis," glass becomes "fused silicate," a crack in a metal support beam becomes a "discontinuity," conservative economic policies become "distributionally conservative notions."

Lawyers and tax accountants speak of an "involuntary conversion" of property when discussing the loss or destruction of property through theft, accident, or condemnation. So if your house burns down, or your car is stolen or destroyed in an accident, you have, in legal jargon, suffered an "involuntary conversion" of your property. This is a legal term with a specific meaning in law and all lawyers can be expected to understand it. But when it is used to communicate with a person outside the group who does not understand such language, it is doublespeak. In 1978 a National Airlines 727 airplane crashed while attempting to land at the Pensacola, Florida, airport, killing three passengers, injuring twenty-one others, and destroying the airplane. Since the insured value of the airplane was greater than its book value, National made an after-tax insurance benefit of $1.7 million on the destroyed airplane, or an extra eighteen cents a share. In its annual report, National reported that this $1.7 million was due to "the involuntary conversion of a 727," thus explaining the profit without even hinting at the crash and the deaths of three passengers.

Gobbledygook or bureaucratese is another kind of doublespeak. Such doublespeak is simply a matter of overwhelming the audience with technical, unfamiliar words. When asked why U.S. forces lacked intelligence information on Grenada before they invaded the island in 1983, Admiral Wesley L. McDonald told reporters that "We were not micromanaging Grenada intelligence-wise until about that time frame."

Some gobbledygook, however impressive it may sound, doesn't even   10
make sense. During the 1988 presidential campaign, vice presidential
candidate Senator Dan Quayle explained the need for a strategic defense
initiative by saying: "Why wouldn't an enhanced deterrent, a more stable
peace, a better prospect to denying the ones who enter conflict in the first
place to have a reduction of offensive systems and an introduction to defensive capability. I believe this is the route the country will eventually go."

In 1974, Alan Greenspan, then chairman of the President's Council of
Economic Advisors, was testifying before a Senate Committee and was in
the difficult position of trying to explain why President Nixon's economic
policies weren't effective in fighting inflation: "It is a tricky problem to
find the particular calibration in timing that would be appropriate to stem
the acceleration in risk premiums created by falling incomes without pre-
maturely aborting the decline in the inflation-generated risk premiums."
In 1988, when speaking to a meeting of the Economic Club of New York,
Mr. Greenspan, [later] Federal Reserve chairman, said, "I guess I should
warn you, if I turn out to be particularly clear, you've probably misunderstood what I've said."

The investigation into the *Challenger* disaster in 1986 revealed the
gobbledygook and bureaucratese used by many involved in the shuttle
program. When Jesse Moore, NASA's associate administrator, was asked
if the performance of the shuttle program had improved with each launch
or if it had remained the same, he answered, "I think our performance in
terms of the liftoff performance and in terms of the orbital performance,
we knew more about the envelope we were operating under, and we have
been pretty accurately staying in that. And so I would say the performance
has not by design drastically improved. I think we have been able to characterize the performance more as a function of our launch experience as
opposed to it improving as a function of time."

A final kind of doublespeak is simply inflated language. Car mechanics
may be called "automotive internists," elevator operators "members of the
vertical transportation corps," and grocery store checkout clerks "career
associate scanning professionals," while television sets are proclaimed to
have "nonmulticolor capability." When a company "initiates a career alternative enhancement program" it is really laying off five thousand workers;
"negative patient care outcome" means that the patient died; and "rapid
oxidation" means a fire in a nuclear power plant.

The doublespeak of inflated language can have serious consequences.
The U.S. Navy didn't pay $2,043 a piece for steel nuts; it paid all that
money for "hexiform rotatable surface compression units," which, by the
way, "underwent catastrophic stress-related shaft detachment." Not to be
outdone, the U.S. Air Force paid $214 apiece for Emergency Exit Lights,
or flashlights. This doublespeak is in keeping with such military doublespeak as "preemptive counterattack" for first strike, "engage the enemy on all
sides" for ambush, "tactical redeployment" for retreat, and "air support" for

bombing. In the doublespeak of the military, the 1983 invasion of Grenada was conducted not by the U.S. Army, Navy, Air Force, and Marines but by the "Caribbean Peace Keeping Forces." But then according to the Pentagon it wasn't an invasion, it was a "predawn vertical insertion."

These last examples of doublespeak should make it clear that doublespeak is not the product of careless language or sloppy thinking. Indeed, serious doublespeak is the product of clear thinking and is carefully designed and constructed to appear to communicate but in fact to mislead. Thus, it's not a tax increase but "revenue enhancement," "tax base broadening," or "user fees," so how can you complain about higher taxes? It's not acid rain, it's just "poorly buffered precipitation," so don't worry about all those dead trees. That isn't the Mafia in Atlantic City, those are just "members of a career-offender cartel," so don't worry about the influence of organized crime in the city. The Supreme Court justice wasn't addicted to the painkilling drug he was taking, it's just that the drug had simply "established an interrelationship with the body, such that if the drug is removed precipitously, there is a reaction," so don't worry that his decisions might have been influenced by his drug addiction. It's not a Titan II nuclear-armed, intercontinental, ballistic missile 630 times more powerful than the atomic bomb dropped on Hiroshima, it's just a "very large, potentially disruptive reentry system," so don't worry about the threat of nuclear destruction. Serious doublespeak is highly strategic, and it breeds suspicion, cynicism, distrust, and, ultimately, hostility.

In his famous and now-classic essay "Politics and the English Language," which was published in 1946, George Orwell wrote that the great enemy of clear language is insincerity. When there is a gap between one's real and one's declared aims, one turns as it were instinctively to long words and exhausted idioms, like a cuttlefish squirting out ink." For Orwell, language was an instrument for "expressing and not for concealing or preventing thought." In his most biting comment, Orwell observes that "in our time, political speech and writing are largely the defense of the indefensible. . . . Political language has to consist largely of euphemism, question-begging, and sheer cloudy vagueness. . . . Political language . . . is designed to make lies sound truthful and murder respectable, and to give an appearance of solidity to pure wind."

Orwell understood well the power of language as both a tool and a weapon. In the nightmare world of his novel *1984*, he depicted language as one of the most important tools of the totalitarian state. Newspeak, the official state language in *1984*, was designed not to extend but to *diminish* the range of human thought, to make only "correct" thought possible and all other modes of thought impossible. It was, in short, a language designed to create a reality which the state wanted.

Newspeak had another important function in Orwell's world of *1984*. It provided the means of expression for doublethink, which Orwell described in his novel as "the power of holding two contradictory beliefs in one's mind simultaneously, and accepting both of them." The classic example of doublethink in Orwell's novel is the slogan "War is Peace." And lest you think doublethink is confined only to Orwell's novel, you need only recall the words of Secretary of State Alexander Haig when he testified before a Congressional Committee in 1982 that a continued weapons build-up by the United States is "absolutely essential to our hopes for meaningful arms reduction." Or the words of Senator Orrin Hatch in 1988: "Capital punishment is our society's recognition of the sanctity of human life."

The more sophisticated and powerful uses of doublespeak can at times be difficult to identify. On 27 July 1981, President Ronald Reagan said in a television speech: "I will not stand by and see those of you who are dependent on Social Security deprived of the benefits you've worked so hard to earn. You will continue to receive your checks in the full amount due you." This speech had been billed as President Reagan's position on Social Security, a subject of much debate at the time. After the speech, public opinion polls recorded the great majority of the public as believing that President Reagan had affirmed his support for Social Security and that he would not support cuts in benefits. Five days after the speech, however, White House spokesperson David Gergen was quoted in the press as saying that President Reagan's words had been "carefully chosen." What President Reagan did mean, according to Gergen, was that he was reserving the right to decide who was "dependent" on those benefits, who had "earned" them, and who, therefore, was "due" them.

During the 1982 Congressional election campaign, the Republican   20
National Committee sponsored a television advertisement which pictured an elderly, folksy postman delivering Social Security checks "with the 7.4 percent cost-of-living raise that President Reagan promised." Looking directly at his audience, the postman then adds that Reagan "promised that raise and he kept his promise, in spite of those sticks-in-the-mud who tried to keep him from doing what we elected him to do."

The commercial was deliberately misleading. The cost-of-living increases had been provided automatically by law since 1975, and President Reagan had tried three times to roll them back or delay them but was overruled by congressional opposition. When these discrepancies were pointed out to an official of the Republican National Committee, he called the commercial "inoffensive" and added, "Since when is a commercial supposed to be accurate? Do women really smile when they clean their ovens?"

In 1986, with the *Challenger* tragedy and subsequent investigation, we discovered that doublespeak seemed to be the official language of NASA, the National Aeronautics and Space Administration, and of the contractors engaged in the space shuttle program. The first thing we learned is that the *Challenger* tragedy wasn't an accident. As Kay Parker of NASA said, experts were "working in the anomaly investigation." The "anomaly" was the explosion of the *Challenger*.

When NASA reported that it was having difficulty determining how or exactly when the *Challenger* astronauts died, Rear Admiral Richard Truly reported that "whether or not a cabin rupture occurred prior to water impact has not yet been determined by a superficial examination of the recovered components." The "recovered components" were the bodies of the astronauts. Admiral Truly also said that "extremely large forces were imposed on the vehicle as evidenced by the immediate breakup into many pieces." He went on to say that "once these forces have been accurately determined, if in fact they can be, the structural analysts will attempt to estimate the effect on the structural and pressure integrity of the crew module." NASA referred to the coffins of the astronauts as "crew transfer containers."

Arnold Aldrich, manager of the national space transportation systems program at Johnson Space Center, said that "the normal process during the countdown is that the countdown proceeds, assuming we are in a go posture, and at various points during the countdown we tag up on the operational loops and face to face in the firing room to ascertain the facts that project elements that are monitoring the data and that are understanding the situation as we proceed are still in the go condition."

In testimony before the commission investigating the *Challenger* 25 accident, Allen McDonald, an engineer for Morton Thiokol (the maker of the rocket), said he had expressed concern about the possible effect of cold weather on the booster rocket's O-ring seals the night before the launch: "I made the comment that lower temperatures are in the direction of badness for both O-rings, because it slows down the timing function."

Larry Mulloy, manager of the space shuttle solid rocket booster program at Marshall Space Flight Center, responded to a question assessing whether problems with the O-rings or with the insulation of the liner of the nozzle posed a greater threat to the shuttle by saying, "The criticality in answering your question, sir, it would be a real foot race as to which one would be considered more critical, depending on the particular time that you looked at your experience with that."

After several executives of Rockwell International, the main contractor to build the shuttle, had testified that Rockwell had been opposed to launching the shuttle because of the danger posed by ice formation on the launch platform, Martin Cioffoletti, vice president for space transportation at Rockwell, said: "I felt that by telling them we did not have a sufficient data base and could not analyze the trajectory of the ice, I felt he understood that Rockwell was not giving a positive indication that we were for the launch."

Officials at Morton Thiokol, when asked why they reversed earlier decisions not to launch the shuttle, said the reversal was "based on the reevaluation of those discussions." The Presidential commission investigating the accident suggested that this statement could be translated to mean there was pressure from NASA.

One of the most chilling uses of doublespeak occurred in 1981 when then Secretary of State Alexander Haig was testifying before congressional committees about the murder of three American nuns and a Catholic lay worker in El Salvador. The four women had been raped and then shot at close range, and there was clear evidence that the crime had been committed by soldiers of the Salvadoran government. Before the House Foreign Affairs Committee, Secretary Haig said, "I'd like to suggest to you that some of the investigations would lead one to believe that perhaps the vehicle the nuns were riding in may have tried to run a roadblock, or may accidentally have been perceived to have been doing so, and there'd been an exchange of fire and then perhaps those who inflicted the casualties sought to cover it up. And this could have been at a very low level of both competence and motivation in the context of the issue itself. But the facts on this are not clear enough for anyone to draw a definitive conclusion."

The next day, before the Senate Foreign Relations Committee, Secretary Haig claimed that press reports on his previous testimony were inaccurate. When Senator Claiborne Pell asked whether Secretary Haig was suggesting the possibility that "the nuns may have run through a roadblock," Secretary Haig replied, "You mean that they tried to violate . . . ? Not at all, no, not at all. My heavens! The dear nuns who raised me in my parochial schooling would forever isolate me from their affections and respect." When Senator Pell asked Secretary Haig, "Did you mean that the nuns were firing at the people, or what did 'an exchange of fire' mean?" Secretary Haig replied, "I haven't met any pistol-packing nuns in my day, Senator. What I meant was that if one fellow starts shooting, then the next thing you know they all panic." Thus did the Secretary of State of the United States explain official government policy on the murder of four American citizens in a foreign land.

The congressional hearings for the IranContra affair produced more doublespeak. During his second day of testimony before the Select Committee on Secret Military Assistance to Iran and the Nicaraguan Opposition, Oliver North admitted that he had on different occasions lied to the Iranians, his colleague Maj. Gen. Richard Secord, congressional investigators, and the Congress, and that he had destroyed evidence and created false documents. North then asserted to the committee that everything he was about to say would be the truth.

North used the words "residuals" and "diversions" to refer to the millions of dollars which were raised for the contras by overcharging Iran for arms. North also said that he "cleaned" and "fixed" things up, that he was "cleaning up the historical record," and that he "took steps to ensure" that things never "came out"—meaning he lied, destroyed official government documents, and created false documents. Some documents weren't destroyed; they were "non-log[ged]" or kept "out of the system so that outside knowledge would not necessarily be derived from having the documents themselves."

North was also careful not to "infect other people with unnecessary knowledge." He explained that the Nicaraguan Humanitarian Assistance Office provided humanitarian aid in "mixed loads," which, according to North, "meant . . . beans and Band-Aids and boots and bullets." For North, people in other countries who helped him were "assets." "Project Democracy" was a "euphemism" he used at the time to refer to the organization that was building an airfield for the contras.

In speaking of a false chronology of events which he helped construct, North said that he "was provided with additional input that was radically different from the truth. I assisted in furthering that version." He mentions "a different version from the facts" and calls the chronology "inaccurate." North also testified that he and William Casey, then head of the C.I.A., together falsified the testimony that Casey was to give to Congress. "Director Casey and I fixed that testimony and removed the offensive portions. We fixed it by omission. We left out—it wasn't made accurate, it wasn't made fulsome, it was fixed by omission." Official lies were "plausible deniability."

While North admitted that he had shredded documents after being   35
informed that officials from the Attorney General's office wanted to inspect some of the documents in his office, he said, "I would prefer to say that I shredded documents that day like I did on all other days, but perhaps with increased intensity."

North also preferred to use the passive to avoid responsibility. When asked "Where are the non-logged documents?" he replied, "I think they were shredded." Again, when asked on what authority he agreed to allow Secord to make a personal profit off the arms sale to Iran, North replied with a long, wordy response filled with such passive constructions as "it was clearly indicated," "it was already known," and "it was recognized." But he never answered the question.

For North, the whole investigation by Congress was just an attempt "to criminalize policy differences between coequal branches of government and the Executive's conduct of foreign affairs." Lying to Congress, shredding official documents, violating laws, conducting unauthorized activities were all just "policy differences" to North. But North was generous with the committee: "I think there's fault to go on both sides. I've said that repeatedly throughout my testimony. And I have accepted the responsibility for my role in it." While North accepts responsibility, he does not accept accountability.

This final statement of North's bears close reading for it reveals the subtlety of his language. North states as fact that Congress was at fault, but at fault for what he doesn't specify. Furthermore, he does not accept responsibility for any specific action, only for his "role," whatever that may have been, in "it." In short, while he may be "responsible" (not guilty) for violating the law, Congress shares in that responsibility for having passed the law.

In Oliver North's doublespeak, then, defying a law is complying with it, noncompliance is compliance. North's doublespeak allowed him to help draft a letter to Congress saying that "we are complying with the letter and spirit" of the Boland Amendment, when what the letter really meant, North later admitted, was that "Boland doesn't apply to us and so we're complying with its letter and spirit."

Contrary to his claim that he was a "stand up guy" who would tell all   40
and take whatever was coming to him, North disclaimed all responsibility for his actions: "I was authorized to do everything that I did." Yet when he was asked who gave him authorization, North replied, "My superiors." When asked which superior, he replied: "Well, who—look who sign—I didn't sign those letters to the—to this body." And North's renowned steel-trap memory went vague or forgetful again.

After North had testified, Admiral John Poindexter, North's superior, testified before the committee. Once again, doublespeak flourished. In the world of Admiral John Poindexter, one does not lie but "misleads" or "withholds information." Likewise, one engages in "secret activities" which are not the same as covert actions. In Poindexter's world, one can "acquiesce" in a shipment of weapons while at the same time not authorize the shipment. One can transfer millions of dollars of government money as a "technical implementation" without making a "substantive decision." One can also send subordinates to lie to congressional committees if one does not "micromanage" them. In Poindexter's world, "outside interference" occurs when Congress attempts to fulfill its constitutional function of passing legislation.

For Poindexter, withholding information was not lying. When asked about Col. North's testimony that he had lied to a congressional committee and that Poindexter had known that North intended to lie, Poindexter replied, "there was a general understanding that he [North] was to withhold information. . . . I . . . did not expect him to lie to the committee. I expected him to be evasive. . . . I'm sure they [North's answers] were very carefully crafted, nuanced. The total impact, I am sure, was one of withholding information from the Congress, but I'm still not convinced . . . that he lied."

Yet Poindexter protested that it is not "fair to say that I have misinformed Congress or other Cabinet officers. I haven't testified to that. I've testified that I withheld information from Congress. And with regard to the Cabinet officers, I didn't withhold anything from them that they didn't want withheld from them." Poindexter did not explain how it is possible to withhold information that a person wants withheld.

The doublespeak of Alexander Haig, Oliver North, and John Poindexter occurred during their testimony before congressional committees. Perhaps their doublespeak was not premeditated but just happened to be the way they spoke, and thought. President Jimmy Carter in 1980 could call the aborted raid to free the American hostages in Tehran an "incomplete success" and really believe that he had made a statement that clearly communicated with the American public. So too could President Ronald Reagan say in 1985 that "ultimately our security and our hopes for success at the arms reduction talks hinge on the determination that we show here to continue our program to rebuild and refortify our defenses" and really believe that greatly increasing the amount of money spent building new weapons will lead to a reduction in the number of weapons in the world. If we really believe that we understand such language and that such language communicates and promotes clear thought, then the world of *1984* with its control of reality through language is upon us.

THINKING CRITICALLY ABOUT THE READING

1. What, according to Lutz, is doublespeak? What are its essential characteristics?

2. What is a euphemism? Are all euphemisms examples of doublespeak? Explain.

3. In his discussion of Oliver North's testimony during the Iran-Contra hearings, Lutz states, "While North accepts responsibility, he does not accept accountability" (37). Explain what Lutz means here. What differences do you draw between responsibility and accountability?

4. Why, according to Lutz, does "doublespeak continue to spread as the official language of public discourse" (1)? In your opinion, is doublespeak as widespread today as it was when Lutz wrote his article? What examples can you provide to back up your opinion?

5. Lutz discusses four basic types or categories of doublespeak—euphemism, jargon, gobbledygook, and inflated language. In what ways does this classification serve to clarify not only the concept of doublespeak but also its many uses? (Glossary: *Classification*)

6. Lutz is careful to illustrate each of the basic types of doublespeak with examples. Why is it important to use plenty of examples in an essay like this? (Glossary: *Examples*) What do his many examples reveal about Lutz's expertise on the subject?

7. Why does Lutz believe that we must recognize doublespeak for what it is and voice our dissatisfaction with those who use it?

LANGUAGE IN ACTION

In an article called "Public Doublespeak," Terence Moran presents the following list of recommended language, which school administrators in Brooklyn gave their elementary school teachers to use when discussing students with their parents.

For Parent Interviews and Report Cards

Harsh Expression (Avoid)	Acceptable Expression (Use)
Does all right if pushed	Accomplishes tasks when interest is stimulated.
Too free with fists	Resorts to physical means of winning his point or attracting attention.

Lies (Dishonest)	Shows difficulty in distinguishing between imaginary and factual material.
Cheats	Needs help in learning to adhere to rules and standards of fair play.
Steals	Needs help in learning to respect the property rights of others.
Noisy	Needs to develop quieter habits of communication.
Lazy	Needs ample supervision in order to work well.
Is a bully	Has qualities of leadership but needs help in learning to use them democratically.
Associates with "gangs"	Seems to feel secure only in group situations; needs to develop sense of independence.
Disliked by other children	Needs help in learning to form lasting friendships.

What are your reactions to these recommendations? Why do you suppose the school administrators made up this list? What purpose does such language serve? Do you believe the "acceptable" language belongs in our nation's schools? Why or why not?

WRITING SUGGESTIONS

1. Think of the ways that you encounter doublespeak every day, whether in school or at work, or while reading a newspaper or watching television. How does it affect you? What do you suppose the speakers' or writers' motives are in using doublespeak? Using your own experiences and observations, write an essay in which you explore the reasons why people use doublespeak. Before starting to write, you may find it helpful to review your Writing to Discover response to the Lutz essay.

2. In his concluding paragraph Lutz states, "If we really believe that we understand [doublespeak] and that such language communicates and promotes clear thought, then the world of *1984* with its control of reality through language is upon us." In an essay, discuss whether or not Lutz is overstating the case and being too pessimistic and whether or not the American public is really unaware of—or apathetic about—how doublespeak manipulates and deceives. Consider also whether or not the American public has reacted to doublespeak with, as Lutz suggests, "suspicion, cynicism, distrust, and, ultimately, hostility."

3. Using resources in your library or on the Internet, write a paper about the language of funeral directors, stockbrokers, college professors, health-care professionals, or some other occupation of your choice. How pervasive is doublespeak in the occupation you selected? Based on the results of your research, why do you think people with this type of job use such language? Do you find this language troublesome? If so, what can be done to change the situation?

Language That Silences

JASON STANLEY

Jason Stanley is a philosopher who specializes in the philosophy of language and linguistics, as well as questions involving cognition, context-dependence, and fallibilism, or the philosophical principle that we could be wrong about our beliefs. Stanley was born in 1969 and earned his B.A. in philosophy and linguistics at the State University of New York at Stony Brook in 1990 and his Ph.D. at the Massachusetts Institute of Technology in 1995. Stanley has taught at a number of colleges and universities, including Rutgers University from 2004 to 2013, and is currently professor of philosophy at Yale University. He has written four books: *Know How* (2011), *Language in Context: Selected Essays* (2007), *Knowledge and Practical Interests* (2005), and *How Propaganda Works* (2015).

In "Language That Silences," first published as "The Ways of Silencing" in the *New York Times* on June 25, 2011, Stanley examines the ways in which language may be supposed to further discussion or shed light on issues but is gradually manipulated and snuffs out the trust necessary for its very existence.

WRITING TO DISCOVER: *Do you think that most news outlets report the news objectively without any biases, or do you think they either give intentionally or unintentionally biased reports? On what evidence do you base your views? Cite examples where possible.*

We might wish politicians and pundits from opposing parties to engage in reasoned debate about the truth, but as we know, this is not the reality of our political discourse.

Instead we often encounter bizarre and improbable claims about public figures. Words are misappropriated and meanings twisted. I believe that these tactics are not really about making substantive claims, but rather play the role of silencing. They are, if you will, linguistic strategies for stealing the voices of others. These strategies have always been part of the arsenal of politics. But since they are so widely used today, it is worth examining their underlying mechanisms, to make apparent their special dangers.

The feminist scholar Catharine MacKinnon famously declared, "Pornography silences women." In the 1990s, the philosophers of language Jennifer Hornsby and Rae Langton developed an account of the mechanisms of silencing that could substantiate MacKinnon's claim. But their basic ideas extend beyond the examples they chose, and can inform us about silencing in our political discourse today.

In her 1993 paper, "Speech Acts and Pornography," Hornsby used an example, credited to Langton: Suppose that men are led to believe that when women refuse a sexual advance they don't mean it. Women, then, will not be understood to be refusing, even when they are. If certain kinds of pornography lead men to think that women are not sincere when they utter the word "no," and women are aware that men think this, those kinds of pornography would rob women of the ability to refuse. Using "no" to refuse a sexual advance is what is known as a speech act—a way of doing something by using words. Hornsby and Langton's work raises the possibility that a medium may undermine the ability of a person or group—in this case, women—to employ a speech act by representing that person or group as insincere in their use of it.

Silencing extends to politics when outlandish claims are made about   5
public figures. Suppose that President Obama really was a secret Islamist agent, or born in Kenya. In that case, he would be grossly insincere. We would have no reason to believe what he said in any situation. The function of disseminating such claims about the president is not to object to his specific arguments or agenda. It is to undermine the public's trust in him, so that nothing he says can be taken at face value.

There are multiple purposes to political speech, only one of which is to assert truths. Nevertheless, we expect a core of sincerity from our leaders. We do not expect a Muammar el-Qaddafi. It is belief in this core of sincerity that bizarre claims about the president are intended to undermine.

It is possible to silence people by denying them access to the vocabulary to express their claims.

Silencing in the sense described by Hornsby and Langton robs others of the ability to engage in speech acts, such as assertion. But there is another kind of silencing familiar in the political domain, not discussed by these authors. It is possible to silence people by denying them access to the vocabulary to express their claims.

One of the best investigations of propaganda was presented by Victor Klemperer, in his book *The Language of the Third Reich*. The data for Klemperer's claims was the language used by the Third Reich. But the points he makes are applicable to propaganda in the service of much more mundane endeavors, be it to pass health care reform or to increase or decrease taxes. The use of propaganda is not limited to a single political affiliation or intent.

As Klemperer writes in *The Language of the Third Reich*, propaganda "changes the value of words and the frequency of their occurrence . . . it commandeers for the party that which was previously common property and in the process steeps words and groups of words and sentence structures in its poison." When writing these words, Klemperer was thinking of the incessant use of the term "heroisch" ("heroic") to justify the military adventures of the National Socialist state. Obviously, the mechanism described by Klemperer is not used for such odious purposes today. Nevertheless, there has been a similar appropriation of the term "freedom" in American political discourse.

Most would agree that heroism and freedom are fundamentally good   10
things. But the terms "heroisch" and "freedom" have been appropriated

for purposes that do not have much connection with the virtues of their original meanings. Whatever one thinks of the wisdom of the 2003 invasion of Iraq, it is difficult to have a reasoned debate about its costs and benefits when the invasion itself is called "Operation Iraqi Freedom." Similarly, whatever one thinks of tax cuts, or the estate tax, it is difficult to engage in reasoned debate when they have been respectively relabeled "tax relief" and "the death tax." It is difficult to have a reasoned debate about the costs and benefits of a policy when one side has seized control of the linguistic means to express all the positive claims. It is easy to say "a tax cut is not always good policy," but considerably more difficult to say "tax relief is not always good policy," even though "tax relief" is just a phrase invented to mean the same as "tax cut."

Silencing is by no means limited to its target. The Fox channel engages in silencing when it describes itself as "fair and balanced" to an audience that is perfectly aware that it is neither. The effect is to suggest that there is no such thing as fair and balanced — that there is no possibility of balanced news, only propaganda. The result is the silencing of every news organ, by suggesting a generalized gross insincerity.

The effects of a belief in general gross insincerity are apparent in societies in which the state media delivers only propaganda. Citizens who grow up in a state in which the authorities deliver propaganda have no experience with trust. So even if the members of that society have access to reliable news, say via the Internet, they do not trust it. They are trained to be suspicious of any organ marketing itself as news.

Silencing is only one kind of propaganda. In silencing, one removes the ability of a target person or group to communicate. As a philosopher of language I am less qualified to make a judgment about the wisdom of Plato, Machiavelli, and Leo Strauss than I am to comment about their favored political tool. However, I do think that given our current environment — of oppression, revolution, intervention, war, pseudo-war and ever-present human power relations — it is worthwhile bearing in mind the dangers of the manipulation of language. What may begin as a temporary method to circumvent reasoned discussion and debate for the sake of a prized political goal may very well end up permanently undermining the trust required for its existence.

THINKING CRITICALLY ABOUT THE READING

1. What is silencing? In your own terms, why does Stanley consider silencing propaganda?

2. Stanley quotes Catharine MacKinnon's statement: "Pornography silences women." What do you think MacKinnon meant by her statement?

3. Does Stanley himself engage in silencing? Explain.

4. Is Stanley an unbiased commentator on the question of silencing?

5. If silencing comes from the right as Stanley seems to believe, can you think of any examples of silencing that have come from the left?

LANGUAGE IN ACTION

Soon after Jason Stanley's article appeared in the *New York Times*, the *Times* published Stanley's response ("Media and Mistrust: A Response," *New York Times*, July 18, 2011) to readers who wrote to the *Times* to comment on his original article. Reprinted below are several of the readers' comments. Choose one for discussion and evaluate its merits.

All of the networks and newspapers engage in some kind of silencing. Some years ago a reporter on a large newspaper explained to me that they [sic] would not report on "extremist" activities such as rallies, meetings and speeches because it help them [sic] get publicity for their message. On the other hand, he admitted, causes that passed muster would be covered and even promoted. He didn't regard this as any kind of censorship but just serving a civic responsibility.

This kind of double standard is everywhere in the media. It's in the *New York Times*, *Washington Post*, and all other newspapers. It's in NBC, Fox News and all the networks. Virtually everyone who complains about the bias of one media outlet ignores or rationalizes the same behavior in others, and that was the case with the original article by Mr. Stanley. He's clearly and obviously partisan on behalf of a point of view. To excoriate Fox News without similarly excoriating MSNBC is simply another form of distortion.

LAIRD WILCOX, Kansas

* * * * *

I read the opinion pages of the local newspaper with a different eye today after having read this. There seem to be some attempts to use language to silence as you have described in this and the previous post, and now I have some tools to help me identify it. Before I was just aware that some words made me uncomfortable, and now I understand why.

Thank you.

GARY, North Carolina

* * * * *

So we should not trust Fox News, but we should trust Rutgers University philosophy professors? Why, exactly? Speaking of trust, how about having a little bit of faith in us news consumers—we know every news writer/broadcaster has his/her own biases that influence their work, and that every news consumer has his own biases that filter what we [sic] read/hear. In the end, it generally balances out.

MORGAN, Philadelphia

WRITING SUGGESTIONS

1. Stanley makes some interesting references in his article to other scholars (e.g., Jennifer Hornsby, Rae Langton, and Victor Klemperer) who have addressed the importance of silencing as a propaganda strategy. Write an essay on silencing based on ideas and examples that you draw from their writings. Be careful to develop an effective thesis, to focus your work, and to include examples of your own in your essay, wherever possible.

2. Some of Stanley's readers have argued that he is guilty in his essay of the same kind of silencing to which he is opposed. Does he write with a political bias? If so, how? Do you find any problems with his examples? Do you also believe that the times we live in are more treacherous than times past, as he argues in paragraph 13? A larger question: Isn't all argumentative writing biased to an extent, even if the writer takes into account opponents' arguments as a way of countering them? Is it possible to write in a totally unbiased manner? Address some of these questions, and others that arise from these questions, in writing an essay on these important issues. You may want to reference comments made by Stanley's readers as well as the comments he has made in response at opinionator.blogs.nytimes.com/2011/07/18/media-and-mistrust-a-response/.

Assassination and the American Language

ELLIOT ACKERMAN

Elliot Ackerman, born in 1980, is an American writer raised in London and Washington, D.C., and currently living in Istanbul. Ackerman attended Tufts University, earning his bachelor's degree and a master's degree in international affairs. His newest work is a novel, *Green on Blue* (2015). His works of short fiction and nonfiction have appeared in the *New Yorker*, the *Atlantic*, the *New Republic*, and *Ecotone*, among others. He is also a member of the Council on Foreign Relations and a contributor to the *Daily Beast*. He has been interviewed in the *Washington Post*, the *New York Times*, and the *Wall Street Journal* and has appeared on *Charlie Rose, The Colbert Report*, and most of the high-profile current events programs on the major broadcast and cable networks. Most recently, he served as a White House fellow in the Obama administration. Ackerman's early career was spent in the military as both an infantry and a special operations officer, serving multiple tours of duty in the Middle East and Southwest Asia, including a role as the primary combat advisor to a commando battalion targeting senior Taliban leadership. He also led a platoon in relief operations in New Orleans after Hurricane Katrina.

In this article, published in the *New Yorker* on November 20, 2014, Ackerman examines the inherent contradictions between Executive Order 12333, an order signed by President Ronald Reagan prohibiting the assassination of foreign targets by U.S. government agencies, and the actions that he and others as members of the C.I.A. undertook in Afghanistan in the wake of the 9/11 attacks. He examines the tortured semantics that separates "assassination" from "targeted killing" and looks at how language can make actions that might be defensible on their own merits into deceptive acts.

WRITING TO DISCOVER: *What euphemisms can you think of in relation to war? Make a list of mild, bland terms and phrases that stand in for more explicit or potentially offensive ones. Which ones seem furthest from the truth? Which ones make light of a situation? Write a paragraph about to what extent we can and should expect accuracy about wartime events, and to what extent we accept the use of euphemisms and other such language to cover over the realities of armed human conflict.*

With the passing of Veterans Day last week, I've been thinking about my first day as a paramilitary officer with the Central Intelligence Agency. I spent it filling out paperwork: a health-care plan, a Roth I.R.A., a parking-pass application, a stipend for child care. It was the summer of 2009, and I'd come to the C.I.A. after a tour in the Marine Corps Special Operations.

Having spent my entire adult life working for the federal government, I'd expected the paper chase, but mixed in with the forms, one stood out — Executive Order 12333, which includes this clause:

> No person employed by or acting on behalf of the United States Government shall engage in, or conspire to engage in, assassination.

This seemed straightforward enough. Silenced pistols and cyanide-laced cocktails were for the movies; they weren't the stuff of real intelligence work. So I signed the order. I was giving more thought to whether a rookie like me could land a decent parking spot at the agency's headquarters, in northern Virginia.

Four months later, I began my initial deployment. I was stationed at a remote outpost in eastern Afghanistan. As a paramilitary officer, I trained and operated alongside a tribal militia, but worked at a base alongside a handful of non-paramilitary case officers. Our workspace was a windowless vault. I spent most of my days in the mountain air with our Afghan partners, shooting on ranges or preparing for raids. My colleagues stayed indoors, the toll of the months they'd been deployed showing in their sallow complexions. They were conducting operations, running agents across the border, to Pakistan's tribal areas, but these occurred at night. By day, they sat at a bank of computers, planning out Predator drone strikes. Dossier upon dossier cluttered their desktops — Taliban senior leaders, Al Qaeda operatives, each one targeted for killing. For assassination.

Silenced pistols and cyanide-laced cocktails were for the movies; they weren't the stuff of real intelligence work.

Granted, lawyers with the C.I.A. and the Administrations of George W. Bush and Barack Obama had drawn up semantic arguments carefully delineating the difference between a targeted killing and an assassination. (Steve Coll wrote about Obama's drone war in Pakistan for the magazine this week.) But when the picture of the person you were trying to kill sat on your desk; when you watched the Predator strikes light up the night sky just across the border; and then, when you took that same picture and moved it into a file for archiving, it sure felt like an assassination.

The discomfort of my colleagues, where it existed, didn't stem from the act itself. Their dossiers were filled with details about Taliban commanders and Al Qaeda operatives — people we had identified as valid targets, who were known to have killed marines and soldiers in Afghanistan, or to have had ambitions to launch attacks in the U.S. or Western Europe. The discomfort existed because it felt like we were doing something, on a large scale, that we'd sworn not to. Most of us felt as though we were violating Executive Order 12333. Everybody knew what was happening — senior intelligence officials, general officers, the Administration, even the American people, who ostensibly would not tolerate assassinations carried out in their name.

America avoids that word, "assassination," because such actions are anathema to our ideals, but, having just marked the thirteenth Veterans Day since the post-9/11 wars began, there seems to be some reckoning with how those conflicts have changed our national identity. Much of that conversation has taken place in the arts, especially literature and film. Books like "Billy Lynn's Long Halftime Walk" and movies like "Lone Survivor" offer widely divergent views of the wars, indicating a second struggle, for a narrative.

An important aspect of that narrative will be the clandestine nature of military action, which has become the hallmark of U.S. involvement abroad. At home, accounts from secret operations are often anecdotal—a raid here or there, a terrorist attack foiled. But in increasingly large swaths of the world, this new type of warfare has come to define America. For people in countries from Syria to Yemen, from Somalia to the Philippines, our clandestine wars have become a part of daily life. The conduct of these campaigns has become a secret we keep only from ourselves.

I don't regret our actions at that remote Afghan outpost. I do regret that, as a nation, we've chosen to cloak such actions in doublespeak, telling a lie of sorts—one that no longer seems to be directed at defeating our adversaries. But maybe by understanding that lie, we'll come a bit closer to understanding the truth.

THINKING CRITICALLY ABOUT THE READING

1. In your opinion, what are the differences between the words "assassination," "murder," and "killing"? Are these words synonymous? If not, what distinguishes one from the other?

2. Ackerman writes about the planning an attack on an enemy: "But when the picture of the person you were trying to kill sat on your desk; when you watched the Predator strikes light up the night sky just across the border; and then, when you took that same picture and moved it into a file for archiving, it sure felt like an assassination" (4). Do you agree with his assessment? Why or why not? What else might you call it?

3. What does Ackerman mean when he says that clandestine operations "have become a hallmark of U.S. involvement abroad" (7)? What are the implications of clandestine operations for a country that prides itself on the openness and transparency of its government?

4. Ackerman writes, "I don't regret our actions at that remote Afghan outpost. I do regret that, as a nation, we've chosen to cloak such actions in doublespeak, telling a lie of sorts—one that no longer seems to be directed at defeating our adversaries" (9). Who, then, is the lie directed at? Who is perpetrating it?

5. In paragraph 9, Ackerman uses the word "doublespeak" to address how the U.S. government defends its actions. Read William Lutz's essay, "The World of Doublespeak" (p. 277). In what ways has doublespeak become prominent in

the language of the U.S. government? What instances of doublespeak would you add to the ones Ackerman discusses?

6. The title of the Ackerman's article, "Assassination and the American Language" deliberately echoes an essay written by George Orwell, "Politics and the English Language" (1946). Search for and read Orwell's essay at your library or on the Web. How do the two works compare? In what ways does Ackerman's article illustrate what Orwell discusses in his essay?

LANGUAGE IN ACTION

Read Robert Yoakum's "Everyspeech," a parody that first appeared in the *New York Times* in November 1994. Yoakum was a speechwriter for John F. Kennedy's successful 1960 campaign. As you read the parody below, identify the features of political speech that are the butt of Yoakum's humor. What connections do you see between Yoakum's use of language and the language abuses that Ackerman criticizes? What language in current political speech fits Yoakum's model? What propaganda devices does Yoakum use (see Cross's essay on pp. 247–257)?

EVERYSPEECH

Ladies and gentlemen. I am delighted to see so many friends from the Third Congressional District. And what better site for some straight talk than at this greatest of all state fairs, where ribbons reward American individual enterprise, whether for the biggest beets or the biggest bull?

Speaking of bull, my opponent has said some mighty dishonest things about me. But what can you expect from a typical politician? I want to address some fundamental issues that set me apart from my opponent and his failed party — the party of gutlessness and gridlock.

The American people are ready for straight talk, although don't count on the press to report it straight. The press, like my opponent, has no respect for the public.

This democracy must return to its roots or it will perish, and its roots are you — the honest, hard-working, God-fearing people who made this the greatest nation on earth. Yes, we have problems. But what problems would not be solved if the press and politicians had faith in the people?

Take crime, for example. Rampant, brutal crime. My rival in this race believes that redemption and rehabilitation are the answers to the lawlessness that is tearing our society apart.

Well, if R and R is what you want for those robbers and rapists, don't vote for me. If pampering the punks is what you want, vote for my opponent.

Do I believe in the death penalty? You bet! Do I believe in three strikes and you're out? No, I believe in *two* strikes and you're out! I believe in three strikes and you're *dead*!

You can count on me to crack down on crime, but I won't ignore the other big C word: character. Character made our nation great. Character, and respect for family values. A belief in children and parents. In brothers and sisters and grandparents.

Oh, sure, that sounds corny. Those cynical inside-the-Beltway journalists will ridicule me tomorrow, but I would rather be guilty of a corny defense of family values than of coddling criminals.

While I'm making myself unpopular with the press and a lot of politicians, I might as well alienate even more Washington wimps by telling you frankly how I feel about taxes. I'm against them! Not just in an election year, like my adversary, but every year!

I'm in favor of slashing wasteful welfare, which is where a lot of your hard-earned tax dollars go. The American people have said "enough" to welfare, but inside the Beltway they don't give a hoot about the industrious folks I see before me today. They're too busy with their cocktail parties, diplomatic functions, and society balls.

My opponent loves those affairs, but I'd rather be with my good friends here than with those fork-tongued lawyers, cookie-pushing State Department fops, and high-priced lobbyists. I promise that when elected, my main office will be right here in the Third District. My branch office will be in D.C. And I promise you this: I shall serve only two terms and then return to live with the folks I love.

So on Nov. 8, if you want someone with an independent mind and the courage to change—to *change back to good old American values*—if you've had enough and want someone tough, vote for me. Thank you, and God bless America.

WRITING SUGGESTIONS

1. Ackerman states, "The conduct of these campaigns has become a secret we keep only from ourselves" (6). Do research on the military actions of the United States around the world in recent years. Write an essay in which you either agree or disagree with Ackerman's statement. To what extent are such military and intelligence campaigns a secret? How is it possible to keep a secret from ourselves?

2. Research Executive Order 12333, signed by Ronald Reagan, especially clauses 2.11 and 2.12, which prohibits assassination or indirect participation in assassination. Write an essay in which you argue that the executive order is correct in that it embraces American values of fairness and due process, or is wrong, in that it unfairly ties the hands of the United States in its defense against enemies. What course of action would you recommend to remedy either the executive order or the actions that seem to betray it? What alternatives, if any, are needed?

9

Language That Changed the World: Words That Made a Difference

Political language is powerful; it is persuasive. At its best political language inspires people and challenges them to make a difference, offering the hope that in working together, we can create a better world. We have all heard stories of how, with powerful words, Franklin D. Roosevelt and Winston Churchill energized and rallied their nations to defeat Nazi Germany during World War II and how Mahatma Gandhi, Martin Luther King Jr., and Nelson Mandela championed nonviolence in leading the fight against oppression and racism in India, America, and South Africa. Few things are more inspiring than a good speech given by an eloquent speaker. A skilled orator is a performer, much like a musician. Instead of a beat, though, the speaker gives words and phrases emphasis and makes them resonate. Like a melody, the speaker's language communicates rich images and compelling thoughts. The words of a speaker are more alive than those of a writer because the speaker can directly communicate the passion and conviction of the words to his or her audience. Nevertheless, the transcript of a good speech can still capture our attention and imagination.

In this chapter, "Language That Changed the World," we include six selections from very different times and places. Despite the widely divergent contexts and issues they address, these writers rely on many of the same rhetorical techniques and strategies to give depth and resonance to their messages. As you read these six selections, look for the writers' use of parallelism, repetition, dramatic short sentences, biblical allusions, and memorable diction to give power and energy to their messages. Martin Luther King Jr.'s "I Have a Dream" speech uses brilliant, rich images and compelling logic to insist on equality for all Americans. Delivered on the steps of the Lincoln Memorial in 1963 during the height of the civil rights movement, this speech is considered by many to be one of the greatest speeches of the last century, and it is now part of our cultural consciousness.

John F. Kennedy, in his "Inaugural Address" in 1961, ushered in a new era of optimism, hope, and exploration. He boldly called upon Americans and the citizens of the world to work together for peace and the freedom of all peoples. As the youngest person elected to serve in the White House, President Kennedy energized the office and willingly accepted the mantle of leadership. In 2013 Malala Yousafzai spoke at the Youth Takeover of the United Nations, less than a year after she had been shot by the Taliban because of her education advocacy work. In her speech she positions herself as an advocate for those without a voice, calling for women around the world to have equal access to education. She uses strong, inclusive language to counter the extremist rhetoric of the Taliban and to show the power of education to affect change.

Toni Morrison also writes about the power of language, and the power of those who wield it. She structures her speech around a metaphor of a blind woman, and through a series of reinterpretations, draws out many ways language can be used and abused. Elie Wiesel uses language as a witness and as a call to action, remembering past atrocities, including his own experience as a Holocaust survivor, and exploring how indifference enabled them. He exhorts his audience to pay attention, to respond, and to intervene in the face of atrocities around the world today.

In "A Modest Proposal," Jonathan Swift uses his wit to attack the wealthy English landlords who were, in his eyes, responsible for the widespread homelessness and poverty among sharecroppers in Ireland. In this classic essay, Swift's narrator uses a logical argument to propose a satiric solution to Ireland's problem: infanticide and cannibalism.

I Have a Dream

MARTIN LUTHER KING JR.

Civil rights leader Martin Luther King Jr. (1929–1968) was the son of a Baptist minister in Atlanta, Georgia. Ordained at the age of eighteen, King went on to earn academic degrees from Morehouse College, Crozer Theological Seminary, Boston University, and Chicago Theological Seminary. He came to prominence in 1955 in Montgomery, Alabama, when he led a successful boycott against the city's segregated bus system. The first president of the Southern Christian Leadership Conference, King became the leading spokesman for the civil rights movement during the 1950s and 1960s, espousing a consistent philosophy of nonviolent direct action or resistance to racial injustice. He also championed women's rights and protested the Vietnam War. Named *Time* magazine's Man of the Year in 1963, King was awarded the Nobel Peace Prize in 1964. King was assassinated in April 1968 after speaking at a rally in Memphis, Tennessee.

"I Have a Dream," the keynote address for the March on Washington in 1963, has become one of the most renowned and recognized speeches of the past century. Delivered from the steps of the Lincoln Memorial to commemorate the centennial of the Emancipation Proclamation, King's speech resonates with hope even as it condemns racial oppression.

WRITING TO DISCOVER: *Most Americans have seen film clips of King delivering the "I Have a Dream" speech in Washington, D.C., on August 28, 1963. What do you know of the speech? What do you know of the events and conditions under which King presented it more than fifty years ago?*

I am happy to join with you today in what will go down in history as the greatest demonstration for freedom in the history of our nation.

Five score years ago, a great American, in whose symbolic shadow we stand today, signed the Emancipation Proclamation. This momentous decree came as a great beacon light of hope to millions of Negro slaves who had been seared in the flames of withering injustice. It came as a joyous daybreak to end the long night of their captivity. But one hundred years later, the Negro still is not free. One hundred years later, the life of the Negro is still sadly crippled by the manacles of segregation and the chains of discrimination. One hundred years later, the Negro lives on a lonely island of poverty in the midst of a vast ocean of material prosperity. One hundred years later, the Negro is still anguished in the corners of American society and finds himself in exile in his own land. And so we have come here today to dramatize a shameful condition.

In a sense we have come to our nation's capital to cash a check. When the architects of our republic wrote the magnificent words of the Constitution and the Declaration of Independence, they were signing a promissory note to which every American was to fall heir. This note was the promise that all men—yes, Black men as well as white men—would be guaranteed the inalienable rights of life, liberty, and the pursuit of happiness.

It is obvious today that America has defaulted on this promissory note insofar as her citizens of color are concerned. Instead of honoring this sacred obligation, America has given the Negro people a bad check, a check which has come back marked "insufficient funds." But we refuse to believe that the bank of justice is bankrupt. We refuse to believe that there are insufficient funds in the great vaults of opportunity of this nation; and so we have come to cash this check, a check that will give us upon demand the riches of freedom and the security of justice.

We have also come to this hallowed spot to remind America of the   5
fierce urgency of *now*. This is no time to engage in the luxury of cooling off or to take the tranquilizing drug of gradualism. *Now* is the time to make real the promises of democracy. *Now* is the time to rise from the dark and desolate valley of segregation to the sunlit path of racial justice. *Now* is the time to lift our nation from the quicksands of racial injustice to the solid rock of brotherhood. *Now* is the time to make justice a reality for all of God's children.

It would be fatal for the nation to overlook the urgency of the moment. This sweltering summer of the Negro's legitimate discontent will not pass until there is an invigorating autumn of freedom and equality. Nineteen sixty-three is not an end, but a beginning. And those who hope that the Negro needed to blow off steam and will now be content will have a rude awakening if the nation returns to business as usual. There will be neither rest nor tranquility in America until the Negro is granted his citizenship rights. The whirlwinds of revolt will continue to shake the foundations of our nation until the bright day of justice emerges.

But there is something that I must say to my people who stand on the warm threshold which leads into the palace of justice. In the process of gaining our rightful place, we must not be guilty of wrongful deeds. Let us not seek to satisfy our thirst for freedom by drinking from the cup of bitterness and hatred. We must forever conduct our struggle on the high plane of dignity and discipline. We must not allow our creative protest to degenerate into physical violence. Again and again we must rise to the majestic heights of meeting physical force with soul force. And the marvelous new militancy which has engulfed the Negro community must not lead us to a distrust of all white people; for many of our white brothers, as evidenced by their presence here today, have come to realize that their destiny is tied up with our destiny, and they have come to realize that their freedom is inextricably bound to our freedom.

We cannot walk alone. And as we walk we must make the pledge that we shall always march ahead. We cannot turn back. There are those who are asking the devotees of civil rights, "When will you be satisfied?" We can never be satisfied as long as the Negro is the victim of the unspeakable horrors of police brutality. We can never be satisfied as long as our bodies, heavy with the fatigue of travel, cannot gain lodging in the motels of the highways and the hotels of the cities. We cannot be satisfied as long as the Negro's basic mobility is from a smaller ghetto to a larger one. We can never be satisfied as long as our children are stripped of their selfhood and robbed of their dignity by signs stating "For Whites Only." We cannot be satisfied as long as the Negro in Mississippi cannot vote and a Negro in New York believes he has nothing for which to vote. No, no, we are not satisfied, and we will not be satisfied until justice rolls down like waters and righteousness like a mighty stream.

I am not unmindful that some of you have come here out of great trials and tribulations. Some of you have come fresh from narrow jail cells. Some of you have come from areas where your quest for freedom left you battered by the storms of persecution and staggered by the winds of police brutality. You have been the veterans of creative suffering. Continue to work with the faith that unearned suffering is redemptive.

Go back to Mississippi, and go back to Alabama. Go back to South Carolina. Go back to Georgia. Go back to Louisiana. Go back to the slums and ghettos of our Northern cities, knowing that somehow this situation can and will be changed. Let us not wallow in the valley of despair.

I say to you today, my friends, even though we face the difficulties of today and tomorrow, I still have a dream. It is a dream deeply rooted in the American dream. I have a dream that one day this nation will rise up and live out the true meaning of its creed: "We hold these truths to be self-evident, that all men are created equal." I have a dream that one day, on the red hills of Georgia, sons of former slaves and the sons of former slave owners will be able to sit down together at the table of brotherhood. I have a dream that one day even the state of Mississippi, a state sweltering with the heat of injustice, sweltering with the heat of oppression, will be transformed into an oasis of freedom and justice. I have a dream that my four little children will one day live in a nation where they will not be judged by the color of their skin, but by the content of their character.

> **I have a dream that my four little children will one day live in a nation where they will not be judged by the color of their skin, but by the content of their character.**

I have a dream today. I have a dream that one day down in Alabama—with its vicious racists, with its governor's lips dripping with the words of interposition and nullification—one day right there in Alabama, little Black boys and Black girls will be able to join hands with little white boys and white girls as sisters and brothers.

I have a dream today. I have a dream that one day every valley shall be exalted and every hill and mountain shall be made low, the rough places will be made plain and the crooked places will be made straight, and the glory of the Lord shall be revealed, and all flesh shall see it together.

This is our hope. This is the faith that I go back to the South with. And with this faith we will be able to hew out of the mountain of despair a stone of hope. With this faith we will be able to transform the jangling discords of our nation into a beautiful symphony of brotherhood. With this faith we will be able to work together, to play together, to struggle together, to go to jail together, to stand up for freedom together, knowing that we will be free one day.

And this will be the day—this will be the day when all of God's chil-   15
dren will be able to sing with new meaning:

My country, 'tis of thee,
Sweet land of liberty,
  Of thee I sing;
Land where my fathers died,
Land of the Pilgrims' pride,
From every mountainside
  Let freedom ring.

And if America is to be a great nation, this must become true.

And so let freedom ring from the prodigious hilltops of New Hampshire. Let freedom ring from the mighty mountains of New York. Let freedom ring from the heightening Alleghenies of Pennsylvania. Let freedom ring from the snow-capped Rockies of Colorado. Let freedom ring from the curvaceous slopes of California.

But not only that. Let freedom ring from Stone Mountain of Georgia. Let freedom ring from Lookout Mountain of Tennessee. Let freedom ring from every hill and molehill of Mississippi. "From every mountainside let freedom ring."

And when this happens—when we allow freedom to ring, when we let it ring from every village and every hamlet, from every state and every city—we will be able to speed up that day when all of God's children, Black men and white men, Jews and Gentiles, Protestants and Catholics, will be able to join hands and sing in the words of the old Negro spiritual: "Free at last! Free at last! Thank God Almighty. We are free at last!"

THINKING CRITICALLY ABOUT THE READING

1. Why does King say that the Constitution and the Declaration of Independence act as a "promissory note" (3) to the American people? In what way has America "defaulted" (4) on its promise?

2. What do you think King means when he says, "In the process of gaining our rightful place [in society] we must not be guilty of wrongful deeds" (7)? Why is this issue so important to him?

3. King uses parallel constructions and repetition throughout his speech. (Glossary: *Parallelism*) Identify the words and phrases that he emphasizes. Explain what these techniques add to the persuasiveness of his argument.

4. King makes liberal use of metaphor—and metaphorical imagery—in his speech. (Glossary: *Figures of Speech*) Choose a few examples, and examine what each adds to the speech. How do they collectively help King engage his listeners' feelings of injustice and give them hope of a better future?

5. In his final paragraph, King claims that by freeing the Negro we will all be free. What exactly does he mean? Is King simply being hyperbolic or does his claim embody an undeniable truth? Explain.

6. What, in a nutshell, is King's dream? What vision does he have for the future?

LANGUAGE IN ACTION

Read the following excerpt from Nelson Mandela's 1994 "Inauguration Speech," which he gave when instated as the first black president of South Africa. His election, coming on the heels of apartheid, was a particular cause for celebration and hope.

What similarities do you see between King's famous speech and Mandela's? Look for similarities in elements like sentence structure, as well as thematic similarities. Are there any points in Mandela's speech that seem to refer directly to King's? Why might Mandela want to remind his listeners of King's address?

> The time for the healing of the wounds has come.
> The moment to bridge the chasms that divide us has come.
> The time to build is upon us.
> We have, at last, achieved our political emancipation. We pledge ourselves to liberate all our people from the continuing bondage of poverty, deprivation, suffering, gender and other discrimination.
> We succeeded to take our last steps to freedom in conditions of relative peace. We commit ourselves to the construction of a complete, just and lasting peace.
> We have triumphed in the effort to implant hope in the breasts of the millions of our people. We enter into a covenant that we shall build the society in which all South Africans, both black and white, will be able to walk tall, without any fear in their hearts, assured of their inalienable right to human dignity—a rainbow nation at peace with itself and the world.
> As a token of its commitment to the renewal of our country, the new Interim Government of National Unity will, as a matter of urgency, address the issue of amnesty for various categories of our people who are currently serving terms of imprisonment.
> We dedicate this day to all the heroes and heroines in this country and the rest of the world who sacrificed in many ways and surrendered their lives so that we could be free.

Their dreams have become reality. Freedom is their reward.

We are both humbled and elevated by the honor and privilege that you, the people of South Africa, have bestowed on us, as the first President of a united, democratic, non-racial and non-sexist government.

We understand it still that there is no easy road to freedom.

We know it well that none of us acting alone can achieve success.

We must therefore act together as a united people, for national reconciliation, for nation building, for the birth of a new world.

Let there be justice for all.

Let there be peace for all.

Let there be work, bread, water and salt for all.

Let each know that for each the body, the mind and the soul have been freed to fulfill themselves.

Never, never and never again shall it be that this beautiful land will again experience the oppression of one by another and suffer the indignity of being the skunk of the world.

Let freedom reign.

The sun shall never set on so glorious a human achievement!

God bless Africa!

Thank you.

WRITING SUGGESTIONS

1. King portrayed an America in 1963 in which there was still systematic oppression of African Americans. What, for you, is oppression? Have you ever felt yourself—or have you known others—to be oppressed or part of a group that is oppressed? Who, if anyone, in America is oppressed today? Who are the oppressors? How can oppression be overcome? Write an essay in which you present your views on how oppression can best be combated in today's world. You may find it helpful to read Martin Luther King Jr.'s "Letter from Birmingham Jail" (95–108) before beginning to write.

2. In using the photograph on page 307 of Martin Luther King Jr. in its "Think Different" advertising campaign, Apple is relying on our cultural memory of King's "I Have a Dream" speech and of King as a person who was creative in his efforts to promote racial justice. To what extent does achieving racial equality depend on "thinking differently"? Write an essay in which you present your position.

3. Martin Luther King Jr. says that his dream is "deeply rooted in the American dream" (11). What is the American dream as you understand it? Can that dream be realized in the twenty-first century? If so, how? If not, why does the dream persist? In an essay, discuss your thoughts on the American dream and its viability today.

4. Traditionally, commencement speakers challenge our nation's high school, college, and university graduates to dream big, to think about what they contribute to making our world a better place for humankind. In 2005

Source: Boston Globe/Contributor/Getty Images

Apple's iconic Steve Jobs was asked to give the commencement address at Stanford University—no small assignment for a man who was a college dropout himself. Jobs framed his talk around three instructive autobiographical stories to show the circuitous route he followed to find his passion. Jobs' message was quite simple: Trust in yourself, don't settle for something you don't love, and follow your heart and intuition no matter what the world around you is telling you to do. You can view Jobs' commencement address on YouTube at http://youtu.be/UF8uR6Z6KLc. After viewing Jobs' speech to the Stanford graduates—and perhaps reading the text of his address online, ask yourself what makes his advice so alluring and yet so challenging. What, if anything, is holding you back from following your heart, doing what you love to do? Write an essay in which you explain what it is you would love to become and then discuss what it will take to achieve your dream.

Inaugural Address

JOHN F. KENNEDY

John Fitzgerald Kennedy (1917–1963), the thirty-fifth president of the United States, was assassinated in Dallas, Texas, on November 22, 1963. After attending the London School of Economics briefly in 1935, Kennedy entered Harvard College in 1936, from which he graduated with honors in 1940. Kennedy's senior thesis, an analysis of the reasons why England failed to rearm before World War II, was published as a book entitled *Why England Slept* (1940). It became an immediate best seller. Kennedy served in the Navy during World War II as the commander of a PT boat in the South Pacific. After the war, Kennedy entered politics and in 1946 was elected to Congress as a representative from Massachusetts, a post he held until 1952 when he successfully campaigned for a seat in the Senate. A moderate liberal in the Democratic Party, Kennedy quickly emerged on the national scene. In 1960 he narrowly defeated the then vice president Richard Nixon for the presidency. During his administration, Kennedy established the Peace Corps, confronted the Soviet Union when it tried to arm Cuba, and supported black Americans in their campaign for civil rights. He was the author of the Pulitzer Prize-winning *Profiles in Courage* (1956), a collection of essays about great congressional leadership at critical moments in our nation's history, and *Strategy of Peace* (1960), a statement of his goals in foreign policy.

Kennedy, the youngest man ever elected president, was known for the youthful and hopeful image he brought to the White House and for the eloquence of his speeches. In his "Inaugural Address" Kennedy used powerful rhetoric to urge people to become involved in their country's affairs and to join the fight against the spread of communism.

WRITING TO DISCOVER: *If we know one thing about Kennedy's "Inaugural Address," it's the oft-quoted statement: "And so, my fellow Americans, ask not what your country can do for you; ask what you can do for your country." How do you think Americans would respond to such a challenge from their president today? In your opinion, what's different about Kennedy's America and the country we live in now?*

We observe today not a victory of party but a celebration of freedom, symbolizing an end as well as a beginning, signifying renewal as well as change. For I have sworn before you and Almighty God the same solemn oath our forebears prescribed nearly a century and three-quarters ago.

The world is very different now. For man holds in his mortal hands the power to abolish all forms of human poverty and all forms of human life. And yet the same revolutionary belief for which our forebears fought is still at issue around the globe, the belief that the rights of man come not from the generosity of the state but from the hand of God.

We dare not forget today that we are the heirs of that first revolution. Let the word go forth from this time and place, to friend and foe alike, that the torch has been passed to a new generation of Americans, born in this century, tempered by war, disciplined by a hard and bitter peace, proud of our ancient heritage, and unwilling to witness or permit the slow undoing of those human rights to which this nation has always been committed, and to which we are committed today at home and around the world.

Let every nation know, whether it wishes us well or ill, that we shall pay any price, bear any burden, meet any hardship, support any friend, oppose any foe to assure the survival and the success of liberty.

This much we pledge—and more.   5

To those old allies whose cultural and spiritual origins we share, we pledge the loyalty of faithful friends. United, there is little we cannot do in a host of co-operative ventures. Divided, there is little we can do, for we dare not meet a powerful challenge at odds and split asunder.

To those new states whom we welcome to the ranks of the free, we pledge our word that one form of colonial control shall not have passed away merely to be replaced by a far more iron tyranny. We shall not always expect to find them supporting our view. But we shall always hope to find them strongly supporting their own freedom, and to remember that, in the past, those who foolishly sought power by riding the back of the tiger ended up inside.

To those peoples in the huts and villages of half the globe struggling to break the bonds of mass misery, we pledge our best efforts to help them help themselves, for whatever period is required, not because the Communists may be doing it, not because we seek their votes, but because it is right. If a free society cannot help the many who are poor, it cannot save the few who are rich.

To our sister republics south of our border, we offer a special pledge: to convert our good words into good deeds, in a new alliance for progress, to assist free men and free governments in casting off the chains of poverty. But this peaceful revolution of hope cannot become the prey of hostile powers. Let all our neighbors know that we shall join with them to oppose aggression or subversion anywhere in the Americas. And let every other power know that this hemisphere intends to remain the master of its own house.

To that world assembly of sovereign states, the United Nations, our   10
last best hope in an age where the instruments of war have far outpaced the instruments of peace, we renew our pledge of support: to prevent it from becoming merely a forum for invective, to strengthen its shield of the new and the weak, and to enlarge the area in which its writ may run.

Finally, to those nations who would make themselves our adversary, we offer not a pledge but a request: that both sides begin anew the quest for peace, before the dark powers of destruction unleashed by science engulf all humanity in planned or accidental self-destruction.

We dare not tempt them with weakness. For only when our arms are sufficient beyond doubt can we be certain beyond doubt that they will never be employed.

But neither can two great and powerful groups of nations take comfort from our present course—both sides over-burdened by the cost of modern weapons, both rightly alarmed by the steady spread of the deadly atom, yet both racing to alter that uncertain balance of terror that stays the hand of mankind's final war.

So let us begin anew, remembering on both sides that civility is not a sign of weakness, and sincerity is always subject to proof. Let us never negotiate out of fear, but let us never fear to negotiate.

My fellow citizens of the world, ask not what America will do for you, but what together we can do for the freedom of man.   15

Let both sides explore what problems unite us instead of belaboring those problems which divide us.

Let both sides, for the first time, formulate serious and precise proposals for the inspection and control of arms, and bring the absolute power to destroy other nations under the absolute control of all nations.

Let both sides seek to invoke the wonders of science instead of its terrors. Together let us explore the stars, conquer the deserts, eradicate disease, tap the ocean depths and encourage the arts and commerce.

Let both sides unite to heed in all corners of the earth the command of Isaiah to "undo the heavy burdens . . . [and] let the oppressed go free."

And if a beachhead of co-operation may push back the jungle of suspicion, let both sides join in creating a new endeavor, not a new balance of power, but a new world of law, where the strong are just and the weak secure and the peace preserved.

All this will not be finished in the first one hundred days. Nor will it   20
be finished in the first one thousand days, nor in the life of this Administration, nor even perhaps in our lifetime on this planet. But let us begin.

In your hands, my fellow citizens, more than mine, will rest the final success or failure of our course. Since this country was founded, each generation of Americans has been summoned to give testimony to its national loyalty. The graves of young Americans who answered the call to service surround the globe.

Now the trumpet summons us again—not as a call to bear arms, though arms we need; not as a call to battle, though embattled we are; but a call to bear the burden of a long twilight struggle, year in and year out, "rejoicing in hope, patient in tribulation," a struggle against the common enemies of men: tyranny, poverty, disease and war itself.

Can we forge against these enemies a grand and global alliance, North and South, East and West, that can assure a more fruitful life for all mankind? Will you join in that historic effort?

In the long history of the world, only a few generations have been granted the role of defending freedom in its hour of maximum danger. I do not shrink from this responsibility; I welcome it. I do not believe that any of us would exchange places with any other people or any other generation. The energy, the faith, the devotion which we bring to this endeavor will light our country and all who serve it, and the glow from that fire can truly light the world.

And so, my fellow Americans, ask not what your country can do for you; ask what you can do for your country. 25

My fellow citizens of the world, ask not what America will do for you, but what together we can do for the freedom of man.

Finally, whether you are citizens of America or citizens of the world, ask of us here the same high standards of strength and sacrifice which we ask of you. With a good conscience our only sure reward, with history that final judge of our deeds, let us go forth to lead the land we love, asking His blessing and His help, but knowing that here on earth God's work must truly be our own.

THINKING CRITICALLY ABOUT THE READING

1. Kennedy's second paragraph begins with the statement, "The world is very different now." In what ways is the world different than what it was at our country's founding?

2. The president makes promises to several groups, not only to the citizens of the United States, but also to groups outside the country. Is it clear which groups Kennedy means? See if you can identify a few of these groups; then, explain what Kennedy gains by not "naming names."

3. Identify several examples of Kennedy's use of parallelism. (Glossary: *Parallelism*) What does this rhetorical strategy add to the strength of his speech?

4. In paragraph 23, Kennedy asks two rhetorical questions. (Glossary: *Rhetorical Questions*) What do you think his purpose is in asking these questions?

5. Kennedy makes clear what he wants to accomplish in his tenure as president; however, he doesn't say how he will achieve these goals. Do you find this problematic, or do you think this lack of specificity is appropriate in a speech of this kind?

LANGUAGE IN ACTION

Long after some speeches have been delivered and the audiences have dispersed, the speakers' words live on. Some thoughts are so compelling or are so well stated that they are quoted years after they were first written and delivered. Have you ever wondered what makes such statements by world leaders and thinkers so compelling and memorable? Carefully read and analyze the following oft-quoted statements:

If you desire many things, many things will seem few.

—BENJAMIN FRANKLIN

A friend to all is a friend to none.

—ARISTOTLE

All great things are simple and many can be expressed in single words: freedom, justice, honor, duty, mercy, hope.

—WINSTON CHURCHILL

Not everything that is faced can be changed. But nothing can be changed until it is faced.

—JAMES BALDWIN

Adopt the pace of nature: her secret is patience.

—RALPH WALDO EMERSON

They don't care how much you know until they know how much you care.

—THEODORE ROOSEVELT

Even the rich are hungry for love, for being cared for, for being wanted, for having someone to call their own.

—MOTHER TERESA

Action expresses priorities.

—MOHANDAS GANDHI

In the practice of tolerance, one's enemy is the best teacher.

—DALAI LAMA

A poem begins in delight and ends in wisdom.

—ROBERT FROST

As a class discuss what these statements have in common. Do any of them suggest or bring to mind other statements that you have heard quoted? What rhetorical techniques or strategies have these speakers used to make their statements memorable? Which ones did you find most memorable? Explain why.

WRITING SUGGESTIONS

1. Both Abraham Lincoln and John F. Kennedy were presidents renowned for the eloquence, simplicity, and brevity of their speeches. Write an essay in which you compare and contrast Lincoln's "Second Inaugural Address" with Kennedy's "Inaugural Address." You can hear and read Lincoln's Second Inaugural Address on YouTube at youtu.be/YhteaxrdmKo.

2. Imagine that you have been elected president of the United States and that your inauguration is three weeks away. Using Kennedy's speech as a model, write an inaugural address in which you identify the chief problems and issues of today and set forth your plan for dealing with them. Consider first what approach to take—for example, you might write an inspirational address to the nation, or you may choose to describe in everyday language the problems that confront the nation and the actions you believe will solve these problems.

Address at the Youth Takeover of the United Nations

MALALA YOUSAFZAI

Malala Yousafzai was born on July 12, 1997, in Mingora, Pakistan, which was once a popular tourist destination before the Taliban began to gain control of the region. Yousafzai, whose father is an anti-Taliban activist, educator, and the founder of her school, recognized from an early age the threat the Taliban posed to her education. As early as 2008 she gave a speech entitled "How Dare the Taliban Take Away My Basic Right to Education?" and by 2009, using a pen name to disguise her identity, she began blogging for the BBC about the effects of Taliban rule. Her identity was revealed soon thereafter and her advocacy for women's rights to an education gained a larger platform, earning her Pakistan's National Youth Peace Prize and a nomination for the International Children's Peace Prize in 2011. But the attention Yousafzai received made her a target, and by the time she was fourteen, the Taliban had issued a death threat against her. Although her family worried for her safety, they did not believe at first that she would be harmed. But on October 9, 2012, when Yousafzai was on her way home from school, the bright and impassioned advocate for girls' education was shot in the head by a member of the Taliban. Incredibly, she survived, becoming not only an international cause célèbre but an even more committed activist for peace and education.

The speech included here was first given at the United Nations in 2013. As a result of the attention the shooting and recovery drew to Yousafzai's activism for women's education, in 2014 Yousafzai was nominated for a Nobel Peace Prize and became the youngest person ever to win the award. She has also written an autobiography entitled *I Am Malala: The Girl Who Stood Up for Education and Was Shot by the Taliban* (2013). Yousafzai is continuing her education in England. She remains a target of the Taliban.

WRITING TO DISCOVER: *How has your family influenced how you think? How you speak? The causes you support or any volunteering you've done? Why and how do you think our families affect our convictions?*

Honorable U.N. Secretary-General Mr. Ban Ki-moon, respected president of the General Assembly Vuk Jeremić, honorable U.N. envoy for global education Mr. Gordon Brown, respected elders and my dear brothers and sisters: *A salaam alaikum.*

Today, it is an honor for me to be speaking again after a long time. Being here with such honorable people is a great moment in my life. And it is an honor for me that today I am wearing a shawl of the late Benazir Bhutto Shaheed.

I don't know where to begin my speech. I don't know what people would be expecting me to say, but first of all thank you to God for whom we all are equal, and thank you to every person who has prayed for my fast recovery and a new life. I cannot believe how much love people have shown me. I have received thousands of good-wish cards and gifts from all over the world. Thank you to all of them. Thank you to the children whose innocent words encouraged me. Thank you to my elders whose prayers strengthened me.

> **We call upon all governments to ensure free, compulsory education all over the world for every child. We call upon all the governments to fight against terrorism and violence. To protect children from brutality and harm.**

I would like to thank my nurses, doctors and the staff of the hospitals in Pakistan and the U.K. and the U.A.E. government, who have helped me to get better and recover my strength.

I fully support Mr. Ban Ki-moon, the Secretary-General, in his Global   5
Education First Initiative, and the work of U.N. Special Envoy Gordon Brown and the respected president of the General Assembly Vuk Jeremić. I thank all of them for their leadership, which they continue to give. They continue to inspire all of us to action.

Dear brothers and sisters, do remember one thing: Malala Day is not my day. Today is the day of every woman, every boy, and every girl who have raised their voice for their rights. There are hundreds of human rights activists and social workers who are not only speaking for their rights, but who are struggling to achieve their goals of peace, education, and equality. Thousands of people have been killed by the terrorists and millions have been injured. I am just one of them.

So here I stand, one girl among many.

I speak not for myself, but so those without a voice can be heard. Those who have fought for their rights. Their right to live in peace. Their right to be treated with dignity. Their right to equality of opportunity. Their right to be educated.

Dear friends, on 9 October 2012, the Taliban shot me on the left side of my forehead. They shot my friends, too. They thought that the bullets would silence us. But they failed. And out of that silence came thousands of voices. The terrorists thought they would change my aims and stop my ambitions. But nothing changed in my life except this: weakness, fear and hopelessness died. Strength, power and courage was born.

I am the same Malala. My ambitions are the same. My hopes are the   10
same. My dreams are the same.

Dear sisters and brothers, I am not against anyone. Neither am I here to speak in terms of personal revenge against the Taliban or any other terrorist group. I am here to speak for the right of education for every child. I want education for the sons and daughters of the Taliban and all the terrorists and extremists.

I do not even hate the Talib who shot me. Even if there was a gun in my hand and he was standing in front of me, I would not shoot him. This is the compassion I have learned from Muhammad, the prophet of mercy, and Jesus Christ, and Lord Buddha. This is the legacy of change I have inherited from Martin Luther King, Nelson Mandela, and Muhammad Ali Jinnah. This is the philosophy of nonviolence that I have learned from Gandhiji, Bacha Khan, and Mother Teresa. And this is the forgiveness that I have learned from my father and from my mother. This is what my soul is telling me: be peaceful and love everyone.

Dear sisters and brothers, we realize the importance of light when we see darkness. We realize the importance of our voice when we are silenced. In the same way, when we were in Swat, the north of Pakistan, we realized the importance of pens and books when we saw the guns.

The wise saying "the pen is mightier than the sword" is true. The extremists are afraid of books and pens. The power of education frightens them. They are afraid of women. The power of the voice of women frightens them. And that is why they killed 14 innocent students in the recent attack in Quetta. And that is why they killed female teachers and polio workers in Khyber Pakhtunkhwa. That is why they are blasting schools every day. Because they were and they are afraid of change, afraid of the equality that we will bring to our society.

And I remember that there was a boy in our school who was asked by 15 a journalist, "Why are the Taliban against education?" He answered very simply. By pointing to his book, he said, "A Talib doesn't know what is written inside this book." They think that God is a tiny little conservative being who would send girls to hell just for going to school. The terrorists are misusing the name of Islam and Pashtun society for their own personal benefit. Pakistan is a peace-loving, democratic country. Pashtuns want education for their daughters and sons. Islam is a religion of peace, humanity, and brotherhood. Islam says it is not only each child's right to get an education, rather it is their duty and responsibility to.

Honorable Secretary-General, peace is a necessity for education. In many parts of the world, especially Pakistan and Afghanistan, terrorism, war and conflicts stop children from going to schools. We are really tired of these wars.

Women and children are suffering in many ways, in many parts of the world. In India, innocent and poor children are victims of child labor. Many schools have been destroyed in Nigeria. People in Afghanistan have been affected by the hurdles of extremism. Young girls have to do domestic child labor and are forced to get married at an early age. Poverty, ignorance, injustice, racism, and the deprivation of basic rights are the main problems faced by both men and women.

Dear fellows, today I am focusing on women's rights and girls' education because they are suffering the most. There was a time when women social activists asked men to stand up for their rights. But this time we will do it by ourselves. I am not telling men to step away from speaking for women's rights, rather I am focusing on women to be independent and fight for themselves.

So dear sisters and brothers, now it is time to speak up. So today, we call upon the world leaders to change their strategic policies in favor of peace and prosperity. We call upon the world leaders that all the peace deals must protect women's and children's rights. A deal that goes against the rights of women is unacceptable.

We call upon all governments to ensure free, compulsory education all over the world for every child. We call upon all the governments to fight against terrorism and violence, to protect children from brutality and harm. We call upon the developed nations to support the expansion of educational opportunities for girls in the developing world. We call upon all communities to be tolerant, to reject prejudice based on caste, creed, sect, color, religion or gender. To ensure freedom and equality for women so they can flourish. We cannot all succeed when half of us are held back. We call upon our sisters around the world to be brave, to embrace the strength within themselves and realize their full potential.

Dear brothers and sisters, we want schools and education for every child's bright future. We will continue our journey to our destination of peace and education. No one can stop us. We will speak up for our rights and we will bring change through our voice. We believe in the power and the strength of our words. Our words can change the whole world, because we are all together, united for the cause of education. And if we want to achieve our goal, then let us empower ourselves with the weapon of knowledge and let us shield ourselves with unity and togetherness.

Dear brothers and sisters, we must not forget that millions of people are suffering from poverty, injustice, and ignorance. We must not forget that millions of children are out of their schools. We must not forget that our sisters and brothers are waiting for a bright, peaceful future.

So let us wage a global struggle against illiteracy, poverty and terrorism. Let us pick up our books and our pens. *They* are our most powerful weapons. One child, one teacher, one book and one pen can change the world.

Education is the only solution. Education first. Thank you.

THINKING CRITICALLY ABOUT THE READING

1. Why do you think Yousafzai uses simple and repeated declarations? What effect does repetition have on listeners and readers? How do simple declarations advance her argument?

2. Why do you think Yousafzai mentions drawing inspiration from a number of different religious and political figures, including many who are not Islamic? Whom does she name, and why might she name these figures in particular? How do you think her initial audience at the United Nations affected her choice?

3. We might characterize Yousafzai's essay as a "call to action," a work meant to stir others to activism. What actions does she call for? Why do you think she makes this type of plea? How does she seem to feel about violence?

4. According to Yousafzai, why are extremists "afraid of books and pens" (8)? Of education? Of women? How does she suggest we address extremists? Must we become extremists?

5. Yousafzai argues that "our words can change the whole world" (13). In what ways does she suggest words can change the world? What words—and whose words—do you think she would have us focus on in addressing extremists and extremisms?

6. Yousafzai makes many grand statements throughout the essay and appeals to her readers for change. What are the most concrete appeals that she makes? What are the most manageable of the grander changes for which she calls? Why might she make such grand statements and appeals, particularly to a young audience? What effect do they have on readers?

LANGUAGE IN ACTION

Malala Yousafzai and her father, Ziauddin, cofounded the Malala Fund to ensure that every girl has access to secondary education. Currently, more than 60 million girls worldwide do not complete their education because of poverty, early marriage, and political crisis and strife. The fund's petition gathered over 1,100,000 signatures, convincing the Global Partnership for Education to expand its focus and support twelve years of safe, quality education for girls around the world. The Malala Fund has invited girls everywhere to stand #withMalala and contribute their creative work—photography, video, drawings, paintings, dance, or spoken word—to an online gallery.

Using your social media outlet of choice, do a search for #withMalala and view some of the stories and artwork that are tagged there. Consider the role of hashtag phrases in contemporary language. How do they operate as tools for human rights advocacy? Does anything you found in your search for #withMalala surprise you?

Discuss in class what you make of the hashtag phrase as a social phenomenon, and the ways you've seen hashtags used. Hashtags lend themselves well to humor and marketing and rallying around a cause, but do they have a dark side, too? If so, where does that come from?

WRITING SUGGESTIONS

1. Yousafzai argues that it is "the power of education" that "frightens" the ultra-conservative Taliban (8). Why is education frightening? What does it offer on a practical level, and what does it represent on an ideological one? Write an essay that explores why education may be "frightening" to some groups. Is frightening the most accurate word? What lies beneath that fear?

2. Yousafzai argues that the Taliban is particularly "afraid of women," that they are "afraid of the equality that we will bring into our society" (8). Can you think of groups in your own nation, region, or community (even your college campus) that could be said to be "afraid of equality"? While few groups act on their fear with the kind of coordinated violence the Taliban uses, there are still repercussions. Choose a group you would argue is "afraid of equality," and write an essay analyzing the effects that group has had on its community. How do people respond to the group? Have any of the changes the group opposes come to be, despite their efforts? What has changed as a result of their stance, and what hasn't?

When Language Dies: 1993 Nobel Prize for Literature Lecture

Toni Morrison

Born Chloe Ardelia Wofford on February 18, 1931, in Lorain, Ohio, Toni Morrison is an American novelist, editor, and professor. Morrison changed her name to Toni while at Howard University because Chloe was difficult to pronounce. She earned her B.A. in English from Howard in 1953 before earning an M.A. in English at Cornell University in 1955. She then taught for two years at Texas Southern University before returning to teach at Howard University. In the early 1960s, Morrison became an editor in the textbooks division of Random House. It would take nearly a decade before her talent was recognized and she became the company's only African American senior editor in trade fiction, where she was instrumental in helping publish the works of African American women writers such as Toni Cade Bambara, June Jordan, and Angela Davis. At the same time, she continued writing her own novels, the first of which, *The Bluest Eye*, was published in 1970.

The Bluest Eye met largely critical reviews, and her first major success as a novelist was *Song of Solomon* (1977), earning Morrison a National Book Critics Circle Award and an American Academy of Arts and Letters Award. But it was *Beloved* (1987) that won her the Pulitzer Prize for fiction, and, ultimately, the Nobel Prize in 1993; for although the Nobel was awarded for her body of work, the committee named *Beloved* in particular as most outstanding.

Morrison gave the speech included here upon receiving her Nobel Prize. Morrison begins with a parable in which a wise, clairvoyant blind woman is asked by a pair of youth eager to disprove her merit to guess whether the bird held in their hands is living or dead. As Morrison explains, the parable shows us not just the blind woman, but the nature of power held by those able to preserve or take a life, a metaphor that Morrison extends to language. Morrison chooses "to read the bird as language and the woman as a practiced writer. She [the blind woman] is worried about how the language she dreams in, given to her at birth, is handled, put into service, even withheld from her." By highlighting this vulnerability—the precariousness of writers and their language—Morrison gestures to her own work and to the work of other African American writers whose language has been "withheld" from the literary canon.

WRITING TO DISCOVER: *Morrison's work was overlooked, even uncredited, early in her career, despite its merit. Have you ever felt overlooked? Why? How did you react? How did this neglect or inattention make you feel? How do you think such a feeling might either fuel or extinguish ambition?*

"Once upon a time there was an old woman. Blind but wise." Or was it an old man? A guru, perhaps. Or a griot soothing restless children. I have heard this story, or one exactly like it, in the lore of several cultures. "Once upon a time there was an old woman. Blind. Wise."

In the version I know the woman is the daughter of slaves, black, American, and lives alone in a small house outside of town. Her reputation for wisdom is without peer and without question. Among her people she is both the law and its transgression. The honor she is paid and the awe in which she is held reach beyond her neighborhood to places far away; to the city where the intelligence of rural prophets is the source of much amusement.

One day the woman is visited by some young people who seem to be bent on disproving her clairvoyance and showing her up for the fraud they believe she is. Their plan is simple: they enter her house and ask the one question the answer to which rides solely on her difference from them, a difference they regard as a profound disability: her blindness. They stand before her, and one of them says, "Old woman, I hold in my hand a bird. Tell me whether it is living or dead."

She does not answer, and the question is repeated. "Is the bird I am holding living or dead?"

Still she doesn't answer. She is blind and cannot see her visitors, let alone what is in their hands. She does not know their color, gender, or homeland. She only knows their motive.   5

The old woman's silence is so long, the young people have trouble holding their laughter.

Finally she speaks and her voice is soft but stern. "I don't know," she says. "I don't know whether the bird you are holding is dead or alive, but what I do know is that it is in your hands. It is in your hands."

Her answer can be taken to mean: if it is dead, you have either found it that way or you have killed it. If it is alive, you can still kill it. Whether it is to stay alive, it is your decision. Whatever the case, it is your responsibility.

For parading their power and her helplessness, the young visitors are reprimanded, told they are responsible not only for the act of mockery but also for the small bundle of life sacrificed to achieve its aims. The blind woman shifts attention away from assertions of power to the instrument through which that power is exercised.

Speculation on what (other than its own frail body) that bird-in-the-hand might signify has always been attractive to me, but especially so now thinking, as I have been, about the work I do that has brought me to this company. So I choose to read the bird as language and the woman as a practiced writer. She is worried about how the language she dreams in, given to her at birth, is handled, put into service, even withheld from her for certain nefarious purposes. Being a writer she thinks of language partly as a system, partly as a living thing over which one has control, but mostly as agency—as an act with consequences. So the question the children put to her: "Is it living or dead?" is not unreal because she thinks of language as susceptible   10 to death, erasure; certainly imperiled and salvageable only by an effort of the will. She believes that if the bird in the hands of her visitors is dead the custodians are responsible for the corpse. For her a dead language is not only one no longer spoken or written, it is unyielding language content to admire its own

Oppressive language does more than represent violence; it is violence; does more than represent the limits of knowledge; it limits knowledge.

paralysis. Like statist language, censored and censoring. Ruthless in its policing duties, it has no desire or purpose other than maintaining the free range of its own narcotic narcissism, its own exclusivity and dominance. However moribund, it is not without effect for it actively thwarts the intellect, stalls conscience, supresses human potential. Unreceptive to interrogation, it cannot form or tolerate new ideas, shape other thoughts, tell another story, fill baffling silences. Official language smitheryed to sanction ignorance and preserve privilege is a suit of armor polished to shocking glitter, a husk from which the knight departed long ago. Yet there it is: dumb, predatory, sentimental. Exciting reverence in schoolchildren, providing shelter for despots, summoning false memories of stability, harmony among the public.

She is convinced that when language dies, out of carelessness, disuse, indifference and absence of esteem, or killed by fiat, not only she herself, but all users and makers are accountable for its demise. In her country children have bitten their tongues off and use bullets instead to iterate the voice of speechlessness, of disabled and disabling language, of language adults have abandoned altogether as a device for grappling with meaning, providing guidance, or expressing love. But she knows tongue-suicide is not only the choice of children. It is common among the infantile heads of state and power merchants whose evacuated language leaves them with no access to what is left of their human instincts for they speak only to those who obey, or in order to force obedience.

The systematic looting of language can be recognized by the tendency of its users to forgo its nuanced, complex, mid-wifery properties for menace and subjugation. Oppressive language does more than represent violence; it is violence; does more than represent the limits of knowledge; it limits knowledge. Whether it is obscuring state language or the faux-language of mindless media; whether it is the proud but calcified language of the academy or the commodity driven language of science; whether it is the malign language of law-without-ethics, or language designed for the estrangement of minorities, hiding its racist plunder in its literary cheek — it must be rejected, altered and exposed. It is the language that drinks blood, laps vulnerabilities, tucks its fascist boots under crinolines of respectability and patriotism as it moves relentlessly toward the bottom line and the bottomed-out mind. Sexist language, racist language, theistic language — all are typical of the policing languages of mastery, and cannot, do not permit new knowledge or encourage the mutual exchange of ideas.

The old woman is keenly aware that no intellectual mercenary, nor insatiable dictator, no paid-for politician or demagogue; no counterfeit journalist would be persuaded by her thoughts. There is and will be rousing language to keep citizens armed and arming; slaughtered and slaughtering in the malls, courthouses, post offices, playgrounds, bedrooms and boulevards; stirring, memorializing language to mask the pity and waste of needless death. There will be more diplomatic language to countenance rape, torture, assassination. There is and will be more seductive, mutant language designed to throttle women, to pack their throats like paté-producing geese with their own unsayable, transgressive words; there will be more of the language of surveillance disguised as research; of politics and history calculated to render the suffering of millions mute; language glamorized to thrill the dissatisfied and bereft into assaulting their neighbors; arrogant pseudo-empirical language crafted to lock creative people into cages of inferiority and hopelessness.

Underneath the eloquence, the glamor, the scholarly associations, however stirring or seductive, the heart of such language is languishing, or perhaps not beating at all—if the bird is already dead.

She has thought about what could have been the intellectual history   15
of any discipline if it had not insisted upon, or been forced into, the waste of time and life that rationalizations for and representations of dominance required—lethal discourses of exclusion blocking access to cognition for both the excluder and the excluded.

The conventional wisdom of the Tower of Babel story is that the collapse was a misfortune. That it was the distraction, or the weight of many languages that precipitated the tower's failed architecture. That one monolithic language would have expedited the building and heaven would have been reached. Whose heaven, she wonders? And what kind? Perhaps the achievement of Paradise was premature, a little hasty if no one could take the time to understand other languages, other views, other narratives period. Had they, the heaven they imagined might have been found at their feet. Complicated, demanding, yes, but a view of heaven as life; not heaven as post-life.

She would not want to leave her young visitors with the impression that language should be forced to stay alive merely to be. The vitality of language lies in its ability to limn the actual, imagined and possible lives of its speakers, readers, writers. Although its poise is sometimes in displacing experience it is not a substitute for it. It arcs toward the place where meaning may lie. When a President of the United States thought about the graveyard his country had become, and said, "The world will little note nor long remember what we say here. But it will never forget what they did here," his simple words are exhilarating in their life-sustaining properties because they refused to encapsulate the reality of 600,000 dead men in a cataclysmic race war. Refusing to monumentalize, disdaining the "final word," the precise "summing up," acknowledging their "poor power to add or detract," his words signal deference to the uncapturability of the life it mourns. It is the deference that moves her, that recognition that language can never live up to life once and for all. Nor should it. Language can never "pin down" slavery, genocide, war. Nor should it yearn for the arrogance to be able to do so. Its force, its felicity is in its reach toward the ineffable.

Be it grand or slender, burrowing, blasting, or refusing to sanctify; whether it laughs out loud or is a cry without an alphabet, the choice word, the chosen silence, unmolested language surges toward knowledge, not its destruction. But who does not know of literature banned because it is interrogative; discredited because it is critical; erased because alternate? And how many are outraged by the thought of a self-ravaged tongue?

Word-work is sublime, she thinks, because it is generative; it makes meaning that secures our difference, our human difference—the way in which we are like no other life.

We die. That may be the meaning of life. But we do language. That may be the measure of our lives.   20

"Once upon a time, . . ." visitors ask an old woman a question. Who are they, these children? What did they make of that encounter? What did they hear in those final words: "The bird is in your hands"? A sentence that gestures towards possibility or one that drops a latch? Perhaps what the children heard was "It's not my problem. I am old, female, black, blind. What wisdom I have now is in knowing I cannot help you. The future of language is yours."

They stand there. Suppose nothing was in their hands? Suppose the visit was only a ruse, a trick to get to be spoken to, taken seriously as they have not been before? A chance to interrupt, to violate the adult world, its miasma of discourse about them, for them, but never to them? Urgent questions are at stake, including the one they have asked: "Is the bird we hold living or dead?" Perhaps the question meant: "Could someone tell us what is life? What is death?" No trick at all; no silliness. A straightforward question worthy of the attention of a wise one. An old one. And if the old and wise who have lived life and faced death cannot describe either, who can?

But she does not; she keeps her secret; her good opinion of herself; her gnomic pronouncements; her art without commitment. She keeps her distance, enforces it and retreats into the singularity of isolation, in sophisticated, privileged space.

Nothing, no word follows her declaration of transfer. That silence is deep, deeper than the meaning available in the words she has spoken. It shivers, this silence, and the children, annoyed, fill it with language invented on the spot.

"Is there no speech," they ask her, "no words you can give us that   25
helps us break through your dossier of failures? Through the education you have just given us that is no education at all because we are paying close attention to what you have done as well as to what you have said? To the barrier you have erected between generosity and wisdom?

"We have no bird in our hands, living or dead. We have only you and our important question. Is the nothing in our hands something you could not bear to contemplate, to even guess? Don't you remember being young when language was magic without meaning? When what you could say, could not mean? When the invisible was what imagination strove to see? When questions and demands for answers burned so brightly you trembled with fury at not knowing?

"Do we have to begin consciousness with a battle heroines and heroes like you have already fought and lost leaving us with nothing in our hands except what you have imagined is there? Your answer is artful, but its artfulness embarrasses us and ought to embarrass you. Your answer is indecent in its self-congratulation. A made-for-television script that makes no sense if there is nothing in our hands.

"Why didn't you reach out, touch us with your soft fingers, delay the sound bite, the lesson, until you knew who we were? Did you so despise our trick, our modus operandi you could not see that we were baffled about how to get your attention? We are young. Unripe. We have heard all our short lives that we have to be responsible. What could that possibly mean in the catastrophe this world has become; where, as a poet said, 'nothing needs to be exposed since it is already barefaced.' Our inheritance is an affront. You want us to have your old, blank eyes and see only cruelty and mediocrity. Do you think we are stupid enough to perjure ourselves again and again with the fiction of nationhood? How dare you talk to us of duty when we stand waist deep in the toxin of your past?

"You trivialize us and trivialize the bird that is not in our hands. Is there no context for our lives? No song, no literature, no poem full of vitamins, no history connected to experience that you can pass along to help us start strong? You are an adult. The old one, the wise one. Stop thinking about saving your face. Think of our lives and tell us your particularized world. Make up a story. Narrative is radical, creating us at the very moment it is being created. We will not blame you if your reach exceeds your grasp; if love so ignites your words they go down in flames and nothing is left but their scald. Or if, with the reticence of a surgeon's hands, your words suture only the places where blood might flow. We know you can never do it properly—once and for all. Passion is never enough; neither is skill. But try. For our sake and yours forget your name in the street; tell us what the world has been to you in the dark places and in the light. Don't tell us what to believe, what to fear. Show us belief's wide skirt and the stitch that unravels fear's caul. You, old woman, blessed with blindness, can speak the language that tells us what only language can: how to see without pictures. Language alone protects us from the scariness of things with no names. Language alone is meditation.

"Tell us what it is to be a woman so that we may know what it is to be a man. What moves at the margin. What it is to have no home in this place. To be set adrift from the one you knew. What it is to live at the edge of towns that cannot bear your company.

"Tell us about ships turned away from shorelines at Easter, placenta in a field. Tell us about a wagonload of slaves, how they sang so softly their breath was indistinguishable from the falling snow. How they knew from the hunch of the nearest shoulder that the next stop would be their last. How, with hands prayered in their sex, they thought of heat, then sun. Lifting their faces as though it was there for the taking. Turning as though there for the taking. They stop at an inn. The driver and his mate go in with the lamp leaving them humming in the dark. The horse's void steams into the snow beneath its hooves and its hiss and melt are the envy of the freezing slaves.

"The inn door opens: a girl and a boy step away from its light. They climb into the wagon bed. The boy will have a gun in three years, but now he carries a lamp and a jug of warm cider. They pass it from mouth to mouth. The girl offers bread, pieces of meat and something more: a glance into the eyes of the one she serves. One helping for each man, two for each woman. And a look. They look back. The next stop will be their last. But not this one. This one is warmed."

It's quiet again when the children finish speaking, until the woman breaks into the silence.

"Finally," she says, "I trust you now. I trust you with the bird that is not in your hands because you have truly caught it. Look. How lovely it is, this thing we have done — together."

THINKING CRITICALLY ABOUT THE READING

1. Morrison begins her speech with a parable, a short story meant to teach a lesson. What is the parable about? What lesson does it teach? Why does Morrison tell us that this story has different versions? How does Morrison link her parable to the writer and her language?

2. What is "official language" (11)? How does Morrison define it? Who speaks it? What problems does it pose?

3. Morrison characterizes language as more than representation; she characterizes it as action. She writes, for example, "oppressive language does more than represent violence; it is violence" (13). What other examples does she give of language as action? What injustices does she suggest are bred by unjust language? How does Morrison suggest that language creates people, or, at the very least, types of people?

4. Morrison argues that "language can never 'pin down' slavery, genocide, war. . . . Nor should it" (18). Why are there things that remain impossible to "pin down"? Why, for Morrison, is it important that some things remain outside of language in this way? What example does she give of this "uncapturability of the life" (18)?

5. Morrison argues that "sexist language, racist language, theistic language" are "all typical of the policing languages of mastery, and cannot, do not permit new knowledge or encourage the mutual exchange of ideas" (13). What does she mean by "policing languages of mastery"? What commonalities do sexist, racist, and theistic language share? How do each of these languages limit the "mutual exchange of ideas"?

6. How does Morrison consistently remind us of African American history throughout the speech? Why do you think she takes this opportunity to tell that history? In what ways is it built into her parable from the start?

7. By the end of her speech, Morrison rewrites the outcome of the introductory parable. The tale is no longer the story of youth holding the fate of a bird in their hands as a demonstration of power, but of youth with empty hands asking for a story. Why do you think Morrison revises this story? What effect does it have on readers? How does it help her to reshape the meaning of the speech?

LANGUAGE IN ACTION

In paragraph 11, Morrison says the writer thinks of language "as partly a system, partly as a living thing over which one has control, but mostly as agency—as an act with consequences." Discuss as a class how each of these ways of thinking about language is accurate. When have you experienced language as a system, as a living thing, or as an act with consequences? Make a list of examples, and discuss what they have in common. Where and when does language act as more than one of these things? When is it most powerful?

WRITING SUGGESTIONS

1. Morrison asks: "But who does not know of literature banned because it is interrogative; discredited because it is critical; erased because alternate?" (19). Here Morrison reminds us that novels and stories are continually banned or challenged, that some histories are routinely silenced by others. Take a look at the American Library Association's list of books most frequently challenged or banned. What reasons are cited for removal? Have you read any of these books? Choose a book that you've read or a story that you know from the list and search for articles or letters calling to ban it. Taking into consideration all that Morrison says about the importance of language and of fostering—rather than silencing—narratives, write a letter in response to the letter or article you find calling to ban the work.

2. Morrison argues that the "policing languages of mastery . . . cannot, do not permit new knowledge or encourage the mutual exchange of ideas" (13). And among these languages she names "sexist language, racist language, theistic language." Choose one of these languages to discuss or another type of speech you would define as a "language of mastery." Spend some time brainstorming how the language both limits knowledge and discourages the exchange of ideas, then make a list of examples that support your points. Write an essay that defines and analyzes the policing language you've chosen, the mastery its users claim, and the mastery it attempts to exert over others. You might look closely at the limitations that language poses to the free and mutual exchange of ideas and the problems those limitations cause.

The Perils of Indifference

Elie Wiesel

Elie Wiesel is a Jewish writer, professor, Nobel Laureate, and Holocaust survivor. Born in Sighet, Transylvania, in 1928, Wiesel and his entire family were taken to the Auschwitz-Birkenau concentration camp in 1944. Separated from his mother and three sisters, Wiesel and his father were sent to the work camp Buna, wherein Wiesel's father was brutally beaten by a Nazi guard for being ill and died shortly thereafter. Wiesel would survive the camp and eventually reunite with two of his sisters, but along with his father, his mother and youngest sister were among the Holocaust's nearly 11 million victims.

After the war, Wiesel worked as a teacher and professional journalist, but for more than a decade did not write about his experiences during the Holocaust. It was not until the early 1950s that French author and Nobel Laureate François Mauriac would become a close friend and persuade Wiesel to write. In 1955 Wiesel moved to the United States and became a citizen, and in 1960 he published *Night*, the first account of his experiences during the Holocaust to gain an audience. It was carved from a nearly nine-hundred-page memoir, *And the World Remained Silent*, originally written and published in Yiddish. Of Wiesel's fifty-seven books, *Night* remains the most widely read and circulated; since its publication it has sold an estimated 10 million copies, been translated into thirty languages, and is among the core works of Holocaust literature.

Beyond his written work, Wiesel has been a tireless educator and activist as well as a professor at the City University of New York, Boston University, Yale University, and Barnard College. Among other causes, Wiesel has spoken on behalf of Soviet and Ethiopian Jews, victims of apartheid in South Africa, and victims of genocide in the former Yugoslavia, and for intervention in Darfur. For his life-long commitment to fighting racism and oppression, Wiesel was awarded the Nobel Peace Prize in 1986, as well as the Congressional Gold Medal, the Presidential Medal of Freedom, and a knighthood, among other honors. In 1999 Wiesel was asked to speak as a part of the Millennium Evenings series at the White House in commemoration of the last century, and he delivered the following speech. As then first-lady Hillary Clinton explained, these evenings were designed to mark the millennium by looking "not just at our noblest achievements" but by confronting "those darkest impulses that have marred this century," including the nadir of the Holocaust and the peril of indifference that Wiesel charges led to such inhumanity.

WRITING TO DISCOVER: *Have you ever experienced moments of pain that were difficult to write or talk about? Did you eventually make a choice to discuss it, or have you remained silent about it? If so, why and in what way have you "talked" about it? If not, why have you remained silent?*

327

Mr. President, Mrs. Clinton, members of Congress, Ambassador Holbrooke, Excellencies, friends:

Fifty-four years ago to the day, a young Jewish boy from a small town in the Carpathian Mountains woke up, not far from Goethe's beloved Weimar, in a place of eternal infamy called Buchenwald. He was finally free, but there was no joy in his heart. He thought there never would be again. Liberated a day earlier by American soldiers, he remembers their rage at what they saw. And even if he lives to be a very old man, he will always be grateful to them for that rage, and also for their compassion. Though he did not understand their language, their eyes told him what he needed to know—that they, too, would remember, and bear witness.

And now, I stand before you, Mr. President—Commander-in-Chief of the army that freed me, and tens of thousands of others—and I am filled with a profound and abiding gratitude to the American people. "Gratitude" is a word that I cherish. Gratitude is what defines the humanity of the human being. And I am grateful to you, Hillary, or Mrs. Clinton, for what you said, and for what you are doing for children in the world, for the homeless, for the victims of injustice, the victims of destiny and society. And I thank all of you for being here.

We are on the threshold of a new century, a new millennium. What will the legacy of this vanishing century be? How will it be remembered in the new millennium? Surely it will be judged, and judged severely, in both moral and metaphysical terms. These failures have cast a dark shadow over humanity: two World Wars, countless civil wars, the senseless chain of assassinations (Gandhi, the Kennedys, Martin Luther King, Sadat, Rabin), bloodbaths in Cambodia and Algeria, India and Pakistan, Ireland and Rwanda, Eritrea and Ethiopia, Sarajevo and Kosovo; the inhumanity in the gulag and the tragedy of Hiroshima. And, on a different level, of course, Auschwitz and Treblinka. So much violence; so much indifference.

Indifference elicits no response. Indifference is not a response. Indifference is not a beginning; it is an end. What is indifference? Etymologically, the word means "no difference." A strange and unnatural state in which the lines blur between light and darkness, dusk and dawn, crime and punishment, cruelty and compassion, good and evil. What are its courses and inescapable consequences? Is it a philosophy? Is there a philosophy of indifference conceivable? Can one possibly view indifference as a virtue? Is it necessary at times to practice it simply to keep one's sanity, live normally, enjoy a fine meal and a glass of wine, as the world around us experiences harrowing upheavals?

Of course, indifference can be tempting—more than that, seductive. It is so much easier to look away from victims. It is so much easier to avoid such rude interruptions to our work, our dreams, our hopes. It is, after all, awkward, troublesome, to be involved in another person's pain and despair. Yet, for the person who is indifferent, his or her neighbors are of no consequence. And, therefore, their lives are meaningless. Their hidden or even visible anguish is of no interest. Indifference reduces the Other to an abstraction.

Over there, behind the black gates of Auschwitz, the most tragic of all prisoners were the "Muselmänner," as they were called. Wrapped in their torn blankets, they would sit or lie on the ground, staring vacantly into space, unaware of who or where they were — strangers to their surroundings. They no longer felt pain, hunger, thirst. They feared nothing. They felt nothing. They were dead and did not know it.

Rooted in our tradition, some of us felt that to be abandoned by humanity then was not the ultimate. We felt that to be abandoned by God was worse than to be punished by Him. Better an unjust God than an indifferent one. For us to be ignored by God was a harsher punishment than to be a victim of His anger. Man can live far from God — not outside God. God is wherever we are. Even in suffering? Even in suffering.

In a way, to be indifferent to that suffering is what makes the human being inhuman. Indifference, after all, is more dangerous than anger and hatred. Anger can at times be creative. One writes a great poem, a great symphony. One does something special for the sake of humanity because one is angry at the injustice that one witnesses. But indifference is never creative. Even hatred at times may elicit a response. You fight it. You denounce it. You disarm it.

Indifference elicits no response. Indifference is not a response. Indifference is not a beginning; it is an end. And, therefore, indifference is always the friend of the enemy, for it benefits the aggressor — never his victim, whose pain is magnified when he or she feels forgotten. The political prisoner in his cell, the hungry children, the homeless refugees — not to respond to their plight, not to relieve their solitude by offering them a spark of hope is to exile them from human memory. And in denying their humanity, we betray our own.

Indifference, then, is not only a sin, it is a punishment.

And this is one of the most important lessons of this outgoing century's wide-ranging experiments in good and evil.

In the place that I come from, society was composed of three simple categories: the killers, the victims, and the bystanders. During the darkest of times, inside the ghettoes and death camps — and I'm glad that Mrs. Clinton mentioned that we are now commemorating that event, that period, that we are now in the Days of Remembrance — but then, we felt abandoned, forgotten. All of us did.

And our only miserable consolation was that we believed that Auschwitz and Treblinka were closely guarded secrets; that the leaders of the free world did not know what was going on behind those black gates and barbed wire; that they had no knowledge of the war against the Jews that Hitler's armies and their accomplices waged as part of the war against the Allies. If they knew, we thought, surely those leaders would have moved

10

heaven and earth to intervene. They would have spoken out with great outrage and conviction. They would have bombed the railways leading to Birkenau, just the railways, just once.

And now we knew, we learned, we discovered that the Pentagon knew,   15
the State Department knew. And the illustrious occupant of the White House then, who was a great leader—and I say it with some anguish and pain, because, today is exactly 54 years marking his death—Franklin Delano Roosevelt died on April the 12th, 1945. So he is very much present to me and to us. No doubt, he was a great leader. He mobilized the American people and the world, going into battle, bringing hundreds and thousands of valiant and brave soldiers in America to fight fascism, to fight dictatorship, to fight Hitler. And so many of the young people fell in battle. And, nevertheless, his image in Jewish history—I must say it—his image in Jewish history is flawed.

The depressing tale of the St. Louis is a case in point. Sixty years ago, its human cargo—nearly 1,000 Jews—was turned back to Nazi Germany. And that happened after the Kristallnacht, after the first state sponsored pogrom, with hundreds of Jewish shops destroyed, synagogues burned, thousands of people put in concentration camps. And that ship, which was already in the shores of the United States, was sent back. I don't understand. Roosevelt was a good man, with a heart. He understood those who needed help. Why didn't he allow these refugees to disembark? A thousand people—in America, the great country, the greatest democracy, the most generous of all new nations in modern history. What happened? I don't understand. Why the indifference, on the highest level, to the suffering of the victims?

But then, there were human beings who were sensitive to our tragedy. Those non-Jews, those Christians, that we call the "Righteous Gentiles," whose selfless acts of heroism saved the honor of their faith. Why were they so few? Why was there a greater effort to save SS murderers after the war than to save their victims during the war? Why did some of America's largest corporations continue to do business with Hitler's Germany until 1942? It has been suggested, and it was documented, that the Wehrmacht could not have conducted its invasion of France without oil obtained from American sources. How is one to explain their indifference?

And yet, my friends, good things have also happened in this traumatic century: the defeat of Nazism, the collapse of communism, the rebirth of Israel on its ancestral soil, the demise of apartheid, Israel's peace treaty with Egypt, the peace accord in Ireland. And let us remember the meeting, filled with drama and emotion, between Rabin and Arafat that you, Mr. President, convened in this very place. I was here and I will never forget it.

And then, of course, the joint decision of the United States and NATO to intervene in Kosovo and save those victims, those refugees, those who were uprooted by a man, whom I believe that because of his crimes, should be charged with crimes against humanity.

But this time, the world was not silent. This time, we do respond. This time, we intervene.

Does it mean that we have learned from the past? Does it mean that   20
society has changed? Has the human being become less indifferent and more human? Have we really learned from our experiences? Are we less insensitive to the plight of victims of ethnic cleansing and other forms of injustices in places near and far? Is today's justified intervention in Kosovo, led by you, Mr. President, a lasting warning that never again will the deportation, the terrorization of children and their parents, be allowed anywhere in the world? Will it discourage other dictators in other lands to do the same?

What about the children? Oh, we see them on television, we read about them in the papers, and we do so with a broken heart. Their fate is always the most tragic, inevitably. When adults wage war, children perish. We see their faces, their eyes. Do we hear their pleas? Do we feel their pain, their agony? Every minute one of them dies of disease, violence, famine.

Some of them—so many of them—could be saved.

And so, once again, I think of the young Jewish boy from the Carpathian Mountains. He has accompanied the old man I have become throughout these years of quest and struggle. And together we walk towards the new millennium, carried by profound fear and extraordinary hope.

THINKING CRITICALLY ABOUT THE READING

1. For Wiesel, indifference is the core of inhumanity. How does he define indifference? What is the problem of human indifference when we live in a world with other people?

2. What feelings does Wiesel discuss other than indifference? How does he distinguish them from indifference?

3. Although Wiesel names four concentration camps—Auschwitz, Treblinka, Birkenau, and Buchenwald—he never identifies them as camps. What does his choice suggest about the power of their names? Do you think he avoids the term "camps" on purpose? If so, why? If not, why not?

4. Wiesel writes about naively believing that "the leaders of the free world did not know what was going on" and that surely, had they known about the camps, they "would have moved heaven and earth to intervene" (14). Why do you think he uses such artful phrasing as "leaders of the free world" and "moved heaven and earth"? What do those images evoke, and what do they show us?

5. Why does Wiesel describe Roosevelt's place in Jewish history as "flawed" (15)? How does he link Roosevelt's actions to indifference? How might having an audience at the White House shape his choice to discuss Roosevelt's actions?

6. Why do you think Wiesel focuses on children and their treatment in remembering this "traumatic century" (18)? Does he note any progress? How would you characterize his conclusion?

LANGUAGE IN ACTION

In a 2015 *New Yorker* article entitled "Carbon Capture," novelist Jonathan Franzen wonders whether climate change has made it more difficult for people to care about conservation. Climate change, he observes, is "a politically more palatable culprit," especially given the government's inability to impose meaningful reform. "Climate change is everyone's fault—in other words, no one's." He points out that for the individual, it's easier to deplore climate change than to focus on more immediate threats to the environment, such as lead ammunition and the overharvesting of horseshoe crabs. Consider the opening paragraphs from Franzen's article.

> Last September, as someone who cares more about birds than the next man, I was following the story of the new stadium that the Twin Cities are building for their football Vikings. The stadium's glass walls were expected to kill thousands of birds every year, and local bird-lovers had asked its sponsors to use a specially patterned glass to reduce collisions; the glass would have raised the stadium's cost by one tenth of one per cent, and the sponsors had balked. Around the same time, the National Audubon Society issued a press release declaring climate change "the greatest threat" to American birds and warning that "nearly half" of North America's bird species were at risk of losing their habitats by 2080. Audubon's announcement was credulously retransmitted by national and local media, including the Minneapolis *Star Tribune*, whose blogger on bird-related subjects, Jim Williams, drew the inevitable inference: Why argue about stadium glass when the real threat to birds was climate change? In comparison, Williams said, a few thousand bird deaths would be "nothing."
>
> I was in Santa Cruz, California, and already not in a good mood. The day I saw the Williams quote was the two hundred and fifty-fourth of a year in which, so far, sixteen had qualified as rainy. To the injury of a brutal drought came the daily insult of radio forecasters describing the weather as beautiful. It wasn't that I didn't share Williams's anxiety about the future. What upset me was how a dire prophecy like Audubon's could lead to indifference toward birds in the present.

Consider your own indifference and its perils. Do you consider climate change when making decisions? Does reading about the potentially massive loss of birdlife motivate you to take action in the present? Do you think the focus on long-term climate action causes us to be more indifferent to conservation efforts today? How does indifference about the environment relate to indifference to the profound human suffering described by Wiesel?

WRITING SUGGESTIONS

1. Early in the essay Wiesel asks: "Can one possibly view indifference as a virtue? Is it necessary at times to practice it simply to keep one's sanity, live normally, enjoy a fine meal and a glass of wine, as the world around us experiences harrowing upheavals?" (5). Although Wiesel's essay overwhelmingly argues that indifference is not a virtue, is there "virtue" in enjoying moments of indifference? Is there, perhaps, a more positive word for what we do when we silence the rest of the world's "harrowing upheavals" to focus on our personal enjoyment? Write an exploratory essay that considers how we balance being an individual and a conscious member of the human race. Can you come up with a word and/or definition for this precarious balance? You might try to devise a set of guidelines for negotiating a balance between citizenship and individuality.

2. Wiesel, writing in 1999, poignantly concludes that he approaches "the new millennium, carried by profound fear and extraordinary hope." Now that we are in the second decade of the new millennium, what do you think Wiesel might characterize as the "fears" and "hopes" these decades have brought? Make a list of events, changes, and developments on the local, national, and international front that you might characterize as a "fear" or a "hope." Choose one of these topics or one of your own to write a reflective essay. Discuss whether or not your topic is a hope or a fear, how it may change in the future, what we might do to quell fear or foster greater hope, and consider, perhaps, how this topic might be seen by those looking back on it at the end of this millennium.

A Modest Proposal

JONATHAN SWIFT

One of the world's greatest satirists, Jonathan Swift was born in 1667 to English parents in Dublin, Ireland, and was educated at Trinity College. When his early efforts at a literary career in England met no success, he returned to Ireland in 1694 and was ordained an Anglican clergyman. From 1713 until his death in 1745, he was dean of St. Patrick's Cathedral in Dublin. A prolific chronicler of human folly, Swift is best known as the author of *Gulliver's Travels* and of the work included here, "A Modest Proposal."

In the 1720s Ireland had suffered several famines, but the English gentry, who owned most of the land, did nothing to alleviate the suffering of tenant farmers and their families; nor would the English government intervene. A number of pamphlets were circulated proposing solutions to the so-called "Irish problem." "A Modest Proposal," published anonymously in 1729, was Swift's ironic contribution to the discussion.

WRITING TO DISCOVER: *Satire is a dramatic literary art form wherein the shortcomings, foibles, abuses, and idiocies of both people and institutions are accentuated and held up for ridicule in order to shame these perpetrators into reforming themselves. Perhaps the very easiest way to see satire around us today is in the work of our political cartoonists. Make a list of individuals and institutions both here and abroad who today might make good subjects for satire. For each individual and institution on your list provide one or two traits or characteristics that might be held up for ridicule.*

A Modest Proposal for Preventing the Children of Poor People in Ireland from Being a Burden to Their Parents or Country, and for Making Them Beneficial to the Public

It is a melancholy object to those who walk through this great town, or travel in the country, when they see the streets, the roads and cabin-doors crowded with beggars of the female sex, followed by three, four, or six children, all in rags, and importuning every passenger for an alms. These mothers, instead of being able to work for their honest livelihood, are forced to employ all their time in strolling, to beg sustenance for their helpless infants, who, as they grow up, either turn thieves for want of work, or leave their dear native country to fight for the Pretender in Spain, or sell themselves to the Barbadoes.

I think it is agreed by all parties that this prodigious number of children, in the arms, or on the backs, or at the heels of their mothers, and frequently of their fathers, is in the present deplorable state of the kingdom a very great additional grievance; and therefore whoever could find out a fair, cheap, and easy method of making these children sound and useful members of the commonwealth would deserve so well of the public as to have his statue set up for a preserver of the nation.

But my intention is very far from being confined to provide only for the children of professed beggars; it is of a much greater extent, and shall take in the whole number of infants at a certain age who are born of parents in effect as little able to support them as those who demand our charity in the streets.

As to my own part, having turned my thoughts for many years upon this important subject, and maturely weighed the several schemes of other projectors, I have always found them grossly mistaken in their computation. It is true a child just dropped from its dam may be supported by her milk for a solar year with little other nourishment, at most not above the value of two shillings, which the mother may certainly get, or the value in scraps, by her lawful occupation of begging, and it is exactly at one year old that I propose to provide for them, in such a manner as, instead of being a charge upon their parents, or the parish, or wanting food and raiment for the rest of their lives, they shall, on the contrary, contribute to the feeding and partly to the clothing of many thousands.

There is likewise another great advantage in my scheme, that it will prevent those voluntary abortions, and that horrid practice of women murdering their bastard children, alas, too frequent among us, sacrificing the poor innocent babes, I doubt, more to avoid the expense than the shame, which would move tears and pity in the most savage and inhuman breast.   5

The number of souls in Ireland being usually reckoned one million and a half, of those I calculate there may be about two hundred thousand couples whose wives are breeders, from which number I subtract thirty thousand couples who are able to maintain their own children, although I apprehend there cannot be so many under the present distresses of the kingdom; but this being granted, there will remain an hundred and seventy thousand breeders. I again subtract fifty thousand for those women who miscarry, or whose children die by accident or disease within the year. There only remain an hundred and twenty thousand children of poor parents annually born: the question therefore is, how this number shall be reared, and provided for, which as I have already said, under the present situation of affairs is utterly impossible by all the methods hitherto proposed, for we can neither employ them in handicraft or agriculture; we neither build houses (I mean in the country), nor cultivate land: they can very seldom pick up a livelihood by stealing until they arrive at six years old, except where they are of towardly parts, although I confess they learn the rudiments much earlier, during which time they can however be properly looked upon only as probationers, as I have been informed by a principal gentleman in the County of Cavan, who protested to me that he never knew above one or two instances under the age of six, even in a part of the kingdom so renowned for the quickest proficiency in that art.

I am assured by our merchants that a boy or girl before twelve years old is no salable commodity, and even when they come to this age, they will not yield above three pounds, or three pounds and half-a-crown at most on the Exchange, which cannot turn to account either to the parents or the kingdom, the charge of nutriment and rags having been at least four times that value.

I shall now therefore humbly propose my own thoughts, which I hope will not be liable to the least objection.

I have been assured by a very knowing American of my acquaintance in London, that a young healthy child well nursed is at a year old a most delicious, nourishing and wholesome food, whether stewed, roasted, baked, or boiled, and I make no doubt that it will equally serve in a fricassee, or a ragout.

I do therefore humbly offer it to public consideration, that of the hundred and twenty thousand children already computed, twenty thousand may be reserved for breed, whereof only one fourth part to be males, which is more than we allow to sheep, black-cattle, or swine, and my reason is that these children are seldom the fruits of marriage, a circumstance not much regarded by our savages, therefore one male will be sufficient to serve four females. That the remaining hundred thousand may at a year old be offered in sale to the persons of quality, and fortune, through the kingdom, always advising the mother to let them suck plentifully in the last month, so as to render them plump, and fat for a good table. A child will make two dishes at an entertainment for friends, and when the family dines alone, the fore or hind quarter will make a reasonable dish, and seasoned with a little pepper or salt will be very good boiled on the fourth day, especially in winter. 10

I have reckoned upon a medium, that a child just born will weigh twelve pounds, and in a solar year if tolerably nursed increaseth to twenty-eight pounds.

I grant this food will be somewhat dear, and therefore very proper for landlords, who, as they have already devoured most of the parents, seem to have the best title to the children.

Infant's flesh will be in season throughout the year, but more plentiful in March, and a little before and after, for we are told by a grave author, an eminent French physician, that fish being a prolific diet, there are more children born in Roman Catholic countries about nine months after Lent than at any other season; therefore reckoning a year after Lent, the markets will be more glutted than usual, because the number of Popish infants is at least three to one in this kingdom, and therefore it will have one other collateral advantage by lessening the number of Papists among us.

I have already computed the charge of nursing a beggar's child (in which list I reckon all cottagers, laborers, and four-fifths of the farmers) to be about two shillings *per annum,* rags included, and I believe no gentleman would repine to give ten shillings for the carcass of a good fat child, which, as I have said, will make four dishes of excellent nutritive meat, when he hath only some particular friend of his own family to dine with him. Thus the Squire will learn to be a good landlord and grow popular among his tenants, the mother will have eight shillings net profit, and be fit for work until she produces another child.

Those who are more thrifty (as I must confess the times require) may 15 flay the carcass; the skin of which artificially dressed, will make admirable gloves for ladies, and summer boots for fine gentlemen.

As to our city of Dublin, shambles may be appointed for this purpose, in the most convenient parts of it, and butchers we may be assured will not be wanting, although I rather recommend buying the children alive, and dressing them hot from the knife, as we do roasting pigs.

A very worthy person, a true lover of his country, and whose virtues I highly esteem, was lately pleased in discoursing on this matter to offer a refinement upon my scheme. He said that many gentlemen of this kingdom having of late destroyed their deer, he conceived that the want of venison might be well supplied by the bodies of young lads and maidens, not exceeding fourteen years of age, nor under twelve, so great a number of both sexes in every county being now ready to starve, for want of work and service: and these to be disposed of by their parents if alive, or otherwise by their nearest relations. But with due deference to so excellent a friend, and so deserving a patriot, I cannot be altogether in his sentiments. For as to the males, my American acquaintance assured me from frequent experience that their flesh was generally tough and lean, like that of our schoolboys, by continual exercise, and their taste disagreeable, and to fatten them would not answer the charge. Then as to the females, it would, I think with humble submission, be a loss to the public, because they soon would become breeders themselves: and besides, it is not improbable that some scrupulous people might be apt to censure such a practice (although indeed very unjustly) as a little bordering upon cruelty, which I confess, hath always been with me the strongest objection against any project, howsoever well intended.

But in order to justify my friend, he confessed that this expedient was put into his head by the famous Psalmanazar, a native of the island Formosa, who came from thence to London, above twenty years ago, and in conversation told my friend that in his country when any young person happened to be put to death, the executioner sold the carcass to persons of quality, as a prime dainty, and that, in his time, the body of a plump girl of fifteen, who was crucified for an attempt to poison the emperor, was sold to his Imperial Majesty's Prime Minister of State, and other great Mandarins of the Court, in joints from the gibbet, at four hundred crowns. Neither indeed can I deny that if the same use were made of several plump young girls in this town who, without one single groat to their fortunes, cannot stir abroad without a chair, and appear at the playhouse and assemblies in foreign fineries which they never will pay for, the kingdom would not be the worse.

Some persons of a desponding spirit are in great concern about that vast number of poor people, who are aged, diseased, or maimed, and I have been desired to employ my thoughts what course may be taken to ease the nation of so grievous an encumbrance. But I am not in the least pain upon that matter, because it is very well known that they are every day dying, and rotting, by cold, and famine, and filth, and vermin, as fast as can be reasonably expected. And as to the younger laborers, they are now in almost as hopeful a condition. They cannot get work, and consequently pine away from want of nourishment, to a degree that if at any time they are accidentally hired to common labor, they have not strength to perform it; and thus the country and themselves are in a fair way of being soon delivered from the evils to come.

I have too long digressed, and therefore shall return to my subject.   20
I think the advantages by the proposal which I have made are obvious and many, as well as of the highest importance.

For first, as I have already observed, it would greatly lessen the number of Papists, with whom we are yearly over-run, being the principal breeders of the nation, as well as our most dangerous enemies, and who stay at home on purpose with a design to deliver the kingdom to the Pretender, hoping to take their advantage by the absence of so many good Protestants, who have chosen rather to leave their country than stay at home and pay tithes against their conscience to an idolatrous Episcopal curate.

Secondly, the poorer tenants will have something valuable of their own, which by law may be made liable to distress, and help to pay their landlord's rent, their corn and cattle being already seized, and money a thing unknown.

Thirdly, whereas the maintenance of an hundred thousand children, from two years old, and upwards, cannot be computed at less than ten shillings a piece *per annum,* the nation's stock will be thereby increased fifty thousand pounds *per annum,* besides the profit of a new dish, introduced to the tables of all gentlemen of fortune in the kingdom, who have any refinement in taste, and the money will circulate among ourselves, the goods being entirely of our own growth and manufacture.

Fourthly, the constant breeders, besides the gain of eight shillings sterling *per annum,* by the sale of their children, will be rid of the charge of maintaining them after the first year.

Fifthly, this food would likewise bring great custom to taverns, where   25
the vintners will certainly be so prudent as to procure the best receipts for dressing it to perfection, and consequently have their houses frequented by all the fine gentlemen, who justly value themselves upon their knowledge in good eating; and a skillful cook, who understands how to oblige his guests, will contrive to make it as expensive as they please.

Sixthly, this would be a great inducement to marriage, which all wise nations have either encouraged by rewards, or enforced by laws and penalties. It would increase the care and tenderness of mothers towards their children, when they were sure of a settlement for life, to the poor babes, provided in some sort by the public to their annual profit instead of expense. We should soon see an honest emulation among the married women, which of them could bring the fattest child to the market. Men would become as fond of their wives, during the time of their pregnancy, as they are now of their mares in foal, their cows in calf, or sows when they are ready to farrow, nor offer to beat or kick them (as it is too frequent a practice) for fear of a miscarriage.

Many other advantages might be enumerated. For instance, the addition of some thousand carcasses in our exportation of barrelled beef; the propagation of swine's flesh, and improvement in the art of making good bacon, so much wanted among us by the great destruction of pigs, too frequent at our tables; which are no way comparable in taste or magnificence to a well-grown, fat yearling child, which roasted whole will make a considerable figure at a Lord Mayor's feast, or any other public entertainment. But this and many others I omit, being studious of brevity.

Supposing that one thousand families in this city would be constant customers for infants' flesh, besides others who might have it at merry meetings, particularly weddings and christenings; I compute that Dublin would take off annually about twenty thousand carcasses, and the rest of the kingdom (where probably they will be sold somewhat cheaper) the remaining eighty thousand.

I can think of no one objection that will possibly be raised against this proposal, unless it should be urged that the number of people will be thereby much lessened in the kingdom. This I freely own, and it was indeed one principal design in offering it to the world. I desire the reader will observe, that I calculate my remedy *for this one individual Kingdom of Ireland, and for no other that ever was, is, or, I think, ever can be upon earth.* Therefore let no man talk to me of other expedients: *Of taxing our absentees at five shillings a pound: Of using neither clothes, nor household furniture except what is of our own growth and manufacture: Of utterly rejecting the materials and instruments that promote foreign luxury: Of curing the expensiveness of pride, vanity, idleness, and gaming in our women: Of introducing a vein of parsimony, prudence, and temperance: Of learning to love our country, wherein we differ even from* Laplanders, *and the inhabitants of* Topinamboo: *Of quitting our animosities and factions, nor act any longer like the* Jews, *who were murdering one another at the very moment their city was taken: Of being a little cautious not to sell our country and consciences for nothing: Of teaching landlords to have at least one degree of mercy towards their tenants.* Lastly, *of putting a spirit of honesty, industry, and skill into our shopkeepers, who, if a resolution could now be taken to buy only our native goods, would immediately unite to cheat and exact upon us in the price, the measure and the goodness, nor could ever yet be brought to make one fair proposal of just dealing, though often and earnestly invited to it.*

Therefore I repeat, let no man talk to me of these and the like expedients, till he hath at least a glimpse of hope that there will ever be some hearty and sincere attempt to put them in practice. 30

But as to myself, having been wearied out for many years with offering vain, idle, visionary thoughts, and at length utterly despairing of success, I fortunately fell upon this proposal, which as it is wholly new, so it hath something solid and real, of no expense and little trouble, full in our own power, and whereby we can incur no danger in disobliging England. For this kind of commodity will not bear exportation, the flesh being of too tender a consistence to admit a long continuance in salt, *although perhaps I could name a country which would be glad to eat up our whole nation without it.*

After all I am not so violently bent upon my own opinion as to reject any offer, proposed by wise men, which shall be found equally innocent, cheap, easy and effectual. But before some thing of that kind shall be advanced in contradiction to my scheme, and offering a better, I desire the author, or authors, will be pleased maturely to consider two points. First, as things now stand, how they will be able to find food and raiment for a hundred thousand useless mouths and backs?

I can think of no one objection that will possibly be raised against this proposal, unless it should be urged that the number of people will be thereby much lessened in the kingdom.

And secondly, there being a round million of creatures in human figure, throughout this kingdom, whose whole subsistence put into a common stock would leave them in debt two millions of pounds sterling; adding those who are beggars by profession, to the bulk of farmers, cottagers, and laborers with their wives and children, who are beggars in effect; I desire those politicians who dislike my overture, and may perhaps be so bold to attempt an answer, that they will first ask the parents of these mortals whether they would not at this day think it a great happiness to have been sold for food at a year old, in the manner I prescribe, and thereby have avoided such a perpetual scene of misfortunes as they have since gone through, by the oppression of landlords, the impossibility of paying rent without money or trade, the want of common sustenance, with neither house nor clothes to cover them from the inclemencies of weather, and the most inevitable prospect of entailing the like, or greater miseries upon their breed for ever.

I profess in the sincerity of my heart that I have not the least personal interest in endeavoring to promote this necessary work, having no other motive than the *public good of my country, by advancing our trade, providing for infants, relieving the poor, and giving some pleasure to the rich.* I have no children by which I can propose to get a single penny; the youngest being nine years old, and my wife past child-bearing.

THINKING CRITICALLY ABOUT THE READING

1. What problem does Swift address in his proposal? What are some of the solutions that he offers? What does Swift see as the "advantages" (20) of his proposal?

2. What "other expedients" (29) are dismissed as "vain, idle, visionary thoughts" (31)? What can you infer about Swift's purpose from paragraphs 29 through 31? (Glossary: *Purpose*) Explain.

3. Describe the "author" of the proposal. Why do you suppose Swift chose such a character or persona to present this plan? At what points in the essay can you detect Swift's own voice coming through?

4. Swift entitles his essay "A Modest Proposal," and in paragraph 2 he talks of making Ireland's "children sound and useful members of the commonwealth." In what ways are Swift's title and statement ironic? Cite several other examples of Swift's irony. (Glossary: *Irony*)

5. In what ways, if any, can the argument presented in this essay be seen as logical? What is the effect, for example, of the complicated calculations in paragraph 6?

6. Satire often has a "stealth quality" about it; that is, the audience for whom it is intended often does not realize at first that the author of the satire is not being serious. At some point in the satire the audience usually catches on and then begins to see the larger issue at the center of the satire. At what point in your reading of "A Modest Proposal" did you begin to catch on to Swift's technique and larger, more important, message?

7. Toward what belief and/or action is Swift attempting to persuade his readers? How does he go about doing so? For example, did you feel a sense of outrage at any point in the essay? Did you feel that the essay was humorous at any point? If so, where and why?

LANGUAGE IN ACTION

Consider the following news item, "Global Food Summit in Rome," by P. P. Rega. The piece, which first appeared on TheSpoof.com on June 8, 2008, reports on a meeting of world leaders to "resolve the present worldwide food crisis."

GLOBAL FOOD SUMMIT IN ROME

P. P. Rega

The Global Food Crisis Summit was held in Rome, Italy, this past week. Agricultural ministers, medical experts, and political activists from around the world convened in the Eternal City to resolve the present worldwide food crisis. Below is a copy of the first day's schedule of lectures and activities that have been sponsored by the United Nation's Food and Agriculture Organization.

Program

0730–0830: Registration at the southwest entrance to The Colosseum

Cappuccino, caffè latte, biscotti anginetti, cenci alla fiorentina e cornetti a piacere

(continued)

0830–0900: Introduction
0900–0930: Uganda: Dehydration, Diarrhea and Death
0930–1000: Malnutrition in Myanmar
1000–1030: Break

Gelati assortiti da Giolitti (cioccolato, nocciole, e crema) con biscotti ed acqua minerale o caffè

1030–1100: Small Farmers in Indonesia: Source of Global Salvation
1100–1200: Introduction of Rice Farming in Haiti: Is It Enough?
1200–1300: Global Epidemic: Drop in Life Expectancy among the
            Poor and Starving
1300–1500: Lunch at Da Piperno

L'antipasto: Carciofi alla giudia

Vino: Verdicchio di Matelica Terre di Valbona 2006

Il Primo: Risotto alla pescatore oppure zuppa napoletana

   Vino: Tommaso Bussola Amarone di Valpolicella 2002

Il Secondo: Coda alla Vaccinara

Il Contorno: Vignarola

   Vino: Cantina Nobile di Montepulciano 1999

Formaggi: Fontina Val d'Aosta, bocconcini alla panna di bufala, pecorino romano

Il Dolce: Aranci in salsa di marsala

Caffè

Sambuca siciliana con tre mosche

1500–1600: Improving Crop Production in Zimbabwe: A Lesson To
            Us All.
1600–1700: Fertilizer or Seeds?
1700–1730: Break

Pizza alla quattro stagione

   Birra: Nastro Azzurro alla spina

1800–1900: Keynote Speaker: Al Gore
            Topic: Doubling Global Food Production in the 21st Century
1900–2100: Dinner at La Pergola

L'antipasto: Mozzarella in carrozza

   Vino: Prosecco Superiore di Locarno 2001

Il Primo: Gnocchetti all'amatriciana
    Vino: Recioto di Soave da Anselmi 2003

Il Secondo: Stufato di manzo con cipolline
Il Contorno: Fritto misto vegetariano
    Vino: Brunello di Montalcino 2001

Formaggi: Gorgonzola, mascarpone di bufala di Battipaglia, Parmigiano-Reggiano
Il Dolce: Cassata alla siciliana
    Caffè
    Limoncello amalfitana

What were your first impressions of Rega's story? What, for you, is Rega's point in presenting "the first day's schedule of lectures and activities"? Do you need to know Italian in order to grasp Rega's message? How do you think Swift would respond to such a meeting? What similarities do you see in the messages of Swift and Rega? Explain.

WRITING SUGGESTIONS

1. Write a modest proposal of your own to solve a difficult social or political problem of the present day or, on a smaller scale, a problem you see facing your school or community.

2. What do you think is the most effective way to bring about social change and to influence societal attitudes? Would Swift's methods work today, or would they have to be significantly modified as Rega has done in "Global Food Summit in Rome"? Write an essay in which you compare and contrast Swift's and Rega's tactics in an effort to determine how a writer can best influence public opinion today.

THE LANGUAGE OF DISCRIMINATION: HATE, PREJUDICE, AND STEREOTYPES

No single issue has absorbed our national consciousness more than prejudice and discrimination. That we are defined by and define others is an inevitability of our human condition, but the manner in which we relate to each other is a measure of our progress as a multiracial, multi-ethnic, and multicultural society. In a larger sense, it is a measure of our growth as a civilization. Not even the most optimistic observers of our society believe that equality is within sight or perhaps even ultimately possible, but implicit in all views of the subject is the notion that we can and must improve our appreciation of each other if we are to better our lives.

Our purpose in this chapter is to introduce you to some ideas on the sources of prejudice and to illustrate the role that language plays in the origin and perpetuation of prejudice and discrimination. We begin with Andrew Sullivan's "What's So Bad about Hate?," an in-depth inquiry into the nature of hatred and its relationship to prejudice, bias, bigotry, malice, anger, and all the emotions in between. Next we present Gordon Allport's classic essay "The Language of Prejudice," acknowledged by scholars for the past fifty years as the definitive word on the subject. Allport's concepts of "nouns that cut slices" and "verbal realism and symbol phobia" demonstrate not only how language encodes prejudice but also how we can use language to escape bias and bigotry. In "The 'F Word'" Firoozeh Dumas uses her wit and good sense of humor to recount what life was like growing up in America as an Iranian immigrant. "All of us immigrants knew that moving to America would be fraught with challenges," she confesses, "but none of us thought that our names would be such an obstacle." How can one's name be seen as an obstacle for an immigrant? Dumas uses examples from her own experience to show how her "identifiably 'ethnic' name" left her vulnerable to taunts and name-calling incidents as a child and clear acts of prejudice and discrimination as an adult. Next, in "Why We Need to Tolerate Hate," Wendy Kaminer makes the case for protecting hate speech as a form of free speech, arguing that you cannot censor bad beliefs without censoring core American values of free speech and civil liberties. Greg Lukianoff continues this argument, looking specifically at debates surrounding hate speech and censorship that have evolved around Twitter. Finally, Akiba Solomon's and Maisha Z. Johnson's essays offer contrasting perspectives on how racist terms, particularly "thug," are used, and what society's response should be.

What's So Bad about Hate?

ANDREW SULLIVAN

Andrew Sullivan was born in 1963 in South Godstone, Surrey, England, to Irish parents. He earned his B.A. degree in modern history at Magdalene College, Oxford, and his M.A. and Ph.D. in government at Harvard University. Sullivan began his career in journalism at the *New Republic,* later wrote for the *New York Times Magazine,* and held an editorial post at the *Atlantic.* A gay, Catholic, conservative, and often controversial commentator, Sullivan is perhaps best known for his blog *The Daily Dish,* which ran from 2000 until 2015 and won the 2008 Weblog Award for Best Blog, and for his pioneering and outspoken advocacy for gay marriage. He has written several books: *Virtually Normal: An Argument about Homosexuality* (1995); *Love Undetectable: Notes on Friendship, Sex and Survival* (1998); and *The Conservative Soul: How We Lost It, How to Get It Back* (2006).

In "What's So Bad about Hate?," first published in the *New York Times Magazine* on September 26, 1999, Sullivan reveals how little we actually know about the emotion that lies at the base of prejudice. As he writes, "For all its emotional punch, 'hate' is far less nuanced an idea than prejudice, or bigotry, or bias, or anger, or even aversion to others."

WRITING TO DISCOVER: *Have you ever been so upset by someone that you could say that you hated the person? If so, what prompted your reaction? How would you characterize the nature of the hatred you felt? Do you think it was an uncontrollable response or a conscious one? Do you think you had your reasons and would react the same way again in similar circumstances?*

I.

I wonder what was going on in John William King's head [in 1997] when he tied James Byrd Jr.'s feet to the back of a pickup truck and dragged him three miles down a road in rural Texas. King and two friends had picked up Byrd, who was black, when he was walking home, half-drunk, from a party. As part of a bonding ritual in their fledgling white supremacist group, the three men took Byrd to a remote part of town, beat him and chained his legs together before attaching them to the truck. Pathologists at King's trial testified that Byrd was probably alive and conscious until his body finally hit a culvert and split in two. When King was offered a chance to say something to Byrd's family at the trial, he smirked and uttered an obscenity.

We know all these details now, many months later. We know quite a large amount about what happened before and after. But I am still drawn, again and again, to the flash of ignition, the moment when fear and loathing became hate, the instant of transformation when King became hunter and Byrd became prey.

What was that? And what was it when Buford Furrow Jr., long-time member of the Aryan Nations, calmly walked up to a Filipino-American mailman he happened to spot, asked him to mail a letter and then shot him at point-blank range? Or when Russell Henderson beat Matthew Shepard, a young gay man, to a pulp, removed his shoes and then, with the help of a friend, tied him to a post like a dead coyote to warn off others?

For all our documentation of these crimes and others, our political and moral disgust at them, our morbid fascination with them, our sensitivity to their social meaning, we seem at times to have no better idea now than we ever had of what exactly they were about. About what that moment means when, for some reason or other, one human being asserts absolute, immutable superiority over another. About not the violence, but what the violence expresses. About what—exactly—hate is. And what our own part in it may be.

I find myself wondering what hate actually is in part because we have   5
created an entirely new offense in American criminal law—a "hate crime"—to combat it. And barely a day goes by without someone somewhere declaring war against it. Last month President Clinton called for an expansion of hate-crime laws as "what America needs in our battle against hate." A couple of weeks later, Senator John McCain used a campaign speech to denounce the "hate" he said poisoned the land. New York's mayor, Rudolph Giuliani, recently tried to stop the Million Youth March in Harlem on the grounds that the event was organized by people "involved in hate marches and hate rhetoric."

For all our zeal to attack hate, we still have a remarkably vague idea of what it actually is.

The media concurs in its emphasis. In 1985, there were 11 mentions of "hate crimes" in the national media database Nexis. By 1990, there were more than a thousand. In the first six months of 1999, there were 7,000. "Sexy fun is one thing," wrote a *New York Times* reporter about sexual assaults in Woodstock '99's mosh pit. "But this was an orgy of lewdness tinged with hate." And when Benjamin Smith marked the Fourth of July this year by targeting blacks, Asians, and Jews for murder in Indiana and Illinois, the story wasn't merely about a twisted young man who had emerged on the scene. As the *Times* put it, "Hate arrived in the neighborhoods of Indiana University, in Bloomington, in the early-morning darkness."

But what exactly was this thing that arrived in the early-morning darkness? For all our zeal to attack hate, we still have a remarkably vague idea of what it actually is. A single word, after all, tells us less, not more. For all its emotional punch, "hate" is far less nuanced an idea than prejudice, or bigotry, or bias, or anger, or even mere aversion to others. Is it to stand in for all these varieties of human experience—and everything in between? If so, then the war against it will be so vast as to be quixotic. Or is "hate" to stand for a very specific idea or belief, or set of beliefs, with a very specific object or group of objects? Then waging war against it is almost certainly unconstitutional. Perhaps these kinds of questions are of no concern to those waging war on hate. Perhaps it is enough for them that they share a sentiment that there is too much hate and never enough vigilance in combating it. But sentiment is a poor basis for law, and a dangerous tool in politics. It is better to leave some unwinnable wars unfought.

II.

Hate is everywhere. Human beings generalize all the time, ahead of time, about everyone and everything. A large part of it may even be hard-wired. At some point in our evolution, being able to know beforehand who was friend or foe was not merely a matter of philosophical reflection. It was a matter of survival. And even today it seems impossible to feel a loyalty without also feeling a disloyalty, a sense of belonging without an equal sense of unbelonging. We're social beings. We associate. Therefore we disassociate. And although it would be comforting to think that the one could happen without the other, we know in reality that it doesn't. How many patriots are there who have never felt a twinge of xenophobia?

Of course, by hate we mean something graver and darker than this kind of lazy prejudice. But the closer you look at this distinction the fuzzier it gets. Much of the time, we harbor little or no malice toward people of other backgrounds or places or ethnicities or ways of life. But then a car cuts you off at an intersection and you find yourself noticing immediately that the driver is a woman, or black, or old, or fat, or white, or male. Or you are walking down a city street at night and hear footsteps quickening behind you. You look around and see that it is a white woman and not a black man, and you are instantly relieved. These impulses are so spontaneous they are almost involuntary. But where did they come from? The mindless need to be mad at someone — anyone — or the unconscious eruption of a darker prejudice festering within?

In 1993, in San Jose, Calif., two neighbors — one heterosexual, one   10
homosexual — were engaged in a protracted squabble over grass clip-pings. (The full case is recounted in *Hate Crimes,* by James B. Jacobs and Kimberly Potter.) The gay man regularly mowed his lawn without a grass catcher, which prompted his neighbor to complain on many occasions that grass clippings spilled over onto his driveway. Tensions grew until one day, the gay man mowed his front yard, spilling clippings onto his neighbor's driveway, prompting the straight man to yell an obscene and common anti-gay insult. The wrangling escalated. At one point, the gay man agreed to collect the clippings from his neighbor's driveway but then later found

them dumped on his own porch. A fracas ensued with the gay man spraying the straight man's son with a garden hose, and the son hitting and kicking the gay man several times, yelling anti-gay slurs. The police were called, and the son was eventually convicted of a hate-motivated assault, a felony. But what was the nature of the hate: anti-gay bias, or suburban property-owner madness?

Or take the Labor Day parade last year in Broad Channel, a small island in Jamaica Bay, Queens. Almost everyone there is white, and in recent years a group of local volunteer firefighters has taken to decorating a pickup truck for the parade in order to win the prize for "funniest float." Their themes have tended toward the outrageously provocative. Beginning in 1995, they won prizes for floats depicting "Hasidic Park," "Gooks of Hazzard" and "Happy Gays." Last year, they called their float "Black to the Future, Broad Channel 2098." They imagined their community a century hence as a largely black enclave, with every stereotype imaginable: watermelons, basketballs and so on. At one point during the parade, one of them mimicked the dragging death of James Byrd. It was caught on videotape, and before long the entire community was depicted as a caldron of hate.

It's an interesting case, because the float was indisputably in bad taste and the improvisation on the Byrd killing was grotesque. But was it hate? The men on the float were local heroes for their volunteer work; they had no record of bigoted activity, and were not members of any racist organizations. In previous years, they had made fun of many other groups and saw themselves more as provocateurs than bigots. When they were described as racists, it came as a shock to them. They apologized for poor taste but refused to confess to bigotry. "The people involved aren't horrible people," protested a local woman. "Was it a racist act? I don't know. Are they racists? I don't think so."

If hate is a self-conscious activity, she has a point. The men were primarily motivated by the desire to shock and to reflect what they thought was their community's culture. Their display was not aimed at any particular black people, or at any blacks who lived in Broad Channel—almost none do. But if hate is primarily an unconscious activity, then the matter is obviously murkier. And by taking the horrific lynching of a black man as a spontaneous object of humor, the men were clearly advocating indifference to it. Was this an aberrant excess? Or the real truth about the men's feelings toward African-Americans? Hate or tastelessness? And how on earth is anyone, even perhaps the firefighters themselves, going to know for sure?

Or recall H. L. Mencken. He shared in the anti-Semitism of his time with more alacrity than most and was an indefatigable racist. "It is impossible," he wrote in his diary, "to talk anything resembling discretion or judgment into a colored woman. They are all essentially childlike, and even hard experience does not teach them anything." He wrote at another time of the "psychological stigmata" of the "Afro-American race." But it is also true that, during much of his life, day to day, Mencken conducted himself with no regard to race, and supported a politics that was clearly integrationist. As the editor of his diary has pointed out, Mencken published many black authors in his magazine, *The Mercury,* and lobbied on their behalf with his publisher, Alfred A. Knopf. The last thing Mencken ever wrote was a diatribe against racial segregation in Baltimore's public parks. He was good friends with leading black writers and journalists, including James Weldon Johnson, Walter White, and George S. Schuyler, and played an underappreciated role in promoting the Harlem Renaissance.

What would our modern view of hate do with Mencken? Probably   15
ignore him, or change the subject. But, with regard to hate, I know lots of people like Mencken. He reminds me of conservative friends who oppose almost every measure for homosexual equality yet genuinely delight in the company of their gay friends. It would be easier for me to think of them as haters, and on paper, perhaps, there is a good case that they are. But in real life, I know they are not. Some of them clearly harbor no real malice toward me or other homosexuals whatsoever.

They are as hard to figure out as those liberal friends who support every gay rights measure they have ever heard of but do anything to avoid going into a gay bar with me. I have to ask myself in the same, frustrating kind of way: are they liberal bigots or bigoted liberals? Or are they neither bigots nor liberals, but merely people?

III.

Hate used to be easier to understand. When Sartre described anti-Semitism in his 1946 essay "Anti-Semite and Jew," he meant a very specific array of firmly held prejudices, with a history, an ideology and even a pseudoscience to back them up. He meant a systematic attempt to demonize and eradicate an entire race. If you go to the Web site of the World Church of the Creator, the organization that inspired young Benjamin Smith to murder in Illinois earlier this year, you will find a similarly bizarre, pseudo-rational ideology. The kind of literature read by Buford Furrow before he rained terror on a Jewish kindergarten last month and then killed a mailman because of his color is full of the same paranoid loopiness. And when we talk about hate, we often mean this kind of phenomenon.

But this brand of hatred is mercifully rare in the United States. These professional maniacs are to hate what serial killers are to murder. They should certainly not be ignored; but they represent what Harold Meyerson, writing in *Salon,* called "niche haters": cold blooded, somewhat deranged, often poorly socialized psychopaths. In a free society with relatively easy access to guns, they will always pose a menace.

But their menace is a limited one, and their hatred is hardly typical of anything very widespread. Take Buford Furrow. He famously issued a "wake-up call" to "kill Jews" in Los Angeles, before he peppered a Jewish community center with gunfire. He did this in a state with two Jewish female senators, in a city with a large, prosperous Jewish population, in a country where out of several million Jewish Americans, a total of 66 were reported by the F.B.I. as the targets of hate-crime assaults in 1997. However despicable Furrow's actions were, it would require a very large stretch to describe them as representative of anything but the deranged fringe of an American subculture.

Most hate is more common and more complicated, with as many vari-   20
eties as there are varieties of love. Just as there is possessive love and needy love; family love and friendship; romantic love and unrequited love; passion and respect, affection and obsession, so hatred has its shadings. There is hate that fears, and hate that merely feels contempt; there is hate that expresses power, and hate that comes from powerlessness; there is revenge, and there is hate that comes from envy. There is hate that was love, and hate that is a curious expression of love. There is hate of the other, and hate of something that reminds us too much of ourselves. There is the oppressor's hate, and the victim's hate. There is hate that burns slowly, and hate that fades. And there is hate that explodes, and hate that never catches fire.

The modern words that we have created to describe the varieties of hate—"sexism," "racism," "anti-Semitism," "homophobia"—tell us very little about any of this. They tell us merely the identities of the victims; they don't reveal the identities of the perpetrators, or what they think, or how they feel. They don't even tell us how the victims feel. And this simplicity is no accident. Coming from the theories of Marxist and post-Marxist academics, these "isms" are far better at alleging structures of power than at delineating the workings of the individual heart or mind. In fact, these "isms" can exist without mentioning individuals at all.

We speak of institutional racism, for example, as if an institution can feel anything. We talk of "hate" as an impersonal noun, with no hater specified. But when these abstractions are actually incarnated, when someone feels something as a result of them, when a hater actually interacts with a victim, the picture changes. We find that hates are often very different phenomena one from another, that they have very different psychological dynamics, that they might even be better understood by not seeing them as varieties of the same thing at all.

There is, for example, the now unfashionable distinction between reasonable hate and unreasonable hate. In recent years, we have become accustomed to talking about hates as if they were all equally indefensible, as if it could never be the case that some hates might be legitimate, even necessary. But when some 800,000 Tutsis are murdered under the auspices of a Hutu regime in Rwanda, and when a few thousand Hutus are killed in revenge, the hates are not commensurate. Genocide is not an event like a hurricane, in which damage is random and universal; it is a planned and often merciless attack of one group upon another. The hate of the perpetrators is a monstrosity. The hate of the victims, and their survivors, is justified. What else, one wonders, were surviving Jews supposed to feel toward Germans after the Holocaust? Or, to a different degree, South African blacks after apartheid? If the victims overcome this hate, it is a supreme moral achievement. But if they don't, the victims are not as culpable as the perpetrators. So the hatred of Serbs for Kosovars today can never be equated with the hatred of Kosovars for Serbs.

Hate, like much of human feeling, is not rational, but it usually has its reasons. And it cannot be understood, let alone condemned, without knowing them. Similarly, the hate that comes from knowledge is always different from the hate that comes from ignorance. It is one of the most foolish clichés of our time that prejudice is always rooted in ignorance, and can usually be overcome by familiarity with the objects of our loathing. The racism of many Southern whites under segregation was not appeased by familiarity with Southern blacks; the virulent loathing of Tutsis by many Hutus was not undermined by living next door to them for centuries. Theirs was a hatred that sprang, for whatever reasons, from experience. It cannot easily be compared with, for example, the resilience of anti-Semitism in Japan, or hostility to immigration in areas where immigrants are unknown, or fear of homosexuals by people who have never knowingly met one.

The same familiarity is an integral part of what has become known as "sexism." Sexism isn't, properly speaking, a prejudice at all. Few men live without knowledge or constant awareness of women. Every single sexist man was born of a woman, and is likely to be sexually attracted to women. His hostility is going to be very different than that of, say, a reclusive member of the Aryan Nations toward Jews he has never met.

In her book *The Anatomy of Prejudices,* the psychotherapist Elisabeth Young-Bruehl proposes a typology of three distinct kinds of hate: obsessive, hysterical, and narcissistic. It's not an exhaustive analysis, but it's a beginning in any serious attempt to understand hate rather than merely declaring war on it. The obsessives, for Young-Bruehl, are those, like the Nazis or Hutus, who fantasize a threat from a minority, and obsessively try to rid themselves of it. For them, the very existence of the hated group is threatening. They often describe their loathing in almost physical terms: they experience what Patrick Buchanan, in reference to homosexuals, once described as a "visceral recoil" from the objects of their detestation. They often describe those they hate as diseased or sick, in need of a cure. Or they talk of "cleansing" them, as the Hutus talked of the Tutsis, or call them "cockroaches," as Yitzhak Shamir called the Palestinians. If you read material from the Family Research Council, it is clear that the group regards homosexuals as similar contaminants. A recent posting on its Web site about syphilis among gay men was headlined, "Unclean."

Hysterical haters have a more complicated relationship with the objects of their aversion. In Young-Bruehl's words, hysterical prejudice is a prejudice that "a person uses unconsciously to appoint a group to act out in the world forbidden sexual and sexually aggressive desires that the person has repressed." Certain kinds of racists fit this pattern. White loathing of blacks is, for some people, at least partly about sexual and physical envy. A certain kind of white racist sees in black America all those impulses he wishes most to express himself but cannot. He idealizes in "blackness" a sexual freedom, a physical power, a Dionysian release that he detests but also longs for. His fantasy may not have any basis in reality, but it is powerful nonetheless. It is a form of love-hate, and it is impossible to understand the nuances of racism in, say, the American South, or in British Imperial India, without it.

Unlike the obsessives, the hysterical haters do not want to eradicate the objects of their loathing; rather they want to keep them in some kind of permanent and safe subjugation in order to indulge the attraction of their repulsion. A recent study, for example, found that the men most likely to be opposed to equal rights for homosexuals were those most likely to be aroused by homoerotic imagery. This makes little rational sense, but it has a certain psychological plausibility. If homosexuals were granted equality, then the hysterical gay-hater might panic that his repressed passions would run out of control, overwhelming him and the world he inhabits.

A narcissistic hate, according to Young-Bruehl's definition, is sexism. In its most common form, it is rooted in many men's inability even to imagine what it is to be a woman, a failing rarely challenged by men's control of our most powerful public social institutions. Women are not so much hated by most men as simply ignored in non-sexual contexts, or never conceived of as true equals. The implicit condescension is mixed, in many cases, with repressed and sublimated erotic desire. So the unawareness of women is sometimes commingled with a deep longing or contempt for them.

Each hate, of course, is more complicated than this, and in any one person hate can assume a uniquely configured combination of these types. So there are hysterical sexists who hate women because they need them so much, and narcissistic sexists who hardly notice that women exist, and sexists who oscillate between one of these positions and another. And there are gay-bashers who are threatened by masculine gay men and gay-haters who feel repulsed by effeminate ones. The soldier who beat his fellow soldier Barry Winchell to death with a baseball bat in July had earlier lost a fight to him. It was the image of a macho gay man—and the shame of being bested by him—that the vengeful soldier had to obliterate, even if he needed a gang of accomplices and a weapon to do so. But the murderers of Matthew Shepard seem to have had a different impulse: a visceral disgust at the thought of any sexual contact with an effeminate homosexual. Their anger was mixed with mockery, as the cruel spectacle at the side of the road suggested.

In the same way, the pathological anti-Semitism of Nazi Germany was obsessive, inasmuch as it tried to cleanse the world of Jews; but also, as

30

Daniel Jonah Goldhagen shows in his book, *Hitler's Willing Executioners,* hysterical. The Germans were mysteriously compelled as well as repelled by Jews, devising elaborate ways, like death camps and death marches, to keep them alive even as they killed them. And the early Nazi phobia of interracial sex suggests as well a lingering erotic quality to the relationship, partaking of exactly the kind of sexual panic that persists among some homosexual-haters and antimiscegenation racists. So the concept of "homophobia," like that of "sexism" and "racism," is often a crude one. All three are essentially cookie-cutter formulas that try to understand human impulses merely through the one-dimensional identity of the victims, rather than through the thoughts and feelings of the haters and hated.

This is deliberate. The theorists behind these "isms" want to ascribe all blame to one group in society—the "oppressors"—and render specific others—the "victims"—completely blameless. And they want to do this in order in part to side unequivocally with the underdog. But it doesn't take a genius to see how this approach, too, can generate its own form of bias. It can justify blanket condemnations of whole groups of people—white straight males, for example—purely because of the color of their skin or the nature of their sexual orientation. And it can condescendingly ascribe innocence to whole groups of others. It does exactly what hate does: it hammers the uniqueness of each individual into the anvil of group identity. And it postures morally over the result.

In reality, human beings and human acts are far more complex, which is why these isms and the laws they have fomented are continually coming under strain and challenge. Once again, hate wriggles free of its definers. It knows no monolithic groups of haters and hated. Like a river, it has many eddies, backwaters, and rapids. So there are anti-Semites who actually admire what they think of as Jewish power, and there are gay-haters who look up to homosexuals and some who want to sleep with them. And there are black racists, racist Jews, sexist women, and anti-Semitic homosexuals. Of course there are.

IV.

Once you start thinking of these phenomena less as the "isms" of sexism/racism and "homophobia," once you think of them as independent psychological responses, it's also possible to see how they can work in a bewildering variety of ways in a bewildering number of people. To take one obvious and sad oddity: people who are demeaned and objectified in society may develop an aversion to their tormentors that is more hateful in its expression than the prejudice they have been subjected to. The F.B.I. statistics on hate crimes throws up an interesting point. In America in the 1990s, blacks were up to three times as likely as whites to commit a hate crime, to express their hate by physically attacking their targets or their property. Just as sexual abusers have often been victims of sexual abuse, and wife-beaters often grew up in violent households, so hate criminals may often be members of hated groups.

Even the Columbine murderers were in some sense victims of hate 33 before they were purveyors of it. Their classmates later admitted that Dylan Klebold and Eric Harris were regularly called "faggots" in the corridors and classrooms of Columbine High and that nothing was done to prevent or stop the harassment. This climate of hostility doesn't excuse the actions of Klebold and Harris, but it does provide a more plausible context. If they had been black, had routinely been called "nigger" in the school and had then exploded into a shooting spree against white students, the response to the matter might well have been different. But the hate would have been the same. In other words, hate-victims are often hate-victimizers as well. This doesn't mean that all hates are equivalent, or that some are not more justified than others. It means merely that hate goes both ways; and if you try to regulate it among some, you will find yourself forced to regulate it among others.

It is no secret, for example, that some of the most vicious anti-Semites in America are black, and that some of the most virulent anti-Catholic bigots in America are gay. At what point, we are increasingly forced to ask, do these phenomena become as indefensible as white racism or religious toleration of anti-gay bigotry? That question becomes all the more difficult when we notice that it is often minorities who commit some of the most hate-filled offenses against what they see as their oppressors. It was the mainly gay AIDS activist group Act Up that perpetrated the hateful act of desecrating Communion hosts at a Mass at St. Patrick's Cathedral in New York. And here is the playwright Tony Kushner, who is gay, responding to the Matthew Shepard beating in *The Nation* magazine: "Pope John Paul II endorses murder. He, too, knows the price of discrimination, having declared anti-Semitism a sin. . . . He knows that discrimination kills. But when the Pope heard the news about Matthew Shepard, he, too, worried about spin. And so, on the subject of gay-bashing, the Pope and his cardinals and his bishops and priests maintain their cynical political silence. . . . To remain silent is to endorse murder." Kushner went on to describe the Pope as a "homicidal liar."

Maybe the passion behind these words is justified. But it seems clear enough to me that Kushner is expressing hate toward the institution of the Catholic Church, and all those who perpetuate its doctrines. How else to interpret the way in which he accuses the Pope of cynicism, lying, and murder? And how else either to understand the brutal parody of religious vocations expressed by the Sisters of Perpetual Indulgence, a group of gay men who dress in drag as nuns and engage in sexually explicit performances in public? Or T-shirts with the words "Recovering Catholic" on them, hot items among some gay and lesbian activists? The implication that someone's religious faith is a mental illness is clearly an expression of contempt. If that isn't covered under the definition of hate speech, what is?

Or take the following sentence: "The act male homosexuals commit is ugly and repugnant and afterwards they are disgusted with themselves. They drink and take drugs to palliate this, but they are disgusted with the act and they are always changing partners and cannot be really happy." The thoughts of Pat Robertson or Patrick Buchanan? Actually that sentence was written by Gertrude Stein, one of the century's most notable lesbians. Or take the following, about how beating up "black boys like that made us feel good inside. . . . Every time I drove my foot into his [expletive], I felt better." It was written to describe the brutal assault of an innocent bystander for the sole reason of his race. By the end of the attack, the victim had blood gushing from his mouth as his attackers stomped on his genitals. Are we less appalled when we learn that the actual sentence was how beating up "white boys like that made us feel good inside. . . . Every time I drove my foot into his [expletive], I felt better?" It was written by Nathan McCall, an African-American who later in life became a successful journalist at the *Washington Post* and published his memoir of this "hate crime" to much acclaim.

In fact, one of the stranger aspects of hate is that the prejudice expressed by a group in power may often be milder in expression than the prejudice felt by the marginalized. After all, if you already enjoy privilege, you may not feel the anger that turns bias into hate. You may not need to. For this reason, most white racism may be more influential in society than most black racism—but also more calmly expressed.

So may other forms of minority loathing—especially hatred within   40
minorities. I'm sure that black conservatives like Clarence Thomas or Thomas Sowell have experienced their fair share of white racism. But I wonder whether it has ever reached the level of intensity of the hatred directed toward them by other blacks? In several years of being an openly gay writer and editor, I have experienced the gamut of responses to my sexual orientation. But I have only directly experienced articulated, passionate hate from other homosexuals. I have been accused over the years by other homosexuals of being a sellout, a hypocrite, a traitor, a sexist, a racist, a narcissist, a snob. I've been called selfish, callous, hateful, self-hating, and malevolent. At a reading, a group of lesbian activists portrayed my face on a poster within the crossfires of a gun. Nothing from the religious right has come close to such vehemence.

I am not complaining. No harm has ever come to me or my property, and much of the criticism is rooted in the legitimate expression of political differences. But the visceral tone and style of the gay criticism can only be described as hateful. It is designed to wound personally, and it often does. But its intensity comes in part, one senses, from the pain of being excluded for so long, of anger long restrained bubbling up and directing itself more aggressively toward an alleged traitor than an alleged enemy. It is the hate of the hated. And it can be the most hateful hate of all. For this reason, hate-crime laws may themselves be an oddly biased category—biased against the victims of hate. Racism is everywhere, but the already victimized might be more desperate, more willing to express it violently. And so more prone to come under the suspicious eye of the law.

V.

And why is hate for a group worse than hate for a person? In Laramie, Wyoming, the now-famous epicenter of "homophobia," where Matthew Shepard was brutally beaten to death, vicious murders are not unknown. In the previous 12 months, a 15-year-old pregnant girl was found east of the town with 17 stab wounds. Her 38-year-old boyfriend was apparently angry that she had refused an abortion and left her in the Wyoming foothills to bleed to death. In the summer of 1998, an 8-year-old Laramie girl was abducted, raped and murdered by a pedophile, who disposed of her young body in a garbage dump. Neither of these killings was deemed a hate crime, and neither would be designated as such under any existing hate-crime law. Perhaps because of this, one crime is an international legend; the other two are virtually unheard of.

But which crime was more filled with hate? Once you ask the question, you realize how difficult it is to answer. Is it more hateful to kill a stranger or a lover? Is it more hateful to kill a child than an adult? Is it more hateful to kill your own child than another's? Under the law before the invention of hate crimes, these decisions didn't have to be taken. But under the law after hate crimes, a decision is essential. A decade ago, a murder was a murder. Now, in the era when group hate has emerged as our cardinal social sin, it all depends.

The supporters of laws against hate crimes argue that such crimes should be disproportionately punished because they victimize more than the victim. Such crimes, these advocates argue, spread fear, hatred and panic among whole populations, and therefore merit more concern. But, of course, all crimes victimize more than the victim, and spread alarm in the society at large. Just think of the terrifying church shooting in Texas only two weeks ago. In fact, a purely random murder may be even more terrifying than a targeted one, since the entire community, and not just a part of it, feels threatened. High rates of murder, robbery, assault, and burglary victimize everyone, by spreading fear, suspicion, and distress everywhere. Which crime was more frightening to more people this summer: the mentally ill Buford Furrow's crazed attacks in Los Angeles, killing one, or Mark Barton's murder of his own family and several random day-traders in Atlanta, killing 12? Almost certainly the latter. But only Furrow was guilty of "hate."

One response to this objection is that certain groups feel fear more   45
intensely than others because of a history of persecution or intimidation.
But doesn't this smack of a certain condescension toward minorities? Why,
after all, should it be assumed that gay men or black women or Jews, for
example, are as a group more easily intimidated than others? Surely in any
of these communities there will be a vast range of responses, from panic to
concern to complete indifference. The assumption otherwise is the kind
of crude generalization the law is supposed to uproot in the first place.
And among these groups, there are also likely to be vast differences. To
equate a population once subjected to slavery with a population of Mexican immigrants or third-generation Holocaust survivors is to equate the
unequatable. In fact, it is to set up a contest of vulnerability in which one
group vies with another to establish its particular variety of suffering, a
contest that can have no dignified solution.

Rape, for example, is not classified as a "hate crime" under most existing laws, pitting feminists against ethnic groups in a battle for recognition. If, as a solution to this problem, everyone, except the white straight
able-bodied male, is regarded as a possible victim of a hate crime, then we
have simply created a two-tier system of justice in which racial profiling is
reversed, and white straight men are presumed guilty before being proven
innocent, and members of minorities are free to hate them as gleefully as
they like. But if we include the white straight male in the litany of potential victims, then we have effectively abolished the notion of a hate crime
altogether. For if every crime is possibly a hate crime, then it is simply
another name for crime. All we will have done is widened the search for
possible bigotry, ratcheted up the sentences for everyone and filled the
jails up even further.

Hate-crime-law advocates counter that extra penalties should be
imposed on hate crimes because our society is experiencing an "epidemic"
of such crimes. Mercifully, there is no hard evidence to support this
notion. The Federal Government has only been recording the incidence
of hate crimes in this decade, and the statistics tell a simple story. In 1992,
there were 6,623 hate-crime incidents reported to the F.B.I., by a total
of 6,181 agencies, covering 51 percent of the population. In 1996, there
were 8,734 incidents reported by 11,355 agencies, covering 84 percent of
the population. That number dropped to 8,049 in 1997. These numbers
are, of course, hazardous. They probably underreport the incidence of
such crimes, but they are the only reliable figures we have. Yet even if they
are faulty as an absolute number, they do not show an epidemic of "hate
crimes" in the 1990s.

Is there evidence that the crimes themselves are becoming more
vicious? None. More than 60 percent of recorded hate crimes in America involve no violent, physical assault against another human being at
all, and, again, according to the F.B.I., that proportion has not budged
much in the 1990s. These impersonal attacks are crimes against property

or crimes of "intimidation." Murder, which dominates media coverage of hate crimes, is a tiny proportion of the total. Of the 8,049 hate crimes reported to the F.B.I. in 1997, a total of eight were murders. Eight. The number of hate crimes that were aggravated assaults (generally involving a weapon) in 1997 is less than 15 percent of the total. That's 1,237 assaults too many, of course, but to put it in perspective, compare it with a reported 1,022,492 "equal opportunity" aggravated assaults in America in the same year. The number of hate crimes that were physical assaults is half the total. That's 4,000 assaults too many, of course, but to put it in perspective, it compares with around 3.8 million "equal opportunity" assaults in America annually.

The truth is, the distinction between a crime filled with personal hate and a crime filled with group hate is an essentially arbitrary one. It tells us

> **The truth is, the distinction between a crime filled with personal hate and a crime filled with group hate is an essentially arbitrary one.**

nothing interesting about the psychological contours of the specific actor or his specific victim. It is a function primarily of politics, of special interest groups carving out particular protections for themselves, rather than a serious response to a serious criminal concern. In such an endeavor, hate-crime-law advocates cram an entire world of human motivations into an immutable, tiny box called hate, and hope to have solved a problem. But nothing has been solved; and some harm may even have been done.

In an attempt to repudiate a past that treated people differently because of the color of their skin, or their sex, or religion or sexual orientation, we may merely create a future that permanently treats people differently because of the color of their skin, or their sex, religion, or sexual orientation. This notion of a hate crime, and the concept of hate that lies behind it, takes a psychological mystery and turns it into a facile political artifact. Rather than compounding this error and extending even further, we should seriously consider repealing the concept altogether.

To put it another way: violence can and should be stopped by the government. In a free society, hate can't and shouldn't be. The boundaries between hate and prejudice and between prejudice and opinion and between opinion and truth are so complicated and blurred that any attempt to construct legal and political fire walls is a doomed and illiberal venture. We know by now that hate will never disappear from human consciousness; in fact, it is probably, at some level, definitive of it. We know after decades of education measures that hate is not caused merely by ignorance; and after decades of legislation, that it isn't caused entirely by law.

To be sure, we have made much progress. Anyone who argues that America is as inhospitable to minorities and to women today as it has been in the past has not read much history. And we should, of course, be vigilant that our most powerful institutions, most notably the government, do not actively or formally propagate hatred; and insure that the violent expression of hate is curtailed by the same rules that punish all violent expression.

But after that, in an increasingly diverse culture, it is crazy to expect that hate, in all its variety, can be eradicated. A free country will always mean a hateful country. This may not be fair, or perfect, or admirable, but it is reality, and while we need not endorse it, we should not delude ourselves into thinking we can prevent it. That is surely the distinction between toleration and tolerance. Tolerance is the eradication of hate; toleration is co-existence despite it. We might do better as a culture and as a polity if we concentrated more on achieving the latter rather than the former. We would certainly be less frustrated.

And by aiming lower, we might actually reach higher. In some ways, some expression of prejudice serves a useful social purpose. It lets off steam; it allows natural tensions to express themselves incrementally; it can siphon off conflict through words, rather than actions. Anyone who has lived in the ethnic shouting match that is New York City knows exactly what I mean. If New Yorkers disliked each other less, they wouldn't be able to get on so well. We may not all be able to pull off a Mencken—bigoted in words, egalitarian in action—but we might achieve a lesser form of virtue: a human acceptance of our need for differentiation, without a total capitulation to it.

Do we not owe something more to the victims of hate? Perhaps we do. But it is also true that there is nothing that government can do for the hated that the hated cannot better do for themselves. After all, most bigots are not foiled when they are punished specifically for their beliefs. In fact, many of the worst haters crave such attention and find vindication in such rebukes. Indeed, our media's obsession with "hate," our elevation of it above other social misdemeanors and crimes, may even play into the hands of the pathetic and the evil, may breathe air into the smoldering embers of their paranoid loathing. Sure, we can help create a climate in which such hate is disapproved of—and we should. But there is a danger that if we go too far, if we punish it too much, if we try to abolish it altogether, we may merely increase its mystique, and entrench the very categories of human difference that we are trying to erase.

For hate is only foiled not when the haters are punished but when the hated are immune to the bigot's power. A hater cannot psychologically wound if a victim cannot psychologically be wounded. And that immunity to hurt can never be given; it can merely be achieved. The racial epithet only strikes at someone's core if he lets it, if he allows the bigot's definition of him to be the final description of his life and his person—if somewhere in his heart of hearts, he believes the hateful slur to be true. The only final answer to this form of racism, then, is not majority persecution of it, but minority indifference to it. The only permanent rebuke to homophobia is not the enforcement of tolerance, but gay equanimity in the face of prejudice. The only effective answer to sexism is not a morass of legal proscriptions, but the simple fact of female success. In this, as in so many other things, there is no solution to the problem. There is only a transcendence of it. For all our rhetoric, hate will never be destroyed. Hate, as our predecessors knew better, can merely be overcome.

THINKING CRITICALLY ABOUT THE READING

1. What does Sullivan mean when he writes in paragraph 8, "A large part of [hate] may even be hard-wired"? If he is correct, what might one conclude about attempts to legislate against hate crimes?

2. In paragraph 21, Sullivan writes that the "modern words we have created to describe the varieties of hate—'sexism,' 'racism,' 'anti-Semitism,' 'homophobia'—tell us very little" about the different kinds of hate he delineates in the paragraph above. What does he mean by this?

3. Some argue that hatred is a result of ignorance. How does Sullivan respond to this argument?

4. What does Sullivan see as the difference between the hatred of the perpetrator and the hatred of the victim in return (24)?

5. Sullivan cites Elisabeth Young-Bruehl's typology of hate in paragraph 26. What three kinds of hate does she identify, and what characterizes each type? How helpful do you find her classification in understanding hate? (Glossary: *Classification*)

6. What problems does Sullivan see with respect to hate-crime legislation (42–56)? What arguments does he present in favor of repealing hate-crime legislation? Do you agree or disagree with his reasons?

7. What does Sullivan find interesting about the hate that has been directed at him by other gay people? How does he explain it?

LANGUAGE IN ACTION

Andrew Sullivan builds a philosophical argument around a single word: hate. Regardless of mainstream dictionary definitions, "hate" is very difficult to define for legal purposes. Without consulting any outside source, work in small groups to come up with a functional, legal definition of hate. Establish criteria that would make an otherwise "ordinary" crime a "hate crime," then provide a list of things that would meet your criteria. Avoid generalizations. For example, if an element of your criteria is a bias against a particular group, what would constitute proof that the offender did in fact have a bias against that group? And what sort of evidence could be provided to prove that the crime itself was motivated "in whole or in part" by that bias?

Once you are able to reach some consensus, join with another group and see in what ways your definitions are alike and in what ways they are different. Where there are differences, try to reach some compromise: try to come up with language that everyone can agree upon.

WRITING SUGGESTIONS

1. Write an essay in which you examine the various terms for hate that Sullivan uses in his essay. How might an examination of these terms help us to understand both the dynamics of prejudice and how we, as individuals and as a society, respond to these dynamics?

2. In paragraph 56, Sullivan writes: "For hate is only foiled not when the haters are punished but when the hated are immune to the bigot's power. A hater cannot psychologically wound if a victim cannot psychologically be wounded. And that immunity to hurt can never be given; it can merely be achieved." Write an essay in which you explore the implications of Sullivan's comments here. Consider in particular how what Sullivan writes here relates to the establishment of hate-crime laws.

The Language of Prejudice

GORDON ALLPORT

Gordon Allport was born in Montezuma, Indiana, in 1897. He attended Harvard College and graduated Phi Beta Kappa in 1919 with majors in philosophy and economics. During his undergraduate years, he also became interested in psychology, and a meeting with Sigmund Freud in Vienna in 1920—during which the founder of psychoanalysis failed to impress him—had a profound influence on him. After studying and teaching abroad, Allport returned to Harvard to teach social ethics and to pursue his Ph.D., which he received in 1922. He went on to become a full professor at Harvard in 1942, served as chairman of the psychology department, and received the Gold Medal Award of the American Psychological Foundation in 1963. He died in 1967.

Allport became known for his outspoken stances regarding racial prejudice, and he was hopeful about efforts being made to eradicate it. His book *The Nature of Prejudice* (1954) is still regarded as one of the most important and influential texts on the subject. The following selection from that book analyzes the connections between language and prejudice and explains some of the specific ways in which language can induce and shape prejudice.

WRITING TO DISCOVER: *While in high school and college, many students are associated with groups that bring together people of disparate racial and religious backgrounds. Labels for these groups often carry many positive or negative associations. You may have made such associations yourself without thinking twice about it, as in "He's just a jock," or "She's with the popular crowd—she'll never go out with me." To what group, if any, did you belong in high school? Briefly write about the effects on you and your classmates of cliques in your school. How did the labels associated with the different groups influence how you thought about the individual members of each group?*

Without words we should scarcely be able to form categories at all. A dog perhaps forms rudimentary generalizations, such as small-boys-are-to-be-avoided—but this concept runs its course on the conditioned reflex level, and does not become the object of thought as such. In order to hold a generalization in mind for reflection and recall, for identification and for action, we need to fix it in words. Without words our world would be, as William James said, an "empirical sand-heap."

NOUNS THAT CUT SLICES

In the empirical world of human beings there are some two and a half billion grains of sand corresponding to our category "the human race." We cannot possibly deal with so many separate entities in our thought, nor can we individualize even among the hundreds whom we encounter in our daily round. We must group them, form clusters. We welcome, therefore, the names that help us to perform the clustering.

The most important property of a noun is that it brings many grains of sand into a single pail, disregarding the fact that the same grains might have fitted just as appropriately into another pail. To state the matter technically, a noun *abstracts* from a concrete reality some one feature and assembles different concrete realities only with respect to this one feature. The very act of classifying forces us to overlook all other features, many of which might offer a sounder basis than the rubric we select. Irving Lee gives the following example:

> I knew a man who had lost the use of both eyes. He was called a "blind man." He could also be called an expert typist, a conscientious worker, a good student, a careful listener, a man who wanted a job. But he couldn't get a job in the department store order room where employees sat and typed orders which came over the telephone. The personnel man was impatient to get the interview over. "But you're a blind man," he kept saying, and one could almost feel his silent assumption that somehow the incapacity in one aspect made the man incapable in every other. So blinded by the label was the interviewer that he could not be persuaded to look beyond it.

Some labels, such as "blind man," are exceedingly salient and powerful. They tend to prevent alternative classification, or even cross-classification. Ethnic labels are often of this type, particularly if they refer to some highly visible feature, e.g., Negro, Oriental. They resemble the labels that point to some outstanding incapacity—*feeble-minded*, *cripple*, *blind man*. Let us call such symbols "labels of primary potency." These symbols act like shrieking sirens, deafening us to all finer discriminations that we might otherwise perceive. Even though the blindness of one man and the darkness of pigmentation of another may be defining attributes for some purposes, they are irrelevant and "noisy" for others.

Most people are unaware of this basic law of language—that every label applied to a given person refers properly only to one aspect of his nature.

Most people are unaware of this basic law of language—that every   5
label applied to a given person refers properly only to one aspect of his nature. You may correctly say that a certain man is *human, a philanthropist, a Chinese, a physician, an athlete*. A given person may be all of these; but the chances are that Chinese stands out in your mind as the symbol of primary potency. Yet neither this nor any other classificatory label can refer to the whole of a man's nature. (Only his proper name can do so.)

Thus each label we use, especially those of primary potency, distracts our attention from concrete reality. The living, breathing, complex individual—the ultimate unit of human nature—is lost to sight. As in the figure, the label magnifies one attribute out of all proportion to its true significance, and masks other important attributes of the individual. . . .

A category, once formed with the aid of a symbol of primary potency, tends to attract more attributes than it should. The category labeled *Chinese* comes to signify not only ethnic membership but also reticence, impassivity, poverty, treachery. To be sure, . . . there may be genuine ethnic-linked traits, making for a certain *probability* that the member of an ethnic stock may have these attributes. But our cognitive process is not cautious. The labeled category, as we have seen, includes indiscriminately the defining attribute, probable attributes, and wholly fanciful, nonexistent attributes.

Even proper names—which ought to invite us to look at the individual person—may act like symbols of primary potency, especially if they arouse ethnic associations. Mr. Greenberg is a person, but since his name is Jewish, it activates in the hearer his entire category of Jews-as-a-whole. An ingenious experiment performed by psychologist Gregory Razran shows this

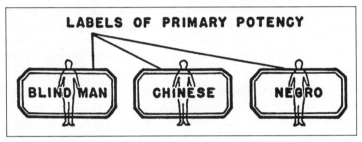

Source: Copyright © 1979 Gordon W. Allport. Reprinted by permission of Basic Books, a member of the Perseus Books Group.

point clearly, and at the same time demonstrates how a proper name, acting like an ethnic symbol, may bring with it an avalanche of stereotypes.

> Thirty photographs of college girls were shown on a screen to 150 students. The subjects rated the girls on a scale from one to five for *beauty, intelligence, character, ambition, general likability*. Two months later the same subjects were asked to rate the same photographs (and fifteen additional ones introduced to complicate the memory factory). This time five of the original photographs were given Jewish surnames (Cohen, Kantor, etc.), five Italian (Valenti, etc.), and five Irish (O'Brien, etc.); and the remaining girls were given names chosen from the signers of the Declaration of Independence and from the Social Register (Davis, Adams, Clark, etc.).
>
> When Jewish names were attached to photographs there occurred the following changes in ratings:
>
> > decrease in liking
> > decrease in character
> > decrease in beauty
> > increase in intelligence
> > increase in ambition

For those photographs given Italian names there occurred:

decrease in liking
decrease in character
decrease in beauty
decrease in intelligence

Thus a mere proper name leads to prejudgments of personal attributes. The individual is fitted to the prejudiced ethnic category, and not judged in his own right.

While the Irish names also brought about depreciated judgment, the depreciation was not as great as in the case of the Jews and Italians. The falling of likability of the "Jewish girls" was twice as great as for "Italians" and five times as great as for "Irish." We note, however, that the "Jewish" photographs caused higher ratings in *intelligence* and in *ambition*. Not all stereotypes of out-groups are unfavorable.

The anthropologist Margaret Mead has suggested that labels of primary potency lose some of their force when they are changed from nouns into adjectives. To speak of a Negro soldier, a Catholic teacher, or a Jewish artist calls attention to the fact that some other group classifications are just as legitimate as the racial or religious. If George Johnson is spoken of not only as a Negro but also as a *soldier,* we have at least two attributes to know him by, and two are more accurate than one. To depict him truly as an individual, of course, we should have to name many more attributes. It is a useful suggestion that we designate ethnic and religious membership where possible with *adjectives* rather than *nouns.*

EMOTIONALLY TONED LABELS

Many categories have two kinds of labels—one less emotional and one   10
more emotional. Ask yourself how you feel, and what thoughts you have, when you read the words *school teacher,* and then *school marm.* Certainly the second phrase calls up something more strict, more ridiculous, more disagreeable than the former. Here are four innocent letters: m-a-r-m. But they make us shudder a bit, laugh a bit, and scorn a bit. They call up an image of a spare, humorless, irritable old maid. They do not tell us that she is an individual human being with sorrows and troubles of her own. They force her instantly into a rejective category.

In the ethnic sphere even plain labels such as Negro, Italian, Jew, Catholic, Irish-American, French-Canadian may have emotional tone for a reason that we shall soon explain. But they all have their higher key equivalents: nigger, wop, kike, papist, harp, canuck. When these labels are employed we can be almost certain that the speaker *intends* not only to characterize the person's membership, but also to disparage and reject him.

Quite apart from the insulting intent that lies behind the use of certain labels, there is also an inherent ("physiognomic") handicap in many terms designating ethnic membership. For example, the proper names characteristic of certain ethnic memberships strike us as absurd. (We compare them, of course, with what is familiar and therefore "right.") Chinese names are short and silly; Polish names intrinsically difficult and outlandish. Unfamiliar dialects strike us as ludicrous. Foreign dress (which, of course, is a visual ethnic symbol) seems unnecessarily queer.

But of all of these "physiognomic" handicaps the reference to color, clearly implied in certain symbols, is the greatest. The word Negro comes from the Latin *niger* meaning black. In point of fact, no Negro has a black complexion, but by comparison with other blonder stocks, he has come to be known as a "black man." Unfortunately *black* in the English language is a word having a preponderance of sinister connotations: the outlook is black, blackball, blackguard, black-hearted, black death, blacklist, blackmail, Black Hand. In his novel *Moby Dick*, Herman Melville considers at length the remarkably morbid connotations of black and the remarkably virtuous connotations of white.

Nor is the ominous flavor of black confined to the English language. A cross-cultural study reveals that the semantic significance of black is more or less universally the same. Among certain Siberian tribes, members of a privileged clan call themselves "white bones," and refer to all others as "black bones." Even among Uganda Negroes there is some evidence for a white god at the apex of the theocratic hierarchy; certain it is that a white cloth, signifying purity, is used to ward off evil spirits and disease.

There is thus an implied value-judgment in the very concept of *white* 15 *race* and *black race*. One might also study the numerous unpleasant connotations of *yellow*, and their possible bearing on our conception of the people of the Orient.

Such reasoning should not be carried too far, since there are undoubtedly, in various contexts, pleasant associations with both black and yellow. Black velvet is agreeable, so too are chocolate and coffee. Yellow tulips are well liked; the sun and moon are radiantly yellow. Yet it is true that "color" words are used with chauvinistic overtones more than most people realize. There is certainly condescension indicated in many familiar phrases: dark as a nigger's pocket, darktown strutters, white hope (a term originated when a white contender was fought against the Negro heavyweight champion, Jack Johnson), the white man's burden, the yellow peril, black boy. Scores of everyday phrases are stamped with the flavor of prejudice, whether the user knows it or not.

We spoke of the fact that even the most proper and sedate labels for minority groups sometimes seem to exude a negative flavor. In many contexts and situations the very terms *French-Canadian*, *Mexican*, or *Jew*, correct and nonmalicious though they are, sound a bit opprobrious. The reason is that they are labels of social deviants. Especially in a culture where uniformity is prized, the name of *any* deviant carries with it *ipso facto* a negative value-judgment. Words like *insane, alcoholic, pervert* are presumably neutral designations of a human condition, but they are more: they are finger-pointing at a deviance. Minority groups are deviants, and for this reason, from the very outset, the most innocent labels in many situations imply a shading of disrepute. When we wish to highlight the deviance and denigrate it still further we use words of a higher emotional key: crackpot, soak, pansy, greaser, Okie, nigger, harp, kike.

Members of minority groups are often understandably sensitive to names given them. Not only do they object to deliberately insulting epithets, but sometimes see evil intent where none exists. Often the word Negro is spelled with a small *n*, occasionally as a studied insult, more often from ignorance. (The term is not cognate with white, which is not capitalized, but rather with Caucasian, which is.) Terms like "mulatto" or "octoroon" cause hard feeling because of the condescension with which they have often been used in the past. Sex differentiations are objectionable, since they seem doubly to emphasize ethnic difference: why speak of Jewess and not of Protestantess, or of Negress and not of whitess? Similar overemphasis is implied in the terms like Chinaman or Scotchman; why not American man? Grounds for misunderstanding lie in the fact that minority group members are sensitive to such shadings, while majority members may employ them unthinkingly.

THE COMMUNIST LABEL

Until we label an out-group it does not clearly exist in our minds. Take the curiously vague situation that we often meet when a person wishes to locate responsibility on the shoulders of some out-group whose nature he cannot specify. In such a case he usually employs the pronoun "they" without an antecedent. "Why don't they make these sidewalks wider?" "I hear they are going to build a factory in this town and hire a lot of foreigners." "I won't pay this tax bill; they can just whistle for their money." If asked "who?" the speaker is likely to grow confused and embarrassed. The common use of the orphaned pronoun *they* teaches us that people often want and need to designate out-groups (usually for the purpose of venting hostility) even when they have no clear conception of the out-group in question. And so long as the target of wrath remains vague and ill-defined specific prejudice cannot crystallize around it. To have enemies we need labels.

Until relatively recently [late 1940s]—strange as it may seem—there was no agreed-upon symbol for *communist*. The word, of course, existed but it had no special emotional connotation, and did not designate a public enemy. Even when, after World War I, there was a growing feeling of economic and social menace in this country, there was no agreement as to the actual source of the menace.

A content analysis of the Boston *Herald* for the year 1920 turned up the following list of labels. Each was used in a context implying some

20

threat. Hysteria had overspread the country, as it did after World War II. Someone must be responsible for the postwar malaise, rising prices, uncertainty. There must be a villain. But in 1920 the villain was impartially designated by reporters and editorial writers with the following symbols:

> alien, agitator, anarchist, apostle of bomb and torch, Bolshevik, communist, communist laborite, conspirator, emissary of false promise, extremist, foreigner, hyphenated-American, incendiary, IWW, parlor anarchist, parlor pink, parlor socialist, plotter, radical, red, revolutionary, Russian agitator, socialist, Soviet, syndicalist, traitor, undesirable.

From this excited array we note that the *need* for an enemy (someone to serve as a focus for discontent and jitters) was considerably more apparent than the precise *identity* of the enemy. At any rate, there was no clearly agreed upon label. Perhaps partly for this reason the hysteria abated. Since no clear category of "communism" existed there was no true focus for the hostility.

But following World War II this collection of vaguely interchangeable labels became fewer in number and more commonly agreed upon. The out-group menace came to be designated almost always as *communist* or *red*. In 1920 the threat, lacking a clear label, was vague; after 1945 both symbol and thing became more definite. Not that people knew precisely what they meant when they said "communist," but with the aid of the term they were at least able to point consistently to *something* that inspired fear. The term developed the power of signifying menace and led to various repressive measures against anyone to whom the label was rightly or wrongly attached.

Logically, the label should apply to specifiable defining attributes, such as members of the Communist Party, or people whose allegiance is with the Russian system, or followers, historically, of Karl Marx. But the label came in for far more extensive use.

What seems to have happened is approximately as follows. Having 25 suffered through a period of war and being acutely aware of devastating revolutions abroad, it is natural that most people should be upset, dreading to lose their possessions, annoyed by high taxes, seeing customary moral and religious values threatened, and dreading worse disasters to come. Seeking an explanation for this unrest, a single identifiable enemy is wanted. It is not enough to designate "Russia" or some other distant land. Nor is it satisfactory to fix blame on "changing social conditions." What is needed is a human agent near at hand: someone in Washington, someone in our schools, in our factories, in our neighborhood. If we *feel* an immediate threat, we reason, there must be a near-lying danger. It is, we conclude, communism, not only in Russia but also in America, at our doorstep, in our government, in our churches, in our colleges, in our neighborhood.

Are we saying that hostility toward communism is prejudice? Not necessarily. There are certainly phases of the dispute wherein realistic social conflict is involved. American values (e.g., respect for the person) and totalitarian values as represented in Soviet practice are intrinsically at odds. A realistic opposition in some form will occur. Prejudice enters only when the defining attributes of *communist* grow imprecise, when anyone who favors any form of social change is called a communist. People who fear social change are the ones most likely to affix the label to any persons or practices that seem to them threatening.

For them the category is undifferentiated. It includes books, movies, preachers, teachers who utter what for them are uncongenial thoughts. If evil befalls—perhaps forest fires or a factory explosion—it is due to communist saboteurs. The category becomes monopolistic, covering almost anything that is uncongenial. On the floor of the House of Representatives in 1946, Representative Rankin called James Roosevelt a communist. Congressman Outland replied with psychological acumen, "Apparently everyone who disagrees with Mr. Rankin is a communist."

When differentiated thinking is at a low ebb—as it is in times of social crises—there is a magnification of two-valued logic. Things are perceived as either inside or outside a moral order. What is outside is likely to be called communist. Correspondingly—and here is where damage is done—whatever is called communist (however erroneously) is immediately cast outside the moral order.

This associative mechanism places enormous power in the hands of a demagogue. For several years Senator McCarthy managed to discredit many citizens who thought differently from himself by the simple device of calling them communist. Few people were able to see through this trick and many reputations were ruined. But the famous senator has no monopoly on the device. As reported in the Boston *Herald:* on November 1, 1946, Representative Joseph Martin, Republican leader in the House, ended his election campaign against his Democratic opponent by saying, "The people will vote tomorrow between chaos, confusion, bankruptcy, state socialism or communism, and the preservation of our American life, with all its freedom and its opportunities." Such an array of emotional labels placed his opponent outside the accepted moral order. Martin was re-elected. . . .

Not everyone, of course, is taken in. Demagogy, when it goes too far, meets with ridicule. Elizabeth Dilling's book, *The Red Network*, was so exaggerated in its two-valued logic that it was shrugged off by many people with a smile. One reader remarked, "Apparently if you step off the sidewalk with your left foot you're a communist." But it is not easy in times of social strain and hysteria to keep one's balance, and to resist the tendency of a verbal symbol to manufacture large and fanciful categories of prejudiced thinking.

30

VERBAL REALISM AND SYMBOL PHOBIA

Most individuals rebel at being labeled, especially if the label is uncomplimentary. Very few are willing to be called *fascistic*, *socialistic*, or *anti-Semitic*. Unsavory labels may apply to others; but not to us.

An illustration of the craving that people have to attach favorable symbols to themselves is seen in the community where white people banded together to force out a Negro family that had moved in. They called themselves "Neighborly Endeavor" and chose as their motto the Golden Rule. One of the first acts of this symbol-sanctified band was to sue the man who sold property to Negroes. They then flooded the house which another Negro couple planned to occupy. Such were the acts performed under the banner of the Golden Rule.

Studies made by Stagner and Hartmann show that a person's political attitudes may in fact entitle him to be called a fascist or a socialist, and yet he will emphatically repudiate the unsavory label, and fail to endorse any movement or candidate that overtly accepts them. In short, there is a *symbol phobia* that corresponds to *symbol realism*. We are more inclined to the former when we ourselves are concerned, though we are much less critical when epithets of "fascist," "communist," "blind man," "school marm" are applied to others.

When symbols provoke strong emotions they are sometimes regarded no longer as symbols, but as actual things. The expressions "son of a bitch" and "liar" are in our culture frequently regarded as "fighting words." Softer and more subtle expressions of contempt may be accepted. But in these particular cases, the epithet itself must be "taken back." We certainly do not change our opponent's attitude by making him take back a word, but it seems somehow important that the word itself be eradicated.

Such verbal realism may reach extreme length.   35

> The City Council of Cambridge, Massachusetts, unanimously passed a resolution (December, 1939) making it illegal "to possess, harbor, sequester, introduce or transport, within the city limits, any book, map, magazine, newspaper, pamphlet, handbill, or circular containing the words Lenin or Leningrad."

Such naiveté in confusing language with reality is hard to comprehend unless we recall that word-magic plays an appreciable part in human thinking. The following examples, like the one preceding, are taken from Hayakawa.

> The Malagasy soldier must eschew kidneys, because in the Malagasy language the word for kidney is the same as that for "shot"; so shot he would certainly be if he ate a kidney.
>
> In May, 1937, a state senator of New York bitterly opposed a bill for the control of syphilis because "the innocence of children might be corrupted by a widespread use of the term. . . . This particular word creates a shudder in every decent woman and decent man."

This tendency to reify words underscores the close cohesion that exists between category and symbol. Just the mention of "communist," "Negro," "Jew," "England," "Democrats," will send some people into a panic of fear or a frenzy of anger. Who can say whether it is the word or the thing that annoys them? The label is an intrinsic part of any monopolistic category. Hence to liberate a person from ethnic or political prejudice it is necessary at the same time to liberate him from *word fetishism*. This fact is well known to students of general semantics who tell us that prejudice is due in large part to verbal realism and to symbol phobia. Therefore any program for the reduction of prejudice must include a large measure of semantic therapy.

THINKING CRITICALLY ABOUT THE READING

1. What is Allport's thesis, and where is it stated? (Glossary: *Thesis*)

2. In paragraph 2, why do you think Allport uses a metaphorical image — grains of sand — to represent people? (Glossary: *Figurative Language*) How does this metaphor help him present his point?

3. In paragraph 3, Allport uses Irving Lee's story of a blind man who was unable to get a job as an example of how powerful certain labels can be. (Glossary: *Examples*) What other quotations does he use as examples? What is the purpose of each one? Do you think they are effective? Why or why not?

4. Nouns, or names, provide an essential service in making categorization possible. Yet according to Allport, nouns are also words that "cut slices." What does he mean by that term? What is inherently unfair about nouns?

5. What are "labels of primary potency" (4)? Why does Allport equate them with "shrieking sirens"? Why are such labels important to his essay?

6. What does the experiment with the nonlabeled and labeled photos demonstrate? How do labels affect the way the mind perceives reality?

7. What does Allport mean by the "orphaned pronoun *they*" (19)? Why is it used so often in conversation?

8. What does Allport mean by *symbol phobia* (33)? How does this concept illustrate the unfairness of labeling others?

9. Allport wrote "The Language of Prejudice" in the early 1950s. Does this help explain why he devotes many paragraphs to the evolution of the label *communist*? What are the connotations of the word *communist* today? (Glossary: *Connotation/Denotation*)

LANGUAGE IN ACTION

Many people and organizations try to promote tolerance and tone down prejudice by suggesting that certain words and phrases be substituted for less respectful or insensitive ones. Consider the following examples that have been put forth in recent years.

Insensitive Words and Phrases	*Respectful Alternatives*
handicap	physical disability
fireman, policeman, postman	firefighter, police officer, letter carrier
illegal alien	undocumented immigrant
anti-abortion	pro-life
pro-abortion	pro-choice
unemployed	nonwaged
Indian	Native American or First Nations
uneducated	lacking formal education
Jew down	negotiate
an autistic person	a person who has autism
half-breed	multi-ethnic
blacklisted	banned
stewardess	flight attendant
old people, elderly	seniors
girls	women
gifted children	advanced learners
wheelchair-bound	a person who uses a wheelchair
BC, AD	BCE, CE
deaf	hearing impaired
mental retardation	intellectual disability
ethnic minority	persons of color
native	inhabitant
underdeveloped country	developing country

In each case, what kind of intolerance or prejudice do you think the language switch is attempting to eliminate or at least minimize? Do you think it's possible to change people's attitudes by simply requiring language changes like the ones suggested above? Discuss why or why not.

WRITING SUGGESTIONS

1. Make an extensive list of the labels that have been or could be applied to you at this time. Write an essay in which you discuss the labels that you find "truly offensive," those you can "live with," and those that you "like to be associated with." Explain your reasons for putting particular labels in each of these categories.

2. Allport states, "Especially in a culture where uniformity is prized, the name of *any* deviant carries with it *ipso facto* a negative value-judgment" (17). This was written in the 1950s. Since then, the turbulent 1960s, the political correctness movement of the 1980s and 1990s and the years since the millennium, and the mainstreaming of "alternative" cultures have all attempted to persuade

people to accept differences and be more tolerant. Write an essay in which you consider Allport's statement today. Which labels that identify someone as different still carry a negative association? Have the social movements of the past decades changed in a fundamental way how we think about others? Do you think there is more acceptance of nonconformity today, or is a nonconformist or member of a minority still subjected to negative, though perhaps more subtle, labeling? Support your conclusions with examples from your own experience and from the depiction of current events in the popular media.

3. Allport wrote *The Nature of Prejudice* before the civil rights movement began in earnest, though he did live to see it grow and reach its climax at the famous 1963 march on Washington. (See Martin Luther King Jr.'s celebrated "I Have a Dream" speech on pp. 301–304.) Obviously, part of the civil rights movement was in the arena of language, and its leaders often used impressive rhetoric to confront the language of prejudice. Write an essay in which you analyze how the kinds of labels and symbols identified by Allport were used in speeches and documents both to justify the continuation of segregation and prejudice and to decry it. How did the leaders of the civil rights movement use language to their advantage? To what emotions or ideas did the language of the opposition appeal? The Internet and your library have vast amounts of information about the movement's genesis and history, so it may be difficult at first to decide on a specific area of research. Start by looking at how language was used by both sides in the battle over civil rights.

The "F Word"

FIROOZEH DUMAS

Firoozeh Dumas was born in Abadan, Iran, in 1965. When she was seven, she and her family moved to Whittier, California. Two years later, they moved back to Iran, living this time in Ahvaz and Tehran, only to return to Southern California after several years. Dumas studied at the University of California, Berkeley, where she met and, after graduation, married François Dumas, who is French. In 2001, she started writing her memoir about life in Iran and the United States as a way of preserving this family history and culture for her children. *Funny in Farsi: A Memoir of Growing Up Iranian in America* was published in 2003. She builds on her first book in *Laughing Without an Accent: Adventures of an Iranian American at Home and Abroad* (2008), a collection of tender and humorous vignettes about the melding of cultures and the struggles of immigrants living in the United States.

In "The 'F Word,'" a chapter from *Funny in Farsi*, Dumas talks about the troubles she and her Iranian family and friends have had with their "identifiably 'ethnic' name[s]." She witnessed the prejudice toward immigrants that came about as a result of the Iranian hostage crisis (1979–1981) and writes about the difficulties she had getting a job interview as a college graduate with an Iranian name.

WRITING TO DISCOVER: *Do you or any of your friends have names that are identifiably ethnic? For example, are the names clearly Hispanic, Jewish, Arabic, Asian, German, Italian, Greek, or some other ethnicity? How do people react to you when they hear your family name? Describe.*

My cousin's name, Farbod, means "Greatness." When he moved to America, all the kids called him "Farthead." My brother Farshid ("He Who Enlightens") became "Fartshit." The name of my friend Neggar means "Beloved," although it can be more accurately translated as "She Whose Name Almost Incites Riots." Her brother Arash ("Giver") initially couldn't understand why every time he'd say his name, people would laugh and ask him if it itched.

All of us immigrants knew that moving to America would be fraught with challenges, but none of us thought that our names would be such an obstacle. How could our parents have ever imagined that someday we would end up in a country where monosyllabic names reign supreme, a land where "William" is shortened to "Bill," where "Susan" becomes "Sue," and "Richard" somehow evolves into "Dick"? America is a great country, but nobody without a mask and a cape has a z in his name. And have Americans ever realized the great scope of the guttural sounds they're missing? Okay, so it has to do with linguistic roots, but I do believe this would be a richer country if all Americans could do a little tongue aerobics and learn to pronounce "kh," a sound more commonly associated in this culture with phlegm, or "gh," the sound usually made by actors in the final moments of a choking scene. It's like adding a few new spices to the kitchen pantry. Move over, cinnamon and nutmeg, make way for cardamom and sumac.

Exotic analogies aside, having a foreign name in this land of Joes and Marys is a pain in the spice cabinet. When I was twelve, I decided to simplify my life by adding an American middle name. This decision serves as proof that sometimes simplifying one's life in the short run only complicates it in the long run.

My name, Firoozeh, chosen by my mother, means "Turquoise" in Farsi. In America, it means "Unpronounceable" or "I'm Not Going to Talk to You Because I Cannot Possibly Learn Your Name and I Just Don't Want to Have to Ask You Again and Again Because You'll Think I'm Dumb or You Might Get Upset or Something." My father, incidentally, had wanted to name me Sara. I do wish he had won that argument.

To strengthen my decision to add an American name, I had just   5
finished fifth grade in Whittier, where all the kids incessantly called me "Ferocious." That summer, my family moved to Newport Beach, where I looked forward to starting a new life. I wanted to be a kid with a name that didn't draw so much attention, a name that didn't come with a built-in inquisition as to when and why I had moved to America and how was it that I spoke English without an accent and was I planning on going back and what did I think of America?

My last name didn't help any. I can't mention my maiden name, because:

"Dad, I'm writing a memoir."

"Great! Just don't mention our name."

Suffice it to say that, with eight letters, including a z, and four syllables, my last name is as difficult and foreign as my first. My first and last name together generally served the same purpose as a high brick wall. There was one exception to this rule. In Berkeley, and only in Berkeley, my name drew people like flies to baklava. These were usually people named Amaryllis or Chrysanthemum, types who vacationed in Costa Rica and to whom lentils described a type of burger. These folks were probably not the pride of Poughkeepsie, but they were refreshingly nonjudgmental.

When I announced to my family that I wanted to add an American   10
name, they reacted with their usual laughter. Never one to let mockery or good judgment stand in my way, I proceeded to ask for suggestions. My father suggested "Fifi." Had I had a special affinity for French poodles or been considering a career in prostitution, I would've gone with that one. My mom suggested "Farah," a name easier than "Firoozeh" yet still Iranian. Her reasoning made sense, except that Farrah Fawcett was at the height of her popularity and I didn't want to be associated with somebody

whose poster hung in every postpubescent boy's bedroom. We couldn't think of any American names beginning with *F*, so we moved on to *J*, the first letter of our last name. I don't know why we limited ourselves to names beginning with my initials, but it made sense at that moment, perhaps by the logic employed moments before bungee jumping. I finally chose the name "Julie" mainly for its simplicity. My brothers, Farid and Farshid, thought that adding an American name was totally stupid. They later became Fred and Sean.

That same afternoon, our doorbell rang. It was our new next-door neighbor, a friendly girl my age named Julie. She asked me my name and after a moment of hesitation, I introduced myself as Julie. "What a coincidence!" she said. I didn't mention that I had been Julie for only half an hour.

Thus I started sixth grade with my new, easy name and life became infinitely simpler. People actually remembered my name, which was an entirely refreshing new sensation. All was well until the Iranian Revolution, when I found myself with a new set of problems. Because I spoke English without an accent and was known as Julie, people assumed I was American. This meant that I was often privy to their real feelings about those "damn I-raynians." It was like having those X-ray glasses that let you see people undressed, except that what I was seeing was far uglier than people's underwear. It dawned on me that these people would have probably never invited me to their house had they known me as Firoozeh. I felt like a fake.

All of us immigrants knew that moving to America would be fraught with challenges, but none of us thought that our names would be such an obstacle.

When I went to college, I eventually went back to using my real name. All was well until I graduated and started looking for a job. Even though I had graduated with honors from UC–Berkeley, I couldn't get a single interview. I was guilty of being a humanities major, but I began to suspect that there was more to my problems. After three months of rejections, I added "Julie" to my résumé. Call it coincidence, but the job offers started coming in. Perhaps it's the same kind of coincidence that keeps African Americans from getting cabs in New York.

Once I got married, my name became Julie Dumas. I went from having an identifiably "ethnic" name to having ancestors who wore clogs. My family and non-American friends continued calling me Firoozeh, while my coworkers and American friends called me Julie. My life became one big knot, especially when friends who knew me as Julie met friends who knew me as Firoozeh. I felt like those characters in soap operas who have an evil twin. The two, of course, can never be in the same room, since they're played by the same person, a struggling actress who wears a wig to play one of the twins and dreams of moving on to bigger and better roles. I couldn't blame my mess on a screenwriter; it was my own doing.

I decided to untangle the knot once and for all by going back to my   15
real name. By then, I was a stay-at-home mom, so I really didn't care
whether people remembered my name or gave me job interviews. Besides,
most of the people I dealt with were in diapers and were in no position to
judge. I was also living in Silicon Valley, an area filled with people named
Rajeev, Avishai, and Insook.

Every once in a while, though, somebody comes up with a new per-
mutation and I am once again reminded that I am an immigrant with a
foreign name. I recently went to have blood drawn for a physical exam.
The waiting room for blood work at our local medical clinic is in the basement of the building, and no matter how early one arrives for an appointment, forty coughing, wheezing people have gotten there first. Apart from
reading *Golf Digest* and *Popular Mechanics,* there isn't much to do except
guess the number of contagious diseases represented in the windowless
room. Every ten minutes, a name is called and everyone looks to see which
cough matches that name. As I waited patiently, the receptionist called
out, "Fritzy, Fritzy!" Everyone looked around, but no one stood up. Usually, if I'm waiting to be called by someone who doesn't know me, I will
respond to just about any name starting with an *F.* Having been called
Froozy, Frizzy, Fiorucci, and Frooz and just plain "Uhhhh . . . ," I am highly
accommodating. I did not, however, respond to "Fritzy" because there
is, as far as I know, no *t* in my name. The receptionist tried again, "Fritzy,
Fritzy DumbAss." As I stood up to this most linguistically original version
of my name, I could feel all eyes upon me. The room was momentarily
silent as all of these sick people sat united in a moment of gratitude for
their own names.

Despite a few exceptions, I have found that Americans are now far
more willing to learn new names, just as they're far more willing to try
new ethnic foods. Of course, some people just don't like to learn. One
mom at my children's school adamantly refused to learn my "impossible"
name and instead settled on calling me "F Word." She was recently transferred to New York where, from what I've heard, she might meet an immigrant or two and, who knows, she just might have to make some room in
her spice cabinet.

THINKING CRITICALLY ABOUT THE READING

1. Dumas confesses that "all of us immigrants knew that moving to America would
   be fraught with challenges, but none of us thought that our names would be
   such an obstacle" (2). What did she and her friends discover was the problem
   with Iranian names like Farbod, Farshid, Neggar, Arash, and Firoozeh?

2. How did Firoozeh reinvent herself when she and her family moved from
   Whittier to Newport Beach, California? How did she happen upon her new
   "American name" (10)?

3. Why do you think that Firoozeh couldn't mention her maiden name? What does she tell you about her last name? What would her last name reveal about her? In what ways did Dumas's "first and last name together generally [serve] the same purpose as a high brick wall" (9)?

4. During the Iranian Revolution, Firoozeh witnessed firsthand some pretty ugly anti-Iranian feelings expressed. Why wasn't she the target of these anti-Iranian sentiments?

5. Why do you think Firoozeh had trouble getting a job interview after graduating from the University of California, Berkeley? What is the problem with "having an identifiably 'ethnic' name" (353)? Explain.

6. Dumas writes about an extremely sensitive subject—personal names and prejudice—with humor. Did you find her humor appropriate for this subject and her audience? Cite several examples where she uses humor effectively.

LANGUAGE IN ACTION

Have you ever thought about changing your name? If so, why? Interestingly, show-business people often change their names to further their careers. Here are the professional names and the original names of a number of celebrities, past and present. Discuss with your classmates any significant associations that the original names might have and the reasons these names might have been changed.

Original Names	*Professional Names*
Demetria Guynes	Demi Moore
Michael Philip	Mick Jagger
Norma Jean Baker	Marilyn Monroe
Madonna Louise Ciccone	Madonna
Eleanor Gow	Elle MacPherson
Caryn Johnson	Whoopi Goldberg
Robert Zimmerman	Bob Dylan
Doris von Kappelhoff	Doris Day
Frederick Austerlitz	Fred Astaire
Marion Michael Morrison	John Wayne
Cassius Marcellus Clay Jr.	Muhammad Ali
Annemaria Italiano	Anne Bancroft
Maurice J. Micklewhite	Michael Caine
Thomas Mapother IV	Tom Cruise
Carlos Ray	Chuck Norris
Leonard Sly	Roy Rogers
Benjamin Kubelsky	Jack Benny

How do you think Firoozeh Dumas would react to some of these name changes? What celebrity name changes can you add to this list?

WRITING SUGGESTIONS

1. Is your surname very common in American society, very rare, or somewhere in between? Do others have difficulty pronouncing or spelling it? What does your surname reveal about your background or family history? Write an essay in which you reflect on the way your surname has affected your life and the way people react to you. Be sure to give examples of the role your name plays in day-to-day life.

2. Do a study of the names of the people in your dormitory or in one of your social groups. Analyze the names in light of Firoozeh Dumas's essay. In your opinion, are any of the names unusual? Why? Do they sound strange to you or others? Do they represent a culture different from your own? Do they remind you of another word that you find humorous? How do each of the people feel about their names? What insights, if any, do these names give you into the state of cultural diversity on your campus? Write an essay in which you discuss your findings. Make sure that you do not simply describe the names you found. Instead, build a context for your essay and provide a thesis for your comments. (Glossary: *Thesis*)

3. Write an essay in which you compare and contrast the experiences that Henry Louis Gates Jr. ("What's in a Name?," p. 14) and Dumas had with names. How did each of them feel when others named and thus defined them? What insights into oppression — namely racial, religious, or ethnic — do their experiences give you?

Why We Need to Tolerate Hate

WENDY KAMINER

Born in 1949, Wendy Kaminer graduated from Smith College in 1971 then earned her law degree from Boston University Law School. She served as a staff attorney for the Legal Aid Society and in the New York City Mayor's office before turning to writing full time. Kaminer is best known as an author and social critic, particularly for her work *I'm Dysfunctional, You're Dysfunctional* (1992), which critiques self-help culture. Her work has appeared in the *New York Times*, the *Atlantic Monthly*, the *Wall Street Journal*, the *Village Voice*, the *American Prospect*, *Dissent*, and the *Nation*. She is also the author of six other books, the most recent of which, *Worst Instincts: Cowardice, Conformity and the ACLU* (2009), looks at the waning ethics of the American Civil Liberties Union (ACLU), where she was once a board member. She is also a former Guggenheim fellow and recipient of the Smith College Medal.

Given her background, Kaminer often writes on the intersections of law and subjects such as feminism, criminal justice, and free speech. Although she is no longer on the board of the ACLU that she critiqued in *Worst Instincts*, Kaminer remains "an ardent civil libertarian," in her own words. In the essay included here, first published in the *Atlantic*, Kaminer reinforces her commitment to civil liberties by defending Americans' right to hate speech. She argues that the alternative, the censure of hate speech, is tantamount to prosecuting "bad thoughts and beliefs" and is fundamentally "in conflict with freedom of speech and belief," which are "quintessential American values."

WRITING TO DISCOVER: *In the communities where you grew up, were you aware of any incidents around hate speech or bigoted language? If so, how did those incidents shape your sense of what is acceptable to say and what isn't? If not, how do you think you would react to such an incident if you were to encounter one now?*

Decorate your house with anti-Semitic slogans or your clothing with swastikas and you engage in protected speech. Paper your neighbor's car with anti-Semitic bumper stickers and you're guilty of vandalism. Hate speech is constitutionally protected (as the Supreme Court confirmed most recently in *Snyder v. Phelps*). Destruction or defacement of someone else's property is legally prohibited.

Advocates of censoring "hate speech" might say that we value property more than the elimination of bigotry. I'd say that we value speech, as well as property, more than inoffensiveness. Besides, protections of presumptively hateful speech are not absolute: A prohibited act, like assault or vandalism, accompanied by vicious expressions of bigotry, may constitute a hate crime under law.

Consider this recent incident at Wheaton College: Anti-Semitic graffiti was scrawled across the back door of the Jewish Life House, where four students reside. The student who discovered it, Molly Tobin, described herself as "shocked, angry, and terrified," according to the *Boston Globe*. But students and faculty members have "come together" in support of diversity, with a potluck and a Facebook campaign. Campus police are investigating the incident, and the school is offering a $1,000 reward for information about it.

Could the vandals in this case be prosecuted for a hate crime? Perhaps. Massachusetts law provides that assaulting someone or damaging her property with "intent to intimidate" on the basis of race, color, or religion, among other characteristics, is punishable by a $5,000 fine and/or a maximum 2 1/2 year prison sentence. Whether or not the graffiti on the door of the Jewish Life House was intentionally intimidating is a question of fact; but you can guess how it might be resolved.

Should the vandals in this case be prosecuted for a hate crime? Fierce   5
free speech advocates, like my friend and colleague Harvey Silverglate, condemn hate crime laws for practically creating thought crimes: "It is foolish and dangerous for the legal system to punish a malefactor on the basis of whatever ideological or personal views or hatreds might, or might not, motivate crimes against person or property," Silverglate says. "The slope from punishing acts to punishing thoughts is very slippery indeed."

People can be mean and stupid. People harbor biases; they always have and always will ...

I tend to agree. Hate crime laws are generally sentence enhancement laws, imposing harsher sentences on crimes motivated by bias. They ensure that assaulting someone you hate because of his personality quirks is a lesser crime than assaulting someone you hate because he belongs to a particular, protected demographic group. In other words, when you're prosecuted for a bias crime, you're prosecuted for your bad thought and beliefs as well as your conduct.

Once convicted of a hate crime, you may even be subject to mandatory thought reform: In Massachusetts, you're required to complete a state sponsored and designed "diversity awareness program" before being released from prison or completing probation. Deface someone's property for the wrong reasons—bigotry or a bad attitude toward a protected group—and your thoughts become the business of the state.

This seems quintessentially un-American, if freedom of speech and belief are quintessential American values. But individual freedom is sometimes valued less, especially on campus, than diversity and the psychic as well as physical security of presumptively disadvantaged groups. FIRE President Greg Lukianoff reports on the lamentable consequences of this values shift in his important new book, *Unlearning Liberty.* "On college campuses today, students are punished for everything from mild satire, to writing politically incorrect short stories, to having the wrong opinion on virtually every hot button issue," he reports, in disturbing detail.

When "mild satire" and arguably offensive jokes are deemed too dangerous or disruptive to tolerate, it's not surprising that anti-Semitic graffiti is "terrifying" and virtually incomprehensible. At Wheaton, Molly Tobin says she remains afraid to walk around the campus at night and describes her reaction to finding the graffiti on her door as "an out of body experience." While appreciative of the strong support offered by Wheaton faculty and students, she considers it "pretty tragic that something on this level has to happen for the campus to respond like this."

Death, disease, war and genocide are tragic; famine is tragic, and climate change is potentially tragic. An isolated incident of anti-Semitic graffiti is unsettling and lamentable, but it's hardly a tragedy. It's human nature. Few of us will go through life without being insulted or disliked on account of race, religion, sex, sexual orientation, or other immutable characteristics. People can be mean and stupid. People harbor biases; they always have and always will, and their right to believe in the inferiority or sinfulness of particular groups is the same as your right to believe in equality.

I'm not suggesting that we should resign ourselves to bigotry. I'm arguing that we should tolerate expressions of it. This doesn't mean tolerating bigoted acts. Vandalism is not a form of protected speech, regardless of the ideas it expresses. Penal laws should punish assaults on people or property that are and aren't motivated by bigotry. Anti-discrimination laws can and do single out bias-motivated acts in employment and education with virtually no opposition from free speech advocates, except in some cases that involve verbal harassment.

Advocates of censoring hateful or offensive speech draw on civil rights laws to assert a right not to be offended or intimidated on account of membership in a protected group. But in the interests of equality, the state can regulate some educational policies (especially in public schools) as well as hiring, firing, and promotion in secular businesses without significantly infringing on the First Amendment. The state can't regulate hate or offensiveness without eviscerating fundamental First Amendment freedoms.

Is this an excuse for vigilantism? When is it necessary, appropriate, or ethical to publicly shame people for their bigoted speech? The Web site *Jezebel* sparked a minor fracas about journalistic ethics by calling out and ratting out to school administrators teenagers who spewed crude, racist tweets in the wake of Barack Obama's re-election:

> We contacted their school's administrators with the hope that, if their educators were made aware of their students' ignorance, perhaps they could teach them about racial sensitivity. Or they could let them know that while the First Amendment protects their freedom of speech, it doesn't protect them from the consequences that might result from expressing their opinions.

10

In fact, because the First Amendment protects the students' freedom of speech it should also protect them from some of the consequences "that might result" from their speech, especially consequences imposed by public school officials. It's true that student speech rights have been significantly limited in recent years, but the girls at *Jezebel* might want to consider whether that's cause for celebration.

In any case, they obviously enjoy their own First Amendment rights   15 to shame teenagers or adults whose speech offends them. They enjoy the right to encourage public school officials to punish students for their racist tweets. But they should perhaps exercise this right with a sense of irony. Instead, the *Jezebel* site is infused with the self-righteousness of people who have little compunction of speaking up in the interests of shutting up their ideological opponents and shutting down speech they find offensive. Freedom of speech respects self-certainty, but requires at least a little self-doubt.

THINKING CRITICALLY ABOUT THE READING

1. What is hate speech? In what ways is hate speech treated as protected speech? In what ways is it criminalized?

2. What are hate crimes? How are they treated differently than other crimes? What effects does this differing treatment have, according to Kaminer?

3. Why does Kaminer "condemn hate crime laws for practically creating thought crimes" (5)? How and why do she and Harvey Silverglate consider this a problem for national values? Do you agree? Why or why not?

4. Kaminer argues that this trend toward policing speech is particularly problematic on college campuses where it seems "individual freedom is sometimes valued less" (8). What examples does she give of how students' speech rights have been challenged? How could such restrictions on campuses begin to shape speech in society at large? What concerns does this phenomenon raise?

5. Kaminer insists that she's "not suggesting that we should resign ourselves to bigotry" but that "we should tolerate expressions of it" (11). How does she explain her position on the language of bigotry? Does guaranteeing freedom of speech also protect us from the consequences of speaking freely, according to Kaminer? If so, how? If not, why not?

6. Why is Kaminer critical of the feminist blog *Jezebel*'s response to racist post-election tweets? How would you characterize Kaminer's language in criticizing *Jezebel*? Does her criticism of *Jezebel* actually call for a censure of *their* free speech? Why or why not?

LANGUAGE IN ACTION

The Federal Bureau of Investigation offers the following definition of hate crimes on its public Web site:

> A hate crime is a traditional offense like murder, arson, or vandalism with an added element of bias. For the purposes of collecting statistics, Congress has defined a hate crime as a "criminal offense against a person or property motivated in whole or in part by an offender's bias against a race, religion, disability, ethnic origin or sexual orientation." Hate itself is not a crime—and the FBI is mindful of protecting freedom of speech and other civil liberties.

How does this definition differ from Kaminer's? How does it complicate Kaminer's argument? How do you think investigators and courts determine whether or not a criminal is motivated by bias? Why do you think the FBI takes a particular interest in hate crimes?

WRITING SUGGESTIONS

1. Kaminer argues that "when you're prosecuted for a bias crime, you're prosecuted for your bad thought and beliefs as well as your conduct" (6). Do you agree that hate crime prosecution is prosecution of thought and belief? If so, why? If not, why not? Kaminer rejects harsher sentences for "bias crime" and is critical of the rehabilitation often required. Do you agree? Write an essay in which you make an argument about the logic of prosecuting hate crimes differently from other crimes.

2. In her essay, Kaminer ties the decline in tolerating hate speech to a decline in student speech rights. She cites FIRE President Greg Lukianoff, who argues that "on college campuses today, students are punished for everything from mild satire, to writing politically incorrect short stories, to having the wrong opinion on virtually every hot button issue" (8). Do you think this is an accurate representation or an exaggeration of the situation? What is your experience of this sort of censorship on campus? Should a college campus support students' rights to any speech—including hate speech—without question? What is unique about the college community that might affect policies and expectations? Write an essay analyzing how controversial and/or bias speech has been protected or censored on your campus. You might research the archives of your school newspaper or speak with a politically active student group.

Twitter, Hate Speech, and the Costs of Keeping Quiet

Greg Lukianoff

Greg Lukianoff is a graduate of American University and of Stanford Law School, where he focused on First Amendment and constitutional law. As an attorney, Lukianoff practiced law in northern California and interned with the ACLU of Northern California. He is now the president and CEO of FIRE, the Foundation for Individual Rights in Education, whose mission is to defend and sustain individual rights at America's colleges and universities. Lukianoff has published articles in a variety of publications including the *Wall Street Journal*, the *Washington Post*, the *New York Times*, the *Los Angeles Times*, *TIME*, the *Boston Globe*, *Forbes*, the *New York Post*, *U.S. News & World Report*, the *Stanford Technology Law Review*, and the *Chronicle of Higher Education*. He has appeared on *CBS Evening News* and *CBS This Morning*, NBC's *Today Show*, and other news programs. He has also testified before both the U.S. Senate and the House of Representatives about free speech issues on America's campuses. In 2008 he became the first ever recipient of the Playboy Foundation Freedom of Expression Award, and in 2010 he received Ford Hall Forum's Louis P. and Evelyn Smith First Amendment Award on behalf of FIRE. He is also the author of *Unlearning Liberty: Campus Censorship and the End of American Debate* (2014) and *Freedom from Speech* (2014), both of which discuss episodes in what he calls his "decade fighting censorship on American college campuses." The essay included here gives a glimpse of that fight, as Lukianoff weighs in on Twitter's important decision to maintain its freedom of hate speech in the wake of a student-led lawsuit against anti-Semitic tweets in France.

WRITING TO DISCOVER: *Have you ever been surprised when someone you knew made a comment or posted a link that indicated a bigoted or hateful perspective? If so, what was surprising about it? How did you react? If not, how do you think you would react? Do you think you are better off knowing the person's opinions, or would you prefer not to know?*

Last month was a bittersweet seventh birthday for Twitter. The Union of Jewish French Students sued the social-media giant for $50 million in a French court in light of anti-Semitic tweets that carried the hashtag *#unbonjuif* ("a good Jew"). In January, Twitter agreed to delete the tweets, but the student group now wants the identities of the users who sent the anti-Semitic messages so that they can be prosecuted under French law against hate speech. Twitter is resisting. It claims that as an American company protected by the First Amendment, it does not have to aid government efforts to control offensive speech.

Forcing hate speech underground by banning it is like taking Xanax for syphilis. You may briefly feel better about your horrible disease, but your sickness will only get worse.

Internationally, America is considered radical for protecting speech that is highly offensive. But even in the U.S., Twitter should not be surprised to discover ambivalence and even outright hostility toward its principled aversion to censorship, especially in that once great institution for the open exchange of ideas: American higher education.

"Hate speech" is constitutionally protected in the United States. But the push against "hurtful" and "blasphemous" speech (primarily speech offensive to Islam) is gaining ground throughout the world. Last fall, for example, when many thought a YouTube video that satirized Mohammed caused a spontaneous attack on our consulate in Benghazi, academics across the country rushed to chide America for its expansive protections of speech. And as someone who has spent more than a decade fighting censorship on American college campuses, I run into antagonism toward free speech on a regular basis, most recently last month, when I spoke at Columbia Law School. After my speech, law professor Frederick Schauer criticized his American colleagues for not being more skeptical about the principle of free speech itself.

This has become a fairly standard refrain, in my experience, as academics who want to limit free speech often paint themselves as a beleaguered, enlightened minority struggling against the unquestioned dogma of free speech. Free speech is certainly alive in U.S. courts. For example, since 1989 more than a dozen courts have declared different politically correct college speech codes unconstitutional. Nevertheless, the idea that hurtful or offensive speech should be banned prevails on American campuses: approximately 63 percent of over 400 top colleges maintain codes that violate First Amendment principles.[1] Meanwhile, prominent professors, such as Jeremy Waldron and Richard Delgado, attempt to seize the moral high ground for "enlightened censorship," and some students even paint themselves as heroes for tearing down campus "free speech walls."

What strikes me about the arguments academics make against free 5 speech is how shallow they tend to be. The critics somehow miss that First Amendment jurisprudence is an extraordinarily thoughtful exposition on what limits are appropriate in a free and diverse society—and, contrary to the meme of America's mindless approach to speech, there are limits (including, for example, libel, as well as threats or incitement to imminent illegal action).

---

1. "Spotlight on Speech Codes 2013: The State of Free Speech on Our Nations Campuses," (Philadelphia: FIRE, 2013). https://www.thefire.org/pdfs/Spotlight_on_Speech _Codes_2013.pdf?direct

The authors of the Constitution also realized that people—flawed, imperfect humans, with biases, blind spots, shortcomings, and agendas—will decide what speech is and is not acceptable. Part of the wisdom of First Amendment law is that it recognizes that we flawed humans will be tempted to ban speech for no better reason than that officials (or voters) simply dislike or disapprove of an idea or a particular speaker. That's why First Amendment doctrine forbids the use of highly subjective standards, which would invite arbitrary punishment of dissenters, oddballs, satirists, or the misunderstood. Too many scholars seem to think a robot could simply apply such standards to produce a perfect outcome every time.

A common academic argument against free speech relies on the idea that the primary, if not sole, justification for freedom of speech is that it is necessary in order for society to discover "objective truth"—what I will call "Big T" Truth. But now, so the fashionable argument goes, the academy has found that objective truth does not exist, so we are free to regulate harmful, hurtful, or hateful speech because the benefit of unfettered speech—revelation of Truth—is illusory. (A revealing preview of today's anti-free speech arguments can be found in the oft-overlooked dissent to Yale's famous 1975 pro-free speech, pro-academic freedom "Woodward Report.")[2]

No doubt the open, anarchical, epistemological system that was celebrated in the Enlightenment—which Jonathan Rauch dubbed "liberal science" in his classic work on the value of freedom of speech, "Kindly Inquisitors"—has resulted in a flowering of creative and scientific thought. It has helped reveal what we consider to be objective facts (e.g., the Earth is an oblate spheroid; gravity is a fundamental force). But the free exchange of ideas benefits society not only by unearthing "Big T" truths; more importantly, it continually exposes mundane yet important pieces of information about the world. I will call this "Little t" truth. "Little t" truths include: who disagrees about what and why, what people feel about a particular issue, what events the newspapers think are important to report. The fact that "Argo" is a movie is truth, whether or not it represents an accurate view of history, as is the fact that some topics of discussion interest no one, while others are radioactive.

Twitter provides a powerful way to view the world. Never before have human beings been able to check the global zeitgeist with such immediacy and on such a massive scale. Its primary service is not to dispense the Platonic ideal of Truth ("the form of beauty = x"), but rather to provide unparalleled access to the peculiar thoughts, ideas, misconceptions, genuine wisdom, fetishes, fads, jokes, obsessions, and problems of a vast sea of people from different cultures, classes, countries, and backgrounds.

---

2. Kenneth J. Barnes, "A Dissenting Statement," (New Haven: Yale, 1975): 37–51. http://www.yale.edu/about/documents/specialdocuments/Freedom_Expression /freedom1975.pdf

In order to be an effective mirror to global society, Twitter thinks   10
of itself primarily as a platform and does its best to get out of the way.
Therefore, we know things we simply would not know otherwise—
from the trivial to the serious. The people who want to scour mass
media and cleanse it of all hateful or hurtful opinions miss that their
purge would deny us important knowledge. Simply put, it is far better to know that there are bigots among us than to pretend all is well.
As Harvey Silverglate, co-founder of FIRE (the Foundation for Individual Rights in Education, where I serve as president), likes to say, he
supports free speech because he thinks it's important that he know if
there's an anti-Semite in the room so he can make sure not to turn his
back to that person.

The idea that society achieves something positive by mandating that
people with bad opinions must hide them, or discuss them only in forums
of the like-minded, is not only extraordinarily naive, it can be dangerous.
Bigots driven into echo chambers may only become more extreme, as
discussed in Cass Sunstein's book, *Going to Extremes*. Meanwhile, what
does society gain from such quarantining? A coerced but false silence that,
if anything at all, plays into the hands of the paranoid and dangerous who
already believe that there is a global conspiracy to shut them up. Forcing
hate speech underground by banning it is like taking Xanax for syphilis.
You may briefly feel better about your horrible disease, but your sickness
will only get worse.

Simply making bigoted speech illegal results in two distortions of reality. First, it can create an overly rosy picture of public sentiment, thus
preventing real and festering social problems from being addressed. Or
second, paradoxically, it may lead people to believe that they live in a far
less tolerant society than they actually do. John L. Jackson, an anthropology professor at the University of Pennsylvania, teased out this idea in
his 2008 book *Racial Paranoia: The Unintended Consequences of Political Correctness*. Jackson argues that if a minority group believes that only
the threats of formal or informal punishments are preventing people from
constantly shouting racial slurs at the top of their lungs, the minority may
conclude that those other people are far more hateful and bigoted than
they may, in fact, be. In this way, attempts to police hateful or hurtful
speech may be making people more paranoid than they need to be about
the feelings most people actually hold in their hearts.

The only lasting fix to the real problem of racism or anti-Semitism is
cultural. A necessarily incomplete attempt to suppress bigotry may well
have far worse unintended consequences, as legal regimes that try to ban
hate speech drive social resentments underground, thus preventing the
right allocation of resources to address social problems openly.

Twitter lets us see people as they are—a mixed lot on any given day,
to be sure. But it is especially important for a free society to learn not just
the good news but the bad news as well.

THINKING CRITICALLY ABOUT THE READING

1. Why does Lukianoff call Twitter's seventh birthday "bittersweet" (1)? Why is there a conflict between the Union of Jewish French Students and the American company?

2. How do American speech laws differ from that of other countries, according to Lukianoff? What criticisms has America's protection of hate speech faced? Do you think those criticisms are valid? Why or why not?

3. What metaphor does Lukianoff use to describe banning hate speech as a means to rid ourselves of hate? Does this comparison seem appropriate, or does it pose problems? Why? What metaphor would you use?

4. Lukianoff is critical of "enlightened censorship" and its proponents (4). What does he suggest this terms means on college campuses? What percentage of campuses "violate" the First Amendment, according to Lukianoff (4)? Why does he see this as a problem? Do you agree?

5. Lukianoff argues against those who would limit hate speech by arguing that "bigots driven into echo chambers may only become more extreme" (11). What does he mean by this phrase? Do you agree? What harm might this cause if we did not have forums such as Twitter where this speech could find an outlet? Conversely, if hate speech were prohibited, do you think the prohibition could be enforced?

6. Why does Lukianoff suggest that "people who want to scour mass media and cleanse it of all hateful or hurtful opinions miss that their purge would deny us important knowledge" (10)? What knowledge are we denied and why is it significant? Why do you think he uses the words "cleanse" and "purge"? What do these words call to mind? How is the reader meant to react?

7. In what way does Lukianoff suggest that Twitter—and forums like it—allow us access to "little t" truths about society? In what ways does censoring speech in these forums "distort reality," according to the author?

LANGUAGE IN ACTION

Lukianoff says that "Twitter provides a powerful way to view the world. Never before have human beings been able to check the global zeitgeist with such immediacy and on such a massive scale" (9).

"Zeitgeist" is a German word that means, basically, "the spirit of the time." What is the spirit of our time? Can it be found on Twitter? Can it be located in words at all? Try to identify features of the contemporary zeitgeist—the spirit of our time. What are some of the dominant values? What words can you think of that express the values of our time? Many of the words you can think of will be abstract: "connectivity," for example. What does it mean? Do we say we want to be "connected" when we mean we want Wi-Fi? Or is a less literal meaning the more common one? Write down some words (on your own or together as a class) that capture the contemporary zeitgeist, then expand on the words as needed to get to a more specific meaning. Fill the board or page with words and see if you can get any closer to the "truth" of our time. How does language shape the zeitgeist?

WRITING SUGGESTIONS

1. Lukianoff criticizes university policies as misguided, as contributing to distorting reality when "approximately 63 percent of over 400 top colleges maintain codes that violate First Amendment principles" (4). Do you agree or disagree with Lukianoff's assessment and its implications? Research your school's code of conduct and any history of the discussion of free speech on your campus. How does your campus's history of engagement with free speech compare to Lukianoff's research? Write an essay analyzing the conflicts you uncover. Does your college's policy violate the First Amendment? What have been the effects of your college's policy, and how do you see those effects in life on campus today?

2. Lukianoff says of FIRE co-founder Harvey Silverglate, "he supports free speech because he thinks it's important that he know if there's an anti-Semite in the room so he can make sure not to turn his back to that person" (10). Write an essay in which you consider the logic of that statement and how it relates to the concept of free speech. What do you see as the dangers of hate speech? What are the dangers of suppressing it? Is there more to fear in hate speech or in the consequences of silencing it? Who is hurt if speech is free, and who is hurt if it isn't?

Thugs. Students. Rioters. Fans: Media's Subtle Racism in Unrest Coverage

AKIBA SOLOMON

Essayist and editor Akiba Solomon is a National Association of Black Journalists Award–winning writer. Solomon was raised in West Philadelphia, lived in Washington, D.C., while earning her B.A. in Communications at Howard University, and now resides in Brooklyn. Solomon is the editorial director of Colorlines.com and writes primarily on gender and race in current events. As a freelance writer she has penned articles for *Redbook*, *Vibe*, *Glamour*, and *Essence* and co-edited an anthology titled *Naked: Black Women Bare All about Their Skin, Hair, Hips, Lips, and Other Parts* (Perigee, 2005), a collection of original essays and memoirs about black women and body image that earned critical acclaim.

Solomon also often writes and lectures about women's and social justice issues, particularly through the lens of hip-hop culture. She has spoken at the Schomburg Center for the Research in Black Culture, Stanford University, Yale University, Harvard University, and the University of Chicago. The essay included here first appeared on Colorlines.com on April 28, 2015, the day after police-brutality victim Freddie Gray's funeral and before another wave of riots in Baltimore to protest Gray's death. Gray's death added to the growing and disproportionate tally of black men and women killed by police using lethal force in otherwise routine arrests or incidents. Here Solomon discusses how the language used to report such incidents in the press highlights the racism of media coverage.

WRITING TO DISCOVER: *Have you ever seen or participated in a protest or demonstration? If so, how would you characterize the participants and their mood? If not, what do you imagine a protest on your campus would look like? What words would you use to describe it?*

Whenever black civilians become enraged enough by police violence toward black men to set fires, loot stores and throw things at police in riot gear, I become this old, conservative black lady who asks annoying, clichéd questions like, "Why are they destroying their own neighborhoods?"

I get my faculties back by reviewing how some media describe arson, looting, and projectile-throwing by predominantly white crowds. I don't do this exercise to condemn individual journalists, but the subtle differences in language and context that emerge are just too jarring to ignore.

Take these excerpts from an April 27, 2015 Associated Press piece that ran in the *New York Times* called "Riots in Baltimore Over Man's Death in Police Custody." Keep in mind that Baltimore is predominantly black and most of images of unrest over Freddie Gray show black men in their late teens and early 20s:

> *Rioters plunged part of Baltimore into chaos Monday,* torching a pharmacy, setting police cars ablaze and throwing bricks at officers hours after thousands mourned the man who died from a severe spinal injury he suffered in police custody.
>
> . . . *Earlier Monday, the smell of burned rubber wafted in the air in one neighborhood where youths were looting a liquor store. Police stood still nearby as people drank looted alcohol.* Glass and trash littered the streets, and other small fires were scattered about. One person from a church tried to shout something from a megaphone as two cars burned.

Now, check out how the *Times* characterized the overwhelmingly white mass of Penn State students who tore up State College, Pa., because they were angry about Joe Paterno—a leader who stood by as his assistant coach, Jerry Sandusky, sexually molested boys—getting fired.

The November 11, 2011 article is titled "Penn State Students Clash   5 With Police in Unrest After Announcement" and describes rioters and their actions:

> After top Penn State officials announced that they had fired Joe Paterno on Wednesday night, *thousands of students stormed the downtown area to display their anger and frustration, chanting the former coach's name, tearing down light poles and overturning a television news van parked along College Avenue.*
>
> . . . *The demonstrators* congregated outside Penn State's administration building before stampeding into the tight grid of downtown streets. *They turned their ire on a news van, a symbolic gesture that expressed a view held by many:* that the news media had exaggerated Mr. Paterno's role in the scandal surrounding accusations that a former assistant coach, Jerry Sandusky, sexually assaulted young boys.

So in Baltimore, "rioters" and "youths" are "plung[ing]" the city into chaos," and drinking liquor they looted. In College Park, "thousands of students" are expressing their anger and making "symbolic gestures" like tipping over news vans.

Let's try another one—a March 2015 Cleveland Plain Dealer story about that riot that mostly white Ohio State fans had to celebrate the Buckeyes championship win.

The piece, "Columbus police use of force against Ohio State crowds reveals training, communication problems," describes some *8,000 to 9,000 people* breaking into the Ohio Stadium, throwing bottles at police, lunging at police, trying to lift police cruisers and setting at least 89 fires. About 200 National Guard members were called in:

Columbus police reported giving differing orders *to a crowd of Ohio State fans celebrating January's championship win* before deploying pepper spray and tear gas, according to reports obtained by Northeast Ohio Media Group.

. . . "The one weakness in our plan, *as Generation Xers planning for a Millennials event,* was that we did not account for everyone to meet at a central location," stated Sgt. Smith Weir in his report.

. . . "Monday we were dealing with **drunk, happy college kids** with a handful of agitators just taking advantage of the situation," Weir wrote.

. . . *Some in the crowd claimed they couldn't hear the police's demands to leave,* [Commander Christopher D.] Bowling stated [in his report], so *he suggested that his department purchase better amplification equipment.*

Compare that to this Associated Press story the *Cleveland Plain Dealer* ran on January 12, 2012 called " 'White Only' swimming pool sign violated girl's civil rights, panel says."

. . . *Racial discrimination has particular resonance in Cincinnati, whose population is 45 percent black,* far higher than the rest of Ohio, which is about 12 percent black. Surrounding Hamilton County is 26 percent black.

Cincinnati was the scene of race riots in April 2001 when police and demonstrators clashed in a blighted neighborhood following the shooting of a black suspect by police.

A white Cincinnati landlord posts a sign that says "Public Swimming   10
Pool, White Only" at his complex's pool to bar a black girl from "clouding" the water with her hair products and that's "discrimination." The April 2001 unrest over a police shooting of a black man amounts to "race riots."

The "racial discrimination has particular resonance" among Cincinnati's black population. But the purposeful, proudly racist landlord literally takes things back to Jim Crow segregation, but racial discrimination doesn't resonate with him?

And then, of course, there's the infamous "who's a looter?" captions from Hurricane Katrina coverage.

> So in Baltimore, "rioters" and "youths" are "plung[ing] the city into chaos," and drinking liquor they looted. In College Park, "thousands of students" are expressing their anger and making "symbolic gestures" like tipping over news vans.

Now I admit that this level of examination does leave me vulnerable to becoming that big-word butchering guy from "In Living Color."

But at the same time, as my late, beloved aunt Kinyozi Yvette Smalls used to say about 15 times a day: "Words are powerful."

If they weren't, everybody would be using the same language.   15

THINKING CRITICALLY ABOUT THE READING

1. How does Solomon argue that the media describes riots involving black crowds? What is Solomon's first reaction to such behavior? Why does her reaction shift?

2. How does Solomon argue that the media describes riots involving white crowds? How does it differ from the descriptions of the rioters in Baltimore? Why does Solomon choose the examples she does?

3. For what reasons do you think Solomon compares descriptions of rioting in Baltimore to those at Penn State in particular? Why might she emphasize twice the sexual assaults involved in the Penn State case? Why do you think she emphasizes the "symbolic gesture" ascribed to the Penn State crowd in comparison to those in Baltimore? How does she suggest these responses are incongruous?

4. How does Solomon suggest race determines the language of media coverage? How does this disparity in media coverage reinforce her Aunt Kinyozi's favorite phrase: "Words are powerful" (14)? What power do the words of the press have to shape the population?

5. What Ohio incidents does Solomon compare? Why are these incidents particularly unnerving? How does the use of language like "racial discrimination has particular resonance" contrast with a phrase like "race riots" (9)?

LANGUAGE IN ACTION

Look up one of the articles Solomon mentions, or another article that uses racially coded language to talk about instances of protest or demonstration. Try replacing the biased language in the articles you find, and rewrite them to follow the opposing model. How drastically do you have to rewrite the articles to avoid the kind of language that Solomon points out? How many times do you have to replace the word "riot" with a phrase like "expressed their anger?" Are you able to find language neutral enough to simply report the events without introducing a racially coded interpretation?

WRITING SUGGESTIONS

1. Solomon makes reference to the now infamous "Who's a Looter?" reactions from Hurricane Katrina coverage, in which a black man with groceries is described as having just looted while a white woman carrying groceries is described as having found food. (Searching the phrase "Who's a Looter?" along with "Hurricane Katrina" will link you to this story and its aftermath.) Is your local press guilty of similarly racist coverage? Search the archives of a local or regional newspaper for coverage of a recent criminal incident involving race. How does the newspaper characterize the police? The victim? The incident? The response? Using Solomon's essay as a model, write an essay analyzing your newspaper's coverage of the story and any biases you notice.

2. Solomon follows her Aunt Kinyozi's adage "Words are powerful" with the explanation, "If they weren't, everybody would be using the same language" (18). What does she mean by this? How do we speak differently in the United States, and how do differences in language reinforce the notion that words are powerful? Spend some time thinking about the relationship between words and power, and research a campus controversy. How was the incident discussed on campus (whether through formal channels like the school paper or a press release, or informally through social media)? What language was used to describe the incident? The parties involved? Do identities—racial, gender, class, or ethnic—play any significant role in how the incident is discussed? If so, how? Write a letter to the editor analyzing the coverage of and conversations about the incident you research; draw attention to the language use and phrasing to comment on the fairness, partiality, or bias of the reporting.

What's Really Going on with the Word "Thug"— And Why I'm Not Ready to Let It Go

Maisha Z. Johnson

Maisha Z. Johnson, an American of Trinidadian descent, self-identifies as a queer, black writer and activist living in the San Francisco Bay Area. She is the founder of Inkblot Arts, an online gallery of written work, and her own work addresses the arts, healing, and social change. Johnson earned her B.A. in Creative Writing from San Francisco State University and an M.F.A. in Poetry from Pacific University, and she notes on her personal blog that it was her father's retellings of Trinidadian folk tales, often stories of everyday magic and resilience, that fostered her interest in the power of storytelling. She writes for publications including *Everyday Feminism, Black Girl Dangerous*, and *Pyragraph*. She has also written a writing guide, *Through Your Own Words: 51 Writing Prompts for Healing and Self-Care* (2014); a full-length collection of poetry, *No Parachutes to Carry Me Home* (2015); and three poetry chapbooks, *Uprooted* (2014), *Queer As In* (2014), and *Split Ears* (2013).

Johnson's activism extends beyond her written work. She is also a facilitator with Fired Up!, a group providing legal advocacy, political education, and re-entry support through the California Coalition for Women Prisoners, and a former member of the staff collective at Community United Against Violence (CUAV), which focuses on helping to prevent and respond to violence within and against LGBTQ communities. In the essay included here, Johnson discusses how words operate in a particular context for people of color. She continues to "explore ways that writing and other creative arts can empower . . . people of color" and asks readers to continue to "call out and fight the efforts" to "erase" and "demonize" people of color through language.

WRITING TO DISCOVER: *What role do you think the arts play in cultural healing? In social change? Have you even experienced art (of any kind) as healing?*

In response to the media coverage of the Baltimore uprising, some are asking if "thug" is "the new n-word." I sure hope it's not.

Declaring "thug" the new n-word might just encourage some white people to say it more. I'll cringe when they gleefully sing along to songs with the word in the lyrics. I might get into a debate about it with one of them, as they find about 300 ways to say the word in the process of defending their right to use it before I walk away. I'll see it cited as an example of "censorship against white people" who suddenly want nothing more than to feel "thug" leap from their mouths.

Having two n-words means twice the headaches.

The sentiment behind the conversation about the word "thug," however, is something everybody should pay attention to—especially those of us who are criminalized. Attitudes that villainize people of color, people defying gender norms, and poor people are the same ones that target us for discrimination, violence, and incarceration. And they're the same attitudes that can add racist undertones to the word "thug."

In this moment, the word is being used in the media to discredit the   5
Black Lives Matter movement—a movement in which we are on the front lines, fighting for our lives. Referring to the Baltimore uprising sparked by the death of Freddie Gray, everyone from journalists to the mayor to the President used the word. And a teenager who damaged a police car during the Baltimore protests—whose photograph is displayed to show an example of these so-called "thugs" —is being punished more severely than most police officers who have killed people of color.

This isn't the first time the word has come up following cases of police brutality—victims of police violence have been described as thugs, too.

There's an atrocious message beneath these descriptions, saying that people more likely to fall victim to law enforcement's deadly force are criminals at fault for our own murders. I can understand the urge to eliminate the use of the word if it's perpetuating that message—so will banning it get to the root of the problem?

I have to be honest: part of the reason I don't want "thug" to be considered the new n-word is because I don't want racist people to take away my power to use it, like they have with the n-word. Just like the n-word, "thug" takes on different meanings depending on if it's hurled at us by white people or used by us, about ourselves. When we say "thug" in the tradition of Tupac Shakur's T.H.U.G. L.I.F.E., we're talking about someone who faces impossible obstacles and doesn't take shit from anyone. There's strength in the word. There's pride in surviving in a way the media tells us we should be ashamed of.

> Just like the n-word, "thug" takes on different meanings depending on if it's hurled at us by white people or used by us, about ourselves.

I'm so sensitive about the n-word's connotations with white people that I hardly utter it even when they're not around (look, I can't even write it out now. Are the white folks looking? I'm afraid they might find a reason to quote this aloud if they are).

But censoring myself alone isn't doing anything to address the sys-   10
tematic racism that makes the n-word so vile from white people. Doing nothing more than avoiding the word misses the point, and even worse, it plays into the respectability politics of the ridiculous claim that it's Black people's responsibility to stop saying the n-word to eliminate racism against us.

So instead of falling into the same mistakes with the word "thug," I'd prefer to address why language matters as a vehicle for anti-Black racism.

If I don't, I might make the error of thinking that eliminating the word means eliminating the harm behind it.

Let's face this facet of white supremacy, instead of letting a word distract us from it.

Here's the thing: language helps anti-Black racism become more pervasive, providing coded words in the place of what we'd think of as overtly racist epithets. The word "angry" is simply a description of emotion, but, often, when white people respond to my experiences of racism with "Why are you so angry?" they're doing more than describing an emotion. They're using the stereotype of the angry Black woman to try and silence me. The word's true meaning depends on who's saying it and of whom it's being said.

Language can also support systems of oppression through myths and misconceptions. Lawmakers say that the War on Drugs locks up "criminals" and that stop and frisk practices locate "suspects," but we all know that such laws violently target poor Black and Latino people who, overwhelmingly, aren't perpetrating any crime.

We know exactly what's happening when the language of white   15 supremacy tries to degrade us. If they can't say the n-word, they'll say "thug," and if not that, they'll find something else. The absence of a word doesn't mean racism has gone away.

As we recognize how words hurt us and push back against them, we can't just stop at removing the words from white people's vocabulary. We also have to call out and fight the efforts to erase us and demonize us through language and more. The word is only the beginning—we need to take down the whole racist system it supports.

THINKING CRITICALLY ABOUT THE READING

1. Why does Johnson argue against aligning the word "thug" with the "n-word"? What detrimental effects does that connection have?

2. Who is Johnson's audience here? To whom is she speaking? Who is the "we" she addresses? If you are not a member of her intended audience, what effect does her essay have?

3. How does Johnson talk about the "n-word"? Why does she refrain from using it? Despite her choice to refrain from using the word, how does she refute the "ridiculous claim" that it's "Black people's responsibility to stop saying the n-word to eliminate racism against us" (10)?

4. Why does Johnson argue that "language matters as a vehicle for anti-Black racism" (11)? How does language's power depend both on who is speaking and on a larger social and historical context? For example, why does "anger" have a different meaning for a Black woman, according to Johnson? Are any other groups of speakers "silenced" by the connotation of certain words? If so, who, what words, and why?

5. How can language "support systems of oppression" (14)? What examples of this does Johnson give? Can you think of others?

6. What does Johnson mean by "the language of white supremacy" (15)? How does this language operate? Why won't removing words change the system, according to Johnson? How does she suggest we change the system, and how does her suggestion depend on language?

LANGUAGE IN ACTION

Comedian Louis C.K., known for his bold and honest stand-up work as well as his television show, *Louie*, brings up issues of power and race in this bit from his 2008 special, "Chewed Up":

> I'm a *white man*. You can't even hurt my feelings! What can you really call a white man that really digs deep?
> "Hey, cracker."
> "Uh, ruined my day. Boy shouldn't have called me a cracker. Bringing me back to owning land and people, what a drag."

Consider C.K.'s point. What derogatory language is applied to people of different races? What historical roles or events gave rise to those terms? How does the power of those words—and the actual number of terms—differ among races? Are there any true equivalents to "thug" or the n-word for someone who isn't black? What do you make of C.K.'s joking assertion that "You can't even hurt my feelings"?

WRITING SUGGESTIONS

1. The loosely veiled use of words like "angry" or "criminal" that carries an overtly racial connotation is a form of coded racism that we've come to call "dog-whistle politics." Research "coded racism" and "dog-whistle politics" to gain a sense of how it operates and maintains what Johnson deems a "language of white supremacy." Then use your understanding of encoded racism and apply it to the last election cycle. What types of language do the political candidates use to talk about gun violence, immigration and immigrants, and minimum wage? What other biases come up around gender, class, and sexuality as part of the same coded language? Write an essay about the use of dog-whistle politics in the last election cycle—and the effect it will have or may have had on voters.

2. Throughout her essay, Johnson is clear that "removing words from white people's vocabulary" will not remove racism and suggests instead that adding words—through awareness, through activism—that "call out and fight the efforts to erase us and demonize us" (16) will help put a stop to systemic racism. How does an essay like Johnson's raise awareness and "call out" racism? What other artists or writers of color "call out" racist language? Johnson mentions Tupac Shakur's use of the word "thug," and others might call attention to the lyrics of N.W.A.; others still might look at the work of visual artist Kara Walker or the novels of Toni Morrison. Spend time with a set of lyrics, work of visual art, or written work by a person of color that "calls out" racism. Analyze the work's activism; discuss how the work responds to dominant white culture and allows for the writer's or artist's own self-definition.

11

THE LANGUAGE OF CONFLICT: ARGUMENT, APOLOGY, AND DIGNITY

The American poet Carl Sandburg in his poem "Primer Lessons" cautioned Americans:

> Look out how you use proud words.
> When you let proud words go, it is not easy to call them back.
> They wear long boots, hard boots; they walk off proud; they can't hear you calling—
> Look out how you use proud words.

His words ring as true for us today as they did for his post-World War I audience almost one hundred years ago. Sandburg had witnessed firsthand the power of words to both start conflicts and to enflame them.

Language often plays a powerful role in the conflict's inception and impacts the trajectory of all conflicts. The way people talk about the problematic group or individual—whether using name-calling or stereotypes—exacerbates conflicts of all kinds. Many conflicts can be positively addressed by examining how we articulate the problem and solution. Inevitably, changing the conflict will require changing the language we use to talk about it. For example, Germany is now called an "ally" and "friend," not an "enemy." Words change as conflicts shift or end.

But once started, conflicts seem to have a life of their own, and at the heart of every conflict one can usually find an argument or disagreement or misunderstanding that centers on how the parties are using or interpreting language. Hardly a day goes by that social media and the news networks do not call out some celebrity, politician, diplomat, organization, or country for starting a fight or escalating one with their sloppy or insensitive use of language. Even on a personal level, we can find ourselves enmeshed in arguments because we express ourselves via social media before we think something out and end up using language indiscriminately.

By analyzing conflicts that have happened in the past or ones that are currently unfolding, we can come to better understand how our words affect others and their words us. During the summer of 2015, demonstrations broke out in Ferguson, Missouri, after white police officer Darren Wilson fatally shot Michael Brown, an unarmed black man, after an altercation. Immediately the finger pointing began and the pent-up anger raged. Dr. Martin Luther King Jr. once observed, "Riots are the language of the unheard." The crowds of protesters taunted the Ferguson Police Department with cries of "racists," "murderers," and "pigs," while the supporters of the police and Officer Wilson retaliated by calling the victim Michael Brown a "thug" and the demonstrators "looters," "rioters," and "a plague of black violence." Such language served one purpose—to drive the two sides further apart in spite of attempts at intervention. Simply changing the words may have an impact, but real change requires deeper shifts. Using politically correct terms may simply disguise deeper beliefs. Looking at language in conflict also requires an examination of who gets to speak and who remains excluded from the conversation. Achieving societal transformation rather than simple change requires deep shifts in how we talk about and listen to one another.

Most people will agree that it seems easier to get into a conflict than it is to get out of one, resolve one, or even find some common ground on which to stand. The acts of apology and forgiving and the concept of dignity—and the language we use to convey an apology and a forgiving and to create or nurture dignity—are all important ingredients in any effort to resolve a conflict or achieve a sense of justice restored.

Our purpose in "The Language of Conflict: Argument, Apology, and Dignity" is to help you think critically about and be sensitive to the language used in ongoing conflicts as well as the language being used to seek resolution so that you can function as a responsible citizen. In the opening selection, "Sorry, Regrets, and More," Edwin L. Battistella analyzes a number of interesting historical examples of public "apologies" to show how important people have used the words *sorry* and *regrets* to avoid giving a sincere apology. By showing readers what is really being said, we can all better understand why the underlying conflict is not really resolved.

In her groundbreaking book *Dignity: The Essential Role It Plays in Resolving Conflict*, Donna Hicks presents us with a new understanding of human dignity. She identifies and examines what she believes are the ten essential elements of dignity as well as ten temptations people have to violate dignity. In "Safety," a chapter from her book, she speaks to the importance of both physical and psychological safety in maintaining dignity. When a person or even a country does not feel this safety, they often feel intimidated, shamed, and humiliated—their dignity has been violated. In "The Dork Police: Further Adventures of Flex Cop," Cincinnati police officer Michael Gardner tells how he and his partner developed strategies to use when called to respond to domestic disputes. After a while they volunteered to take all the domestic violence calls so that they could refine their strategies for defusing hostile situations. Gardner and his partner learned how the creative use of language and an ability to be spontaneous and untraditional in critical situations often resulted in magical solutions to dangerous disputes. Sportswriter Rick Reilly lampoons the public apologies of sports and entertainment celebrities in "Regret-lessly Yours: The No-Fault Apology." His spoof "apology" shows how formulaic and insincere many public apologies are and how the apologizer avoids taking responsibility for his or her actions. In "Tarring Opponents as Extremists Really Can Work," Emily Badger enters the political arena and discusses how people and organizations use labels such as "socialist," "right-winger," "racist," "radical," "Christian fundamentalist," "Islamic extremist," and "high-booted feminist" to tarnish or call into question an opponent's positions, especially when American values are at issue. This tactic, she finds, is surprisingly more effective that one might expect. In the final selection "Letting Go," Amy Westervelt uses the example of herself and her friend Leah to explore the nature and value of forgiveness. In the process she discovers that even though we know how good it is for us to both forgive ourselves and to forgive others, forgiveness requires a degree of selflessness as well as practice and hard work. She advises to "feel the feelings you need to feel, express them, then leave them in the past where they can no longer have power over you."

Sorry, Regrets, and More

Edwin Battistella

Edwin A. Battistella is a professor of English and writing at Southern Oregon University in Ashland, Oregon, where he has also served as the dean of the School of Arts and Letters and as the interim provost. Battistella studied linguistics at the City University of New York and received his Ph.D. in 1981. Prior to teaching in Oregon, he held academic positions at the University of Alabama in Birmingham, the Thomas J. Watson Research Center, and Wayne State College. From 1995 to 2001 Battistella served as the book review editor for *Language*, the journal of the Linguistic Society of America, and in 2014 began a term on the society's Executive Committee.

Battistella is the author of five books on varying aspects of linguistics, including two books on linguistic markedness, two on nineteenth- and twentieth-century language attitudes, and a book on public apologies. *Sorry About That: The Language of Public Apology* (2014) examines the public apologies offered by politicians, entertainers, and others, to analyze how certain language is perceived as creating sincere or insincere apologies. The essay here, which focuses on analyzing both the grammar and reception of notorious public apologies, is excerpted from *Sorry About That*.

WRITING TO DISCOVER: *Have you apologized recently? To whom? Why? Spend a few minutes trying to recall your apology. What language did you use? How did you convey your sincerity? Could your language or tone have been misconstrued as insincere? Why or why not?*

"I'M VERY SORRY FOR THAT"

When he became president in 1993, Bill Clinton quickly set up the Task Force on National Health Care Reform. Headed by first lady Hillary Clinton, the task force was intended to make good on Clinton's campaign promise to enact universal health care. The effort failed, as had previous efforts beginning with Theodore Roosevelt, and health-care reform became a major factor in Democratic losses in the 1994 midterm elections. Opponents personalized the failure by portraying the task force as an intrusive bureaucracy being imposed by the first lady. They called it HillaryCare.

After the 1994 midterm losses, Bill Clinton began to adjust his priorities and adapt his approach. Hillary Clinton also began to think about her role, at one point organizing an off-the-record lunch with a group of columnists and journalists that included syndicated columnist Ann Landers,

Cindy Adams and Louis Romano of the *New York Post,* Marian Burros of the *New York Times,* and others. At the lunch, Clinton described how she believed her health-care efforts had been twisted by opponents and how she herself had been portrayed. She told the journalists, "I regret very much that the efforts on health care were badly misunderstood, taken out of context and used politically against the Administration. I take responsibility for that, and I'm very sorry for that." What Clinton was saying was that the fault lay with others who were distorting her efforts on health care and that she should have better understood the political machinations.

Was Clinton apologizing? She regrets three grammatically passive actions—efforts on health care being misunderstood by the public, efforts being taken out of context, and efforts being used by political opponents—and she says she is sorry. However, her sorry refers to the actions of others who misunderstood or misrepresented health-care reform. Sorry indicates regret for a situation, not regret for an offense. Taken alone, her sorry is more like the usage in "I'm sorry that I missed your call" than "I'm sorry that I lost your book."

Clinton confused matters somewhat by also saying "I take responsibility for that." With that phrasing she also asserted responsibility for the public's misunderstandings and her opponents' misrepresentations. She treated what happened as something she might have prevented with different actions—in other words she treated it as a transgression. Her "I'm very sorry for that" was thus ambiguous, carrying both the sense of reporting on a regrettable situation and that of taking the blame for that situation. The conversational logic of her statement was unresolved.

When Clinton's comments came out, she was criticized for apologizing. The *Chicago Sun Times* headline was "Hillary 'Sorry' About Health Care," and the article led with the statement that "over a plate of heart-healthy American cuisine, Hillary Rodham Clinton took full responsibility for the failure of the health-care program she helped design . . . and said she was 'sorry.'" The *Arkansas Democrat-Gazette* wrote "First Lady Says She's Sorry, But Insists She Won't Hide For Next 2 Years" and the *New York Times*—which broke the story—wrote that "Mrs. Clinton put most of the fault on herself."

As the story developed, others commented on the first lady's words and whether or not saying sorry was a stereotypical feature of women's speech. One state legislator said, "When [Clinton] says she is responsible for the failure of health care, that is the woman trying to take all the burdens on herself. She could have been Mother Teresa and that health care bill still would have failed." Linguist Deborah Tannen even discussed the incident and its relationship to gender in a *New York Times Magazine* article, quoting an unnamed political scientist saying, "To apologize for substantive things you've done raises the white flag. There's a school of thought in politics that you never say you're sorry."

Ironically, Clinton had noted, "I can only guess that people are getting perceptions about me from things I am saying or doing in ways that don't correspond with things I am trying to get across." Were her words treated as an apology because she was woman? Let's start by taking a closer look at the grammar of *sorry* and how it differs from *apologize*.

THE GRAMMAR OF *SORRY*

Saying "I'm sorry" is different from saying "I apologize." The former reports on an internal state of the speaker but does not literally perform an apology. Instead, speakers and hearers use the conversational maxims of quality, quantity, relation, and manner to imply or infer an apology. By itself, the minimal report "I'm sorry" (or, the simple "Sorry" used for minor transgressions) doesn't tell us much. Much of the meaning-making comes from the complements that follow *sorry*.

Like *apologize, sorry* can occur with a gerund complement or a conditional (*if*) complement—I can be sorry for speaking out of turn or I can be sorry if I have offended you. Unlike *apologize, sorry* can occur with an infinitive complement. If the following infinitive is *to be, sorry* is understood as an apology ("I'm sorry to be such a bother"), while if the verb is one of perception it is often understood as report of empathy ("I'm sorry to hear about your loss").

Sorry differs from *apologize* in that it frequently occurs with a noun clause. Noun clauses, you'll recall, are tricky because the choice of the subject of the clause can affect the meaning: I can be sorry that I was so inconsiderate or I can be sorry that you were offended. When the subjects of both clauses are the first person *I* (or *we*), the speaker is sorry for something he or she has done. But when the subordinate clause subject does not match the first-person subject of the main clause, then the speaker is sorry for something that happened. So "I'm sorry that it's raining" expresses disappointment but not apology. *Sorry* also differs from *apologize* in not allowing an expressed indirect object. That means that the grammar of *sorry* does not indicate to whom the apology is addressed. An apology using *sorry* must either rely on context (by uttering the expression face to face or in a person-to-person communication like a letter or email) or on making the recipient of the apology clear by mentioning it elsewhere.

Sorry provides somewhat more grammatical flexibility than *apologize* and somewhat more semantic flexibility. When a speaker says "I'm sorry," he or she may be implying an apology or making a report. Thus, when businesswoman Martha Stewart was convicted of several charges related to insider stock trading in March 2004, she said she was sorry. In court she told the judge:

Today is a shameful day. It is shameful for me, for my family, and for my beloved company and all of its employees and partners. What was a small personal matter became over the last two and a half years an almost fatal circus event of unprecedented proportions spreading like oil over a vast landscape, even around the world. I have been choked and almost suffocated to death.

She ended by saying "I'm very sorry it has come to this." Was Stewart apologizing? Perhaps she intended it to be taken that way. But her ambiguous language can also be understood as meaning that she regrets the unfortunate situation she is in. And both the abstractness of the shame ("Today is a shameful day") and the vague passiveness of the language ("a small personal matter . . . has become," "I have been choked . . ." ". . . it has come to this") suggest that she is not performing an apology but merely reporting her feelings.

The distinction between performing an apology by saying "I apologize" and reporting a mental state by saying "I'm sorry" provides insight into another aspect of apologetic discourse—apologies sometimes combine the two expressions. Thus when England's Prince Harry apologized for dressing in a Nazi uniform for a 2005 costume party, he said this: "I am very sorry if I caused any offense or embarrassment to anyone. It was a poor choice of costume and I apologize." The use of "I apologize" extends and supplements the conditional "I am very sorry if" in the first sentence. There is also a bit of a verbal trick in the positioning of the word *apologize*. The prince is apologizing for an abstraction—a poor choice of costume—not for offensive behavior or the values implied in dressing as a Nazi. Putting the apology last allows the speaker to shape the transgression in a more innocuous way. A similar verbal trick arises with the positioning of *sorry* in our next example, from the 2004 presidential election.

RATHER SORRY

Shortly before the 2004 presidential election, CBS broadcast a *Sixty Minutes* segment calling into doubt President George W. Bush's National Guard record. The September 8 report by Dan Rather aired on *Sixty Minutes Wednesday* and showed four documents that appeared to have been written by Bush's commanding officer. The documents created the impression that Bush had disobeyed orders to report for a physical, had been grounded from flying, and had used political influence to receive more positive evaluations than he deserved. The presumed author of the memos, Lieutenant Colonel Jerry Killian, had died in 1984, and the memos were provided to a CBS producer by another retired National Guard lieutenant colonel, Bill Burkett, who claimed to have burned the originals after faxing them to CBS. Prior to airing the segment, CBS producers consulted with several document experts and interpreted the results in the most positive light for the potential news story, but failed to contact a crucial typography expert.

Immediately after the story aired, bloggers and then the print news media began to question the authenticity of the documents. For a time, CBS and Rather defended the segment, but soon they had to disavow it. On the September 20 *CBS Evening News,* Rather explained that in light of additional research on the authenticity and source of the documents:

> I no longer have the confidence in these documents that would allow us to continue vouching for them journalistically. I find we have been misled on the key question of how our source for the documents came into possession of these papers. That, combined with some of the questions that have been raised in public and in the press, leads me to a point where—if I knew then what I know now—I would not have gone ahead with the story as it was aired, and I certainly would not have used the documents in question.
>
> But we did use the documents. We made a mistake in judgment, and for that I am sorry.

Dan Rather first explains the situation and concludes that he would have acted differently if he had more information. At the end, he names the offense—a mistake in judgment—and he explains that he is sorry, inviting viewers to infer an apology. Because an apology was in order, *sorry* was indeed understood as implying an apology instead of simply regrets that something happened. Conversational logic suggests that Rather would not be saying CBS made a mistake and that he was sorry if he did not intend an apology.

I hope you noticed how Rather used the plural *we* in the last two sentences cited above, switching from an earlier *I.* He switches from "I no longer have confidence," "I find we have been misled," and "I would not have gone ahead," to "we did use" and "we made a mistake." He depersonalizes the naming of the offense then switches back to *I* at the end to personalize his regret. Rather uses pronouns to ever so slightly separate himself from the offense.

Following the incident, CBS commissioned an independent review panel whose report led to several executive- and producer-level firings. The panel's report noted that Rather still felt the documents were accurate and that he had merely "delivered the apology" in support of the corporate decision to back off the story. Two months after the panel report was issued, Rather left the CBS anchor position, a year ahead of his planned retirement, and sued the network. In the lawsuit, Rather argued that he was forced to apologize by CBS, that he was not responsible for the errors in the reporting, and that he was being made a scapegoat. The seventy-million-dollar suit was unsuccessful.

Soon after the original story aired, CBS also issued a separate statement saying, "Based on what we now know, CBS News cannot prove that the documents are authentic, which is the only acceptable journalistic standard to justify using them in the report. We should not have used them. That was a mistake, which we deeply regret." Here CBS makes its apology with *regret* rather than *sorry*. But how does *regret* differ from *sorry*?

REGRETS

The sorries expressed by Hillary Clinton and Dan Rather illustrate   20
self-reports of speakers' attitudes about their actions or inactions. Just as common is the verb *regret,* which also reports on a speaker's internal state. The grammar of *regret* largely parallels that of *sorry. Regret* does not allow indirect objects, but it does take direct object nouns and pronouns, conditionals, noun clauses, gerunds, and infinitives as complements. I can regret my actions, regret it if anyone was offended, regret that I behaved so poorly, regret calling him mean, or regret to have to tell you bad news. Again, a gerund can provide an especially strong grammatical foundation for an implied apology: "I regret calling him mean" aligns the subject of the main clause with the understood subject of the gerund. A noun clause can similarly invite interpretation as an apology when the subjects match, as in "I regret that I behaved so poorly." Both gerunds and noun clauses, however, can complement *regret* in ways that merely report on situations without assuming agency for them: "I regret your being inconvenienced" and "We regret that they feel that way." Here, the speaker regrets a situation but does not assume responsibility for it.

Regret also occurs with noun phrases, as we have seen: "I sincerely regret the unfortunate choice of language" (Harry Truman), "I . . . profoundly regret my horrific relapse" (Mel Gibson), and "I deeply regret any offense my remark in the *New York Observer* might have caused anyone" (Joe Biden). And *regret* of course may be a noun, which provides a further option for apologies: "I always put the victim first but here I didn't follow my principle and that is my greatest regret" (said by Scotland Yard assistant commissioner John Yates on his decision not to reopen an investigation into *News International* in 2009) or "I'm very disappointed and want to express my regret to The Open fans" (Tiger Woods commenting on his performance at the 2011 British Open). Having or expressing regrets makes the attitude more abstract—it is more a thing than a mental action—and distances the regretter from the regret.

Like *sorry, regret* is ambiguous. Literally, *regret* refers to one's attitudes toward an event or action. It can be used to indicate an apologetic stance toward one's own actions but can also merely comment on a disagreeable state of affairs. Often the difference is clear. When a Soviet court sentenced captured pilot Francis Gary Powers to a ten-year sentence in 1960, President Dwight Eisenhower's press secretary released a statement that Eisenhower "deplored the Soviet propaganda activity associated with the episode beginning last May and regrets the severity of the sentence." Eisenhower was not apologizing. He was expressing disapproval. When President John F. Kennedy sent troops to oversee the integration of the University of Mississippi, he noted that it was his responsibility to enforce the court decision even though the government had not been a part of the court case. Kennedy said: "I deeply regret the fact that any action by the executive branch was necessary in this case, but all other avenues and alternatives, including persuasion and conciliation, had been tried and exhausted." Kennedy was explaining and regretting that circumstances made federal action necessary. But he was not apologizing.

Like *sorry, regret* is ambiguous.

Sometimes in partisan politics there is public debate about whether an expression of regret implies apology. This was the case when secretary of state William Jennings Bryan presented a treaty to the Senate expressing "sincere regret" to the nation of Colombia. Was this an apology? We will get to this controversy in just a moment. First, one last question.

Does "I regret" mean the same thing as "I'm sorry"? There is overlap of course, but as we have seen, *sorry* reports on internal emotional states and de-emphasizes the calculus of acts and consequences. *Regret,* on the other hand, places more weight on situations and on the analysis of acts and consequences. Thus, *sorry* is typically used for mild transgressions (jostles and spills) and *regret* for more formal, serious, and detached situations. Of course, as speakers of English, we use and understand the nuances intuitively. The overlap and distinction between regretting and being sorry are evident in fixed expressions like "I regret to inform you that we selected another applicant" as opposed to "I'm sorry for your loss." *Sorry* is too personal for some professional and business exchanges, while *regret* is usually too impersonal and detached for condolences.

DID THE WILSON ADMINISTRATION APOLOGIZE TO COLOMBIA?

In the early part of the twentieth century, US relations with Colombia 25 deteriorated because of the Panama Canal conflict. The geographically strategic state of Panama had been a part of Colombia since 1821. Panamanian secession efforts had repeatedly failed, most notably during the Thousand Days War of 1899 to 1902. At the same time, the United States was negotiating with the Colombian government to gain rights to a five-hundred-square-mile area for a canal.

Events turned when the Colombian Senate rejected the Hay-Herrán Treaty, which would have given the United States rights to the canal zone in perpetuity in return for a $10 million initial payment and annual payments of $250,000. Determined to have the canal, the Roosevelt administration threw its support behind the Panamanian independence movement. American ships, ordered to the area by President Roosevelt, blockaded Colombian forces. In November 1903, Panama proclaimed its independence and was immediately recognized by the United States. American troops landed with the stated role of keeping order and protecting American lives and property, but also to interfere with and intimidate Colombian forces. Five days after independence was declared, the treaty the United States had sought was signed, and in 1904, work began on the five-hundred-mile-long canal.

The Colombians, and many Americans as well, insisted that the separation of Panama was an immoral and illegal action instigated by American commercial interests and abetted by Roosevelt. Later in the Roosevelt administration and through the Taft years, efforts were made to repair the rift. Diplomatic contacts continued, and when Woodrow Wilson became president, one of his priorities was to improve relations with the strategic region of Central and Latin America. By 1914, a treaty had been negotiated to ensure full recognition of Panama. The Thomson-Urrutia Treaty proposed to pay Colombia twenty-five million dollars and to grant special canal privileges in return for Colombia's recognition of Panama's independence and sovereignty. The treaty also included this sentence:

> The government of the United States of America, wishing to put at rest all controversies and differences with the Republic of Colombia arising out of which the present situation on the Isthmus of Panama have resulted on its own part and in the name of the people of the United States expresses sincere regret that anything should have occurred to interrupt or to mar the relations of cordial friendship that had so long subsisted between the two nations.

When the treaty was presented in April of 1914, it met with strong opposition from Roosevelt's supporters in the Senate. Roosevelt himself lobbied against it, calling the payment "blackmail." And some senators objected to the words *sincere regret* as an apology to Colombia. California senator George Perkins, for example, said, "I do not believe that the United States Senate will ever ratify this treaty, which implies an apology to Colombia and payment of $25,000,000 in reparations. Colombia should apologize to the United States." The *New York Times* added its opinion that "a formal apology is uncalled for," since the Colombians were trying to prevent construction of the canal.

James Du Bois, the minister to Colombia under William Howard Taft, argued that the treaty was not an apology at all but rather a "simple expression of regret." Du Bois reported telling the Colombian negotiators that the United States "would never apologize for a political act" and noted that neither he nor the Colombian negotiators viewed the statement as an apology. The apology claim was, he said, "only the cry of the Roosevelt people to defeat the treaty." Woodrow Wilson too denied that the treaty had an apology, describing that view as "pure guff." Nebraska senator Gilbert Hitchcock elaborated: "The language of the treaty falls very far short of an apology, and an apology in this case is not called for."

The wording of the treaty supports the view that there was no apol- 30 ogy. Look back at the phrase "expresses sincere regret that anything should have occurred to interrupt or to mar the relations of cordial friendship." The noun clause following *regret* is nonspecific. Expressing regret for "anything that might have occurred" does not name any particular transgression. An apology might be inferred, but the implication is weak given the vagueness in the sentence and in the context. Nevertheless, those who argued against the treaty carried the day through the Wilson administration. The treaty would not have included the word *regret,* they argued, unless apology was implied. By 1915, it was clear that the treaty would not be ratified with the expression of regret included. Wilson was soon occupied by other issues and never returned to the treaty. But in 1921, two years after Theodore Roosevelt had died, the new Harding administration succeeded in passing the treaty, with the expression of regret omitted.

SHORTCUTS

The expressions "I was wrong" and "Forgive me" are also sometimes taken to imply apologies. "I was wrong" concedes error. "Forgive me" asks for reconciliation. To conversationally cooperative listeners, either can imply the full apology process. Recall our earlier modeling of the apology process as made up of a call to apologize, a two-part expressed apology (a naming and a regretting), and a response. When we shortcut a full apology by merely saying "I was wrong," we are relying on the naming of the offense to perform the work of the apology without the sorry-saying. And when we shortcut a full apology with "Forgive me," we are jumping directly to the response step of the process.

Sometimes such shortcuts are sufficient, especially if the person apologizing is sufficiently contrite or if the audience is particularly receptive. Consider this terse public admission by Senator John McCain: "It was the wrong thing to do, and I have no excuse for it." McCain was referring to a joke he had made about Chelsea Clinton's appearance and parentage, which he characterized as a "very unfortunate and insensitive remark." Saying he was wrong suggests regret, and saying he had no excuse condemns the behavior. The statement thus contains two key elements of an apology: regret and condemnation of one's behavior. McCain was not literally apologizing here, but his statement uses conversational logic to invite the inference.

Shortcutting the apology process is understandable. John McCain had apologized privately to the Clinton family, so he perhaps felt no need to apologize expansively in public. But for a serious offense, a shortcut apology often seems like a verbal trick to gain the social benefits of apolo gizing without having to say you are sorry. Thus, McCain seems to be not quite apologizing. And the converse is true as well. Admitting a mistake can be treated as an apology, even when no apology is intended.

For very minor offenses, of course, a shortcut is often exactly what is called for. For the stepped-on foot or jostled elbow, a linguistically elaborate process is overkill. For small social offenses, we may skip the call to apologize and the naming of the offense, Both are apparent from the immediate situation, so we move right to a quickly spoken "Sorry," "'Scuse me," "Pardon," or "My fault" which may or may not be followed by a response from the person harmed. The French-derived counterparts of "Forgive me," "Excuse me," and "Pardon me" are especially common for very minor transgressions. And they are conventionally used to pre-apologize for an imposition. We say "Pardon me, do you have the time?," or "Excuse me, can I ask you a question?"

Just as we take a shortcut by saying "I was wrong," we can also imply an apology with the simple possessive phrase *my fault*. Even shorter is the phrase *my bad*, used as a tic of adolescent speech in the 1995 movie *Clueless*. Lexicographers have traced the origin of the phrase to basketball. Ben Zimmer, who for a time wrote the On Language column at the *New York Times*, favors the view that *my bad* originated on playgrounds in the 1970s and 1980s. He cites *Oxford English Dictionary* examples from the 1980s as proof, including a 1986 guide which gives this definition: "My bad, an expression of contrition uttered after making a bad pass or missing an opponent." Today, *my bad* lends itself to any quick expressions of apology where the call to apologize is apparent and no response is expected.

35

THINKING CRITICALLY ABOUT THE READING

1. How does Battistella analyze Hillary Clinton's 1994 apology? What grammatical voice does she use? How is the text of the apology different than the way it is received?

2. What role may Clinton's gender have played in how her words were received? Why? Why might women, stereotypically, apologize more in our society?

3. How does "I'm sorry" differ from "I apologize," according to Battistella? Which focuses on one's own feelings or "mental state"? Which focuses on the feelings of the other and performs an act showing regret? Why and how do these words work? Why is their difference important?

4. In what ways can "I'm sorry" be manipulated or changed in meaning? Can the phrase actually convey the opposite of its proposed meaning? If so, how?

5. How does regret differ from "I'm sorry" and "I apologize" in public apologies? What are the limitations of "regret"?

LANGUAGE IN ACTION

Though the percentage varies depending on circumstance, some social scientists estimate that nonverbal communication makes up as much as 93 percent of our communication. This means that our body language—the way we carry ourselves, our facial expressions, our gestures, etc.—constitutes the vast majority of what we actually say. With that in mind, why does Battistella say so very little about body language in the context of public apologies?

To decide whether you think body language should have bearing on how apologies are perceived, search for video of famous public apologies. Compare what you notice about body language to Battistella's written analysis. Does what you see affect how you interpret the words said, and should Battistella have accounted for visual cues? Based on what you see versus what you read, what percentage of communication is nonverbal? Does 93 percent seem like an accurate number?

WRITING SUGGESTIONS

1. Battistella usefully diagrams the difference between "I'm sorry," "I apologize," and "I regret" in speeches perceived as public apologies, and he models a pattern for analyzing these words and their effect in the public forum. Choose a public figure's recent "apology" to closely analyze as Battistella does. Although you do not need to focus, as the linguist does, on parsing and identifying the parts of speech in operation, his approach should help you identify the "quirks" within the apology you choose to analyze. What words of apology does the speech use? Does the apology focus on an action or on the speaker's feelings? What words seem to limit the apology? Does the speaker deflect blame in any way? Write an essay analyzing how these aspects of the apology affect denotative meaning (the meaning of the words as used in the sentence) and connotative meaning (the meaning implied by the context of the speech and what readers infer about it). Be sure to weigh in on whether or not the speaker has actually apologized.

2. Choose a public "apology" that appears insincere or evasive, and rewrite it to convey an actual apology. Read and compare the original version with your own and write a reflective essay. What are the differences between the actual apology and your version? Why do those differences matter? What do you think the consequences would have been if your version had been the one used publicly—both for the perpetrator and the victims of the offense?

Dignity

DONNA HICKS

Donna Hicks is an associate at the Weatherhead Center for International Affairs at Harvard University and has taught courses at Harvard, Clark, and Columbia universities. Hicks earned her B.A. in educational psychology (1983) and her M.S. (1987), M.S.W. (1988), and Ph.D. (1991) from the University of Wisconsin before completing a post-doctoral fellowship at Harvard University with Herbert Kelman, director of the Program on International Conflict Analysis, which largely shaped her career in international conflict resolution. Hicks has more than twenty years of experience as a facilitator during international conflicts in the Middle East, Sri Lanka, Colombia, Cuba, Northern Ireland, and the United States. As her personal Web site explains, "her unique focus on dignity, and the essential role it plays in resolving conflict, has transformed work environments for the world's most prominent companies, non-profits, and governmental agencies," and past clients have included the World Bank, United Nations, and the U.S. Navy.

She is the author of *Dignity: The Essential Role It Plays in Resolving Conflict* (2011), a best-selling book that was also the New England Book Festival's 2011 runner-up for best nonfiction title. Hicks and the subjects she discusses in *Dignity* have been featured on the BBC, *Fox News*, NPR, and radio stations across the country, as well as in *Psychology Today* and *Newsday*. The essay here, which focuses on the relationship between dignity and psychological safety, is excerpted from her book.

WRITING TO DISCOVER: *How would you define dignity? Have you ever thought of it as playing a role in how you resolve conflicts with others? Consider a recent upheaval in your own life. Did dignity, as you've defined it here, play any role in how the conflict was resolved?*

Put people at ease at two levels: physically, so they feel safe from bodily harm, and psychologically, so they feel safe from being humiliated. Help them to feel free to speak without fear of retribution.

My husband, Rick, and I were invited to the home of new friends for dinner to celebrate the seventh birthday of their youngest child, Seth (not his real name). When we pulled into the driveway, we saw about a dozen children playing soccer in their big backyard. The house and gardens were beautiful—our friends had spent time and effort on landscaping—and because it was such a warm night, they had decided to have the party outside. The dinner table was set underneath a huge maple tree strung with little white lights.

417

Before we got out of our car, we sat for a while watching the children play. Not able to have children ourselves, we both get a little wistful at times like these. After a minute, still staring at the children, my husband said, "They have it all, don't they?"

We joined the other adults on the patio. Our hosts, Margot and Tom (not their real names), gave us a warm welcome, then introduced us to the other guests, most of whom were the parents of Seth's friends.

When Margot announced that dinner was nearly ready, Rick and I volunteered to help bring the food outside. Seth came running into the kitchen, out of breath, unsuccessfully trying to hold back tears. Tom looked at him and said. "What's the matter? Why are you crying? You look like a baby."

Seth burst into tears and ran into his mother's arms. He told her that   5
one of his friends had yelled at him in front of everybody because he had messed up a goal.

Tom said to Margot, "Don't baby him."

"What are you talking about? He's hurting."

Tom walked up to her and said, his face only inches from hers, "You have made him into a sissy. So what if his feelings are hurt? He needs to toughen up. He can't come running to you every time something goes wrong."

With her hands on her hips and her chest heaving, she said to Tom, "I'll tell you what's wrong; you're what's wrong. Don't you dare talk to me like that." Margot stormed out of the room.

Tom turned to Seth and said, "Get back out there with the other kids   10
and stop being a mama's boy."

Seth left the room with his chin on his chest and with arm across his face, wiping away tears. Tom said to us with a nervous laugh, "A little shaming always works." He picked up a tray of food and headed for the patio.

Rick turned to me and said, "Never trust appearances."

This story shows what a violation of dignity's essential element of safety looks like. Specifically, Seth's psychological safety was at stake. Seth experienced a double hit. He was publicly humiliated when one of his friends yelled at him, in front of everybody, for not making a goal—which he must have felt bad about already. Having attention drawn to his mistake made flubbing the goal even worse, to the point where he bolted. Flight is a typical reaction to being humiliated, as we have seen. Seth fled into the house for consolation. But he did not get the nurturing and acknowledgment he needed. Instead, he was hit again. His father called him a sissy, and he did it in front of others. Humiliating someone in front of other people can be devastating.

When we are psychologically injured, the area of our brain that is activated is the same area that is activated when we experience a physical injury, as research by Naomi Eisenberger and Matthew Lieberman has shown. We wouldn't think twice about rushing our child to an emergency room if he broke his arm or leg; the pain and suffering of a physical injury is acknowledged immediately. When his spirit is broken by shame or humiliation, when damage is done to his sense of worth, there was, in Seth's case, nowhere to go to take care of the wound. Running to his mother was his best option. But being told, as Seth was, to "be tough" and "stop being a mama's boy," makes it a fairly sure bet that the internal injury will grow and fester, contaminating his sense of worth. We humans need acknowledgment for what we have suffered, and when we don't get it, the temptation to think we deserved our misfortune comes naturally. Safety and vulnerability share a complex connection.

Listening to parents yell at each other also undermines a child's sense   15
of security, and it models undignified behavior. Sad to say, both parents felt justified in saying hurtful things to one another. Each felt the other was wrong. Our need to be right is a powerful motivation for inflicting psychological harm on another—for violating another's dignity. Righteous indignation is used to justify bad behavior all too frequently.

I once heard William Sloane Coffin, pastor of the Riverside Church in New York, being interviewed on the radio. He said that self-righteousness was a scourge because it didn't leave room for self-criticism. In the heat of the moment, neither Tom nor Margot stopped to reflect on their own behavior. They were both overtaken by their fight instincts. Their Me's were in combat. Their reactions were so strong that the presence of other adults, who were not close friends, did not deter them.

Tom and Margot are not bad people. They have good intentions; they both want the best for their youngest child. But like so many of us, they are not aware of their blind spots—in this case, their instinctive violations of each other's dignity and the dignity of their child, especially under stressful circumstances.

What would it have looked like if Tom and Margot had handled their son's emergency with dignity? Margot was on the right track—she acknowledged how hurtful it was for Seth to be shamed in front of his friends. After the acknowledgment, she could have reminded him that he was a wonderful boy and that he shouldn't take his friend's outburst to mean that he himself had something wrong with him. His friend was upset because his team hadn't won the game, that's all. And Seth had missed a goal, which anyone could have done.

After she was sure that she had successfully helped Seth reinterpret the event, Margot could have encouraged him to go back out and play. She could have also encouraged him to go to his friend and say that he was sorry he had missed the goal—he had wanted to win the game, too.

Most people, young or old, respond positively to a comment like that.   20
It is a way to acknowledge the experience of the other, even the one who inflicted the wound. It is a way to say that the victim, too, has a perspective on the situation, one that he is capable of seeing now that he is no longer

hurting. A gesture of acknowledgment doesn't let the perpetrator off the hook, but it gives the victim a chance to regain his own wounded dignity and open up his perspective to include the experience of the other.

It would not be surprising to discover that Tom suffered crippling shame as a child. His father probably shamed him and told him to toughen up, too. This is how ignorance and the pain it causes get passed down like a dominant gene. Old childhood injuries create blind spots for us unless we get the help we need to recover from them.

Tom's blind spot was not being aware of how intolerable shaming can be to a child. He had dissociated pain from shame long ago to survive. A little education about how not to violate the dignity of children could have helped Tom, not only with his parenting but also with his self-knowledge. He could have understood the effects that extreme shame had on him when he was growing up. These early imprints of indignity—the memories of being painfully shamed early in childhood—continue to affect us and our dealings with others throughout our lives. Unless we become aware of them, heal from them, and make a conscious decision not to let them determine our actions, we continue to hurt others, jeopardizing their and our own dignity and threatening all our relationships.

The early imprints of dignity and indignity have a profound effect on our developing understanding of our value and worth.

The early imprints of dignity and indignity have a profound effect on our developing understanding of our value and worth. During childhood, when we are vulnerable and dependent on others for our sense of well-being, we need our caretakers' ongoing love and attention to set the stage for the development of our fledgling dignity. If we experience the opposite—abuse and neglect in its myriad forms—we start our lives doubting our worth. Instead of developing a sense that we are good, valuable, loveable, and worthy, our inner world becomes dominated by a sense of inadequacy, badness, and fears of being defective. This primitive and childlike way of making meaning about ourselves becomes embedded and lasts into adulthood. Unless we do the work necessary to replace the childlike understanding of what happened to us early in our lives with an adult perspective on it, we can remain haunted by self-doubt and continue to feel uncertain of our worth.

The way we treat our children matters. Their brains are vulnerable to abuse and neglect because they are in a constant state of development. Bruce Perry, a specialist in child trauma who trained both as a psychiatrist and as a neuroscientist, has documented his findings of the effects of childhood trauma on brain development and the quality of life of abused and neglected children. He was one of the first researchers to debunk the myth that children are naturally resilient and bounce back no matter what they suffer. When undergoing treatment, traumatized children often used to be medicated for depression or anxiety disorders, but what they had gone through was neglected. Perry has spent his career developing innovative treatment protocols informed by his knowledge of neuroscience and the effects trauma has on normal brain development. Admittedly, a majority of the children he has cared for suffered severe abuse and neglect—some were raped or witnessed the murder of a parent—but he tells us that from their experiences we can learn an enormous amount about the psychological needs of children in general.

Although most of us have not suffered such severe psychological   25
trauma, most of us did experience wounds to our dignity during the psychologically formative years of our childhood. Because of pervasive ignorance about the fragility of humans' emotional worlds, few of us have developed an awareness of the lasting effects of the psychological harm done to us or of the psychological harm that we have done, especially to our own children, who need our care and loving attention.

Children's awareness of their worth begins with the way they are treated early on by their caretakers. If their dignity is violated more than it is honored, they will live in a constant state of doubt about their worth.

Let me be clear. When we are ignorant of the effects that our behavior has on others, and if our culture perpetuates and enables that ignorance, we will unknowingly do harm to one another. Even if we know that we are doing harm, in the absence of explicit societal norms to correct our behavior, we may continue to do harm. Because of this complex interaction of ignorance, denial, and societal taboos against discussing emotional trauma, it is no wonder that we have all experienced some kind of violation in our early lives. And it is no wonder that the caretakers who are responsible for violations of children's dignity are either unaware of the violations or are ignorant of how to nurture it.

What is important here is to know the dignity violations we experienced. To know them is to name them, to give them legitimacy and validation. And knowing them is the first step toward healing. The problem, as Jennifer Freyd points out, is our strong loyalty to our caretakers, especially if they are parents, which makes it difficult to view them as anything but good. Breaking through this loyalty is crucial if we want to get to do the healing necessary for us to recognize and accept the harm that was done to us and that distorts our understanding of our inherent worth.

The purpose of examining our early experiences is not to place blame or to make our caretakers feel bad. The purpose is to uncover the truth about what happened to us or, more the point, to uncover the untruth about our unworthiness.

Having an awareness of our early imprints of indignity enables us to   30
identify vulnerabilities in our adult relationships. The early wounds set the stage for our relationships later in life. If we think of relationships as a source of pain (violations of our dignity) rather than a source of safety and comfort, we will have a hard time with intimacy. We become preoccupied

with protecting ourselves from others (the default reaction) rather than connecting with them.

The purpose of identifying our early experiences with indignities is to show us where we may have problems in our relationships later on and, in particular, where we may run the risk of unknowingly violating the dignity of others. Our early violations often create blind spots that enable us to unconsciously justify hurting others.

Add to these default reactions the experiences we have all had growing up in a time when most socializing agents (parents, teachers, religious leaders) are blind to the negative impact they have on children, and it is no wonder that our relationships are a mess. No matter what culture we were raised in, the awareness and practice of what is acceptable treatment of one human being by another is at a fairly primitive level. The combination of our evolutionary (genetic) predispositions and the negative and traumatic experiences that we have all endured leaves us with much to learn about healthy and dignified relationships.

As important as it is to know about childhood violations of our dignity, it is just as important to identify the ways in which our dignity was honored and nurtured throughout our childhood. I have found that people are more aware of the ways their dignity has been violated than the ways it has been recognized, honored, and nurtured. Painful, demeaning treatment apparently makes a more lasting imprint than being treated well does. If we start out feeling unworthy and never have an opportunity to challenge that childlike way of making meaning about who we are and the truth of our worthiness, we can unconsciously carry around that distorted belief throughout our lives. Early emotional wounds to our dignity have tremendous power to keep us locked into a perpetual state of self-doubt, even when there is evidence to the contrary.

I heard recently about a man who was awarded a prestigious employee-recognition award for his contributions to his company; by all accounts, the award was a clear affirmation of his dignity. Yet when asked how he felt about receiving the award, he said that he still felt like a number, that he wasn't really seen or recognized for who he was. Without an internalized belief in his own worthiness, unless his wounds from the early imprints to his dignity were cleansed and healed, he would not be able to appreciate any validation of his worth from the outside, no matter how much recognition he was accorded. The uncared-for and untreated wounds to his dignity demand acknowledgment and attention. Recognizing the need for professional help — from a therapist or counselor of some sort — is the first step on the road to recovery.

After dignity wounds and their effects are tended to, it seems to help to develop an awareness of the forgotten ways our dignity was honored during childhood. Perhaps a special aunt or uncle, teacher, or next-door neighbor, or, for that matter, a much-loved childhood pet, provided validation and recognition. My experience has shown that once people have

35

taken care of the internal wounds, they can even recall times that the perpetrators of violations treated them well. Those experiences were obscured by the overwhelmingly negative emotions that violations to our dignity create.

The negative power of unhealed wounds to out dignity can keep us in a frozen state of self-doubt, preventing us from accessing the positive power that is at our disposal once we see and accept our value and worth. We must tend to our dignity wounds if we want to grow and develop, if we want to abandon a self-protective stance in order to move forward and be open to creating relationships in which we feel safe.

THINKING CRITICALLY ABOUT THE READING

1. How does Hicks explain the relationship between dignity and safety? Why might she want to link dignity to a basic human need in this way?

2. Why do you think Hicks spends time creating an idyllic image of the party? How does the scene of relative comfort, happiness, and devotion abruptly shift? How is Seth first humiliated? How does Seth's father violate Seth's dignity? What is the difference between humiliation and a violation of dignity?

3. What role does Hicks suggest that narration—or storytelling—could play in helping us to "reinterpret" events (19) and process our feelings? How might Seth have benefited from such reinterpretation and reassurance of his safety?

4. How does Hicks reinforce the notion that physical pain and psychological pain are related? How does she also dispel the myth that kids are resilient? Why might she focus on childhood?

5. What effect does Hicks suggest our lack of adult understanding of the wounds we suffered as children can have on our treatment of others? On our own feelings of worth and validation? How have you seen this play out elsewhere?

6. Hicks makes important connections between how the indignity one has suffered affects both one's feelings of unworthiness and the indignities one goes on to perpetrate. What might she imply about our culture? Why might it be important to tie cultural action to individual actions in this way?

LANGUAGE IN ACTION

Pope Francis, in a 2015 General Audience address on the role of fathers, shared the following anecdote:

> Once I heard a father at a meeting on marriage say: "Sometimes I have to strike the children lightly . . . but never in the face so as not to humiliate them." How beautiful! He has a sense of dignity. He must punish, but he does it in a just way, and moves on.

This statement caused a media frenzy, with news outlets across the globe reporting that Pope Francis condoned spanking, or worse, child abuse. *Did* he condone child abuse? Do you think it's possible to physically punish a child while preserving his or her dignity? How might Hicks respond to this idea? What alternatives might she suggest?

WRITING SUGGESTIONS

1. Hicks argues that unexamined individual indignities create a culture of individuals who "become preoccupied with protecting ourselves from others . . . rather than connecting with them" (28). And she argues that this culture "enable[s] us to unconsciously justify hurting others" (29) and perpetuates the cycle of indignity on a personal and societal level. How might we use this theory to explain injustice or inequalities? Could it help to explain bigotry or discrimination? Are we as a culture in need of therapy? Spend some time thinking about the degree to which Hicks's assessment of individuals might be applicable to the social problems we face as a nation. Could we, for example, reframe personal and cultural narratives for those who show bigoted or discriminatory behavior? Write an exploratory essay considering one way to apply Hicks's assessment on a cultural level.

2. For many readers, Hicks's work offers a new way of thinking about the word "dignity." She considers what enables and disables dignity, what dignity means to our sense of self, and how a lack of dignity compels us to compensate. Do you think there are other words that we need to reconsider in terms of their effect on our self-worth? For example, Hicks suggests at least two other words that are misinterpreted or misapplied: "resilience" (mistaken notion that children don't register harm long-term) and "vulnerability" (mistaken as showing weakness). Can you think of others? Choose a quality that seems to be misunderstood or unfairly saddled with a negative association in our culture. Try to consider the effects of this misinterpretation on both individual experience and cultural understanding. Write a definitional essay that seeks to redefine the term in a more complete way. As Hicks does, offer real life examples as evidence.

The Dork Police: Further Adventures of Flex Cop

MICHAEL GARDNER

Michael Gardner is a twenty-eight-year veteran sergeant of the Cincinnati Police Department, where he served as the department's legal liaison, expert witness for use of force issues, and academy instructor. He and his wife, Debbie, met at the police academy in 1973, where they were both students, but it was an incident the following year that would alter their careers. In 1974, Debbie, despite all her physical and martial arts training, was assaulted with a gun. It was this "dramatic failure," as the couple calls it on their Web site, that led them to rethink their traditional police training and refocus on "visual and verbal persuasion." This tactic, which they felt was most crucial to their survival as officers, was also the most under-emphasized in the police academy, which focused on physical preparedness and weaponry. The assault compelled Debbie to found the Survive Institute in 1981 and Mike to continue working on the police force to conduct real-life research into innovative visual and verbal tactics that focused on self-control and de-escalation. His tactics worked. As Gardner explains in the essay included here, "during my 30 year police career, I never fired my gun." In fact, he reports that he only had to use mace—once.

In 1990 Gardner's approach was formally recognized when he was named Officer of the Year by the Cincinnati Police Department. His ideas about crisis control were not only deployed in Cincinnati's police academy but have been featured in newspapers all over the United States. After serving as the commander of the police academy and retiring from the Warren County Sheriff's Office, he and Debbie co-authored *Raising Kids That Can Protect Themselves* (2004). Gardner continues to work with the Survive Institute and serve as a professional consultant for a number of law enforcement agencies.

WRITING TO DISCOVER: *Have you ever been so profoundly persuaded by language that you changed your belief or position? If so, why and how did this language affect you? What made it extraordinarily convincing? Do you think it would have been equally effective if you had been in mental or emotional distress?*

Everyone in the field knows that the most dangerous part of police work is handling domestic disputes. Roughly one third of the police officer assaults and killings in this country occur during domestic disputes. A cop may go in to arrest the attacker and suddenly the spouse turns on him with the frying pan when she sees he's making an arrest. There's no telling who may be a problem, and people are much more likely to fight to defend their homes against intruders.

A lot of the calls we got on night shift were domestic violence runs. Cops hate making domestic runs because they're so dangerous, but for research purposes my partner and I asked other cops, "Do you mind if we start taking over your domestic runs so we can experiment with defusing hostile situations?" Of course we got no objections.

Traditionally, police officers are limited to only four choices for controlling situations—visual and verbal persuasion, chemical irritant, impact weapon, and deadly force. In training, most emphasis was on weaponry defense, without nearly enough on visual and verbal defense. My partner and I saw the need to stretch our flexibility to hundreds of choices in this uncharted territory.

The traditional approach in police work for a domestic run was to show up at an apartment and bang on the door using a raid-type knock with the police night stick, BAM BAM BAM BAM! I even hate it when the UPS or mail carrier bangs on my door to give me something I *want*, so I tried to imagine how someone already in emotional distress would be angered even more with a raid-type bang on their door. To be less intrusive and confrontational we started showing up and doing the "shave and haircut" knock, a very light "Rap ta-ta tap tap, tap tap." Even if the people inside didn't catch on to the jingle, it was a less invasive knock, and its association with a harmless advertisement was more to relax *us* than the people inside. It kept us at a condition orange—alert, but not the red of alarmed. We would even joke sometimes going into an apartment, "Hey let's be condition purple." What we were really saying was, "Hey let's not get red, because if we go in there red, we're going to have a fight."

The usual question police were trained to ask when entering a home   5
was, "What's the problem here?" Well, if you enter after a loud raid-type knock and ask them, "What's the problem here?" They'll give you a problem, usually several. They may tell you their problems from twenty years ago.

Instead we'd ask something like, "What have you decided to do between the time you called us and the time we got here?" That put them in solution mode. Other times we'd ask people to step out into the hallway so they wouldn't feel the need to defend their turf. We also purposely wore our hats when we approached, so when we did enter their house or apartment we could take them off as a sign of respect.

My partner and I became known to our fellow officers as the Dork Police, because no one knew what crazy thing we were going to do next. They were equally amazed at our success in non-violent control of tense situations. We experimented daily with ways of startling subjects into confusion in order to interrupt their dangerous mental patterns and provide a space for something more positive.

For example, we would sometimes approach potentially dangerous domestic disputes with our jackets purposely buttoned improperly, or with our caps pulled down so our ears stuck out. Other times we'd say "no" while nodding our heads up and down. Unless the combatants were too intoxicated or high to observe this odd behavior, they stopped, at least temporarily. They couldn't help responding to what they saw. Then it was hard for them to pick up their fight where they had left off.

> **All we were trying to do was get them to refocus out of their anger and onto something else.**

Sometimes we'd walk into a shouting match between a couple, and we'd just run over and switch the channel on the TV set. If one of them said, "Hey, what the hell are you doing?" We'd say cheerfully, "Hey, you're not going to listen to us anyway, so we're going to watch some TV."

All we were trying to do was get them to refocus out of their anger and onto something else. We would do anything to create a change. Once that was accomplished, we'd offer suggestions for where couples could go for longer-term help.

Using humor was particularly useful when performing routine, uncomfortable tasks like patting down or frisking a suspect. While maintaining physical control, we would like to say, "You don't have any hand grenades, swords, or bazookas hidden on you, do you?" Subjects generally laughed it off. Now and then, one would disclose that he had a knife or razor.

When couples were screaming at each other we'd start sniffing and shouting out. "Oh, do you smell gas? Where's your stove? There must be a burner on!" While the fight was temporarily stopped, my partner and I would go to the kitchen and pretend to check the stove for gas leaks. After a few minutes of sniffing the stove and kitchen area, we would advise the people that everything was OK, then ask "What else can we help you with?" The response was amazing. Often they said, "Nothing, officer . . . " If the argument did begin again, all my partner and I had to do was to sniff with a concerned look on our faces. With this pattern interruption, the subjects' personal fighting became secondary to the threat of a gas explosion in their home. They may even start getting an unconscious connection of, *Every time I start getting nasty there's danger, maybe I should try something else.*

Other times, we would enter a residence and be greeted by someone standing in a fighting position and shouting, "You two think you can take me? Come on!" We would mirror his stance, but hold our palms up instead of making fists, saying, "No way. We heard how tough you are. We can't beat you, we'd have to call ten more guys in here." If that statement had any effect, we would follow up with, "Why don't we talk first, then you can kick our butts." On several occasions the potentially violent subject changed his mind. And if he didn't respond to our initial

10

statement, that signaled us to try something else. Initially it was hard for us to give this kind of "pull" statement when a violent subject "pushed" us verbally. We instinctively wanted to "push" back with an "attack" statement. Yet the patience of our "pull" statement always minimized the force of our arrest.

One time we had a husband and wife close to killing each other. They were shouting countless obscenities at each other, and their hand gestures were disjointed and out of sync with the tone and tempo of their verbal language. I remembered the metaphor of an orchestra conductor—when people talk in rhythm with their gestures it tends to be good venting; letting their anger come out verbally rather than physically. But when their gestures are short, choppy, stab-like motions, disconnected from their language, it is likely that they're about to explode physically. This couple was actually making verbal threats like, "I'm going to kill you, you son of a bitch!" "You're dead, mother-fucker!"

In a flash I said, "In all my years of police work, I've never seen some- 15
body able to express their anger like you can! I appreciate that, because sometimes things really piss me off and I wish I could express my anger like you are!" I was empathizing with them to bring their attention to me and to the importance of what they were feeling, and away from a fight.

Another time we came into an argument with the woman yelling and screaming at her husband. I said to her, "I bet you don't talk to the mailman this way, do you?"

"What? Of course not!"

"And I bet you don't talk to your car mechanic that way, do you?"

"No, of course not!"

"Well the reason you talk to your husband like that is obviously 20
because you care a whole lot more about what he says than what the mailman or the mechanic says."

"Yeah, well I guess so."

My questions first took her attention away from her emotions and what she was mad about. Then I offered her a new meaning for her outburst—it was because she *cared* about her husband. After about 15-20 minutes of me telling them how frustrated I was at not being able to express my feelings the way they could, they started counseling me. Soon it was apparent by the way they were sitting next to each other and looking at each other that they were eager to be left alone. I think we reframed their anger toward each other to such an extent that they wanted us gone so they could make up!

Once we came into a heated dispute and I said to the man, "Hey, you don't work for the city, do you?"

"NO!"

"That car out there with the lights on, that's not your car, is it?"   25

"NO!"

"You don't want us here, do you?"

"NO!"

"You'll be happy when we leave here, won't you?"

"Fuck yeah!"

This way I matched him and let him express himself. He was in the mood to disagree, so I started with questions all of which let him say "No." Then I shifted to a "Yes" question, leading him to a more positive place and getting his explicit agreement that when we left he'd be happy. It might sound like a small thing, but it made a huge difference. Now we were on the same page and he was more relaxed—no longer disagreeing with everything we said.

We'd also do a thing I called "word salad." I never did it in a disrespectful way, but when people get violent they're behaving worse than childish. Sometimes I'd say, "What you're saying here sounds like a phonological ambiguity to me, so rather than jeopardize any other litigation circumstances why don't you just take a walk and let things cool off?"

They got so confused by the first part of my sentence, they would jump on the first thing that made sense, usually responding. "I'll just take a walk and cool off a bit."

I'd say, "Great, I appreciate that."

Often we would use many of these different tactics one after the other, until we found what worked. By systematically attempting to stop violence by using our appearance or words, we put ourselves in a position where we would be much more justified—both emotionally and legally—if we ended up having to resort to a higher degree of force. Yet in all these experiments on permanent night shift, and during my thirty-year police career, I never fired my gun. I had to use mace on a person only once, simply because the man was so intoxicated I couldn't communicate with him. We had tried many things, but he just wasn't there because of the alcohol. He had a little paring knife that he wouldn't drop. Technically I could have shot him, but I had been relaxed and aware enough to keep a table between us, so I was able to subdue him with the mace. As amazing as these techniques were for defusing violence in the moment, our biggest success was that we stopped getting return calls from the places we visited. Before we started using these techniques, it was common to get calls from the same location two or three times a night. Sometimes my partner and I would spend 15 or 30 minutes out on a call, and we'd get in trouble from our supervisor because he wanted us in and out. If they didn't straighten up right away he wanted us to simply arrest them. But we knew we could save time in the long run by coming to a peaceful resolution.

Probably our most interesting encounter came in June of 1984. My partner and I were patrolling our beat on a Saturday afternoon, when the dispatcher's voice crackled over our radio:

"Car 405, Car 405, respond to 755 East McMillan Street, reference a man with a gun. The only description we have is he's male, black, and his last name is Large. He threatened to kill a person and stated he would kill the police. Car 405."

We replied, "Car 405, OK."

Our sergeant came on the air with, "Car 422, advise Car 405 to wait for my arrival before they approach the address. I'll respond with a taser gun."

Unfortunately for us, my partner and I happened to be on the one-way McMillan Street heading for that very address when the dispatch came out. Other police units were coming over the air advising that they would also respond. Since we were so close already, we parked near the location and advised our dispatcher that we were on the scene. Needless to say, our adrenaline was pumping. We often got calls where the details sounded frightening, but this one was different. We were afraid. As we approached an alley between two buildings, we observed a man in an army coat arguing with a woman. Without thinking, I blurted out, "Anyone here order a *large* pizza?"

The male subject turned and looked at me with a puzzled expression. Even my partner was looking at me funny. I could see the man's hands were empty. He said, "My name is Large..."

With that we knew who he was. We quickly handcuffed him and put him in the back seat of our car. Fortunately, he did not have a gun — something we did not know until after we had him under control. It turned out that he was a walk-away mental patient from the Veteran's Hospital Psychiatric Unit. He had been walking around threatening to kill people, hoping to force the police to kill him. Who knows what might have happened if Mr. Large hadn't been caught off guard. I sincerely believe that on this particular day the flexibility that I'd learned saved the life of a mentally disturbed veteran — and perhaps my life as well.

My partner, himself a Vietnam veteran, was able to chat with Mr. Large on the way to the Veteran's Hospital. Upon our arrival, the hospital staff was shocked that we didn't have to struggle with Mr. Large. I can't thank the people enough who taught me how to use these skills. Even though we may have been justified legally with some tactical force, we could never have lived with ourselves if we had hurt Mr. Large.

Unfortunately, it's very difficult to measure what *doesn't* happen, but I can say confidently that I was involved in hundreds of peaceful resolutions that would have ended up in arrests or fights had we used traditional police procedure. Ever since my eyes were opened to what is possible, I've been studying and researching how police officers everywhere can increase their choices by using visual and verbal persuasion to prevent, or at least minimize, their use of force in violent situations. Believe me, police officers all over this country need new tools for accomplishing their duties. They are hungry for positive education that will enhance their control over themselves and others. No group of professionals needs flexibility more than police officers.

THINKING CRITICALLY ABOUT THE READING

1. From the beginning of the essay, Gardner's focus is on changing his interactions as a police officer from more intrusive to more inquisitive. What are some of the verbal and non-verbal tactics Gardner and his partner change? What do they use instead? Why does the method require "flexibility," as Gardner concludes?

2. What do Gardner's colleagues call him and his partner? Is it a flattering moniker? Despite such a handle, do their tactics work? How successful are they?

3. How do Gardner's tactics rely on "visual and verbal" persuasion (3)? How do some of the visual tactics Gardner describes compare with our typical idea of how a police officer looks or moves?

4. What is a "word salad," and how does it work (32)? Why do you think it's successful? Do you think it could have ever been seen as disrespectful?

5. In what ways does Gardner suggest the pattern of one's language use is connected to or predictive of behavior? How did he and his partner work with the sound or rhythm of language to defuse tense situations?

6. What does Gardner's experience suggest about the power of language, observation, and flexibility in police work?

LANGUAGE IN ACTION

Much of Michael Gardner's approach to conflict resolution has to do with body language. Experiment with your own body language using the concept of "power poses" made popular by a 2012 TED Talk by social scientist Amy Cuddy. Cuddy reports a direct connection between body language and physiological responses in our bodies: when subjects deliberately adopted "power poses"—positions which take up space in the room and give the impression of openness and control—subsequent saliva tests revealed raised testosterone and lowered cortisol levels, two hormones important in risk-taking and stress management. Likewise, subjects who deliberately held "low-power poses"—positions which take up little space and give the impression of being closed and turned inward—actually had lowered levels of testosterone and raised cortisol.

Try out what Cuddy suggests together as a class. (You may want to watch Cuddy's TED Talk, which can be found online, if time permits.) Have each member of the class pick a pose and hold it for two minutes. Did the poses feel particularly unnatural or uncomfortable for anyone, or does the pose seem particularly out of sync with your impression of others in the class? If you had to translate these positions into actual words, what might each one say? What might Gardner say about power poses as related to the unique approaches to conflict resolution he advocates for law enforcement?

WRITING SUGGESTIONS

1. As a police officer, Gardner observes that "most emphasis was on weaponry defense, without nearly enough on visual and verbal defense" (3), a tool that he and his partner saw as underutilized and misunderstood. In the last several years, police forces across the nation have been under scrutiny for their questionable use of force and inability to verbally defuse situations, such as in the highly publicized deaths of Michael Brown in 2014 and Sandra Bland in 2015. According to Gardner, officers "are hungry for positive education that will enhance their control over themselves and others" (44), yet these tactics do not seem to be widespread. Research phrases like "excessive force" and "police brutality," and choose a specific case for further research and discussion. How did the situation go awry? Do you think police training in Gardner's tactics would have helped create a different outcome? If so, how? If not, why not? Write an informative essay discussing how you would use the case you've chosen as a training scenario for future officers using Gardner's tactics. Which tactics might work best? Which might have unintended consequences? How would you get future officers thinking about the power their words might hold in protecting themselves and their suspects in threatening situations?

2. Gardner states, "As amazing as these techniques were for defusing violence in the moment, our biggest success was that we stopped getting return calls from places we visited. . . . [W]e knew we could save time in the long run by coming to a peaceful resolution" (35). Why do you think Gardner's tactics resulted in fewer return calls for domestic disputes? How might couples and families benefit from Gardner's approach even after the police have left? Write an essay in which you explore the ways in which Gardner's tactics might help couples resolve their own problems or keep the situation from escalating again.

Regretlessly Yours: The No-Fault Apology

RICK REILLY

Rick Reilly began his thirty-five-year career as a sportswriter and television personality in 1979, working for the *Boulder Daily Camera* while a sophomore at the University of Colorado. A Colorado native, Reilly stayed on at the *Camera* for two more years and then moved to the *Denver Post* before leaving to work at the *Los Angeles Times*, and, eventually, at *Sports Illustrated* in 1985. His twenty-two-year tenure at *Sports Illustrated*, from 1985 to 2007, defined his career. He wrote the popular feature "Life of Reilly," which ran on the magazine's last page and from which this essay is taken.

In 2007 Reilly was not only inducted into the National Sportswriters and Sportscasters Hall of Fame, but he moved to ESPN where he was a regular on *SportsCenter*, hosted the one-hour interview show *Homecoming with Rick Reilly*, and reprised his "Life of Reilly" column for *ESPN The Magazine* until 2010. He also won the 2009 Damon Runyon Award for Outstanding Contributions to Journalism. On March 12, 2014, he announced his retirement from sports writing but has continued working for ESPN, appearing on programs such as *SportsCenter* and *Sunday NFL Countdown*.

Reilly is also the author of eleven books on sports-related topics, including *Sports from Hell: My Search for the World's Dumbest Competition* (2010), which was a finalist for the 2011 Thurber Prize, and he was voted National Sportswriter of the Year eleven times. In addition to novels and nonfiction, Reilly co-authored the screenplay for the film *Leatherheads* (2008), about the 1924 Duluth Eskimos and the nascent NFL, starring George Clooney. As his writing attests, Reilly has a remarkable ability to tell a good human interest story, but the popularity of his work is said to lie in his sharp wit, as shown in the essay included here on the formulaic sports "no-pology."

WRITING TO DISCOVER: *What kind of response or apology do you expect when a public figure, such as an athlete or a celebrity, has committed a crime or transgression? What factors shape that expectation? Do you think we hold some public figures to higher standards than others—or even ourselves?*

Star athletes tend to get themselves in more hot water than Top Ramen. Last week alone Keith Hernandez, Kenyon Martin and Delmon Young all had to do major damage control for bad behavior. But now, thanks to the discount law firm of Wheezle, Wangle and Dodge, stars can save boatloads of p.r. and legal fees with the first-ever Do It Yourself Athletic Apology—the No-pology™. It's the best way to say "I'm sorry" without really meaning it. Try it next time you're busted! (Clear throat and read sincerely.)

THE NO-FAULT APOLOGY

Ladies and gentlemen, let me begin by saying I'm acutely aware of the accusations that I (pick from Menu A). Let me state categorically and on the record that (one from Menu B). What everybody involved needs to clearly understand is that (Menu C). And I refuse to let the (Menu D) win. Still, if (Menu E), then I would definitely like to take this opportunity to (Menu F). But I'll tell you one thing, I (Menu G). Peace. Out.

Menu A Offenses

- tested positive for every chemical on the element chart
- insulted an entire (race/gender/religion)
- beat the bejesus out of that meter maid
- groped most of the Rockettes
- threatened to kneecap my coach
- kneecapped my coach

Menu B Excuses

- I have no recollection of doing any of that
- it is what it is
- my meds were way off
- that's just (my name) being (my name)
- it was the arthritic rub
- I had to do something; they dissed my peeps

Menu C Rationalizations

- people just build you up to knock you down
- things got blown way out of proportion
- I didn't know that the damn thing was loaded
- people should be curing cancer, not hassling me

- nobody would've said a word if I were (name different race)
- nobody told me cops can dress like hookers

Menu D Scapegoats

- media
- haters
- liberals
- terrorists
- Girl Scouts
- voices in my head

Menu E Distancing Phrase

- my actions were somehow misinterpreted
- my T-shirt was taken out of context
- people are that PC
- one little flag-burning offended the mouth-breathers
- my Rosie O'Donnell impression bothered anybody
- the wildfires have become a distraction

Menu F No-Pology™

- turn the page and move forward
- in a way, apologize, up to a point-ish

<table>
<tr><td>

- express regret that it even happened
- feel bad for these morons
- ask you what you want me to say
- leave it in (Jesus/Allah/Vishnu)'s hands

Menu G The Last Word

- sure as hell ain't apologizing to that nun

</td><td>

- will pick a batboy next time who can take a punch
- didn't even know those people were considered a minority
- won't ever ride my Harley in Nordstrom again
- will not torpedo any more Smirnoff/Zoloft shooters ever again
- had my fingers crossed

</td></tr>
</table>

THINKING CRITICALLY ABOUT THE READING

1. How does Reilly use humor to criticize star athletes and those involved in such "damage control"? What effect does Reilly's means of criticism have? Do you think the form letter scolds, in earnest, the actions of the athletes he names? Of those supporting or sponsoring the athlete?

2. What does Reilly's form letter suggest about athletes' feelings about their transgressions? What does he suggest about the nature of public apologies? About "damage control" as opposed to showing remorse or feeling regret?

3. What does Reilly mean by the neologism "No-pology"? What do the words "wheezle," "wangle," and "dodge" connote, and why might he choose that as the law firm's name? How do these words emphasize the performance involved in public apologies? How else does Reilly draw attention to public apology as a performance?

4. What are the titles of the menu categories? How do these single words characterize the "No-pology"? How do these words serve to criticize these athletes, their handlers, and the process of the No-Fault Apology?

5. Why do you think Reilly uses hyperbole to define the offenses in each of the menu categories? How might it emphasize the absurdity of the formulaic apology? What does Reilly's language say about the nature of the offenses that actual athletes have committed?

6. In order for satire to work, we need to be able to recognize ourselves and/or our society within the work. What menu items most accurately reflect the actual offenses of the athletes named? How does the inclusion of these items help Reilly to make a critical point rather than just an elaborate joke?

LANGUAGE IN ACTION

Examine this guide to effective apology by Aaron Lazare, professor of psychiatry and author of the book *On Apology* (2004). How does Reilly's humorous guide nod to Lazare's sincere list of requirements? What do the two have in common, and where exactly do they part ways? Use the template of Reilly's apology but discard his "menus" and instead fill in the blanks using Lazare's recommendations, writing the sincerest apology you can write. Do you think Lazare is right about what's required? What, if anything, does he miss?

There are up to four parts to an effective apology, though not every apology requires all four parts. They are as follows.

1. A valid acknowledgment of the offense that makes clear who the offender is and who is the offended. The offender must clearly and completely acknowledge the offense.
2. An effective explanation, which shows an offense was neither intentional nor personal, and is unlikely to recur.
3. Expressions of remorse, shame, and humility, which show that the offender recognizes the suffering of the offended.
4. A reparation of some kind, in the form of a real or symbolic compensation for the offender's transgression.

WRITING SUGGESTIONS

1. Are athletes the only people in the public eye to use the No-Fault Apology? Think about other public apologies you've read about or witnessed offered by politicians, musicians, or celebrities. What phrases and moves do you associate with apologies from disgraced public figures? How do you think the words used by politicians, sports figures, and celebrities differ? Do they follow the same formula? What is each group trying to convey to its audience? Are there different patterns for each group? Write an essay that first identifies the pattern of apology for one of the groups listed above, compares it to Reilly's model, and then discusses whether or not these types of public "No-pologies" have any meaning.

2. Write your own "No-Pology" to a family member, significant other, friend, or teacher for a real offense, recent or past, using the narrative structure Reilly creates and menu items you've created for your offense. Read your "No-pology." Would you give it to the person for whom you wrote it? Why or why not? How does it differ from a genuine apology? From the apology you (presumably) offered for your own transgression? Does it reflect your offense accurately or make light of it? Write a reflection on how the "No-pology" differs from the apology you made or would make. Is an apology just about saying the right words? About the language we use? About delivery? What makes an apology genuine?

Tarring Opponents as Extremists Really Can Work

EMILY BADGER

Emily Badger grew up in Chicago where, as she writes, she "first learned to think about architecture, inequality and the value of public transit." After earning a bachelor's degree in journalism from Northwestern University, she earned a master's degree in nonfiction writing from Johns Hopkins University. Previously a staff writer for *Atlantic CityLab*, the *Atlantic*'s Web site devoted to original reporting on urban life, she now covers urban policy at the *Washington Post*.

As her Web site explains, although "she writes frequently about urban planning, housing, transportation, poverty and inequality—and why we can't talk about any of these topics without mentioning the others as well," the essay included here discusses how "extremist" language is used as a political tactic to manipulate readers and voters when two sides are in conflict over an issue. The essay was first published in *Pacific Standard* magazine in 2011.

WRITING TO DISCOVER: *Has anyone ever characterized you using a term you were surprised to hear, or one that assumed you were part of a group with which you don't identify? What do you think was the person's intent in using the term? How did you react?*

Back in 2002, when the male-only, members-only Augusta National golf club was picked to host the Masters Tournament, advocates of equality for women were taken aback. They wanted the tournament moved or the storied golf club opened to women. And their cause resonated with many Americans in an age when the public supports little outright gender discrimination.

The campaign ran into a hitch, though: for many people, it became synonymous with Martha Burk, a feminist leader whose name frequently appeared in the national press alongside words like "radical," "extreme," and "dogmatic."

That story is a classic example of a tactic prevalent in politics. Tar a policy's proponents as "extreme," and maybe the policy will start to look that way, too. Political strategists clearly bank on this idea. And new political science research reveals that it works on many of us.[1]

Researchers Thomas Nelson, Gregory Gwiasda, and Joseph Lyons studied the strategy in a paper published in the journal *Political Psychology*.

---

1. Thomas E. Nelson, Gregory Gwiasda, and Joseph Lyons, "Vilification and Values," *Political Psychology* 32, no. 5 (2011): 813–835.

To understand their findings, it's helpful to view political disputes—even the Augusta National story—as a clash of conflicting values, in this case gender equality and the rights of private organizations to determine their own rules.

Most values are generally thought to be positive, although people may   5
rank them with different priorities. Most of us are on the same page about freedom, security, equality, and even the environment. No one *dislikes* those things.

"We think of [values] as kind of rules that can never be violated, sacred rules that must be protected," Nelson said. "The problem, of course, is you can't have everything. Sooner or later those things are going to come into conflict. This happens in our everyday lives."

And it happens constantly in politics.

When two of these values come into conflict—in, say, a policy question pitting national security against personal liberties—strategists must figure out how to advocate one at the expense of the other. No one wants to go on record attacking the value of security, or liberty. But you can do the next best thing: attack the people standing near it.

Nelson offers this example: "Everybody loves national parks, everybody loves the environment, nobody wants to be perceived as anti-environment. So if you are, say, the snowmobile manufacturer, and you want to push for greater access to public land for snowmobiles, you can't say, 'Well, the environment is stupid, nobody cares about the environment. The only thing that's important is riding a snowmobile.'"

> **Tar a policy's proponents as "extreme," and maybe the policy will start to look that way, too.**

You could, however, say, "Sporting outdoorsmen may not get to   10
enjoy our national parks this winter because radical environmentalists care more about owls than the local economy."

Such rhetoric helps ambivalent voters find their way out of a conflict between competing values.

In their study, the researchers had undergraduate students read and respond to an account of the Augusta National dispute with three small changes: one referred to critics of the policy as "people" and "citizens"; another as "radical feminists," "militant feminists" and "extremists"; and the third with extended descriptions of the type of world such radical feminists advocate (one with co-ed locker rooms!). The policy itself remained constant as these descriptions changed. As a result, the students exposed to the extremist language were less likely to support moving the tournament or welcoming female members to the club—even though a self-assessment of their values would suggest that they might.

The researchers performed similar experiments with opinion pieces and blog posts about environmental issues and immigration.

Most surprising to them was their discovery that sometimes the label itself is enough. Sometimes, simply calling advocates "feminists" or "environmentalists" is sufficient to tap into extremist associations people already have about those groups (perhaps the same negative associations that underlie the odd phenomenon that many people who care about the environment and gender equality don't want to be called "environmentalists" or "feminists"). Other times, it's apparently necessary to dress up that label, maybe "wild-eyed radical feminists," or even "extreme feminists who would go so far as to advocate unisex toilets."

The authors don't know where that line is drawn. They also don't   15
know what distinguishes the people unfazed by this trick from those who are persuaded by it. In their studies, only some of the students were lulled by extremist labels into opposing policies that otherwise align with their values.

Perhaps other voters know the tactic when they see it, or they've seen it so many times that extremist labels themselves become off-putting (Nelson calls this the "tactic tactic," calling out an opponent for using just such a tactic).

"For a lot of people, that does raise a red flag. This looks like a last desperate measure of somebody who doesn't have anything better to say," he said. "But what distinguishes those people from others who are susceptible to it?"

THINKING CRITICALLY ABOUT THE READING

1. What types of words were used to describe feminist activist Martha Burk? How did researchers test the effects of such words on reception of the Augusta National story? What were the results?

2. How do Nelson and his co-researchers, whom Badger cites, suggest "extremist" branding works (12)? Why do they argue that it works in this way?

3. How does the essay define "values"? What are some of the values named in the essay? How is the language of values related to the language of extremes?

4. What does Badger mean by a "conflict between competing values" (11)? What example does the text offer? How can this kind of conflict escalate?

5. What is meant by the term "tactic tactic" (16)? What does it accomplish? Why might some people be unaffected by extremist rhetoric?

LANGUAGE IN ACTION

In her essay "Bad Feminist," from the book of the same name, writer Roxane Gay admits the following:

> I sometimes cringe when someone refers to me as a feminist, as if I should be ashamed of my feminism or as if the word *feminist* is an insult. The label is rarely offered in kindness. I am generally called a feminist when I have the nerve to suggest that the misogyny deeply embedded in our culture is a real problem, requiring relentless vigilance. . . .
>
>   I'm not the only outspoken woman who shies away from the feminist label, who fears the consequences of accepting the label.

What do you think are some of the consequences of accepting labels like the one Gay describes here — or like the ones Badger lists in her essay? Are such labels ever "offered in kindness"? Can they be used to empower individuals or groups instead of tearing them down?

WRITING SUGGESTIONS

1. Online satirical news sites like *Clickhole* and *The Onion* successfully use extremist language to render mundane topics comically absurd. Do you think the effectiveness of satire in American culture depends on an understanding of the "tactic tactic" Badger discusses? Why or why not? Visit a satirical news site and read some of the articles to get a sense of how the rhetoric of extremism operates. Then find a local mundane report — minor road construction, a change in cafeteria offerings, a shift in library hours — to render as a similar satire for your campus newspaper. Be sure to use the language of extremes to color your outrage at the mundane occurrence you've chosen.

2. Badger suggests that to "tar a policy's proponents as 'extreme'" in order to make the "policy . . . look that way, too" (3) is rather an old tactic and one that has long worked in American politics. Select a contemporary controversial political issue to research, and compare coverage of that issue. It will be most be useful to consider how one specific incident is reported across several sources rather than how a broader topic is discussed. Look at local and national coverage in newspapers whose bias tends toward both conservatism and liberalism. Does one side seem to use extreme language more than the other? Do particular media sources tend toward extreme language more than the other? How are values addressed in this coverage? What sites and genres seem to be the most guilty of using the language of extremes to discuss this issue? Why? After narrowing your selection of coverage to five or six sources reporting on the same incident, write a research essay that analyzes the media's use of extreme language about your topic.

Letting Go

AMY WESTERVELT

Amy Westervelt is a freelance journalist who lives in California with her husband, son, cat, and dog. Westervelt graduated from the University of California, Berkeley, in 2000 and has been involved in regional environmental writing in California. Her research into the prospects and challenges of biofuels, "Algae Arms Race," won a 2007 Folio Award, and in 2015 she won a Rachel Carson Award from the Audubon Society, celebrating "women greening journalism." She is also the co-founder of the Boxwood Bureau, a crowd-funded collective of journalists with a focus on environmental protection.

As a contributor to the *Wall Street Journal*, the *Guardian*, *Forbes*, *Slate*, and *Aeon*, where this essay first appeared, she has primarily written about technology, the environment, and health issues. The essay included here considers the effect of forgiveness on physical and mental health though a compelling personal narrative about the death of a friend.

WRITING TO DISCOVER: *What, if anything, have you been taught about forgiveness? Where did you learn about forgiveness, and what kind of importance does it hold for you? How have you seen forgiveness portrayed in songs, stories, and films?*

In the cleanest college library I've ever seen, women of various ages and ethnicities were seated around a long wooden table. A few were chatting, but most were nervously shuffling notebooks and pens or staring at the floor. The men—there were five, ranging in age from early 20s to mid-50s—showed up just before class began. I tried to divine, one by one, what horrible tragedy had brought them all there.

This was the Tuesday night forgiveness course at Stanford University. I was there strictly to observe. Formalized forgiveness training—complete with a reading list, lectures, practice sessions, and homework—was for people who had survived genocide, not for me with my garden-variety baggage (even if I had read everything I could about forgiveness training, developing a not-unhealthy obsession with the topic). Professor Frederic Luskin told me I could sit in on his class, but would have to participate so it wouldn't seem weird. No problem. I prepared an almost-true story about a fight with my mother.

Then, his large eyes flashing and greying hair standing on end, Luskin held his hands out in front of him like a zombie, palms down and spaced about a foot apart. "Most of our disappointment in life stems from wanting this," he jabbed at the air with his left hand, the higher of the two, for emphasis, "and getting this," he said, jiggling the lowered right hand. Then he stared at all of us, intently. "OK? And forgiveness is about what you decide to do with this space in the middle. Are you going to adjust what you expect and let the rest go, or are you going to live in this space? Because I'll tell you what, living in there is miserable."

Shit. Now all I could think about was living in that terrible, empty space between his two giant hands. How I'd been stuck there for years, waiting for things to change and then being angry and disappointed when nothing happened.

When we got paired off to share our stories, my fake mom story   5 was running through my head on rapid repeat, but my mouth rebelled, blurting out to the nice man on my left: "My best friend died and now I hate everyone for not being her and I really need to let it go. And actually this is really weird because Leah died here. Not right here in this library, but over there at the university hospital. This is the first time I've been back since."

It was a moment I'd read about—this sudden shift when the need to forgive outweighs the drive for revenge. I felt weightless, nauseous, sad, the prospect of letting go of all those years of anger finally opening up a space for grief. It is this rare freedom for the soul that has made forgiveness a cornerstone of all major world religions for hundreds of years as well as an increasingly popular subject in modern psychology—both the traditional and pop varieties. But while its benefits have been proved, forgiveness remains a thorny subject, bound up in ideas about everything from doctrinal religion to justice.

My research began when I stumbled across a story about Robert Enright, a psychologist at the University of Wisconsin. Enright was raised Catholic, but abandoned religion for academia early in his career. "I became a professor and thought I knew who God was—it was me," he said.

By the time he returned to his faith, Enright had established himself as "the father of forgiveness," creating a therapeutic protocol for how to practice it that was officially sanctioned by the American Psychology Association and the United Nations. He thought the Catholic Church could be doing more to emphasize its deep history in the subject, and spreading the gospel of forgiveness to the masses, and said so in a speech at the Vatican.

As a lapsed Catholic myself, Enright's story resonated with me. Forced to attend church and Catholic school in my youth, I'd rebelled in my teens and twenties, not because I didn't believe in God but because I didn't like the self-righteous way in which most of the religious people I knew behaved. I didn't really miss religion, apart from those moments at the end of Mass where Holy Communion absolved me of my sins and I'd be given a few moments of silence to pray in gratitude. I'd looked forward to those moments—and the peace they brought me—every week. Few other experiences delivered a similar relief from daily worries, and when I read about Enright and his work I wondered if forgiveness might be the thing.

Each of the Abrahamic faiths—Islam, Judaism, Christianity—include   10
teachings on forgiveness, both the sort that God doles out and the sort
that human beings can (and should) bestow on each other. The Torah,
the Bible, and the Qur'an are all filled with dictates about forgiveness,
and rules about what God can and cannot, or will not, forgive. The non-
Abrahamic faiths, meanwhile, have a wellness-focused approach to forgiveness that's not so different from modern, secular treatments of the
subject in the context of the positive psychology movement. Buddhism,
for example, teaches that people who hold on to the wrongs done to them
create an identity around that pain, and it is that identity that continues
to be reborn.

But what about the nuts and bolts of forgiveness, about which all the
Catholic rituals around penance and confession had taught me nothing?
I knew exactly how to ask God for forgiveness, but I had no idea how to
forgive, or ask forgiveness from the people in my life. This turns out to be
an important distinction: University of Michigan researchers have found
that forgiveness between people tends to have more reliably positive physical benefits than any perceived forgiveness from God.

Forgiveness is a relatively new academic research area, studied in earnest only since Enright began publishing on the subject in the 1980s. The
first batch of studies were medical in focus. Forgiveness was widely correlated with a range of physical benefits, including better sleep, lower blood
pressure, lower risk of heart disease, even increased life expectancy; really,
every benefit you'd expect from reduced stress. The late Kathleen Lawler,
while working as a researcher in the psychology department at the University of Tennessee in Knoxville, studied the effects of both hostility and
forgiveness on the body's systems fairly extensively. "Forgiveness is aptly
described as 'a change of heart,'" she wrote, in summarizing a series of
studies focused on the impact of forgiveness on heart health. Meanwhile,
Duke University researchers found a strong correlation between improved
immune system function and forgiveness in HIV-positive patients, and
between forgiveness and improved mortality rates across the general
population.

More recently, the subject has surged in popularity as everyone from
the United Nations to the victims of mass shootings espouses the virtues
of forgiveness for everything from mental health to managing war zones.
Even Oprah Winfrey has gotten in on the forgiveness game: her favorite
life coach, Iyanla Vanzant, frequently spotlighted the subject in her Oprah
Winfrey Network show *Iyanla: Fix My Life*, and launched an e-learning
class entitled"How to Forgive Everyone for Everything."

In her book, *Forgiveness: 21 Days to Forgive Everyone for Everything*,
Vanzant lays out a 21-day program to set readers on the path to forgiveness. Perhaps unsurprisingly (Winfrey is the queen of self-improvement,
after all), the book is focused largely on self-forgiveness. Vanzant is also
a proponent of Progressive Energy Field Tapping (Pro EFT)—tapping

specific energy points just under the surface of the skin, "releasing emotions trapped in our energy system," according to the official Pro EFT Web site. It's a bit New Age-y for my taste, but hey, it's a process and a lot of people are saying it works.

It's not just Oprah who's promoting the self-improvement side of   15
forgiveness. The rise of popular interest in forgiveness has coincided with a second wave of academic studies, focused on self-forgiveness. After investigating the relationship between forgiveness and health, Jon R. Webb at East Tennessee State University found that "it may be that forgiveness of self is relatively more important to health-related outcomes" than other forms of forgiveness. Sara Pelucchi, at the Catholic University in Milan, claims that it is beneficial to romantic relationships, and Thomas Carpenter at Baylor University found that we have an easier time forgiving ourselves if those we have hurt forgive us first.

Enright has also examined self-forgiveness, although he's more measured about it than Vanzant. "The issue of self-forgiveness is much more complicated than forgiveness in general and here's why: when you offend yourself, you are both the victim and the perpetrator," he told me. "The problem is compounded by the fact that we rarely offend ourselves in isolation from offending others."

Enright recommends that people struggling with self-forgiveness learn to forgive others first, before offering that same compassion to themselves. "Otherwise it can be tricky: If you're a compulsive gambler and keep squandering the family's money, for example, you could forgive yourself and keep doing it, but true self-forgiveness requires stopping the behavior that led to the offense in first place."

It's the "learn to forgive" part that's key to making forgiveness stick. According to Luskin, religion might help to motivate or oblige people to forgive, but it's the secular realm that is bringing the idea of forgiveness to the masses. It's also teaching us precisely how to do it.

Feel the feelings you need to feel, express them, then leave them in the past where they can no longer have power over you.

While researchers have spent the past 20 years proving the physical and mental benefits of forgiveness, it's the step-by-step forgiveness guides they've developed that might turn out to be academia's most important contribution to the subject. Like Vanzant's pop-psych version, the protocols that Enright and Luskin have developed offer specific steps towards forgiveness rooted in decades of research and clinical experience. While the various approaches differ, all include practical guidance and the basics are consistent: feel the feelings you need to feel, express them, then leave them in the past where they can no longer have power over you.

When I first met my friend Leah, it was all off-color jokes and dares.   20
Then she invited me to her ex-boyfriend's funeral and things got real. I met her mother, who was sweet and funny and cooked us dinner in an

apron, but also smoked around Leah even though it was likely to trigger an asthma attack. Her father, a retired physician, and the sort of stiff grown-up that people like me (and Leah) loved to get a rise out of, patted Leah's shoulder and tousled her hair as we got into the car to leave.

Later Leah said that was the most affection he had ever shown her in public. Then she told me how, when she was about five, her father had killed her cat because it was annoying him, and had buried it in the carrot patch. Telling her to go find it there, he had then laughed gleefully when the horrified child uncovered her dead pet. We traded unpleasant stories the whole ride home, and after that our friendship was sealed.

Shortly after that outing, I barged into her apartment and found her on her living-room floor wheezing in and out of a massive steroid inhaler. She explained that she had cystic fibrosis and that her brother had died from it, but that she, the beneficiary of various trial drugs, would most likely be OK.

A couple years later, after we graduated from college, I got Leah a job at the magazine where I worked. When I had to fire her because she showed up late every day and spent hours hanging out under my desk, sipping lattes, I didn't make up excuses or lie. I just called her at the end of the day and, before she could even say "Hello?" I yelled: "You're fired!"

She erupted in laughter.

"No, but seriously, you're fired. I mean, come on, I don't think you've   25
made it to the office on time once. Plus you spend most of that time under my desk. AND you really blew that call the other day."

Our boss had asked her to make some advertising sales calls. Leah's technique had been to play it cool and say: "I know the last thing you want to do is advertise, especially in this lousy magazine." She thought they'd find it refreshing and humorous, but our boss, overhearing her, did not appreciate her creativity.

"Ach. Yeah, OK, I get it. I'm sorry—did I get you into trouble?"

"No, but I think having me fire you is some sort of test."

"Well, tell that egg-shaped douche you passed."

In my first conversation with Enright, he explained that he'd started   30
researching forgiveness in 1985, "when no one in the social sciences would even touch the topic. It was either totally off their radar or just too scary because it is really rooted in the monotheistic traditions. I thought that was folly. Forgiveness might be important to the human condition and scientists have the obligation to go where the ideas lead, no matter what."

That conversation led to other scholars who had waded into forgiveness research, Luskin among them. Like Enright, Luskin had worked with civil war survivors (in Sierra Leone), various factions within Northern Ireland, and death row inmates in the United States. When I found him, Luskin had been running forgiveness classes at Stanford for about a decade, and had moved away from what he called the "big, dramatic" forms of forgiveness, to which youth and media attention had drawn him early in his career.

"Even the stuff that forgiveness was supposed to be good for—stuff like murders . . . it's so rare," he told me. "More important is can you forgive your brother-in-law for being annoying? Can you forgive traffic? Those things happen every day. Big things? They happen once in a life-time, maybe twice. It's a waste of forgiveness. That's my perspective. But forgiveness is really important for smoothing over the normal, interper-sonal things that rub everyone the wrong way."

Part of what makes the word—and practice—tough for people, in Luskin's view, is that it requires a degree of selflessness. "For me to say, 'Even though you were a shithead, it's not my problem; it's your problem, and I'm not going to stay mad at you, because that's you, not me,' that's a huge renunciation of self," he said. "And I don't know whether it's our [Western] culture or a human thing, but it's hard."

Plus it requires acknowledgement of our fundamental human vulnera-bility, without getting angry or bitter about it. "A lot of times people start with this idea that 'I shouldn't have been harmed,'" Luskin said. "Why not? We live on a planet where harm happens all the time, where children are murdered and horrible things happen; to think that you should escape that is a mammoth overstatement of your own importance and a lack of sensitivity to everyone else on the planet."

But even for those who might find themselves nodding along with Luskin's sentiments, walking the walk is another story. What all of the researchers and pop-psych proponents of forgiveness agree on is that it takes practice and that it is hard work. Vanzant compares it to pulling out a tooth without Novocaine. Luskin described it as re-training the brain. "You can get upset about anything—you can also get un-upset about anything, it's just a matter of learning how," he said.   35

In the eight years since Leah died, I've married, had a child and made new friends, yet I still miss her desperately. If I had a bad experience at work, Leah thought I should quit. Screw them. If I argued with a boy-friend, he was an asshole. Period. Even when everyone, including me, knew I was the asshole. It was the kind of backup she craved, too, which is why it's been so hard to shake the feeling that ultimately I failed her.

Toward the end of her life, Leah's doctors said the only way she'd be able to continue living was on a ventilator. Knowing she wouldn't want to live that way, her parents decided to take her off life support. I agreed with their choice, difficult as it would be to lose her. When I went to be with her on that last night, she was alone. Her parents couldn't bear to see Leah suffer the same slow, painful death they'd watched their son endure. I couldn't imagine doing otherwise.

When the nurse took Leah off the machines, she panicked, opened her eyes wide, clenched my hand and mouthed, "Help me." Several hours later, when the nurse came to check on her, she reported with surprise that Leah's blood oxygenation levels were normal. When I asked what that meant, she said, "Well, it means she didn't really need to be on that ventilator." At that point, I asked if we shouldn't reconsider things, but the nurse was quick to squash that idea. "I've probably just had her on too much oxygen," she said. "I'll turn it down."

It is the biggest regret of my life that I didn't make a huge fuss in that moment, and demand to see the doctor. That I did not call Leah's parents and beg them to reconsider. That I did not wait until the nurse left the room, then jack the oxygen back up. That I did precisely nothing but hold my friend's hand while she died.

In the weeks following Luskin's forgiveness seminar, it all clicked. I'd   40
been waiting for a magical moment in which I would forgive myself for failing Leah—and the rest of the world for being around when she wasn't. That moment never came and in the meantime, I had justified a lot of my own bad behavior.

After reading everything from religious scripture to academic studies, I finally realized that's not at all how forgiveness works, and that's what makes it so damn hard. Time does not heal all wounds. This too shall not pass. Letting go of hurt and anger is a grind, and forgiveness only works if you practice it regularly, and are prepared to fail often without giving up. But the pay-off is so huge it just might be worth it.

THINKING CRITICALLY ABOUT THE READING

1. How does Westervelt describe the space, atmosphere, and participants of the forgiveness workshop? How does she describe Professor Luskin? What effect do his words have on her? Why might she begin the story this way?

2. Although the essay links forgiveness with religion, "University of Michigan researchers have found that forgiveness between people tends to have more reliably positive physical benefits than any perceived forgiveness from God" (11). What are the health benefits of forgiveness? What do you make of the idea that forgiveness from others trumps forgiveness from a higher power? Why might that be true?

3. Why does forgiveness require "a degree of selflessness" (32)? Why might this requirement pose problems in our culture?

4. What metaphors have forgiveness researchers used to describe the act of learning to forgive? Why is it important to see forgiveness as a quality we can learn? Do you think we can get better at forgiving?

5. Westervelt discusses her friend Leah and Leah's death in the essay. How does Westervelt link this story to forgiveness? What is the purpose of including a personal story? What kind of language does it allow into the essay, and how does that language affect the reader?

6. In the conclusion of her essay, Westervelt contradicts well-known adages that many accept as truth. She writes: "time does not heal all wounds" and "this too shall not pass." What do these adages mean? How do they overlook the role of forgiveness? How might they keep us from the work of forgiveness?

LANGUAGE IN ACTION

In line with Westervelt's discovery that forgiveness can have positive impacts on health, the Mayo Clinic Web site—a significant resource for health information maintained by one of the leading research hospitals in the world—includes an article (excerpted below) on the benefits of forgiveness.

FORGIVENESS: LETTING GO OF GRUDGES AND BITTERNESS

When someone you care about hurts you, you can hold on to anger, resentment and thoughts of revenge—or embrace forgiveness and move forward.

BY MAYO CLINIC STAFF

Nearly everyone has been hurt by the actions or words of another. Perhaps your mother criticized your parenting skills, your colleague sabotaged a project or your partner had an affair. These wounds can leave you with lasting feelings of anger, bitterness or even vengeance.

But if you don't practice forgiveness, you might be the one who pays most dearly. By embracing forgiveness, you can also embrace peace, hope, gratitude and joy. Consider how forgiveness can lead you down the path of physical, emotional and spiritual well-being.

What Is Forgiveness?

Generally, forgiveness is a decision to let go of resentment and thoughts of revenge. The act that hurt or offended you might always remain a part of your life, but forgiveness can lessen its grip on you and help you focus on other, more positive parts of your life. Forgiveness can even lead to feelings of understanding, empathy and compassion for the one who hurt you.

Forgiveness doesn't mean that you deny the other person's responsibility for hurting you, and it doesn't minimize or justify the wrong. You can forgive the person without excusing the act. Forgiveness brings a kind of peace that helps you go on with life.

What Are the Benefits of Forgiving Someone?

Letting go of grudges and bitterness can make way for happiness, health and peace. Forgiveness can lead to:

- Healthier relationships
- Greater spiritual and psychological well-being
- Less anxiety, stress and hostility
- Lower blood pressure
- Fewer symptoms of depression
- Stronger immune system
- Improved heart health
- Higher self-esteem

What does it mean when a hospital Web site includes information on how and why we ought to forgive? As a society, we generally accept the idea that there is a connection between our emotional and physical health, but do we use that knowledge well? How might an article like this one—or like Westervelt's—make it easier to incorporate that understanding into our lives? In what other places have you seen a similar message?

WRITING SUGGESTIONS

1. We are taught to think of forgiveness as a kind thing to do for someone else, but it also has some benefits for the forgiver. In her essay, Westervelt cites some real physical benefits: "Forgiveness was widely correlated with a range of physical benefits, including better sleep, lower blood pressure, lower risk of heart disease, even increased life expectancy; really, every benefit you'd expect from reduced stress" (12). How do these findings affect our idea of forgiveness? What do you see as the relationship between forgiveness (or lack of it) and stress? Is it more selfish to forgive or to withhold forgiveness? Who suffers, in each case? Write an essay in which you analyze a situation in which you were able to give or felt compelled to withhold forgiveness. What effects did that decision have on you? On the person you did or did not forgive? How did you handle other situations in the future as a result?

2. In addition to briefly addressing religious traditions and teachings about forgiveness, Westervelt discusses a few popular, secular paths to forgiveness: "While the various approaches differ, all include practical guidance and the basics are consistent: feel the feelings you need to feel, express them, then leave them in the past where they can no longer have power over you" (19). Write a process analysis in which you lay out the steps of offering someone forgiveness in a specific situation (say, forgiving a cheating partner or a thieving roommate). Expand on Westervelt's overview here to offer specific advice and practical advice on the situation you've chosen. What considerations might you add to Westervelt's list of steps?

12

LANGUAGE AND GENDER: POWER, ABUSE, EQUALITY

When one considers the range of topics and the variety of approaches taken by scholars in the general field of gender studies, there is an astounding body of work that one can access and analyze, and perhaps research even further. When one adds to the mix the scholarly efforts occurring in the study of language, the conjoined field of language and gender offers one of the most vibrant and revealing areas of intellectual pursuit available today. From the various definitions of gender itself to questions of usage, stylistics, ethnography, race, power, education, sociology, folklore, communication, pragmatics, literature, queer culture, and sexuality—to name just a few areas of research in play—the intersecting studies of language and gender have offered some amazing insights into who we are and how we communicate with one another.

The essays in Language and Gender are but a small sampling of the ways gender and language interact. Roxane Gay's piece "The Careless Language of Sexual Violence" begins the conversation by questioning the language that popular culture and the media use to talk and write about rape and exploring the ramifications of the language we choose to use. Next, the novelist Chimamanda Ngozi Adichie talks about calling herself a "Happy Feminist" and confronts and explores people's discomfort with the term. In "The Social Harms of 'Bitch,'" Sherryl Kleinman, Matthew B. Ezzell, and A. Corey Frost examine how "bitch" is used as a term of abuse and examine whether it can be reclaimed. Joanna Schroeder continues this focus on the language we use, looking at the words that boys need to learn in order to express themselves socially and emotionally. Next, Michael Kimmel examines the "Guy Code" that he claims prescribes what it means to be a man in our society and how language aids and abets in the formation and preservation of that strange cultural phenomenon. Finally, Ben Crair looks at how linguistic trends on the Internet reflect typically feminine speech patterns and the implications of this for how we understand gender.

The Careless Language of Sexual Violence

Roxane Gay

Born in 1974 in Nebraska, Roxane Gay is a professor of writing at Purdue University in West Lafayette, Indiana. Gay attended the prestigious Phillips Exeter Academy in New Hampshire and has a doctorate degree in rhetoric and technical communication from Michigan Technological University. Gay's work has appeared in *Best American Mystery Stories* (2014), *Best American Short Stories* (2012), *Best Sex Writing* (2012), *A Public Space, McSweeney's, Tin House, Oxford American, American Short Fiction, West Branch, Virginia Quarterly Review, NOON*, the *New York Times Book Review, Bookforum, Time*, the *Los Angeles Times*, the *Nation*, the *Rumpus, Salon*, and many others. She is the co-editor of *PANK Magazine*. She is also the author of the books *Ayiti* (2011), *An Untamed State* (2014), *Bad Feminist (2014)*, and *Hunger* (2016). Gay has said that in her work, she wants to get at deeper issues about society and feminism while still "admitting to our humanity and enjoying sometimes inappropriate things."

In the following essay, which appeared on the Web site *Rumpus* on March 10, 2011, Gay uses the media story of a gang rape in Cleveland, Texas, as the starting point for an honest discussion about rape. She examines how the horror of rape can be lessened with the use of language. Gay calls for the use of the language that brings to the reader the visceral, physical, brutal impact of rape instead of hiding behind vague language such as "sexual assault."

WRITING TO DISCOVER: *The language used to describe "rape" is often couched in easier to handle terms, such as "sexual assault" and "sexual violence." How is language connected to perceptions of reality? In what sense does a phrase create an acceptance of what is unacceptable? What other phrases are used to ease the reality of a particularly bad situation, such as death, murder, illness, or injury?*

There are crimes and then there are crimes and then there are atrocities. These are, I suppose, matters of scale. I read an article in the *New York Times* about an eleven-year old girl who was gang raped by eighteen men in Cleveland, Texas.[1] The levels of horror to this story are many, from the victim's age to what is known about what happened to her, to the number of attackers, to the public response in that town, to how it is being reported. There is video of the attack too, because this is the future. The unspeakable will be televised.

---

1. James McKinley, "Vicious Assault Shakes Texas Town," *New York Times* (New York: NY), March 8, 2011. http://www.nytimes.com/2011/03/09/us/09assault.html?_r=2

The *Times* article was entitled, "Vicious Assault Shakes Texas Town," as if the victim in question was the town itself. James McKinley Jr., the article's author, focused on how the men's lives would be changed forever, how the town was being ripped apart, how those poor boys might never be able to return to school. There was discussion of how the eleven-year-old girl, the child, dressed like a twenty-year-old, implying that there is a realm of possibility where a woman can "ask for it" and that it's somehow understandable that eighteen men would rape a child. There were even questions about the whereabouts of the mother, given, as we all know, that a mother must be with her child at all times or whatever ill may befall the child is clearly the mother's fault. Strangely, there were no questions about the whereabouts of the father while this rape was taking place.

The overall tone of the article was what a shame it all was, how so many lives were affected by this one terrible event. Little addressed the girl, the child. It was an eleven-year-old girl whose body was ripped apart, not a town. It was an eleven-year-old girl whose life was ripped apart, not the lives of the men who raped her. It is difficult for me to make sense of how anyone could lose sight of that and yet it isn't.

We live in a culture that is very permissive where rape is concerned. While there are certainly many people who understand rape and the damage of rape, we also live in a time that necessitates the phrase "rape culture." This phrase denotes a culture where we are inundated, in different ways, by the idea that male aggression and violence toward women is acceptable and often inevitable. As Lynn Higgins and Brenda Silver ask in their book *Rape and Representation*, "How is it that in spite (or perhaps because) of their erasure, rape and sexual violence have been so ingrained and so rationalized through their representations as to appear 'natural' and inevitable, to women as men?" It is such an important question, trying to understand how we have come to this. We have also, perhaps, become immune to the horror of rape because

We live in a culture that is very permissive where rape is concerned.

we see it so often and discuss it so often, many times without acknowledging or considering the gravity of rape and its effects. We jokingly say things like, "I just took a rape shower," or "My boss totally just raped me over my request for a raise." We have appropriated the language of rape for all manner of violations, great and small. It is not a stretch to imagine why James McKinley Jr. is more concerned about the eighteen men than one girl.

The casual way in which we deal with rape may begin and end with television and movies where we are inundated with images of sexual and domestic violence. Can you think of a dramatic television series that has not incorporated some kind of rape storyline? There was a time when these storylines had a certain educational element to them, *ala A Very Special Episode*. I remember, for example, the episode of *Beverly Hills 90210*

5

where Kelly Taylor discussed being date raped at a slumber party, surrounded, tearfully, by her closest friends. For many young women that episode created a space where they could have a conversation about rape as something that did not only happen with strangers. Later in the series, when the show was on its last legs, Kelly would be raped again, this time by a stranger. We watched the familiar trajectory of violation, trauma, disillusion, and finally vindication, seemingly forgetting we had sort of seen this story before.

Every other movie aired on Lifetime or Lifetime Movie Network features some kind of violence against women. The violence is graphic and gratuitous while still being strangely antiseptic where more is implied about the actual act than shown. We consume these representations of violence and do so eagerly. There is a comfort, I suppose, to consuming violence contained in 90-minute segments and muted by commercials for household goods and communicated to us by former television stars with feathered bangs.

While once rape as entertainment fodder may have also included an element of the didactic, such is no longer the case. Rape, these days, is good for ratings. *Private Practice*, on ABC, recently aired a story arc where Charlotte King, the iron-willed, independent, and sexually adventurous doctor was brutally raped. This happened, of course, just as February sweeps were beginning. The depiction of the assault was as graphic as you might expect from prime time network television. For several episodes we saw the attack and its aftermath, how the once vibrant Charlotte became a shell of herself, how she became sexually frigid, how her body bore witness to the physical damage of rape. Another character on the show, Violet, bravely confessed she too had been raped. The show was widely applauded for its sensitive treatment of a difficult subject.

The soap opera *General Hospital* is currently airing a rape storyline, and the height of that story arc occurred, yes, during sweeps. *General Hospital*, like most soap operas, incorporates a rape storyline every five years or so when they need an uptick in viewers. Before the current storyline, Emily Quartermaine was raped and before Emily, Elizabeth Webber was raped, and long before Elizabeth Webber, Laura of Luke and Laura was raped by Luke but that rape was okay because Laura ended up marrying Luke so her rape doesn't really count. Every woman, *General Hospital* wanted us to believe, loves her rapist. The current rape storyline has a twist. This time the victim is a man, Michael Corinthos Jr., son of Port Charles mob boss Sonny Corinthos, himself no stranger to violence against women. While it is commendable to see the show's producers trying to address the issue of male rape and prison rape, the subject matter is still handled carelessly, is still a source of titillation, and is still packaged neatly between commercials for cleaning products and baby diapers.

Of course, if we are going to talk about rape and how we are inundated by representations of rape and how, perhaps, we've become numb to rape, we have to discuss *Law & Order: SVU*, which deals, primarily, in all manner of sexual assault against women, children, and once in a great while, men. Each week the violation is more elaborate, more lurid, more unspeakable. When the show first aired, Rosie O'Donnell, I believe, objected quite vocally when one of the stars appeared on her show. O'Donnell said she didn't understand why such a show was needed. People dismissed her objections and the incident was quickly forgotten. The series is in its 12th season and shows no signs of ending anytime soon. When O'Donnell objected to *SVU*'s premise, when she dared to suggest that perhaps a show dealing so explicitly with sexual assault was unnecessary, was too much, people treated her like she was the crazy one, the prude censor. I watch *SVU* religiously, have actually seen every single episode. I am not sure what that says about me.

I am trying to connect my ideas here. Bear with me.   10

It is rather ironic that only a couple weeks ago, the *Times* ran an editorial about the War on Women.[2] This topic is, obviously, one that matters to me. I recently wrote an essay about how, as a writer who is also a woman, I increasingly feel that to write is a political act whether I intend it to be or not because we live in a culture where McKinley's article is permissible and publishable.[3] I am troubled by how we have allowed intellectual distance between violence and the representation of violence. We talk about rape but we don't talk about rape, not carefully.

We live in a strange and terrible time for women. There are days, like today, where I think it has always been a strange and terrible time to be a woman. It is nothing less than horrifying to realize we live in a culture where the "paper of record" can write an article that comes off as sympathetic to eighteen rapists while encouraging victim blaming. Have we forgotten who an eleven-year-old is? An eleven-year-old is very, very young, and somehow, that amplifies the atrocity, at least for me. I also think, perhaps, people do not understand the trauma of gang rape. While there's no benefit to creating a hierarchy of rape where one kind of rape is worse than another because rape is, at the end of day, rape, there is something particularly insidious about gang rape, about the idea that a pack of men feed on each other's frenzy and both individually and collectively believe it is their right to violate a woman's body in such an unspeakable manner.

Gang rape is a difficult experience to survive physically and emotionally. There is the exposure to unwanted pregnancy and sexually transmitted diseases, vaginal and anal tearing, fistula and vaginal scar tissue. The reproductive system is often irreparably damaged. Victims of gang

---

2. "The War on Women" *New York Times* (New York: NY), February 25, 2011.
3. Roxane Gay, "To Write As a Woman Is Political," *HTML GIANT*, February 23, 2011, http://htmlgiant.com/random/to-write-as-a-woman-is-political/

rape, in particular, have a higher chance of miscarrying a pregnancy. Psychologically, there are any number of effects including PTSD, anxiety, fear, coping with the social stigma, and coping with shame, and on and on. The actual rape ends but the aftermath can be very far reaching and even more devastating than the rape itself. We rarely discuss these things, though. Instead, we are careless. We allow ourselves [to believe] that rape can be washed away as neatly as it is on TV and in the movies where the trajectory of victimhood is neatly defined.

I cannot speak universally but given what I know about gang rape, the experience is wholly consuming and a never-ending nightmare. There is little point in pretending otherwise. Perhaps McKinley Jr. is, like so many people today, anesthetized or somehow willfully distanced from such brutal realities. Perhaps it is that despite this inundation of rape imagery, where we are immersed in a rape culture, that not enough victims of gang rape speak out about the toll the experience exacts. Perhaps the right stories are not being told or we're not writing enough about the topic of rape. Perhaps we are writing too many stories about rape. It is hard to know how such things come to pass.

I am approaching this topic somewhat selfishly. I write about sexual   15
violence a great deal in my fiction. The why of this writerly obsession doesn't matter but I often wonder why I come back to the same stories over and over. Perhaps it is simply that writing is cheaper than therapy or drugs. When I read articles such as McKinley's, I start to wonder about

How do you get this sort of thing right? How do you write violence authentically without making it exploitative?

my responsibility as a writer. I'm finishing my novel right now. It's the story of a brutal kidnapping in Haiti and part of the story involves gang rape. Having to write that kind of story requires going to a dark place. At times, I have made myself nauseous with what I'm writing and what I am capable of writing and imagining, my ability to *go there*.

As I write any of these stories, I wonder if I am being gratuitous. I want to *get it right*. How do you get this sort of thing right? How do you write violence authentically without making it exploitative? There are times when I worry I am contributing to the kind of cultural numbness that would allow an article like the one in the *Times* to be written and published, that allows rape to be such rich fodder for popular culture and entertainment. We cannot separate violence in fiction from violence in the world no matter how hard we try. As Laura Tanner notes in her book *Intimate Violence*, "the act of reading a representation of violence is defined by the reader's suspension between the semiotic and the real, between a representation and the material dynamics of violence which it evokes, reflects, or transforms." She also goes on to say that, "The distance and detachment of a reader who must leave his or her body behind in order to enter imaginatively into the scene of violence make it possible for representations of violence to obscure the material dynamics of bodily violation, erasing not only the victim's body but his or her pain." The way we currently represent rape, in books, in newspapers, on television, on the silver screen, often allows us to ignore the material realities of rape, the impact of rape, the meaning of rape.

While I have these concerns, I also feel committed to telling the truth, to saying these violences happen even if bearing such witness contributes to a spectacle of sexual violence. When we're talking about race or religion or politics, it is often said we need to speak carefully. These are difficult topics where we need to be vigilant not only in what we say but how we express ourselves. That same care, I would suggest, has to be extended to how we write about violence, and sexual violence in particular.

In the *Times* article, the phrase "sexual assault" is used, as is the phrase "the girl had been forced to have sex with several men." The word "rape" is only used twice and not really in connection with the victim. That is not the careful use of language. Language, in this instance, and far more often than makes sense, is used to buffer our sensibilities from the brutality of rape, from the extraordinary nature of such a crime. Feminist scholars have long called for a rereading of rape. Higgins and Silver note that "the act of rereading rape involves more than listening to silences; it requires restoring rape to the literal, to the body: restoring, that is, the violence—the physical, sexual violation." I would suggest we need to find new ways, whether in fiction or creative nonfiction or journalism, for not only rereading rape but rewriting rape as well, ways of rewriting that restore the actual violence to these crimes and that make it impossible for men to be excused for committing atrocities and that make it impossible for articles like McKinley's to be written, to be published, to be considered acceptable.

An eleven-year-old girl was raped by eighteen men. The suspects ranged in age from middle-schoolers to a 27-year-old. There are pictures and videos. Her life will never be the same. The *New York Times*, however, would like you to worry about those boys, who will have to live with this for the rest of their lives. That is not simply the careless language of violence. It is the criminal language of violence.

THINKING CRITICALLY ABOUT THE READING

1. Gay opens with the line, "There are crimes and then there are crimes and then there are atrocities" (1). What does she mean by this? Where do you think she would draw the line between a crime and an atrocity?

2. Gay says, "We live in a culture that is very permissive where rape is concerned" (4). What causes her to make that claim? Do you agree with her statement? Why or why not?

3. In paragraph 4, Gay writes, we "have also, perhaps, become immune to the horror of rape because we see it so often and discuss it so often. . . . We have appropriated the language of rape for all manner of violations, great

and small." Why do you think Gay focuses on the seemingly joking uses of words like "rape"? How is such usage different from using a word like "kill" or "murder" as hyperbole?

4. Gay mentions a number of television shows in which rape is depicted (*Beverly Hills 90210, Private Practice, General Hospital*). In your opinion, what responsibilities, if any, does television have in the representation of rape? Consider that the audience for television can be much bigger than for many other types of media. Who is affected by television portrayals of rape, and how? What ideas do viewers take away from such portrayals?

5. Gay brings up the term "rape culture," which she defines as "a culture where we are inundated, in different ways, by the idea that male aggression and violence toward women is acceptable and often inevitable" (4). Where do you see examples of rape culture? How do small instances of aggression (sometimes called micro-aggressions) connect to physical and sexual violence?

6. In paragraph 16, Gay writes, " How do you write violence authentically without making it exploitative?" What is the connection between the two? Is it possible to use language to describe violence without exploitation? What is the writer's responsibility to the victims of such violence?

LANGUAGE IN ACTION

Graphic design student Emma Sulkowicz spent the last months of her senior year at Columbia University carrying a mattress everywhere she went on campus (see p. 459). She did so as a performance art piece titled "Carry That Weight," and as a public protest against the university's lack of attention to her reported rape, promising she would carry it until her alleged rapist was expelled. She even carried it at graduation, though Columbia administrators made it clear they wanted her to leave it out of the ceremonies.

If you were to put Sulkowicz's protest into words, what might those words be? Why do you think she choose a visual, physical protest, and what statements do the details of her protest make? Why a mattress? Why *carry* it, and for so many months? Sulkowicz urged other women to do the same, and many on campuses across the country took her up on the challenge. Why do you think others were convinced to join her? What points from Gay's article shed light on Sulkowicz's action, and how does Sulkowicz reinforce Gay's argument?

WRITING SUGGESTIONS

1. Gay points out that we often gloss over the lasting effects of rape, saying "We allow ourselves [to believe] that rape can be washed away as neatly as it is on TV and in the movies where the trajectory of victimhood is neatly defined" (13). What other experiences are given too neat a trajectory in typical media portrayals? Where else do we shy away from the complicated and long-lasting effects of trauma? Write an essay about a specific movie or television portrayal of a traumatic experience (rape, war, terrorist attack, serious injury, etc.) and analyze the portrayal of the victim. To what extent is the person's "trajectory

Source: Andrew Burton/Staff/Getty Images

of victimhood" made too neat? Which experiences are emphasized, and which are minimized? Why?

2. Write an essay in which you examine the use of euphemism to cover the unpleasant physical realities of violence in all its forms, including rape, assault, and murder. Investigate the role of language in creating or manipulating language to convey a desired impression. What terms do we rely on when describing violence? What do we shy away from discussing explicitly, and why? Are there ever good reasons for using such euphemisms?

Happy Feminist

CHIMAMANDA NGOZI ADICHIE

Chimamanda Ngozi Adichie was born in 1977 in Nigeria, where she was raised in the house formerly occupied by famous Nigerian writer Chinua Achebe. Her father, the country's first professor of statistics, taught at the University of Nigeria, and her mother was the first female registrar at the university. Adichie excelled in her studies of medicine and pharmacy while also editing the *Compass,* a magazine published by the university's Catholic medical students. Eventually, she left Nigeria for the United States to study at Drexel University in Philadelphia, transferring later to Eastern Connecticut University. After her graduation, she earned a master's degree in Creative Writing from Johns Hopkins University. As an undergraduate, she began working on her first novel, *Purple Hibiscus,* which was released late in 2003 to great critical acclaim, winning the Commonwealth Writer's Prize for Best First Book in 2005. She has also written *Half of a Yellow Sun* (2006), *The Thing Around Your Neck* (2009), and *Americanah* (2013). She has received numerous awards and recognitions, including a MacArthur Foundation "Genius" grant in 2008. Her writing displays a strong sense of humor and strength, and she has said, "I didn't choose writing, writing chose me." She is a popular writer, educator, and speaker. For Adichie, writing fiction is a way "to turn fact into truth."

In this essay, Adichie speaks about the negative connotations surrounding the word "feminist." She speaks of the importance of confronting directly the oppression of women and the role that gender plays in society. She does so with her typical humor and charm, but she also makes a strong case that "culture is not people, people are culture," and that we must do more to improve the position of women in our culture.

WRITING TO DISCOVER: *Think of important women you have known in your life. They could include your mother, sister, friend, teacher, partner, or any other woman. Which of those women would you describe as feminists? Why or why not? Be specific in your response. Are your associations with the word "feminist" positive or negative? What do you think is behind those associations?*

In 2003, I wrote a novel called *Purple Hibiscus,* about a man who, among other things, beats his wife, and whose story doesn't end too well. While I was promoting the novel in Nigeria, a journalist, a nice, well-meaning man, told me he wanted to advise me. (Nigerians, as you might know, are very quick to give unsolicited advice.) He told me that people were saying my novel was feminist, and his advice to me—he was shaking his head sadly as he spoke—was that I should never call myself a feminist, since feminists are women who are unhappy because they cannot find husbands.

So I decided to call myself a Happy Feminist.

Then an academic, a Nigerian woman, told me that feminism was not our culture, that feminism was un-African and I was only calling myself a feminist because I had been influenced by western books. (Which amused me, because much of my early reading was decidedly unfeminist: I must have read every single Mills & Boon romance published before I was 16. And each time I try to read those books called "classic feminist texts," I get bored, and I struggle to finish them.)

But it is time we should begin to dream about and plan for a different world. A fairer world. A world of happier men and women who are truer to themselves.

Anyway, since feminism was un-African, I decided I would now call myself a Happy African Feminist. Then a dear friend told me that calling myself a feminist meant that I hated men. So I decided I would now be a Happy African Feminist Who Does Not Hate Men. At some point I was a Happy African Feminist Who Does Not Hate Men And Who Likes To Wear Lip Gloss And High Heels For Herself And Not For Men.

Gender matters everywhere in the world. But it is time we should   5
begin to dream about and plan for a different world. A fairer world. A world of happier men and happier women who are truer to themselves.

Gender is not an easy conversation to have. It makes people uncomfortable, sometimes even irritable. Both men and women are resistant to talk about gender, or are quick to dismiss the problems of gender. Because thinking of changing the status quo is always uncomfortable.

Some people ask, "Why the word *feminist*? Why not just say you are a believer in human rights, or something like that?" Because that would be dishonest. Feminism is, of course, part of human rights in general—but to choose to use the vague expression *human rights* is to deny the specific and particular problem of gender. It would be a way of pretending that it was not women who have, for centuries, been excluded. It would be a way of denying that the problem of gender targets women. That the problem was not about being human, but specifically about being a female human. For centuries, the world divided human beings into two groups and then proceeded to exclude and oppress one group. It is only fair that the solution to the problem should acknowledge that.

Some men feel threatened by the idea of feminism. This comes, I think, from the insecurity triggered by how boys are brought up, how their sense of self-worth is diminished if they are not "naturally" in charge as men.

Other men might respond by saying, "Okay, this is interesting, but I don't think like that. I don't even think about gender."

Maybe not.   10

And that is part of the problem. That many men do not *actively* think about gender or notice gender. That many men say that things might have been bad in the past but everything is fine now. And that many men do nothing to change it. If you are a man and you walk into a restaurant and the waiter greets just you, does it occur to you to ask the waiter, "Why have you not greeted her?" Men need to speak out in all of these ostensibly small situations.

Because gender can be uncomfortable, there are easy ways to close this conversation. Some people will bring up evolutionary biology and apes, how female apes bow to male apes—that sort of thing. But the point is this: we are not apes. Apes also live in trees and eat earthworms. We do not. Some people will say, "Well, poor men also have a hard time." And they do.

But that is not what this conversation is about. Gender and class are different. Poor men still have the privileges of being men, even if they do not have the privileges of being wealthy. I learned a lot about systems of oppression and how they can be blind to one another by talking to black men. I was once talking about gender and a man said to me, "Why does it have to be you as a woman? Why not you as a human being?" This type of question is a way of silencing a person's specific experiences. Of course I am a human being, but there are particular things that happen to me in the world because I am a woman. This same man, by the way, would often talk about his experience as a black man. (To which I should probably have responded, "Why not your experiences as a man or as a human being? Why a black man?")

So, no, this conversation is about gender. Some people will say, "Oh, but women have the real power: bottom power." (This is a Nigerian expression for a woman who uses her sexuality to get things from men.) But bottom power is not power at all, because the woman with bottom power is actually not powerful; she just has a good route to tap another person's power. And then what happens if the man is in a bad mood or sick or temporarily impotent?

Some people will say a woman is subordinate to men because it's our culture. But culture is constantly changing. I have beautiful twin nieces who are 15. If they had been born a hundred years ago, they would have been taken away and killed. Because a hundred years ago, Igbo culture considered the birth of twins to be an evil omen. Today that practice is unimaginable to all Igbo people. 15

What is the point of culture? Culture functions ultimately to ensure the preservation and continuity of a people. In my family, I am the child who is most interested in the story of who we are, in ancestral lands, in our tradition. My brothers are not as interested as I am. But I cannot participate, because Igbo culture privileges men, and only the male members of the extended family can attend the meetings where major family decisions are taken. So although I am the one who is most interested in these things, I cannot attend the meeting. I cannot have a formal say. Because I am female.

Culture does not make people. People make culture. If it is true that the full humanity of women is not our culture, then we can and must make it our culture.

My great-grandmother, from stories I've heard, was a feminist. She ran away from the house of the man she did not want to marry and married the man of her choice. She refused, protested, spoke up whenever she felt she was being deprived of land and access because she was female. She did not know that word *feminist*. But it doesn't mean she wasn't one. More of us should reclaim that word. My own definition of a feminist is a man or a woman who says, "Yes, there's a problem with gender as it is today and we must fix it, we must do better."

All of us, women and men, must do better.

THINKING CRITICALLY ABOUT THE READING

1. Adichie opens her speech with a story about a man who advises her not to identify herself as a feminist. What does he see as the danger behind the word "feminist"?

2. What is the point of Adichie calling herself a "Happy Feminist" (2)? Why does she proceed to refer to herself as a "Happy African Feminist Who Does Not Hate Men And Who Likes To Wear Lip Gloss And High Heels For Herself And Not For Men" (4)? What point is she making overall about her identity as a feminist? About others' expectations of her as a woman and as a feminist?

3. What is the importance of the distinction that Adichie makes between "human rights" (7) and women's rights specifically?

4. Adichie says that many men "feel threatened by the idea of feminism" (8). Why is this so? Note that she uses the word "idea." How is the actual reality of feminism different than what many might imagine? Be specific in your response.

5. Adichie talks about the "blindness" of systems of oppression (13). What does she mean by this? In what ways does oppression by gender follow the same processes as other types of oppression, such as that based on race or class? In what ways might they be different?

6. Adichie states, "Culture does not make people. People make culture" (17). Do you agree with her? Why or why not?

7. How does the use of humor help Adichie to advance her points? In particular, how does Adichie's tone in this essay refute some of the ideas she encounters about feminists? Point to specific lines when possible.

LANGUAGE IN ACTION

At a 2014 United Nations event for the HeForShe Campaign, Emma Watson, the actor who played Hermione Granger in the Harry Potter films, gave a speech. She spoke in her capacity as U.N. Women Goodwill Ambassador about how her identification with the word "feminist" developed and the pushback she experienced as she decided to adopt it for herself. Consider the excerpt below. (You can find her full speech online.)

> I am from Britain and think it is right that as a woman I am paid the same as my male counterparts. I think it is right that I should be able to make decisions about my own body. I think it is right that women be involved on my behalf in the policies and decision-making of my country. I think it is right that socially I am afforded the same respect as men. But sadly I can say that there is no one country in the world where all women can expect to receive these rights.
>
> No country in the world can yet say they have achieved gender equality.
>
> These rights I consider to be human rights but I am one of the lucky ones. My life is a sheer privilege because my parents didn't love me less because I was born a daughter. My school did not limit me because I was a girl. My mentors didn't assume I would go less far because I might give birth to a child one day. These influencers were the gender equality ambassadors that made me who I am today. They may not know it, but they are the inadvertent feminists who are changing the world today. And we need more of those.

What does Watson's story have in common with Adichie's experience? Why do you think there is so much opposition to the term "feminist"? Do you think you might be what Watson calls an "inadvertent feminist," or do you know anyone who is? Is the term important, if it's possible to advocate for women without connecting one's actions or identity to the word specifically? Why or why not?

WRITING SUGGESTIONS

1. Write an essay in which you examine how language has been used to manipulate attitudes towards women. For instance, describe how slanted or biased language promotes or argues against measures that ensure equality for women, or against the goals of feminists. Be sure to include specific examples.

2. A key idea in Adichie's essay is that not only will women benefit from feminism, but men will, too. Consider the points she makes within her speech about gender roles that men are forced to conform to, and how feminism will free men as well as women from stereotypical gendered expectations. Write an essay in which you show how men will or will not benefit from feminism. You may wish to watch Adichie's entire speech online, called "We Should All Be Feminists," on TED Talks to get a fuller understanding of her argument.

The Social Harms of "Bitch"

SHERRYL KLEINMAN, MATTHEW B. EZZELL, AND A. COREY FROST

Sherryl Kleinman is a professor of sociology at the University of North Carolina at Chapel Hill, where she has been teaching since 1980. Her research focuses on gender and identity and often takes a feminist approach. In addition to scholarly articles, Kleinman has published personal essays and creative nonfiction. Matthew B. Ezzell graduated from University of North Carolina at Chapel Hill with an undergraduate degree in women's studies. After working as a rape crisis counselor and community educator, he returned to UNC for his PhD in sociology. He is currently an associate professor at James Madison University, where he does research on masculinity and teaches courses on the sociology of race, ethnicity, and gender. A. Corey Frost received his B.A. in sociology at the University of North Carolina at Chapel Hill in 2008. He studied with Sherryl Kleinman and served as an undergraduate teaching assistant in her "Sex and Gender in Society" course. Frost worked as a public health researcher for several years before entering the University of North Carolina School of Law, where he will graduate this year.

The reading below comes from a longer article Kleinman, Ezzell, and Frost co-authored and published in 2009 in the journal *Sociological Analysis*. In this excerpt, the authors discuss how the epithet "bitch" is used to express dominance over a person or object. They analyze how some have recently attempted to "reclaim" the term in popular culture and question whether it is possible to endow a sexist term with a positive connotation.

WRITING TO DISCOVER: *Make a list of words that you use that you associate with feminine characteristics. Then make a list of words that you use that you associate with masculine characteristics. Which group of words do you think convey more positive impressions? Why?*

We used to believe that feminists found the term "bitch" unacceptable. . . . Unlike "you guys," "bitch" is a slur; and there's no doubt that the word has a female referent, and a non-human one at that. Feminists knew that women could act in mean-spirited ways, but we also knew that using "bitch" to describe them reinforced sexism. If women liked the feel of "bitch" in their mouths more than "jerk," feminists analyzed that preference as internalized oppression, whereby members of an oppressed group learn to enjoy using the dominant group's term for them. And the pleasure of saying "bitch" keeps women from building solidarity, dividing

> As feminists taught us long ago, the personal is political; women who normalize "bitch" also normalize sexism.

them, as so many other words do, into good women and bad women. Yet, in the last several years, we've heard "bitch" used increasingly among college students, including women who affectionately greet one another with "Hey, bitches, how're you doing?" And this includes women who call themselves feminists. . . .

Despite anyone's intentions, putting "bitches" into the atmosphere, over and again, sends the message that it is acceptable for men to use the term. After all, members of the oppressed group are using it to describe themselves! Even in the case of "nigger," a word considered so vile that jobs have been lost by white people who use it among themselves, there are some whites who have used it among black people (especially black men) after hearing blacks use it with each other in a friendly way (Kennedy 2002). Most white people know better than to do so, or at least fear the consequences of using it, especially if they are white men interacting with black men. Men calling each other on racist terms has the real threat of violence. "Bitch" is much more widely accepted—who uses euphemisms like the "B-word" or the "B-bomb"? And unlike the N-word, men don't worry that women who get upset with them for using "bitches" will react violently, so there is less incentive for men to drop it. By and large, women accept men's use of the term "bitch." A woman who is the target of "bitch" by a man might reject the application of the word to her, but not to other women. The rare woman who sarcastically says "thank you" in response to a man who calls her a bitch, still makes the word acceptable. She might say instead, "No, I'm a feminist."

We're convinced that women feel good when they say "Hey, bitches!" to their friends, just as women accept saying "you guys" and "freshman." But experiencing what we say or do as pleasurable does not make it harmless. The pleasure they derive from using the term, whether as a female generic or as the old-fashioned putdown ("She's a bitch!"), is an instance of false power (Kleinman et al. 2006). The person in the subordinate group may feel good about adopting an oppressive practice, but that feeling does not challenge an oppressive system. The pleasure, after all, is about enjoying the feel of dominance, something that systematically belongs to the privileged group.

"Bitch" is everywhere, so people have become desensitized to its harms, some even enjoying its use. Our point is not that these words are offensive (though they may offend some), but that they unintentionally hurt women as a group. That most people aren't bothered by them is disturbing, indicating that sexism is the water we swim in, and we are the fish who cannot see it. How can people be motivated to make change if nothing seems to be the matter? As one of us wrote (Kleinman 2000: 7), "If we [women] aren't even deserving of our place in humanity in language, why should we expect to be treated as human beings otherwise?"

False power can provide feelings of empowerment among members   5
of the oppressed group (in this case, women), the same feelings that

make it difficult for oppressed people to see their lack of empowerment in society. "Bitch," when uttered by women and girls, masks inequality, deflects attention from its harm, or provides meager compensation for sexism. And if a woman believes that "some" sexism exists, false power allows her to believe that other women might be dupes of sexism, but not her. After all, she can say "bitches" in a friendly way, or spit out "Bitch!" as well as a man. Sexist language, then, reinforces individual "solutions" (e.g., "sexy bitch") to social problems, which ultimately do not threaten the status quo.

The normalizing of bitch indicates the lack of imagination that results from living under conditions of entrenched inequalities. Why is "bitch" a preferred tool of women's empowerment? That women would rather call themselves or other women bitches—rather than feminists—suggests that domination and subordination have become the only legitimate options in U.S. society. Even if women who proclaim themselves "bitches" could be taken seriously, that would hardly be a feminist solution; we'd have women divided into the categories of "bitches" (honorary men) and "doormats" (all other women). Sound familiar?

A woman who enjoys the honorary status of man by using "bitch" may have fun with "the girls" or win temporary acceptance from "the guys." But this individual gain ultimately is part of a collective loss for women. That women use "bitch" reinforces the idea that women are essentially different from men, and in a negative way: men may act like jerks, but women are "bitches." And only men who act "like women" (members of the subordinate category) will be accused of "bitching." Women using men's pejoratives for women is flattering to men; at the same time, those terms legitimate sexist ideas about women.

We envision feminism as a movement in which women and male allies work together to end patriarchy. Our goal would be to replace it with a humane society in which "bitch"—and other terms that repro-duce sexism, and every other inequality—would become relics of our patriarchal past.

REFERENCES

Kennedy, Randall. 2002. *Nigger: The Strange Career of a Troublesome Word*. New York: Vintage.

Kleinman, Sherryl. 2000. "Why Sexist Language Matters," The Center Line, a Newsletter of the Orange County Rape Crisis Center, Sep-tember edition, 6–7.

_____, Martha Copp, and Kent Sandstrom. 2006. "Making Sexism Visible: Birdcages, Martians, and Pregnant Men," *Teaching Sociology* 34: 126–142.

THINKING CRITICALLY ABOUT READING

1. Kleinman, Ezzell, and Frost suggest that a woman who is called a "bitch" by a man might respond by saying, "No, I'm a feminist" (2). Do you think this is an appropriate response? Are the terms "bitch" and "feminist" opposites?

2. The article mentions the "false power" that some women feel when they reclaim the term "bitch" (5). Why is this power "false"? Do you agree with that this power is illusory?

3. In paragraph 2, the authors contrast the gendered epithet "bitch" with the racial epithet "nigger." Is this is an apt contrast? How are the terms similar, and how are they different?

4. The authors are disturbed that "bitch" is not considered universally offensive, arguing that "sexism is the water we swim in, and we are the fish who cannot see it" (4). What metaphor is being used here? Is it successful?

5. In the original article, Kleinman, Ezzell, and Frost discuss the roots of the epithet "bitch." ("Bitch" is the English word for a female dog, and it was used as early as the 1400s to insult a woman as sexually promiscuous.) Do the origins of the word matter when considering how it is used today? Why or why not? Language in Action

LANGUAGE IN ACTION

Read the following letter to the editor of the *New York Times*. In it Nancy Stevens, president of a small Manhattan advertising agency, argues against using the word "guys" to address women. How do you think Kleinman, Ezzell, and Frost would feel about it? At the end of their essay, the authors argue for replacing "terms that reproduce sexism—and every other inequality." Does "guys" fall into this category? What do our objections about language reveal about our perspective on gender?

WOMEN AREN'T GUYS

A young woman, a lawyer, strides into a conference room. Already in attendance, at what looks to be the start of a high-level meeting, are four smartly dressed women in their 20's and 30's. The arriving woman plunks her briefcase down at the head of the polished table and announces, "O.K., guys, let's get started."

On "Kate and Allie," a television show about two women living together with Kate's daughter and Allie's daughter and son, the dialogue often runs to such phrases as, "Hey, you guys, who wants pizza?" All of the people addressed are female, except for Chip, the young son. "Come on, you guys, quit fighting," pleads one of the daughters when there is a tiff between the two women.

Just when we were starting to be aware of the degree to which language affects people's perceptions of women and substitute "people working" for "men working" and "humankind" for "mankind," this "guy" thing happened. Just when people have started becoming aware that a 40 year old woman shouldn't be called a girl, this "guy" thing has crept in.

Use of "guy" to mean "person" is so insidious that I'll bet most women don't notice they are being called "guys," or, if they do, find it somehow flattering to be one of them.

Sometimes, I find the courage to pipe up when a bunch of us are assembled and are called "guys" by someone of either gender. "We're not guys," I say. Then everyone looks at me funny.

One day, arriving at a business meeting where there were five women and one man, I couldn't resist. "Hello, ladies," I said. Everyone laughed embarrassedly for the blushing man until I added, "and gent." Big sigh of relief. Wouldn't want to call a guy a "gal" now, would we?

Why is it not embarrassing for a woman to be called "guy"? We know why. It's the same logic that says women look sexy and cute in a man's shirt, but did you ever try your silk blouse on your husband and send him to the deli? It's the same mentality that holds that anything male is worthy (and to be aspired toward) and anything female is trivial.

We all sit around responding, without blinking, "black with one sugar, please," when anyone asks, "How do you guys like your coffee?"

What's all that murmuring I hear?

"Come on, lighten up."

"Be a good guy."

"Nobody means anything by it."

Nonsense.

WRITING SUGGESTIONS

1. Write an essay in which you investigate the use of language in the depiction of both prominent male and female figures. You might look at popular news sources, talk shows, or political blogs and news feeds. What words are used to show approval of men? What words are used to show disapproval? What words show approval of women? What words show disapproval of women? What can you conclude from your research?

2. In the final paragraph, the authors conclude, "We envision feminism as a movement in which women and male allies work together to end patriarchy." Has this always been the approach of the feminist movement? Write an essay in which you research the history of feminism, and in particular, the role that "male allies" have played in advancing women's rights and equality.

11 Words You Need to Teach Your Son Before He Turns 6

JOANNA SCHROEDER

Joanna Schroeder was an executive editor and now serves as director of media relations for *The Good Men Project,* a Web site that "examines what it means to be a good man in today's society." She is also a writer whose work has appeared on *Redbook, Yahoo!, xoJane, MariaShriver.com,* and *TIME.com,* among others. She and her husband are outdoor sports enthusiasts raising very active sons. She describes herself as a "fervent feminist with an eye on men's issues."

In this article, published by *The Good Men Project* on January 15, 2015, Schroeder argues that young boys should be taught certain words in order to learn to accept certain values and behaviors that, in a society defined by rigid gender stereotypes, boys are seldom allowed to express. Schroeder looks at their development from boys to men, in that if young boys can be taught to embrace the words, so too can adult men, and their lives improved for it—as well as the lives of those around them.

WRITING TO DISCOVER: *Most of us have heard the expression "boys don't cry." But what else are boys not allowed to do? In your experience, what sorts of emotions, feelings, and problems are boys—and men—not allowed to express? What are some of the consequences of that stifled expression?*

Recently, while helping in my youngest son's art camp, I noticed one little boy falling behind the others and no longer participating.

> **I think it's crucial that we make a conscious choice to arm all of our kids with words that can give them important social skills or the ability to describe feelings.**

I touched his shoulder and pointed at the teacher, as a reminder to pay attention. He ignored me and looked around the room. A few minutes later, his head was down and he wasn't even trying.

I knelt in front of him and asked, "Why aren't you doing the project?" He started crying.

"Everyone's ahead. I can't do it now. It's too late."

Thing was, he *could* have done it. They were simple steps and all laid out in front of him. He also could've asked for help. But he shook his head and said he couldn't. He just couldn't.

"Oh," I said. "Do you feel overwhelmed?"

He looked at me funny and asked what "overwhelmed" means. When I explained that it's a feeling you get when there's so much happening and you just don't know where to start, so you sort of freeze up.

5

His eyes lit up. "Yes!" he said, and seemed excited that someone understood exactly how he felt.

When his mom arrived to pick him up, he ran to her and said, "I was overwhelmed today, but then I got all caught up." He shoved the craft into her hands and beamed. At that moment, it occurred to me how important it is for kids (and adults, too) to have a wide variety of words to describe feelings and situations.

As a parent, and someone who pays close attention to social issues   10 around gender, I think it's crucial that we make a conscious choice to arm all of our kids with words that can give them important social skills or the ability to describe feelings. This list is for parents of kids of any gender, but I am focusing a bit on what words boys need to know, so we can help them describe things we don't typically think of as manly or boyish.

1. LONELY

Loneliness often happens when you feel like nobody cares about you. As adults, we can often reason with ourselves about this feeling, but for a child it can be awfully hard to understand why people aren't giving us what we need, emotionally, at the moment we need it.

Your kid may be resisting bedtime and say that he gets scared or sad in his room. He may actually be scared, or just sad, or he may feel very alone. Maybe you watch TV on the couch after he goes to bed, or you and your spouse sleep in the same bed without him. Being excluded from those things could be a lonely feeling for a kid.

Once you understand the nature of his feelings, you can better explain that even though he's by himself in his bed, he's very much loved by his family and in the morning you can all be together again.

2. FRUSTRATED

It's not angry. It's not sad. It's something else, and young children feel this sensation regularly. Imagine having to follow every command of somebody else all the time, even when their demands feel illogical. How frustrating would it be to watch other kids get to do stuff you aren't allowed to do, just because of your size? These are the challenges kids face every day. And it's frustrating.

And yet most little kids don't know that word, so when they start   15 to feel that way, they can only define it as mad. I suspect that's why tantrums often look like little rage-fests. So get down to eye-level with your child and describe that frustration is when you get upset because you just can't seem to do what you want to do, and maybe you don't even know why you can't.

Try teaching them the word, explaining the definition, and asking them to say "I'm so frustrated!" next time. Once you understand, then you can walk him through the problem and help him solve it—or at least understand the "why."

3. INTIMIDATED

I remember arriving at a park to play with a bunch of our preschool buddies with my son and he turned and said, "I want to go home."

I'd driven thirty minutes to get there, and we weren't going home. I asked him why, and all he'd say was, "Because."

"Because what?"

Nothing.   20

Finally he said, "I'm scared."

There was nothing to be scared of, and I told him that, not realizing that I was invalidating his feelings at that moment. He was safe, he'd played there before, and I was right next to him.

Finally he explained that he felt like his friends were all together and he didn't know what they were playing. I realized then that he wasn't scared, he was intimidated. He felt unprepared and unworthy. Once I understood that, I was able to solve the problem. And once he knew the word, he used it frequently in situations like that.

4. THAT'S JUST NOT MY THING

This is a funny one, but it's something we've evolved in our family after a lot of trial and error.

Saying, "that's just not my thing," is a way for kids to back out of   25
socially-pressured situations without seeming like they're judging others or making a big deal out of something. This can be anything from, "Hey, why don't you play basketball with us at recess like the other guys?" to something that he or she's not ready to handle, like a roller coaster or a scary movie.

It can also be used to diffuse a dangerous or amoral situation like bullying or excessive risk-taking. Of course when kids are being cruel or harming someone (or themselves), you should empower your kid to stop or report them to a trusted grown-up, but he may also need an "out" for the situation that's handy in a pinch so he can take a moment to figure out how to proceed next.

5. HANGRY

Things we know about kids: They act out and get more emotional when they're hungry. But oftentimes, they don't realize they're hungry! They just feel mad, and will tell you that in no uncertain terms!

We joke about the word "hangry" with our kids, but it's a useful term because hungry anger is a pretty specific feeling, and having a word for it may help your kid feel empowered to explain exactly what he or she is feeling, and remind them to stop and eat a nutritious snack like a string cheese or some almonds, that will help stabilize his or her blood sugar *and* mood.

6-8. PROPER NAMES FOR THEIR BODY PARTS

Specifically: Penis, Vagina (or vulva), and anus.

I know, there's nothing cute or fun about talking about the accurate   30 terminology for body parts, but it's necessary. Being able to accurately describe parts of our own bodies empowers us to speak openly and honestly about them. Using these terms without shame teaches our kids that they can come to us with questions or concerns, and this is important for their health and their emotional development.

By not using cutesy terms, we raise kids who are empowered about their own bodies. We can then discuss that their genitals are their own private business, and that nobody gets to touch them without permission. Likewise, we don't touch other people's genitals or make people feel uncomfortable.

Christopher Anderson, Executive Director of MaleSurvivor.org—an advocacy and support group for men and boys (and their loved ones) who have been sexually abused—explains further why accurate terminology is important:

> Many child protection experts strongly urge parents to empower children with the proper terminology for all body parts. Doing so can greatly improve a child's understanding of their own bodies, which can in turn improve their self-image and confidence. Confident, well-educated children are also less at risk for abuse, especially sexual abuse, at the hands of perpetrators who often seek out children who are more vulnerable and less informed.

This is, of course, part of a much larger conversation, but it's one that can help prevent your child from being abused or abusing others. This conversation has to start at age 1 and continue into their college years. For more specific instructions, see *The Healthy Sex Talk, Teaching Consent Ages 1-21*, which I co-authored.

I want to note that I think following your child's lead in what they call   35 their genitals is okay, as long as they are clear on the technical terms too.

I wouldn't stop a boy from calling his penis a "weenie" or something, as long as it was very clear he knew the word penis was accurate and totally fine to say, as well.

9. TOUCHED-OUT

This term has become synonymous with new parents who have babies climbing all over them all the time, but it's useful in a lot of different ways, too.

Sometimes, as a parent, you just feel like you need some personal space. Maybe you're in a bad mood, or maybe you have had a baby on you all day long. Regardless, it's okay to lovingly tell someone — even your own child — that you're feeling "touched out" and would like a little time where nobody is touching you. Reassure him or her that pretty soon you'll feel like snuggling or wrestling again, but for now you need everyone to honor your "space bubble." I always use my hands to show my kids how far around me my space bubble is, and ask them not to pop it.

Not only are you teaching them to honor others' bodily autonomy, but if you also offer this as an option for your child, then you're empowering him or her to say "no" to touching, even loving or innocent touch. If his little brother or sister is poking him or trying to snuggle, then he can say to you or them, "I feel touched out" and you can help advocate for his personal space.

10. OVERWHELMED

I talked about this at the beginning, but I want to underline the way I see this word helping kids, especially boys, in classroom settings.

Often, when we see a kid drifting or fidgeting in class we may default 40 (even if only subconsciously) to assuming that the kid has an attention issue or just doesn't care about school.

But what if there's another issue? What if he really wants to engage but is overwhelmed because he's behind, or because he can't hear the teacher, has a distraction, or see the board well? I really do think this feeling-word could be of great service in young elementary school classrooms.

11. MAY I PLEASE ...?

At the top of my list of things kids do that drive me crazy is when kids make demands. It drives me absolutely bonkers to hear a kid say, "Get me some milk" or "Give me that toy." I know kids are naturally very selfish creatures, and being demanding is a part of development, but part of teaching your child empathy is asking them to consider how it feels to have someone demand something from them.

"Dad, may I please have a glass of milk?" or "Mom, could you please get me the Lego bin?" are questions that require your child to consider how you feel, what you're doing, and how their request might affect you. If my arms are full of groceries, I hope my sons will see that and not tell me at that exact moment to open the door for them. But if we don't teach them to ask people for things nicely, they may not learn to consider the feelings of the person they're imposing upon.

And trust me, your child's teacher will appreciate the good habit.

Becoming comfortable with asking for things with respect, as well as   45
learning to be kind and gracious when someone says "no" are lessons that will carry forward into their lives as older kids, too, especially when they start dating.

THINKING CRITICALLY ABOUT THE READING

1. What kind of pressure did the young boy at the start of the article feel that caused him to stop working and burst into tears? How did the author's use of language help change the boy's understanding of and attitude towards his problem?

2. As you look over Schroeder's list of words and phrases, are there any that you disagree with? Why or why not? Are there any you would add? What emotions did you experience as a kid that you didn't have the right words for? How would it have helped you to have those words?

3. The fourth item on Schroeder's list is a phrase: "That's just not my thing." In your opinion, are children under six old enough to understand the concepts she's speaking about, such as peer-pressure or bullying? Or, is this advice that might be more appropriate for older children? Defend your answer.

4. Schroeder's list collects words to teach sons. How many words can you think of that we ought to teach daughters? Or how might you recast some of Schroeder's words for daughters instead of sons? Do you think we need to teach different words to boys and girls at all?

5. Were you uncomfortable with the naming of the body parts in items 6 through 8? What value is there in using the proper terms rather than euphemisms that parents in past generations used with their children?

6. The term "touched-out" is unusual in that it's designed as a term for parents to use when speaking with their children. Did you find this term odd or strange? Especially if you have young children of your own, or you're around young children, do you find this to be a useful term? Have you ever experienced the kind of feeling that Schroeder describes as being "touched-out"?

7. The phrase in item 11 seems almost old-fashioned in its proper use of "may" as in "May I please . . . ?" How does the author defend her inclusion of this phrase on her list? Do you find her reasoning convincing or not? Explain.

LANGUAGE IN ACTION

In an article titled "10 Simple Words Every Girl Should Learn," writer and activist Soraya Chemaly states,

> People often ask me what to teach girls or what they themselves can do. "What can I do if I encounter sexism? It's hard to say anything, especially at school." I tell them to practice these words, every day:
> "Stop interrupting me," "I just said that," and "No explanation needed."
> It will do both boys and girls a world of good.

What is your reaction to this list? What do you think prompted Chemaly to create it? How would you compare it to Schroeder's? Do you agree that using the phrases Chemaly sets forth will benefit both boys and girls? Why or why not?

WRITING SUGGESTIONS

1. Write an essay in which you examine the ability of language not simply to convey reality but to shape reality. You may wish to refer not only to this essay, but also to William Lutz's "The World of Doublespeak" (p. 277) or George Orwell's "Politics and the English Language" (searchable online), among others. How does the language we use shape our world?

2. The acquisition of a native language by children can be fascinating. (Note that Steven Pinker, who wrote "Good Writing" on p. 208, has studied and written about children's language acquisition.) Do some research of your own on how children acquire language, and how the words they hear and speak can form their resulting attitudes towards the world. Write an essay in which you argue for or against Schroeder's premise that words and phrases can be taught to young children to alter not only their behavior but also their self-image.

"Bros Before Hos": The Guy Code

MICHAEL KIMMEL

Michael Kimmel has an international reputation as a researcher, lecturer, and writer on men and masculinity. Born in 1951, he earned his B.A. with distinction from Vassar College in 1972, his M.A. from Brown University in 1974, and his Ph.D. from the University of California, Berkeley, in 1981. Among his many published works are *Changing Men: New Directions in Research on Men and Masculinity* (1987), *Men Confront Pornography* (1990), *Manhood in America: A Cultural History* (1996), *The Gendered Society* (2nd ed., 2003), *The History of Men: Essays on American and British Masculinities* (2005), and *The Gender of Desire: Essays on Masculinity and Sexuality* (2005). Kimmel has taught at Bryant University, New York University, Rutgers University, the University of Oslo, and at Stony Brook University where he is presently Distinguished Professor of Sociology.

In "'Bros Before Hos': The Guy Code," taken from his book *Guyland: The Perilous World Where Boys Become Men* (2008), Kimmel defines the term "Guy Code" as a "collection of attitudes, values, and traits that together composes what it means to be a man" in American society today. Notice how language is skillfully utilized to encourage compliance with the code by its members and to discourage wandering from its demands by any independent thinkers.

WRITING TO DISCOVER: *Think about the groups that you belong to and how language has been used to unify its members and to characterize those who either do not belong or fail to conform to its requirements.*

Whenever I ask young women what they think it means to be a woman, they look at me puzzled, and say, basically, "Whatever I want." "It doesn't mean anything at all to me," says Nicole, a junior at Colby College in Maine. "I can be Mia Hamm, I can be Britney Spears, I can be Madame Curie or Madonna. Nobody can tell me what it means to be a woman anymore."

For men, the question is still meaningful — and powerful. In countless workshops on college campuses and in high-school assemblies, I've asked young men what it means to be a man. I've asked guys from every state in the nation, as well as about fifteen other countries, what sorts of phrases and words come to mind when they hear someone say, "Be a man!"

The responses are rather predictable. The first thing someone usually says is "Don't cry," then other similar phrases and ideas — never show your feelings, never ask for directions, never give up, never give in, be strong, be aggressive, show no fear, show no mercy, get rich, get even, get laid, win — follow easily after that.

477

Here's what guys say, summarized into a set of current epigrams. Think of it as a "Real Guy's Top Ten List."

1. "Boys Don't Cry"
2. "It's Better to Be Mad than Sad"
3. "Don't Get Mad—Get Even"
4. "Take It Like a Man"
5. "He Who Has the Most Toys When He Dies, Wins"
6. "Just Do It," or "Ride or Die"
7. "Size Matters"
8. "I Don't Stop to Ask for Directions"
9. "Nice Guys Finish Last"
10. "It's All Good"

The unifying emotional subtext of all these aphorisms involves never   5
showing emotions or admitting to weakness. The face you must show to the world insists that everything is going just fine, that everything is under control, that there's nothing to be concerned about (a contemporary version of Alfred E. Neuman of *MAD* Magazine's "What, me worry?"). Winning is crucial, especially when the victory is over other men who have less amazing or smaller toys. Kindness is not an option, nor is compassion. Those sentiments are taboo.

This is "The Guy Code," the collection of attitudes, values, and traits that together composes what it means to be a man. These are the rules that govern behavior in Guyland, the criteria that will be used to evaluate whether any particular guy measures up. The Guy Code revisits what psychologist William Pollack called "the boy code" in his bestselling book *Real Boys*—just a couple of years older and with a lot more at stake. And just as Pollack and others have explored the dynamics of boyhood so well, we now need to extend the reach of that analysis to include late adolescence and young adulthood.

In 1976, social psychologist Robert Brannon summarized the four basic rules of masculinity:

1. "No Sissy Stuff!" Being a man means not being a sissy, not being perceived as weak, effeminate, or gay. Masculinity is the relentless repudiation of the feminine.
2. "Be a Big Wheel." This rule refers to the centrality of success and power in the definition of masculinity. Masculinity is measured more by wealth, power, and status than by any particular body part.
3. "Be a Sturdy Oak." What makes a man is that he is reliable in a crisis. And what makes him so reliable in a crisis is not that he is able to respond fully and appropriately to the situation at hand, but rather that he resembles an inanimate object. A rock, a pillar, a species of tree.

4. "Give 'em Hell." Exude an aura of daring and aggression. Live life out on the edge. Take risks. Go for it. Pay no attention to what others think.

Amazingly, these four rules have changed very little among successive generations of high-school and college-age men. James O'Neil, a developmental psychologist at the University of Connecticut, and Joseph Pleck, a social psychologist at the University of Illinois, have each been conducting studies of this normative definition of masculinity for decades. "One of the most surprising findings," O'Neil told me, "is how little these rules have changed."

BEING A MAN AMONG MEN

Where do young men get these ideas? "Oh, definitely, my dad," says Mike, a 20-year-old sophomore at Wake Forest. "He was always riding my ass, telling me I had to be tough and strong to make it in this world."

"My older brothers were always on my case," says Drew, a 24-year-old   10
University of Massachusetts grad. "They were like, always ragging on me, calling me a pussy, if I didn't want to play football or wrestle. If I just wanted to hang out and like play my Xbox, they were constantly in my face."

"It was subtle, sometimes," says Warren, a 21-year-old at Towson, "and other times really out front. In school, it was the male teachers, saying stuff about how explorers or scientists were so courageous and braving the elements and all that. Then, other times, it was phys-ed class, and everyone was all over everyone else talking about 'He's so gay' and 'He's a wuss.'"

"The first thing I think of is my coach," says Don, a 26-year-old former football player at Lehigh. "Any fatigue, any weakness, any sign that being hit actually hurt and he was like 'Waah! [fake crying] Widdle Donny got a boo boo. Should we kiss it guys?' He'd completely humiliate us for showing anything but complete toughness. I'm sure he thought he was building up our strength and ability to play, but it wore me out trying to pretend all the time, to suck it up and just take it."

The response was consistent: Guys hear the voices of the men in their lives—fathers, coaches, brothers, grandfathers, uncles, priests—to inform their ideas of masculinity.

This is no longer surprising to me. One of the more startling things I found when I researched the history of the idea of masculinity in America for a previous book was that men subscribe to these ideals not because they want to impress women, let alone any inner drive or desire to test themselves against some abstract standards. They do it because they want to be positively evaluated by other men. American men want to be a "man among men," an Arnold Schwarzenegger-like "man's man," not a Fabio-like "ladies' man." Masculinity is largely a "homosocial" experience: performed for, and judged by, other men.

Noted playwright David Mamet explains why women don't even   15
enter the mix. "Women have, in men's minds, such a low place on the social ladder of this country that it's useless to define yourself in terms of a woman. What men need is men's approval." While women often become a kind of currency by which men negotiate their status with other men, women are for possessing, not for emulating.

THE GENDER POLICE

Other guys constantly watch how well we perform. Our peers are a kind of "gender police," always waiting for us to screw up so they can give us a ticket for crossing the well-drawn boundaries of manhood. As young men, we become relentless cowboys, riding the fences, checking the boundary line between masculinity and femininity, making sure that nothing slips over. The possibilities of being unmasked are everywhere. Even the most seemingly insignificant misstep can pose a threat or activate that haunting terror that we will be found out.

On the day the students in my class "Sociology of Masculinity" were scheduled to discuss homophobia, one student provided an honest and revealing anecdote. Noting that it was a beautiful day, the first day of spring after a particularly brutal Northeast winter, he decided to wear shorts to class. "I had this really nice pair of new Madras shorts," he recounted. "But then I thought to myself, these shorts have lavender and pink in them. Today's class topic is homophobia. Maybe today is not the best day to wear these shorts." Nods all around.

Our efforts to maintain a manly front cover everything we do. What we wear. How we talk. How we walk. What we eat (like the recent flap over "manwiches"—those artery-clogging massive burgers, dripping with extras). Every mannerism, every movement contains a coded gender language. What happens if you refuse or resist? What happens if you step outside the definition of masculinity? Consider the words that would be used to describe you. In workshops it generally takes less than a minute to get a list of about twenty terms that are at the tip of everyone's tongues: wimp, faggot, dork, pussy, loser, wuss, nerd, queer, homo, girl, gay, skirt, Mama's boy, pussy-whipped. This list is so effortlessly generated, so consistent, that it composes a national well from which to draw epithets and put-downs.

Ask any teenager in America what is the most common put-down in middle school or high school? The answer: "That's so gay." It's said about anything and everything—their clothes, their books, the music or TV shows they like, the sports figures they admire. "That's so gay" has become a free floating put down, meaning bad, dumb, stupid, wrong. It's the generic bad thing.

Listen to one of America's most observant analysts of masculinity,   20
Eminem. Asked in an MTV interview in 2001 why he constantly used "faggot" in every one of his raps to put down other guys, Eminem told the interviewer, Kurt Loder,

> The lowest degrading thing you can say to a man when you're battling him is to call him a faggot and try to take away his manhood. Call him a sissy, call him a punk. "Faggot" to me doesn't necessarily mean gay people. "Faggot" to me just means taking away your manhood.

But does it mean homosexuality? Does it really suggest that you suspect the object of the epithet might actually be attracted to another guy? Think, for example, of how you would answer this question: If you see a man walking down the street, or meet him at a party, how do you "know" if he is homosexual? (Assume that he is not wearing a T-shirt with a big pink triangle on it, and that he's not already holding hands with another man.)

When I ask this question in classes or workshops, respondents invariably provide a standard list of stereotypically effeminate behaviors. He walks a certain way, talks a certain way, acts a certain way. He's well dressed, sensitive, and emotionally expressive. He has certain tastes in art and music—indeed, he has *any* taste in art and music! Men tend to focus on the physical attributes, women on the emotional. Women say they "suspect" a man might be gay if he's interested in what she's talking about, knows something about what she's talking about, or is sensitive and a good listener. One recently said, "I suspect he might be gay if he's looking at my eyes, and not down my blouse." Another said she suspects he might be gay if he shows no sexual interest in her, if he doesn't immediately come on to her.

Every mannerism, every movement contains a coded gender language.

Once I've established what makes a guy "suspect," I ask the men in the room if any of them would want to be thought of as gay. Rarely does a hand go up—despite the fact that this list of attributes is actually far preferable to the restrictive one that stands in the "Be a Man" box. So, what do straight men do to make sure that no one gets the wrong idea about them?

Everything that is perceived as gay goes into what we might call the Negative Playbook of Guyland. Avoid everything in it and you'll be all right. Just make sure that you walk, talk, and act in a different way from the gay stereotype; dress terribly; show no taste in art or music; show no emotions at all. Never listen to a thing a woman is saying, but express immediate and unquenchable sexual interest. Presto, you're a real man, back in the "Be a Man" box. Homophobia—the fear that people might *misperceive* you as gay—is the animating fear of American guys' masculinity. It's what lies underneath the crazy risk-taking behaviors practiced by boys of all ages, what drives the fear that other guys will see you as weak, unmanly, frightened. The single cardinal rule of manhood, the one from which all the other characteristics—wealth, power, status, strength, physicality—are derived is to offer constant proof that you are not gay.

Homophobia is even deeper than this. It's the fear *of* other men—that   25
other men will perceive you as a failure, as a fraud. It's a fear that others will see you as weak, unmanly, frightened. This is how John Steinbeck put it in his novel *Of Mice and Men*:

> "Funny thing," [Curley's wife] said. "If I catch any one man, and he's alone, I get along fine with him. But just let two of the guys get together an' you won't talk. Jus' nothin' but mad." She dropped her fingers and put her hands on her hips. "You're all scared of each other, that's what. Ever'one of you's scared the rest is goin' to get something on you."

In that sense, homosexuality becomes a kind of shorthand for "unmanliness"—and the homophobia that defines and animates the daily conversations of Guyland is at least as much about masculinity as it is about sexuality.

But what would happen to a young man if he were to refuse such limiting parameters on who he is and how he's permitted to act? "It's not like I want to stay in that box," says Jeff, a first-year Cornell student at my workshop. "But as soon as you step outside it, even for a second, all the other guys are like, 'What are you, dude, a fag?' It's not very safe out there on your own. I suppose as I get older, I'll get more secure, and feel like I couldn't care less what other guys say. But now, in my fraternity, on this campus, man, I'd lose everything."

The consistency of responses is as arresting as the list is disturbing: "I would lose my friends." "Get beat up." "I'd be ostracized." "Lose my self-esteem." Some say they'd take drugs or drink. Become withdrawn, sullen, a loner, depressed. "Kill myself," says one guy. "Kill them," responds another. Everyone laughs, nervously. Some say they'd get mad. And some say they'd get even. "I dunno," replied Mike, a sophomore at Portland State University. "I'd probably pull a Columbine. I'd show them that they couldn't get away with calling me that shit."

Guys know that they risk everything—their friendships, their sense of self, maybe even their lives—if they fail to conform. Since the stakes are so enormous, young men take huge chances to prove their manhood, exposing themselves to health risks, workplace hazards, and stress-related illnesses. Here's a revealing factoid. Men ages 19 to 29 are three times less likely to wear seat belts than women the same age. Before they turn nineteen though, young men are actually *more* likely to wear seat belts. It's as if they suddenly get the idea that as long as they're driving the car, they're completely in control, and therefore safe. Ninety percent of all driving offenses, excluding parking violations, are committed by men, and 93 percent of road ragers are male. Safety is emasculating! So they drink too much, drive too fast, and play chicken in a multitude of dangerous venues.

The comments above provide a telling riposte to all those theories of   30
biology that claim that this definition of masculinity is "hard-wired," the result of millennia of evolutionary adaptation or the behavioral response to waves of aggression-producing testosterone, and therefore inevitable. What these theories fail to account for is the way that masculinity is coerced and policed relentlessly by other guys. If it were biological, it would be as natural as breathing or blinking. In truth, the Guy Code fits as comfortably as a straightjacket.

THINKING CRITICALLY ABOUT THE READING

1. In your own words what is the "Guy Code"? Do you believe it actually exists? Explain.

2. How is language used to support the Guy Code and ward off threats to it?

3. If you are a man, what are the consequences of violating the Guy Code?

4. According to Kimmel, is the Guy Code hard-wired into us biologically or do we create it ourselves? Why is the question and how we answer it important?

5. What does Kimmel mean when he writes in paragraph 26, "In that sense, homosexuality becomes a kind of shorthand for 'unmanliness'—and the homophobia that defines and animates the daily conversations of Guyland is at least as much about masculinity as it is about sexuality"?

6. How appropriate is Kimmel's title?

LANGUAGE IN ACTION

In an essay entitled "The Common Guy" written by Audrey Bilger and published in 2002 in the feminist publication *Bitch Magazine,* she argues that women need to stop referring to groups of two or more women as "guys." Here is what Bilger has to say in the next to last paragraph of her essay:

> Most of us have probably had the experience of pointing out some type of sexist expression or behavior to acquaintances and being accused of being "too sensitive" or "too pc" and told to "lighten up." It's certainly easier just to go along with things, to avoid making people uncomfortable, to accept what we think will do no harm. If you feel this way about "you guys," you might want to consider Alice Walker's view of the expression: "I see in its use some women's obsequious need to be accepted, at any cost, even at the cost of erasing their own femaleness, and that of other women. Isn't it at least ironic that after so many years of struggle for women's liberation, women should end up calling themselves this?"

What relationship, if any, do you see between how Kimmel has characterized "Guyland" and its inhabitants and what Bilger and Alice Walker find so wrong with referring to groups of women as "guys"? Has your opinion about the use of the term changed as a result of your reading of both Kimmel and Bilger? If so, how?

WRITING SUGGESTIONS

1. Write an essay in which you describe your own experiences in growing into manhood—or growing up around men. Has Kimmel opened your eyes to what you are experiencing or observing but perhaps not realizing? Do the examples he uses to support his argument sound familiar? What examples and insights of your own can you add? Of course, even more interesting is a thesis to the contrary, one in which you paint an entirely different, perhaps more benign, picture of what it means to be a man. Most important is the role language plays in either approach to manhood. Be sure to use examples of the kind of language involved in the process, examples that shed light because they are both authentic and revealing.

2. The women's movement has sought since the nineteenth century in modern times, and most especially from the 1950s in the twentieth century to the present day, to affirm the independence of women and their desire for self-actualization. Read Audrey Bilger's essay (available online) and write an essay of your own on how the phrase "you guys" demonstrates the power of language in undermining those efforts. Why is it not such an innocuous phrase and why have women surprisingly embraced the term, sometimes willfully and happily? Is there some sense in which the phrase can be seen to be empowering but, like a Trojan Horse, is not what it's assumed to be? How can women stop trying to be the "common guy"? What advice can you offer to discourage such usage?

The Internet Talks Like a Woman

BEN CRAIR

A graduate of the University of Pennsylvania, Ben Crair, born in 1985, is a freelance writer. He has also served as an editor for the *New Republic,* the *Daily Beast,* and *Salon,* as well as publishing articles in *Slate, Grantland,* the *Awl,* and *New York Magazine.* Regarding the subject of language and technology, Crair says, "My main interest in this subject is the way in which technology is forcing people to demand of writing the expressiveness they expect of speech, and the formal innovation that has resulted."

In this article, originally published May 17, 2015, on *NYMag.com,* the online version of *New York Magazine,* Crair looks at how men and women communicate differently on the Internet. Citing various studies on the use of language, emoticons, and emoji, Crair concludes that men show more emotion in their online writing than what is typical in offline or traditional writing—in other words, men write more like women when they write online.

WRITING TO DISCOVER: *Think about your use of language when you are writing online, such as tweets, texts, posts, and emails. How often do you use emoticons and emoji? How do you use abbreviations and acronyms? How does the use of symbols and linguistic shorthand enhance your ability to communicate? To what extent does it limit you?*

Long before "mansplaining" became a cliché, linguists observed that men tended to dominate public conversations. They hogged the floor, asserted more opinions, and interrupted more frequently than women. One study from 1975 found, for instance, that men were responsible for 96 percent of all interruptions in conversations with women.[1] In the early '90s, some scholars hoped that the internet, with its promise of anonymity, would offer women more equal footing.[2] But the fantasy proved short-lived. When linguists like Susan C. Herring at the University of Indiana looked at online discussion groups, they discovered the same

> **Despite the boys'-club atmosphere that often seems to permeate the Internet, so much of what seems fun today about online writing is, in fact, thanks to women.**

1. Don H. Zimmerman and Candace West, "Sex Roles, Interruptions and Silences in Conversation," in Language and Sex: Difference and Dominance, ed. Barrie Thorne and Nancy Henley, 105–129 (New York: Newbury House Publishers, 1975).
2. Susan C. Herring, Deborah A. Johnson, and Tamra DiBenedetto, "Participation in Electronic Discourse in a "Feminist" Field," *Language and Gender: A Reader,* 2nd edition, ed. J. Coates & P. Pichler, 171–182 (Wiley-Blackwell, 2011).

old pattern.[3] Despite anonymity, women posted less than men, received fewer responses when they did post, and struggled to influence the topic of conversation. Men were also more antagonistic (and worse, downright harassing), relishing the absence of rules, while women were more polite and considerate of others.[4] Gender still influenced the way people wrote online.

As technology evolved, gender manifested itself not just in participation patterns, but also in writing styles. Women tended to use more emoticons, exclamation points, and lexical features like homophones, complex capitalization, phonetic spellings, repetition, and extra letters.[5] These quirks—known (sometimes derisively) as Netspeak—emerged as users of text and instant messages began to demand from writing the nimbleness of speech, even though old-fashioned writing lacked the paralinguistic elements, like tone and body language, that shaped the meaning of our spoken words. And so instead of a level playing field, the Web proved to be a petri dish for linguistic theories about gender. When linguists analyzed IM conversations in 2006, they found that women's messages were more expressive than men's.[6] A 2009 analysis of Italian text messages found similarly that women, as compared to men, had crafted "a highly expressive style."[7]

The advent of the smartphone, with all the extra opportunities it offers for constant, compressed communication, may have exacerbated these trends. Witness, for instance, the recent *New York Times* article: "Should Grown Men Use Emoji?"[8] The headline suggested that not only do emoji characters seem girly to your average guy, but also that they

3. Susan C. Herring, "Gender and Power in Online Communication," CSI Working Paper No. WP-01-05, October 2001, https://scholarworks.iu.edu/dspace/bitstream /handle/2022/1024/WP01-05B.html.

4. Susan C. Herring, "Posting in a Different Voice: Gender and Ethics in Computer-Mediated Communication," in *Philosophical Perspectives on Computer-Mediated Communication,* ed. Charles Ess, 115–145 (Albany: State University of New York Press, 1996); Amanda Hess, "Why Women Aren't Welcome on the Internet," *Pacific Standard,* January 6 2014, http://www.psmag.com/health-and-behavior/women-arent-welcome-internet-72170.

5. Alecia Wolf, "Emotional Expression Online: Gender Differences in Emoticon Use," *CyberPsychology & Behavior* 3, no. 5 (2000): 827–833; Carol Waseleski, Gender and the Use of Exclamation Points in Computer-Mediated Communication: An Analysis of Exclamations Posted to Two Electronic Discussion Lists," *Journal of Computer-Mediated Communication* 11, no. 4 (2006): 1012–1024, DOI: 10.1111/j.1083-6101.2006.00305.x; Susan C. Herring and Asta Zelenkauskaite, "Symbolic Capital in a Virtual Heterosexual Market: Abbreviation and Insertion in Italian iTB SMS," *Written Communication* 26, no. 1 (2009): 5–31, doi: 10.1177/0741088308327911.

6. Annie B. Fox, Danuta Bukatko, Mark Hallahan, and Mary Crawford, "The Medium Makes a Difference: Gender Similarities and Differences in Instant Messaging," *Journal of Language and Social Psychology 26,* no. 4 (2007): 389–397.

7. Herring and Zelenkauskaite, "Symbolic Capital in a Virtual Heterosexual Market," 5–31.

8. Matt Haber, "Should Grown Men Use Emoji?" *New York Times,* April 3, 2015, http://www.nytimes.com/2015/04/03/fashion/mens-style/should-grown-men-use-emoji.html.

tempt him. Despite the boys'-club atmosphere that often seems to permeate the internet, so much of what seems fun today about online writing is, in fact, thanks to women.

Many of these differences mirror ones that already exist IRL. In the 1980s, Deborah Tannen, a professor at Georgetown, studied the differences between male and female communication strategies and observed what she called "report style" versus "rapport style."[9] Men generally used conversation to exhibit knowledge, coordinate activities, and convey concrete information, while women used conversation to build and maintain relationships. "For girls and women, talk is the glue that holds the relationship together," Tannen says. Not surprisingly, women also write longer messages than men in private communications, like texting, and exchange messages at a higher volume.

There's a tendency to interpret stylistic flourishes in Netspeak as signs of emotionality—for instance, an emoji to indicate happiness or sadness—but their actual use is usually more sophisticated: They clarify the intention of the writing they accompany, like tone in spoken conversation. One study, for instance, found that women most frequently used smiley faces to indicate not that they were happy, but that they were being humorous (e.g., "That was dumb of me :)").[10] "It's a question of style," says Naomi S. Baron, the author of *Words Onscreen: The Fate of Language in a Digital World*. "Sometimes we choose to do things to have a certain style to them. That takes an effort. Statistically, women are more likely to make the effort than men."

One sign of that style's acceptance is how quickly its conventions have become standard. Nowadays, "it's almost obligatory to use an exclamation point," says Susan Herring—but more owing to the fear of being seen as unfriendly than an actual outpouring of friendliness. Tannen has written that much of women's stylistic embellishment "does not signal literal enthusiasm, but rather is necessary to avoid the impression of negativity or apathy." One of Tannen's students once showed some peers an exchange between two women, where one answered the other with short one- or two-word answers ending in a period. Six of the seven female students said the respondent was angry. All five male students said the respondent was probably busy or just indifferent.

But men are conscious of these subtleties, too—in some situations more than others. Men are more likely to spruce up their writing when they converse with women, a finding that surprised some linguists because, in spoken public conversations, women typically use more standardized language. In 2000, for instance, a study found that male use of emoticons soared when mostly male discussion groups were compared to gender-balanced discussion groups.[11] In the mixed-gender groups, men and women

5

---

9. Deborh Tannen, *You Just Don't Understand* (Ballantine Books, 1990).
10. Wolf, "Emotional Expression Online," 832.
11. Ibid, 831.

used emoticons almost equally, confounding the expectations of the study's author, Alecia Wolf. "Rather than the females adopting the offline male standard of *less* emotional expression, the opposite occurs: both males and females display an increase in emoticon use," she wrote. Although not always creatively: In the *Times* article about men and emoji, a woman complained about men's frequent flirtatious use of the winking face with its tongue sticking out: "It seems like that's the go-to if a guy can't come up with something else to say." Meanwhile, in focus groups with teenagers, Baron discovered that the boys were more willing to experiment with style when texting with women—or, as one teenage boy put it, to "play the game." In other words, far from enabling total anonymity, the internet may have actually helped make people more aware of gender differences.

THINKING CRITICALLY ABOUT THE READING

1. In paragraph 1, Crair uses the term "mansplaining." What does he mean by that? How might mansplaining reflect gender-based attitudes towards the use of language?

2. Crair cites a study from 1975, showing some of the history of research regarding the differences in how men and women communicate, not just in the use of particular vocabulary, but in body language, verbal style, willingness to interrupt, and assertion of opinions. How might these differences reflect society's expectations of gender roles? What other aspects of communication would you add to that list?

3. Why did some people believe the Internet might be a place to provide "more equal footing" (1) for men and women? Why didn't that happen? What might this say about how new technologies are integrated into existing culture?

4. Crair points out that written language doesn't have what he calls the "paralinguistic elements, like tone and body language, that shaped the meaning of our spoken words" (2). What has happened in our online communications to compensate for that lack? How has technology evolved to accommodate our own ways of working around the need for tone and body language in online communication?

5. Paragraph 4 begins with the following sentence: "Many of these differences mirror ones that already exist IRL." What does the term "IRL" mean? Why did Crair use it? Did you even notice its use the first time you read this article, or are you attuned enough to such language that it didn't even strike you as out of place? Does Crair use an acronym or online abbreviation anywhere else in the article?

6. Crair quotes Alecia Wolf, the author of a study that looked at the use of emoticons by gender: "Rather than the females adopting the offline male standard of less emotional expression, the opposite occurs: both males and females display an increase in emoticon use . . . " (7). In your opinion, is it fair to attribute emotional content to the use of emoticons in writing? Or are they just a shortcut? Are emoticons and emoji more likely to express emotion or hide true feeling? Support your answer.

LANGUAGE IN ACTION

Using the text messages in your own phone or the phone of a partner, test Crair's assertions about male vs. female expressiveness in digital conversation. Do men use more or fewer emojis? Do men, as some women complain, rely too heavily on the "flirtatious use of the winking face with the tongue sticking out" (7)? If you wrote the text, or you remember the context well, did you use emojis or exclamation points because you genuinely meant them, or because of "the fear of being seen as unfriendly" (5)? Discuss your findings with classmates. What observations do you have in common? Do your findings support or contradict Crair's argument?

WRITING SUGGESTIONS

1. Research the use of language as based on gender. You might start with the list of references for Crair's article, which includes experts such as Deborah Tannen and Naomi S. Baron. Write an essay in which you analyze how a specific technology (a device, an app, or a platform, for instance) has influenced the traditional communication styles of men and women. Are we more likely to express ourselves differently depending on which app or device we use? To what extent do gendered expectations about language carry through to communications using your chosen technology?

2. An underlying thread that runs throughout the article is how much, or how little, emotion appears in a written work. The stereotypical division based on gender is that women are more emotional, men less. Are these stereotypes accurate? Consider the many forms of writing, including song lyrics, poetry, fiction, or letters, in addition to online communications discussed in Crair's article. Write an essay in which you defend or refute those stereotypes. How do we measure and quantify emotion in writing? Does it depend on who is doing the quantifying?

13

CURRENT LANGUAGE
CONTROVERSIES

HOW DOES TECHNOLOGY IMPACT COMMUNICATION IN RELATIONSHIPS?

Much has happened in recent years at the intersection of language and technology, and the promise of the future is that we will see even more inventions and developments that dramatically change our lives. More advancements are coming our way, but their accelerating rate of turnover will test our ability to adjust to them technically, psychologically, intellectually, and behaviorally. The authors of the readings in this chapter have already begun to assess how we and our language are responding and adjusting, preferring quite naturally to focus on the perceived problems rather than the obvious benefits of the new technologies. After all, we know what cell phones, texting, and social media are doing for us. What they are doing to us still needs to be examined.

The three readings in this section have a fairly narrow focus in that they examine, as our title indicates, the impact of technology on communication in relationships. We begin with an article by the noted MIT sociologist and technology expert Sherry Turkle, in which she examines the ways that the Internet and smartphones are changing the ways people interact. Younger people in particular seem to be using the technology to escape from "real world" communication and interactions. In an ironic turnabout, we seem to be communicating more but connecting less. As Turkle puts it, we now have "the ability to hide from each other as we are constantly connected to each other." She further observes, "But there is no simple story here of monolithic negative effects," and she offers a variety of fascinating examples of the ways in which she believes personalities are being altered. Have the new technologies made it easier for us to be rude to one another? Journalist David Carr thinks so. In "Keep Your Thumbs Still When I'm Talking to You," he expresses his disbelief and dismay at people who decide to text or talk to someone on the phone when they are presumably having a conversation with him. What message is actually being sent when one chooses to talk to someone who isn't there over the person who is standing two feet away? Finally, in a somewhat similar vein, Alison J. Stein describes how much we have lost when face-to-face communication is supplanted by e-mail and people are able to hide from one another.

The Tethered Self: Technology Reinvents Intimacy and Solitude

SHERRY TURKLE

Sherry Turkle, born 1948 in Brooklyn, New York, is the Abby Rockefeller Mauzé Professor of the Social Studies of Science and Technology at the Massachusetts Institute of Technology. She has a B.A. in social studies from Harvard University and went on to earn her Ph.D. from Harvard in sociology and personal psychology. Turkle's more popular books include *The Second Self: Computers and the Human Spirit* (1984), *Identity and the Age of the Internet* (1995), and *Simulation and Its Discontents* (2009). Turkle says that she writes "on the subjective side" of how people relate to technology, most importantly computers. She has been frequently published in periodicals such as the *New York Times, Scientific American*, and *Wired*. She was named Woman of the Year by *Ms. Magazine* in 1984, among other numerous awards and accolades. Most recently, she published, *Reclaiming Conversation: The Power of Talk in the Digital Age* (2015).

In this article, which is an excerpt from a Harvard Extension School Centennial Lowell Lecture delivered on May 14, 2010, Turkle points out how the Internet, and accompanying technology like smartphones, have changed the way people interact in real life. Indeed, especially for younger users, this new technology provides an escape from "real world" interactions, which are deemed as too difficult and too revealing. Technologies change how we interact, and in doing so, they also change us.

WRITING TO DISCOVER: *What is your experience of social technology? How is your personal identity revealed, confirmed, or distorted in social media Web sites such as Facebook, Twitter, Instagram, or others? How often do you use your phone to send texts rather than talk?*

When I first came to MIT, in 1976, at the very birth of the personal computer culture, even the most cutting-edge faculty did not know what the new "home computers" would do. It did not seem that many people would want them for writing; they could be used for tax preparation, certainly, and there would be a market for simple games. But beyond that? I have been a witness to the birth of the personal computer culture, with its intense one-on-one relationships with machines, and then to the development of the networked culture, with people using the computer to communicate with each other. In my most recent work on the revolutions in

> Often, our new digital connections offer the illusion of companionship without the demands of friendship.

social networking and sociable robotics, I see a world of new possibilities as well as perils. Technology is the architect of our intimacies, but this means that as we text, Twitter, e-mail, and spend time on Facebook, technology is not just doing things for us, but to us, changing the way we view ourselves and our relationships.

These days, we are on our e-mail, our games, our virtual worlds, and social networks. We text each other at family dinners, while we jog, while we drive, as we push our children on swings in the park. We don't want to intrude on each other, so instead we totally intrude on each other, but not in "real time," some of us sending many thousands of texts a month. And that's not counting our Twitters, e-mail, instant messages, or social networking messages and postings. When we misplace our mobile devices we become anxious, impossible. We archive our own lives as we upload photos to the Web. Indeed, many young people tell me they feel guilty, remiss, if they do not do so. Teenagers say that they sleep with their cell phones, and even when their phones are put away—relegated, say, to a school locker—they know when their phones are vibrating. The technology has become like a phantom limb, it is so much a part of us.

In technology's volume and velocity, we are not being satisfied. Often, our new digital connections offer the illusion of companionship without the demands of friendship. We become accustomed to connection at a distance and in amounts we can control. Teenagers say they would rather text than talk. Like Goldilocks—not too close, not too far, just right. In other words, we become accustomed to connection made to measure: the ability to hide from each other even as we are constantly connected to each other.

But there is no simple story here of monolithic negative effects. Connectivity offers new possibilities for experimenting with identity and, particularly in adolescence, the sense of a free space, what Erik Erikson called the moratorium. This is a time, relatively consequence free, for doing what adolescents need to do: fall in and out of love with people and ideas. Real life does not always provide this kind of space, but the Internet does. No handle cranks, no gear turns, to have us leave a stage of life and move on to another. So, adults, too, use the Internet as a useful place for experimentation—indeed, as an identity workshop. But there is a point in focusing on "discontents." They point us to what we miss, what we hold dear and don't want to lose. They point us to our "sacred spaces." In particular, the "nostalgia" of the young illustrates how young people try to reach for something they never fully knew as they dream the future. Young people reach, for example, for the idea of telephone calls made—as one 18-year-old puts it—"sitting down and giving each other full attention." Teenagers grew up in a culture of distraction. They remember that their parents were on cell phones when they were pushed on swings as toddlers. Now, their parents text at the dinner table and don't look up from their Black-Berries when they pick them up after school. From the moment this generation met technology, it was the competition. And significantly, young people imagine a world in which information is not taken from them auto-matically, just as the cost of doing business.

One 16-year-old tells me that when he really wants privacy, he uses a   5
pay phone, "the kind that takes coins . . . and that is really hard to find in Boston!" Another says she feels safe because "who would care about me and my little life." These are not empowering mantras.

Of technology's current effects on our experience of the self, perhaps the most important is how it redraws the boundaries between intimacy and solitude. We talk of getting "rid" of our e-mails, as though these notes were so much excess baggage. Teenagers avoid the telephone, fearful that it reveals too much. Besides, it takes too long; they would rather text than talk. Adults, too, choose keyboards over the human voice. Tethered to technology, we are shaken when that world "unplugged" does not signify, does not satisfy. After an evening of avatar-to-avatar talk in a networked game, we feel at one moment in possession of a full social life, and in the next curiously isolated, in tenuous complicity with strangers. We build a following on Facebook and wonder to what degree our followings are friends. We re-create ourselves as online personae in games or in a virtual world and give ourselves new bodies, homes, jobs, and romances. Yet, suddenly, in the half-light of virtual community, we may feel utterly alone. As we distribute ourselves, do we abandon ourselves? Sometimes people tell me they experience no sense of having connected after hours of com-munication. And they report feelings near communion when they thought they were paying hardly any attention at all.

Distinctions blur. We are not sure whom to count on. Virtual friend-ships and worlds offer connection with uncertain claims to commitment. We know this, and yet the emotional charge of the online world is very high. People talk about it as the place for hope, the place where something new will come to them, the place where loneliness can be defeated. A woman in her late 60s describes her new iPhone: "It's like having a little Times Square in my pocketbook. All lights. All the people I could meet." People are lonely. Connectivity is seductive. But what do we have, now that we have what we say we want, now that we have what technology makes easy? We can communicate when we wish and disengage at will. We can choose not to see or hear our interlocutors. What we have is a technol-ogy that makes it easy to hide.

Mandy, 13, tells me she "hates the phone and never listens to voice-mail." She presents a downbeat account of a telephone call: "You wouldn't want to call because then you would have to get into a conversation." And conversation, "Well, that's something where you only want to have them when you want to have them." For Mandy, this would be "almost never. . . . It [that is, conversation] is almost always too prying, it takes too long, and it is impossible to say 'goodbye.'"

Stan, 16, will not speak on the telephone except when his mother makes him call a relative. "When you text," he says, "you have more time to think about what you're writing. On the telephone, too much might show."

This is not a teen problem. In corporations, among friends, within   10
academic departments, people readily admit that they would rather leave
a voicemail or send an e-mail than talk face-to-face. Some who say, "I live
my life on my BlackBerry," are forthright about avoiding the "real time"
commitment of a phone call. Here, we use technologies to dial down
human contact, to titrate its nature and extent. People are comforted by
being in touch with a lot of people whom they also keep at bay.

THINKING CRITICALLY ABOUT READING

1. Turkle says, "Technology is the architect of our intimacies" (1). What does
   that mean? Do you agree with her statement? Why or why not?

2. Turkle suggests that our daily lives and in-person interactions with our friends
   and loved ones have been superseded by the Internet and social media in particular. Do you agree or disagree with this assessment? Why?

3. Turkle argues that in today's world, technology offers "the illusion of companionship without the demands of friendship" (3). In your experience, is this
   true? Why or why not?

4. The Internet, with social media sites such as Facebook, Twitter, Instagram,
   and many others, as well as other functions such as e-mail and instant messaging, seems to have exposed its users to the entire world. Yet, Turkle says,
   "What we have here is a technology that makes it easy to hide" (7). How
   do you explain this paradox? In what ways do we deliberately expose or hide
   ourselves online?

5. Turkle says, "Here we use technologies to dial down human contact, to titrate
   its nature and extent" (10). What does she mean by this? Look up the word
   "titrate" in a dictionary if you're unfamiliar with it. How is Turkle using that
   as a metaphor in this sentence?

Keep Your Thumbs Still
When I'm Talking to You

David Carr

David Carr was a journalist and author who wrote about media and culture for the *New York Times*. He was born and raised in 1956 in Hopkins, Minnesota, where he attended grade school and high school. Later, he attended the University of Wisconsin–River Falls and then the University of Minnesota, all the while working at odd jobs to pay for his education. In all, as he put it in an interview for a series about unconventional educations, it took him seven years to get through college. Carr was the former editor of the *Twin Cities Reader*, and he wrote for the alternative weekly *Washington City Paper*, the *Atlantic Monthly*, and *New York Magazine* before moving to the *Times*. In addition to being one of the writers featured in *Page One: Inside the New York Times*, a documentary about how and why the *New York Times* wouldn't relinquish its esteemed position in the journalistic world to Facebook and Twitter, Carr was the author of the best-selling memoir *The Night of the Gun*. In the book he recounts the story of his own cocaine addiction by interviewing the people he associated with during that period of his life. In his review of the memoir, Corby Kummer, his former editor at the *Atlantic*, referred to Carr's "joyous peculiarity." Carr died of pneumonia and complications of lung cancer in February 2015, after collapsing in the newsroom.

In "Keep Your Thumbs Still When I'm Talking to You," which was first published in the *New York Times* on April 15, 2011, Carr argues that our digital age "has made it fashionable to be rude."

WRITING TO DISCOVER: *When someone you are conversing with answers a call or takes out a phone to make a call, what has been your response? How did you feel? Unimportant? Understanding, especially if there might be an emergency? Angry or disgusted when you realized the call was trivial chit-chat? Have you changed the way you react to such situations over time?*

You are at a party and the person in front of you is not really listening to you. Yes, she is murmuring occasional assent to your remarks, or nodding at appropriate junctures, but for the most part she is looking beyond you, scanning in search of something or someone more compelling.

Here's the funny part: If she is looking over your shoulder at a room full of potentially more interesting people, she is ill-mannered. If, however, she is not looking over your shoulder, but into a smartphone in her hand, she is not only well within modern social norms, but is also a wired, well-put-together person.

Add one more achievement to the digital revolution: It has made it fashionable to be rude.

I thought about that a lot at South by Southwest Interactive, the annual campfire of the digitally interested held in Austin, Tex., the second week of March; inside, conference rooms brimmed with wireless connections, and the people on the dais competed with a screen in almost every seat: laptops, or even more commonly, tablets. In that context, the live presentation that the people in the audience had ostensibly come many miles to see was merely companion media.

But even more remarkably, once the badge-decorated horde spilled   5 into the halls or went to the hundreds of parties that mark the ritual, almost everyone walked or talked with one eye, or both, on a little screen. We were adjacent but essentially alone, texting and talking our way through what should have been a great chance to engage flesh-and-blood human beings. The wait in line for panels, badges, or food became one more chance to check in digitally instead of an opportunity to meet someone you didn't know.

I moderated a panel there called "I'm So Productive, I Never Get Anything Done," which was ostensibly about how answering e-mail and looking after various avatars on Facebook, Twitter and Tumblr left little time to do what we actually care about or get paid for. The biggest reaction in the session by far came when Anthony De Rosa, a product manager and programmer at Reuters and a big presence on Twitter and Tumblr, said that mobile connectedness has eroded fundamental human courtesies.

"When people are out and they're among other people they need to just put everything down," he said. "It's fine when you're at home or at work when you're distracted by things, but we need to give that respect to each other back."

His words brought sudden and tumultuous applause. It was sort of a moment, given that we were sitting amid some of the most digitally devoted people in the hemisphere.

Add one more achievement to the digital revolution: It has made it fashionable to be rude.

Perhaps somewhere on the way to the merger of the online and offline world, we had all stepped across a line without knowing it.

In an e-mail later, Mr. De Rosa wrote: "I'm fine with people stepping aside to check something, but when I'm standing in front of someone and in the middle of my conversation they whip out their phone, I'll just stop talking to them and walk away. If they're going to be rude, I'll be rude right back."

After the panel, one of the younger people in the audience came   10 up to me to talk earnestly about the importance of actual connection, which was nice, except he was casting sidelong glances at his iPhone while we talked. I'm not even sure he knew he was doing it. It's not just conferences full of inforati where this happens. In places all over America (theaters, sports arenas, apartments), people gather in groups only to disperse into lone pursuits between themselves and their phones.

Every meal out with friends or colleagues represents a negotiation between connectedness to the grid and interaction with those on hand. "Last year, for my friend's birthday, my gift to her was to stay off my phone at her birthday dinner," said Molly McAleer, who blogs and sends Twitter messages under the name Molls. "How embarrassing."

If South by Southwest is, as its attendees claim, an indicator of what is to come, we won't be seeing a lot of one another even if we happen to be in the same room. Anthony Breznican, a reporter for *Entertainment Weekly*, said all it takes is for one person at a dinner to excuse himself into his phone, and the race is on among everyone else.

"Instead of continuing with the conversation, we all take out our phones and check them in earnest," he said. "For a few minutes everybody is typing away. A silence falls over the group and we all engage in a mass thumb-wrestling competition between man and little machine. Then the moment passes, the BlackBerrys and iPhones are reholstered, and we return to being humans again after a brief trance."

In the instance of screen etiquette, sharing is not always caring, and sometimes, the bigger the screen, the larger the faux pas: On an elevator in the Austin Convention Center, some crazed social media promoter jammed his iPad under my nose and started demo-ing his hideously complicated social networking app that was going to change the world. I leaped to safety as soon as the door opened.

Still, many are finished apologizing for what has become a very natural mix of online and offline pursuits. In an essay on *TechCrunch* entitled "I Will Check My Phone at Dinner and You Will Deal With It," MG Siegler wrote, "Forgive me, but it's Dinner 2.0."   15

He added: "This is the way the world works now. We're always connected and always on call. And some of us prefer it that way."

It scans as progress, but doesn't always feel that way. There are a number of reasons why people at conferences and out in the world treat their phones like a Tamagotchi, the digital pet invented in Japan that died if it wasn't constantly looked after and fed.

To begin with, phones glow. It is a very normal impulse to stare at something in your hand that is emitting light.

Beyond the gadget itself, the screen offers a data stream of many people, as opposed to the individual you happen to be near. Your e-mail, Twitter, Facebook, and other online social groups all offer a data stream of many individuals, and you can choose the most interesting one, unlike the human rain delay you may be stuck with at a party. Then there is also a specific kind of narcissism that the social Web engenders. By grooming and updating your various avatars, you are making sure you remain at the popular kid's table. One of the more seductive data points in real-time media is what people think of you. The metrics of followers and retweets beget a kind of always-on day trading in the unstable currency of the self.

"My personal pet peeve is people who live-tweet every interaction," said Roxanna Asgarian, a student at the CUNY Graduate School of Journalism who attended South by Southwest this year. "I prefer to experience the thing itself over the experience of telling people I'm doing the thing." 20

Still, for those of us who are afraid of missing something, having the grid at our fingertips offers reassurance that we are in the right spot or gives indicators of heat elsewhere.

But all is not vanity. For anybody with children, a job, or a significant other, the expectation these days is that certain special people, usually beginning with our bosses, can reach us at any minute of any day. Every once in a while something truly important tumbles into our in-box that requires immediate attention.

Mobile devices do indeed make us more mobile, but that tether is also a leash, letting everyone know that they can get you at any second, most often to tell you they are late, but on their way. (Another bit of bad manners that the always-on world helps facilitate, by the way.)

At the conference, I saw people who waited 90 minutes to get into a party with a very tough door, peering into their phones the whole while, only to breach the door finally and resume staring into the same screen and only occasionally glancing up. In that sense, the scenery never really changes when you are riding with your digital wingman. I saw people who were sitting on panels surfing or e-mailing during lulls, and then were taken by surprise when it was their turn to talk. (And it's not just those children. I was hosting a discussion at another conference with Martha Stewart, no slouch when it comes to manners, and she kept us all waiting while she checked "one more thing" on her Twitter.)

I should sheepishly mention I was on highest alert for electronic 25 offense because I switched out my smartphone before South by Southwest and was on a new Droid that I'm pretty sure could guide the next mission to Mars, but it was clunky when it came to sending texts and Twitter messages. Digital natives (read "young people") will tell you that they can easily toggle between online and offline. My colleague Brian Stelter can almost pull it off, in part because he always seems to be creating media and consuming it. And in Austin I saw Andy Carvin, NPR's one-man signal tower of North African revolution on Twitter, sitting in front of a screen while the British band Yuck played a killer outdoor set at Stubb's. He sent Twitter messages about the show, and about Bahrain as well.

William Powers, the author of *Hamlet's BlackBerry*, a book about getting control of your digital life, appeared on a panel at South by Southwest and wrote that he came away thinking he had witnessed "a gigantic competition to see who can be more absent from the people and conversations happening right around them. Everyone in Austin was gazing into their little devices—a bit desperately, too, as if their lives depended on not missing the next tweet."

In a phone conversation a few weeks afterward, Mr. Powers said that he is far from being a Luddite, but that he doesn't "buy into the idea that digital natives can do both screen and eye contact."

"They are not fully present because we are not built that way," he said.

Where other people saw freedom—from the desktop, from social convention, from the boring guy in front of them—Mr. Powers saw "a kind of imprisonment."

"There is a great deal of conformity under way, actually," he added.   30

And therein lies the real problem. When someone you are trying to talk to ends up getting busy on a phone, the most natural response is not to scold, but to emulate. It's mutually assured distraction.

THINKING CRITICALLY ABOUT THE READING

1. In paragraph 4 Carr discusses his experience at the South by Southwest Interactive conference. What did he find ironic about the presentations by people on the dais? (Glossary: *Irony*)

2. Why, according to Carr, do we find it more attractive to reach for our phone than talk to the person we are with? What's the allure?

3. What does Carr mean when he writes in paragraph 19: "The metrics of followers and retweets beget a kind of always-on day trading in the unstable currency of the self"? Explain the metaphor that Carr uses in paragraph 24 when he writes: "In that sense, the scenery never really changes when you are riding with your digital wingman." (Glossary: *Figures of Speech*)

4. Author William Powers thought he had witnessed at the South by Southwest show "a gigantic competition to see who can be more absent from the people and conversations happening right around them" (26). In your opinion, is he correct? If so, what does that observation say about how we are changing as a result of the digital revolution?

5. How well does Carr's title reflect his topic and thesis? (Glossary: *Thesis*)

Lost in Translation

Alison J. Stein

Alison J. Stein is an award-winning writer who serves as the culinary travel editor for *About.com*, a New York Times Company-owned Web magazine for original ideas and advice. Stein grew up in New York City and, as she puts it, "ate her way through its great neighborhoods." Passionate about traveling, eating, and writing, she revels in what she regards as the ideal life. Her writing has appeared in many publications, including *Business Week*, *Chicago Tribune*, *New York Magazine*, *Glamour*, *Ladies' Home Journal*, *Money*, *Mother Jones*, *The Smart Set*, the *Toronto Star*, and *USA Weekend*. Stein is also the author of *(Like) Riding a Bike: On Learning as an Adult* (2011), a book about how at nearly thirty-four years of age she finally decided to learn to ride a bicycle. Her writing has been anthologized in *Best Women's Travel Writing 2010*, and you can follow her on Twitter.

In "Lost in Translation," first published on *Inc.com* on September 1, 2005, Stein extols the virtues of face-to-face communication over e-mail.

WRITING TO DISCOVER: *Is it better to meet people face-to-face or simply send an e-mail, or does it depend on what you have to say? How do you decide? What are the advantages and disadvantages of meeting or e-mailing?*

When employees report to work on Fridays at Roberts Golden Consulting in San Francisco, they're greeted with a gentle reminder from president Sara Roberts: Remember, today is No E-mail Friday.

From Monday through Thursday at this management consultancy, as at most companies, e-mail reigns as the primary form of communication — whether with colleagues, clients, or suppliers. But on the fifth day of the workweek, Roberts's employees give their keyboards a rest. Too much e-mail, says Roberts, makes it harder to build rapport, and that threatens to derail effective business relationships. "People hide behind e-mail," she says. "For just one day a week, I want us to pick up the phone or talk to someone face-to-face."

Uneasiness about e-mail is almost as old as e-mail itself. But until now, most of the complaints have focused on things like e-mail overload, or the damage and embarrassment caused when messages go to the wrong people, or the need, for legal reasons, to be careful about what is put into writing. But those concerns just scratch the surface. New research indicates that overreliance on e-mail can degrade an organization's interpersonal communications. If it's not used properly, instead of making your company quicker and more efficient, too much text-based communicating can actually make it stupider.

To be sure, e-mail is not inherently evil. But it can be the kiss of death when it's used to communicate anything sensitive, important, or complicated, says Ron McMillan, who is co-author of *Crucial Conversations: Tools for Talking When Stakes Are High* and who spent 10,000 hours observing how companies nationwide communicate. As text messages fly between desktops, laptops, and hand-helds, McMillan says, they arrive without the rich stew of nonverbal information, such as tone of voice, facial expressions, and eye gaze, that we typically rely on to figure out what someone really means. One study by UCLA psychology professor Albert Mehrabian found that 55 percent of meaning in an interaction comes from facial and body language and 38 percent comes from vocal inflection. Only 7 percent of an interaction's meaning is derived from the words themselves. Since e-mail is, by definition, just the words themselves, it's more easily misunderstood than an actual conversation. Yet managers and employees rely increasingly on text messages for nuanced conversations that really ought to be handled face-to-face, or at least voice-to-voice, says McMillan.

New research indicates that overreliance on e-mail can degrade an organization's interpersonal communications.

The results range from the merely comical to the truly horrifying, as Sara Roberts observed during a 10-year career in corporate America prior to founding her company. In one case, a colleague interacted on a near daily basis with a client over e-mail—without ever figuring out whether the person was male or female.

More seriously, text messages often touch off needless conflict. At one company, Roberts witnessed an explosive turf battle sparked when one employee left another off a "reply all" e-mail chain. Battles started over e-mail often rage longer, and more dramatically, than face-to-face disputes. People tend to be less inhibited over e-mail and more prone to conflict, according to Barry Wellman at the University of Toronto. Indeed, several studies comparing e-mail with face-to-face communication found that e-mail was more blunt and included more swearing and insults. "Everyone has an e-mail that they wish they hadn't sent," says Wellman.

That's why the 40 employees at MSCO, a marketing firm based in Purchase, N.Y., are not allowed to use e-mail or their BlackBerrys if they plan to criticize one another. It's just too easy for an exchange to escalate out of control, says CEO Mark Stevens. A few months ago, one employee complained about another's work performance via BlackBerry—and copied four others, including Stevens, on the message. "The person doing the criticizing was two offices down from the person being criticized, so what was that about?" wondered Stevens, who dropped what he was doing, sat down with the e-critic, and let him know that what he'd done was inappropriate.

Of course, there's no reason to go office to office looking deep into the eyes of every staffer whenever you send an e-mail. But periodic in-person

5

check-ins will let you know when you need to do some damage control. In fact, if you make the time for old-fashioned face-to-face encounters on a regular basis, e-mail and IM actually may strengthen your working relationships, says University of Toronto's Wellman. "The face-to-face world and the bit-to-bit world can fit together," he says.

JoAnne Yates, a professor at MIT's Sloan School of Management who studies e-mail usage in the workplace, advises people to use electronic communication only to transmit and confirm simple information, and have actual conversations for anything that could possibly be sensitive. At the same time, flexibility is key. Sara Roberts, for example, knows she can't force her employees to ignore a message from a client who expects an immediate written response—even on No E-mail Friday. The point isn't to achieve perfect adherence, she says, but rather to remind people of the importance of communicating face-to-face. "No E-mail Friday helps us to remember we really could go over to that person sitting right over there and collaborate more," she says. In a wired world, it's worth remembering that there's still no technology more powerful than an actual meeting of minds.

ALL E-MAIL (ALL THE TIME)

Sometimes, face-to-face communication simply is not possible. That's   10
the case at Alpine Access, a provider of outsourced call-center services based in Golden, Colo. Senior executives at the company log zero face time with their 7,500 employees—including call-center agents, managers, and trainers, nearly all of whom work from their homes scattered across the country. Hiring, training, day-to-day management, and strategic planning all are handled electronically or over the phone. "There's no opportunity to look into someone's eyes to make sure they understand what's being said," says co-founder Jim Ball. So the company has developed a number of practices to compensate—practices that will boost the effectiveness of e-mail at any company.

Clarity Is Everything

Important messages, such as word that everyone needs to work harder to meet a monthly target, are vetted by several people for everything from grammar to nuance.

Trust but Verify

When employees get an e-mail, they're required to acknowledge receipt and are immediately offered the opportunity to ask questions. Managers check back regularly to ensure that employees are on track and not missing any critical info.

Know When Not to Type

For truly difficult conversations—such as performance reviews—forget the bits and bytes. "You can be just as empathetic over the phone as you would be in person," Ball insists. "It's more difficult, but it can be done."

THINKING CRITICALLY ABOUT THE READING

1. In paragraph 2, Stein quotes Sara Roberts as saying, "People hide behind e-mail." What does she mean?

2. In paragraph 4, Stein reports that Professor Mehrabian found "only 7 percent of an interaction's meaning is derived from the words themselves." Does that statistic seem accurate to you? Why or why not?

3. Stein writes in paragraph 6 "text messages often touch off needless conflict." What evidence does she provide for her claim?

4. According to Stein in paragraph 6, there are several studies that "found that e-mail was more blunt and included more swearing and insults." Why might that be true?

5. In paragraph 10, Stein cites the example of Alpine Access in Golden, Colorado, where face-to-face communication is impossible. Assess the advice Alpine Access offers its employees to improve e-mail effectiveness. Do you think the company's advice could help improve communication? Explain.

WRITING SUGGESTIONS: DEBATING THE ISSUE

1. Sherry Turkle notes, "Teenagers grew up in a culture of distraction. They remember that their parents were on cell phones when they were pushed on swings as toddlers. Now, their parents text at the dinner table and don't look up from their BlackBerries when they pick them up after school. From the moment this generation met technology, it was the competition" (2). David Carr makes a similar point with anecdotes in "Keep Your Thumbs Still While I'm Talking to You" (p. 496). Write an essay in which you analyze the effects of technology on family interactions. In your experience, is Turkle's portrayal correct? How have you seen families (your own or others) manage the intrusion that technology represents? To what extent does it even need to be managed?

2. Turkle writes, "We re-create ourselves as online personae in games or in a virtual world and give ourselves new bodies, homes, jobs, and romances. Yet, suddenly, in the half-light of virtual community, we may feel utterly alone. As we distribute ourselves, do we abandon ourselves?" (6). Write an essay in which you explore the question of personal identity today. How does the presence of social media affect one's identity? Can a distinction be fairly made between one's online presence and one's personal presence, or have the two become irrevocably blurred? Is it possible to have an online presence that is completely divorced from one's real life, or vice versa?

3. In "Keep Your Thumbs Still When I'm Talking to You," David Carr raises the issue of rudeness. What is rudeness, anyway? Is the possibility of rudeness always present but made more obvious by our interactive media? Or are we all fighting for more recognition and a desire to be in the center of things and caring less for how we might offend each other? Write an essay in which you define rudeness and how our smartphones and the language they carry are encouraging the disrespect we see for each other wherever people gather today. Finally, if you disagree with the assumptions just presented, write an essay in which you define rudeness but argue that rudeness is not new, just made easier and more visible by recent innovations and methods of communicating.

4. Write an essay in which you examine your own behavior when talking on your cell phone or texting. Are you conscious of when and where to use your cell phone? Have your habits changed over the time you have been making calls and texting? Do you talk on the phone in public places such as restaurants, lectures, sporting events, and parties? What distinctions do you and your friends make about the proper etiquette to use in various situations? What determines the principles you abide by, and how do you react to those who violate generally accepted practices?

5. In our culture we tend to think that any kind of personal communication can be accomplished over the phone or through texts or e-mail. If you have traveled, however, you soon realize that such might not be the case in other cultures. One student realized that when she traveled through France, Spain, and Italy, she needed to present herself in person to discuss complicated or involved matters and that it was almost disrespectful to do otherwise. Showing up in person legitimized the discussion, whereas attempting to discuss matters on the telephone trivialized them. If you have traveled abroad, write an essay describing your experiences in this regard. What cultural differences did you notice and how did you learn to communicate within them? If you have not traveled abroad, what cultural norms have you learned to abide by in this country? Would you text your history professor explaining why work on your research project is not going well? Would you call your professor at home? Would you ask permission to send a draft of your project proposal to your professor beforehand? What advice can you offer as to how to decide when and by what means and under what circumstances people should communicate with colleagues?

6. Write an essay in which you describe the particular dangers in miscommunication that can arise when using e-communication. Alison J. Stein in "Lost in Translation" (p. 502) quotes Barry Wellman at the University of Toronto as saying, "Everyone has an e-mail that they wish they hadn't sent." What e-mail(s) do you wish you hadn't sent? Have you ever sent a traditional or snail mail letter that you wish you hadn't sent? Have you ever misaddressed a text or e-mail message? What problems arose? Of special interest when discussing this topic is what happens when you text a message and the autocorrect feature of your phone sends a message you did not intend. Such messages can be funny and appreciated for their humor or they can offend with their inadvertent crudeness. Most are easily excused as a by-product of our digital age. Does that make them all right, in your opinion? What do all miscommunications say about the need to carefully proofread?

HOW DOES LANGUAGE WORK IN ADVERTISING?

Advertising is big business and a very real part of our daily lives. We hear a steady stream of ads on the radio; see them on television, the Web, and our phones; read them in newspapers and magazines; and even wear them on our clothing. Advertising is so ever-present in our lives that we often take it for granted, never thinking about the impact that it has on each of us every day. In the next decades American businesses will spend well over $150 billion a year on print ads and television and Internet commercials. Appealing to our fantasies of wealth, good looks, power, social acceptance, healthy living, love, and happiness, advertising tries to persuade us to purchase particular products or services. Though every business hopes that its ads will be memorable and work effectively, we know that not all of them are successful. What makes one advertisement more effective than another? To answer such a question, we need to become more sensitive to advertising language and the ways advertisers combine words and images.

The articles in this section cover a range of views on the power of advertising in our lives. In the opening selection, "The Hard Sell: Advertising in America," Bill Bryson provides a historical perspective and context for the world of advertising, whose roots he locates in the late nineteenth and early twentieth centuries. William Lutz challenges advertisers and their manipulative language in "Weasel Words" and exposes some of the secrets of successful advertising language and what it really means. Next, Kiera Butler focuses on the deceptive language practices of one well-known fast food chain, Taco Bell. She bases her observations on the recent and influential book *The Language of Food: A Linguist Reads the Menu* by linguist Dan Jurafsky. Finally, in "Is the 'Natural' Label 100 Percent Misleading?" Deena Shanker examines the debate surrounding a term found on so many food products: "natural." Shanker's research sheds light on how advertisers exploit the ambiguity of a term that seems self-explanatory.

The Hard Sell: Advertising in America

BILL BRYSON

Journalist and author Bill Bryson was born in Des Moines, Iowa, in 1951, and spent two years at Drake University before dropping out in 1972. He spent most of his adult life in Great Britain, beginning with a backpacking trip to Europe in 1973. He settled in England with his wife in 1977, where he worked as a journalist, eventually becoming chief copy editor of the business section of the *Times,* and then national news editor for the *Independent.* Bryson's interest in language is reflected in his *A Dictionary of Troublesome Words* (1987), *The Mother Tongue: English and How It Got That Way* (1990), *Shakespeare: The World as Stage* (2007), and *Bryson's Dictionary for Writers and Editors* (2008). Among his many books on travel are *The Lost Continent: Travels in Small-Town America* (1989), *Neither Here Nor There: Travels in Europe* (1992), *A Walk in the Woods: Rediscovering America on the Appalachian Trail* (1998), and *Bill Bryson's African Diary* (2002). Bryson's 2003 book on science, *A Short History of Nearly Everything,* won the prestigious Royal Society Aventis Prize for science writing. His memoir, *The Life and Times of the Thunderbolt Kid,* was published in 2006. Most recently he served as Chancellor of Durham University in Durham, England.

The following essay is a chapter in Bryson's *Made in America: An Informal History of the English Language in the United States* (1994). In it, he provides a historical perspective on advertising and explores some of the trends that have appeared over the years. It may surprise many people to learn that advertising as we know it is a modern invention, spanning only about a century. During that time, however, the influence of advertisements has grown so much that they now shape the way we see the world.

WRITING TO DISCOVER: *Reactions to advertising vary, but most people would say that ads are a necessary evil and that they ignore them whenever possible. Yet advertising is a multibillion-dollar industry, which is financed by what we buy and sell. Think about some recent TV shows you've watched or newspapers you've read. Jot down the names of the products you saw advertised. Do you buy any of these products? Write about the influences, if any, advertising seems to have on the way you spend your money.*

In 1885, a young man named George Eastman formed the Eastman Dry Plate and Film Company in Rochester, New York. It was rather a bold thing to do. Aged just thirty-one, Eastman was a junior clerk in a bank on a comfortable but modest salary of $15 a week. He had no background in business. But he was passionately devoted to photography and had become increasingly gripped with the conviction that anyone who could develop a simple, untechnical camera, as opposed to the cumbersome, outsized, fussily complex contrivances then on the market, stood to make a fortune.

Eastman worked tirelessly for three years to perfect his invention, supporting himself in the meantime by making dry plates for commercial photographers, and in June 1888 produced a camera that was positively dazzling in its simplicity: a plain black box just six and a half inches long by three and a quarter inches wide, with a button on the side and a key for advancing the film. Eastman called his device the *Detective Camera*. Detectives were all the thing—Sherlock Holmes was just taking off with American readers—and the name implied that it was so small and simple that it could be used unnoticed, as a detective might.

The camera had no viewfinder and no way of focusing. The *photographer* or *photographist* (it took a while for the first word to become the established one) simply held the camera in front of him, pressed a button on the side, and hoped for the best. Each roll took a hundred pictures. When the roll was fully exposed, the anxious owner sent the entire camera to Rochester for developing. Eventually he received the camera back, freshly loaded with film, and—assuming all had gone well—one hundred small circular pictures, two and a half inches in diameter.

Often all didn't go well. The film Eastman used at first was made of paper, which tore easily and had to be carefully stripped of its emulsion before the exposures could be developed. It wasn't until the invention of celluloid roll film by a sixty-five-year-old Episcopal minister named Hannibal Goodwin in Newark, New Jersey—this truly was the age of the amateur inventor—that amateur photography became a reliable undertaking. Goodwin didn't call his invention *film* but *photographic pellicule,* and, as was usual, spent years fighting costly legal battles with Eastman without ever securing the recognition or financial payoff he deserved—though eventually, years after Goodwin's death, Eastman was ordered to pay $5 million to the company that inherited the patent.

In September 1888, Eastman changed the name of the camera to *Kodak*—an odd choice, since it was meaningless, and in 1888 no one gave meaningless names to products, especially successful products. Since British patent applications at the time demanded a full explanation of trade and brand names, we know how Eastman arrived at his inspired name. He crisply summarized his reasoning in his patent application: "First. It is short. Second. It is not capable of mispronunciation. Third. It does not resemble anything in the art and cannot be associated with anything in the art except the Kodak." Four years later the whole enterprise was renamed the Eastman Kodak Company.

Despite the considerable expense involved—a Kodak camera sold for $25, and each roll of film cost $10, including developing—by 1895, over 100,000 Kodaks had been sold and Eastman was a seriously wealthy man. A lifelong bachelor, he lived with his mother in a thirty-seven-room mansion with twelve bathrooms. Soon people everywhere were talking about snapshots, originally a British shooting term for a hastily executed shot. Its photographic sense was coined by the English astronomer Sir John Herschel, who also gave the world the terms *positive* and *negative* in their photographic senses.

From the outset, Eastman developed three crucial strategies that have been the hallmarks of virtually every successful consumer goods company since. First, he went for the mass market, reasoning that it was better to make a little money each from a lot of people rather than a lot of money from a few. He also showed a tireless, obsessive dedication to making his products better and cheaper. In the 1890s, such an approach was widely perceived as insane. If you had a successful product, you milked it for all it was worth. If competitors came along with something better, you bought them out or tried to squash them with lengthy patent fights or other bullying tactics. What you certainly did not do was create new products that made your existing lines obsolescent. Eastman did. Throughout the late 1890s, Kodak introduced a series of increasingly cheaper, niftier cameras—the Bull's Eye model of 1896, which cost just $12, and the famous slimline Folding Pocket Kodak of 1898, before finally in 1900 producing his eureka model: the little box Brownie, priced at just $1 and with film at 15 cents a reel (though with only six exposures per reel).

Above all, what set Eastman apart was the breathtaking lavishness of his advertising. In 1899 alone, he spent $750,000, an unheard-of sum, on advertising. Moreover, it was *good* advertising: crisp, catchy, reassuringly trustworthy. "You press the button—we do the rest" ran the company's first slogan, thus making a virtue of its shortcomings. Never mind that you couldn't load or unload the film yourself. Kodak would do it for you. In 1905, it followed with another classic slogan: "If It Isn't an Eastman, It Isn't a Kodak."

Kodak's success did not escape other businessmen, who also began to see virtue in the idea of steady product refinement and improvement. AT&T and Westinghouse, among others, set up research laboratories with the idea of creating a stream of new products, even at the risk of displacing old ones. Above all, everyone everywhere began to advertise.

Advertising was already a well-established phenomenon by the turn of   10
the twentieth century. Newspapers had begun carrying ads as far back as the early 1700s, and magazines soon followed. (Benjamin Franklin has the distinction of having run the first magazine ad, seeking the whereabouts of a runaway slave, in 1741.) By 1850, the country had its first *advertising agency*, the American Newspaper Advertising Agency, though its function was to buy advertising space rather than come up with creative campaigns. The first advertising agency in the modern sense was N. W. Ayer & Sons of Philadelphia, established in 1869. *To advertise* originally carried the sense of to broadcast or disseminate news. Thus a nineteenth-century newspaper that called itself the *Advertiser* meant that it had lots of news, not lots of ads. By the early 1800s the term had been stretched to accommodate

the idea of spreading the news of the availability of certain goods or services. A newspaper notice that read "Jos. Parker, Hatter" was essentially announcing that if anyone was in the market for hats, Jos. Parker had them. In the sense of persuading members of the public to acquire items they might not otherwise think of buying—items they didn't know they needed—advertising is a phenomenon of the modern age.

By the 1890s, advertising was appearing everywhere—in newspapers and magazines, on *billboards* (an Americanism dating from 1850), on the sides of buildings, on passing streetcars, on paper bags, even on matchbooks, which were invented in 1892 and were being extensively used as an advertising medium within three years.

Very early on, advertisers discovered the importance of a good slogan. Many of our more venerable slogans are older than you might think. Ivory Soap's "99 44/100 percent pure" dates from 1879. Schlitz has been calling itself "the beer that made Milwaukee famous" since 1895, and Heinz's "57 varieties" followed a year later. Morton Salt's "When it rains, it pours" dates from 1911, the American Florist Association's "Say it with flowers" was first used in 1912, and the "good to the last drop" of Maxwell House coffee, named for the Maxwell House Hotel in Nashville, where it was first served, has been with us since 1907. (The slogan is said to have originated with Teddy Roosevelt, who pronounced the coffee "good to the last drop," prompting one wit to ask, "So what's wrong with the last drop?")

Sometimes slogans took a little working on. Coca-Cola described itself as "the drink that makes a pause refreshing" before realizing, in 1929, that "the pause that refreshes" was rather more succinct and memorable. A slogan could make all the difference to a product's success. After advertising its soap as an efficacious way of dealing with "conspicuous nose pores," Woodbury's Facial Soap came up with the slogan "The skin you love to touch" and won the hearts of millions. The great thing about a slogan was that it didn't have to be accurate to be effective. Heinz never actually had exactly "57 varieties" of anything. The catchphrase arose simply because H. J. Heinz, the company's founder, decided he liked the sound of the number. Undeterred by considerations of verity, he had the slogan slapped on every one of the products he produced, already in 1896 far more than fifty-seven. For a time the company tried to arrange its products into fifty-seven arbitrary clusters, but in 1969 it gave up the ruse altogether and abandoned the slogan.

The great thing about a slogan was that it didn't have to be accurate to be effective.

Early in the 1900s, advertisers discovered another perennial feature of marketing—the *giveaway*, as it was called almost from the start. Consumers soon became acquainted with the irresistibly tempting notion that if they bought a particular product they could expect a reward—the chance to receive a prize, a free book (almost always ostensibly dedicated to the general improvement of one's well-being but invariably a thinly disguised plug for the manufacturer's range of products), a free sample, or a rebate in the form of a shiny dime, or be otherwise endowed with some gratifying bagatelle. Typical of the genre was a turn-of-the-century tome called *The Vital Question Cook Book*, which was promoted as an aid to livelier meals, but which proved upon receipt to contain 112 pages of recipes all involving the use of Shredded Wheat. Many of these had a certain air of desperation about them, notably the "Shredded Wheat Biscuit Jellied Apple Sandwich" and the "Creamed Spinach on Shredded Wheat Biscuit Toast." Almost all involved nothing more than spooning some everyday food on a piece of shredded wheat and giving it an inflated name. Nonetheless the company distributed no fewer than four million copies of *The Vital Question Cook Book* to eager consumers.

The great breakthrough in twentieth-century advertising, however, came with the identification and exploitation of the American consumer's Achilles' heel: anxiety. One of the first to master the form was King Gillette, inventor of the first safety razor and one of the most relentless advertisers of the early 1900s. Most of the early ads featured Gillette himself, who with his fussy toothbrush mustache and well-oiled hair looked more like a caricature of a Parisian waiter than a captain of industry. After starting with a few jaunty words about the ease and convenience of the safety razor—"Compact? Rather!"—he plunged the reader into the heart of the matter: "When you use my razor you are exempt from the dangers that men often encounter who allow their faces to come in contact with brush, soap, and barbershop accessories used on other people."

Here was an entirely new approach to selling goods. Gillette's ads were in effect telling you that not only did there exist a product that you never previously suspected you needed, but if you *didn't* use it you would very possibly attract a crop of facial diseases you never knew existed. The combination proved irresistible. Though the Gillette razor retailed for a hefty $5—half the average workingman's weekly pay—it sold by the millions, and King Gillette became a very wealthy man. (Though only for a time, alas. Like many others of his era, he grew obsessed with the idea of the perfectibility of mankind and expended so much of his energies writing books of convoluted philosophy with titles like *The Human Drift* that he eventually lost control of his company and most of his fortune.)

By the 1920s, advertisers had so refined the art that a consumer could scarcely pick up a magazine without being bombarded with unsettling questions: "Do You Make These Mistakes in English?"; "Will Your Hair Stand Close Inspection?"; "When Your Guests Are Gone—Are You Sorry You Ever Invited Them?" (because, that is, you lack social polish); "Did Nature fail to put roses in your cheeks?"; "Will There be a Victrola in Your Home This Christmas?"[1] The 1920s truly were the Age of Anxiety. One

15

---

1. The most famous 1920s ad of them all didn't pose a question, but it did play on the reader's anxiety: "They Laughed When I Sat Down, but When I Started to Play . . ." It was originated by the U.S. School of Music in 1925.

ad pictured a former golf champion, "now only a wistful onlooker," whose career had gone sour because he had neglected his teeth. Scott Tissues mounted a campaign showing a forlorn-looking businessman sitting on a park bench beneath the bold caption "A Serious Business Handicap—These Troubles That Come from Harsh Toilet Tissue." Below the picture the text explained "65 percent of all men and women over 40 are suffering from some form of rectal trouble, estimates a prominent specialist connected with one of New York's largest hospitals. 'And one of the contributing causes,' he states, 'is inferior toilet tissue.'" There was almost nothing that one couldn't become uneasy about. One ad even asked: "Can You Buy a Radio Safely?" Distressed bowels were the most frequent target. The makers of Sal Hepatica warned: "We rush to meetings, we dash to parties. We are on the go all day long. We exercise too little, and we eat too much. And, in consequence, we impair our bodily functions—often we retain food within us too long. And when that occurs, poisons are set up—*Auto-Intoxication begins.*"

In addition to the dread of auto-intoxication, the American consumer faced a gauntlet of other newly minted maladies—*pyorrhea, halitosis* (coined as a medical term in 1874, but popularized by Listerine beginning in 1922 with the slogan "Even your best friend won't tell you"), *athlete's foot* (a term invented by the makers of Absorbine Jr. in 1928), *dead cuticles, scabby toes, iron-poor blood, vitamin deficiency* (*vitamins* had been coined in 1912, but the word didn't enter the general vocabulary until the 1920s, when advertisers realized it sounded worryingly scientific), *fallen stomach, tobacco breath,* and *psoriasis,* though Americans would have to wait until the next decade for the scientific identification of the gravest of personal disorders—*body odor,* a term invented in 1933 by the makers of Lifebuoy soap and so terrifying in its social consequences that it was soon abbreviated to a whispered *B.O.*

The white-coated technicians of American laboratories had not only identified these new conditions, but—miraculously, it seemed—simultaneously come up with cures for them. Among the products that were invented or rose to greatness in this busy, neurotic decade were *Cutex* (for those deceased cuticles), *Vick's VapoRub, Geritol, Serutan* ("Natures spelled backwards," as the voiceover always said with somewhat bewildering reassurance, as if spelling a product's name backward conferred some medicinal benefit), *Noxema* (for which read: "knocks eczema"), *Preparation H, Murine* eyedrops, and *Dr. Scholl's Foot Aids.*[2] It truly was an age of miracles—one in which you could even cure a smoker's cough by smoking, so long as it was Old Golds you smoked, because, as the slogan proudly if somewhat

---

2. And yes, there really was a Dr. Scholl. His name was William Scholl; he was a real doctor, genuinely dedicated to the well-being of feet, and they are still very proud of him in his hometown of La Porter, Indiana.

untruthfully boasted, they contained "Not a cough in a carload." (As late as 1953, L&M cigarettes were advertised as "just what the doctor ordered!")

By 1927, advertising was a $1.5-billion-a-year industry in the United   20
States, and advertising people were held in such awe that they were asked not only to mastermind campaigns but even to name the products. An ad man named Henry N. McKinney, for instance, named *Keds* shoes, *Karo* syrup, *Meadow Gold* butter, and *Uneeda Biscuits.*

Product names tended to cluster around certain sounds. Breakfast cereals often ended in *-ies (Wheaties, Rice Krispies, Frosties);* washing powders and detergents tended to be gravely monosyllabic (*Lux, Fab, Tide, Duz*). It is often possible to tell the era of a product's development by its termination. Thus products dating from the 1920s and early 1930s often ended in *-ex (Pyrex, Cutex, Kleenex, Windex)*, while those ending in *master (Mixmaster, Toastmaster)* generally betray a late 1930s or early-1940s genesis. The development of *Glo-Coat* floor wax in 1932 also heralded the beginning of American business's strange and long-standing infatuation with illiterate spellings, a trend that continued with *ReaLemon* juice in 1935, *Reddi-Wip* whipped cream in 1947, and many hundreds of others since, from *Tastee-Freez* drive-ins to *Toys 'Я' Us*, along with countless others with a *Kwik, E-Z,* or *U* (as in *While-U-Wait*) embedded in their titles. The late 1940s saw the birth of a brief vogue for endings in *matic,* so that car manufacturers offered vehicles with *Seat-O-Matic* levers and *Cruise-O-Matic* transmissions, and even fitted sheets came with *Ezy-Matic* corners. Some companies became associated with certain types of names. Du Pont, for instance, had a special fondness for words ending in *-on.* The practice began with *nylon*—a name that was concocted out of thin air and owes nothing to its chemical properties—and was followed with *Rayon, Dacron, Orlon,* and *Teflon,* among many others. In recent years the company has moved on to what might be called its *Star Trek* phase with such compounds as *Tyvek, Kevlar, Sontara, Condura, Nomex,* and *Zemorain.*

Such names have more than passing importance to their owners. If American business has given us a large dose of anxiety in its ceaseless quest for a healthier *bottom line* (a term dating from the 1930s, though not part of mainstream English until the 1970s), we may draw some comfort from the thought that business has suffered a great deal of collective anxiety over protecting the names of its products.

A certain cruel paradox prevails in the matter of preserving brand names. Every business naturally wants to create a product that will dominate its market. But if that product so dominates the market that the brand name becomes indistinguishable in the public mind from the product itself—when people begin to ask for a *thermos* rather than a "Thermos brand vacuum flask"—then the term has become generic and the owner faces the loss of its trademark protection. That is why advertisements and labels so often carry faintly paranoid-sounding lines like "Tabasco is the registered trademark for the brand of pepper sauce made by McIlhenny

Co." and why companies like Coca-Cola suffer palpitations when they see a passage like this (from John Steinbeck's *The Wayward Bus*):

> "Got any coke?" another character asked.
> "No," said the proprietor. "Few bottles of Pepsi-Cola. Haven't had any coke for a month. . . . It's the same stuff. You can't tell them apart."

An understandable measure of confusion exists concerning the distinction between patents and trademarks and between trademarks and trade names. A *patent* protects the name of the product and its method of manufacture for seventeen years. Thus from 1895 to 1912, no one but the Shredded Wheat Company could make shredded wheat. But because patents require manufacturers to divulge the secrets of their products—and thus make them available to rivals to copy when the patent runs out—companies sometimes choose not to seek their protection. *Coca-Cola*, for one, has never been patented. A *trademark* is effectively the name of a product, its *brand name*. A *trade name* is the name of the manufacturer. So *Ford* is a trade name, *Taurus* a trademark. Trademarks apply not just to names, but also to logos, drawings, and other symbols and depictions. The MGM lion, for instance, is a trademark. Unlike patents, trademark protection goes on forever, or at least as long as the manufacturer can protect it.

Few really successful brand names of today were not just as familiar to your grandparents or even great-grandparents, and a well-established brand name has a sort of self-perpetuating power.

For a long time, it was felt that this permanence gave the holder an unfair advantage. In consequence, America did not enact its first trademark law until 1870, almost a century after Britain, and then it was declared unconstitutional by the Supreme Court. Lasting trademark protection did not begin for American companies until 1881. Today, more than a million trademarks have been issued in the United States and the number is rising by about thirty thousand a year.

A good trademark is almost incalculably valuable. Invincible-seeming brand names do occasionally falter and fade. *Pepsodent, Rinso, Chase & Sanborn, Sal Hepatica, Vitalis, Brylcreem,* and *Burma-Shave* all once stood on the commanding heights of consumer recognition but are now defunct or have sunk to the status of what the trade calls "ghost brands"—products that are still produced but little promoted and largely forgotten. For the most part, however, once a product establishes a dominant position in a market, it is exceedingly difficult to depose it. In nineteen of twenty-two categories, the company that owned the leading American brand in 1925 still has it today— *Nabisco* in cookies, *Kellogg's* in breakfast cereals, *Kodak* in film, *Sherwin Williams* in paint, *Del Monte* in canned fruit, *Wrigleys* in chewing gum, *Singer* in sewing machines, *Ivory* in soap, *Campbell's* in soup, *Gillette* in razors. Few really successful brand names of today were not just as familiar to your grandparents or even great-grandparents, and a

25

well-established brand name has a sort of self-perpetuating power. As *The Economist* has noted: "In the category of food blenders, consumers were still ranking General Electric second twenty years after the company had stopped making them."

An established brand name is so valuable that only about 5 percent of the sixteen thousand or so new products introduced in America each year bear all-new brand names. The others are variants on an existing product— *Tide with Bleach, Tropicana Twister Light Fruit Juices,* and so on. Among some types of product a certain glut is evident. At last count there were 220 types of branded breakfast cereal in America. In 1993, according to an international business survey, the world's most valuable brand was *Marlboro,* with a value estimated at $40 billion, slightly ahead of *Coca-Cola.* Among the other ten brands were *Intel, Kellogg's, Budweiser, Pepsi, Gillette,* and *Pampers. Nescafé* and *Bacardi* were the only foreign brands to make the top ten, underlining American dominance.

Huge amounts of effort go into choosing brand names. General Foods reviewed 2,800 names before deciding on *Dreamwhip.* (To put this in proportion, try to think of just ten names for an artificial whipped cream.) Ford considered more than twenty thousand possible car names before finally settling on *Edsel* (which proves that such care doesn't always pay), and Standard Oil a similar number of names before it opted for *Exxon.* Sometimes, however, the most successful names are the result of a moment's whimsy. *Betty Crocker* came in a flash to an executive of the Washburn Crosby Company (later absorbed by General Mills), who chose *Betty* because he thought it sounded wholesome and sincere and *Crocker* in memory of a beloved fellow executive who had recently died. At first the name was used only to sign letters responding to customers' requests for advice or information, but by the 1950s, Betty Crocker's smiling, confident face was appearing on more than fifty types of food product, and her loyal followers could buy her recipe books and even visit her "kitchen" at the General Foods headquarters.

Great efforts also go into finding out why people buy the brands they do. Advertisers and market researchers bandy about terms like *conjoint analysis technique, personal drive patterns, Gaussian distributions, fractals,* and other such arcana in their quest to winnow out every subliminal quirk in our buying habits. They know, for instance, that 40 percent of all people who move to a new address will also change their brand of toothpaste, that the average supermarket shopper makes fourteen impulse decisions in each visit, that 62 percent of shoppers will pay a premium for mayonnaise even when they think a cheaper brand is just as good, but that only 24 percent will show the same largely irrational loyalty to frozen vegetables.

To preserve a brand name involves a certain fussy attention to linguistic and orthographic details. To begin with, the name is normally expected to be treated not as a noun but as a proper adjective—that is, the name should be followed by an explanation of what it does: *Kleenex facial tissues,*

30

Q-Tip cotton swabs, Jell-O brand gelatin dessert, Sanka brand decaffeinated coffee. Some types of products—notably cars—are granted an exemption, which explains why General Motors does not have to advertise *Cadillac self-propelled automobiles* or the like. In all cases, the name may not explicitly describe the product's function, though it may hint at what it does. Thus *Coppertone* is acceptable; *Coppertan* would not be.

The situation is more than a little bizarre. Having done all they can to make their products household words, manufacturers must then in their advertisements do all in their power to imply that they aren't. Before trademark law was clarified, advertisers positively encouraged the public to treat their products as generics. Kodak invited consumers to "Kodak as you go," turning the brand name into a dangerously ambiguous verb. It would never do that now. The American Thermos Product Company went so far as to boast, "Thermos is a household word," to its considerable cost. Donald F. Duncan, Inc., the original manufacturer of the *Yo-Yo*, lost its trademark protection partly because it was amazingly casual about capitalization in its own promotional literature. "In case you don't know what a yo-yo is . . ." one of its advertisements went, suggesting that in commercial terms Duncan didn't. Duncan also made the elemental error of declaring, "If It Isn't a Duncan, It Isn't a Yo-Yo," which on the face of it would seem a reasonable claim, but was in fact held by the courts to be inviting the reader to consider the product generic. Kodak had long since stopped saying "If it isn't an Eastman, it isn't a Kodak."

Because of the confusion, and occasional lack of fastidiousness on the part of their owners, many dozens of products have lost their trademark protection, among them *aspirin, linoleum, yo-yo, thermos, cellophane, milk of magnesia, mimeograph, lanolin, celluloid, dry ice, escalator, shredded wheat, kerosene,* and *zipper.* All were once proudly capitalized and worth a fortune.

On July 1, 1941, the New York television station WNBT-TV interrupted its normal viewing to show, without comment, a Bulova watch ticking. For sixty seconds the watch ticked away mysteriously, then the picture faded and normal programming resumed. It wasn't much, but it was the first television *commercial.*

Both the word and the idea were already well established. The first commercial—the term was used from the very beginning—had been broadcast by radio station WEAF in New York on August 28, 1922. It lasted for either ten or fifteen minutes, depending on which source you credit. Commercial radio was not an immediate hit. In its first two months, WEAF sold only $550 worth of airtime. But by the mid-1920s, sponsors were not only flocking to buy airtime but naming their programs after their products—*The Lucky Strike Hour, The A&P Gypsies, The Lux Radio Theater,* and so on. Such was the obsequiousness of the radio networks that by the early 1930s, many were allowing the sponsors to take complete artistic and production control of the programs. Many of the most popular shows were actually written by the advertising agencies, and the agencies naturally seldom missed an opportunity to work a favorable mention of the sponsor's products into the scripts.

With the rise of television in the 1950s, the practices of the radio   35
era were effortlessly transferred to the new medium. Advertisers inserted their names into the program title — *Texaco Star Theater, Gillette Cavalcade of Sports, Chesterfield Sound-Off Time, The U.S. Steel Hour, Kraft Television Theater, The Chevy Show, The Alcoa Hour, The Ford Star Revue, Dick Clark's Beechnut Show,* and the arresting hybrid *The Lux-Schlitz Playhouse,* which seemed to suggest a cozy symbiosis between soapflakes and beer. The commercial dominance of program titles reached a kind of hysterical peak with a program officially called *Your Kaiser Dealer Presents Kaiser-Frazer "Adventures in Mystery" Starring Betty Furness in "Byline."* Sponsors didn't write the programs any longer, but they did impose a firm control on the contents, most notoriously during a 1959 *Playhouse 90* broadcast of *Judgment at Nuremberg,* when the sponsor, the American Gas Association, managed to have all references to gas ovens and the gassing of Jews removed from the script.

Where commercial products of the late 1940s had scientific-sounding names, those of the 1950s relied increasingly on secret ingredients. Gleem toothpaste contained a mysterious piece of alchemy called *GL-70*.[3] There was never the slightest hint of what GL-70 was, but it would, according to the advertising, not only rout odor-causing bacteria but "wipe out their enzymes!"

A kind of creeping illiteracy invaded advertising, too, to the dismay of many. When Winston began advertising its cigarettes with the slogan "Winston tastes good like a cigarette should," nationally syndicated columnists like Sydney J. Harris wrote anguished essays on what the world was coming to — every educated person knew it should be "as a cigarette should" — but the die was cast. By 1958, Ford was advertising that you could "travel smooth" in a Thunderbird Sunliner and the maker of Ace Combs was urging buyers to "comb it handsome" — a trend that continues today with "pantihose that fits you real comfortable" and other grammatical manglings too numerous and dispiriting to dwell on.

We may smile at the advertising ruses of the 1920s — frightening people with the threat of "fallen stomach" and "scabby toes" — but in fact such creative manipulation still goes on, albeit at a slightly more sophisticated level. The *New York Times Magazine* reported in 1990 how an advertising copywriter had been told to come up with some impressive labels for a putative hand cream. She invented the arresting and healthful-sounding term *oxygenating moisturizers* and wrote accompanying copy with

---

3. For purposes of research, I wrote to Procter & Gamble, Gleem's manufacturer, asking what GL-70 was, but the public relations department evidently thought it eccentric of me to wonder what I had been putting in my mouth all through childhood and declined to reply.

references to "tiny bubbles of oxygen that release moisture into your skin." This done, the advertising was turned over to the company's research and development department, which was instructed to come up with a product that matched the copy.

If we fall for such commercial manipulation, we have no one to blame but ourselves. When Kentucky Fried Chicken introduced "Extra Crispy" chicken to sell alongside its "Original" chicken, and sold it at the same price, sales were disappointing. But when its advertising agency persuaded it to promote "Extra Crispy" as a premium brand and to put the price up, sales soared. Much the same sort of verbal hypnosis was put to work for the benefit of the fur industry. Dyed muskrat makes a perfectly good fur, for those who enjoy cladding themselves in dead animals, but the name clearly lacks stylishness. The solution was to change the name to *Hudson seal*. Never mind that the material contained not a strand of seal fur. It sounded good, and sales skyrocketed.

Truth has seldom been a particularly visible feature of American 40 advertising. In the early 1970s, Chevrolet ran a series of ads for the Chevelle boasting that the car had "109 advantages to keep it from becoming old before its time." When looked into, it turned out that these 109 vaunted features included such items as rearview mirrors, backup lights, balanced wheels, and many other components that were considered pretty well basic to any car. Never mind; sales soared. At about the same time, Ford, not to be outdone, introduced a "limited edition" Mercury Monarch at $250 below the normal list price. It achieved this, it turned out, by taking $250 worth of equipment off the standard Monarch.

And has all this deviousness led to a tightening of the rules concerning what is allowable in advertising? Hardly. In 1986, as William Lutz relates in *Doublespeak,* the insurance company John Hancock launched an ad campaign in which "real people in real situations" discussed their financial predicaments with remarkable candor. When a journalist asked to speak to these real people, a company spokesman conceded that they were actors and "in that sense they are not real people."

During the presidential campaign [in 1982], the Republican National Committee ran a television advertisement praising President Reagan for providing cost-of-living pay increases to federal workers "in spite of those sticks-in-the-mud who tried to keep him from doing what we elected him to do." When it was pointed out that the increases had in fact been mandated by law since 1975 and that Reagan had in any case three times tried to block them, a Republican official responded: "Since when is a commercial supposed to be accurate?" Quite.

In linguistic terms, perhaps the most interesting challenge facing advertisers today is that of selling products in an increasingly multicultural society. Spanish is a particular problem, not just because it is spoken over such a widely scattered area but also because it is spoken in so many different forms. Brown sugar is *azucar negra* in New York, *azucar prieta* in

Miami, *azucar morena* in much of Texas, and *azucar pardo* pretty much everywhere else—and that's just one word. Much the same bewildering multiplicity applies to many others. In consequence, embarrassments are all but inevitable.

In mainstream Spanish, *bichos* means *insects*, but in Puerto Rico it means *testicles*, so when a pesticide maker promised to bring death to the *bichos*, Puerto Rican consumers were at least bemused, if not alarmed. Much the same happened when a maker of bread referred to its product as *un bollo de pan* and discovered that to Spanish-speaking Miamians of Cuban extraction that means a woman's private parts. And when Perdue Chickens translated its slogan "It takes a tough man to make a tender chicken" into Spanish, it came out as the slightly less macho "It takes a sexually excited man to make a chick sensual."

Never mind. Sales soared.   45

THINKING CRITICALLY ABOUT THE READING

1. Why do you think Bryson begins his essay with an extensive passage on George Eastman before even mentioning advertising, the focus of his essay? Why is this background information important to the rest of the essay? (Glossary: *Beginnings and Endings*) What do you need to consider when writing an introduction to an essay?

2. What is Bryson's purpose in this essay—to express personal thoughts and feelings, to inform his audience, or to argue a particular position? (Glossary: *Purpose*) What in his essay leads you to this conclusion?

3. Bryson peppers his essay with examples from the world of business and advertising. (Glossary: *Examples*) These examples serve not only to illustrate the points he makes but also to help establish his authority on the subject. Which examples do you find most effective? Least effective? Explain why.

4. It is important for companies to prevent their trademarks from becoming household words because they could lose their trademark protection. For example, advertisements for Kleenex and Xerox urge people to ask for a *tissue* or say they're going to *copy* a paper. Identify two or three current trademarks that you think could lose their trademark protection in the future, and explain your reasoning for choosing each trademark.

5. Bryson discusses what he calls a "creeping illiteracy" (37) that has invaded advertising. What form does this illiteracy take? In what ways might using poor English benefit advertisers?

6. In talking about the powers of advertising to persuade, Bryson discusses "commercial manipulation" and "verbal hypnosis" (39). What exactly does he mean by each term? How have advertisers used these techniques to sell their products? How do you think you as a consumer can guard against such advertising practices?

7. According to Bryson, what is one of the more interesting linguistic challenges facing today's advertisers?

Weasel Words: The Art of Saying Nothing at All

William Lutz

William Lutz was born in 1940 in Racine, Wisconsin. An emeritus professor of English at Rutgers University at Camden, Lutz holds a Ph.D. in Victorian literature, linguistics and rhetoric, and a law degree from the Rutgers School of Law. Lutz is the author or coauthor of numerous books having to do with language, including *Webster's New World Thesaurus* (1985) and *The Cambridge Thesaurus of American English* (1994). Considered an expert on language, Lutz has worked with many corporations and government agencies to promote clear, "plain" English. A member of the Pennsylvania bar, he was awarded the Pennsylvania Bar Association Clarity Award for the Promotion of Plain English in Legal Writing in 2001.

Lutz is best known for his series of books on "doublespeak": *Doublespeak: From Revenue Enhancement to Terminal Living* (1989), *The New Doublespeak: Why No One Knows What Anyone's Saying Anymore* (1996), and *Doublespeak Defined: Cut Through the Bull**** and Get to the Point* (1999). Lutz edited the *Quarterly Review of Doublespeak* from 1980 to 1994.

The term *doublespeak* comes from the Newspeak vocabulary of George Orwell's novel *1984*. It refers to speech or writing that presents two or more contradictory ideas in such a way that an unsuspecting audience is not consciously aware of the contradiction and is likely to be deceived. As chair of the National Council of Teachers of English's Committee on Public Doublespeak, Lutz has been a watchdog of public officials and business leaders who use language to "mislead, distort, deceive, inflate, circumvent, and obfuscate." Each year the committee presents the Orwell Awards, recognizing the most outrageous uses of public doublespeak in government and business.

In the following excerpt from his book *Doublespeak*, Lutz reveals some of the ways that advertisers use language to imply great things about products and services without promising anything at all. With considerable skill, advertisers can produce ads that make us believe a certain product is better than it is without actually lying about it. Lutz's word-by-word analysis of advertising claims reveals how misleading—and ridiculous—these slogans and claims can be.

WRITING TO DISCOVER: *Imagine what it would be like if you were suddenly transported to a world in which there were no advertisements and no one trying to sell you a product. Write about how you would decide what to buy. How would you learn about new products? Would you prefer to live in such a world? Why or why not?*

WEASEL WORDS

One problem advertisers have when they try to convince you that the product they are pushing is really different from other, similar products is that their claims are subject to some laws. Not a lot of laws, but there are some designed to prevent fraudulent or untruthful claims in advertising. Even during the happy years of nonregulation under President Ronald Reagan, the FTC did crack down on the more blatant abuses in advertising claims. Generally speaking, advertisers have to be careful in what they say in their ads, in the claims they make for the products they advertise. Parity claims are safe because they are legal and supported by a number of court decisions. But beyond parity claims there are weasel words.

Advertisers use weasel words to appear to be making a claim for a product when in fact they are making no claim at all. Weasel words get their name from the way weasels eat the eggs they find in the nests of other animals. A weasel will make a small hole in the egg, suck out the insides, then place the egg back in the nest. Only when the egg is examined closely is it found to be hollow. That's the way it is with weasel words in advertising: Examine weasel words closely and you'll find that they're as hollow as any egg sucked by a weasel. Weasel words appear to say one thing when in fact they say the opposite, or nothing at all.

"Help"—The Number One Weasel Word

The biggest weasel word used in advertising doublespeak is "help." Now "help" only means to aid or assist, nothing more. It does not mean to conquer, stop, eliminate, end, solve, heal, cure, or anything else. But once the ad says "help," it can say just about anything after that because "help" qualifies everything coming after it. The trick is that the claim that comes after the weasel word is usually so strong and so dramatic that you forget the word "help" and concentrate only on the dramatic claim. You read into the ad a message that the ad does not contain. More importantly, the advertiser is not responsible for the claim that you read into the ad, even though the advertiser wrote the ad so you would read that claim into it.

The next time you see an ad for a cold medicine that promises that it "helps relieve cold symptoms fast," don't rush out to buy it. Ask yourself what this claim is really saying. Remember, "help" means only that the medicine will aid or assist. What will it aid or assist in doing? Why, "relieve" your cold "symptoms." "Relieve" only means to ease, alleviate, or mitigate, not to stop, end, or cure. Nor does the claim say how much relieving this medicine will do. Nowhere does this ad claim it will cure anything. In fact, the ad doesn't even claim it will *do* anything at all. The ad only claims that it will aid in relieving (not curing) your cold symptoms, which are probably a runny nose, watery eyes, and a headache. In other words, this medicine probably contains a standard decongestant and some aspirin. By the way, what does "fast" mean? Ten minutes, one hour, one day? What is fast to one person can be very slow to another. Fast is another weasel word.

Ad claims using "help" are among the most popular ads. One says, 5 "Helps keep you young looking," but then a lot of things will help keep you young looking, including exercise, rest, good nutrition, and a facelift. More importantly, this ad doesn't say the product will keep you young, only "young *looking*." Someone may look young to one person and old to another.

A toothpaste ad says, "Helps prevent cavities," but it doesn't say it will actually prevent cavities. Brushing your teeth regularly, avoiding sugars in food, and flossing daily will also help prevent cavities. A liquid cleaner ad says, "Helps keep your home germ free," but it doesn't say it actually kills germs, nor does it even specify which germs it might kill.

"Help" is such a useful weasel word that it is often combined with other action-verb weasel words such as "fight" and "control." Consider the claim, "Helps control dandruff symptoms with regular use." What does it really say? It will assist in controlling (not eliminating, stopping, ending, or curing) the *symptoms* of dandruff, not the cause of dandruff nor the dandruff itself. What are the symptoms of dandruff? The ad deliberately leaves that undefined, but assume that the symptoms referred to in the ad are the flaking and itching commonly associated with dandruff. But just shampooing with *any* shampoo will temporarily eliminate these symptoms, so this shampoo isn't any different from any other. Finally, in order to benefit from this product, you must use it regularly. What is "regular use"—daily, weekly, hourly? Using another shampoo "regularly" will have the same effect. Nowhere does this advertising claim say this particular shampoo stops, eliminates, or cures dandruff. In fact, this claim says nothing at all, thanks to all the weasel words.

Look at ads in magazines and newspapers, listen to ads on radio and television, and you'll find the word "help" in ads for all kinds of products. How often do you read or hear such phrases as "helps stop . . . ," "helps overcome . . . ," "helps eliminate . . . ," "helps you feel . . . ," or "helps you look . . ."? If you start looking for this weasel word in advertising, you'll be amazed at how often it occurs. Analyze the claims in the ads using "help," and you will discover that these ads are really saying nothing.

There are plenty of other weasel words used in advertising. In fact, there are so many that to list them all would fill the rest of this book. But, in order to identify the doublespeak of advertising and understand the real meaning of an ad, you have to be aware of the most popular weasel words in advertising today.

Virtually Spotless

One of the most powerful weasel words is "virtually," a word so 10 innocent that most people don't pay any attention to it when it is used in an advertising claim. But watch out. "Virtually" is used in advertising claims that appear to make specific, definite promises when there is no promise. After all, what does "virtually" mean? It means "in essence or effect, although not in fact." Look at that definition again. "Virtually" means *not in fact*. It does *not* mean "almost" or "just about the same as," or anything else. And before you dismiss all this concern over such a small word, remember that small words can have big consequences.

In 1971 a federal court rendered its decision on a case brought by a woman who became pregnant while taking birth control pills. She sued the manufacturer, Eli Lilly and Company, for breach of warranty. The woman lost her case. Basing its ruling on a statement in the pamphlet accompanying the pills, which stated that, "When taken as directed, the tablets offer virtually 100 percent protection," the court ruled that there was no warranty, expressed or implied, that the pills were absolutely effective. In its ruling, the court pointed out that, according to *Webster's Third New International Dictionary*, "virtually" means "almost entirely" and clearly does not mean "absolute" (*Whittington* v. *Eli Lilly and Company*, 333 F. Supp. 98). In other words, the Eli Lilly company was really saying that its birth control pill, even when taken as directed, *did not in fact* provide 100 percent protection against pregnancy. But Eli Lilly didn't want to put it that way because then many women might not have bought Lilly's birth control pills.

The next time you see the ad that says that this dishwasher detergent "leaves dishes virtually spotless," just remember how advertisers twist the meaning of the weasel word "virtually." You can have lots of spots on your dishes after using this detergent and the ad claim will still be true, because what this claim really means is that this detergent does not *in fact* leave your dishes spotless. Whenever you see or hear an ad claim that uses the word "virtually," just translate that claim into its real meaning. So the television set that is "virtually trouble free" becomes the television set that is not in fact trouble free, the "virtually foolproof operation" of any appliance becomes an operation that is in fact not foolproof, and the product that "virtually never needs service" becomes the product that is not in fact service free.

New and Improved

If "new" is the most frequently used word on a product package, "improved" is the second most frequent. In fact, the two words are almost always used together. It seems just about everything sold these days is "new and improved." The next time you're in the supermarket, try counting the number of times you see these words on products. But you'd better do it while you're walking down just one aisle, otherwise you'll need a calculator to keep track of your counting.

Just what do these words mean? The use of the word "new" is restricted by regulations, so an advertiser can't just use the word on a product or in an ad without meeting certain requirements. For example, a product is considered new for about six months during a national advertising campaign. If the product is being advertised only in a limited test market area, the word can be used longer, and in some instances has been used for as long as two years.

What makes a product "new"? Some products have been around for a 15 long time, yet every once in a while you discover that they are being advertised as "new." Well, an advertiser can call a product new if there has been "a material functional change" in the product. What is "a material functional change," you ask? Good question. In fact it's such a good question it's being asked all the time. It's up to the manufacturer to prove that the product has undergone such a change. And if the manufacturer isn't challenged on the claim, then there's no one to stop it. Moreover, the change does not have to be an improvement in the product. One manufacturer added an artificial lemon scent to a cleaning product and called it "new and improved," even though the product did not clean any better than without the lemon scent. The manufacturer defended the use of the word "new" on the grounds that the artificial scent changed the chemical formula of the product and therefore constituted "a material functional change."

Which brings up the word "improved." When used in advertising, "improved" does not mean "made better." It only means "changed" or "different from before." So, if the detergent maker puts a plastic pour spout on the box of detergent, the product has been "improved," and away we go with a whole new advertising campaign. Or, if the cereal maker adds more fruit or a different kind of fruit to the cereal, there's an improved product. Now you know why manufacturers are constantly making little changes in their products. Whole new advertising campaigns, designed to convince you that the product has been changed for the better, are based on small changes in superficial aspects of a product. The next time you see an ad for an "improved" product, ask yourself what was wrong with the old one. Ask yourself just how "improved" the product is. Finally, you might check to see whether the "improved" version costs more than the unimproved one. After all, someone has to pay for the millions of dollars spent advertising the improved product.

Of course, advertisers really like to run ads that claim a product is "new and improved." While what constitutes a "new" product may be subject to some regulation, "improved" is a subjective judgment. A manufacturer changes the shape of its stick deodorant, but the shape doesn't improve the function of the deodorant. That is, changing the shape doesn't affect the deodorizing ability of the deodorant, so the manufacturer calls it "improved." Another manufacturer adds ammonia to its liquid cleaner and calls it "new and improved." Since adding ammonia does affect the cleaning ability of the product, there has been a "material functional change" in the product, and the manufacturer can now call its cleaner "new," and "improved" as well. Now the weasel words "new and improved" are plastered all over the package and are the basis for a multimillion-dollar ad campaign. But after six months the word "new" will have to go, until someone can dream up another change in the product. Perhaps it will be adding color to the liquid, or changing the shape of the package, or maybe adding a new dripless pour spout, or perhaps a___. The "improvements" are endless, and so are the new advertising claims and campaigns.

"New" is just too useful and powerful a word in advertising for advertisers to pass it up easily. So they use weasel words that say "new" without really saying it. One of their favorites is "introducing," as in, "Introducing improved Tide," or "Introducing the stain remover." The first is simply saying, here's our improved soap; the second, here's our new advertising campaign for our detergent. Another favorite is "now," as in, "Now there's Sinex," which simply means that Sinex is available. Then there are phrases like "Today's Chevrolet," "Presenting Dristan," and "A fresh way to start the day." The list is really endless because advertisers are always finding new ways to say "new" without really saying it. If there is a second edition of [my] book, I'll just call it the "new and improved" edition. Wouldn't you really rather have a "new and improved" edition of [my] book rather than a "second" edition?

Acts Fast

"Acts" and "works" are two popular weasel words in advertising because they bring action to the product and to the advertising claim. When you see the ad for the cough syrup that "Acts on the cough control center," ask yourself what this cough syrup is claiming to do. Well, it's just claiming to "act," to do something, to perform an action. What is it that the cough syrup does? The ad doesn't say. It only claims to perform an action or do something on your "cough control center." By the way, what and where is your "cough control center"? I don't remember learning about that part of the body in human biology class.

Ads that use such phrases as "acts fast," "acts against," "acts to pre-   20 vent," and the like are saying essentially nothing, because "act" is a word empty of any specific meaning. The ads are always careful not to specify exactly what "act" the product performs. Just because a brand of aspirin claims to "act fast" for headache relief doesn't mean this aspirin is any better than any other aspirin. What is the "act" that this aspirin performs? You're never told. Maybe it just dissolves quickly. Since aspirin is a parity product, all aspirin is the same and therefore functions the same.

Works Like Anything Else

If you don't find the word "acts" in an ad, you will probably find the weasel word "works." In fact, the two words are almost interchangeable in advertising. Watch out for ads that say a product "works against," "works like," "works for," or "works longer." As with "acts," "works" is the same meaningless verb used to make you think that this product really does something, and maybe even something special or unique. But "works," like "acts," is basically a word empty of any specific meaning.

Like Magic

Whenever advertisers want you to stop thinking about the product and to start thinking about something bigger, better, or more attractive than the product, they use that very popular weasel word "like." The word "like" is the advertiser's equivalent of a magician's use of misdirection. "Like" gets you to ignore the product and concentrate on the claim the advertiser is making about it. "For skin like peaches and cream" claims the ad for a skin cream. What is this ad really claiming? It doesn't say this cream will give you peaches-and-cream skin. There is no verb in this claim, so it doesn't even mention using the product. How is skin ever like "peaches and cream"? Remember, ads must be read literally and exactly, according to the dictionary definition of words. (Remember "virtually" in the Eli Lilly case.) The ad is making absolutely no promise or claim whatsoever for this skin cream. If you think this cream will give you soft, smooth, youthful-looking skin, you are the one who has read that meaning into the ad.

The wine that claims "It's like taking a trip to France" wants you to think about a romantic evening in Paris as you walk along the boulevard after a wonderful meal in an intimate little bistro. Of course, you don't really believe that a wine can take you to France, but the goal of the ad is to get you to think pleasant, romantic thoughts about France and not about how the wine tastes or how expensive it may be. That little word "like" has taken you away from crushed grapes into a world of your own imaginative making. Who knows, maybe the next time you buy wine, you'll think those pleasant thoughts when you see this brand of wine, and you'll buy it. Or, maybe you weren't even thinking about buying wine at all, but now you just might pick up a bottle the next time you're shopping. Ah, the power of "like" in advertising.

> **The word "like" is the advertiser's equivalent of a magician's use of misdirection.**

How about the most famous "like" claim of all, "Winston tastes good like a cigarette should"? Ignoring the grammatical error here, you might want to know what this claim is saying. Whether a cigarette tastes good or bad is a subjective judgment because what tastes good to one person may well taste horrible to another. Not everyone likes fried snails, even if they are called escargot. (*De gustibus non est disputandum,* which was probably the Roman rule for advertising as well as for defending the games in the Colosseum.) There are many people who say all cigarettes taste terrible, other people who say only some cigarettes taste all right, and still others who say all cigarettes taste good. Who's right? Everyone, because taste is a matter of personal judgment.

Moreover, note the use of the conditional, "should." The complete claim is, "Winston tastes good like a cigarette should taste." But should cigarettes taste good? Again, this is a matter of personal judgment and probably depends most on one's experiences with smoking. So, the Winston ad is simply saying that Winston cigarettes are just like any   25 other cigarette: Some people like them and some people don't. On that statement R. J. Reynolds conducted a very successful multimillion-dollar advertising campaign that helped keep Winston the number-two-selling cigarette in the United States, close behind number one, Marlboro.

CAN IT BE UP TO THE CLAIM?

Analyzing ads for doublespeak requires that you pay attention to every word in the ad and determine what each word really means. Advertisers try to wrap their claims in language that sounds concrete, specific, and objective, when in fact the language of advertising is anything but. Your job is to read carefully and listen critically so that when the announcer says that "Crest can be of significant value . . ." you know immediately that this claim says absolutely nothing. Where is the doublespeak in this ad? Start with the second word.

Once again, you have to look at what words really mean, not what you think they mean or what the advertiser wants you to think they mean. The ad for Crest only says that using Crest "can be" of "significant value." What really throws you off in this ad is the brilliant use of "significant." It draws your attention to the word "value" and makes you forget that the ad only claims that Crest "can be." The ad doesn't say that Crest *is* of value, only that it is "able" or "possible" to be of value, because that's all that "can" means.

It's so easy to miss the importance of those little words, "can be." Almost as easy as missing the importance of the words "up to" in an ad. These words are very popular in sale ads. You know, the ones that say, "Up to 50% Off!" Now, what does that claim mean? Not much, because the store or manufacturer has to reduce the price of only a few items by 50 percent. Everything else can be reduced a lot less, or not even reduced. Moreover, don't you want to know 50 pecent off of what? Is it 50 percent off the "manufacturer's suggested list price," which is the highest possible price? Was the price artificially inflated and then reduced? In other ads, "up to" expresses an ideal situation. The medicine that works "up to ten times faster," the battery that lasts "up to twice as long," and the soap that gets you "up to twice as clean" all are based on ideal situations for using those products, situations in which you can be sure you will never find yourself.

UNFINISHED WORDS

Unfinished words are a kind of "up to" claim in advertising. The claim that a battery lasts "up to twice as long" usually doesn't finish the comparison— twice as long as what? A birthday candle? A tank of gas? A cheap battery made in a country not noted for its technological achievements? The implication is that the battery lasts twice as long as batteries made by other battery makers, or twice as long as earlier model batteries made by the advertiser, but the ad doesn't really make these claims. You read these claims into the ad, aided by the visual images the advertiser so carefully provides.

Unfinished words depend on you to finish them, to provide the words   30
the advertisers so thoughtfully left out of the ad. Pall Mall cigarettes were once advertised as "A longer finer and milder smoke." The question is, longer, finer, and milder than what? The aspirin that claims it contains "Twice as much of the pain reliever doctors recommend most" doesn't tell you what pain reliever it contains twice as much of. (By the way, it's aspirin. That's right; it just contains twice the amount of aspirin. And how much is twice the amount? Twice of what amount?) Panadol boasts that "nobody reduces fever faster," but, since Panadol is a parity product, this claim simply means that Panadol isn't any better than any other product in its parity class. "You can be sure if it's Westinghouse," you're told, but just exactly what it is you can be sure of is never mentioned. "Magnavox gives you more" doesn't tell you what you get more of. More value? More television? More than they gave you before? It sounds nice, but it means nothing, until you fill in the claim with your own words, the words the advertiser didn't use. Since each of us fills in the claim differently, the ad and the product can become all things to all people, and not promise a single thing.

Unfinished words abound in advertising because they appear to promise so much. More importantly, they can be joined with powerful visual images on television to appear to be making significant promises about a product's effectiveness without really making any promises. In a television ad, the aspirin product that claims fast relief can show a person with a headache taking the product and then, in what appears to be a matter of minutes, claiming complete relief. This visual image is far more powerful than any claim made in unfinished words. Indeed, the visual image completes the unfinished words for you, filling in with pictures what the words leave out. And you thought that ads didn't affect you. What brand of aspirin do you use?

Some years ago, Ford's advertisements proclaimed "Ford LTD— 700 percent quieter." Now, what do you think Ford was claiming with these unfinished words? What was the Ford LTD quieter than? A Cadillac? A Mercedes Benz? A BMW? Well, when the FTC asked Ford to substantiate this unfinished claim, Ford replied that it meant that the inside of the LTD was 700 percent quieter than the outside. How did you finish those unfinished words when you first read them? Did you even come close to Ford's meaning?

COMBINING WEASEL WORDS

A lot of ads don't fall neatly into one category or another because they use a variety of different devices and words. Different weasel words are often combined to make an ad claim. The claim, "Coffee-Mate gives coffee more body, more flavor," uses unfinished words ("more" than what?) and also uses words that have no specific meaning ("body" and "flavor"). Along with "taste" (remember the Winston ad and its claim to taste good), "body" and "flavor" mean nothing because their meaning is entirely subjective. To you, "body" in coffee might mean thick, black, almost bitter coffee, while I might take it to mean a light brown, delicate coffee. Now, if you think you understood that last sentence, read it again, because it said nothing of objective value; it was filled with weasel words of no specific meaning: "thick," "black," "bitter," "light brown," and "delicate." Each of those words has no specific, objective meaning, because each of us can interpret them differently.

Try this slogan: "Looks, smells, tastes like ground-roast coffee." So, are you now going to buy Taster's Choice instant coffee because of this ad? "Looks," "smells," and "tastes" are all words with no specific meaning and depend on your interpretation of them for any meaning. Then there's that great weasel word "like," which simply suggests a comparison but does not make the actual connection between the product and the quality. Besides, do you know what "ground-roast" coffee is? I don't, but it sure sounds good. So, out of seven words in this ad, four are definite weasel words, two are quite meaningless, and only one has clear meaning.

Remember the Anacin ad—"Twice as much of the pain reliever doc-   35
tors recommend most"? There's a whole lot of weaseling going on in this ad. First, what's the pain reliever they're talking about in this ad? Aspirin, of course. In fact, any time you see or hear an ad using those words "pain reliever," you can automatically substitute the word "aspirin" for them. (Makers of acetaminophen and ibuprofen pain relievers are careful in their advertising to identify their products as nonaspirin products.) So, now we know that Anacin has aspirin in it. Moreover, we know that Anacin has twice as much aspirin in it, but we don't know twice as much as what. Does it have twice as much aspirin as an ordinary aspirin tablet? If so, what is an ordinary aspirin tablet, and how much aspirin does it contain? Twice as much as Excedrin or Bufferin? Twice as much as a chocolate chip cookie? Remember those unfinished words and how they lead you on without saying anything.

Finally, what about those doctors who are doing all that recommending? Who are they? How many of them are there? What kind of doctors are they? What are their qualifications? Who asked them about recommending pain relievers? What other pain relievers did they recommend? And there are a whole lot more questions about this "poll" of doctors to which I'd like to know the answers, but you get the point. Sometimes, when I call my doctor, she tells me to take two aspirin and call her office in the morning. Is that where Anacin got this ad?

THINKING CRITICALLY ABOUT THE READING

1. What are weasel words? How, according to Lutz, did they get their name?
2. Lutz is careful to illustrate each of the various kinds of weasel words with examples of actual usage. (Glossary: *Examples*) What do these examples add to his essay? Which ones do you find most effective? Explain.

3. According to Lutz, why is "help" the biggest weasel word used by advertisers (3–8)? In what ways does it help them present their products without having to make promises about actual performance?

4. Why is "virtually" a particularly effective weasel word (10–12)? Why can advertisers get away with using words that literally mean the opposite of what they want to convey?

5. When advertisers use the word "like," they often create a simile—"Ajax cleans *like* a white tornado." (Glossary: *Figures of Speech*) What, according to Lutz, is the power of similes in advertising (22–24)? Explain by citing several examples of your own.

6. What kinds of claims fit into Lutz's "unfinished words" category (29–32)? Why are they weasels? What makes them so difficult to detect?

7. Lutz uses the strategy of division and classification to develop this essay. (Glossary: *Division and Classification*) Explain how he uses this strategy. Why do you suppose Lutz felt the need to create the "Combining Weasel Words" category? Did the headings in the essay help you follow his discussion? What would be lost had he not included them?

The Creepy Language Tricks Taco Bell Uses to Fool People into Eating There

Kiera Butler

Born in 1980, Kiera Butler is a senior editor at *Mother Jones* and the author of *Raise: What 4-H Teaches 7 Million Kids—and How Its Lessons Could Change Food and Farming Forever* (2014). One critic stated, "*Raise* masterfully combines vivid accounts from a little-known subculture with a broader analysis of agriculture education today, using 4-H as a lens through which to view the changing landscape of farming in America and the rest of the world." At *Mother Jones*, Butler writes and edits stories about the environment, nutrition, health, and agriculture, including her award-winning column, "Econundrums." She earned her master's degree in journalism at Columbia University. Her piece about a dietitians' convention sponsored by McDonald's was featured on National Public Radio's *All Things Considered*. Butler's work has also been published in the *Atlantic*, *Wired.com*, *Slate*, and *Grist*.

In this article, which appeared in *Mother Jones* on September 29, 2014, Butler presents some of the findings of Dan Jurafsky of Stanford University. In his book, *The Language of Food: A Linguist Reads the Menu* (2014), Jurafsky examines the food menus of one of America's biggest fast food chains, Taco Bell, and reads through the subtle messages presented. He compares Taco Bell's use of language to the same company's higher-end restaurant, U.S. Taco Co., to see the subtle differences—and the messages those subtle differences reveal about food, audience, and culture.

WRITING TO DISCOVER: *What kind of places do you eat at when you eat out? A campus cafeteria? An off-campus eatery? Fast food restaurants? Somewhere else? How does where you eat affect what you eat, in terms of price, nutritional value, taste, and types of food?*

What can you tell about a restaurant from its menu? A lot more than what's cooking. That's what linguist Dan Jurafsky reveals in his new book, *The Language of Food: A Linguist Reads the Menu*.

Jurafsky, a professor of linguistics at Stanford, looked at hundreds of examples of food language—from menus to marketing materials to restaurant reviews. Along the way, he uncovered some fascinating patterns. For example: In naming foods, he explains, marketers often appeal to the associations that we already have with certain sounds. Crackers and other crispy foods tend to have names with short, front-of-the-mouth vowels (Ritz, Cheez-Its, Triscuits), while rich and heavy foods have longer vowels that we form in the back of our mouth (Rocky Road, Jamoca Almond Fudge). He also describes the shared linguistic heritage of some of the most common food words. Take salad, sauce, slaw, and salsa: All come from the Latin word *sal*, meaning "salted."

[W]e often use sex metaphors to talk about fancy food, while for cheaper food, the metaphor of choice is often drugs.

But it's Jurafsky's menu analysis that really stands out. Where most of us see simply a list of dishes, Jurafsky identifies subtle indicators of the image that a restaurant is trying to project—and which customers it wants to lure in. I asked Jurafsky to examine the menus of Taco Bell and its new upscale spinoff, US Taco Co., whose first location just opened in Southern California.

We started with Taco Bell's breakfast menu. Of course, everyone knows that the Tex-Mex fast food chain isn't exactly fine dining, but Jurafsky pointed to some hidden hallmarks of down-market eateries' menus.

The first thing that Jurafsky noticed about Taco Bell's menu was its size: There are dozens, if not hundreds of items. "The very, very fancy restaurants, many of them have no menu at all," Jurafsky says. "The waiter tells you what you're going to eat, kind of. If you want, they'll email you a menu if you really want it." 5

Next, Jurafsky picked up on descriptors. "So there's all of those adjectives and participles," he says. "'Fluffy.' 'Seasoned.'" That's one thing that's common on cheaper restaurant menus—as if the restaurant feels the need to try and convince its diners of the quality of the food. A fancier restaurant, he explains, would take it as a given that the diner expects the eggs to be fluffy and the pico de gallo to be freshly prepared.

"Notice the word 'flavorful,'" Jurafsky says. "The cheapest restaurants use these vague, positive adjectives. 'Delicious.' 'Tasty.' 'Scrumptious.' 'Wonderful.' Again, more expensive restaurants take all that as a given."

"The description specifies 'real cheddar cheese.' Just like all the other adjectives, 'real' tells you that they think customers are assuming that the cheese is not real, so they have to tell you that it is." Also, note that the word "jalapeño" is missing its tilde—the little squiggle over the "n" that signifies a "nye" pronunciation in Spanish words. Jurafsky isn't sure whether the missing "ñ" is linguistically meaningful, but keep it in mind, because it will become important when we look at US Taco Co.'s menu.

The words "double portion" and "lots" are also typical on the menus of cheap restaurants, says Jurafsky. "They want you to know you're getting enough food for your money."

Next, we turned to US Taco Co.: 10

"This is a hipster menu," Jurafsky says. "This isn't a linguistics thing, but there's a Day of the Dead skull on top and the desserts are served in mason jars. I mean, how hipster can you get?"

Let's take a closer look at some of the menu items:

"What the really upscale restaurants these days are doing is just listing their ingredients. They don't say "and" or "with." It's just a list. They're also using nonstandard capitalization, everything lower case or everything upper case, for example. Here they're making everything upper case. On the Taco Bell menu, they used standard capitalization."

Also, in "Wanna Get Lei'd" there's a reference to sex. Jurafsky explains that we often use sex metaphors to talk about fancy food, while for cheaper food, the metaphor of choice is often drugs. "The wings are addictive, or the chocolate must have crack," he says. "There's something about inexpensive foods that make us feel guilty. Talking about it in terms of drugs lets us put the responsibility on the food, not on ourselves."

"There are more unusual Spanish words on this menu," he says. Taco   15
Bell has "burrito" and "taco." Everyone knows those. But "here we have 'molcajete' and 'cotija.' Every item has at least one Spanish word. And there's the "ñ" in jalapeño! For Taco Bell, there might be tension between English and Spanish. In a hipster place, it's okay to be authentic."

Of course, says Jurafsky, language trends are always evolving. What we consider hipster menu language now is not the same as it was a few decades ago. In his book, Jurafsky notes that for most of the last century, trendy restaurants used French words to signify their status (think *au jus, a la mode*, and *sur le plat*). To the modern ear, these sound pretentious. Today's fashionable restaurant menus have replaced French phrases with "carefully selected obscure food words and pastoral images of green pastures and heirloom vegetables," he writes. That is, "if they offer you a menu at all."

THINKING CRITICALLY ABOUT THE READING

1. Why might a type of food be connected to the sound of its name (2)? What sort of marketing advantage might that give a product?

2. In paragraph 4, Butler uses the term "fine dining." What does that mean? How does fine dining differ from other types, such as fast food restaurants, family-style restaurants, or other lower-end eateries?

3. In analyzing the menu of Taco Bell, Dan Jurafsky notes that such restaurants need to stress that they have quality food, but high end restaurants can consider that as a given. What are some of the associations many people have with lower-end eateries that make such claims necessary?

4. Jurafsky makes an observation about the presence of the Spanish tilde in "jalapeño" on the menu at U.S. Taco Co., but its absence on the menu at lower-end Taco Bell. In your opinion, what does this suggest that Taco Bell thinks of its customers? What does Taco Bell itself take seriously, and what does it overlook?

5. Jurafsky refers to the menu at the U.S. Taco Co., as a "hipster menu" (11). What does he mean by this? How is seeing dessert in a mason jar a signal of the hipster? Examine also the tone associated with the word "hipster," as Jurafsky uses it.

6. Jurafsky notes that the language of both sex and drugs are used in connection with food. Why are higher-end foods associated with sex and lower-end foods associated with drugs?

Is the "Natural" Label 100 Percent Misleading?

Deena Shanker

Deena Shanker, based in New York, is the food and consumer goods reporter at Quartz, a digital news outlet focused on the global economy. Her work has appeared on *Salon* and *Fortune*. She was also the Healthy Food Editor at BuzzFeed. Shanker graduated from the University of Pennsylvania Law School and was a corporate litigator before embarking on her reporting career.

This article first appeared on September 6, 2012 on Grist, an environmental news and analysis Web site. In the selection, Shanker analyzes the hard-to-define "natural" label on food packages. Although there is little official regulation of the term, consumers are more likely to buy a product with the label "natural." Many well-known food companies make this claim despite—or perhaps because—the term means something different to every consumer.

WRITING TO DISCOVER: *How much attention do you pay to language on food labels? Do words such as "healthy" or "natural" make you more likely to buy a product? Do you assume that there is government regulation behind the use of such words? How often do you think that companies creating these products adhere to such regulations?*

What do Juicy Juice fruit punch, Tyson chicken, and Nature Valley granola bars have in common? They're all branded with the same mysterious, ubiquitous term: natural.

The natural label's takeover is not just anecdotal. In 2008, Mintel's Global New Products Database found that "all-natural" was the second most used claim on new American food products. And a recent study by the Shelton Group, an advertising company focusing on sustainability, found that it's also the most popular. When asked, "Which is the best description to read on a food label?" 25 percent of consumers answered, "100 percent natural."

So what does natural mean? Well, that depends on who you're asking. A salesperson in the meat department at Shoprite in Chester, N.Y., told me that Tyson's all natural chicken is "basically the same thing" as organic. At General Mills, 100 percent natural means "that all ingredients used are from a natural source and a natural process," though when I asked for clarification on what counts as a "natural process," the customer service agent was out of answers.

According to Rachel Saks, co-founder of the Brooklyn-based nutrition consulting company tABLE health, for her health-conscious clients, natural "means whatever they want it to mean." Clients with high blood pressure, for example, "tend to interpret natural as good for their blood pressure, maybe not too high in salt." Clients looking to lose weight, meanwhile, read the claim to mean the food is low-calorie. "It solves whatever problem they want to solve."

With all of these disparate interpretations of a once-straightforward word, it may come as a surprise that there is, at least on principle, some official government guidance to how the word should be used.

What confuses most people, however, is that the two agencies that regulate food in this country—the U.S. Department of Agriculture (USDA) and the Food and Drug Administration (FDA)—have very different approaches to the term.

A meaty approach

The USDA, which is tasked with regulating meat and poultry, says that a product is "natural" if it contains "no artificial ingredient or added color and is only minimally processed. Minimal processing means that the product was processed in a manner that does not fundamentally alter the product."

As little as this definition really tells us, Stephen Gardner, director of litigation for the Center of Science in the Public Interest (CSPI), says it beats the FDA's definition hands down. "Meat is an easy one. Natural, at a minimum, should be what you get off the cow, or the pig, or the chicken. It shouldn't be treated." And for the most part, that is what natural means when used on meat products. It says nothing about what happened to the animal before slaughter, what it was fed or treated with while alive (read: GMO corn or grass, antibiotics or not), or under what kinds of conditions it was raised. But it does mean that between the slaughterhouse and the supermarket, nothing was added or done to it. (Gardner notes that there are some outliers that seem to have escaped the USDA's eye, like chicken that is pumped with salt water to give it a healthier appearance and better taste.)

Everything else

The real problem, according to Gardner, is the lack of regulation on non-meat products, which, despite being called "natural," are often highly processed. Gardner and CSPI are taking this issue to the courts in a lawsuit against General Mills for marketing its Nature Valley granola bars, which contain additives like maltodextrin, as "100% Natural." The suit challenges the practice as misleading advertising, not as running afoul of FDA rules—probably because the rules themselves allow the practice to continue.

The FDA says on its website, "from a food science perspective, it is difficult to define a food product that is 'natural' . . . [The] FDA has not developed a definition for use of the term natural or its derivatives.

However, the agency has not objected to the use of the term if the food does not contain added color, artificial flavors, or synthetic substances."

How's that for hard-lined? Seriously, though, "natural" can mean anything a food producer wants it to, no matter how misleading, and the FDA won't "object." Even though the agency is aware of how misunderstood the term is, it has been willfully avoiding opportunities to define it since the late 1970s.

"What should happen is that the FDA should just adopt, as first the Sugar Association and then CSPI asked it to do about five years ago, the USDA definition of natural, which is minimally processed," says Gardner. The term "minimally processed" refers to "stuff you could do in your own kitchen." General Mills, on the other hand, claims that "natural" means the ingredients are derived from a "natural process"—a vague phrase if there is one.

Saks encounters this "natural" misunderstanding with as much as 15 percent of her clientele, who are often, but not always, well-educated and concerned with the quality of their food. While she'd like to see stricter standards for the term, she admits, "that's tough too, because you'd have to be defining it by something that it's not," as in not made with corn derivatives, genetically modified organisms, or other synthesized ingredients.

So what does natural mean? Well, that depends on who you're asking. Even among the food lawyers there is a debate about what "natural" should mean on a food label and whether the FDA should step in. Yve Golan, founding partner of The Golan Firm and a specialist in food labeling law, has disagreed with Gardner's contention that the FDA should define the term. Pointing to loopholes in the organic label, she worries that an FDA definition will lead to "a hypertechnical definition riddled with needless exceptions."

That, of course, brings us back to the original problem Saks pointed to: "Natural" currently means something different to every consumer. And, if that's really the case, how can it mean anything at all?

THINKING CRITICALLY ABOUT THE READING

1. Were you surprised to read that a company as well-known as General Mills was making a specific claim about their products that was in fact untrue? What does this suggest about the nature of American business and marketing in particular? Why did the suit challenge the practice as "misleading advertising" rather than breaking FDA rules?

2. Shanker cites several people in the food industry—a salesperson, the co-founder of a nutrition consulting company, and a customer service agent— who all have different takes on what "natural" means. What seems to be the common thread?

3. In paragraph 4, Shanker quotes nutrition consultant Rachel Saks, who observes that consumers interpret "natural" in different ways. It "means whatever they want it to mean . . . It solves whatever problem they want to solve.'" What does Saks's observation suggest about the American consumer? Who benefits most from the ambiguity of the term—consumers or industry?

4. One of the problems that Shanker notes is that the FDA and the USDA have "very different approaches" to the term "natural" (6). What are the differences in how these two government agencies address "natural" food? What are the legal implications of such different approaches?

5. Stephen Gardner argues in the article that "The FDA should just adopt, as first the Sugar Association and the CSPI asked it to do about five years ago, the USDA definition of natural, which is minimally processed" (12). Do you think this is an adequate definition? Would improving the accuracy of the label result in any change in consumer behavior? Why or why not?

WRITING SUGGESTIONS: DEBATING THE ISSUE

1. Think of a product that you have used and been disappointed by, one that has failed to live up to its advertising claims. Write a letter to the manufacturer in which you describe your experience with the product and explain why you believe the company's advertisements have been misleading. Send your letter to the president of the company or to the director of marketing.

2. Many product names are chosen because of their connotative or suggestive values (Glossary: *Connotation/Denotation*) For example, the name *Tide* for a detergent suggests the power of the ocean tides and the rhythmic surge of cleansing waters; the name *Pride* for the wax suggests how the user will feel after using the product; the name *100% Natural* for the cereal suggests that the consumer is getting nothing less than nature's best; and the name *Taurus* for the Ford car suggests the strength and durability of a bull. Test what Bill Bryson has said about brand names in "The Hard Sell: Advertising in America" (p. 507) by exploring the connotations of the brand names in one of the following categories: cosmetics, deodorants, candy, paint, car batteries, fast food sandwiches, pain relievers, disposable diapers, or cat food. Report your findings in an essay.

3. In paragraph 12 of "The Hard Sell: Advertising in America," Bryson reminds us that successful advertisers have always known the importance of good slogans. Some early slogans, such as the American Florist Association's "Say it with flowers," are still in use today even though they were coined years ago. Research five or six current product slogans that Bryson doesn't mention and write an essay in which you discuss the importance of slogans to advertising campaigns. How, for example, do slogans serve to focus, direct, and galvanize advertising campaigns? What do you think makes some slogans work and others fail? What makes a slogan memorable? As you start this project, you may find it helpful to search out materials in your library or on the Internet relating to slogans in general and how they engage people.

4. Choose something that you own and like—a mountain bike, luggage, a comfortable sofa, a guitar, or anything else that you are glad you bought. Imagine that you need to sell it to raise some money for a special weekend, and to do so you need to advertise online. Write copy for an online ad in which you try to sell your item. Include a slogan or make up a product name and use it in the ad. Then write a short essay about your ad in which you discuss the features of the item you chose to highlight, the language you used to make it sound as appealing as possible, and how your slogan or name makes the advertisement more memorable.

5. Pay attention to the ads for companies that offer rival products or services (for example, Apple and Microsoft, Coca-Cola and Pepsi-Co, Burger King and McDonald's, Charles Schwab and Raymond James, and AT&T and Verizon). Focusing on a single pair of ads, analyze the different appeals that companies make when comparing their products or services to those of the competition. To what audience does each ad appeal? How many weasel words can you detect? How does each ad use the strategies described by William Lutz in "Weasel Words: The Art of Saying Nothing at All" (p. 520) to its product's advantage? Based on your analysis, write an essay about the advertising strategies companies use when in head-to-head competition with the products of other companies. You might look at Deena Shanker's article (p. 534) for inspiration.

6. Look at several issues of one popular women's or men's magazine (such as *Cosmopolitan, Vogue, Elle, Glamour, Sports Illustrated, GQ, Maxim, Car and Driver, Field and Stream*), and analyze the advertisements they contain. What types of products or services are advertised? Which ads caught your eye? Why? Are the ads made up primarily of pictures, or do some have a lot of text? Do you detect any relationship between the ads and the editorial content of the magazine? Write an essay in which you present the findings of your analysis.

7. In Kiera Butler's "The Creepy Language Tricks Taco Bell Uses to Fool People into Eating There" (p. 531), Dan Jurafsky examines the menus at Taco Bell and its higher-end cousin, U.S. Taco Co., to make a point about the language restaurants use to give impressions about their food. Research a menu from a different low-end eatery (fast food or other type) and compare that to the menu of a higher-end restaurant serving similar cuisine. Write an essay in which you examine the use of language of both restaurants' menus. Do your findings agree with Jurafsky's, or are they different? How so? Do either of the menus use any of the "weasel words" described by William Lutz in "Weasel Words: The Art of Saying Nothing at All"?

8. In paragraph 15 of Butler's "The Creepy Language Tricks Taco Bell Uses to Fool People into Eating There," Jurafsky comments on the absence of the Spanish tilde in the Taco Bell menu as an indication of a possible "tension between English and Spanish." So much of the food consumed in America traces its heritage to cultures from other countries (e.g., Italian, Mexican, French, Chinese, and so on), but has the language around those foods accompanied them? Write an essay in which you report on how immigration has affected American cuisine. (You might narrow your topic by focusing on a specific region in the U.S. or a specific community of immigrants.) Which

dishes that we think of as "American" are borrowed from other cultures? How does acceptance of a type of cuisine affect society's impression of immigrants of that culture?

9. Deena Shanker notes in her article "Is the 'Natural' Label 100 Percent Misleading?" that the FDA "has not developed a definition for the term natural or its derivatives" (10). Write a possible definition for the term "natural" as it relates to food labeling and advertisement. What separates "natural" food from "unnatural" food? Then, in an essay, defend your definition. How will your definition prevent companies from using "natural" as a "weasel word," as William Lutz might say?

WHY DO WE LIE?

When one considers the trouble lying causes, it is difficult to fathom why we do it. We are all too familiar with the practice nonetheless. Richard Gunderman tells us in "Is Lying Bad for Us?" that "it has been estimated that the average American tells 11 lies per week" (1). If so many of us are lying so often, might we consider lying normal rather than aberrant behavior? And what's wrong with lying anyhow? Plenty. From the little white lies we tell as children, and more often as adults, to the perjury we commit before a court of law, lies inflict pain and emotional distress, not just on those we deceive but on ourselves as well. Perhaps Fyodor Dostoyevsky in his novel *The Brothers Karamazov* put it best: "Above all, don't lie to yourself. The man who lies to himself and listens to his own lie comes to a point that he cannot distinguish the truth within him, or around him, and so loses all respect for himself and for others. And having no respect he ceases to love." We lie to get ourselves out of trouble, to cope, to avoid punishment, and for about as many reasons as the human condition presents us.

In "The Truth about Lying," the first article we present in this section, veteran author Judith Viorst classifies, describes, and gives examples of the various kinds of lies we commit. Her classification establishes a solid foundation for the discussions that follow. Next, Po Bronson, author of "Learning to Lie," examines why kids lie and how they grow out of lies, or sadly double down as they grow older. Richard Gunderson, in "Is Lying Bad for Us?" writes clearly, succinctly, and cogently why lying is very bad behavior, indeed. Finally, Chana Joffe-Walt and Alix Spiegel in "Psychology of Fraud: Why Good People Do Bad Things" offer a causal analysis of how ethical and business decisions can be divorced from one another with disastrous consequences. The authors offer tangible evidence of Sir Walter Scott's famous warning: *Oh, what a tangled web we weave, / When first we practice to deceive!*

The Truth about Lying

JUDITH VIORST

Judith Viorst, poet, journalist, author of children's books, and novelist, was born in New Jersey in 1931. She has chronicled her life in such books as *It's Hard to Be Hip over Thirty and Other Tragedies of Married Life* (1968), *How Did I Get to Be Forty and Other Atrocities* (1976), and *When Did I Stop Being Twenty and Other Injustices: Selected Prose from Single to Mid-Life* (1987). In 1981, she went back to school, taking courses at the Washington Psychoanalytic Institute. This study, along with her personal experience of psychoanalysis, helped to inspire *Necessary Losses* (1986), a popular and critical success. She wrote the very popular children's book, *Alexander and the Horrible, No Good, Very Bad Day* (1972). Her stories about Alexander, which also include *Alexander, Who Used to Be Rich Last Sunday* (1986) and *Alexander, Who's Not (Do You Hear Me? I Mean It!) Going to Move* (1995) deal with the general nature of emotions. Combining theory, poetry, interviews, and anecdotes, Viorst approaches personal growth as a shedding of illusions. Her recent work includes *I'm Too Young to Be Seventy: And Other Delusions* (2005), and *Unexpectedly Eighty: And Other Adaptations* (2010).

In the following essay, first published in the March 1981 issue of *Redbook*, the author approaches lying with delicacy and candor as she carefully classifies the different types of lies we all encounter.

WRITING TO DISCOVER: What is your attitude toward lying? Do you allow yourself "little white lies" or no lies at all, or a lot of lies in order to get you out of awkward situations? What have been the consequences of lying in your life?

I've been wanting to write on a subject that intrigues and challenges me: the subject of lying. I've found it very difficult to do. Everyone I've talked to has a quite intense and personal but often rather intolerant point of view about what we can—and can never *never*—tell lies about. I've finally reached the conclusion that I can't present any ultimate conclusions, for too many people would promptly disagree. Instead, I'd like to present a series of moral puzzles, all concerned with lying. I'll tell you what I think about them. Do you agree?

SOCIAL LIES

Most of the people I've talked with say that they find social lying acceptable and necessary. They think it's the civilized way for folks to behave. Without these little white lies, they say, our relationships would

541

be short and brutish and nasty. It's arrogant, they say, to insist on being so incorruptible and so brave that you cause other people unnecessary embarrassment or pain by compulsively assailing them with your honesty. I basically agree. What about you?

Will you say to people, when it simply isn't true, "I like your new hairdo," "You're looking much better," "It's so nice to see you," "I had a wonderful time"?

Will you praise hideous presents and homely kids?

Will you decline invitations with "We're busy that night—so sorry we   5
can't come," when the truth is you'd rather stay home than dine with the So-and-sos?

And even though, as I do, you may prefer the polite evasion of "You really cooked up a storm" instead of "The soup"—which tastes like warmed-over coffee—"is wonderful," will you, if you must, proclaim it wonderful?

There's one man I know who absolutely refuses to tell social lies. "I can't play that game," he says; "I'm simply not made that way." And his answer to the argument that saying nice things to someone doesn't cost anything is, "Yes, it does—it destroys your credibility." Now, he won't, unsolicited, offer his views on the painting you just bought, but you don't ask his frank opinion unless you want *frank*, and his silence at those moments when the rest of us liars are muttering, "Isn't it lovely?" is, for the most part, eloquent enough. My friend does not indulge in what he calls "flattery, false praise, and mellifluous comments." When others tell fibs he will not go along. He says that social lying is lying, that little white lies are still lies. And he feels that telling lies is morally wrong. What about you?

PEACE-KEEPING LIES

Many people tell peace-keeping lies; lies designed to avoid irritation or argument; lies designed to shelter the liar from possible blame or pain; lies (or so it is rationalized) designed to keep trouble at bay without hurting anyone.

I tell these lies at times, and yet I always feel they're wrong. I understand why we tell them, but still they feel wrong. And whenever I lie so that someone won't disapprove of me or think less of me or holler at me, I feel I'm a bit of a coward, I feel I'm dodging responsibility, I feel . . . guilty. What about you?

Do you, when you're late for a date because you overslept, say that   10
you're late because you got caught in a traffic jam?

Do you, when you forget to call a friend, say that you called several times but the line was busy?

Do you, when you didn't remember that it was your father's birthday, say that his present must be delayed in the mail?

And when you're planning a weekend in New York City and you're not in the mood to visit your mother, who lives there, do you conceal—with a lie, if you must—the fact that you'll be in New York? Or do you have the courage—or is it the cruelty?—to say, "I'll be in New York, but sorry—I don't plan on seeing you"?

(Dave and his wife Elaine have two quite different points of view on this very subject. He calls her a coward. She says she's being wise. He says she must assert her right to visit New York sometimes and not see her mother. To which she always patiently replies: "Why should we have useless fights? My mother's too old to change. We get along much better when I lie to her.")

Finally, do you keep the peace by telling your husband lies on the subject of money? Do you reduce what you really paid for your shoes? And in general do you find yourself ready, willing and able to lie to him when you make absurd mistakes or lose or break things? 15

"I used to have a romantic idea that part of intimacy was confessing every dumb thing that you did to your husband. But after a couple of years of that," says Laura, "have I changed my mind!"

And having changed her mind, she finds herself telling peace-keeping lies. And yes, I tell them, too. What about you?

PROTECTIVE LIES

Protective lies are lies folks tell—often quite serious lies—because they're convinced that the truth would be too damaging. They lie because they feel there are certain human values that supersede the wrong of having lied. They lie, not for personal gain, but because they believe it's for the good of the person they're lying to. They lie to those they love, to those who trust them most of all, on the grounds that breaking this trust is justified.

They may lie to their children on money or marital matters.

They may lie to the dying about the state of their health. 20

They may lie about adultery, and not—or so they insist—to save their own hide, but to save the heart and the pride of the men they are married to.

They may lie to their closest friend because the truth about her talents or son or psyche would be—or so they insist—utterly devastating.

> We never can be sure, once we start to juggle lies, just where they'll land, exactly where they'll roll.

I sometimes tell such lies, but I'm aware that it's quite presumptuous to claim I know what's best for others to know. That's called playing God. That's called manipulation and control. And we never can be sure, once we start to juggle lies, just where they'll land, exactly where they'll roll.

And furthermore, we may find ourselves lying in order to back up the lies that are backing up the lie we initially told.

And furthermore—let's be honest—if conditions were reversed, we   25
certainly wouldn't want anyone lying to us.

Yet, having said all that, I still believe that there are times when protective lies must nonetheless be told. What about you?

If your Dad had a very bad heart and you had to tell him some bad family news, which would you choose: to tell him the truth or lie?

If your former husband failed to send his monthly child-support check and in other ways behaved like a total rat, would you allow your children—who believed he was simply wonderful—to continue to believe that he was wonderful?

If your dearly beloved brother selected a wife whom you deeply disliked, would you reveal your feelings or would you fake it?

And if you were asked, after making love, "And how was that for   30
you?" would you reply, if it wasn't too good, "Not too good"?

Now, some would call a sex lie unimportant, little more than social lying, a simple act of courtesy that makes all human intercourse run smoothly. And some would say all sex lies are bad news and unacceptably protective. Because, says Ruth, "a man with an ego that fragile doesn't need your lies—he needs a psychiatrist." Still others feel that sex lies are indeed protective lies, more serious than simple social lying, and yet at times they tell them on the grounds that when it comes to matters sexual, everybody's ego is somewhat fragile.

"If most of the time things go well in sex," says Sue, "I think you're allowed to dissemble when they don't. I can't believe it's good to say, 'Last night was four stars, darling, but tonight's performance rates only a half.' "

I'm inclined to agree with Sue. What about you?

TRUST-KEEPING LIES

Another group of lies are trust-keeping lies, lies that involve triangulation, with A (that's you) telling lies to B on behalf of C (whose trust you'd promised to keep). Most people concede that once you've agreed not to betray a friend's confidence, you can't betray it, even if you must lie. But I've talked with people who don't want you telling them anything that they might be called on to lie about.

"I don't tell lies for myself," says Fran, "and I don't want to have   35
to tell them for other people." Which means, she agrees, that if her best friend is having an affair, she absolutely doesn't want to know about it.

"Are you saying," her best friend asks, "that if I went off with a lover and I asked you to tell my husband I'd been with you, that you wouldn't lie for me, that you'd betray me?"

Fran is very pained but very adamant. "I wouldn't want to betray you, so . . . don't ask me."

Fran's best friend is shocked. What about you?

Do you believe you can have close friends if you're not prepared to receive their deepest secrets?

Do you believe you must always lie for your friends?

Do you believe, if your friend tells a secret that turns out to be quite immoral or illegal, that once you've promised to keep it, you must keep it?   40

And what if your friend were your boss—if you were perhaps one of the President's men—would you betray or lie for him over, say, Watergate?

As you can see, these issues get terribly sticky.

It's my belief that once we've promised to keep a trust, we must tell lies to keep it. I also believe that we can't tell Watergate lies. And if these two statements strike you as quite contradictory, you're right—they're quite contradictory. But for now they're the best I can do. What about you?

Some say that truth will out and thus you might as well tell the truth. Some say you can't regain the trust that lies lose. Some say that even though the truth may never be revealed, our lies pervert and damage our relationships. Some say . . . well, here's what some of them have to say.

"I'm a coward," says Grace, "about telling close people important,   45
difficult truths. I find that I'm unable to carry it off. And so if something is bothering me, it keeps building up inside till I end up just not seeing them anymore."

"I lie to my husband on sexual things, but I'm furious," says Joyce, "that he's too insensitive to know I'm lying."

"I suffer most from the misconception that children can't take the truth," says Emily. "But I'm starting to see that what's harder and more damaging for them is being told lies, is not being told the truth."

"I'm afraid," says Joan, "that we often wind up feeling a bit of contempt for the people we lie to."

And then there are those who have no talent for lying.

"I'm willing to lie. But just as a last resort—the truth's always better."   50

"Over the years, I tried to lie," a friend of mine explained, "but I always got found out and I always got punished. I guess I gave myself away because I feel guilty about any kind of lying. It looks as if I'm stuck with telling the truth."

For those of us, however, who are good at telling lies, for those of us who lie and don't get caught, the question of whether or not to lie can be a hard and serious moral problem. I liked the remark of a friend of mine who said, "I'm willing to lie. But just as a last resort—the truth's always better."

"Because," he explained, "though others may completely accept the lie I'm telling, I don't."

I tend to feel that way, too.

What about you?   55

THINKING CRITICALLY ABOUT THE READING

1. Viorst divides lying into a series of classifications. Do you find these classifications convincing, or do you think she has overlooked other types of lying? Why or why not?

2. Viorst talks about different kinds of lies: social lies, peace-keeping lies, protective lies, and trust-keeping lies. Which lies is she most in favor of? Why? Do you agree with her assessments? Why or why not?

3. Of the categories of lies that Viorst writes about in this essay, which sort are you most likely to commit? Why?

4. What is the difference between yourself accepting a lie that you tell, and others accepting it? Is the difference between the two significant? Explain.

5. Some lies may be considered by some to be relatively inconsequential (e.g., "No, honey, that dress does not make you look fat.") while others are more significant (e.g., being cheated on by a lover). What attitude does Viorst reveal towards these differences, and do you agree with her? Why or why not?

Learning to Lie

PO BRONSON

Born in 1964 in Seattle, Washington, and educated at Stanford University
and San Francisco State, Po Bronson has a long career as a professional
writer of both fiction and nonfiction. He has published six books and
has written for television, magazines, and newspapers, including the *New
York Times* and the *Wall Street Journal*, and for National Public Radio's
Morning Edition. Bronson's book of social documentary, *What Should
I Do with My Life?*, was a number one *New York Times* best seller and
remained in the Top 10 for nine months. His first novel, *Bombardiers*, was
a number one best seller in the United Kingdom. His books have been
translated into nineteen languages. In regard to writing as a career, Bronson states, "Most writers, rather unglamorously, are really just people who
find some solace in expression. Combined with some tenacity, or refusal
to give up, we spend years learning the skills of writing. One day we get
published and expression becomes our profession. We continue to seek
an elusive mastery of our art. What makes us good writers is our constant
devotion to this craft, a willingness to keep learning. More tenacity."

In this article, published in *New York Magazine* on February 10, 2008,
Bronson writes about how children, even from the very young ages of three
or four, learn to lie. Rather than growing out of lying, as many parents
hope—and parenting guidebooks assure them—children in fact become
better liars. By the time they reach their young teenage years, many have
become quite proficient at lying, often as a means of social coping.

WRITING TO DISCOVER: *How important is lying as a means of getting along
in society? Think of different kinds of lies: lying to your grandmother about how much
you like her present when actually don't like it; lying about how you spent your time
when you were supposed to be studying for a test; lying about the quality of a meal
someone special cooked for you. Is it really possible to get along with others without
the occasional lie?*

In the last few years, a handful of intrepid scholars have decided it's
time to try to understand why kids lie. For a study to assess the extent of
teenage dissembling, Dr. Nancy Darling, then at Penn State University,
recruited a special research team of a dozen undergraduate students, all
under the age of 21. Using gift certificates for free CDs as bait, Darling's
Mod Squad persuaded high-school students to spend a few hours with
them in the local pizzeria.

Each student was handed a deck of 36 cards, and each card in this
deck listed a topic teens sometimes lie about to their parents. Over a slice
and a Coke, the teen and two researchers worked through the deck, learning what things the kid was lying to his parents about, and why.

"They began the interviews saying that parents give you everything and yes, you should tell them everything," Darling observes. By the end of the interview, the kids saw for the first time how much they were lying and how many of the family's rules they had broken. Darling says 98 percent of the teens reported lying to their parents.

Out of the 36 topics, the average teen was lying to his parents about twelve of them. The teens lied about what they spent their allowances on, and whether they'd started dating, and what clothes they put on away from the house. They lied about what movie they went to, and whom they went with. They lied about alcohol and drug use, and they lied about whether they were hanging out with friends their parents disapproved of. They lied about how they spent their afternoons while their parents were at work. They lied about whether chaperones were in attendance at a party or whether they rode in cars driven by drunken teens.

Being an honors student didn't change these numbers by much; nor   5 did being an overscheduled kid. No kid, apparently, was too busy to break a few rules. And lest you wonder if these numbers apply only to teens in State College, Pennsylvania, the teens in Darling's sample were compared to national averages on a bevy of statistics, from academics to extracurriculars. "We had a very normal, representative sample," Darling says.

For two decades, parents have rated "honesty" as the trait they most wanted in their children. Other traits, such as confidence or good judgment, don't even come close. On paper, the kids are getting this message. In surveys, 98 percent said that trust and honesty were essential in a personal relationship. Depending on their ages, 96 to 98 percent said lying is morally wrong.

So when do the 98 percent who think lying is wrong become the 98 percent who lie?

It starts very young. Indeed, bright kids—those who do better on other academic indicators—are able to start lying at 2 or 3. "Lying is related to intelligence," explains Dr. Victoria Talwar, an assistant professor at Montreal's McGill University and a leading expert on children's lying behavior.

Although we think of truthfulness as a young child's paramount virtue, it turns out that lying is the more advanced skill. A child who is going to lie must recognize the truth, intellectually conceive of an alternate reality, and be able to convincingly sell that new reality to someone else. Therefore, lying demands both advanced cognitive development and social skills that honesty simply doesn't require. "It's a developmental milestone," Talwar has concluded.

This puts parents in the position of being either damned or blessed,   10 depending on how they choose to look at it. If your 4-year-old is a good liar, it's a strong sign she's got brains. And it's the smart, savvy kid who's most at risk of becoming a habitual liar.

By their 4th birthday, almost all kids will start experimenting with lying in order to avoid punishment. Because of that, they lie indiscriminately—whenever punishment seems to be a possibility. A 3-year-old will say, "I didn't hit my sister," even if a parent witnessed the child's hitting her sibling.

> **[K]ids who grasp early the nuance between lies and truth use this knowledge to their advantage, making them more prone to lie when given a chance.**

Most parents hear their child lie and assume he's too young to understand what lies are or that lying's wrong. They presume their child will stop when he gets older and learns those distinctions. Talwar has found the opposite to be true—kids who grasp early the nuances between lies and truth use this knowledge to their advantage, making them more prone to lie when given the chance.

Many parenting Web sites and books advise parents to just let lies go—they'll grow out of it. The truth, according to Talwar, is that kids grow into it. In studies where children are observed in their natural environment, a 4-year-old will lie once every two hours, while a 6-year-old will lie about once every hour and a half. Few kids are exceptions.

By the time a child reaches school age, the reasons for lying become more complex. Avoiding punishment is still a primary catalyst for lying, but lying also becomes a way to increase a child's power and sense of control—by manipulating friends with teasing, by bragging to assert status, and by learning he can fool his parents.

Thrown into elementary school, many kids begin lying to their peers 15 as a coping mechanism, as a way to vent frustration or get attention. Any sudden spate of lying, or dramatic increase in lying, is a danger sign: Something has changed in that child's life, in a way that troubles him. "Lying is a symptom—often of a bigger problem behavior," explains Talwar. "It's a strategy to keep themselves afloat."

In longitudinal studies, a majority of 6-year-olds who frequently lie have it socialized out of them by age 7. But if lying has become a successful strategy for handling difficult social situations, a child will stick with it. About half of all kids do—and if they're still lying a lot at 7, then it seems likely to continue for the rest of childhood. They're hooked.

"My son doesn't lie," insisted Steve, a slightly frazzled father in his mid-thirties, as he watched Nick, his eager 6-year-old, enthralled in a game of marbles with a student researcher in Talwar's Montreal lab. Steve was quite proud of his son, describing him as easygoing and very social. He had Nick bark out an impressive series of addition problems the boy had memorized, as if that was somehow proof of Nick's sincerity.

Steve then took his assertion down a notch. "Well, I've never heard him lie." Perhaps that, too, was a little strong. "I'm sure he must lie some, but when I hear it, I'll still be surprised." He had brought his son to the lab after seeing an advertisement in a Montreal parenting magazine that asked, "Can Your Child Tell the Difference Between the Truth and a Lie?"

Steve was curious to find out if Nick would lie, but he wasn't sure he wanted to know the answer. The idea of his son's being dishonest with him was profoundly troubling.

But I knew for a fact his son did lie. Nick cheated, then he lied, and 20 then he lied again. He did so unhesitatingly, without a single glimmer of remorse.

Nick thought he'd spent the hour playing a series of games with a couple of nice women. He had won two prizes, a cool toy car and a bag of plastic dinosaurs, and everyone said he did very well. What the first-grader didn't know was that those games were really a battery of psychological tests, and the women were Talwar's trained researchers working toward doctorates in child psychology.

One of Talwar's experiments, a variation on a classic experiment called the temptation-resistance paradigm, is known in the lab as "the Peeking Game." Through a hidden camera, I'd watched Nick play it with another one of Talwar's students, Cindy Arruda. She told Nick they were going to play a guessing game. Nick was to sit facing the wall and try to guess the identity of a toy Arruda brought out, based on the sound it made. If he was right three times, he'd win a prize.

The first two were easy: a police car and a crying baby doll. Nick bounced in his chair with excitement when he got the answers right. Then Arruda brought out a soft, stuffed soccer ball and placed it on top of a greeting card that played music. She cracked the card, triggering it to play a music-box jingle of Beethoven's *Für Elise*. Nick, of course, was stumped.

Arruda suddenly said she had to leave the room for a bit, promising to be right back. She admonished Nick not to peek at the toy while she was gone. Nick struggled not to, but at thirteen seconds, he gave in and looked.

When Arruda returned, she could barely come through the door 25 before Nick—facing the wall again—triumphantly announced, "A soccer ball!" Arruda told Nick to wait for her to get seated. Suddenly realizing he should sound unsure of his answer, he hesitantly asked, "A soccer ball?"

Arruda said Nick was right, and when he turned to face her, he acted very pleased. Arruda asked Nick if he had peeked. "No," he said quickly. Then a big smile spread across his face.

Without challenging him, or even a note of suspicion in her voice, Arruda asked Nick how he'd figured out the sound came from a soccer ball.

Nick cupped his chin in his hands, then said, "The music had sounded like a ball." Then: "The ball sounded black and white." Nick added that the music sounded like the soccer balls he played with at school: They squeaked. And the music sounded like the squeak he heard when he kicked a ball. To emphasize this, his winning point, he brushed his hand against the side of the toy ball.

This experiment was not just a test to see if children cheat and lie under temptation. It was also designed to test a child's ability to extend a lie, offering plausible explanations and avoiding what the scientists call "leakage"—inconsistencies that reveal the lie for what it is. Nick's whiffs at covering up his lie would be scored later by coders who watched the videotape. So Arruda accepted without question the fact that soccer balls play Beethoven when they're kicked and gave Nick his prize. He was thrilled.

Seventy-six percent of kids Nick's age take the chance to peek during   30 the game, and when asked if they peeked, 95 percent lie about it.

But sometimes the researcher will read the child a short storybook before she asks about the peeking. One story read aloud is "The Boy Who Cried Wolf"—the version in which both the boy and the sheep get eaten because of his repeated lies. Alternatively, they read "George Washington and the Cherry Tree," in which young George confesses to his father that he chopped down the prized tree with his new hatchet. The story ends with his father's reply: "George, I'm glad that you cut down the tree after all. Hearing you tell the truth instead of a lie is better than if I had a thousand cherry trees."

Now, which story do you think reduced lying more? When we surveyed 1,300 people, 75 percent thought "The Boy Who Cried Wolf" would work better. However, this famous fable actually did not cut down lying at all in Talwar's experiments. In fact, after hearing the story, kids lied even a little more than normal. Meanwhile, hearing "George Washington and the Cherry Tree"—even when Washington was replaced with a nondescript character, eliminating the potential that his iconic celebrity might influence older kids—reduced lying a sizable 43 percent in kids. Although most kids lied in the control situation, the majority hearing George Washington told the truth.

The shepherd boy ends up suffering the ultimate punishment, but the fact that lies get punished is not news to children. Increasing the threat of punishment for lying only makes children hyperaware of the potential personal cost. It distracts children from learning how their lies affect others. In studies, scholars find that kids who live in threat of consistent punishment don't lie less. Instead, they become better liars, at an earlier age—learning to get caught less often.

Ultimately, it's not fairy tales that stop kids from lying—it's the process of socialization. But the wisdom in "The Cherry Tree" applies: According to Talwar, parents need to teach kids the worth of honesty, just like George Washington's father did, as much as they need to say that lying is wrong.

The most disturbing reason children lie is that parents teach them to.   35 According to Talwar, they learn it from us. "We don't explicitly tell them to lie, but they see us do it. They see us tell the telemarketer, 'I'm just a guest here.' They see us boast and lie to smooth social relationships."

Consider how we expect a child to act when he opens a gift he doesn't like. We instruct him to swallow all his honest reactions and put on a polite smile. Talwar runs an experiment where children play games to win a present, but when they finally receive the present, it's a lousy bar of soap. After giving the kids a moment to overcome the shock, a researcher asks them how they like it. About a quarter of preschoolers can lie that they like the gift—by elementary school, about half. Telling this lie makes them extremely uncomfortable, especially when pressed to offer a few reasons *why* they like the bar of soap. Kids who shouted with glee when they won the Peeking Game suddenly mumble quietly and fidget.

Meanwhile, the child's parent usually cheers when the child comes up with the white lie. "Often, the parents are proud that their kids are 'polite'—they don't see it as lying," Talwar remarks. She's regularly amazed at parents' seeming inability to recognize that white lies are still lies.

When adults are asked to keep diaries of their own lies, they admit to about one lie per every five social interactions, which works out to one per day, on average. The vast majority of these lies are white lies, lies to protect yourself or others, like telling the guy at work who brought in his wife's muffins that they taste great or saying, "Of course this is my natural hair color."

Encouraged to tell so many white lies and hearing so many others, children gradually get comfortable with being disingenuous. Insincerity becomes, literally, a daily occurrence. They learn that honesty only creates conflict, and dishonesty is an easy way to avoid conflict. And while they don't confuse white-lie situations with lying to cover their misdeeds, they bring this emotional groundwork from one circumstance to the other. It becomes easier, psychologically, to lie to a parent. So if the parent says, "Where did you get these Pokémon cards?! I told you, you're not allowed to waste your allowance on Pokémon cards!" this may feel to the child very much like a white-lie scenario—he can make his father *feel better* by telling him the cards were extras from a friend.

Now, compare this with the way children are taught not to tattle.   40 What grown-ups really mean by "Don't tell" is that we want children to learn to work it out with one another first. But tattling has received some scientific interest, and researchers have spent hours observing kids at play. They've learned that nine out of ten times, when a kid runs up to a parent to tell, that kid is being completely honest. And while it might seem to a parent that tattling is incessant, to a child that's not the case—because for every time a child seeks a parent for help, there are fourteen instances when he was wronged but did not run to the parent for aid. So when the frustrated child finally comes to tell the parent the truth, he hears, in effect, "Stop bringing me your problems!"

By the middle years of elementary school, a *tattler* is about the worst thing a kid can be called on the playground. So a child considering reporting a problem to an adult not only faces peer condemnation as a traitor but also recalls the reprimand "Work it out on your own." Each year, the problems they deal with grow exponentially. They watch other kids cut class, vandalize walls, and shoplift. To tattle is to act like a little kid. Keeping their mouth shut is easy; they've been encouraged to do so since they were little.

The era of holding back information from parents has begun.

By withholding details about their lives, adolescents carve out a social domain and identity that are theirs alone, independent from their parents or other adult authority figures. To seek out a parent for help is, from a teen's perspective, a tacit admission that he's not mature enough to handle it alone. Having to tell parents about it can be psychologically emasculating, whether the confession is forced out of him or he volunteers it on his own. It's essential for some things to be "none of your business."

Many books advise parents to just let lies go—they'll grow out of it. The truth is, kids grow into it.

The big surprise in the research is when this need for autonomy is strongest. It's not mild at 12, moderate at 15, and most powerful at 18. Darling's scholarship shows that the objection to parental authority peaks around ages 14 to 15. In fact, this resistance is slightly stronger at age 11 than at 18. In popular culture, we think of high school as the risk years, but the psychological forces driving deception surge earlier than that.

Many books advise parents to just let lies go—they'll grow out of it. The truth is, kids grow into it.   45

In her study of teenage students, Darling also mailed survey questionnaires to the parents of the teenagers interviewed, and it was interesting how the two sets of data reflected on each other. First, she was struck by parents' vivid fear of pushing their teens into outright hostile rebellion. "Many parents today believe the best way to get teens to disclose is to be more permissive and not set rules," Darling says. Parents imagine a trade-off between being informed and being strict. Better to hear the truth and be able to help than be kept in the dark.

Darling found that permissive parents don't actually learn more about their children's lives. "Kids who go wild and get in trouble mostly have parents who don't set rules or standards. Their parents are loving and accepting no matter what the kids do. But the kids take the lack of rules as a sign their parents don't care—that their parent doesn't really want this job of being the parent."

Pushing a teen into rebellion by having too many rules was a sort of statistical myth. "That actually doesn't happen," remarks Darling. She found that most rules-heavy parents don't actually enforce them. "It's too much work," says Darling. "It's a lot harder to enforce three rules than to set twenty rules."

A few parents managed to live up to the stereotype of the oppressive parent, with lots of psychological intrusion, but those teens weren't rebelling. They were obedient. And depressed.

"Ironically, the type of parents who are actually most consistent in   50
enforcing rules are the same parents who are most warm and have the
most conversations with their kids," Darling observes. They've set a few
rules over certain key spheres of influence, and they've explained why the
rules are there. They expect the child to obey them. Over life's other
spheres, they supported the child's autonomy, allowing them freedom to
make their own decisions.

The kids of these parents lied the least. Rather than hiding twelve
areas from their parents, they might be hiding as few as five.

In the thesaurus, the antonym of *honesty* is *lying,* and the opposite of
arguing is *agreeing.* But in the minds of teenagers, that's not how it works.
Really, to an adolescent, arguing is the opposite of lying.

When Nancy Darling's researchers interviewed the teenagers from
Pennsylvania, they also asked the teens when and why they told the truth
to their parents about things they knew their parents disapproved of. Occasionally they told the truth because they knew a lie wouldn't fly—they'd
be caught. Sometimes they told the truth because they just felt obligated,
saying, "They're my parents, I'm supposed to tell them." But one important motivation that emerged was that many teens told their parents the
truth when they were planning on doing something that was against the
rules—in hopes their parents might give in and say it was okay. Usually,
this meant an argument ensued, but it was worth it if a parent might
budge.

The average Pennsylvania teen was 244 percent more likely to lie than
to protest a rule. In the families where there was less deception, however,
there was a much higher ratio of arguing and complaining. The argument
enabled the child to speak honestly. Certain types of fighting, despite the
acrimony, were ultimately signs of respect—not of disrespect.

But most parents don't make this distinction in how they perceive   55
arguments with their children. Dr. Tabitha Holmes of SUNY–New Paltz
conducted extensive interviews asking mothers and adolescents, separately, to describe their arguments and how they felt about them. And
there was a big difference.

Forty-six percent of the mothers rated their arguments as being destructive to their relationships with their teens. Being challenged was stressful,
chaotic, and (in their perception) disrespectful. The more frequently they
fought, and the more intense the fights were, the more the mother rated
the fighting as harmful. But only 23 percent of the adolescents felt that
their arguments were destructive. Far more believed that fighting *strengthened* their relationship with their mothers. "Their perception of the fighting was really sophisticated, far more than we anticipated for teenagers,"
notes Holmes. "They saw fighting as a way to see their parents in a new
way, as a result of hearing their mother's point of view be articulated."

What most surprised Holmes was learning that for the teens, fighting often, or having big fights, did not cause them to rate the fighting

as harmful and destructive. Statistically, it made no difference at all. Certainly, there is a point in families where there is too much conflict, Holmes notes. "But we didn't have anybody in our study with an extreme amount of conflict." Instead, the variable that seemed to really matter was how the arguments were resolved.

It will be many years before my own children become teenagers, but having lying on my radar screen has changed the way things work around the Bronson household. No matter how small, lies no longer go unnoticed. The moments slow down, and I have a better sense of how to handle them.

Just the other day, my 6-year-old son, Luke, came home from school having learned a new phrase and a new attitude—quipping "I don't care" snidely, and shrugging his shoulders to everything. He repeated "I don't care" so many times I finally got frustrated and demanded to know if someone at school had taught him this dismissive phrase.

He froze. And I could suddenly intuit the debate running through   60
his head—should he lie to his dad, or rat out his friend? Recognizing the conflict, I told him that if he learned the phrase at school, he did not have to tell me who taught him the phrase. Telling me the truth was not going to get his friends in trouble.

"Okay," he said, relieved. "I learned it at school." Then he told me he did care, and he gave me a hug. I haven't heard it again.

Does how we deal with a child's lies really matter down the road in life? The irony of lying is that it's both normal and abnormal behavior at the same time. It's to be expected, and yet it can't be disregarded.

Dr. Bella DePaulo of the University of California, Santa Barbara, has devoted much of her career to adult lying. In one study, she had both college students and community members enter a private room equipped with an audiotape recorder. Promising them complete confidentiality, DePaulo's team instructed the subjects to recall the worst lie they ever told—with all the scintillating details.

"I was fully expecting serious lies," DePaulo remarks. "Stories of affairs kept from spouses, stories of squandering money, or being a salesperson and screwing money out of car buyers." And she did hear those kinds of whoppers, including theft and even one murder. But to her surprise, a lot of the stories told were about when the subject was a mere child—and they were not, at first glance, lies of any great consequence. "One told of eating the icing off a cake, then telling her parents the cake came that way. Another told of stealing some coins from a sibling." As these stories first started trickling in, DePaulo scoffed, thinking, "C'mon, that's the worst lie you've ever told?" But the stories of childhood kept coming, and DePaulo had to create a category in her analysis just for them. "I had to reframe my understanding to consider what it must have been like as a child to have told this lie," she recalls. "For young kids, their lie challenged their self-concept that they were a good child, and that they did the right thing."

Many subjects commented on how that momentous lie early in life   65
established a pattern that affected them thereafter. "We had some who
said, 'I told this lie, I got caught, and I felt so badly, I vowed to never do it
again.' Others said, 'Wow, I never realized I'd be so good at deceiving my
father, I can do this all the time.' The lies they tell early on are meaningful.
The way parents react can really affect lying."

Talwar says parents often entrap their kids, putting them in positions
to lie and testing their honesty unnecessarily. Last week, I put my 3½-year-
old daughter in that exact situation. I noticed she had scribbled on the
dining table with a washable marker. Disapprovingly, I asked, "Did you
draw on the table, Thia?" In the past, she would have just answered honestly, but my tone gave away that she'd done something wrong. Immediately, I wished I could retract the question. I should have just reminded
her not to write on the table, slipped newspaper under her coloring book,
and washed the ink away. Instead, I had done just as Talwar had warned
against.

"No, I didn't," my daughter said, lying to me for the first time.

For that stain, I had only myself to blame.

THINKING CRITICALLY ABOUT THE READING

1. The article begins with a discussion of a study done at Penn State University
    with college-age students under the age of twenty-one who then recruited
    high school students to get involved in a study about honesty and lying. Why
    do you think the professors themselves did not perform the study directly
    with the high schoolers? Do you believe proximity in age ensured more hon-
    esty among the participants? Why or why not?

2. Were you surprised by the topics the high school students admitted to lying
    about the most? Why or why not? How does that compare with your sense of
    your own patterns of lying?

3. Bronson quotes Dr. Victoria Talwar as saying, "Lying is related to intelli-
    gence" (8). How is this so? Were you surprised by these findings? Why or why
    not?

4. How does lying give a child a sense of control or power? In what circum-
    stances would this sense of power be useful to a child? Does this mean that
    children learn to see honesty as a losing strategy? Why or why not?

5. Beginning with paragraph 17, Bronson tells the story of Steve and his
    six-year-old son Nick. Steve doesn't believe his son lies, but Nick tells
    quite the whopper: that a soccer ball being kicked makes the sound of a
    Beethoven musical composition. Nick does this to get a prize. To an adult,
    of course, Nick's lie is absurd, but in what ways might adults lie in order to
    get something they value? Make a list of lies you've seen or heard of adults
    telling in order to get ahead (perhaps some you've told yourself). What
    does this say about the difference between adult lying and the lies children
    tell?

6. Talwar did an experiment in which children were told two classic stories: the Aesop's fable "The Boy Who Cried Wolf" and the story of George Washington and the cherry tree. What is the difference in the lies in the two tales? Why is the story about George Washington more effective at stopping lying than "The Boy Who Cried Wolf"? Were you surprised by the results? Why or why not?

7. Talwar notes that parents unwittingly teach children to lie. Parents serve as role models, and children see their own parents lie, perhaps to avoid annoyances like a telemarketer or to "smooth social relationships" (35). What are the consequences of this learning? Is there any realistic way around this problem? Should there be?

8. How is not "tattling" a form of lying (40)? According to Bronson, how do parents react to tattling? How do children interpret that reaction? What are the consequences for the children?

Is Lying Bad for Us?

RICHARD GUNDERMAN

Richard Gunderman, born in 1961, is professor of radiology, pediatrics, medical education, philosophy, liberal arts, philanthropy, and medical humanities and health studies at Indiana University. He received his A.B. summa cum laude from Wabash College, his M.D. and Ph.D. (Committee on Social Thought) with honors from the University of Chicago, and his M.P.H. from Indiana University. He was a Chancellor Scholar of the Federal Republic of Germany and received an honorary doctorate of humane letters from Garrett Theological Seminary at Northwestern University. He was also the Spinoza Professor at the University of Amsterdam. He has received the Indiana University Trustees Teaching Award nine times. He is the author of more than five hundred articles and has published eight books, including *We Make a Life by What We Give* (2008), *Leadership in Healthcare* (2009), *Achieving Excellence in Medical Education* (second edition, 2011), *X-ray Vision* (2013), and *Essential Radiology* (third edition, 2014). On the importance of writing, Gunderman says, "Writing is thinking, and thinking is living. By learning to write better we can think better, and by learning to think better we can live better. And what could be more important than leading the best lives of which we are capable?"

In this article, published in the *Atlantic* on February 13, 2013, Gunderman examines the problem of lying. Not only does the average American lie, but he or she lies on average more than once a day. Gunderman examines the causes and the consequences of this, not only in terms of social interaction, but also in terms of physical health. Ultimately, when we lie, not only are we deceiving others, but we are also deceiving ourselves.

WRITING TO DISCOVER: *How often do you lie? What sorts of lies do you tell: little white lies you hope harm no one? Bigger lies that you hope will get some advantage? Big lies that if exposed you ruin personal relationships, cost your job, or even potentially decimate your future? Why do you lie?*

It has been estimated that the average American tells 11 lies per week. Is this bad for us? Suppose we knew that a lie would never be detected, nor would we be punished. Suppose we had some means of ensuring that the lie would never cause us any physical or psychological harm through loss of sleep or the like. Suppose even that telling the lie would actually redound to our benefit, at least in the sense that it would secure us the pleasure, status, wealth, or power that those fudging the truth commonly seek. Under these circumstances, would it still make sense to tell the truth? Or would lying becoming the prudent course of action?

In his 2005 runaway philosophy best seller, *On Bullshit,* Princeton University's Harry Frankfurt distinguishes between lying and what he called "bullshit." Though liars do not tell the truth, they care about it, while the bullshitter does not even care about the truth and seeks merely to impress. Liars tell deliberate untruths, while bullshitters merely do not admit

> **Liars tell deliberate untruths, while bullshitters merely do not admit when they do not know something.**

when they do not know something. This is a particularly pervasive form of untruth in my own orbits, medicine and academia, where people wish others to believe that we know more than we do. So instead of saying, "I don't know," we make things up, merely giving the appearance of knowledge while actually saying nothing.

We live in a culture where it is increasingly common to encourage lying, and even to suppose that there is nothing problematic about doing so. In his new book, *Heads in Beds,* former hospitality industry employee Jacob Tomsky encourages hotel guests to bend the truth to their own advantage. For example, he states that guests need never pay for in-room movies. Here is how: "Watch and enjoy any movie. Call down and say you accidentally clicked on it. Or it froze near the end. Or it never even started. If the desk attendant offers to restart the movie, say you are about to go to bed or leave, and ask them instead just to remove the charges." Voila!

This bit of advice has been presented under the rubric, "Things every guest must know." It is only one of many points at which Tomsky shows guests how, by saying things that are not true, it is possible to avoid all manner of hotel charges. Ever pay for using items in a minibar? "These are the most often disputed charges on any hotel bill." After enjoying your snack or beverage, just say, "I never used these items." Worried about a same-day cancellation penalty? Call the property and tell the front desk you've had a personal emergency and won't arrive till next week. They will change the reservation. Then call back later and cancel next week's reservation at no penalty.

The implicit message? Honesty is for the unsophisticated.

One recent study laid the groundwork of a case for honesty by suggesting that liars are less healthy. Researchers at the University of Notre Dame followed 110 people over a period of ten weeks. Half of the participants were asked to stop lying over this period of time, and the other half were not. Both groups took weekly polygraph tests to determine how many times they had lied in the previous week. Those who were able to reduce by three the number of lies they told had four fewer mental health complaints (such as feeling tense) and three fewer physical health complaints (such as headaches) than those who did not.

Why might this be? A number of explanations might be invoked. One would be that it takes more work to lie, because liars need to think through everything they say to a much greater degree in order to avoid detection.

5

Another might be that it is more stressful to lie. This is likely to be particularly true when lies are exposed, resulting in shame, embarrassment, and other unpleasantries. But even if the lying is never detected, the piling up of lies tends to make relationships with colleagues, friends, and family members shallower and less meaningful. And it could be that living with the guilt of lying is toxic in itself, especially in extreme cases where we are "living a lie." Could we lower our blood pressure, narrow our waistline, reduce our dependence on antidepressants, and perhaps even prolong our lives merely by exaggerating less about our accomplishments and making up fewer excuses when we are late or fail to complete tasks? Suppose the answer to this question is yes. Suppose that those who reduce their weekly lies by one-half lose on average ten pounds, report feeling more confident and content, and end up living on average an additional three years, compared to those who continue lying at the same rate. Would this reduce the level of mendacity in America?

I suspect the answer is a resounding yes. Many of us would tell fewer lies if we thought doing so would make us healthier. Of course, it would not be good news for some sectors of the health care industry, which have a vested interest in collecting revenue from efforts to improve health. What if the sales of antidepressants, the number psychologist and psychiatrist office visits, and the number of heart surgeries all declined? On the other hand, perhaps pharmaceuticals could be developed that would reduce the impulse to tell falsehoods, and mental health professionals and hospitals could offer tuition-generating courses on how to stop lying.

> **Do we want to live in families, communities, or societies where truth telling needs to be incentivized?**

Whether the health care industry can monetize honesty or not, however, a more fundamental problem remains. Do we want to live in families, communities, or societies where truth telling needs to be incentivized? Do we want our spouses and children, our friends and neighbors, and our colleagues and associates to be asking themselves on a regular basis, "Really, why shouldn't I lie?" Surely most of us wish to live in a community where people can be relied on to tell the truth, regardless its effects on waistlines, pocketbooks, social standing, career prospects, and even our general level of happiness. Isn't there something inherently wrong with lying?

Perhaps the most powerful moral argument for honesty has to do with   10
what the French philosopher Jean-Paul Sartre called "bad faith." Liars deceive others, but in a sense, liars also deceive themselves. When we lie we tend to distort our own view of reality, and the more often we lie, the more habitual this distortion becomes. Over time, the habit of lying divorces us further and further from reality, so we see less and less clearly the choices before us and what is at stake in them. Eventually, we may find ourselves unable to see what we are really doing and how it is affecting others and ourselves. We end up leading inauthentic and irresponsible lives.

To tell the truth is to live authentically and responsibly, to really live. At times we may make honest mistakes, misperceiving what is really happening, failing to see things in appropriate context, or even operating unknowingly on deliberate untruths. Whenever possible, however, we should be honest with others and ourselves. When we are honest, we ground ourselves most completely in the world we actually inhabit, being as real as we can with others, and reducing as much as possible the distance between the way things seem to be and the way they really are. In the final analysis, honesty means avoiding illusion and unreality, instead keeping life as real as we possibly can.

THINKING CRITICALLY ABOUT THE READING

1. In paragraph 3, Gunderman says, "We live in a culture where it is increasingly common to encourage lying. . . ." Do you agree with this statement? Why or why not?

2. Gunderman concludes, based on the advice given by Jacob Tomksy on how to cheat a hotel out of money, that the lesson is "Honesty is for the unsophisticated" (5). How does this go against basic moral values held in our society? Or, has this society changed to the point where only suckers— "the unsophisticated"—are honest?

3. What is Gunderman's argument about the relationship between honesty and physical health? Did you find his argument convincing? Why or why not? What would make it more persuasive?

4. In paragraph 7, Gunderman states that ". . . the piling up of lies tends to make relationships with colleagues, friends, and family members shallower and less meaningful." Why is this so? If this is true, why then do people continue to lie? Is our ability to manage people's impressions of us more important than the depth of our relationships with them?

5. There is a certain cynicism in Gunderman's comment about the ability of the healthcare industry to "monetize honesty" (9), but his observation gets at the larger question of why people need an extra incentive (e.g., financial, medical) to be honest. Why, beyond securing more money and good health, should we tell the truth? Why do we feel as though telling the truth is an act worthy of special reward? What does that say about our expectations of ourselves and others?

6. In paragraph 10, Gunderman concludes by saying that telling the truth is "to live authentically and responsibly, to really live." What does that last phrase mean, "to really live"? Can a frequent liar not claim that he or she "really lives"? How does Gunderman's conclusion relate to his question in the headnote preceding his essay: "And what could be more important than leading the best lives of which we are capable?"

Psychology of Fraud: Why Good People Do Bad Things

CHANA JOFFE-WALT AND ALIX SPIEGEL

Chana Joffe-Walt is a reporter for *This American Life* on National Public Radio (NPR), and she previously worked as a reporter for NPR and radio station KPLU, based in Seattle, Washington. Alix Spiegel grew up in Baltimore, Maryland, and graduated from Oberlin College in Ohio. Spiegel has worked on NPR's Science Desk for ten years covering psychology and human behavior. She began her career in 1995 as one of the founding producers of *This American Life*. While there, Spiegel produced her first psychology story, which ultimately led to her focus on human behavior. It was a piece called "81 Words," and it examined the history behind the removal of homosexuality from the *Diagnostic and Statistical Manual of Mental Disorders*. Over the course of her career in public radio, Spiegel has won many awards, including a George Foster Peabody Award, a Livingston Award, an Alfred I. duPont-Columbia University Award, a Scripps Howard National Journalism Award, and a Robert F. Kennedy Journalism Award. Her work has also appeared in the *New Yorker* and the *New York Times*. She is currently co-host of the NPR program *Invisibilia*.

The following article was initially broadcast as a segment on NPR'S *All Things Considered* and then posted as a Web story on May 1, 2012. The authors examine the psychology of fraud, questioning the assumption that those who commit fraud are always conscious of wrongdoing. The work focuses primarily on the story of Toby Groves, who — despite a promise to his father — committed fraud some twenty years after his older brother had done the exact same thing. His story serves as a challenge to the belief that those committing fraud are simply thieves.

WRITING TO DISCOVER: *What is your relationship with fraud? Have you had direct experience with being defrauded by someone, or is your experience confined to reading or hearing about it on the news? In your opinion, what seems to be at the root of most fraud? Greed? Incompetence? Desperation?*

Enron, Worldcom, Bernie Madoff, the subprime mortgage crisis.

Over the past decade or so, news stories about unethical behavior have been a regular feature on TV, a long, discouraging parade of misdeeds marching across our screens. And in the face of these scandals, psychologists and economists have been slowly reworking how they think about the cause of unethical behavior.

In general, when we think about bad behavior, we think about it being tied to character: Bad people do bad things. But that model, researchers say, is profoundly inadequate.

Which brings us to the story of Toby Groves.

CHAPTER 1: The Promise

Toby grew up on a farm in Ohio. As a kid, the idea that he was a   5
person of strong moral character was very important to him. Then one
Sunday in 1986, when Toby was around 20, he went home for a visit
with his family, and he had an experience that made the need to be good
dramatically more pressing.

Twenty-two years after Toby made that promise to his father, he found himself standing in front of the *exact same judge* who had sentenced his brother, being sentenced for the *exact same crime*: fraud.

And not just any fraud—a massive bank fraud involving millions of dollars that drove several companies out of business and resulted in the loss of about a hundred jobs.

In 2008, Toby went to prison, where he says he spent two years staring at a ceiling, trying to understand what had happened.

Was he a bad character? Was it genetic? "Those were things that haunted me every second of every day," Toby says. "I just couldn't grasp it."

This very basic question—what causes unethical behavior?—has been   10
getting a fair amount of attention from researchers recently, particularly those interested in how our brains process information when we make decisions.

And what these researchers have concluded is that most of us are capable of behaving in profoundly unethical ways. And not only are we capable of it—without realizing it, we do it all the time.

CHAPTER 2: The First Lie

Consider the case of Toby Groves.

In the early 1990s, a couple of years after graduating from college, Toby decided to start his own mortgage loan company—and that promise to his father was on his mind.

So Toby decided to lie.

He told the bank that he was making $350,000, when in reality he was making nowhere near that.   15

This is the first lie Toby told—the unethical act that opened the door to all the other unethical acts. So, what was going on in his head at the time?

"There wasn't much of a thought process," he says. "I felt like, at that point, that was a small price to pay and almost like a cost of doing business. You know, things are going to happen, and I just needed to do whatever I needed to do to fix that. It wasn't like . . . I didn't think that I

was going to be losing money forever or anything like that."

Consider that for a moment.

Here is a man who stood with his heartbroken father and pledged to behave ethically. Anyone involved in the mortgage business knows that it is both unethical and illegal to lie on a mortgage application.

CHAPTER 3: Why We Don't See The Ethical Big Picture

How could that promise be so easily broken?   20

To understand, says Ann Tenbrunsel, a researcher at Notre Dame who studies unethical behavior, you have to consider what this looks like from Toby's perspective.

There is, she says, a common misperception that at moments like this, when people face an ethical decision, they clearly understand the choice that they are making.

"We assume that they can see the ethics and are consciously choosing not to behave ethically," Tenbrunsel says.

This, generally speaking, is the basis of our disapproval: They knew. They *chose* to do wrong.

But Tenbrunsel says that we are frequently blind to the ethics of a   25 situation.

Over the past couple of decades, psychologists have documented many different ways that our minds fail to see what is directly in front of us. They've come up with a concept called "bounded ethicality": That's the notion that cognitively, our ability to behave ethically is seriously limited, because we don't always see the ethical big picture.

One small example: the way a decision is framed. "The way that a decision is presented to me," says Tenbrunsel, "very much changes the way in which I view that decision, and then eventually, the decision it is that I reach."

Essentially, Tenbrunsel argues, certain cognitive frames make us blind to the fact that we are confronting an ethical problem at all.

Tenbrunsel told us about a recent experiment that illustrates the problem. She got together two groups of people and told one to think about a business decision. The other group was instructed to think about an ethical decision. Those asked to consider a business decision generated one mental checklist; those asked to think of an ethical decision generated a different mental checklist.

Tenbrunsel next had her subjects do an unrelated task to distract them. Then she presented them with an opportunity to cheat.   30

Those cognitively primed to think about business behaved radically different from those who were not—no matter who they were, or what their moral upbringing had been.

"If you're thinking about a business decision, you are significantly more likely to lie than if you were thinking from an ethical frame," Tenbrunsel says.

According to Tenbrunsel, the business frame cognitively activates one set of goals—to be competent, to be successful; the ethics frame triggers other goals. And once you're in, say, a business frame, you become really focused on meeting those goals, and other goals can completely fade from view.

BUSINESS DECISION
mental checklist:
☐ What might I gain?
☐ How will it affect the future?

ETHICAL DECISION
mental checklist:
☐ Is this fair?
☐ Will people be hurt?

Tenbrunsel listened to Toby's story, and she argues that one way to understand Toby's initial choice to lie on his loan application is to consider the cognitive frame he was using.

"His sole focus was on making the best business decision," she says, which made him blind to the ethics.   35

Obviously we'll never know what was actually going through Toby's mind, and the point of raising this possibility is not to excuse Toby's bad behavior, but simply to demonstrate in a small way the very uncomfortable argument that these researchers are making:

That people can be genuinely unaware that they're making a profoundly unethical decision.

It's not that they're evil—it's that they *don't see.*

And if we want to attack fraud, we have to understand that *a lot of fraud is unintentional.*

 CHAPTER 4: Fraud Spreads

Tenbrunsel's argument that we are often blind to the ethical dimen-   40
sions of a situation might explain part of Toby's story, his first unethical
act. But a bigger puzzle remains: How did Toby's fraud spread? How did
a lie on a mortgage application balloon into a $7 million fraud?

According to Toby, in the weeks after his initial lie, he discovered
more losses at his company—huge losses. Toby had already mortgaged
his house. He didn't have any more money, but he needed to save his
business.

The easiest way for him to cover the mounting losses, he reasoned,
was to get more loans. So Toby decided to do something that is much
harder to understand than lying on a mortgage application: He took out a
series of entirely false loans—loans on houses that didn't exist.

Creating false loans is not an easy process. You have to manufacture
from thin air borrowers and homes and the paperwork to go with them.

Toby was CEO of his company, but this was outside of his skill set. He
needed help—people on his staff who knew how loan documents should
look and how to fake them.

And so, one by one, Toby says, he pulled employees into a room.   45

"Maybe that was the most shocking thing," Toby says. "Everyone
said, 'OK, we're in trouble, we need to solve this. I'll help you. You know,
I'll try to have that for you tomorrow.'"

According to Toby, no one said no.

Most of the people who helped Toby would not talk to us because
they didn't want to expose themselves to legal repercussions.

Of the four people at his company Toby told us about, we were
able to speak about the fraud with only one—a woman on staff named
Monique McDowell. She was involved in fabricating documents, and her
description of what happened and how it happened completely conforms
to Toby's description.

If you accept what they're saying as true, then that raises a troubling   50
scenario, because we expect people to protest when they're asked to do
wrong. But Toby's employees didn't. What's even more troubling is that
according to Toby, it wasn't just his employees: "I mean, we had to have
assistance from other companies to pull this off," he says.

To make it look like a real person closed on a real house, Toby needed
a title company to sign off on the fake documents his staff had generated.
And so after he got his staff onboard, Toby says he made some calls and
basically made the same pitch he'd given his employees.

"It was, 'Here is what happened. Here is the only way I know to fix
it, and if you help me, great. If you won't, I understand.' Nobody said,
'Maybe we'll think about this. . . .' Within a few minutes [it was], 'Yes,
I'll help you.'"

So here we have people outside his company, agreeing to do things
completely illegal and wrong.

Again, we contacted several of the title companies. No one would
speak to us, but it's clear from the legal cases that title companies were
involved. One title company president ended up in jail because of his dealings with Toby; another agreed to a legal resolution.

So how could it be that easy?   55

CHAPTER 5: We Lie Because We Care

Typically when we hear about large frauds, we assume the perpetrators were driven by financial incentives. But psychologists and economists
say financial incentives don't fully explain it. They're interested in another
possible explanation: Human beings commit fraud because human beings
like each other.

We like to help each other, especially people we identify with. And
when we are helping people, we really don't see what we are doing as
unethical.

Lamar Pierce, an associate professor at Washington University in
St. Louis, points to the case of emissions testers. Emissions testers are
supposed to test whether or not your car is too polluting to stay on the
road. If it is, they're supposed to fail you. But in many cases, emissions
testers lie.

"Somewhere between 20 percent and 50 percent of cars that should
fail are passed—are *illicitly* passed," Pierce says.

Financial incentives can explain some of that cheating. But Pierce and   60
psychologist Francesca Gino of Harvard Business School say that doesn't
fully capture it.

They collected hundreds of thousands of records and were actually
able to track the patterns of individual inspectors, carefully monitoring

those they approved and those they denied. And here is what they found:

If you pull up in a fancy car—say, a BMW or Ferrari—and your car is polluting the air, you are likely to fail. But pull up in a Honda Civic, and you have a much better chance of passing.

Why?

"We know from a lot of research that when we feel empathy towards others, we want to help them out," says Gino.

Emissions testers—who make a modest salary—see a Civic and iden-   65
tify, they feel empathetic.

Essentially, Gino and Pierce are arguing that these testers commit fraud not because they are greedy, but because they are *nice*.

"And most people don't see the harm in this," says Pierce. "That is the problem."

Pierce argues that cognitively, emissions testers can't appreciate the consequences of their fraud, the costs of the decision that they are making in the moment. The cost is abstract: the global environment. They are literally being asked to weigh the costs to the global environment against the benefits of passing someone who is right there who needs help. We are not cognitively designed to do that.

"I've never talked to a mortgage broker who thought, 'When I help someone get into a loan by falsifying their income, I deeply consider whether or not I would destabilize the world economy,' " says Pierce. "You are helping someone who is real."

Gino and Pierce argue that Toby's staff was faced with the same kind   70
of decision: future abstract consequences, or help out the very real person in front of them.

And so without focusing on the ethics of what they were doing, they helped out a person who was not focusing on the ethics, either. And together they perpetrated a $7 million fraud.

CHAPTER 6: Searching for Resolution

As for Toby, he says that maintaining the giant lie he'd created was exhausting day in and day out.

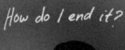

So in 2006, when two FBI agents showed up at his office, he quickly confessed everything. He says he was relieved.

Two years later, he was standing in front of the same judge who had sentenced his brother. A short time after that, he was in jail, grateful that his father wasn't alive to see him, wondering how he ended up where he did.

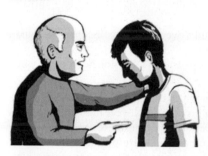

"The last thing in the world that   75 I wanted to do in my life would be to break that promise to my father," he says. "It haunts me."

Now if these psychologists and economists are right, if we are all capable of behaving profoundly unethically without realizing it, then our workplaces and regulations are poorly organized. They're not designed to take into account the cognitively flawed human beings that we are. They don't attempt to structure things around our weaknesses.

Some concrete proposals to do that are on the table. For example, we know that auditors develop relationships with clients after years of working together, and we know that those relationships can corrupt their audits without them even realizing it. So there is a proposal to force businesses to switch auditors every couple of years to address that problem.

Another suggestion: A sentence should be placed at the beginning of every business contract that explicitly says that lying on this contract is unethical and illegal, because that kind of statement would get people into the proper cognitive frame.

And there are other proposals, of course.

Or, we could just keep saying what we've always said—that right is   80 right, and wrong is wrong, and people should know the difference.

THINKING CRITICALLY ABOUT THE READING

1. The article begins with a list of frauds that have all made the front page of national newspapers and the lead in television news programs: "Enron, Worldcom, Bernie Madoff, the subprime mortgage crisis." Why list famous frauds to start the article? Do the authors expect their readers (and listeners) to have been personally affected or morally outraged by at least one of these frauds? If not, what is the advantage of leading with this list?

2. In recounting the story of Toby Groves, the authors begin by letting the reader (or listener) know the conclusion: that Groves committed fraud just like this older brother. What is the advantage of giving away the ending at the beginning? How does this better set up the reader to understand the details about Toby's fraud?

3. The authors tell about the results of a research study about decision making: that when asked to make decisions on an ethical basis, people choose one course of action; when asked to make decisions based on business concerns, people choose a different course, even if that course crosses ethical boundaries. What are the larger implications of this in a country in which economic success is driven by successful businesses? Are there places where business concerns and ethical concerns might overlap? If so, where? If not, why not?

4. In the case of Toby Groves, one fraud (overstating his income on a loan application) led to additional frauds. Why do you suppose Groves didn't stop? What drove his decision to keep going—and his decision to confess when confronted by the FBI?

5. One surprising element to the story is how much help Groves received in continuing to commit fraud, not just from his own employees but from people in other companies and other parts of the mortgage business. Why would they agree to go along with his scheme even as they were putting themselves in legal jeopardy? What was it about Groves that made them want to help him? To what extent did Groves tell them the truth?

6. Professor Lamar Pierce of Washington University contributes the example of the emissions testers who pass sub-performing vehicles. According to Pierce, why does this ethical lapse occur? Have you ever witnessed—or perhaps benefited from—such an occurrence yourself? Pierce makes the point that people tend to base ethical decisions based on what they see in front of them (e.g., a modestly paid worker with a polluting car) rather than larger abstractions (e.g., the global environment). Where might similarly skewed ethical decisions happen in other industries with even larger implications?

7. One feature of this article is that it uses cartoon panels to illustrate actions, especially the actions of Toby Groves. Why? What do the illustrations add to the article? Why choose to illustrate a story that was also put forth in audio form via radio?

WRITING SUGGESTIONS: DEBATING THE ISSUE

1. Research the records of recent national political leaders—presidents, senators, and other prominent persons—and find out how often leaders lie in order to promote their own goals. In your opinion, how often do our leaders lie or mislead the public, and what are the consequences of this failure to be truthful? Be sure to back up your assertions with evidence from sources. What effect, if any, do you think a leader's record of truthfulness has on his or her ability to gain votes? What kinds of lies are considered fatal to a career in the public eye, and which are merely politically expedient? Do you think leaders should be held to a different standard than the average citizen? Why or why not?

2. In paragraph 7 of "Learning to Lie," Po Bronson (p. 547) writes, "So when do the 98 percent who think lying is wrong become the 98 percent who lie?" Virtually everyone lies. However, not all lies (or liars) appear to be equal: some

lies we use for social cohesion, while other lies—particularly ones told to avoid censure or punishment—we are more apt to condemn. Write an essay in in which you argue whether a certain degree of lying is necessary to get along in society or not. Use the terms Judith Viorst uses in "The Truth about Lying" (p. 541) to describe the different kinds of lying as you consider the following questions: Which kinds of lies, if any, are necessary and which are not? What do we gain by lying, and what do we risk losing?

3. Po Bronson's essay "Learning to Lie" ends with a discussion of parents and the choices they face about rules and restrictions. When is a parent too strict or too permissive? Do further research on the relationship between parent-imposed rules and the behavioral responses of children. Consider how rules and restrictions lead (or don't lead) to lying, obedience, rebellion, aggression, passivity, depression, or self-confidence. Write an essay in which you present your findings.

4. In paragraph 10 of "Is Lying Bad for Us?" Richard Gunderman (p. 558) asks, "Isn't there something inherently wrong with lying?" Using the examples and conclusions set forth by Viorst, Bronson, and Joffe-Walt and Spiegel, write an essay that shapes an argument in response to Gunderman's question. Be sure to support your claims with evidence from these essays or your own research. If you agree with Gunderman, then what, exactly, is wrong with lying, and why? If you disagree, what is it that keeps lying from being inherently wrong? Be sure to address counterarguments that could disprove your claims.

5. In "Is Lying Bad for Us?" Gunderman writes: "Over time, the habit of lying divorces us further and further from reality, so we see less and less clearly the choices before us and what is at stake in them. Eventually, we may find ourselves unable to see what we are really doing and how it is affecting others and ourselves" (10). Write an essay in which you apply this idea to the story of Toby Groves. What would Gunderman say about the series of lies and frauds Groves committed? What physical and mental toll did the fraud take? Why did Groves continue to lie and even draw others into perpetrating fraud? What larger conclusions can you draw from Groves's story and Gunderman's ideas about lying?

6. In "Is Lying Bad for Us?" Gunderman asks the following questions: "Do we want to live in families, communities, or societies where truth telling needs to be incentivized? Do we want our spouses and children, our friends and neighbors, and our colleagues and associates to be asking themselves on a regular basis, 'Really, why shouldn't I lie?'" (9) Write an essay in which you explore and analyze Gunderman's idea of "incentives" for truth-telling. Is there something wrong with considering the tangible rewards of avoiding lies? What other kinds of incentives—beyond physical or monetary ones—exist for telling the truth? Are there incentives for lying? Which are more compelling? You might consider the story of Toby Groves as you consider these issues. What kind of incentives did Groves have to avoid lying or committing fraud? Why do you think he ignored those incentives?

7. Research an instance of large-scale fraud—corporate, political, personal, artistic, or whatever interests you. Write an essay in which you examine how the fraud began, what the motivation was for the fraud, how it grew, how it was

discovered, and what the results were. What kinds of lies served as the foundation for the fraud?

8. Toby Groves's story is one in which honor and truthfulness lose out to the dire circumstances of a particular situation. According to the authors, we tend to believe that "Bad people do bad things. But that model, researchers say, is profoundly inadequate" (2). Indeed, when Groves is finally caught by the FBI, he seems relieved. On the other hand, his actions not only led to his own imprisonment but the loss of over one hundred jobs and the liberty of at least one co-conspirator. His story suggests that our concept of good and bad might need revision. The other option, given at the end of the essay, is that " . . . we could just keep saying what we've always said—that right is right, and wrong is wrong, and people should know the difference." Do some research the psychology of wrong-doing, and write an essay in which you criticize or defend the authors' statement about the complexity of human criminal behavior. What kinds of stories do we hear (in the media, in literature, in our lives) that reinforce the idea that "bad people do bad things"? How might we convince people to revisit that assumption?

14

A BRIEF GUIDE TO WRITING A RESEARCH PAPER

The research paper is an important part of a college education for good reason. In writing such a paper, you acquire a number of indispensable research skills that you can adapt to other college assignments and, after graduation, to important life tasks.

The real value of writing a research paper, however, goes beyond acquiring basic skills; it is a unique hands-on learning experience. The purpose of a research paper is not to present a collection of quotations that show you can report what others have said about your topic. Rather, your goal is to analyze, evaluate, and synthesize the materials you research—and thereby learn how to do so with any topic. You learn how to view the results of research from your own perspective and arrive at an informed opinion of a topic.

Writing a researched essay is not very different from the other writing you will be doing in your college writing course. You will find yourself drawing heavily on what you have learned in "Writing in College and Beyond" (pp. 21–42). First you determine what you want to write about. Then you decide on a purpose, consider your audience, develop a thesis, collect your evidence, write a first draft, revise and edit, and prepare a final copy. What differentiates the researched paper from other kinds of papers is your use of outside sources and how you acknowledge them.

Your library research will involve working with print and electronic sources. Your aim is to select the most appropriate sources for your research from the many that are available on your topic. (See also Chapter 3, "Writing with Sources.")

In this chapter, you will learn some valuable research techniques:

- How to establish a realistic schedule for your research project
- How to conduct research on the Internet using directory and keyword searches
- How to evaluate sources
- How to analyze sources
- How to develop a working bibliography
- How to take useful notes

- How to acknowledge your sources using Modern Language Association (MLA) and American Psychological Association (APA) style in-text citations and a list of works cited
- How to present your research paper using MLA and APA manuscript format

ESTABLISH A REALISTIC SCHEDULE

A research project easily spans several weeks. So as not to lose track of time and find yourself facing an impossible deadline at the last moment, establish a realistic schedule for completing key tasks. By thinking of the research paper as a multi-staged process, you avoid becoming overwhelmed by the size of the whole undertaking.

Your schedule should allow at least a few days to accommodate unforeseen needs and delays. Use the following template, which lists the essential steps in writing a research paper to plan your own research schedule:

Research Paper Schedule

Task	Completion Date
1. Choose a research topic and pose a worthwhile question.	/ /
2. Locate print and electronic sources.	/ /
3. Develop a working bibliography.	/ /
4. Evaluate your sources.	/ /
5. Read your sources, taking complete and accurate notes.	/ /
6. Develop a preliminary thesis and make a working outline.	/ /
7. Write a draft of your paper, integrating sources you have summarized, paraphrased, and quoted.	/ /
8. Visit your college writing center for help with your revision.	/ /
9. Decide on a final thesis and modify your outline.	/ /
10. Revise your paper and properly cite all borrowed materials.	/ /
11. Prepare a list of works cited.	/ /
12. Prepare the final manuscript and proofread.	/ /
13. Submit research paper.	/ /

LOCATE AND USE PRINT AND ONLINE SOURCES

The distinction between print sources and electronic sources is fast disappearing. Many sources that used to appear only in print are now available in electronic format as well; some, in fact, are moving entirely to electronic format, as a more efficient and in many cases less expensive means of distribution.

There are, however, still important distinctions between print sources (or their electronic equivalent) and Internet sources. Many of the sources you will find through an Internet search will not be as reliable as those that traditionally appeared in print. For this reason, in most cases you should use print sources or their electronic versions (books, newspapers, journals, periodicals, encyclopedias, pamphlets, brochures, and government publications) as your primary tools for research. These sources, unlike many Internet sources, are often reviewed by experts in the field before they are published, are generally overseen by a reputable publishing company or organization, and are examined by editors and fact checkers for accuracy and reliability. Unless you are instructed otherwise, you should try to use these sources in your research.

The best place to start any search for sources is your college library's home page. Here you will find links to the computerized catalog of book holdings, online reference works, periodical databases, electronic journals, and a list of full-text databases. You'll also find links for subject study guides and for help conducting your research.

To get started, decide on some likely search terms and try them out. (For tips on conducting and refining keyword searches, see pages 580–581.) Search through your library's reference works, electronic catalog, periodical indexes, and other databases to generate a

preliminary listing of books, magazine and newspaper articles, public documents and reports, and other sources that may be helpful in exploring your topic. At this early stage, it is better to err on the side of listing too many sources. Then, later on, you will not have to backtrack to find sources you discarded too hastily.

Sources that you find through an Internet search can also be informative and valuable additions to your research. The Internet is especially useful in providing recent data, stories, and reports. For example, you might find a just-published article from a university laboratory, or a news story in your local newspaper's online archives. Generally, however, Internet sources should be used alongside sources you access through your college library and not as a replacement for them. Practically anyone with access to a computer and an Internet connection can put text and pictures on the Internet; there is often no governing body that checks for content or accuracy. Therefore, while the Internet offers a vast number of useful and carefully maintained resources, it also contains much unreliable information. It is your responsibility to determine whether a given Internet source should be trusted. (For advice on evaluating sources, see pages 582–584.)

If you need more instruction on conducting Internet searches, go to your on-campus learning center or library for more information, or consult one of the many books written for Internet research beginners.

Conduct Keyword Searches

When searching for sources about your topic in an electronic database, in the library's computerized catalog, or on the Internet, you should start with a keyword search. To make the most efficient use of your time, you will want to know how to conduct a keyword search that is likely to yield solid sources and leads for your research project. As obvious or simple as it may sound, the key to a successful keyword search is the quality of the keywords you generate about your topic. You might find it helpful to start a list of potential keywords as you begin your research and add to it as your work proceeds. Often you will discover combinations of keywords that will lead you right to the sources you need.

Databases and library catalogs index sources by author, title, and year of publication, as well as by subject headings assigned by a cataloger who has previewed the source. The key here is to find a keyword that matches one of the subject headings. Once you begin to locate sources that are on your topic, be sure to note the subject headings listed for each source. You can use these subject headings as keywords to lead you to additional book sources or to articles in periodicals, using full-text databases like *Info Trac, LexisNexis, Expanded Academic ASAP,* or *JSTOR* to which your library subscribes.

The keyword search process is somewhat different—more wide open—when you are searching on the Web. It is always a good idea to look for search tips on the help screens or advanced search instructions for the search engine you are using before initiating a keyword search.

When you type a keyword in the "Search" box on a search engine's home page, the search engine goes looking for Web sites that match your term. One problem with keyword searches is that they can produce tens of thousands of matches, making it difficult to locate sites of immediate value. For that reason, make your keywords as specific as you can, and make sure that you have the correct spelling. Once you start a search, you may want to narrow or broaden it depending on the number of hits, or matches, you get.

Refining Keyword Searches on the Web

While some variation in command terms and characters exists among electronic databases and popular search engines on the Internet, the following functions are almost universally accepted. If you have a particular question about refining your keyword search, seek assistance by clicking on "Help" or "Advanced Search."

- Use quotation marks or parentheses to indicate that you are searching for words in exact sequence—e.g., "bilingual education"; (college slang).
- Use AND or a plus sign (+) between words to narrow your search by specifying that all words need to appear in a document—e.g., prejudice AND Asians; doublespeak + advertisements.
- Use NOT or a minus sign (−) between words to narrow your search by eliminating unwanted words–e.g., advertisements NOT public service; natural–organic.
- Use an asterisk (*) to indicate that you will accept variations of a term—e.g., euphemism*.

Use Subject Directories to Define and Develop Your Research Topic

If you are undecided as to exactly what you want to write about, the subject directories on the home pages of search engines make it easy to browse the Web by various subjects and topics for ideas that interest you. Subject directories can also be a big help if you have a topic but are undecided about your exact research question or if you simply want to see if there is enough material to supplement your research work with print sources. Once you choose a subject area in the directory, you can select more specialized subdirectories, eventually arriving at a list of sites closely related to your topic.

The most common question students have at this stage of a Web search is, "How can I tell if I'm looking in the right place?" There is no straight answer; if more than one subject area sounds plausible, you will have to dig more deeply into each of their subdirectories, using logic and the process of elimination to determine which one is likely to produce the best leads for your topic. In most cases, it doesn't take long—usually just one or two clicks—to figure out whether you're searching in the right subject area. If you click on a subject area and none of the topics listed in its subdirectories seems to pertain even remotely to your research topic, try a different subject area. As you browse through various subject directories and subdirectories, keep a running list of keywords associated with your topic that you can use in subsequent keyword searches.

EVALUATE YOUR SOURCES

You will not have to spend much time in the library to realize that you do not have time to read every print and online source that appears relevant. Given the abundance of print and Internet sources, the key to successful research is identifying those books, articles, Web sites, and other online sources that will help you most. You must evaluate your potential sources to determine which materials you will read, which you will skim, and which you will simply eliminate. Here are some evaluation strategies and questions to assist you in identifying your most promising sources.

Strategies for Evaluating Print and Online Sources

EVALUATING A BOOK

- Read the dust jacket or cover copy for insights into the book's coverage and currency as well as the author's expertise.
- Scan the table of contents and identify any promising chapters.
- Read the author's preface, looking for his or her thesis and purpose.
- Check the index for key words or key phrases related to your research topic.
- Read the opening and concluding paragraphs of any promising chapter; if you are unsure about its usefulness, skim the whole chapter.

- Ask yourself: Does the author have a discernable bias? If so, you must be aware that this bias will color his or her claims and evidence.

EVALUATING AN ARTICLE

- Ask yourself what you know about the journal or magazine publishing the article:

  - Is the publication scholarly or popular? Scholarly journals (*American Economic Review, Journal of Marriage and the Family, The Wilson Quarterly*) publish articles about original research written by authorities in the field. Research essays always cite their sources in footnotes or bibliographies. Popular news and general interest magazines (*National Geographic, Smithsonian, Time, Ebony*), on the other hand, publish informative, entertaining, and easy-to-read articles written by editorial staff or freelance writers. Popular essays sometimes cite sources but often do not.
  - What is the reputation of the journal or magazine? Determine the publisher or sponsor. Is it an academic institution or a commercial enterprise or individual? Does the publisher or publication have a reputation for accuracy and objectivity?
  - Who are the readers of this journal or magazine?

- What are the author's credentials?
- Consider the title or headline of the article as well as the opening paragraph or two and the conclusion. Does the source appear to be too general or too technical for your needs and audience?
- For articles in journals, read the abstract (a summary of the main points) if there is one.
- Examine any photographs, charts, graphs, or other illustrations that accompany the article. Determine how useful they might be for your research purposes.

EVALUATING A WEB SITE

- Consider the type of Web site. Is this site a personal blog or a professional publication? Often the URL, especially the top-level domain name, can give you a clue about the kinds of information provided and the type of organization behind the site. Common suffixes include:

    .com — business/commercial/personal

.edu—educational institution
.gov—government sponsored
.net—various types of networks
.org—nonprofit organization, but also some commercial/
personal

- Be advised that *.org* is not regulated like *.edu* and *.gov*, for example. Most nonprofits use *.org*, but many commercial and personal sites do as well.
- Examine the home page of the site.

  - Does the content appear to be related to your research topic?
  - Is the home page well maintained and professional in appearance?
  - Is there an *About* link on the home page that takes you to background information on the site's sponsor? Is there a mission statement, history, or statement of philosophy? Can you verify whether the site is official—actually sanctioned by the organization or company?

- Identify the author of the site. What are the author's qualifications for writing on this subject?
- Determine whether a print equivalent is available. Is the Web version more or less extensive than the print version?
- Determine when the site was last updated. Is the content current enough for your purposes?

You can find sources on the Internet itself that offer useful guidelines for evaluating electronic sources. One excellent example was created by reference librarians at the Wolfgram Memorial Library of Widener University. Type *Wolfgram evaluate Web pages* into a search engine to access that site.

On the basis of your evaluation, select the most promising books, articles, and Web sites to pursue in depth for your research project.

ANALYZE YOUR SOURCES

Before beginning to take notes, it is essential that you carefully analyze your sources for their thesis, overall argument, amount and credibility of evidence, bias, and reliability in helping you explore your research topic. Look for the writers' main ideas, key examples, strongest arguments, and conclusions. Read critically. While it is easy to become absorbed in sources that support your own beliefs, always seek out several sources with opposing viewpoints, if only to test your own position. Look for information about the authors themselves—information that will help you determine their authority and where they position themselves in the broader conversation on the issue. You should also know the reputation and special interests of book publishers and magazines, because you are likely to get different views—conservative, liberal, international, feminist—on the same topic depending on the publication you read. Use the following checklist to assist you in analyzing your print and online sources.

Checklist for Analyzing Print and Online Sources

- What is the writer's thesis or claim?
- How does the writer support this thesis? Does the evidence seem reasonable and ample, or is it mainly anecdotal?
- Does the writer consider opposing viewpoints?
- Does the writer have any obvious political or religious biases? Is the writer associated with any special-interest groups such as Planned Parenthood, Greenpeace, Amnesty International, or the National Rifle Association?
- Is the writer an expert on the subject? Do other writers mention this author in their work?
- Does the publisher or publication have a reputation for accuracy and objectivity?
- Is important information documented through footnotes or links so that it can be verified or corroborated in other sources?
- What is the author's purpose—to inform or to argue for a particular position or action?
- Do the writer's thesis and purpose clearly relate to your research topic?
- Does the source appear to be too general or too technical for your needs and audience?
- Does the source reflect current thinking and research in the field?

DEVELOP A WORKING BIBLIOGRAPHY OF YOUR SOURCES

As you discover books, journal and magazine articles, newspaper stories, and Web sites that you think might be helpful, you need to start maintaining a record of important information about each source. This record, called a working bibliography, will enable you to know where sources are located as well as what they are when it comes time to consult them or acknowledge them in your list of works cited or final bibliography (for MLA Works Cited list, see pp. 590–600; for APA References list, see pp. 603–608.). In all likelihood, your working bibliography will contain more sources than you actually consult and include in your list of works cited.

One method for creating a working bibliography is to make a separate bibliography card, using a 3- by 5-inch index card, for each work that you think might be helpful to your research. As your collection of cards grows, alphabetize them by the authors' last names. By using a separate card for each book, article, or Web site, you can continually edit your working bibliography, dropping sources that did not prove helpful for one reason or another and adding new ones.

With the computerization of most library resources, you now have the option to copy and paste bibliographic information from the library computer catalog and periodical indexes or from the Internet into a document on your computer that you can edit/add/delete/search throughout the research process. The advantage of the copy/paste option over the index card method is accuracy, especially in punctuation, spelling, and capitalization — details that are essential in accessing Internet sites.

Checklist for a Working Bibliography

FOR BOOKS

- Library call number
- Names of all authors, editors, and translators
- Title and subtitle
- Publication data:

  > Place of publication (city and state)
  > Publisher's name
  > Date of publication

- Edition (if not first) and volume number (if applicable)

FOR PERIODICAL ARTICLES

- Names of all authors
- Name and subtitle of article
- Title of journal, magazine, or newspaper

- Publication data:
    Volume number and issue number
    Date of issue
    Page numbers

FOR INTERNET SOURCES

- Names of all authors, editors, compilers, or sponsoring agents
- Title and subtitle of the document
- Title of the longer work to which the document belongs (if applicable)
- Title of the site or discussion list
- Author, editor, or compiler of the Web site or online database
- Name of company or organization that owns the Web site
- Date of release, online posting, or latest revision
- Name and vendor of database or name of online service or network
- Medium (online, CD-ROM, etc.)
- Format of online source (Web page, .pdf, podcast)
- Date you accessed the site
- Electronic address (URL)

FOR OTHER SOURCES

- Name of author, government agency, organization, company, recording artist, personality, etc.
- Title of the work
- Format (pamphlet, unpublished diary, interview, television broadcast, etc.)
- Publication or production data:
    Name of publisher or producer
    Date of publication, production, or release
    Identifying codes or numbers (if applicable)

TAKE NOTES

As you read, take notes. You're looking for ideas, facts, opinions, statistics, examples, and other evidence that you think will be useful as you write your paper. As you read through books and articles, look for recurring themes, and notice where writers are in agreement and where they differ. Try to remember that the effectiveness of your paper is largely determined by the quality—not necessarily the quantity—of your notes. Your purpose is not to present a collection of quotes that show that you've read all the material and know what others have said about your topic. Your goal is to analyze, evaluate, and synthesize the information you collect—in other words, to enter into the discussion of the issues and thereby take ownership of your topic. You want to view the results of your research from your own perspective and arrive at an informed opinion of your topic. (For more information on writing with sources, see Chapter 3.)

Now for some practical advice on taking notes. First, be systematic in your note-taking. As a rule, write one note on a card, and include the author's full name, the complete title of the source, and a page number indicating the origin of the note. Use cards of uniform size, preferably 4- by 6-inch index cards because they are large enough to accommodate even a long note on a single card and yet small enough to be easily handled and conveniently carried. If you keep notes electronically, consider creating a separate file for each topic or source, or using an electronic research manager like Zotero (zotero.org) or OneNote. If you keep your notes organized, when you get to the planning and writing stage, you will be able to sequence them according to the plan you have envisioned for your paper. Furthermore, should you decide to alter your organizational plan, you can easily reorder your notes—whether on cards or in digital files—to reflect those revisions.

Second, try not to take too many notes. One good way to control your note-taking is to ask yourself, "How exactly does this material help prove or disprove my thesis?" Try to envision where in your paper you will use the information. If it does not seem relevant to your thesis, don't bother to take a note.

Once you decide to take a note, you must decide whether to summarize, paraphrase, or quote directly. The approach you take should be determined by the content of the passage and the way you plan to use it in your paper. For detailed advice on summaries, paraphrases, and quotations, see Chapter 3, pages 46–50.

DOCUMENT YOUR SOURCES

Whenever you summarize, paraphrase, or quote a person's thoughts and ideas and whenever you use facts or statistics that are not commonly known or believed, you must properly acknowledge the source of your information. If you do not properly acknowledge ideas and information created by someone else, you are guilty of *plagiarism*, or using someone else's material but making it look as if it were your own. (For more information on plagiarism and how to avoid it, see pages 53–56.) You must document the source of your information whenever you do the following:

- Quote a source word for word
- Refer to information and ideas from another source that you present in your own words as either a paraphrase or a summary
- Cite statistics, table, charts, graphs, or other visuals

You do not need to document these types of information:

- Your own observations, experiences, and ideas
- Factual information available in a number of reference works (information known as "common knowledge")
- Proverbs, sayings, and familiar quotations

A reference to the source of your borrowed information is called a *citation*. There are many systems for making citations, and your citations must consistently follow one of these systems. The documentation style recommended by the Modern Language Association (MLA) is commonly used in English and the humanities and is the style used throughout this book. Another common system is the American Psychological Association (APA) style, which is generally used in the social sciences. Your instructor will probably tell you which style to use. For more information on documentation styles, consult the appropriate manual or handbook.

There are two components of documentation. *In-text citations* are placed in the body of your paper, and the *list of works cited* provides complete publication data for your in-text citations and is placed on a separate page at the end of your paper. Both of these components are necessary for complete documentation.

MLA IN-TEXT CITATIONS

In-text citations, also known as *parenthetical citations*, give the reader citation information immediately, at the point at which it is most meaningful. Rather than having to find a footnote or an endnote, the reader sees the citation as a part of the writer's text.

Most in-text citations consist of only the author's last name and a page reference. Usually the author's name is given in an introductory signal phrase at the beginning of the borrowed material, and the page reference is given in parentheses at the end. If the author's name is not given at the beginning, put it in parentheses along with the page reference. When you borrow material from two or more works by the same author, you must include the title of the work in the signal phrase or parenthetically at the end. (For examples of signal phrases and in-text citations, see pages 50–53.) The parenthetical reference signals the end of the borrowed material and directs your readers to the list of works cited should they want to pursue a particular source. Treat electronic sources as you do print sources, keeping in mind that some electronic sources use paragraph numbers instead of page numbers. Consider the following examples of in-text citations, taken from student Richard Carbeau's paper on the debate over whether or not to make English America's official language.

Many people are surprised to discover that English is not the official

language of the United States. Today, even as English literacy becomes

a necessity for people in many parts of the world, some people in the

United States believe its primacy is being threatened right at home. Much

of the current controversy focuses on Hispanic communities with large

Spanish-speaking populations who may feel little or no pressure to learn

English. Columnist and cultural critic Charles Krauthammer believes English   Citation with
                                                                                author's name in
should be America's official language. He notes that this country has been   the signal phrase

"blessed . . . with a linguistic unity that brings a critically needed cohesion

to a nation as diverse, multiracial and multiethnic as America" and that

communities such as these threaten the bond created by a common

language (112). There are others, however, who think that "Language

does not threaten American unity. Benign neglect is a good policy for any

country when it comes to language, and it's a good policy for America"   Citation with
                                                                          author's name
(King 64).   in parentheses

Works Cited

King, Robert D. "Should English Be the Law?" *Atlantic Monthly* Apr. 1997:

    55-64. Print.

Krauthammer, Charles. "In Plain English: Let's Make It Official." *Time* 12

    June 2006: 112. Print.

In the preceding example, the student followed MLA style guidelines
for his Works Cited list. When constructing the list of works cited page
for your paper, consult the following MLA guidelines, based on the *MLA
Handbook for Writers of Research Papers*, seventh edition (2009), where
you will find model entries for periodical print publications, nonperiodical
print publications, Web publications, and other common sources.

MLA LIST OF WORKS CITED

In this section, you will find general MLA guidelines for creating a
works cited list followed by sample entries that cover the citation situations you are most likely to encounter. Make sure that you follow the
formats as they appear on the following pages.

1. Begin the list on a fresh page following the last page of text.
2. Center the title *Works Cited* at the top of the page.
3. Double-space both within and between entries on your list.
4. Alphabetize your sources by the authors' last names. If you have two or more authors with the same last name, alphabetize first by last names and then by first names.
5. If you have two or more works by the same author, alphabetize by the first word of the titles, not counting *A, An,* or *The.* Use the author's name in the first entry and three unspaced hyphens followed by a period in subsequent entries:

   > Twitchell, James B. *Branded Nation: When Culture Goes Pop.* New York: Simon, 2004. Print.

   > ---. "The Branding of Higher Ed." *Forbes* 25 Nov. 2002: 50. Print.

   > ---. *Living It Up: America's Love Affair with Luxury.* New York: Columbia UP, 2002. Print.

6. If no author is known, alphabetize by title.
7. Begin each entry at the left margin. If the entry is longer than one line, indent the second and subsequent lines five spaces or one-half inch.
8. Italicize the titles of books, journals, magazines, and newspapers. Use quotation marks with titles of periodical articles, chapters and essays within books, short stories, and poems.
9. Provide the medium of the source (i.e., Print, Web, Film, Television, Performance).

Periodical Print Publications: Journals, Magazines, and Newspapers

1. Name of the author of the work; for anonymous works, begin entry with title of work
2. Title of the work, in quotation marks
3. Name of the periodical, italicized
4. Series number or name, if relevant
5. Volume number (for scholarly journals that use volume numbers)
6. Issue number (if available, for scholarly journals)
7. Date of publication (for scholarly journals, year; for other periodicals, day, month, and year, as available)
8. Page numbers
9. Medium of publication (for print sources, use *Print*)

ARTICLE IN A SCHOLARLY JOURNAL

For all scholarly journals—whether they paginate continuously throughout a given year or not—provide the volume and issue numbers (if both are given) separated by a period, the year, the page numbers, and the medium.

Gazzaniga, Michael S. "Right Hemisphere Language Following Brain Bisection: A Twenty-Year Perspective." *American Psychologist* 38.5 (1983): 528-49. Print.

If the journal does not use volume numbers, cite the issue number alone.

Harpham, Geoffrey Galt. "Roots, Races, and the Return to Philology." *Representations* 106 (2009): 34-62. Print.

ARTICLE IN A MAGAZINE

When citing a weekly or biweekly magazine, give the complete date (day, month, year).

Begley, Sharon. "What's in a Word?" *Newsweek* 20 July 2009: 31. Print.

When citing a magazine published every month or every two months, provide the month or months and year.

Bernstein, Charles. "Sounding the Word." *Harper's Magazine* Mar. 2011: 15-18. Print.

If an article in a magazine is not printed on consecutive pages—for example, an article might begin on page 45, then skip to 48—include only the first page followed by a plus sign.

ARTICLE IN DAILY OR WEEKLY NEWSPAPER

Carney, Heather. "Unlocking English." *Naples Daily News* 18 Dec. 2011, final ed.: A1+. Print.

Evelyn, Jamilah. "The 'Silent Killer' of Minority Enrollments." *Chronicle of Higher Education* 20 June 2003: A17-18. Print.

REVIEW (BOOK/FILM)

Morozov, Evgeny. "Sharing It All." Rev. of *I Know Who You Are and I Saw What You Did: Social Networks and the Death of Privacy*, by Lori Andrews. *New York Times Book Review* 29 Jan. 2012: 18. Print.

Dargis, Manohla. "The King's English, Albeit with Twisted Tongue." Rev. of *The King's Speech*, dir. Mike Leigh. *New York Times* 25 Nov. 2010, nat. ed.: AR18. Print.

If the review has no title, simply begin with *Rev.* after the author's name. If there is neither title nor author, begin with *Rev.* and alphabetize by the title of the book or film being reviewed.

ANONYMOUS ARTICLE

When no author's name is given, begin the entry with the title.

"Pompeii: Will the City Go from Dust to Dust?" *Newsweek* 1 Sept. 1997: 8. Print.

EDITORIAL (SIGNED/UNSIGNED)

Jackson, Derrick Z. "The Winner: Hypocrisy." Editorial. *Boston Globe* 6 Feb. 2004: A19. Print.

"Beginning of the End." Editorial. *New York Times* 19 Feb. 2012, national ed.: SR10. Print.

LETTER TO THE EDITOR

Lakind, Alexandra. "Constructive Criticism." Letter. *New Yorker* 13 & 20 Feb. 2012: 8. Print.

Nonperiodical Print Publications: Books, Brochures, and Pamphlets

BOOK BY A SINGLE AUTHOR

Metcalf, Allan. *OK: The Improbable Story of America's Greatest Word.* New York: Oxford UP, 2011. Print.

Use a shortened version of the publisher's name—for example, *Houghton* for Houghton Mifflin, or *Cambridge UP* for Cambridge University Press.

ANTHOLOGY

Eggers, Dave, ed. *The Best American Nonrequired Reading, 2002.* New York: Houghton, 2002. Print.

BOOK BY TWO OR MORE AUTHORS

For a book by two or three authors, list the authors in the order in which they appear on the title page.

Perry, Theresa, and Lisa Delpit. *The Real Ebonics Debate.* Ypsilanti, MI: Beacon, 1998. Print.

For a book by four or more authors, list the first author in the same way as for a single-author book, followed by a comma and the abbreviation *et al.* ("and others").

Chomsky, Noam, et al. *Acts of Aggression.* New York: Seven Stories, 1999. Print.

BOOK BY A CORPORATE AUTHOR

Carnegie Foundation for the Advancement of Teaching. *Campus Life: In Search of Community*. Princeton, NJ: Princeton UP, 1990. Print.

WORK IN AN ANTHOLOGY

Smith, Seaton. "'Jiving' with Your Teen." *The Best American Nonrequired Reading, 2002*. Ed. Dave Eggers. New York: Houghton, 2002. 217-20. Print.

ARTICLE IN A REFERENCE BOOK

Baugh, John. "Dialect." *The World Book Encyclopedia*. 2009 ed. Print.

If an article is unsigned, begin with the title.

"Dictionary of the English Language." *Benet's Reader's Encyclopedia*. 5th ed. 2008. Print.

INTRODUCTION, PREFACE, FOREWORD, OR AFTERWORD TO A BOOK

McCourt, Frank. Foreword. *Eats, Shoots & Leaves: The Zero Tolerance Approach to Punctuation*. By Lynne Truss. New York: Gotham Books, 2004. xi-xiv. Print.

TRANSLATION

Chaucer, Geoffrey. *The Canterbury Tales: A Complete Translation into Modern English*. Trans. Ronald L. Ecker and Eugene J. Crook. Palatka, FL: Hodge & Braddock, 1993. Print.

CHAPTER OR SECTION IN A BOOK

Lamott, Anne. "Shitty First Drafts." *Bird by Bird: Some Instructions on Writing and Life*. New York: Pantheon, 1994. 21-27. Print.

BOOK PUBLISHED IN A SECOND OR SUBSEQUENT EDITION

Aitchison, Jean. *Language Change: Process or Decay?* 2nd ed. Cambridge: Cambridge UP, 1991. Print.

Modern Language Association of America. *MLA Handbook for Writers of Research Papers*. 7th ed. New York: MLA, 2009. Print.

BROCHURE/PAMPHLET

Harry S. Truman Library and Museum. *Museum Guide*. Independence, MO: Truman Library, 2008. Print.

GOVERNMENT PUBLICATION

United States. Dept. of Justice. *Hate Crime Statistics, 1990: A Resource Book*. Washington: GPO. 1991. Print.

Give the government, the agency, and the title with a period and a space after each. The publisher is the Government Printing Office (GPO).

Web Publications

The following guidelines and models for citing information retrieved from the Internet have been adapted from the most recent advice of the MLA, as detailed in the *MLA Handbook for Writers of Research Papers*, seventh edition (2009), and from the "MLA Style" section on the MLA's Web site (mla.org). You will quickly notice that citations of Web publications have some common features with both print publications and reprinted works, broadcasts, and live performances. Standard information for all citations of online materials includes:

1. Name of the author, editor, or compiler of the work. The guidelines for print sources for works with more than one author, a corporate author, or unnamed author apply. For anonymous works, begin your entry with the title of the work.
2. Title of the work. Italicize the title, unless it is part of a larger work. Titles that are part of a larger work should be presented within quotation marks.
3. Title of the overall Web site in italics if this is distinct from item 2 above.
4. Version or edition of the site, if relevant.
5. Publisher or sponsor of the site. This information is often found at the bottom of the Web page. If this information is not available, use *N.p.* (for *no publisher*).
6. Date of publication (day, month, and year, if available). If no date is given, use *n.d.*
7. Medium of publication. For online sources, the medium is *Web*.
8. Date of access (day, month, and year).

MLA does not require you to include URLs in works cited entries. However, if your instructor wants you to include URLs in your citations or if you believe readers will not be able to locate the source without the URL, insert the URL as the last item in an entry, immediately after the date of access. Enclose the URL in angle brackets, followed by a period. The following example illustrates an entry with the URL included:

> Finley, Laura L. "How Can I Teach Peace When the Book Only Covers War?" *The Online Journal of Peace and Conflict Resolution* 5.1 (2003): n. pag. Web. 12 Feb. 2012. <http://www.trinstitute.org/ojpcr/5_1finley.htm>.

MLA style requires that you break URLs extending over more than one line only after a slash. Do *not* add spaces, hyphens, or any other punctuation to indicate the break.

ONLINE SCHOLARLY JOURNALS. To cite an article, a review, an editorial, or a letter to the editor in a scholarly journal existing only in electronic form on the Web, provide the author, the title of the article, the title of the journal, the volume and issue, and the date of issue, followed by the page numbers (if available), the medium, and the date of access.

ARTICLE IN AN ONLINE SCHOLARLY JOURNAL

Donner, Jonathan. "The Rules of Beeping: Exchanging Messages Via Intentional 'Missed Calls' on Mobile Phones." *Journal of Computer-Mediated Communication* 7.1 (2007): n. pag. Web. 28 Feb. 2012.

BOOK REVIEW IN ONLINE SCHOLARLY JOURNAL

Opongo, Elias Omondi. Rev. of *Responsibility to Protect: The Global Effort to End Mass Atrocities,* by Alex J. Bellamy. *Journal of Peace, Conflict, and Development* 14.14 (2009): n. pag. Web. 7 Mar. 2011.

EDITORIAL IN ONLINE SCHOLARLY JOURNAL

"Writing Across the Curriculum and Writing Centers." Editorial. *Praxis: A Writing Center Journal* 6.2 (2009): n. pag. Web. 10 Jan. 2011.

PERIODICAL PUBLICATIONS IN ONLINE DATABASES. Here are some model entries for periodical publications collected in online databases.

JOURNAL ARTICLE FROM AN ONLINE DATABASE OR SUBSCRIPTION SERVICE

Johnstone, Barbara, and Dan Baumgardt. "'Pittsburghese' Online: Vernacular Norming in Conversation." *American Speech* 79.2 (2004): 115-45. *Project Muse*. Web. 29 Feb. 2012

McEachern, William Ross. "Teaching and Learning in Bilingual Countries: The Examples of Belgium and Canada." *Education* 123. 1 (2002): 103. *Expanded Academic ASAP Plus*. Web. 17 Mar. 2011.

MAGAZINE ARTICLE FROM AN ONLINE DATABASE OR SUBSCRIPTION SERVICE

Keizer, Garret. "Sound and Fury: The Politics of Noise in a Loud Society." *Harper's Magazine*. Mar. 2001: 39-48. *Expanded Academic ASAP Plus*. Web. 27 Mar. 2011.

NEWSPAPER ARTICLE FROM AN ONLINE DATABASE OR SUBSCRIPTION SERVICE

Sanders, Joshunda. "Think Race Doesn't Matter? Listen to Eminem." *San Francisco Chronicle* 20 July 2003. *LexisNexis*. Web. 18 Mar. 2011.

NONPERIODICAL WEB PUBLICATIONS. Nonperiodical Web publications includes all Web-delivered content that does not fit into one of the previous two categories—scholarly journal Web publications and periodical publication in an online database or subscription service.

ARTICLE IN AN ONLINE MAGAZINE

Green, Joshua. "Elusive Green Economy." *Atlantic.com*. Atlantic Monthly Group, July-Aug. 2009. Web. 3 Mar. 2012.

Grossman, Samantha. "British School Bans Students from Using Slang and 'Text Speak.'" *Time.com*. Time, 15 Feb. 2012. Web. 10 Mar. 2012.

Hitchings, Henry. "What's the Language of the Future?" *Salon.com*. 6 Nov. 2011. Web. 23 Feb. 2012.

ARTICLE IN AN ONLINE NEWSPAPER

Peach, Gary. "Latvians Reject Russian as an Official National Language." *Seattletimes. com*. Seattle Times, 18 Feb. 2012. Web. 22 Feb. 2012.

"Immigration and the Campaign." Editorial. *New York Times*. New York Times, 20 Feb. 2012. Web. 7 Mar. 2012.

ARTICLE IN ONLINE SCHOLARLY PROJECT

Driscoll, Dana Lynn. "Irregular Verbs." Chart. *The OWL at Purdue*. Purdue U Online Writing Lab, 13 May 2007. Web. 8 Mar. 2011.

BOOK OR PART OF A BOOK ACCESSED ONLINE

For a book available online, provide the author, the title, the editor (if any), original publication information, the name of the database or Web site, the medium (*Web*), and the date of access.

Sapir, Edward. *Language: An Introduction to the Study of Speech*. New York: Harcourt, 1921. *Bartleby.com: Great Books Online*. Web. 1 Mar. 2012.

If you are citing only part of an online book, include the title or name of the part directly after the author's name.

Johnson, Samuel, and John Walker. "Sounds of the Vowels." *Dictionary of the English Language*. London: Pickering, 1828. *Google Book Search*. Web. 15 Jan. 2012.

SPEECH, ESSAY, POEM, OR SHORT STORY FROM ONLINE SITE

Faulkner, William. "On Accepting the Nobel Prize." 10 Dec. 1950. *The History Place: Great Speeches Collection*. Web. 12 Mar. 2011.

ARTICLES AND STORIES FROM ONLINE NEWS SERVICES

Pressman, Gabe. "Eminent Domain: Let the Public Beware!" *NBCNewYork.com*. NBC New York, 5 Dec. 2009. Web. 6 Mar. 2012.

"Americans Urged to Live MLK's Ideals at Memorial Dedication." *CNN.com*. Cable News Network, 17 Oct. 2011. Web. 18 Mar. 2012.

ARTICLE IN ONLINE ENCYCLOPEDIA OR OTHER REFERENCE WORK

"Etymology." *Encyclopaedia Britannica Online*. Encyclopaedia Britannica, 2012. Web. 13 Mar. 2012.

"Semantics." *Merriam-Webster Online Dictionary*. Merriam-Webster. 2012. Web. 23 Mar. 2012.

ONLINE CHARTS, MAPS, ARTWORK, PHOTOGRAPHS, AND OTHER IMAGES

Ager, Simon. "Braille: Basic Letters." Chart. *Omniglot.com*. 12 Jan. 2007. Web. 29 Feb. 2012.

da Vinci, Leonardo. *Mona Lisa*. 1503-06. Musee du Louvre, Paris. *WebMuseum*, 19 June 2006. Web. 22 Mar. 2011.

Short, Daniel M. "World Distribution of Indo-European Languages." Map. *Danshort. com*. 25 Sept. 2008. Web. 5 Mar. 2012.

ONLINE GOVERNMENT PUBLICATION

United States. Dept. of Justice. Federal Bureau of Investigation. *Hate Crime Statistics, 2010*. Nov. 2011. Web. 2 Apr. 2012.

HOME PAGE FOR ACADEMIC DEPARTMENT

Dept. of English. Home page. Arizona State U, n.d. Web. 29 Mar. 2012.

WIKI ENTRY

"Sign Language." *Wikipedia*. Wikimedia Foundation. 17 Feb. 2012. Web. 4 Mar. 2012.

No author is listed for a Wiki entry because the content is written collaboratively.

POSTING ON A BLOG

Broadway Bob. "Defining Home." *babblebob*. By Robert M. Armstrong, 24 Aug. 2009. Web. 10 Feb. 2012.

VIDEO RECORDING POSTED ONLINE

Jeanroustan. "Alyssa Talking Backwards." *YouTube*. YouTube, 30 Jan. 2012. Web. 29 Feb. 2012.

Additional Common Sources

TELEVISION OR RADIO BROADCAST

"Everyone's Waiting." *Six Feet Under*. Dir. Alan Ball. Perf. Peter Krause, Michael C. Hall, Frances Conroy, and Lauren Ambrose. Writ. Alan Ball. HBO. 21 Aug. 2005. Television.

SOUND RECORDING

Muri, John T., and Ravin I. McDavid Jr. *American's Speaking*. NCTE, 1967. LP Record.

Shakespeare, William. *Macbeth*. Ed. A. R. Branmuller. New York: Voyager, 1994. CD.

FILM OR VIDEO RECORDING

The Gods Must Be Crazy, I & II. Dir. Jamie Uys. Perf. N!xau, Marius Weyers, Sandra Prinsloo. 1990. Sony. 2004. DVD.

INTERVIEW

Handke, Peter. Interview. *New York Times Magazine* 2 July 2006: 13. Print.

For interviews that you conduct, provide the name of the person interviewed, the type of interview (personal, telephone, e-mail), and the date.

Clark, Virginia P. Telephone interview. 30 Jan. 2012.

CARTOON OR COMIC STRIP

Luckovich, Mike. Cartoon. *Atlanta Journal Constitution* 21 Nov. 2009. Print.

ADVERTISEMENT

Rosetta Stone. Advertisement. *Smithsonian* Mar. 2012: 42. Print.

LECTURE, SPEECH, ADDRESS, READING

England, Paula. "Gender and Inequality: Trends and Causes." President's Distinguished Lecture Series. U. of Vermont. Memorial Lounge, Burlington. 12 Mar. 2015. Lecture.

LETTER, MEMO, OR E-MAIL MESSAGE

Britto, Marah. Letter to the author. 22 Jan. 2016. MS.

Macomber, Sarah. "New Online Language Options." Message to the author. 10 Feb. 2015. E-mail.

Indicate the medium using MS (handwritten manuscript), TS (typescript), or E-mail.

DIGITAL FILE

A number of different types of work can come to you as a digital file—a book, typescript, photograph, or sound recording. It is important that you record the format of the digital file in the space reserved for medium of publication (JPEG file, PDF file, Microsoft Word file, MP3 file).

> Dengle, Isabella. *Eben Peck Cabin*. ca. 1891. Wisconsin Historical Society, Madison.
> JPEG file.

> Federman, Sarah. "The Language of Conflict: Seeking Resolution." 2015. Microsoft Word file.

MLA MANUSCRIPT FORMAT

The following guidelines for formatting manuscripts have been adapted from Modern Language Association recommendations.

Paper and Type

For academic papers use 8½- by-11-inch, twenty-pound white paper, and print in black on one side of each sheet. Use a standard type style such as Times New Roman or Courier. Use a paper clip (do not staple) to secure the pages unless instructed otherwise. Finally, be sure you keep both a paper copy and an electronic copy of your paper.

Title, Name, and Course Information

Beginning at the left margin one inch from the top of the first page, type your name, your instructor's name, the name and number of the course, and the date on separate lines, double-spaced. Double-space again, and center your title. Double-space between your title and the first sentence of your paper. For example, see page 39.

Margins, Line Spacing, and Paragraph Indentation

Leave a one-inch margin on all sides of the page. Double-space the text of the paper including long, set-off quotations, information notes, and the entries on the Works Cited page. Do not justify (make even) the right-hand margin. Indent the first line of each paragraph one-half inch (or five spaces).

Page Numbers

Place your last name and the page number (e.g., DeAngelus 1) in the upper right corner of each page, approximately one-half inch from the top and one inch from the right edge of the page. Do not use the word *page* or its abbreviation *p*; do not use a period or any other mark of punctuation with your name and page number. Number all pages of your paper, including the first and last. For example, see pages 39–42.

Long Quotations

Set off prose quotations that are longer than four lines to help your reader more clearly see the quotation as a whole. Poetry quotations are set off when longer than three lines. Set-off quotations are indented ten spaces from the left margin and are double-spaced; no quotation marks are necessary because the format itself indicates that the passage is a quotation. When you are quoting two or more paragraphs from the same source, indent the first line of each paragraph three additional spaces. Note that, unlike an integrated quotation in which the parenthetical citation is inside the end punctuation, with a long, set-off quotation the parenthetical citation is placed outside the final punctuation. For example, see page 59.

Spacing for Punctuation

Leave one space after a comma, colon, or semicolon and between the three periods in an ellipsis. MLA recommends one space after a period, question mark, or exclamation point at the end of a sentence. Form dashes by using two hyphens with no space between them. Do not leave a space before or after a dash. Most word processors will convert your two hyphens into a dash, as seen in the sample student paper on pages 58–63.

Web Addresses

Should you have occasion to divide a Web address at the end of a line in the text of your paper, MLA recommends that you break only after a slash. Never insert a hyphen to mark the break.

Works Cited Page

The list of Works Cited is placed on a separate page at the end of your paper and titled *Works Cited*. Place your last name and page number in the upper right-hand corner, one-half-inch from the top and one inch from the right edge of the page. Double-space and then center the words *Works Cited*. For a model Works Cited page from a student paper, see page 63. For the specific requirements of the format of each entry in the list of Works Cited, refer to the model entries on pages 591–600.

To assemble a Works Cited list for your paper, follow the guidelines given on page 591.

APA IN-TEXT CITATIONS

In-text citations in the American Psychological Association (APA) style generally consist of the author's last name, the year of publication, and a page reference. Usually the author's name and year of publication are given in an introductory signal phrase at the beginning of the borrowed material, and the page reference is given in parentheses at the end. If the author's name and publication year are not given at the beginning, put them in parentheses along with the page reference. When you borrow material from two or more works by the same author, you must include the title of the work in the signal phrase or parenthetically at the end. (For examples of signal phrases and in-text citations, see pages 50–53.) The parenthetical reference signals the end of the borrowed material and directs your readers to the list of References should they want to pursue a particular source. Treat electronic sources as you do print sources, keeping in mind that some electronic sources use paragraph numbers instead of page numbers. Consider the following examples of in-text citations, taken from student Richard Carbeau's paper on the debate over whether or not to make English America's official language.

Many people are surprised to discover that English is not the official language of the United States. Today, even as English literacy becomes a necessity for people in many parts of the world, some people in the United States believe its primacy is being threatened right at home. Much of the current controversy focuses on Hispanic communities with large Spanish-speaking populations who may feel little or no pressure to learn English. Columnist and cultural critic Charles Krauthammer believes English should be America's official language.

Krauthammer (2006) noted that this country has been "blessed . . . with a linguistic unity that brings a critically needed cohesion to a nation as diverse, multiracial and multiethnic as America" and that communities such as these threaten the bond created by a common language (p. 112).

Citation with author's name and publication year in the signal phrase

There are others, however, who think that "Language does not threaten American unity. Benign neglect is a good policy for any country when it comes to language, and it's a good policy for America" (King, 1997, p. 64).

Citation with author's name and publication year in parentheses

References

King, R. D. (1997, April). Should English be the law? *The Atlantic*

    Monthly, 55-64.

Krauthammer, C. (2006, June 12). In plain English: Let's make it official.

    Time, 112.

In the preceding example, the student followed APA style guidelines for his References list. When constructing the References list page for your paper, consult the following APA guidelines, based on the *Publication Manual of the American Psychological Association*, sixth edition (2010), where you will find model entries for periodical print publications, nonperiodical print publications, Web publications, and other common sources.

APA LIST OF REFERENCES

In this section, you will find general APA guidelines for creating a list of References followed by sample entries that cover the citation situations you are most likely to encounter. Make sure that you follow the formats as they appear on the following pages.

GUIDELINES FOR CONSTRUCTING YOUR LIST OF REFERENCES

1. Begin the list on a fresh page following the last page of text.
2. Center the title *References* at the top of the page.
3. Double-space both within and between entries on your list.
4. Capitalize only the first word in a title or subtitle. Do not capitalize other words within titles unless they are proper nouns.
5. Alphabetize your sources by the authors' last names. If you have two or more authors with the same last name, alphabetize first by last names and then by first names. Use only initials for first and middle names.
6. Multiple authors should be separated by commas, with *&* before the final author.
7. If you have two or more works by the same author, list in chronological order. For two works from the same year, add letters after the year to indicate different sources:

    Twitchell, J. B. (2002a, 25 November). The branding of higher ed. *Forbes*, 50.
    Twitchell, J. B. (2002b). Science friction. In *Living it up: America's love affair with*
        luxury. New York, NY: Columbia University Press.
    Twitchell, J. B. (2004). *Branded nation: When culture goes pop*. New York, NY: Simon
        and Schuster.

8. If no author is known, alphabetize by title.

9. Begin each entry at the left margin. If the entry is longer than one line, indent the second and subsequent lines five spaces or one-half inch.

10. Italicize the titles of books, journals, magazines, and newspapers.

Periodical Print Publications: Journals, Magazines, and Newspapers

STANDARD INFORMATION FOR PERIODICAL PRINT PUBLICATIONS

1. Name of the author of the work; for anonymous works, if "Anonymous" is cited as author, use that; otherwise, begin entry with title of work

2. Date of publication (use month and day if citing a newspaper or magazine)

3. Title of the work, and subtitle if applicable; capitalize only the first word and any proper nouns

4. Name of the periodical, italicized; capitalize all major words

5. Volume number and issue number (if available)

6. Page numbers in full

ARTICLE IN A SCHOLARLY JOURNAL

For all scholarly journals—whether they paginate continuously throughout a given year or not—provide the date of publication, volume and issue numbers (if both are given) with the volume number italicized and the issue number (in parentheses if each issue starts with page 1), and the page numbers.

> Ziegler, N. A. (2014). Fostering self-regulated learning through the European language portfolio: An embedded mixed methods study. *The Modern Language Journal, 98*, 4, 921-936.

If the journal does not use volume numbers, cite the issue number alone.

> Harpham, G. G. (2009). Roots, races, and the return to philology. *Representations,* 106, 34-62.

ARTICLE IN A MAGAZINE

When citing a weekly or biweekly magazine, give the complete date (day, month, year).

> French, P., & Stevens, L. (2012, November). Anything you say may be given in evidence. . . . *Babel*, 12-15.

ARTICLE IN DAILY OR WEEKLY NEWSPAPER

Carney, H. (2011, December 18). Unlocking English. *Naples Daily News*, p. A1.

Evelyn, J. (2003, June 20). The "silent killer" of minority enrollments. *Chronicle of Higher Education*, pp. A17-18.

REVIEW (BOOK/FILM)

Morozov, E. (2012, January 29). Sharing it all. [Review of the book *I know who you are and I saw what you did: Social networks and the death of privacy*, by L. Andrews]. *New York Times Book Review*, p. 18.

If the review has no title, simply begin with "Review of" *before* the title of the work and author(s), in brackets.

Black, K. (2014, October 8). [Review of the book *The language of food*, by D. Jurafsky]. *The Boston Globe*, p. 27.

UNSIGNED ARTICLE

When no author's name is given, begin the entry with the title.

Pompeii: Will the city go from dust to dust? (1997, September 1). *Newsweek*, p. 8.

LETTER TO THE EDITOR

Ninuaai, N. M. (2015, August 15). Tracking police use of force [Letter to the editor]. *The New York Times*, p. A22.

Nonperiodical Print Publications: Books, Conference Proceedings, and Dissertations

BOOK BY A SINGLE AUTHOR

Metcalf, A. (2011). *OK: The improbable story of America's greatest word*. New York, NY: Oxford University Press.

Use the publisher's full name, but do not include words like *Inc.* or *Co.*

ANTHOLOGY

Eggers, D. (Ed.). (2013) *The best American nonrequired reading 2013*. New York, NY: Mariner Books.

BOOK BY TWO OR MORE AUTHORS

For a book by two or more authors, list the authors in the order in which they appear on the title page. Use an ampersand before the final author's name.

> Levitt, S. D., & Dubner, S. J. (2014). *Think like a freak: The authors of* Freakonomics *offer to retrain your brain.* New York, NY: William Morrow.

For a book by eight or more authors, list the first six authors as above, followed by a comma, three ellipsis dots (. . .), and the final author's name, with no ampersand.

BOOK BY A CORPORATE AUTHOR

> World Health Organization. (2015). *Handbook for the assessment of capacities at the human-animal interface.* Geneva, Switzerland: WHO Press.

WORK IN AN ANTHOLOGY OR CHAPTER IN EDITED BOOK

> Gorney, C. (2013). Cuba's new now. In D. Eggers (Ed.), *Best American nonrequired reading 2013* (pp. 180-196). New York, NY: Mariner Books.

INTRODUCTION, PREFACE, FOREWORD, OR AFTERWORD TO A BOOK

> McCourt, F. (2004). Foreword. In L. Truss, *Eats, shoots & leaves: The zero tolerance approach to punctuation* (pp. xi-xiv]. New York, NY: Gotham Books.

TRANSLATION

> Chaucer, G. (2003). *The Canterbury tales: A complete translation into modern English* (R. L. Ecker and E. J. Crook, Trans.). Palatka, FL: Hodge & Braddock.

BOOK PUBLISHED IN A SECOND OR SUBSEQUENT EDITION

> Lightbown, P. M. & Spada, N. (2013). *How languages are learned* (4th ed.). Oxford, UK: Oxford University Press.

PUBLISHED CONFERENCE PROCEEDINGS

> Hunter, G. (2014). *AMA winter marketing educators' conference 2014: Engaging customers.* Red Hook, NY: Curran Associates Proceedings.

DISSERTATION

If applicable, include database information in your citation of a published thesis or dissertation.

> Smith, A. H. (2009). *Language learning in adulthood: Why some have more trouble than others* (Doctoral dissertation, Stanford University). Retrieved from http://dissexpress.umi.com/dxweb/doc/304999890.html?FMT=AI&desc=Language+learning+in+adulthood%3A+Why+some+have+more+trouble+than+others

Web Publications

The following guidelines and models for citing information retrieved from the Internet have been adapted from the most recent advice of the APA, as detailed in the *APA Style Guide to Electronic References*. Standard information for all citations of online materials includes:

1. Name of the author, editor, or compiler of the work. The guidelines for print sources for works with more than one author, a corporate author, or unnamed author apply.
2. Date of publication (day, month, and year, if available).
3. Title of the work. Italicize the title, unless it is part of a larger work.
4. Title of the overall Web site or online publication in italics if this is distinct from item 2 above.
5. Volume number, issue number, and page number, as relevant.
6. Unique DOI (digital object identifier), if available. If you include a DOI, you can omit the retrieval date, database name, or URL; if no DOI, then include "Retrieved from" and a URL for the Web page or journal. If your citation ends with the URL, do not use a closing period after the URL.

ONLINE SCHOLARLY JOURNAL ARTICLES AND PERIODICALS. To cite an article, a review, an editorial, or a letter to the editor in a scholarly journal existing only in electronic form on the Web, provide the author, the date of issue, the title of the article, the title of the journal, the volume and issue (if applicable), and the retrieval URL. For periodical and journal articles without a DOI accessed through a database, give the URL of the homepage of the article.

ARTICLE WITH A DOI

Ruppel, E. K. & Burke, T. J. (2014). Complementary channel use and the role of social competence. *Journal of Computer-Mediated Communication, 20,* 37-51. doi: 10.1111/jcc4.12090

ARTICLE WITHOUT A DOI

Winter, Y. (2014). On the grammar of a Senegalese drum language. *Language, 90,* 644-668. Retrieved from http://muse.jhu.edu/login?auth=0&type=summary&url=/journals/language/v090/90.3.winter.html

ARTICLE FROM AN ONLINE PERIODICAL

McWhorter, J. (2013, April 25). Is texting killing the English language? *Time.* Retrieved from http://ideas.time.com

NONPERIODICAL WEB PUBLICATIONS. Nonperiodical Web publications includes all Web-delivered content that does not fit into one of the previous two categories—scholarly journal Web publications and periodical publication in an online database or subscription service.

NONPERIODICAL WEB DOCUMENT

Mayo Clinic. (2013, May 9). *Childhood apraxia of speech.* Retrieved from http://www.mayoclinic.org/diseases-conditions/childhood-apraxia-of-speech/basics/definition/con-20031147

WIKI ENTRY

Sign language. (n.d.). In *Wikipedia*. Retrieved March 12, 2015, from http://en.wikipedia.org/wiki/Sign_language

Be sure to include a retrieval date, as content in a wiki changes frequently.

POSTING ON A BLOG

Armstrong, R. M. (2009, August 24). Defining home [Web log post]. Retrieved from http://www.babblebob.com/2009/08/defining-home.html

VIDEO RECORDING POSTED ONLINE

Jeanroustan. (2012, January 30). Alyssa talking backwards [Video file]. Retrieved from http://www.youtube.com/watch?v=CRse-IePpbE

APA MANUSCRIPT FORMAT

The following guidelines for formatting manuscripts have been adapted from American Psychological Association recommendations.

Paper and Type

For academic papers use 8½-by-11-inch paper, and use a standard type style such as Times New Roman in 12-point font. On each page be sure to include a running head, which consists of the title of your paper abbreviated to fifty characters, in all capital letters on the left side of the upper margin; also include a page number on the right side of the upper margin. Finally, be sure you keep both a paper copy and an electronic copy of your paper.

Title Page

The title page should include a special running head in the upper left margin of the page:

Running head: TITLE OF PAPER

In the center of the page, in double-spaced type, include the full paper title, your name, and the name of your institution.

Margins, Line Spacing, and Paragraph Indentation

Leave a one-inch margin on all sides of the page. Double-space the text of the paper including long, set-off quotations, information notes, and the entries in the list of References. Do not justify (make even) the right-hand margin. Indent the first line of each paragraph one-half inch (or five spaces).

Page Numbers

Place the page number (e.g., 1) in the upper right corner of each page, approximately one inch from the top and one inch from the right edge of the page. Do not use the word *page* or its abbreviation *p*; do not use a period or any other mark of punctuation with your name and page number. Number all pages of your paper, including the first and last.

Spacing for Punctuation

Leave one space after a comma, colon, or semicolon, and between the three periods in an ellipsis. APA recommends one space after a period, question mark, or exclamation point at the end of a sentence. Form dashes by using two hyphens with no space between them. Do not leave a space before or after a dash. Most word processors will convert your two hyphens into a dash.

Web Addresses

Should you have occasion to divide a Web address at the end of a line in the text of your paper, break only after a slash. Never insert a hyphen to mark the break.

References Page

The list of References is placed on a separate page at the end of your paper and titled *References*. Continue the running head and page numbering on this page. Double-space and then center the words *References*. For the specific requirements of the format of each entry in the list of References, refer to the model entries on pages 604–608.

GLOSSARY OF RHETORICAL AND LINGUISTIC TERMS

Abstract See *Concrete/Abstract.*

Accent Characteristics of pronunciation that reflect regional or social identity.

Acronym A word made from the initial letters (in some cases, the first few letters) of a phrase or organization; for example, NATO (North Atlantic Treaty Organization) and scuba (self-contained underwater breathing apparatus).

Allusion A passing reference to a familiar person, place, or thing drawn from history, the Bible, mythology, or literature. An allusion is an economical way for a writer to capture the essence of an idea, atmosphere, emotion, or historical era, as in "The scandal was his Watergate," "He saw himself as a modern Job," or "Everyone there held those truths to be self-evident."

American Sign Language (ASL, Ameslan) A system of communication used by deaf people in the United States, consisting of hand symbols that vary in the shape of the hands, the direction of their movement, and their position in relation to the body. It is different from finger spelling, in which words are signed in the order in which they are uttered, thus preserving English structure and syntax.

Analogy A special form of comparison in which the writer explains something complex or unfamiliar by comparing it to something familiar: "A transmission line is simply a pipeline for electricity. In the case of a water pipeline, more water will flow through the pipe as water pressure increases. The same is true of a transmission line for electricity." When a subject is unobservable or abstract, or when readers may have trouble understanding it, analogy is particularly useful.

Argument A strategy for developing an essay. To argue is to attempt to convince a reader to agree with a point of view, to make a given decision, or to pursue a particular course of action. Logical argument is based on reasonable explanations and appeals to the reader's intelligence. See also *Persuasion, Logical Fallacies, Deduction,* and *Induction.*

Attitude A writer's opinion of a subject, which may be very positive, very negative, or somewhere between these two extremes. See also *Tone.*

Audience The intended readership for a piece of writing. For example, the readers of a national weekly newsmagazine come from all walks of life and have diverse opinions, attitudes, and educational experiences. In contrast, the readership for an organic chemistry journal may be comprised of people with similar scientific interests and educational backgrounds. The essays in this book are intended for general readers, intelligent people who may lack specific information about the subjects being discussed.

Beginnings and Endings A *beginning* is the sentence, group of sentences, or section that introduces an essay. Good beginnings usually identify the thesis or main idea, attempt to interest the reader, and establish a tone. Some effective ways to begin essays include (1) telling an anecdote that illustrates the thesis, (2) providing a controversial statement or opinion that engages the reader's interest, (3) presenting startling statistics or facts, (4) defining a term that is central to the discussion that follows, (5) asking thought-provoking questions, (6) providing a quotation that illustrates the thesis, (7) referring to a current event that helps to establish the thesis, or (8) showing the significance of the subject or stressing its importance to the reader.

An *ending* is the sentence or group of sentences that brings an essay to closure. Good endings are well planned; they are the natural outgrowths of the essays themselves and give readers a sense of finality or completion. Some of the techniques mentioned above for beginnings may be effective for endings as well.

Biased Language Language that is used by a dominant group within a culture to maintain its supposed superior position and to disempower others. See also *Racist Language* and *Sexist Language*.

Bidialectalism The use of two dialects of the same language.

Bilingual Education Teaching in a child's primary language, which may or may not be the language of the dominant population.

Black English A vernacular variety of English used by some black people; it may be divided into Standard Black English and Black English Vernacular (BEV). See also *Ebonics*.

Brainstorming A discovery technique in which writers list everything they know about a topic, freely associating one idea with another. When writers brainstorm, they also make lists of questions about aspects of the topic for which they need information. See also *Clustering* and *Freewriting*.

Cause and Effect Analysis A strategy for developing an essay. Cause and effect analysis answers the question *why*. It explains the reasons for an occurrence or the consequences of an action. Whenever a question asks *why*, answering it will require discovering a *cause* or series of causes for a particular *effect*; whenever a question asks *what if*, its answer will point out the effect or effects that can result from a particular cause.

Classification See *Division and Classification*.

Cliché An expression that has become ineffective through overuse, such as *quick as a flash, dry as dust, jump for joy,* and *slow as molasses*. Writers normally avoid such trite expressions and seek instead to express themselves in fresh and forceful language. See also *Figures of Speech*.

Clustering A discovery technique in which a writer puts a topic or keyword in a circle at the center of a blank page and then generates main ideas about that topic, circling each idea and connecting it with a line to the topic in the center circle. Writers often repeat the process in order to add specific examples and details to each main idea. This technique allows writers to generate material and sort it into meaningful clusters at the same time. See also *Brainstorming* and *Freewriting*.

Coherence A quality of good writing that results when all of the sentences, paragraphs, and longer divisions of an essay are naturally connected. Coherent writing is achieved through (1) a logical sequence of ideas (arranged in chronological order, spatial order, order of importance, or some other appropriate order), (2) the thoughtful repetition of keywords and ideas, (3) a pace suitable for your topic and your reader, and (4) the use of transitional words and expressions. Coherence should not be confused with unity. See also *Unity* and *Transitions*.

Colloquial Expressions Informal expressions that are typical of a particular language. In English, phrases such as *come up with, be at loose ends,* or *get with the program* are colloquial expressions. Such expressions are acceptable in formal writing only if they are used for a specific purpose.

Comparison and Contrast A strategy for developing an essay. In comparison and contrast, the writer points out the similarities and differences between two or more subjects in the same class or category. The function of any comparison and contrast is to clarify — to reach some conclusion about the items being compared and contrasted. An effective comparison and contrast does not dwell on obvious similarities or differences; instead, it tells readers something significant that they may not already know.

Conclusions See *Beginnings and Endings*.

Concrete/Abstract A *concrete word* names a specific object, person, place, or action that can be directly perceived by the senses: *car, bread, building, book, John F. Kennedy, Chicago,* or *hiking*. An *abstract word,* in contrast, refers to general qualities, conditions, ideas, actions, or relationships that cannot be directly perceived by the senses: *bravery, dedication, excellence, anxiety, friendship, thinking,* or *hatred*.

Although writers must use both concrete and abstract language, good writers avoid using too many abstract words. Instead, they rely on concrete words to define and illustrate abstractions. Because concrete words appeal to the senses, they are easily comprehended by a reader.

Connotation/Denotation Both terms refer to the meanings of words. *Denotation* is the dictionary meaning of a word, its literal meaning. *Connotation,* on the other hand, is a word's implied or suggested meaning. For example, the denotation of *lamb* is a "a young sheep." The connotations of lamb are numerous: *gentle, docile, weak, peaceful, blessed, sacrificial, blood, spring, frisky, pure, innocent,* and so on. Good writers are sensitive to both the denotations and the connotations of words and use these meanings to advantage in their writing.

Deduction The process of reasoning that moves from stated premises to a conclusion that follows necessarily. This form of reasoning moves from the general to the specific. See also *Induction* and *Syllogism*.

Definition A strategy for developing an essay. A definition, which states the meaning of a word, may be either brief or extended; it may be part of an essay or an entire essay itself.

Denotation See *Connotation/Denotation*.

Description A strategy for developing an essay. Description tells how a person, place, or thing is perceived by the five senses. Objective description reports these sensory qualities factually, whereas subjective description gives the writer's interpretation of them.

Descriptivism   A school of linguistic analysis that seeks to describe linguistic facts as they are. See also *Prescriptivism.*

Dialect   A variety of language, usually regional or social, that is set off from other varieties of the same language by differences in pronunciation, vocabulary, and grammar.

Diction   A writer's choice and use of words. Good diction is precise and appropriate—the words mean exactly what the writer intends, and the words are well suited to the writer's subject, intended audience, and purpose. The word-conscious writer knows, for example, that there are differences among *aged, old,* and *elderly; blue, navy,* and *azure;* and *disturbed, angry,* and *irritated.* Furthermore, this writer knows when to use each word. See also *Connotation/ Denotation.*

Direct Quotation   A writer's use of the exact words of a source. Direct quotations, which are put in quotation marks, are normally reserved for important ideas stated memorably, for especially clear explanations by authorities, and for proponents' arguments conveyed in their own words. See also *Paraphrase, Summary,* and *Plagiarism.*

Division and Classification   A strategy for developing an essay. *Division* involves breaking down a single large unit into smaller subunits, or separating a group of items into discrete categories. *Classification,* on the other hand, involves arranging or sorting people, places, or things into categories according to their differing characteristics, thus making them more manageable for the writer and more understandable for the reader. Division, then, takes apart, while classification groups together. Although the two processes can operate separately, most often they work hand in hand.

Doublespeak   According to doublespeak expert William Lutz, "Doublespeak is a blanket term for language which pretends to communicate but doesn't, language which makes the bad seem good, the negative appear positive, the unpleasant attractive, or at least tolerable. It is language which avoids, shifts, or denies responsibility."

Ebonics   A term coined in 1973 for African American Vernacular English (AAVE). Public debate centers on whether it is a dialect of English or a separate language with its own grammatical rules and rhythms. See also *Black English.*

Endings   See *Beginnings and Endings.*

English-Only Movement   The ongoing attempts, which began in the Senate in 1986, to declare English the official language of the United States. Although these attempts have failed thus far at the federal level, a number of states have passed various forms of English-only legislation.

Essay   A relatively short piece of nonfiction in which the writer attempts to make one or more closely related points. A good essay is purposeful, informative, and well organized.

Ethnocentricity   The belief that one's culture (including language) is at the center of things and that other cultures (and languages) are inferior.

Euphemism   A pleasing, vague, or indirect word or phrase that is substituted for one that is considered harsh or offensive. For example, *pacify* is a euphemism for *bomb, pavement deficiency* for *pothole, downsize* or *release from employment* for *fire.*

Evidence   The data on which a judgment or an argument is based or by which proof or probability is established. Evidence usually takes the form of statistics, facts, names, examples or illustrations, and opinions of authorities.

Examples   Ways of illustrating, developing, or clarifying an idea. Examples enable writers to show and not simply to tell readers what they mean. The terms *example* and *illustration* are sometimes used interchangeably. An example may be anything from a statistic to a story; it may be stated in a few words or go on for several pages. An example should always be *relevant* to the idea or generalization it is meant to illustrate. An example should also be *representative*. In other words, it should be typical of what the writer is trying to show.

Exemplification   A strategy for developing an essay. In exemplification, the writer uses examples—facts, opinions, anecdotes, or statistics—to make ideas more vivid and understandable. Exemplification is used in all types of essays. See also *Examples*.

Fallacy   See *Logical Fallacies*.

Figurative Language   Language that uses figures of speech, especially metaphor, to convey or emphasize a particular meaning.

Figures of Speech   Brief, imaginative comparisons that highlight the similarities between things that are basically dissimilar. They make writing vivid and interesting and therefore more memorable. Following are the most common figures of speech:

Simile: An implicit comparison introduced by *like* or *as*. "The fighter's hands were like stone."

Metaphor: An implied comparison that uses one thing as the equivalent of another. "All the world's a stage."

Onomatopoeia: The use of words whose sound suggests the meaning, as in *buzz, hiss,* and *meow.*

Personification: A special kind of simile or metaphor in which human traits are assigned to an inanimate object. "The engine coughed and then stopped."

Freewriting   A discovery technique that involves writing for a brief uninterrupted period of time—ten or fifteen minutes—on anything that comes to mind. Writers use freewriting to discover new topics, new strategies, and other new ideas. See also *Brainstorming* and *Clustering*.

Gobbledygook   The use of technical or unfamiliar words that confuse rather than clarify an issue for an audience.

Grammar   The system of a language including its parts and the methods for combining them.

Idiom   A word or phrase that is used habitually with a particular meaning in a language. The meaning of an idiom is not always readily apparent to nonnative speakers of that language. For example, *catch cold, hold a job, make up your mind,* and *give them a hand* are all idioms in English.

Illustration   See *Examples*.

Indo-European Languages   A group of languages descended from a supposed common ancestor and now widely spoken in Europe, North and South America, Australia, New Zealand, and parts of India.

Induction   A process of reasoning whereby a conclusion about all members of a class is reached by examining only a few members of the class. This form of reasoning moves from a set of specific examples to a general statement or principle. As long as the evidence is accurate, pertinent, complete, and sufficient to represent the assertion, the conclusion of the inductive argument can be regarded as valid; if, however, readers can spot inaccuracies in the evidence or point to contrary evidence, they have good reason to doubt the assertion as it stands. Inductive reasoning is the most common of argumentative structures. See also *Deduction*.

Introductions   See *Beginnings and Endings*.

Irony   The use of words to suggest something different from their literal meaning. A writer can use irony to establish a special relationship with the reader and to add an extra dimension or twist to the meaning.

Jargon   See *Technical Language*.

Language   Words, their pronunciation, and the conventional and systematic methods for combining them as used and understood by a community.

Lexicography   The art of dictionary-making.

Linguistic Relativity Hypothesis   The belief that the structure of a language shapes the way speakers of that language view reality. Also known as the Sapir-Whorf Hypothesis after Edward Sapir and Benjamin Lee Whorf.

Logical Fallacies   Errors in reasoning that render an argument invalid. Some of the more common logical fallacies are listed here:

Oversimplification: The tendency to provide simple solutions to complex problems. "The reason we have inflation today is that OPEC has unreasonably raised the price of oil."

Non sequitur ("It does not follow"): An inference or a conclusion that does not follow from established premises or evidence. "It was the best movie I saw this year, and it should get an Academy Award."

Post hoc, ergo propter hoc ("After this, therefore because of this"): Confusing chance or coincidence with causation. Because one event comes after another one, it does not necessarily mean that the first event caused the second. "I won't say I caught cold at the hockey game, but I certainly didn't have it before I went there."

Begging the question: Assuming in a premise that which needs to be proven. "If American autoworkers built a better product, foreign auto sales would not be so high."

False analogy: Making a misleading analogy between logically unconnected ideas. "He was a brilliant basketball player; therefore, there's no question in my mind that he will be a fine coach."

Either/or thinking: The tendency to see an issue as having only two sides. "Used car salesmen are either honest or crooked."

Logical Reasoning   See *Deduction* and *Induction*.

Metaphor   See *Figures of Speech*.

Narration   A strategy for developing an essay. To narrate is to tell a story, to tell what happened. Although narration is most often used in fiction, it is also important in nonfiction, either by itself or in conjunction with other strategies. A good narrative essay has four essential features. The first is *context:* The writer makes clear when the action happened, where it happened, and to whom. The second is *point of view:* The writer establishes and maintains a consistent relationship to the action, either as a participant or as a reporter simply looking on. The third is *selection of detail:* The writer carefully chooses what to include, focusing on those actions and details that are most important to the story while merely mentioning or actually eliminating others. The fourth is *organization:* The writer organizes the events of the narrative into an appropriate sequence, often a strict chronology with a clear beginning, middle, and end.

Objective/Subjective *Objective writing* is factual and impersonal, whereas *subjective writing,* sometimes called impressionistic writing, relies heavily on personal interpretation.

Onomastics The study of the meaning and origins of proper names of persons and places.

Onomatopoeia See *Figures of Speech.*

Organization In writing, the thoughtful arrangement and presentation of one's points or ideas. Narration is often organized chronologically, whereas other kinds of essays may be organized point by point or from most familiar to least familiar. Argument may be organized from least important to most important. There is no single correct pattern of organization for a given piece of writing, but good writers are careful to discover an order of presentation suitable for their subject, audience, and purpose.

Paradox A seemingly contradictory statement that may nonetheless be true. For example, *we little know what we have until we lose it* is a paradox.

Paragraph A series of closely related sentences and the single most important unit of thought in an essay. The sentences in a paragraph adequately develop its central idea, which is usually stated in a topic sentence. A well-written paragraph has several distinguishing characteristics: a clearly stated or implied topic sentence, adequate development, unity, coherence, and an appropriate organizational pattern.

Parallelism The arrangement of words, phrases, or sentences in similar grammatical and stylistic form, often to emphasize important ideas.

Paraphrase A restatement of the information a writer is borrowing. A paraphrase closely parallels the presentation of the ideas in the original, but it does not use the same words or sentence structure. See also *Direct Quotation, Summary,* and *Plagiarism.*

Personification See *Figures of Speech.*

Persuasion An attempt to convince readers to agree with a point of view, to make a given decision, or to pursue a particular course of action. See also *Argument, Induction,* and *Deduction.*

Phonetics The study of speech sounds.

Phonology The study of sound patterns in languages.

Plagiarism The use of someone else's ideas in their original form or in an altered form without proper documentation. Writers avoid plagiarism by (1) putting direct quotations within quotation marks and properly citing them and (2) documenting any idea, explanation, or argument that is borrowed and presented in a summary or paraphrase, making it clear where the borrowed material begins and ends. See also *Direct Quotation, Paraphrase,* and *Summary.*

Point of View The grammatical person of the speaker in an essay. For example, a first-person point of view uses the pronoun *I* and is commonly found in autobiography and the personal essay; a third-person point of view uses the pronouns *he, she,* or *it* and is commonly found in objective writing.

Prescriptivism   A grammar that seeks to explain linguistic facts as they should be. See also *Descriptivism.*

Process Analysis   A strategy for developing an essay. Process analysis answers the question *how* and explains how something works or gives step-by-step directions for doing something.

Propaganda   Ideas, facts, or rumors purposely spread to further one's cause or to damage the cause of an opponent.

Purpose   What a writer wants to accomplish in a particular composition—his or her reason for writing. The three general purposes of writing are *to express* thoughts and feelings and lessons learned from life experiences, *to inform* readers about something about the world around them, or *to persuade* readers to accept some belief or take some action.

Racist Language   A form of biased language that makes distinctions on the basis of race and deliberately or subconsciously suggests that one race is superior to all others.

Rhetorical Questions   Questions that are asked but require no answer from the reader. "When will nuclear proliferation end?" is such a question. Writers use rhetorical questions to introduce topics they plan to discuss or to emphasize important points.

Sapir-Whorf Hypothesis   See *Linguistic Relativity Hypothesis.*

Semantics   The study of meanings in a language.

Sexist Language   A form of biased language that makes distinctions on the basis of sex and shows preference for one sex over the other.

Signal Phrase   A phrase alerting the reader that borrowed information is to follow. A signal phrase usually consists of the author's name and a verb (for example, "Keesbury argues") and helps to integrate direct quotations, paraphrases, and summaries into the flow of a paper.

Simile   See *Figures of Speech.*

Slang   The unconventional, very informal language of particular subgroups in a culture. Slang words such as *zonk, split, rap, cop,* and *stoned* are acceptable in formal writing only if they are used for a specific purpose. A writer might use slang, for example, to re-create authentic dialogue in a story.

Specific/General   *General words* name groups or classes of objects, qualities, or actions. *Specific words,* on the other hand, name individual objects, qualities, or actions within a class or group. To some extent the terms *general* and *specific* are relative. For example, *dessert* is a class of things. *Pie,* however, is more specific than *dessert* but more general than *pecan pie* or *chocolate cream pie.* Good writing judiciously balances the general with the specific. Writing with too many general words is likely to be dull and lifeless because general words do not create vivid responses in the reader's mind. On the other hand, writing that relies exclusively on specific words may lack focus and direction, which more general statements provide.

Standard English   A variety of English that is used by the government and the media and that is taught in the schools. It is often best expressed in written form.

Style   The individual manner in which a writer expresses his or her ideas. Style is created by the author's particular selection of words, construction of sentences, and arrangement of ideas.

Subjective   See *Objective/Subjective.*

Summary   A condensed form of the essential idea of a passage, an article, or an entire chapter. A summary is always shorter than the original. See also *Paraphrase, Direct Quotation*, and *Plagiarism.*

Syllogism   An argument that utilizes deductive reasoning and consists of a major premise, a minor premise, and a conclusion. For example,

All trees that lose leaves are deciduous. (major premise)

Maple trees lose their leaves. (minor premise)

Therefore, maple trees are deciduous. (conclusion)

See also *Deduction.*

Symbol   A person, place, or thing that represents something beyond itself. For example, the eagle is a symbol of America, and the bear is a symbol of Russia.

Syntax   The way words are arranged to form phrases, clauses, and sentences. Syntax also refers to the grammatical relationships among the words themselves.

Taboo Language   Language that is avoided in a given society. Almost all societies have language taboos.

Technical Language   The special vocabulary of a trade or profession. Writers who use technical language do so with an awareness of their audiences. If the audience is a group of peers, technical language may be used freely. If the audience is a more general one, technical language should be used sparingly and carefully so as not to sacrifice clarity. Technical language that is used only to impress, hide the truth, or cover insecurities is termed *jargon* and is not condoned. See also *Diction.*

Thesis   A statement of the main idea of an essay, the point the essay is trying to make. A thesis may sometimes be implied rather than stated directly.

Tone   The manner in which a writer relates to an audience, the "tone of voice" used to address readers. Tone may be described as friendly, serious, distant, angry, cheerful, bitter, cynical, enthusiastic, morbid, resentful, warm, playful, and so forth. A particular tone results from a writer's diction, sentence structure, purpose, and attitude toward the subject. See also *Attitude.*

Topic Sentence   The sentence that states the central idea of a paragraph and thus limits and controls the subject of the paragraph. Although the topic sentence normally appears at the beginning of the paragraph, it may appear at any other point, particularly if the writer is trying to create a special effect. See also *Paragraph.*

Transitions   Words or phrases that link the sentences, paragraphs, and larger units of an essay in order to achieve coherence. Transitional devices include parallelism, pronoun references, conjunctions, and the repetition of key ideas, as well as the many transitional expressions such as *moreover, on the other hand, in addition, in contrast,* and *therefore.* See also *Coherence.*

Unity   A quality that is achieved in an essay when all the words, sentences, and paragraphs contribute to its thesis. The elements of a unified essay do not distract the reader. Instead, they all harmoniously support a single idea or purpose.

Usage   The way in which words and phrases are actually used in a language community. See also *Descriptivism* and *Prescriptivism.*

Rhetorical Contents

ANALOGY

Gordon Allport, *The Language of Prejudice*   364
Raffaella Zanuttini, *Our Language Prejudices Don't Make
    No Sense*   137

ARGUMENT AND PERSUASION

Raffaella Zanuttini, *Our Language Prejudices Don't Make
    No Sense*   137
Martin Luther King Jr., *I Have a Dream*   301
John F. Kennedy, *Inaugural Address*   309
Malala Yousafzai, *Address at the Youth Takeover of the
    United Nations*   314
Elie Wiesel, *The Perils of Indifference*   327
Jonathan Swift, *A Modest Proposal*   334
Andrew Sullivan, *What's So Bad about Hate?*   347
Wendy Kaminer, *Why We Need to Tolerate Hate*   382
Greg Lukianoff, *Twitter, Hate Speech, and the Cost of Keeping
    Quiet*   387
Roxane Gay, *The Careless Language of Sexual Violence*   452
Sherryl Kleinman, Matthew B. Ezzell, A. Corey Frost,
    The Social Harms of "Bitch"   465
David Carr, *Keep Your Thumbs Still When I'm Talking to You*   496

CAUSE AND EFFECT ANALYSIS

Susanne K. Langer, *Language and Thought*   112
Eric C. Miller, *Talk the Talk*   186
Donna Hicks, *Safety*   417
Sherry Turkle, *The Tethered Self: Technology Reinvents Intimacy
     and Solitude*   492
Po Bronson, *Learning to Lie*   547
Chana Joffe-Walt and Alix Spiegel, *Psychology of Fraud: Why
     Good People Do Bad Things*   562

COMPARISON AND CONTRAST

Lou Ann Walker, *Losing the Language of Silence*   168
Akiba Solomon, *Thugs. Students. Rioters. Fans: Media's Subtle Racism in
     Unrest Coverage*   393
Ben Crair, *The Internet Talks Like a Woman*   485
Kiera Butler, *The Creepy Language Tricks Taco Bell Uses to Fool People
     into Eating There*   531

DEFINITION

Chimamanda Ngozi Adichie, *Happy Feminist*   460
William Lutz, *Weasel Words: The Art of Saying Nothing at All*   520
Elie Wiesel, *The Perils of Indifference*   327
Akiba Solomon, *Thugs. Students. Rioters. Fans: Media's Subtle Racism in
     Unrest Coverage*   393
Maisha Z. Johnson, *What's Really Going on with the Word "Thug"—And
     Why I'm Not Ready to Let It Go*   398
Michael Kimmel, *"Bros Before Hos": The Guy Code*   477
Elliott Ackerman, *Assassination and the American Language*   294
Deena Shanker, *Is the "Natural" Label 100 Percent
     Misleading?*   534

DESCRIPTION

Paul Roberts, *Speech Communities*   148
Lou Ann Walker, *Losing the Language of Silence*   168
Toni Morrison, *When Language Dies: 1993 Nobel Prize for Literature
     Lecture*   319

DIVISION AND CLASSIFICATION

Donna Woolfolk Cross, *Propaganda: How Not to Be Bamboozled*   247
William Lutz, *The World of Doublespeak*   277
Martin Luther King Jr., *Letter from Birmingham Jail*   95
Melissa Fay Greene, *Word Power for Babies*   126
Jason Stanley, *Language That Silences*   289
Lera Boroditsky, *Lost in Translation*   141
Richard Lederer, *All-American Dialects*   159
Edwin Battistella, *Sorry, Regrets, and More*   406
Amy Tan, *Mother Tongue*   179
Judith Viorst, *The Truth about Lying*   541
Kiera Butler, *The Creepy Language Tricks Taco Bell Uses to Fool People into Eating There*   531

EXAMPLE AND ILLUSTRATION

Natalie Goldberg, *Be Specific*   5
Emily Parker, *You Can Keep Quiet, You Can Emigrate, or You Can Stay Here and Fight*   88
Melissa Fay Greene, *Word Power for Babies*   126
Steven Pinker, *Words Don't Mean What They Mean*   120
Maria Konnikova, *The Lost Art of the Unsent Angry Letter*   272
William Zinsser, *Simplicity*   233
Roxane Gay, *The Careless Language of Sexual Violence*   452
Newman P. Birk and Genevieve B. Birk, *Selection, Slanting, and Charged Language*   261
Michael Gardner, *The Dork Police: Further Adventures of Flex Cop*   425
Rick Reilly, *Regretlessly Yours: The No-Fault Apology*   433
Joanna Schroeder, *11 Words You Need to Teach Your Son Before He Turns 6*   470
Alison J. Stein, *Lost in Translation*   501
Bill Bryson, *The Hard Sell: Advertising in America*   507

NARRATION

Henry Louis Gates Jr., *What's in a Name?*   14

Malcolm X, *Coming to an Awareness of Language*   67

Helen Keller, *The Day Language Came into My Life*   72

Sherman Alexie, *Superman and Me*   77

Mary Pipher, *Writing to Change the World*   82

Emily Parker, *You Can Keep Quiet, You Can Emigrate, or You Can Stay Here and Fight*   88

Amy Westervelt, *Letting Go*   441

Bharati Mukherjee, *Two Ways to Belong in America*   174

Firoozeh Dumas, *The "F Word"*   376

PROCESS AND ANALYSIS

Ben Zimmer, *Chunking*   133

Bill Hayes, *On Not Writing*   239

Anne Lamott, *Shitty First Drafts*   221

Annie Dillard, *Write Till You Drop*   202

Steven Pinker, *Good Writing*   208

Emily Badger, *Tarring Opponents as Extremists Really Can Work*   437

Amy Westervelt, *Letting Go*   441

Donald M. Murray, *The Maker's Eye: Revising Your Own Manuscripts*   226

Stephen King, *Reading to Write*   196

Acknowledgments (continued from page ii)

CHAPTER 1

Page 3, From *Writing Down the Bones: Freeing the Writer Within*, by Natalie Goldberg, © 1986 by Natalie Goldberg. Reprinted by arrangement with The Permissions Company, Inc., on behalf of Shambhala Publications Inc., Boston, MA. www.shambhala.com.

Page 14, Henry Louis Gates Jr., "'What's in a Name?' Some Meanings of Blackness," from *Dissent*, 36.4, Fall 1989. Reprinted with permission of the University of Pennsylvania Press.

Page 18, By permission Esther P. Lederer Trust and Creators Syndicate, Inc.

CHAPTER 3

Page 44, From *The Boston Globe*, May 5 © 2011 Boston Globe. All rights reserved. Used by permission and protected by the Copyright Laws of the United States. The printing, copying, redistribution, or retransmission of this Content without express written permission is prohibited.

Page 45, Janet Holmes, "Women Talk Too Much." Reprinted with permission of the author.

Page 46, From *The New York Times*, October 31 © 2010 The New York Times. All rights reserved. Used by permission and protected by the Copyright Laws of the United States. The printing, copying, redistribution, or retransmission of this Content without express written permission is prohibited.

CHAPTER 4

Page 67, "Saved" from *Autobiography of Malcolm X* by Malcolm X as told to Alex Haley, copyright © 1964 by Alex Haley and Malcolm X. Copyright © 1965 by Alex Haley and Betty Shabazz. Used by permission of Ballantine Books, an imprint of Random House, a division of Penguin Random House LLC. All rights reserved.

Page 70, "It Pays to Enrich Your Word Power," originally published in *Reader's Digest*. Copyright © 1999 by Trusted Media Brands, Inc. Used by permission. All rights reserved.

Page 78, Originally published in Milkweed Editions, *The Most Wonderful Books: Writers on Discovering the Pleasures of Reading*. Copyright © 1997 Sherman Alexie. Reprinted by permission of Nancy Stauffer Associates Literary Agents.

CHAPTER 5

CHAPTER 6

CHAPTER 7

Page 239, From *The New York Times*, August 24 © 2014 The New York Times. All rights reserved. Used by permission and protected by the Copyright Laws of the United States. The printing, copying, redistribution, or retransmission of this Content without express written permission is prohibited.

CHAPTER 8

Page 247, Donna Woolfolk Cross, "Propaganda: How Not to Be Bamboozled" from *Speaking of Words: A Language Reader* © 1977. Reprinted by permission of the author.
Page 261, Birk/Birk, *Understanding and Using English*, 5th Edition, © 1972. Reprinted by permission of Pearson Education, Inc., Upper Saddle River, NJ.
Page 272, From *The New York Times*, March 23 © 2014 The New York Times. All rights reserved. Used by permission and protected by the Copyright Laws of the United States. The printing, copying, redistribution, or retransmission of this Content without express written permission is prohibited.
Page 277, "The World of Doublespeak" © 1989. *Doublespeak* by William Lutz. Used by permission of William Lutz, in care of the Jean V. Naggar Literary Agency, Inc.
Page 289, From *The New York Times*, June 26 © 2011 The New York Times. All rights reserved. Used by permission and protected by the Copyright Laws of the United States. The printing, copying, redistribution, or retransmission of this Content without express written permission is prohibited.
Page 292, From *The New York Times*, July 18 © 2011 The New York Times. All rights reserved. Used by permission and protected by the Copyright Laws of the United States. The printing, copying, redistribution, or retransmission of this Content without express written permission is prohibited.
Page 294, Elliot Ackerman/The New Yorker; © Conde Nast.
Page 297, Robert Yoakum, "Everyspeech." Reprinted by permission of the author.

CHAPTER 9

Page 301, Reprinted by arrangement with The Heirs to the Estate of Martin Luther King Jr., c/o Writers House as agent for the proprietor New York, NY. Copyright 1963 Dr. Martin Luther King Jr; copyright renewed 1991 Coretta Scott King.

Page 305, Reprinted by permission of The Nelson Mandela Foundation.

Page 314, Reproduced with permission of Curtis Brown Group Ltd, London, on behalf of Malala Yousafzai. Copyright © Malala Yousafzai 2013.

Page 320, "When Language Dies:" 1993 Nobel Prize for Literature Lecture by Toni Morrison. Used by Permission. All rights reserved.

Page 328, "On the Perils of Indifference" by Elie Wiesel. Originally given as a speech, April 12, 1999. Copyright © 1999 by Elie Wiesel. Reprinted by permission of Georges Borchardt, Inc., on behalf of Elie Wiesel.

CHAPTER 10

Page 347, Andrew Sullivan, "What's So Bad About Hate," *The New York Times*, September 26, 1999. © Andrew Sullivan, reprinted by permission of The Wylie Agency.

Page 364, From *The Nature of Prejudice* by Gordon W. Allport. Copyright © 1979 Gordon W. Allport. Reprinted by permission of Basic Books, a member of the Perseus Books Group.

Page 376, "The F Word" from *Funny in Farsi: A Memoir of Growing Up Iranian in America* by Firoozeh Dumas, copyright © 2003 by Firoozeh Dumas. Used by permission of Villard Books, an imprint of Random House, a division of Penguin Random House LLC. All rights reserved.

Page 382, Wendy Kaminer, "Why We Need To Tolerate Hate," from *The Atlantic*. Copyright © Wendy Kaminer. Reprinted by permission.

Page 387, Greg Lukianoff, "Twitter, Hate Speech, and the Costs of Keeping Quiet," from CNET. Reprinted by permission of the YGS Group.

Page 393, Akiba Solomon, "Thugs. Students. Rioters. Fans: Media's Subtle Racism in Unrest Coverage." Copyright © Akiba Solomon. Reprinted by permission of Race Forward.

Page 398, Maisha Johnson, "What's Really Going on with the Word 'Thug'—And Why I'm Not Ready To Let It Go," *Black Girl Dangerous* (5/18/15). Reprinted by permission of the author.

CHAPTER 11

Page 406, *Sorry About That* by Edwin L Battistella (2014): pp. 56–75. © Oxford University Press 2014. Reprinted by permission.

CHAPTER 12

CHAPTER 13

Index of Authors and Titles

Ackerman, Elliot
"Assassination and the American Language," 246, 294–298
"Address at the Youth Takeover of the United Nations" (YOUSAFZAI), 299–300, 314–318
Adichie, Chimamanda Ngozi
"Happy Feminist," 451, 460–464
Alexie, Sherman, 52
"Superman and Me," 65, 77–81
"All-American Dialects" (LEDERER), 147, 159–167
Allport, Gordon
"The Language of Prejudice," 47–48, 345, 364–375
"Alone Together; Why We Expect More from Technology and Less from Each Other" (TURKLE), 44–52
"A Loss for Words: The Story of Deafness in a Family" (WALKER), 168
"A Modest Proposal" (SWIFT), 300, 334–343
"Assassination and the American Language" (ACKERMAN), 246, 294–298
"The Autobiography of Malcolm X" (MALCOLM X), 67–71

Badger, Emily
"Tarring Opponents as Extremists Really Can Work," 405, 437–440
Battistella, Edwin A.
"Sorry About That: The Language of Public Apology," 404, 406–416
"Be Specific" (GOLDBERG), 3–6

Birk, Genevieve B.
"Selection, Slanting, and Charged Language," 48–49, 245, 261–271
Birk, Newman P.
"Selection, Slanting, and Charged Language," 48–49, 245, 261–271
Boroditsky, Lera, 44
"Lost in Translation," 111, 141–146
Bronson, Po
"Learning to Lie," 540, 547–557
" 'Bros Before Hos': The Guy Code" (KIMMEL), 451, 477–484
Bryson, Bill
"The Hard Sell: Advertising in America," 507–519
Butler, Kiera, 25
"The Creepy Language Tricks Taco Bell Uses to Fool People into Eating There," 531–533

"The Careless Language of Sexual Violence" (GAY), 451–459
Carr, David
"Keep your Thumbs Still While I'm Talking to You," 491, 496–500
"Chunking" (ZIMMER), 111, 133–136
"Coming to an Awareness of Language" (MALCOLM X), 65–71
Crair, Ben
"The Internet Talks Like a Woman," 451, 485–489
"Creeper! Rando! Sketchball!" (ZIMMER), 45–46
"The Creepy Language Tricks Taco Bell Uses to Fool People into Eating There" (BUTLER), 531–533

Cross, Donna Woolfolk, 20
"Propaganda: How Not to Be
Bamboozled," 245, 247–260

"The Day Language Came Into My
Life" (KELLER), 65, 72–76
"Dignity" (HICKS), 404, 417–424
Dillard, Annie
"Write Till You Drop," 195,
202–207
"Don't Let Stereotypes Warp Your
Judgment" (HEILBRONER), 55–56
"The Dork Police: Further Adventures
of Flex Cop" (GARDNER), 404,
425–432
Dumas, Firoozeh
"The 'F Word'," 345, 376–381

Ezzell, Matthew B.
"The Social Harms of 'Bitch'," 451,
465–469

"Feeling and Form" (LANGER), 111–119
"Freedom from Speech" (LUKIANOFF),
387
Friend, Tad
"You Can't Say That: The Networks
Play Word Games," 54–55
Frost, A. Corey
"The Social Harms of 'Bitch'," 451,
465–469
"Funny in Farsi" (DUMAS), 376–381
"The 'F Word'" (DUMAS), 345,
376–381

Gardner, Michael
"The Dork Police: Further
Adventures of Flex Cop," 404,
425–432
Gates, Henry Louis Jr.
"What's in a Name?," 14–18
Gay, Roxane
"The Careless Language of Sexual
Violence," 451–459
Goldberg, Natalie, 3–4
"Be Specific," 3–6
"Good Writing" (PINKER), 195,
208–220
Greene, Melissa Fay
"Word Power for Babies," 111,
126–132

Gunderman, Richard
"Is Lying Bad for Us?," 540,
558–561

"Happy Feminist" (ADICHIE), 451,
460–464
"The Hard Sell: Advertising in
America" (BRYSON), 507–519
Hayes, Bill
"On Not Writing," 195,
239–243
Heilbroner, Robert L.
"Don't Let Stereotypes Warp Your
Judgment," 55–56
Hicks, Donna
"Dignity," 404, 417–424
"The High Price of Facebook"
(LYONS), 52–53
Holmes, Janet
"Women Talk Too Much," 45

"I Have a Dream" (KING), 29, 299,
301–308
"Inaugural Address" (KENNEDY), 299,
309–313
"The Internet Talks Like a Woman"
(CRAIR), 451, 485–489
"Is Lying Bad for Us?" (GUNDERMAN),
540, 558–561
"Is the 'Natural' Label 100 Percent
Misleading?" (SHANKER), 534–539
Jamieson, Jake, 33
"The 'Official English' Movement,"
57–63
Jimenez, Marta, 44
Joffe-Walt, Chana
"Psychology of Fraud: Why Good
People Do Bad Things," 540,
562–576
Johnson, Maisha K.
"What's Really Going on with the
Word 'Thug'—And Why I'm
Not Ready to Let It Go," 346,
398–401

Kahn, Joseph P.
"What Does Friend Mean Now?,"
44
Kaminer, Wendy
"Why We Need to Tolerate Hate,"
345–346, 382–386

"Keep your Thumbs Still While I'm
Talking to You" (CARR), 491,
496–500
Keller, Helen
"The Day Language Came into My
Life," 65, 72–76
Kennedy, John F.
"Inaugural Address," 299, 309–313
Kimmel, Michael
" 'Bros Before Hos': The Guy
Code," 451, 477–484
King, Martin Luther Jr.
"I Have a Dream," 29, 299, 301–308
"Letter from Birmingham Jail," 50,
65, 95–110
King, Stephen
"Reading to Write," 195–201
Kleinman, Sherryl
"The Social Harms of 'Bitch'," 451,
465–469
Konnikova, Maria
"The Lost Art of the Unsent Angry
Letter," 245–246, 272–276

Lamott, Anne, 52
"Shitty First Drafts," 195, 221–225
Landers, Ann
"Refusal to Use Name Is the
Ultimate Insult," 18–19
Langer, Susanne K., 20
"Language and Thought," 111–119
"Language and Thought" (LANGER),
111–119
"Language Learnability and Language
Development" (PINKER), 120
"The Language of Prejudice"
(ALLPORT), 47–48, 345, 364–375
"Language That Silences" (STANLEY),
246, 289–293
"Learning to Lie" (BRONSON), 540,
547–557
Lederer, Richard, 20
"All-American Dialects," 147, 159–167
"Letter from Birmingham Jail" (KING),
50, 65, 95–110
"Letting Go" (WESTERVELT), 405,
441–449
"Losing the Language of Silence"
(WALKER), 147, 168–173
"The Lost Art of the Unsent Angry
Letter" (KONNIKOVA),
245–246, 272–276

"Lost in Translation" (BORODITSKY),
111, 141–146
"Lost in Translation" (STEIN), 491,
501–506
Lukianoff, Greg, 25
"Twitter, Hate Speech, and the
Costs of Keeping Quiet," 346,
387–392
Lutz, William
"The World of Doublespeak," 246,
277–288
"Weasel Words: The Art of Saying
Nothing at All," 520–530
Lyons, Daniel
"The High Price of Facebook,"
52–53

"The Maker's Eye: Revising Your Own
Manuscripts" (MURRAY), 195,
226–232
Malcolm X, 25
"The Autobiography of Malcolm X,"
67–71
"Coming to an Awareness of
Language," 65, 67–71
Miller, Eric C.
"Talk the Talk," 147, 186–193
Morrison, Toni
"When Language Dies: 1993 Nobel
Prize for Literature Lecture," 300,
319–326
"Mother Tongue" (TAN), 147,
179–185
Mujica, Mauro E.
"Why the U.S. Needs an Official
Language," 44–45
Mukherjee, Bharati, 20
"Two Ways to Belong in America,"
147, 174–178
Murray, Donald M.
"The Maker's Eye: Revising Your Own
Manuscripts," 195, 226–232

"The 'Negro Revolt' in Me' "
(SANDLIN), 39–42
The 'Official English' Movement"
(JAMIESON), 57–63
"On Not Writing" (HAYES), 195,
239–243
"Our Language Prejudices Don't Make
No Sense" (ZANUTTINI), 111,
137–140

Parker, Emily
  "You Can Keep Quiet, You Can
    Emigrate, or You Can Stay Here
    and Fight," 66, 88–94
"The Perils of Indifference" (WIESEL),
    300, 327–333
Pinker, Steven
  "Good Writing," 195, 208–220
  "Words Don't Mean What They
    Mean," 111, 120–125
Pipher, Mary
  "Writing to Change the World,"
    65–66, 82–86
"Primer Lessons" (SANDBURG), 403
"Propaganda: How Not to Be
    Bamboozled" (CROSS), 245,
    247–260
"Psychology of Fraud: Why Good
    People Do Bad Things" (JOFFE-
    WALT), 562–576
"Psychology of Fraud: Why Good
    People Do Bad Things" (SPIEGEL),
    562–576

"Reading to Write" (KING),
    195–201
"Refusal to Use Name Is the Ultimate
    Insult" (LANDERS), 18–19
"Regretlessly Yours: The No-Fault
    Apology" (REILLY), 404–405,
    433–436
Reichman, Henry, 32
Reilly, Rick
  "Regretlessly Yours: The No-Fault
    Apology," 404–405, 433–436
Roberts, Paul
  "Speech Communities," 147–158

Sanburg, Carl
  "Primer Lessons," 403
Sandlin, Rebekah, 23–24, 39–42
  "The 'Negro Revolt' in Me'," 39–42
Schroeder, Joanna
  "11 Words You Need to Teach Your
    Son Before He Turns 6," 451,
    470–476
"Selection, Slanting, and Charged
    Language" (BIRK), 48–49, 245,
    261–271
Shanker, Deena
  "Is the 'Natural' Label 100 Percent
    Misleading?," 534–539

"Shitty First Drafts" (LAMOTT), 195,
    221–225
"Simplicity" (ZINSSER), 49–50, 195,
    233–238
"The Social Harms of 'Bitch' "
    (EZZELL), 451, 465–469
"The Social Harms of 'Bitch' " (FROST),
    451, 465–469
"The Social Harms of 'Bitch' "
    (KLEINMAN), 451, 465–469
Solomon, Akiba
  "Thugs. Students. Rioters. Fans:
    Media's Suble Racism in Unrest
    Coverage," 346, 393–397
"Sorry, Regrets, and More"
    (BATTISTELLA), 404, 406–416
"Sorry About That: The Language of
    Public Apology" (BATTISTELLA),
    404, 406–416
"Speech Communities" (ROBERTS),
    147–158
Spiegel, Alix
  "Psychology of Fraud: Why Good
    People Do Bad Things," 540,
    562–576
"Sports From Hell: My Search for the
    World's Dumbest Competition"
    (REILLY), 433
Stanley, Jason
  "Language That Silences," 246,
    289–293
"The Story of My Life" (KELLER), 72–76
Stein, Alison J.
  "Lost in Translation," 491, 501–506
Sullivan, Andrew, 52
  "What's So Bad about Hate?," 345,
    347–363
"Superman and Me" (ALEXIE), 65,
    77–81
Swift, Jonathan
  "A Modest Proposal," 300, 334–343

"Talk the Talk" (MILLER), 147,
    186–193
Tan, Amy
  "Mother Tongue," 147, 179–185
"Tarring Opponents as Extremists
    Really Can Work" (BADGER), 405,
    437–440
"The Tethered Self: Technology
    Reinvents Intimacy and Solitude"
    (TURKLE), 491–495

"Thugs. Students. Rioters. Fans: Media's Subtle Racism in Unrest Coverage" (SOLOMON), 346, 393–397

"The Truth About Lying" (VIORST), 540–546

Turkle, Sherry, 52
"Alone Together; Why We Expect More from Technology and Less from Each Other," 44–52
"The Tethered Self: Technology Reinvents Intimacy and Solitude," 491–495

"Twitter, Hate Speech, and the Costs of Keeping Quiet" (LUKIANOFF), 346, 387–392

"Two Ways to Belong in America" (MUKHERJEE), 147, 174–178

"Understanding and Using Language" (BIRK), 261–271

"Understanding Grammar" (ROBERTS), 148

Viorst, Judith
"The Truth About Lying," 540–546

Walker, Lou Ann
"Losing the Language of Silence," 147, 168–173

"Weasel Words: The Art of Saying Nothing at All" (LUTZ), 520–530

Westervelt, Amy
"Letting Go," 405, 441–449

"What Does Friend Mean Now?" (KAHN), 44

"What's in a Name?" (GATES), 14–18

"What's Really Going on with the Word 'Thug'—And Why I'm Not Ready to Let It Go" (JOHNSON), 346, 398–401

"What's So Bad about Hate?" (SULLIVAN), 345, 347–363

"When Language Dies: 1993 Nobel Prize for Literature Lecture" (MORRISON), 300, 319–326

"Why the U.S. Needs an Official Language" (MUJICA), 44–45

"Why We Need to Tolerate Hate" (KAMINER), 345–346, 382–386

Wiesel, Elie
"The Perils of Indifference," 300, 327–333

"Women Talk Too Much" (HOLMES), 45

"Word Power for Babies" (GREENE), 111, 126–132

"Words Don't Mean What They Mean" (PINKER), 111, 120–125

"11 Words You Need to Teach Your Son Before He Turns 6" (SCHROEDER), 451, 470–476

"The World of Doublespeak" (LUTZ), 246, 277–288

"Write Till You Drop" (DILLARD), 195, 202–207

"Writing to Change the World" (PIPHER), 65–66, 82–86

"You Can Keep Quiet, You Can Emigrate, or You Can Stay Here and Fight" (PARKER), 66, 88–94

"You Can't Say That: The Networks Play Word Games" (FRIEND), 54–55

Yousafzai, Malala
"Address at the Youth Takeover of the United Nations," 299–300, 314–318

Zanuttini, Raffaella
"Our Language Prejudices Don't Make No Sense," 111, 137–140

Zimmer, Ben
"Chunking," 111, 133–136
"Creeper! Rando! Sketchball!," 45–46

Zinsser, William
"Simplicity," 49–50, 195, 233–238